# Game-Based Approaches to Language Teaching and Learning

Millicent Ngema
https://orcid.org/0000-0002-6760-5907
*University of South Africa, South Africa*

Nkidi Phatudi
*University of South Africa, South Africa*

IGI Global
Scientific Publishing
Publishing Tomorrow's Research Today

| | |
|---|---|
| Vice President of Editorial | Melissa Wagner |
| Director of Acquisitions | Mikaela Felty |
| Director of Book Development | Jocelynn Hessler |
| Production Manager | Mike Brehm |
| Cover Design | Jose Rosado |

Published in the United States of America by
IGI Global Scientific Publishing
701 East Chocolate Avenue
Hershey, PA, 17033, USA
Tel: 717-533-8845 | Fax: 717-533-7115
Website: https://www.igi-global.com E-mail: cust@igi-global.com




Library of Congress Cataloging-in-Publication Data

Names: Ngema, Millicent editor | Phatudi, Nkidi editor
Title: Game-based approaches to language teaching and learning / edited by: Millicent Ngema and Nkidi Phatudi.
Description: Hershey, PA : IGI Global Scientific Publishing, [2026] | Includes bibliographical references and index. | Summary: "This book advocates for the intentional incorporation of games including traditional ones into language curricula to create dynamic and inclusive learning experiences"-- Provided by publisher.
Identifiers: LCCN 2025044736 (print) | LCCN 2025044737 (ebook) | ISBN 9798337343228 hardcover | ISBN 9798337343235 paperback | ISBN 9798337343242 ebook
Subjects: LCSH: Educational games
Classification: LCC LB1029.G3 G26 2026 (print) | LCC LB1029.G3 (ebook) | DDC 371.337--dc23/eng/20260129
LC record available at https://lccn.loc.gov/2025044736
LC ebook record available at https://lccn.loc.gov/2025044737

British Cataloguing in Publication Data
A Cataloguing in Publication record for this book is available from the British Library.

# Table of Contents

# Detailed Table of Contents



This study examines contemporary folklore and puppetry as strategies to strengthen mother tongue instruction in Namibian early grades. The chapter is grounded in socio-cultural and semiotic perspectives. It uses multimodal analysis of a shadow puppet performance and teacher focus group interviews. Findings show puppetry enhances oral expression, literacy, and cultural identity but faces resource and training barriers. Professional development and culturally responsive practices are recommended to support mother tongue education.



Folklore is a wide phenomenon among different cultures and languages across the globe. In isiZulu, more particularly, folklore is vital for developing and enhancing language and critical thinking skills, and these are useful for primary school teachers and learners, as learners learn while they enjoy. Language and critical thinking skills are both vital for effective communication and problem-solving. While language skills incorporate listening, speaking, reading, and writing skills, critical thinking involves analysing information and solving problems. Both these skills are interconnected, and they contribute to the learner's ability to understand and interact with the world effectively. This chapter aims to demonstrate how folktales and riddles can be used as techniques to enhance a primary school learner's language and critical language skills. Such skills play a vital role in the learner's academic achievement throughout their academic life, thus need to be adopted by primary school language teachers for effective teaching.

This chapter foregrounds the pedagogical value of parental involvement and indigenous game-based practices in fostering early language development within diverse and resource-constrained South African communities. Despite growing acknowledgement of culturally embedded forms of learning in language practices, mainstream pedagogical frameworks often overlook the everyday educational contributions of parents and Indigenous Knowledge Systems (IKS). Grounded in a Pedagogy-in-Participation approach, Vygotsky's Sociocultural Theory, and transformative pedagogy, the chapter explores how traditional activities such as kgati, storytelling, clapping games, and rhythmic play serve as rich literacy and cognitive developmental resources. Drawing on empirical data from six mothers' narratives, it repositions parents as co-educators and showcases how indigenous practices support vocabulary, narrative, and culture. The chapter advocates for contextually grounded, community-based approaches that honour children's full linguistic ecologies and promote equitable early language education.



This chapter investigates the preservation of Indigenous languages in Zimbabwe through interactive digital experiences, particularly language-focused games. The colonial legacy has entrenched English as the dominant language, marginalizing Indigenous tongues and contributing to cultural erosion. Despite government efforts, progress remains insufficient, highlighting the need for innovative solutions. Using a gamification framework informed by community engagement, this research enhances the learning of selected Indigenous languages. Collaborating with cultural experts, we developed engaging game narratives and features, showing gamification's potential as a transformative tool for linguistic preservation. The findings suggest that interactive experiences can revitalize Indigenous languages, addressing challenges in implementation and cultural nuances.

This chapter explores the intersection of game-based learning, cultural responsiveness, and literacy development in marginalized communities. Drawing on sociocultural theory and digital pedagogy frameworks, we examine how culturally-responsive game-based interventions can address persistent literacy gaps while honoring students' linguistic and cultural assets. Through analysis of empirical studies, theoretical frameworks, and implementation models, this chapter demonstrates that game-based learning environments, when designed with cultural responsiveness at their core, offer transformative potential for literacy education in underserved populations. We discuss design principles, pedagogical approaches, assessment strategies, and policy implications for scaling culturally-responsive game-based literacy interventions. The chapter concludes with recommendations for researchers, educators, and policymakers seeking to bridge literacy gaps through culturally-sustaining digital pedagogies.



Integrating culturally relevant content from the indigenous knowledge systems (IKS) and languages can enhance engagement and understanding of language teaching and learning. Although South Africa's Constitution (1996) recognises 12 official languages and encourages the documentation, preservation, and promotion of minority languages and dialects, the commitment to promoting cultural diversity and inclusion of these languages is still meagre, especially among the marginalized indigenous rural communities. This chapter argues that folk songs as part of the IKS can help to improve language and other creative skills since they incorporate poetic elements such as rhythm, metaphor, and wordplay. The chapter adopted a decolonial lens and the repetition as a rhetorical tool for emphasis and persuasion, rhythm, balance, memory, and learning to explore the Lobedu folk song "Ka totoma".

This study was conducted in township schools in the Ekurhuleni South District of Gauteng province, South Africa. Its purpose was to explore how game-based approaches can help sustain the Sesotho language in a multilingual society. The study was grounded in the interpretivism paradigm, informed by the Zone of Proximal Development theory. A qualitative approach was used, employing interviews and observations to gather data. Purposive sampling was used to select six Grade 4 Sesotho teachers; four were male and two were female. The data collected were categorised into codes and themes. It was revealed that game-based strategies foster engagement, collaboration, and a sense of cultural ownership, thereby strengthening the use of the home language among children. The study concludes that integrating games into the curriculum can be a powerful tool for celebrating and sustaining linguistic heritage in a multilingual context. It is recommended that teacher training and curriculum designers integrate culturally appropriate game-based strategies into the home language curriculum.



In traditional biliteracy instruction, biliteracy is taught as Home Language and First Additional Language literacies, following Eurocentric monolingualising ideologies. Curricula and pedagogy in these classrooms reject discourses about play-based and multimodal pedagogical approaches for highly pedagogised and decontextualised instruction that excludes African oral literature and art. Drawing on language ideologies, and multiliteracies as theoretical frameworks this study aims to challenge the narrow literacy approaches and nation-state ideologies that determine how language is used. The study draws on auto-ethnographic case study of 60 grade 3-6 children who were members the Stars of Today Literacy Club#. The study focuses on the selected gamesongs and the related art activities. It draws on interactional and multimodal analysis as analytic tools. Findings show that using gamesongs can enhance vocabulary, rhyme and rhythm. Finally, multilingual and multimodal pedagogies enhance biliteracy development and positions children as competent emergent bilinguals

# Preface

## INTRODUCTION

As Editors of this volume, we are pleased to present *Game-Based Approaches to Language Teaching and Learning*, a collection that brings together emerging scholarship and practice at the intersection of language education and game-based pedagogy. Language development remains a foundational aspect of cognitive growth, social interaction, and academic success. Increasingly, research has highlighted the powerful role that games can play in supporting language acquisition, not only as engaging tools for learners but also as promising components in the evolution of intelligent tutoring systems within educational environments.

This book explores a wide spectrum of game-based approaches, encompassing both traditional and digital forms. We intentionally include indigenous knowledge systems (IKS), such as dances, role-playing, and folktales, alongside contemporary digital games. By doing so, we aim to foreground diverse epistemologies and practices that have long supported language learning across cultures, while also acknowledging innovations shaped by technological advancement. Across age groups and linguistic contexts, games offer immersive and low-anxiety environments that foster communication, vocabulary development, grammatical awareness, and narrative competence.

One of the defining strengths of game-based learning lies in its capacity to engage learners meaningfully. When learners are actively involved, motivation increases, anxiety is reduced, and opportunities for authentic language use expand. The chapters in this volume draw on case studies and empirical research to demonstrate how such approaches support both first and additional language acquisition, while also encouraging collaboration and social interaction among learners.

A central aim of this book is to advocate for the intentional integration of games—including traditional and culturally grounded practices—into language curricula.

Such integration is especially important in contexts where languages are marginalized or underrepresented, as game-based approaches can revitalize interest in initial reading and literacy development in ways that are culturally relevant and inclusive.

This volume also contributes practical and theoretical insights for educators. It offers an array of strategies designed to enhance language teaching by strengthening learner motivation, engagement, and self-regulation. Teachers will find guidance on how to create dynamic, responsive, and contextually meaningful learning environments that reflect the diverse backgrounds of their learners. In doing so, the book underscores the importance of aligning pedagogy with learners' lived experiences and cultural contexts.

Furthermore, the book speaks to a broad audience that includes teachers, parents, guardians, and researchers. For educators working in resource-constrained settings, it provides adaptable and accessible approaches to integrating games into language instruction. For researchers, it opens pathways for future inquiry into the evolving role of games in language education, including their intersection with technology, culture, and pedagogy.

The chapters collectively examine how game-based language enhancement strategies—particularly those rooted in indigenous practices—operate across diverse contexts and how they impact learning outcomes. In bringing these perspectives together, we hope to inspire continued dialogue, innovation, and collaboration in the field.

We extend our gratitude to the contributors for their insightful work and to the readers who seek to reimagine language teaching and learning through creative, inclusive, and evidence-based approaches.

## ORGANIZATION OF THE BOOK

As Editors, we are pleased to introduce the chapters in this volume, each of which offers a distinctive yet interconnected perspective on the role of games, play, and culturally grounded practices in language teaching and learning across diverse contexts.

Chapter 1, authored by Annaly Strauss, foregrounds the pedagogical value of folklore and puppetry in early grade classrooms in Namibia. Drawing on socio-cultural and semiotic frameworks, the chapter demonstrates how storytelling through shadow puppetry can meaningfully support mother tongue instruction. Through multimodal analysis and teacher insights, it reveals how such approaches enhance oral language development, early literacy, and cultural identity, while also highlighting the structural challenges of limited resources and teacher training. The chapter ultimately calls for sustained professional development and culturally responsive pedagogies to strengthen foundational language learning.

In Chapter 2, Zinhle Nkosi examines the use of isiZulu folktales and riddles as dynamic tools for enhancing both language and critical thinking skills among primary school learners. The chapter underscores the interconnectedness of linguistic competence and cognitive development, illustrating how storytelling and riddling practices foster listening, speaking, reading, and writing alongside analytical and problem-solving abilities. It positions folklore as an engaging and effective pedagogical strategy that supports learners' holistic academic development.

Chapter 3 by Salmita Khumalo shifts attention to the home and community as vital sites of language learning. Through a Pedagogy-in-Participation lens and sociocultural theory, the chapter highlights the role of parents and indigenous games—such as kgati, clapping games, and storytelling—in supporting early language development. Drawing on narratives from mothers in South African communities, it repositions parents as co-educators and emphasizes the importance of recognizing Indigenous Knowledge Systems as rich resources for vocabulary development, narrative skills, and cultural continuity.

Chapter 4, by Onias Matumbu and Nomatter Kufarimani, explores the intersection of language preservation and digital innovation in Zimbabwe. Addressing the marginalization of Indigenous languages due to colonial legacies, the chapter presents an applied research study on the development of language-focused digital games. Through collaboration with cultural experts, the authors demonstrate how gamified, interactive experiences can revitalize Indigenous languages, offering a promising pathway for culturally grounded and technologically enhanced language learning.

In Chapter 5, Sohom Saha and Mahendra Singh examine how culturally responsive game-based learning can address literacy gaps in marginalized communities. Drawing on sociocultural and digital pedagogy frameworks, the chapter presents both theoretical and practical insights into designing inclusive learning environments that honor learners' linguistic and cultural identities. It offers implementation strategies, assessment considerations, and policy recommendations, positioning game-based learning as a transformative approach to equitable literacy education.

Chapter 6, authored by Maletšema Emsley and Mantsha Modiba, explores the role of indigenous Lobedu folk songs in enhancing language learning. Using a decolonial lens, the chapter illustrates how musical and poetic elements—such as rhythm, repetition, and metaphor—support memory, engagement, and linguistic development. Through analysis of the folk song "Ka totoma," the authors demonstrate how culturally embedded artistic expressions can enrich language teaching while affirming learners' identities and heritage.

Chapter 7 by Margaret Maja and Lerato Motaung investigates the use of game-based approaches to sustain the Sesotho language within multilingual township schools in South Africa. Grounded in interpretivist and sociocultural perspectives, the study highlights how games foster learner engagement, collaboration, and a sense of cultural ownership. The findings reinforce the importance of integrating culturally relevant games into the curriculum as a means of preserving linguistic heritage and strengthening home language use.

Chapter 8, authored by Xolisa Guzula, challenges traditional, monolingual approaches to biliteracy instruction through an exploration of gamesongs and multimodal pedagogies. Drawing on an auto-ethnographic case study of the Stars of Today Literacy Club, the chapter demonstrates how bilingual languaging, music, and art-based activities enhance vocabulary, rhythm, and overall biliteracy development. It positions learners as capable emergent bilinguals and advocates for more inclusive, play-based literacy practices.

Chapter 9 by Fortunate Madondo and Thaddeus Mahoso presents a strategic framework for integrating game-based learning into language instruction. Drawing on constructivist, self-determination, and cognitive load theories, the chapter highlights how carefully designed game mechanics can enhance motivation, engagement, and self-regulation. Through a case study in a rural context, it underscores the importance of aligning games with instructional goals and incorporating culturally responsive elements, including indigenous games.

In Chapter 10, Oindrilla Ghosh and Binod Kumar synthesize key theoretical frameworks that underpin game-based language learning. The chapter provides a comprehensive overview of constructivism, sociocultural theory, experiential learning, and flow theory, among others. It offers critical insights into how these frameworks inform the design of meaningful, engaging, and effective game-based learning environments, emphasizing scaffolding, feedback, and learner agency.

Chapter 11, authored by Kenan Cetin, focuses on digital game-based language learning within teacher education. Using the case of *Discovery Tour: Ancient Egypt*, the chapter illustrates how immersive digital environments can support preservice teachers in designing innovative, culturally enriched language lessons. It highlights the role of structured support in maximizing the pedagogical potential of digital games and fostering creativity and engagement among future educators.

In Chapter 12, Ayushi Zina and colleagues examine the complementary roles of digital and non-digital games in language teaching. Through empirical investigation, the chapter reveals how both forms enhance motivation, participation, and communicative competence, while also identifying practical challenges such as limited resources and training. It advocates for a blended approach that leverages the strengths of both formats to create inclusive and sustainable learning environments.

Finally, Chapter 13 by Moleboheng Mokhele-Ramulumo expands the discussion to early childhood education through the design of the *Renewable Rangers* wordless picture book. Integrating Indigenous Knowledge Systems with Global Citizenship

Education, the chapter presents a design-based approach to fostering self-directed learning, creativity, and environmental awareness. It illustrates how multimodal storytelling can support not only language development but also broader cognitive and social growth, positioning the resource as both a pedagogical tool and a model for transformative education.

Together, these chapters reflect the richness and diversity of game-based approaches to language teaching and learning. They collectively affirm the importance of culturally responsive, contextually grounded, and theoretically informed practices in shaping the future of language education.

## CONCLUSION

As Editors, we conclude this volume with a strong sense of the transformative potential that game-based approaches hold for language teaching and learning across diverse contexts. The chapters presented in this book collectively affirm that language development is most effective when it is meaningful, culturally grounded, and engaging for learners. By drawing on both traditional and contemporary forms of play—including folklore, indigenous games, music, storytelling, and digital innovations—this volume demonstrates that language learning can be both rigorous and joyful.

A key thread that runs throughout the book is the importance of context. Whether situated in rural, urban, or resource-constrained environments, the contributions emphasize that effective language pedagogy must be responsive to learners' linguistic, cultural, and social realities. Indigenous Knowledge Systems, in particular, emerge as powerful and often underutilized resources that not only support language acquisition but also affirm identity, heritage, and community belonging. At the same time, digital technologies and gamified learning environments offer new and exciting possibilities for expanding access, creativity, and interaction in language education.

Equally significant is the role of educators, parents, and communities as active agents in the learning process. This volume highlights the need for sustained teacher development, collaborative practices, and supportive policy frameworks to ensure that game-based learning is not treated as an occasional addition, but as an integral part of curriculum design and instructional practice. The insights offered across chapters underscore that meaningful integration requires thoughtful alignment between pedagogy, content, and context.

Importantly, this book also points toward future directions for research and practice. It calls for continued exploration of how game-based approaches can be adapted, scaled, and evaluated across varied educational settings. It invites scholars and practitioners to further examine the intersections of language, culture, technology, and play, and to develop innovative strategies that address persistent inequities in language and literacy education.

In bringing this collection together, we hope to contribute to a growing body of work that reimagines language education as inclusive, dynamic, and responsive to the needs of all learners. We trust that this volume will serve as a valuable resource for educators, researchers, policymakers, and communities seeking to harness the power of games to enrich language teaching and learning.

**Millicent Ngema**
*University of South Africa, South Africa*

**Nkidi Phatudi**
*University of South Africa, South Africa*

# Chapter 1
# The Use of Folklore/Folktales in Language Development (Teaching and Learning):
## Using Storytelling With Puppets to Promote Mother Tongue in the Early Grades

**Annaly M. Strauss**
http://orcid.org/0000-0003-2992-1885
*University of Namibia, Namibia*

**Jessica Mary-Ann Jansen**
*University of Namibia, Namibia*

## ABSTRACT

*This study examines contemporary folklore and puppetry as strategies to strengthen mother tongue instruction in Namibian early grades. The chapter is grounded in socio-cultural and semiotic perspectives. It uses multimodal analysis of a shadow puppet performance and teacher focus group interviews. Findings show puppetry enhances oral expression, literacy, and cultural identity but faces resource and training barriers. Professional development and culturally responsive practices are recommended to support mother tongue education.*

DOI: 10.4018/979-8-3373-4322-8.ch001

## INTRODUCTION

This chapter explores the use of contemporary folklore and puppetry as a teaching and learning strategy to support mother tongue instruction in early years. Highlighting the importance of the mother tongue, puppetry provides an engaging and culturally responsive approach to promoting language development in early-grade classrooms. Puppetry, an instructional art form that combines entertainment with education, acts as an effective medium for communication across diverse cultures and languages (Remer & Tzuriel, 2015). The mother tongue (first language) is vital in learning a second language (Cummins, 2000; Begi, 2014). In the multilingual Namibian society, Afrikaans and Khoekhoegowab as mother tongues are increasingly at risk of becoming endangered. However, scholars have emphasised that deliberate and mindful teaching is essential for providing diverse experiences and enabling children's active engagement in oral language (Amorsen & Wilson, 2020). Preserving the mother tongue requires intentional cultural and linguistic practices. Reinforcing the importance of the mother tongue, puppetry provides an engaging, culturally sensitive approach to supporting language development in early-grade classrooms.

## BACKGROUND

The mother tongue plays a crucial role in everyday life, supporting effective communication, social bonds, and cultural engagement. Elya et al. (2019) outline three key stages in developing speaking skills: word pronunciation, vocabulary learning, and sentence formation. In Namibia, however, indigenous mother tongues such as Afrikaans and Khoekhoegowab face notable decline. According to national census data (Namibia Statistics Agency, 2014), the percentage of households speaking Afrikaans has fallen from 11.4% in 2001 to 10.4% in 2011, while Khoekhoegowab experienced a slight decrease from 11.5% to 11.3% over the same period. Worsening this decline, Khoekhoegowab faces a shortage of qualified teachers, which restricts opportunities for meaningful instruction in schools (NBC Online, 2025, September).

## PUPPETRY IN EARLY LANGUAGE LEARNING

Using puppets in children's learning can capture their attention, foster interaction, and motivate participation. The use of puppets as a learning tool has a long-standing tradition in early childhood education and care (ECEC) classrooms, yet their application as a pedagogical resource remains limited in both ECEC institutions and teacher training (Forsberg Ahlcrona, 2012; Kröger & Nupponen, 2019). Puppets create a playful and engaging learning environment for early language development. One advantage of using puppets with young children is their visual appeal and their ability to both amuse and stimulate imagination in an engaging way (Tierney, 1995). Despite the recognised benefits of puppetry for early language development, there is a notable gap in its systematic use to support mother tongue instruction within Namibian ECEC settings and teacher training programmes. Hand puppets serve as a visual medium in storytelling, supporting children's oral language development by conveying messages through visual interaction. Over time, puppetry designers have adapted to advancing technologies by creating new forms, including stop-motion animation, digital manipulation (Kaplin, 2001), and virtual puppets. These various forms of puppetry have the potential to enrich storytelling and improve language learning experiences for young children. Kröger & Nupponen (2019) highlight how puppetry fosters meaningful communication, creative expression, collaboration, and positive classroom dynamics. Rolling (2012) urged educators to facilitate opportunities for pupils to articulate their narratives both visually and verbally within the classroom environment. In the same vein, the long-held belief is that we are beings who tell stories, and that the tales we tell move us and impact who we are and the world around us (Romanski, 2019).

## FOLKLORE AND CULTURAL LEARNING

Integrating puppetry with folklore offers a means to revive oral traditions while also supporting language and cultural learning. Folklore is defined as a narrative story, which can be categorised as an oral tradition (Kaltsum & Utami, 2015). Contemporary folklore and puppetry may serve as practical approaches to revitalising oral traditions in both teacher training and early language education during the initial grades. Folklore, exemplified by the Jakkals en Wolf stories, originates from Khoi oral traditions and has been subsequently adapted into Afrikaans children's literature (Van Niekerk, 2018). Folklore, as oral storytelling and communication, is essential for the development of learners' native language (Mzimela, 2016). Incorporating folklore into early childhood education in Namibia, whether in Afrikaans or Khoekhoegowab, may present valuable opportunities for language development and cultural education.

## THEORETICAL FRAMEWORK

Bakhtin (1981) explored the idea of dialogism, which creates imagined or figured worlds. Likewise, playful dialogue through storytelling with puppets illustrates

Bruner's (1985) view that young children develop meaning through interactive social contexts. Communication and folklore, such as folktales, are common ways of social interaction that create frameworks for encouraging social participation and sharing culture and values. These methods, including rhyme, rhythm, song, repetition, substitution, and verbal humour, lay an essential foundation for language learning in the early years. For instance, songs like Twinkle, Twinkle, Little Star use rhyme and repetition to help build vocabulary and phonological awareness. Bruner's (1985) theory aligns with Vygotsky's (1978) socio-cultural theory regarding the zone of proximal development (ZPD), scaffolding, and learning within a social community. When children listen to stories, they imagine unseen characters, form mental images based on what they hear, and think about experiences they have not personally had (Vygotsky, 1978). Therefore, storytelling allows teachers to support children's understanding and vocabulary by encouraging visualisation, discussion, and connections to personal experiences, while fostering language development within the zone of proximal development (Vygotsky, 1978; Bruner, 1985).

In early primary classrooms, children's ability to regulate speech and language is essential for literacy development (Reed & Lee, 2020). Puppetry in storytelling, conducted in the mother tongue, incorporates multisensory elements such as movement, dialogue, and gestures to enhance vocabulary, sentence structure, and understanding, supporting language learning in culturally relevant contexts. Telling stories in children's mother tongue, enriched with puppetry and cultural artefacts, may promote language development and active, multisensory engagement in early primary classrooms. Based on socio-cultural and dialogic theories, storytelling can be further improved through multisensory strategies that strengthen learning and participation.

## MULTI-SENSORY ENGAGEMENT ENHANCES LEARNING

Sensory processing involves the ability to take in information through the senses (such as touch, movement, smell, taste, vision, and hearing), organise and interpret that information, and respond appropriately (Murray et al., 2009). Through various sensory experiences, individuals learn to manage and regulate their behaviour as well as react to different stimuli. In early-year classrooms, activities like storytelling are more effective when they involve multisensory stimulation, as this enhances children's learning and memory compared to using only one sensory channel (Shams & Seitz, 2008). Additionally, creating spaces that help children regulate their senses and teach them strategies to recognise and communicate their difficulties can boost participation in the classroom and encourage social play within the school environment (Schramm, 2021). Cultural probes, such as artefacts, images, or objects from children's own communities, can be added to storytelling to make the activity more meaningful and culturally relevant, thereby increasing engagement and learning.

Furthermore, using modern teaching strategies, especially in multilingual settings, can enhance learning outcomes when applied effectively in early years. However, it is not enough for children to passively observe an activity, such as a teacher using hand puppets during storytelling; they should also have chances to retell the story using the same aids. In practice, teachers are encouraged to develop their own teaching materials, like stories, and to adjust the cognitive load of multisensory engagement by utilising tools such as silhouettes. A recent study by Aprilianti and Baa (2024) demonstrates that code-switching in multilingual classrooms improves comprehension, confidence, and participation by enabling learners to draw on their home language when necessary. While multisensory storytelling enhances vocabulary and understanding, multilingual classrooms often depend on strategic language choices, like code-switching, to support comprehension and participation.

## LANGUAGE EXPOSURE AND VOCABULARY DEVELOPMENT

Multisensory storytelling keeps children engaged while enhancing language skills and broadening vocabulary. Vocabulary can be defined as the words an individual recognises and uses, or those within a language or subject (Cambridge University Press, n.d.). In this context, oral storytelling, singing, rhyming, and reading aloud are recognised as essential practices in supporting language development (Stephens, 2018) and expanding vocabulary. Evidence further indicates that multisensory storytelling positively influences vocabulary growth (Walisundara, & Ranaweera, 2020), while explicit vocabulary teaching during storytelling improves children's word acquisition (Strauss & Bipath, 2020). Additionally, pointing to and tracking words during shared reading promotes print awareness and helps internalise word features (Ehri & Sweet, 1991), ultimately encouraging natural vocabulary development through interactive experiences. Loy et al. (2021) find that puppetry fosters vocabulary development and listening-speaking skills by creating engaging, non-threatening interactions, which are crucial for learners facing learning challenges.

## PRACTICAL APPLICATION OF CODE-SWITCHING AND LANGUAGE CHOICES

Teachers frequently employ code-switching to clarify concepts, grammar, and give instructions in multilingual classrooms. Conversely, Leoanak & Amalo (2018) emphasised its role in managing classrooms, motivating participation, and clarifying vocabulary. In a recent study, Strauss and Marshal (2024) observed that students preferred code-switching, noting that they sometimes find it easier to understand when lecturers switch to a local language, such as Afrikaans or Khoekhoegowab. Code-switching involves alternating between two or more languages within a single interaction. Research by Datokarama et al. (2020) confirms that when used strategically, code-switching serves as an effective pedagogical scaffold. It improves comprehension, reduces learner anxiety, and boosts confidence, especially among lower-proficiency students in EFL or multilingual classrooms. Children supporting peers who are less knowledgeable in language learning, for example, through translating and explaining concepts, help create a shared peer learning experience for all (Strauss & Marshall, 2024).

## ENHANCEMENT OF LEARNER PARTICIPATION AND BEHAVIOUR

In many cultures, including Namibia, folklore is a vital part of storytelling, reflecting a community's shared wisdom, traditions, and moral lessons. Effective teaching and learning depend not only on cognitive engagement but also on students' behavioural, emotional, and social involvement. Research shows how folktales, storytelling, and play nurture children's social imagination, creativity, and language development (Hajisoteriou, Angelides, & Nicolaou, 2021; Holmes, Rees, & Guillemin, 2017). Incorporating sounds, gestures, poses, and movements enhances the storytelling experience while supporting key educational goals such as improving attention, engagement, and understanding (Noviana et al., 2023). Moreover, storytelling with puppets promotes learners' emotional engagement and social participation, positively affecting classroom behaviour. However, empirical evidence of its impacts in diverse early-grade classrooms remains limited (Xiao et al., 2023). Although interactive storytelling encourages engagement, resource limitations and challenges in teacher training in Namibia restrict the effective implementation of these methods.

## TEACHER TRAINING AND RESOURCE CHALLENGES

Within a South African context, multiple constraints have been reported regarding the adequacy of teacher training and in-service teachers at rural schools in the foundation phase (Ang et al., 2025). These challenges include insufficient knowledge and skills, as well as a trivialised attitude among some in-service teachers when utilising valuable learning and teaching support material (LTSM) in learning environments (e.g., visual media displayed above eye level, locked-away literacy resources, educational toys, and creative materials). Furthermore, these authors revealed that limited understanding of the national curriculum, unsuitable pedagogical approaches, reciting stories in a choir, limited child-teacher interactions, and various other challenges hinder language learning. Namibia's Junior Primary education faces similar challenges. Jansen and Ngema (2024) alluded that teachers teach phonics and reading but lack curricular guidelines on creative writing and feel ill-equipped to teach it effectively.

Integrating imaginative and creative thinking into children's educational experiences builds a strong foundation for shaping future worlds (Leggett, 2017). In a study, Oktaviani, Sari, and Situmorang (2024) examined the effectiveness of show-and-tell, role-play, and storytelling techniques in improving English speaking skills. The study found that storytelling had a very high effect size (1.34), indicating its significant influence on enhancing speaking abilities. Although storytelling and interactive techniques support language development, limited training, curricular guidance, and resources may hinder their implementation in Namibian Junior Primary classrooms. Challenges in teacher training, pedagogy, and classroom resources can restrict interactive storytelling, especially when parental and community support for early literacy is absent.

## PARENTAL AND COMMUNITY ENGAGEMENT IN EARLY LITERACY

In a study, Strauss and Bipath (2020) found that in Namibia, the impact of demographic factors, especially socioeconomic status, on parents' reading practices and children's emergent literacy remains insufficiently explored. Reading skills go beyond simply decoding individual words, phrases, or passages; their main goal is to extract and develop meaningful understanding from a broad range of texts, known as reading comprehension (Smith et al., 2021). Parents who are strongly inclined towards reading tend to read often, have larger collections of books, and engage regularly in reading activities with their children, thereby supporting early literacy development (Niklas & Schneider, 2017). However, limited parental participation and weak school–community partnerships have been shown to impede the promotion of storytelling and reading, especially in rural and resource-limited settings. Enhancing teacher preparation and classroom practices is therefore crucial to address gaps in home and community support for children's early literacy development.

## METHODOLOGY

This chapter adopts a generic qualitative approach to examine how puppetry is used in storytelling with pre-primary and Grade 1 learners and to gather insights from teachers in two regions of Namibia. A multimodal analysis was conducted on shadow puppet performances. The puppet silhouettes were projected from inside a backlit box to tell the story, titled Ansare's Big Ears by Fritzina Stein (B. ED final-year student). For Kress (2010), "the social semiotic theory is interested in meaning in all forms and meaning arises in social environments and social interactions" (p.54). Kress (2010) explains that the core unit of semiotics is the sign, a fusion of form and meaning. Kress offers a broader perspective on communication in general, which is especially relevant to language learning.

A sample of 13 teachers from the Khomas region and 17 teachers from the Hardap region of Namibia participated in four focus groups, to explore how storytelling can support mother tongue development and how puppets might serve as an effective teaching and learning strategy. The interviews also asked teachers about the advantages and challenges of using storytelling with puppets. The interview transcripts were analysed through a qualitative data analysis process (Strauss & Corbin, 2008), which involves three stages: open coding, axial coding, and selective or analytical coding (Bogdan & Biklen, 1998).

By combining qualitative research with multimodality and semiotic analysis, this chapter emphasises both the pedagogical value and practical challenges of using puppets to promote mother tongue development, employing puppetry and storytelling as strategies to enhance language learning. The data included audiotaped recordings and field notes that were transcribed into text. From this data, themes were identified. This generic qualitative approach, mixing methods, enabled data triangulation, thereby increasing the credibility and trustworthiness of the findings. In the Hardap region, Afrikaans and Khoekhoegowab are the main languages, with English serving as the primary medium of communication within these multilingual settings, where several other local languages, including Oshiwambo, Otjiherero, and Damara/Nama, are also spoken. Afrikaans and Khoekhoegowab reflect the linguistic diversity of the communities involved in data collection.

The Hardap region was selected as a research site because it exemplifies a semi-rural educational setting. In contrast, the Khomas region provides an urban context for analysing language use and teaching methods across different socio-linguistic environments. The presence of multilingual learners and the use of English as a medium of instruction in various language contexts make these regions suitable for examining the impact of teaching strategies on language learning outcomes.

## BIOGRAPHIC INFORMATION OF THE PARTICIPANTS

### Teacher Demographics

The demographic profile of teachers provides insights into their professional backgrounds, training routes, and linguistic skills, which in turn shape their instructional methods. Recognising these factors is crucial, as teachers' experience, education, and language use directly affect how effectively they can support early literacy and mother tongue development in diverse classrooms.

*Table 1. Years of experience*

| Region | No of teachers | Years of teaching in years | Region | No. of teachers | Years of teaching in years |
|---|---|---|---|---|---|
| Hardap | 17 | | Khomas | 13 | |
| | 6 | 0-5 | | 0-5 | 2 |
| | 5 | 6-7 | | 6-7 | 3 |
| | 3 | 8-12 | | 8-12 | 4 |
| | 2 | 13-15 | | 13-15 | 4 |
| | 1 | More | | More | |

Table 1 displays the teaching experience of the participants. The educators demonstrated a variety of experience levels, ranging from newcomers to highly experienced teachers. Most teachers (8) had between 6 and 7 years of experience, followed by seven teachers with 0-5 and 8-12 years respectively, six with 13–15 years, and one with over 15 years of teaching experience in the Hardap region. In the Khomas region, two teachers had 0-5 years of experience, while two had between 10 and 14 years.

### Teacher training institutions

Most of the teachers in both regions, a total of twenty (20), completed their training at the University of Namibia, in Windhoek and Keetmanshoop. Other institutions included Montessori in Walvis Bay (three teachers), IOL (three teachers), IUM (five teachers), and the UNAM-INSET programme (two teachers). Training institutions play a crucial role in shaping teachers' pedagogical approaches and preparing them to address the linguistic and cultural diversity in their classrooms.

## Languages of the Participants

Participants were asked about the languages they grew up speaking at home. Responses from the two groups were as follows:

**Hardap region 1:** Afrikaans, Khoekhoegowab, Rukwangali, and Otjiherero

**Khomas region 2:** Khoekhoegowab, Afrikaans

While most teachers mainly use English and Afrikaans in instruction, the learners come from various linguistic backgrounds, including Oshiwambo, Afrikaans, Khoekhoegowab, and other local languages. The difference between teachers' languages and learners' home languages underscores the need for instructional strategies such as puppetry to leverage learners' full linguistic repertoires.

## Observed Changes in School Community and Classroom Language Practices

Teachers observed several changes in language practices within the school community over time. The teachers from Khomas indicated that learners are eager to participate during lessons, but their mother tongue can sometimes pose a barrier, creating difficulties. Both groups observed a significant trend: children are becoming more aware of English through watching TV and accessing multimedia content on YouTube in Afrikaans and English. Unfortunately, these resources are not available in Khoekhoegowab (KKG). Teachers are unable to translate the sources into the mother tongue of KKG learners.

Furthermore, a participant revealed that

*There are many new and engaging stories for young children. Old stories, such as 'Sleeping Beauty', are outdated and no longer culturally relevant. We need exciting, fresh stories for Afrikaans and KKG that are affordable. Although new trends exist for storytelling, the Ministry of Education does not support teachers in providing materials.*

A teacher observed, "Code-switching has emerged as an important strategy to engage learners who may struggle to understand lesson content, helping them participate more effectively in classroom activities." This reflects a common classroom practice where bilingual teachers alternate between languages in separate sentences or clauses without blending them. For example: *"We will read a story. Ons lees nou n storie."* In this instance, the teacher switches between English and Afrikaans while keeping the meaning intact, to illustrate traditional code-switching.

Participants in a focus group observed a lack of pride in speaking Khoekhoegowab. Learners tend to use the language only in classrooms where it is formally taught. Additionally, parents are often hesitant to send their children to mother tongue classrooms, which affects the consistent use and transmission of local languages within the school community and beyond. Parents' language preference often leads to reluctance to enrol children in mother tongue classrooms, despite national policies supporting mother tongue instruction in the early grades. As a result, the consistent use and transmission of local languages within the school community are compromised, limiting opportunities for learners to develop strong literacy skills in their home language.

## Role of the Mother Tongue in Early Grade Learners' Development

Recognising the mother tongue as the foundation of early education is vital, as it fosters cognitive, language, and socio-cultural development, while enabling learners to expand their understanding based on their existing knowledge.

A participating teacher emphasised this point,

*"That is the language they know. The foundation must be established. They come to school with the knowledge of their mother tongue. When they arrive at school, they understand and can relate to what they are taught."*

Another participant complained about the lack of resources in all Namibian languages, which hampers the teaching of mother tongue in schools.

## Integrating Learners' Mother Tongue in Storytelling and Reading Lessons

Ollerhead and Pennington (2024) emphasise that multilingual storytelling, which affirms children's home languages and cultural identities, greatly enhances their oral language development. This supports the idea that incorporating both standard language and dialect, as well as orality, in early literacy settings can promote stronger language skills.

A teacher remarked,

*We read stories, do vocabulary or theme words, and explain them in both English and the mother tongue." Another said, "I read stories aloud, show pictures in sequence, sometimes use puppets, and ask learners to role-play the story. Children retell the story in their own words. "*

A participating teacher stated, "These days, schools are no longer provided with any resources." Another teacher confirmed that in the past, they were supplied with flashcards, sentence strips, and games to support early grades in learning their mother tongue. Currently, there are no resources.

Teachers observed that the Ministry of Education provides them with a Teacher's Manual, which they use as a resource to tell the stories outlined in the manual. These stories, such as The Three Little Pigs (Halliwell-Phillipps, 1843) and Little

Red Riding Hood (Grimm & Grimm, 1812), originate from language teaching of Namibia's colonial past and are not necessarily suitable for mother tongue instruction or engaging for learners. Moreover, these prescribed stories are culturally distant from the learners' lived experiences, reducing their relevance and weakening the potential of storytelling as a pedagogical strategy. However, teachers also miss more interactive and culturally relevant resources that could support language or mother tongue learning. They mentioned that the Ministry of Education does not allocate a budget for resources, which forces teachers to improvise. This lack of materials limits the potential of storytelling and reduces opportunities for mother-tongue literacy development.

## Engaging Families and Caregivers in Storytelling Through Their Home Language

Storytelling is a practice found across cultures, serving as a means through which communities safeguard their beliefs, values, wisdom, and cultural experiences, while passing them on to future generations (Ntwalana & Matiso, 2024). By inviting families to participate in storytelling, teaching can foster a meaningful language experience rooted in the child's home culture. Parents and caregivers can share traditional folktales, personal anecdotes, or songs in the mother tongue, whether during classroom visits or through recorded media. They can also assist in selecting or creating bilingual books that reflect the child's heritage, ensuring the content is both accessible and culturally relevant. This collaborative approach not only enhances children's language comprehension and expression but also nurtures their cultural identity and strengthens the bond between home and school. Ollerhead and Pennington (2024) describe how a "multilingual storytelling" initiative, specifically their "multilingual story box" project, increased oral language engagement among emergent bilingual Year 1 learners by integrating children's home languages and cultural knowledge into classroom literacy activities.

In both regions, Khomas and Hardap, participants observed that involving parents during lessons is difficult. Parents are often busy or working during the day. However, a teacher stated that "stories are told from generation to generation, but we are not around the fire anymore, but on smartphones."

Using puppets to share traditional stories in early grade teaching may help pass vital knowledge and cultural wisdom from one generation to the next, engagingly and memorably.

## Multimodality

*Figure 1. Puppet boxes*

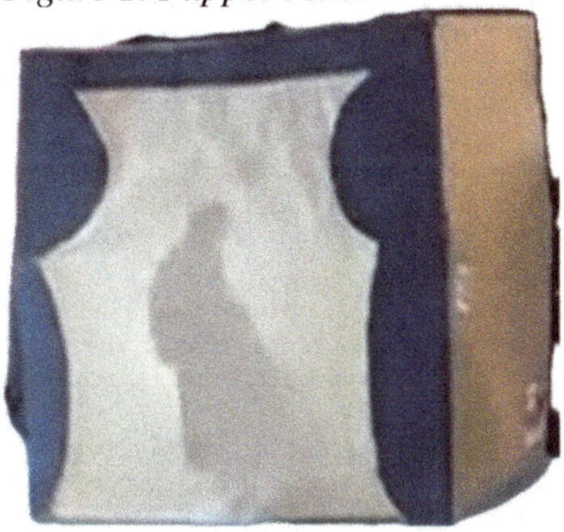

Based on the story, 'Ansare's Big Ears' by Fritzina Stein (Unpublished), the images depict shadow puppet theatres made from a box and cut-out figures representing Ansare first and then Ansare and the elderly woman. The two figures appear human-like. In the second picture, the elder woman is bent forward, and Ansare stands upright, wearing a large hat. These character outlines foster children's curiosity and use of imagination, which are essential for storytelling and language development.

These puppets were used to retell the story in Khoekoegowab and Afrikaans, outlining the beginning, middle and end.

*Box 1.*

| | |
|---|---|
| Khoekoegowab | **Gao\gôas Ansares di Kai ǂGaedi**<br>**Xoa-aos:** Fritzina Stein<br>Gaxu, gaxu ǁaeb !kharu hâse, sorexa !nū !hūbaib ais ge îsa tsî khoexa!nâ gao\gôas Ansare ti \on hâsa gere ǁan. Xawe Ansares ge ge ǂkhî tama hâ ī.<br>''Tita ge ti ǂgaedi xa !gâibahe tama hâ, kaise ǂkhari'' tis ge ra mî. ǁÎs ge \gapade gere tani. ǁÎs ge !gaidī-ūhe ra ǁgamron tsîna gere ā tsâ, \gui xū-i tsîn ge ge hui tama hâ ī. ǁÎs ge \guitsē gā-ai kaira taras tawa ra sī. ''Hui te ǁkhās a?'' tis ge Ansaresa ra dî. ''Î'' tis ge kaira tarasa ra mî, ''xawe sa ǂgaedi ge kaise kaise nî kai!'' Ansares ge danas \kha î ti ra ǁgau. ''Dītsâ ǂgao ta ra'' Nē kaira taras ge amrosa ra ǁnae ,....''Kai ǂgaedi, kai ǂgaedi, ge !gâise ra !gâ'' POEF!Ansares ge nēsisa kai!gâ hāgū ǂgaede ūhâ! ǁÎs ge mûnaixūs !nâ ra kōsen. ''Ae, titse!'' tis ge ra !au. ''Shhhhh, !gâ re'' tis ge kaira tarasa ra mî.<br>Ansares ge !nō tsî !auga ra ǂoa. ǁÎs ge ra ǁnâu ǂoab ta ǁnae \gausa, tsî ǂnuiwǂgoagu ra !hoa \gausa. ǁÎs ge ǁkhāti haidi ra tuwu \gaus tsîna ra ǁnâu. ǂGui \gôan ge !haese \khā-e xu ra \khī, ''Mîba da tarenas ta ǁnâu?'' tin ge ra dî. Ansares ge \nom tsî ra mî ,''Hoaraga xūna ta ge ra ǁnâu'' ti.<br>ǁÎs ge nēsisa kaise ǂnīsa ǁîs kai ǂgaera ai. ǁÎs ge ǁîs ǂgaera \kha ǂhôarona ǁgam tsî khoena gere hui. ǁNā tsēsa xus ge Gao\gôa Ansaresa ǂoaǂoaǂamsa !gâ-aos ase !hūbaib !nâ ge ǂansa ī.<br>**ǁKhāǁkhās:** Mâ \gui\guibe khoe-i hoa-i ge ǁî-i di \gaub ai a \ō-aisa.<br>(\Ō-aisase !Gao!gaos ǁgau!nâs \gôaron !aroma Dr. Annaly Strauss<br>(Khoekhoegowab ǂnûi!khunis !Gôahesab Donald Casius Jossob) |
| Afrikaans | **Prinses Ansare se Groot Ore**<br>**Skrywer:** Fritzina Stein<br>Lank, lank gelede, in 'n sonnige land ver van hier, het daar 'n mooi en vriendelike prinses met die naam Ansare gewoon. Maar Ansare was nie gelukkig nie.<br>"Ek hou nie van my ore nie," sê sy. "Hulle is te klein!" Sy het hoede probeer dra. Sy het towerdrankies probeer.... Niks het gewerk nie. Eendag het sy na 'n wyse ou vrou gegaan. "Kan jy my help?" vra Ansare. "Ja," sê die ou vrou, "maar jou ore sal baie, baie groot wees!" Ansare knik. "Ek wil probeer." Die ou vrou het 'n liedjie gesing...."Groot ore, groot ore, luister mooi..."<br>POEF! Ansare het nou reuse-varkore gehad! Sy kyk in die spieël. "O nee!" gil sy. "Shhh," sê die ou vrou. "Luister!"<br>Ansare gaan toe buite toe. Sy hoor die wind sing. Sy hoor die miere praat. Sy hoor selfs hoe die bome fluister! Gou het kinders van oral gekom. "Vertel vir ons wat jy hoor!" sê hulle. Ansare glimlag. "Ek hoor alles!"<br>Nou was sy trots op haar groot ore. Sy het dit gebruik om stories te vertel en mense te help. En van daardie dag af was Prinses Ansare die beste luisteraar in die hele wye wêreld.<br>**Les:** Almal is spesiaal op hulle eie manier!<br>*(Vertaal en aangepas vir voorskoolse kinders deur Dr. Annaly Strauss)* |

Essentially, using puppetry in multiple languages not only brought Ansare's Big Ears story to life but also created an engaging, culturally rich, and participatory learning environment that enhanced learners' imagination, language skills, and appreciation of their mother tongue. Research by Nkomo, Magxala, and Lebopa (2023) demonstrates that reading and storytelling with children fosters brain development and imagination, teaches children about language and emotions, and strengthens the relationship between the child and the caregiver.

*Figure 2. Narrating the story in the mother tongue*

The figure depicts a storytelling session in Khoekoegowab, using puppet silhouettes to engage pre-primary learners. The two teachers, foregrounded in the figure, narrated the story. Speaking in the learners' mother tongue helps them to understand, build cultural bonds, and strengthen their linguistic identity. This method supports early literacy and language development, while also connecting the story to the learners' personal lives, experiences, and prior knowledge.

The shadow puppets provide a visual representation of the story. The learners observed the characters and imagined their actions. They stayed engaged with the puppets throughout the story. They took part in prediction, promoting play-based learning and involvement.

The seating arrangement allowed the learners to concentrate on the shadow puppet box, demonstrating a high level of interest. Some learners raised their hands when asking questions, displaying their enthusiasm and willingness to participate in their mother tongue. The dual role of the teachers was to facilitate the story session smoothly and support each other in encouraging learners' participation.

## Benefits for Mother Tongue Development

Previous studies, Mujahidah, Damayanti, and Afiif (2021), show that using hand puppets in storytelling provides significant benefits for young learners' language development. Puppetry not only captures children's attention and encourages active participation in lessons but also enhances their oral expression, listening comprehension, and receptive language skills. Additionally, puppets offer opportunities for children to expand their vocabulary, improve early literacy, and build self-confidence in communication. Notably, the interactive nature of puppetry allows learners to retell stories in their own words, thereby strengthening word recognition, narrative sequencing, and overall oral language abilities (Mujahidah et al., 2021). In storytelling, using puppets helps support mother tongue development, which can enhance comprehension, meaning-making, and memory retention. As a result, oral language, cultural connections, and socio-emotional bonds are strengthened. Puppetry is a culturally responsive and developmentally appropriate teaching method. When teachers include the mother tongue alongside puppets during storytelling, it engages learners, encourages participation, and makes lessons more enjoyable. Furthermore, learners' linguistic and cultural backgrounds can be recognised within a multilingual setting.

## Technology and Mother Tongue Language Learning

On the question of how the use of technology supports mother tongue learning and audio stories in local languages, a teacher revealed that "I try, but the school's WIFI is far, unless I download something to show the learners when I have data. Sometimes I bring my laptop to school, or maybe I bring a USB with songs downloaded from YouTube for the learners to sing." Another teacher said, "It is a struggle, and the school do not have LCD projectors in classes." Laudari and Maher (2019) argue that the school-level barriers include the absence of ICT infrastructure, old or poorly maintained hardware, and a lack of suitable educational software. Similarly, the teacher-level barriers include a lack of teacher ICT skills, a lack of teacher confidence, and a lack of pedagogical teacher training.

In Namibia, two recent digital tools supporting mother tongue instruction are the Nam Read app (Smart Kidz Club, 2020), launched during Namibia Reads on March 21, 2020, and the e-Tale website (https://dev.taleafrica.com/), designed for teachers. Nam Read offers learners interactive stories, phonics exercises, and vocabulary activities in their mother tongue, helping to develop foundational literacy skills and fostering a love of reading from an early age. Conversely, e-Tale functions as a resource hub for teachers, providing access to a wide array of digital storybooks and instructional materials that can be utilised to plan lessons and engage learners in classroom practice. Together, these tools provide promising support for promoting multilingual literacy and enhancing language learning by connecting learners' home languages with English in meaningful ways. However, teachers in these focus groups were unaware of both the Nam Read app and e-Tale, reflecting a broader challenge of limited computer literacy and lack of exposure to digital platforms and ICTs (Strauss & Bipath, 2021). While innovative digital tools for mother tongue learning exist, their potential impact remains limited unless infrastructural barriers are addressed and teachers are adequately trained and supported to integrate them into everyday classroom practice.

## SOLUTIONS AND RECOMMENDATIONS

To address the lack of culturally relevant resources in local languages, the study introduced puppetry as a creative and contextually adaptable teaching strategy. Puppetry enables teachers to engage learners in their mother tongue while promoting imagination, participation, and oral language development without relying on costly or unavailable resources.

This chapter recommends professional development for teachers on the integration of puppetry and technology to strengthen their capacity to support mother tongue instruction. In addition, it advocates for the inclusion of interactive and culturally relevant literacy practices that can enhance learning outcomes across diverse regions.

## CONCLUSION

This chapter illustrates how teachers' training, experience, and linguistic skills shape their support for early literacy and mother tongue development in Namibia's multilingual classrooms. Teachers employ strategies such as storytelling, code-switching, and puppetry to engage learners and build on their cultural and linguistic backgrounds. However, these efforts are constrained by limited resources, parental preferences, and insufficient institutional support. While digital tools hold promises for strengthening multilingual literacy, their potential remains underutilised due to infrastructural and training gaps. Addressing these challenges through targeted teacher preparation, culturally relevant materials, and stronger collaboration with families and policymakers is vital to sustaining mother tongue literacy and promoting inclusive, equitable learning opportunities.

## REFERENCES

Amorsen, A., & Wilson, D. (2020). Intentional teaching to support oral language development. *Practical Literacy: The Early and Primary Years, 25*(1), 35–37.

Ang, L., Du Preez, H., Du Plessis, A., Basson, L., Ebersöhn, L., & Gu, Q. (2025). The role of early childhood development and education (ECDE) in supporting learning and well-being in rural early childhood and primary schools in South Africa. *International Journal of Early Years Education, 33*(2), 272–289. DOI: 10.1080/09669760.2023.2259953

Aprilianti, R., & Baa, D. (2024). Code-switching in multilingual classrooms helps students feel more included by enabling them to express themselves in a language they are comfortable with. *American Journal of Teacher Education, 45*(2), 112–125.

Bakhtin, M. M. (1981). *The dialogic imagination: Four essays*. University of Texas Press.

Begi, N. (2014). The use of the mother tongue as a language of instruction in the early years of school is to preserve Kenyan culture. *Journal of Education and Practice, 5*(3), 37–49.

Bogdan, R. C., & Biklen, S. K. (1998). *Qualitative education research* (3rd ed.). Allyn & Bacon.

Bruner, J. (1985). Models of the Learner. *Educational Researcher, 14*(6), 5–8. DOI: 10.3102/0013189X014006005

Cambridge University Press. (n.d.). Vocabulary. In the Cambridge Dictionary. Cambridge University Press. Retrieved 6 September 2025, from https://dictionary.cambridge.org/dictionary/english/vocabulary

Cummins, J. (2000). *Language, Power and Pedagogy: Bilingual Children in the Crossfire*. Multilingual Matters.

Datokarama, A. S., Abbas, H., & Patak, A. A. (2020). Teachers' and students' perceptions of the use of code-switching in the English classroom. Exposure. *Journal of English Language Education, 9*(2), 235–248. DOI: 10.26618/exposure.v9i2.3832

Ehri, L. C., & Sweet, J. (1991). Fingerpoint-reading of memorized text: What enables beginners to process the print? *Reading Research Quarterly*, 442-462.
**ADDITIONAL RESOURCES** https://youtube.com/shorts/7XQo7haQOxw?si=OBAHl4WHk1xVg-C7 https://youtu.be/kIXnbkY8xsE?feature=shared

Forsberg Ahlcrona, M. (2012). The puppet's communicative potential as a mediating tool in preschool education. *International Journal of Early Childhood, 44*(2), 171–184. DOI: 10.1007/s13158-012-0060-3

Hajisoteriou, C., Angelides, P., & Nicolaou, C. (2021). Empowering children to speak out and take action on social justice issues: The use of folktales and collaborative storytelling as tools of social imagination. *British Educational Research Journal, 48*(2), 253–271. DOI: 10.1002/berj.3765

Holmes, R. M., Rees, A., & Guillemin, D. (2017). The relationship between young children's language abilities, creativity, play, and storytelling. *Early Child Development and Care, 189*(2), 244–254. DOI: 10.1080/03004430.2017.1314274

Jansen, J. M. A., & Ngema, M. (2024). Challenges Experienced by Teachers in Implementing the Creative Writing Curriculum. *Reading and Writing, 15*(1), 1–11.

Kaltsum, H. U., & Utami, R. D. (2015). Folklore as an English teaching medium for young learners. *Proceedings of ISETH (International Summit on Science, Technology, and Humanity)*, 386–392.

Kaplin, S. (2001). A Puppet Tree, A Model for the Field of Puppet Theatre, in *Puppets, Masks, and Performing Objects*, Ed. by John Bell (TDR Books; The MIT Press, 2001), pp. 18–25

Kress, G. (2010). *Multimodality: A social semiotic approach to contemporary communication*. Routledge.

Kröger, T., & Nupponen, A. M. (2019). Puppet as a pedagogical tool: A literature review. *International Electronic Journal of Elementary Education, 11*(4), 393–401. DOI: 10.26822/iejee.2019450797

Laudari, S., & Maher, D. (2019). Barriers of ICT use in EFL teacher education courses in Nepal: An activity-theory perspective. *J. NELTA, 24*(1-2), 77–94. DOI: 10.3126/nelta.v24i1-2.27681

Leggett, N. (2017). Early childhood creativity: Challenging educators to intentionally develop creative thinking in children. *Early Childhood Education Journal, 45*(6), 845–853. DOI: 10.1007/s10643-016-0836-4

Leoanak, S. P. P., & Amalo, B. K. (2018). Teachers' beliefs and perceptions of code-switching in English as a foreign language classroom. *SHS Web of Conferences, 42*, 00034. EDP Sciences. https://doi.org/DOI: 10.1051/shsconf/20184200034

Mujahidah, N., Damayanti, E., & Afiif, A. (2021). The role of storytelling methods using hand puppets in early children's language development. *Child Education Journal, 3*(2), 78–91. DOI: 10.33086/cej.v3i2.2129

Murray, E. A., Lane, S. J., & Murray, D. G. (2009). Physiological and behavioural differences in sensory processing. *Frontiers in Integrative Neuroscience, 3*(29). Advance online publication. DOI: 10.3389/neuro.07.029.2009

Mzimela, J. (2016). Exploring the role of teaching using folklore in developing grade R learners' mother tongue. *Studies of Tribes and Tribals, 14*(2), 129–137. DOI: 10.1080/0972639X.2016.11886740

Namibia Statistics Agency. (2014). *Languages spoken in Namibian households* [Census data].

Niklas, F., & Schneider, W. (2017). Home learning environment and development of child competencies from kindergarten until the end of elementary school. *Contemporary Educational Psychology, 49*, 263–274. DOI: 10.1016/j.cedpsych.2017.03.006

Nkomo, S. A., Magxala, X. P., & Lebopa, N. (2023). Early literacy experiences of two children during the COVID-19 lockdown in South Africa: A semi-ethnographic study. *Journal of Early Childhood Literacy, 23*(1), 141–174. DOI: 10.1177/14687984231154351

Noviana, E., Syahza, A., Putra, Z. H., Hadriana, Y., Erlinda, S., Putri, D. R., Rusandi, M. A., & Biondi Situmorang, D. D. (2023). Why is didactic transposition in disaster education needed by prospective elementary school teachers? *Heliyon, 9*(4), e15413. DOI: 10.1016/j.heliyon.2023.e15413

Ntwalana, Y., & Matiso, N. H. (2024). Preserving Human Culture in Schools Through Oral Storytelling: Perspectives From Teachers in Eastern Cape, South Africa.

Ollerhead, S., & Pennington, C. (2024). Multilingual storytelling as culturally sustaining pedagogy: Reimagining early literacy in diverse classrooms. *Ethnography and Education, 19*(1), 1–18. DOI: 10.1177/14687984241303390

Ollerhead, S., & Pennington, G. (2024). Starting small: Engaging young learners with literacy through multilingual storytelling. *Journal of Early Childhood Literacy*. Advance online publication. DOI: 10.1177/14687984241303390

NBC Online. (2025, September). *Shortage of qualified teachers for Khoekhoegowab, Setswana, and Afrikaans persists.* Retrieved from NBC News.

Reed, J., & Lee, E. L. (2020). The Importance of Oral Language Development in Young Literacy Learners: Children Need to Be Seen and Heard. *Dimensions of Early Childhood*, *48*(3), 6–9.

Remer, R., & Tzuriel, D. (2015). "I teach better with the puppet"–Use of puppet as a mediating tool in Kindergarten Education–An evaluation. *American Journal of Educational Research*, *3*(3), 356–365. DOI: 10.12691/education-3-3-15

Rolling, J. H.Jr. (2012). Sacred structures: Narrating lifeworlds and implications for urban arts education practice. *Studies in Art Education*, *53*(2), 112–124. DOI: 10.1080/00393541.2012.11518856

Romanski, N. M. (2019). Reigniting the transformative power of puppets through narrative pedagogy, contemporary art, and transdisciplinary approaches in art education. *Art Education*, *72*(4), 36–42. DOI: 10.1080/00043125.2019.1602496

Schramm, H. (2021). *Implementing a sensory room for preschoolers* [Capstone project, Creighton University]. Creighton University.

Shams, L., & Seitz, A. R. (2008). Benefits of multisensory learning. *Trends in Cognitive Sciences*, *12*(11), 411–417. DOI: 10.1016/j.tics.2008.07.006

Smart Kidz Club, Inc. (2020, March 21). *Namibia Reads* [Mobile app]. Launched on Namibia's Independence Day. https://www.smartkidzclub.app/

Smith, R., Snow, P., Serry, T., & Hammond, L. (2021). The role of background knowledge in reading comprehension: A critical review. *Reading Psychology*, *42*(3), 214–240. https://www.creighton.edu/sites/default/files/2021-12/SPAHP-schrammhannah-3402420-59866244-schramm-hannah-capstone-presentation-2.pdf. DOI: 10.1080/02702711.2021.1888348

Stephens, V. (2018). National Library of New Zealand. Feel the rhythm: developing language through rhythm and rhyme. Available at: https://natlib.govt.nz/blog/posts/feel-the-rhythm-developing-language-throughrhythm-and-rhyme (accessed 06 September 2025).

Strauss, A., & Corbin, J. (2008). *Basics of qualitative research* (3rd ed.). Sage.

Strauss, A. M., & Bipath, K. (2020). Exploring the influence of parents' home reading practices on emergent literacy. *Journal for Language Teaching = Ijenali Yekufundzisa Lulwimi =. Tydskrif vir Taalonderrig*, *54*(1), 195–213. DOI: 10.4314/jlt.v54i1.5

Strauss, A. M., & Bipath, K. (2021). Evolving trends of distance learning for basic education in Namibia: A parental perspective during COVID-19 lockdown. *Journal for Language Teaching= Ijenali Yekufundzisa Lulwimi=. Tydskrif vir Taalonderrig*, *55*(1), 57–75. DOI: 10.4314/jlt.v55i1.3

Strauss, A. M., & Marshall, J. (2024). *Rural Undergraduate Students' Narratives of English Language Learning Within Multilingual Classroom Contexts: A Namibian Perspective.* Rural Education Journal. DOI: 10.55533/2643-9662.1517

Tierney, J. L. (1995). *Puppetry in Early Childhood Education*" (Doctoral Thesis), University of Massachusetts Amherst.

Van Niekerk, J. (2018). Afrikaans stories of Jackal and Hyena: Oral and written traditions. *Tydskrif vir Letterkunde*, *55*(3), 80–97. DOI: 10.17159/2309-9070/tvl.v.55i3.5511

Vygotsky, L. (1978). *Mind in Society*. Harvard University Press.

Walisundara, D. C., & Ranaweera, M. (2020). Shyamani Hettiarachchi. *Journal of Intellectual Disabilities*, *1*, 19.

Xiao, M., Amzah, F., & Rong, W. (2023). Experience of beauty: Valuing emotional engagement and collaboration in teacher-child storytelling activities. *International Journal of Learning. Teaching and Educational Research*, *22*(2), 165–187. DOI: 10.26803/ijlter.22.2.10

Chapter 2

# The Use of IsiZulu Folktales and Riddles in Enhancing Language and Critical Thinking Skills for Primary School Learners

**Zinhle Primrose Nkosi**
http://orcid.org/0000-0001-6086-3252
*University of KwaZulu-Natal, South Africa*

## ABSTRACT

*Folklore is a wide phenomenon among different cultures and languages across the globe. In isiZulu, more particularly, folklore is vital for developing and enhancing language and critical thinking skills, and these are useful for primary school teachers and learners, as learners learn while they enjoy. Language and critical thinking skills are both vital for effective communication and problem-solving. While language skills incorporate listening, speaking, reading, and writing skills, critical thinking involves analysing information and solving problems. Both these skills are interconnected, and they contribute to the learner's ability to understand and interact with the world effectively. This chapter aims to demonstrate how folktales and riddles can be used as techniques to enhance a primary school learner's language and critical language skills. Such skills play a vital role in the learner's academic achievement throughout their academic life, thus need to be adopted by primary school language teachers for effective teaching.*

DOI: 10.4018/979-8-3373-4322-8.ch002

## INTRODUCTION

Learning in the twenty-first century requires that teachers are able to use pedagogies that will make learning fun, and should try to move away from traditional methods of teaching, especially when teaching challenging topics (Mzimela, 2016; Pham, 2016; Wiysahnyuy & Valentine, 2023). Approaches like game-based pedagogy are significant and others have been found to be more fruitful when compared with the old traditional methods of teaching. Teachers therefore, play a crucial role in creating game-based learning procedures, enhancing learning, and improving learner motivation (Hamral, 2017). In language teaching, diverse literary forms like poem, novel, short story, essay, drama, and folklore are used for the purpose of developing reading for comprehension and critical thinking skills.

The use of folklore has been found to be significant in the teaching of language and critical thinking skills (Maledu, 2024; Wiysahnyuy & Valentine, 2023; Maruma & Molotja, 2018). While folklore is a broad field of study, this paper explores more particularly the use of folktales and riddles in isiZulu language teaching, to enhance language and critical thinking skills for primary school learners. The study focuses on the primary school teachers teaching Grades 4 in the Clermont area, in Pinetown District. This chapter aims to demonstrate how folktales and riddles can be used as techniques when teaching language and critical thinking skills. The section below discusses folklore.

### What is Folklore?

The term folklore includes the traditional beliefs, traditional stories, customs, expressions transmitted orally, that are passed down from generation to generation within a specific culture or community (Adipat, 2021, Pham, 2016). In isiZulu, folklore is called *ubuciko bomlomo*, and it comprises a wide range of oral traditions, such as folktales, riddles, idioms, proverbs and traditional poetry (Mishra & Satpathy, 2020). It involves belief systems, for example, rites and rituals surrounding coupling, childbirth, initiation into adulthood, and ideas about the afterlife. In this paper, we will however focus on the folktales and the riddles. The section below discusses folktales.

### What are Folktales?

A folktale is an old story that has been told from generation to generation. Such a story is entertaining and contains some teachings to the child who is the listener of the story. Dahal and Bhatta (2021), state that folk tales are narratives formed by the integration and narration of a real event with imaginative adventures. Other writers believe that listening to books is more effective than reading them (Foster, 1967). During storytelling, the taleteller directly communicates with children who are listening to the story. The responsibility of a tale teller is to narrate the story well, ensuring they stay true to its original. During the olden days, folktales were told by the elderly to the youth, at night time, around the fire, after the day chores were finished, and everyone who would come to listen had completed their chores. However, they were also told by children to each other, and everyone would like to participate in the game. This was a way of encouraging the youth to ensure they finish their daily chores, so they would have a story told to them.

## The Use of Folktales

According to Dahal and Bhatta (2021), folktales are used to entertain, instruct, and preserve cultural heritage across generations, and any language that exists, has folktales that are passed down from generation to generation. These folktales function as educational tools to teach the youth moral lessons, social behaviour, and values, such as honesty and kindness.

Key aspects of the use of folktales include:

- ***Educational and Moral Instruction*:** Folk tales are more than just entertaining. They are often used to teach the youth about consequences on conducting certain behaviour, for example, teaching them about what is right or wrong, so as to discourage anti-social behaviour. Unlike direct moral lessons, these stories allow kids to uncover values like kindness, honesty, and courage on their own.
- ***Development of language skills*:** When children listen to or read particular stories, this helps in enhancing their language development, imagination, and critical thinking skills. Through the adventures of characters, children learn to think critically about actions and their consequences.
- ***Social Cohesion*:** Through sharing stories, communities from the same or different cultures are able to strengthen their bonds, which helps in fostering a sense of unity.
- ***Build Empathy***: Stories from diverse cultures encourage understanding and respect for differences.
- ***Entertainment and Imagination*:** Folktales help in providing imaginative narratives that often feature magical, supernatural, or animal characters.
- ***Cultural Preservation*:** Folktales are used to pass down customs, beliefs, and history from generation to generation, and this always connects the present to the past.

Nowadays, folklore is vital for developing and enhancing language and critical thinking skills in learners (Adipat, 2021; Maruma & Molotja, 2018). Therefore, folklore is useful for primary school language teachers to help learners develop language and critical thinking skills (Yuliarsih, 2022; Rahmawati et al., 2022; Szalkiewicz, 2017). Language and critical thinking skills are both vital for effective communication and problem-solving. While language skills incorporate listening, speaking, reading, and writing skills, critical thinking involves analysing information and solving problems. Both these skills are interconnected and they contribute to the learner's ability to understand and interact with the world effectively. Therefore, these skills play a vital role in the primary school learner's language and critical language skills development (Yuliarsih, 2022; Rahmawati et al., 2022). The section below discusses the types of folktales.

## Types of Folktales

In isiZulu, the three most popular folktales are myths, legends and fairy tales (Dundes, 2007). Fairy tales are short stories featuring fantasy or magical events and characters and are explicitly moral tales. They consist of fictional tales about people or animals, often involving superstitions and unfounded beliefs. They may involve fairies, giants, dragons, witches, dwarves, and other imaginary forces (Rahman, 2017). The names of the characters are often associated with recognizable traits or values in the cultural environment in which the children are immersed. Prominent examples include the story of a rock hyrax, also called the dassie or rock rabbit[1] and why it does not have a tail while the other animals do. The other one is that of a mouse and a pig, which tries to explain why the mouse has a sharp mouth and why a pig has a flat snout. Also, the story of *Demane* (who was a boy child) and *Demazane* (who was a girl child) and the cannibal is one of the most popular Zulu folktales.

The other type of folktale is the legend. Legends are stories purported to be historical in nature but that are without substantiation. They include no happenings that are outside the realm of 'possibility,' but may include miracles. Legends may be transformed over time, in order to keep them relevant and realistic. Many legends operate within the realm of uncertainty, and are not entirely to be believed by the participants, but also are not decisively distrusted." (Yumnam, 2021). They can tell about historical events, legends, who are known in history, but they contain unrealistic events, that make the narrative untrusted, even if it may contain characters known in history. The example of such stories is the one of Mpeza and the crow.

The third type of folktale is the myth. Myths are traditional stories that may answer life's overarching questions, such as the origins of the world (the creation myth) or the creation of humankind. A myth can also be an attempt to explain mysteries, supernatural events, and cultural traditions. These are meant to contain the theme of faith, therefore could involve God, gods or other creatures. It presents reality in dramatic ways. Examples include the story of a woman in the moon (inkosikazi esenyangeni), and the story of a lizard and a chameleon (intulo nonwabu). Also, the other common myth that spans multiple cultures is that of a great flood, and Noah's ark (uzamcolo nomkhumbi kaNowa).

## The Importance of Folktales in a Child's Language Development

Folktales are crucial for children's language development because they expand vocabulary, improve comprehension and narrative skills, and foster crucial literacy foundations like understanding story structure and sequential events through engaging language and interactive storytelling (Yumnam, 2021). These orally transmitted stories introduce children to new words and complex narrative techniques, while also promoting creative thinking, critical analysis, and cultural understanding in a fun and meaningful context (Dundes, 2007).

From a very young age children are told folktales at home by adults (their parents, grandparents and even older siblings), and they grow up knowing these stories. Studies have emphasized the vital role stories play in a child development (Scott & Ytreberg, 2001). Stories, especially folktales, provoke their imaginations and provide them with material from which children create their understanding of origins and purposes of the world and form abstract concepts and values of society. For example, they can learn about the benefits of being good to others, empathy, honesty, hard-work bravery, respect and love for other people (Ningrum et al., 2019).

Children also learn how being bad to others, theft, stubbornness, disrespect, laziness, betrayal, and dishonesty are punished. These stories stimulate their imagination about the world, allow them to visualize the world outside their homes, help them distinguish between what is right and wrong, and what can be acceptable and unacceptable behaviour (Kaliwal, 2024; Faraj & Joshi, 2025).

According to Kaliwal (2024) "Folktales also model the elements of effective decision-making. Characters in folktales invariably encounter a conflict that requires them to make difficult decisions and act to resolve it. These decisions then lead to clear consequences that carry a message: making a good or more responsible decision results in positive outcomes while making a poor or irresponsible decision inevitably leads to negative outcomes. As a result, folktales can demonstrate the importance of making difficult decisions under challenging circumstances."

## Folktales as a Pedagogic Tool

Wiysahnyuy and Valentine (2023) in their study of folktales as indigenous pedagogic tools for educating school children in Cameroon, found that most teachers and parents believed that integrating folktales in language teaching was potentially significant. In their study, they found that all teachers used folktales during lessons. Participating parents indicated that folktales should be used in schools, mentioning that folktales were pedagogical tools for teaching children morality and the ways of their ancestors. Also, Mzimela (2016) studied the role of teaching using folklore in developing grade R learners' mother tongue. The results showed the great significance on improving the learners' isiZulu mother tongue competence. She also states that the use of folktales fosters creativity and imagination to the learners, as well as "encourages students to think outside the box, explore different perspectives, and develop original ideas. This creative thinking is essential not only for language learning but also for problem-solving and critical analysis in various academic disciplines" (Mzimela, 2016).

Pham (2016) states that "folktales provide an opportunity for teachers to design activities which engage learners and create a stress-free, non-threatening environment for learning to occur. As young learners, primary school children can immerse themselves in stories, find the stories interesting to read or to listen to and be excited by being involved in related activities or tasks provided by the teacher" (Maluleke & Smith, 2025).

Pham (2016) argues that "through folktales, young language learners are exposed to a wide range of authentic vocabulary. This vocabulary can be nouns of concrete objects, verbs, adjectives or adverbs. Young learners also have the chance to listen to meaningful input in chunks, rather than just single words. This gives them more chances to learn vocabulary incidentally (Ningrum et al., 2019). When teachers read stories aloud, children are exposed to patterns of language that are not commonly found in their everyday communication. As children listen to stories being read aloud they build up a relationship between the printed word and its meaning" (Yuliarsih, 2022; Pham, 2016). The section below discusses the riddles.

## WHAT ARE RIDDLES?

According to Kaivola-Bregenhoj (2018), riddles are an exchange of words in which people are deliberately misled because the correct answer is usually completely unexpected. Also, according to the Oxford online dictionary, a riddle is a question or statement intentionally phrased so as to require ingenuity in ascertaining its answer or meaning. Toshtemirova (2021) mentions that riddles can be a verbal game, a challenge to the mind, or a type of puzzle that promotes critical thinking. They use words to describe something which requires that the solver thinks creatively. They often use metaphors or descriptions of objects, people, or animals in a puzzling manner. Riddles therefore are a verbal game which challenges one's mind, or they are a type of puzzle that promotes critical thinking. The solution to a riddle requires a thoughtful answer (Danesi (2018).

Each riddle contains a question, either explicit or implicit. To guess a riddle means to find a solution to a problem, which demands a complex mental operation (Mai et al, 2004). According to Mai et al. (2004), "The subject in question in the riddle is hidden, encrypted, and the encryption methods are different. The type of logical task, its complexity, and, subsequently, the nature of the mental operation to be performed by the guessing one depends on the method of encryption. "

## The Use of Riddles in Teaching the Language Skills

Riddles can be used as a technique for creating engaging activities to study language skills, particularly vocabulary, comprehension, and critical thinking (Kaivola-Bregenho 2018). In the classroom, riddles can be used to stimulate group discussion, enhance memory, and build confidence, making them a valuable instructional tool for students of all ages. Ningrum et al. (2019) state that riddles game is an interesting technique used to teach vocabulary because they make the students enjoy while they learn. He further states that using riddles games is an advantage because learners are fond of games. They always play game in their lives. Playing games helps in easing shyness and nervousness.

Language lessons, particularly for primary school learners, should be inspiring and permit learners to think, create, and imagine (Banaji, Cranmer, & Perrotta, 2010). Educational games such as riddles, enhance creativity in language learners (Ott & Pozzi, 2012). The teacher or learners challenges others with puzzles and counterintuitive questions, so as to stimulate creative thought, enhance comprehension, and boost memory. A teacher who utilizes a game-based pedagogy can use riddles to foster critical thinking, problem-solving, and active learner participation in the classroom.

Toshtemirova (2021) mentions that riddles enhance critical and logical thinking. He further mentions that riddles require students to think differently, and they encourage divergent thinking and the ability to analyze and interpret information. The enjoyable and challenging nature of solving riddles increases student interest and motivation to learn. The following section presents the conceptual framework of the research.

## CONCEPTUAL FRAMEWORK

While several studies have used game-based pedagogy as a teaching approach, in this study it was employed as a conceptual framework. Definitions of game-based pedagogy mostly emphasize that it is a type of game play with defined learning outcomes (Plass et al. 2015; Shaffer et al., 2005). Numerous studies describe game-based pedagogy as "a teaching method that motivates teachers to attract learners' attention by using types of games (Thangjai & Worapun, 2022); an educational entertaining tool to cultivate knowledge and practice skills (Azhar & Jalil, 2022); support or tool for learning in educational settings" (Pinedo et al., 2021). Thangjai and Worapun (2022), state that "games could be non-technology-based, for example, flashcards, board games, crosswords, or technology-based using consoles, computers, and network technology."

Some scholars have queried what in essence defines a game, and what does not (Salen & Zimmerman, 2004). Some have defined a game as "a system in which players engage in an artificial conflict, defined by rules, that results in a quantifiable outcome" (Salen & Zimmerman, 2004, p. 80). For example, the gamification of a reading comprehension homework, which may involve giving learners points and stars for the completion of learning activities that they consider boring or difficult. Game-based learning would involve redesigning the homework activities, using artificial conflict and rules of play, to make them more interesting and engaging.

With Game-based pedagogy students learn while they enjoy the lesson (Chen & Chang, 2020) because "it mimics the experience of playing a game, which is characterised by curiosity and enjoyment" (Liu et al., 2021). According to Wang & Zheng (2021), game-based pedagogy has been found to be effective in increasing learner motivation and engagement.

Games have the potential to be a primary means of instruction for complex, sensitive and difficult topics (Wang & Zheng, 2021; Hsiao et al., 2022). Studies have confirmed that many learners perceive language teaching to be more engaging when taught through the use of game-based pedagogy. Shaham et al. (2013) state that teaching "must focus on the creation of opportunities for the development of learning abilities through active learning, the development of critical thinking using tasks, and the adjustment of learning styles to thinking styles." This conceptual framework is relevant in this study as the focus is on the use of indigenous games, which are folktales and riddles in teaching language and critical thinking skills to a primary school learner, who at this stage is a young learner, who should learn the content while enjoying the lesson. The following section will discuss the research methodology used.

## RESEARCH METHODOLOGY

The study adopted the qualitative research approach and it operated under the interpretivist paradigm. Qualitative research is an approach for scientific inquiry that emphasizes the depth and richness of context and voice in understanding social phenomena (Cohen *et al.*, 2018; Lim, 2025). Hence, qualitative research approach can be used for understanding complex phenomena. Such a research approach aims to unveil the "what," "why," "when," "where," "who," and "how" (or the "5W1H") behind social behaviours and interactions, rather than merely quantifying occurrences (Lim, 2023; 2025). Lim (2025) further accentuates that the value of qualitative research lies in its capacity to generate rich, contextualized insights, offering a human-centred understanding of the world. Also, Ugwu and Eze (2023) emphasize that qualitative research is concerned with feelings, ideas, or experiences. These researchers further explain that the main goal of qualitative research is finding insights that can result in testable hypotheses, which is frequently done in narrative form, as researchers tend to find patterns in the data produced. Choosing this approach allowed me to delve deeper into the generated data, trying to uncover the broad themes emerging from it.

Nickerson (2024) states that the interpretivist paradigm aims to understand how people create and interpret meaning within their social worlds, emphasizing subjective experiences over objective measurement. Also, such a paradigm is grounded in the belief that reality is socially constructed and that knowledge arises from the interaction between researcher and participants. The goal is to uncover how certain people make sense of events, relationships, and cultural practices rather than to test hypotheses (Bertram & Christiansen, 2019). The interpretivist paradigm was suitable for this research because I wanted to understand how the teachers teach isiZulu home language learners at primary school where they were teaching.

The study also adopted a case study research design. According to Coombs (2022), "a case study is a detailed analysis of a single person, group, or event that allows researchers to report in-depth information." In this study, participants were four isiZulu Home Language Grade 4 primary school teachers from one school in the Pinetown District area. These were experienced teachers who have taught isiZulu as a home language for over ten years. One of them was a master teacher[2] while the other three were post level 1[3] teachers. Three of these teachers (those at post level 1) had a Bachelor of Education (B Ed) Degree as the highest qualification, while the other one (the master teacher) had a Master's Degree. Since the study involved a small sample of teachers from a single setting, the findings cannot be generalized as they are primarily relevant to this context.

These teachers were purposively selected because the study focused on the teaching of isiZulu home language learners at primary school where they were teaching. Adeoye (2023) and Cohen (2018), agree that purposive sampling is a type of non-probability sampling technique widely used in qualitative research, and it involves the deliberate selection of particular units on the premise that they have certain elements that representatively characterize the population.

Data was generated from the teachers through semi-structured interviews as well as observation methods. All the interviews took place in the school, in an unused classroom. Each interview took about 45 minutes long, and questions asked were those in the semi-structured interview schedule. However, probing questions were used where required. Also, with regard to observation of lessons, I developed an observation schedule, and opted to be a non-participant observer when the participating teachers delivered their lessons. Three lessons for each teacher were observed, in order to understand how they teach language and critical thinking skills to Grade 4 isiZulu home language learners. After data was generated, it was analysed through the use of thematic analysis. Thematic analysis is a qualitative data analysis method that involves reading through a data set, such as transcripts from in depth interviews, and identifying patterns in meaning across the data to derive themes. I looked for patterns, organized them, then derived major themes.

Before the study was conducted, all ethical procedures were observed and participants' consent was obtained and the University granted ethical clearance approval for the study, with the following Protocol Number: HSSREC/00008680/2025. The following section presents the findings and discussion.

## FINDINGS AND DISCUSSION

This section presents the findings of the study. The discussion will be organized according to the themes that emerged from the generated data through observations and semi-structured interviews. These are: (i)The benefits of using folktales in teaching isiZulu language and critical thinking skills; (ii) teacher competency in using folktales to teach language to primary school learners; (iii) the disadvantages of using folktales in the language classroom; (iv) and benefits of using riddles for the development of language and critical thinking skills. Below is a discussion under the sub-topic "The benefits of using folktales in teaching isiZulu language and critical thinking skills."

The benefits of using folktales as a traditional game in teaching isiZulu language and critical thinking skills

Under this heading, the following sub-topics emerged: Speaking and listening skills learner improvement; learner active participation; vocabulary and comprehension skills enhancement; moral lessons and critical thinking benefit.

## Speaking and Listening Skills Learner Improvement

All four participating teachers remarked that the use of folktales in the primary school isiZulu classroom improves learner listening and speaking skills. For example, teacher Sonto said:

*Although I cannot say all my learners are fluent speakers and have good listening skills, but many are very good, ever since I started to pay more attention on the use of folktales. I have noted that they have drastically improved in all the language skills, more particularly speaking and listening.*

The same sentiments were shared by the other three participating teachers. This shows that all of them agree that the use of folktales in the language classroom is pivotal. Mantra and Maba (2018) and Syafii et al. (2021) have reported that using folktales to teach language skills can be of great benefit as it enhances listening and speaking skills. This is further elucidated by Pham (2016) who observes that using folktales in teaching a primary school language learner "enhances their ability to articulate ideas clearly and confidently, which is vital for effective communication. By engaging with stories, students learn to organize their thoughts logically and express them in a coherent manner."

## Learner Active Participation

All the four teachers remark that the use of folktales in the classroom increases learner participation, as they enjoy when they are taught through the use of folktales. For example, teacher Khethiwe stated: "For me, using folktales not only makes them enjoy the lesson, but their engagement in the lesson becomes fabulous!" Also, teacher Thanda said: "They participate much better in a lesson where there is use of folktale." Mzimela (2016) asserts that the use of folktales in the classroom increases learner engagement. When they are emotionally invested in a story, they are more likely to participate actively in class discussions and activities. This is also supported by Syafii et al. (2021) and Simon et al. (2008) who affirm that the teacher who uses a folktale, motivates the leaners to participate actively while enjoying the lesson.

## Vocabulary and Comprehension Skills Enhancement

The four participating teachers in the study all expressed that using folktales assists in enhancing vocabulary and comprehension skills in a language classroom. Some mentioned that learners find it easy to understand and utilise the vocabulary gained from the folktale used, and their comprehension improves. The following statements are testament to this:

*The use of folktales in teaching vocabulary and comprehension skills cannot be overemphasized. There is no folktale that I have used and they struggled with vocabulary. (Khethiwe)*

*Folktales are very useful when teaching a Zulu language lesson, no matter which skill I want to focus on. Their appreciation of folktales plays a great role in their vocabulary and comprehension development - this is not an exaggeration!" (Pat)*

Yusuf (2015) confirms that the use of folktales in language classroom increases vocabulary and comprehension skills. He states that using folktales helps students develop their language and reading comprehension skills. Yusuf (2015) proclaims that there are some educational benefits to reading children's folktales aloud, for example, improving speaking, listening, vocabulary and reading comprehension. By using folktales, the teacher catches the students' interest in the reading material, while they also benefit the other language skills development. Ishak et al. (2020) mention that success in reading for comprehension can positively affect academic progress. Also, some studies advocate the introduction of suitable, relatable reading materials and strategies in promoting vocabulary and comprehension (Yusuf, 2015; Ishak et al., 2020; Hamral, 2017).

## Moral Lessons and Critical Thinking

Participants in this study reported that besides learning the language for academic purposes, learners also acquire moral lessons that contribute in shaping them to become responsible citizens of society, who can think critically. Fauzia et al. (2023) remark that teachers play a vital role in guiding students to develop critical thinking skills through various innovative and problem-solving-oriented teaching methods, for example, the use of folktales when teaching a language lesson to primary school learners. The following are excerpts from the participants' statements:

*It gives them another opportunity to learn about what is wrong and what is not, because the characters behave like human beings. So, one learns that by doing so, I might be doing bad to others. (Kelly)*

*My learners enjoy story time a lot, and each time when I give them some questions based on the folktale, it shows they did not only enjoy, but they have learnt something, particularly good or bad conduct. (Thanda)*

The above statements are congruent with Tan and Teo (2021), who affirm that while folktales are used for entertainment, they also teach children about what is right or wrong. "Through the adventures of characters, children learn to navigate moral dilemmas and think critically about actions and their consequences. Unlike straightforward moral lessons, these stories allow children to uncover values like kindness, honesty, and courage on their own" (Fauzia et al, 2023).

The moral lessons in folktales often seem simple on the surface, but they encourage thoughtful engagement. For instance, stories about good triumphing over evil give children a clear sense of justice while prompting deeper discussions about fairness and empathy. Wiysahnyuy and Valentine (2023) state that parents and teachers can "amplify these benefits by talking through the stories with children. Asking questions about a character's choices or imagining alternative endings helps children apply the lessons to their own lives, sharpening their critical thinking skills."

## Teacher Competency in Using Folktales as a Benefit to the Learners

Teacher competency was identified as one of the fundamentals on teaching isi-Zulu home language to primary school learners, particularly when using indigenous games. Participants in this study revealed:

*The teacher's pedagogical knowledge especially when using folktales is vital for teaching a language learner. Not many teachers are sure about how this can be used effectively in teaching a language learner. (Sonto)*

*I do not have much experience in the field but learning from experienced teachers who possess great pedagogical skills and content knowledge have benefitted me a lot. You cannot be a good language teacher if your pedagogical knowledge is shaky. (Khethiwe)*

*Language development for a primary school learner requires a good teacher, who is a mother tongue speaker or a highly proficient in the language, who also knows how to teach and relate well with young people so they [teachers] can be in their [learners] shoes. You need to know your stuff to be able to teach a native language learner." (Kelly)*

The statements above emphasize the importance of a teacher to have certain competencies so they are relevant in teaching a primary school language learner. Rulyansah et al (2023) studied competencies of teachers in game-based pedagogy. Their research aimed at determining what kind of "expertise educators could require to effectively use game-based education (GBP). The fields of pedagogy, technology, collaboration, and creativity were defined as the four key domains of competency. These researchers found that teachers' collaborative skills (whether intra-school or inter-school collaborations or networks with other teachers and key actors) were crucial to the success of the GBP's implementation."

## The Disadvantages of Using Folktales

Of the four teachers, two noted that although using folktales to teach in a language classroom is significant, it also has some disadvantages. Such disadvantages include: the rise of the level of noise in the classroom, as learners sometimes forget that they are in class, for they keep talking, laughing, even if they are told to stop so the lesson continues. For example:

> *Children can sometimes overdo something, you know! You see, sometimes you regret why you have chosen a folktale in your lesson...they will just laugh or make annoying noise, even if you tell them to stop. In this way, definitely you aren't going to finish your lesson on time, because your lesson has been disrupted. Perhaps one needs to select a boring story - I don't know. (Kelly)*

Besides the comment above, also, teacher Khethiwe stated that the themes of cultural identity content for children are usually a reflection of social values, customs and beliefs. What becomes a problem is that many animal characters are always presented negatively, for example the snake, the crocodile, the baboon, and the owl. For this reason, the children may develop negative attitudes towards these animals and may not identify with them. For instance, in many folktales, the snake is always presented as cruel, merciless, evil, an enemy to humans, therefore, children may not identify with the snake, resulting in unfounded hate of such animals, which contributes to their killings or torturing (Opondo, 2022). Some people, both children and adults, still believe that the snake is one of humans' biggest enemies, therefore it must be killed whenever it emerges.

## Benefits of Using Riddles for the Development of Language and Critical Thinking Skills

Under this heading, are the following sub-headings: Improved problem-solving skills; teamwork encouragement; active learner participation through the use of riddles; and improved vocabulary. Below will be the discussion under the sub-heading "Improved problem-solving skills."

## Improved Problem-Solving Skills

All the participating teachers cited that using riddles improves learners' problem-solving skills. Also, all of them mentioned that teaching riddles improves learners' logical and critical thinking skills. For example, teacher Pat stated "I have noted that through the use of riddles my students have improved drastically in problem-solving skills." Also, teacher Khethiwe mentioned that "the strategy is useful as learners are able to present ideas logically, while also their critical thinking becomes incredible. When you give them a riddle, they will not spend time to solve it." (Sonto)

Guneri-Yoyen et al (2017) note that a learner with good problem-solving skills grows up as a self-confident individual who can think creatively and independently. Therefore, such learners are able to overcome societal problems easily when they grow up. Also, Szalkiewicz (2017) remarks that successfully solving riddles can build students' confidence in their abilities. This researcher further states that no matter in which field an individual may be, greatness is demonstrated by turning problems into opportunity and confidently overcoming adversity. It does not matter what the problem is, how much knowledge or how many skills a learner has, confidence is key to achieving the results they desire. In line with Szalkiewicz (2017) cited above, Tukhtasinova (2024) also emphasized that the ability to solve a riddle increases self-esteem and confidence in the learner. This is because when children solve a riddle, they are content of their accomplishments and skills. This coincides well with game-based learning which has been used in language learning which includes difficult subject matter (Oktovianus, 2020; Neri et al., 2020). Therefore, the use of riddles in the lessons, as part of game-based learning, was found to increase learners' interest and desire to learn, which improving language and critical thinking skills (Ke et al., 2022).

## Teamwork Encouragement

Based on the observation of lessons and interviews data, the use of riddles to teach the isiZulu lesson to the Grade 4 learners is indispensable as it encourages teamwork. Participants mentioned that riddle games are often played in pairs or small groups. Each group is given a different riddle to solve, and the one which comes up with the solution first will be the 'king' of the day. For example, teacher Thanda stated:

*I use some flash cards where I write riddles, and give them to individual groups. Each group gets a different riddle. Such an activity requires that learners work in groups. It depends on the types of riddles for that day. For example, there are descriptive riddles, paradoxical riddles and wordplay riddles. To clarify by means of examples, I will say, (1) A red cow surrounded by white cows. (Answer: A tongue. This is because it is red in colour, and is surrounded by white teeth). (2) "What grows bigger the more you take from it" (Answer: a hole). This is a paradoxical riddle, and (3) "When a duck is on the fence, and you hit it with a stone, in which side is it going to fall? Will it fall inside of the yard or outside?" (This one does not require a straight forward answer. What will happen is that you will need to know what the duck is, and how does it live. A learner who is clever, will say, no, there is no such, because a duck cannot climb on top of the fence. (Thanda)*

As evidenced in the statement by teacher Thanda quoted above, the use of riddles encourages teamwork to primary school learners. Tukhtasinova (2024) states that using riddles in the classroom encourages teamwork and collaboration amongst learners. Notably, many riddles can be solved in teams, which fosters learners to collaborate, leading to improved social relationships within the classroom.

## Active Learner Participation Through the Use of Riddles

The participating teachers in the study all concur with each other regarding the value of using riddles to teach a language lesson. For example, teacher Pat said: "When your learners make their own examples, they are keen to participate in the lesson, and this makes me happy because it shows they understand." Also, teacher Sonto said: "Active participation is key to effective learning. When learners are engaged through activities they are more likely to remember and understand the material. This is what happens when we play riddles. They really enjoy riddles. Everyone wants to be a star!"

The above statements concur with Ikhsanudin et al. (2019), who mention that riddles help to increase the students' involvement in the lessons. Randle (2024) states that the aim of using a riddle game in the lesson is to critically challenge the mind of the gamer and to serve as a tool to learn new events within a space. In this way, learners in the classroom become active participants. No learner would want to be excluded or to remain passive when it comes to games. This coincides with Du et al. (2025), who declare that active learner participation is important for academic success and increased motivation. He states that the lesson outcomes can be significantly improved when learners engage actively in the learning process. This aligns well with game-based pedagogy, which was chosen as the study theoretical framework.

## Improved vocabulary

The study also found that playing riddle games in the language classroom improves learner vocabulary. All the four teachers state that riddles are an important tool in improving learner vocabulary. Below are examples:

*I find it very useful to use riddles as the strategy improves their vocabulary. (Sonto)*

*I heavily recommend the use of riddles whenever one teaches language skills because it enhances student vocabulary, which makes it easier for them to grasp the lesson taught. (Khethiwe)*

Rahmawati et al. (2022) state that the use of riddle games can engage students and help them retain terminology based on the subject presented. These researchers further state that riddle games can be an effective method in teaching vocabulary. Similar to Rahmawati et al. (2022), Ningrum et al. (2019) state that students can acquire vocabulary by playing riddle games, and this can help them identify the meaning and spelling of words. Students can retain word meanings in their schemata, and correct spellings by employing the riddle technique. This assertion is also supported by Mina et al. (2021) and Yuliarsih (2022) who acknowledge that through the use of riddles in the classroom, learners improve their ability to study the language and acquire certain unfamiliar terms, which improves their vocabulary.

In the same vein, Ningrum et al. (2019) remark that vocabulary is important in language learning because without mastering vocabulary, a learner cannot articulate their thoughts effectively.

## CONCLUSION

The study concludes that through the use of folktales and riddles, learners learn while they enjoy the lesson, which helps in improving their language and critical thinking skills. Such skills include speaking, listening, comprehension, critical thinking, analysis skills, and problem-solving skills. Participation in the lesson improves when learners learn while they enjoy. However, their enjoyment in class needs to be controlled by the teacher because they may disrupt the lesson when they over-enjoy, thus diverting the lesson, leading to the primary aim of the lesson being lost. This means that, while being an important tool to teach, folktales and riddles should be used for the benefit of the learner, who should gain knowledge and feel comfortable with the lesson, and should not be used to disrupt the lesson. Also, the use of folktales and riddles requires a skilful teacher, who should possess some competencies, for example, classroom management skills, subject content knowledge, as well as the pedagogic knowledge. It may also be useful to the teacher to be able to choose the folktale or the riddle that will match the learners' age, which also cannot perpetuate hatred towards certain creatures as this may endanger certain species, owing to the lack of awareness about them.

## REFERENCES


Adeoye, M. A. (2023). Review of sampling techniques for education. *ASEAN Journal for Science Education, 2*(2), 87–94.

Azhar, S. A. F. J., & Jalil, H. A. (2022). Comparison of individual and collaborative game-based learning using tablet in improving students' knowledge in primary classroom environment. *Asian Journal of University Education, 18*(1), 205–216. DOI: 10.24191/ajue.v18i1.17188

Bertram, C., & Christiansen, I. (2019). *Understanding Research: An Introduction to Reading Research.* Van Schaik.

Chen, S. Y., & Chang, Y. M. (2020). The impacts of real competition and virtual competition in digital game-based learning. *Computers in Human Behavior, 104*, 106171. DOI: 10.1016/j.chb.2019.106171

Cohen, L., Manion, L., & Morrison, K. (2018). *Research Methods in Education* (8th ed.). Routledge., DOI: 10.4324/9781315456539

Coombs, H. (2022). *Case study research: Single or multiple* [White paper]. Southern Utah University. DOI: 10.5281/zenodo.7604301

Dahal, H., & Bhatta, B. (2021). Folktales: A Moral Message from the Past to the Future Generation. [NJMR]. *Nepal Journal of Multidisciplinary Research, 4*(1), 31–43. DOI: 10.3126/njmr.v4i1.36618

Danesi, M. (2018). *What is a riddle? Psychology Today.* https://www.psychologytoday.com/za/blog/brain-workout/201808/what-is- riddle

Du, W., Wijaya, T. T., Cao, Y., & Li, X. (2025). What factors influence secondary students' active participation in mathematics classrooms: A theory of planned behaviour perspective. *Acta Psychologica, 253*, 1–14. DOI: 10.1016/j.actpsy.2025.104694

Dundes, A. (2007). *The Meaning of Folklore.* Utah State University Press.

Faraj, I. H., & Joshi, J. (2025). A Cognitive View on the Impact of Folktales on Children's Thinking. *International Journal of Multidisciplinary Comprehensive Research, 4*(2), 18–20. DOI: 10.54660/IJMCR.2025.4.2.18-20

Fauzia, N., Kuswardani, R., Rosyid, A, Abida, F.I.N., Budi, D & Darma, D.B. (2023). Employing Traditional Stories to Enhance Critical Thinking Skills of Junior High School Students. *Humanitatis: Journal of Language and Literature*, 147- 158.

Foster, F. P. (1967). *Literature and the Young Child.* State of New Jersey Department of Health, Education & Welfare Office of Education.

Guneri-Yoyen, E., Azaklı, A., Uney, R., & Demirci, O. (2017). Ergenlerin Kişilik Ozelliklerinin Problem Çozme Becerisi Uzerine Etkisi [in Turkish]. *Dogu Anadolu Sosyal Bilimlerde Egilimler Dergisi, 1*(1), 75–93.

Hamral, A. 2017. *The role of folktales as learning source to support vocabulary mastery for senior high school students.* (MA Dissertation). Graduate Program State University of Makassar.

Hsiao, H. S., Lin, Y. W., Lin, K. Y., Lin, C. Y., Chen, J. H., & Chen, J. C. (2022). Using robot-based practices to develop an activity that incorporated the 6E model to improve elementary school students' learning performances. *Interactive Learning Environments, 30*(1), 85–99. DOI: 10.1080/10494820.2019.1636090

Ishak, N., Maulan, S., Dellah, N. F., Zabidin, N., & Nordin, N. A. (2020). Using folklore in enhancing primary school students' reading comprehension. 5th international conference on education. *Islamic Studies and Social Sciences Research* (iceisr).

Kaivola-Bregenho, A. (2018). The Riddle: Form and Performance. *Humanities (Washington), 7*(2), 1–17.

Kaliwal, A. (2024). The effects of stories on children's cognitive and intellectual development. *Journal of Social Sciences, 7*(2), 179–192. DOI: 10.62810/jss.v7i2.42

Ke, F., Moon, J., & Sokolikj, Z. (2022). Designing and deploying a virtual social sandbox for autistic children. *Disability and Rehabilitation. Assistive Technology,* •••, 1–32.

Lim, W. M. (2023). Philosophy of science and research paradigm for business research in the transformative age of automation, digitalization, hyperconnectivity, obligations, globalization and sustainability. *Journal of Trade Science, 11*(2/3), 3–30. DOI: 10.1108/JTS-07-2023-0015

Lim, W. M. (2025). What Is Qualitative Research? An Overview and Guidelines. *Australasian Marketing Journal, 33*(2), 199–229. DOI: 10.1177/14413582241264619

Liu, Y. C., Wang, W. T., & Lee, T. L. (2021). An integrated view of information feedback, game quality, and autonomous motivation for evaluating game- based learning effectiveness. *Journal of Educational Computing Research, 59*(1), 3–40. DOI: 10.1177/0735633120952044

Mai, X. Q., Luo, J., Wu, J. H., & Luo, Y. J. (2004). Aha! effects in a guessing riddle task: An event-related potential study. *Human Brain Mapping*, *22*(4), 261–270. DOI: 10.1002/hbm.20030

Maluleke, V. L., & Smith, C. (2025). Cultural Perceptions of Folklore in the Grade Nine EFAL Classroom. *Southern African Journal for Folklore Studies*, *34*(1), 1–22. DOI: 10.25159/2663-6697/18867

Mantra, I. B. N., & Maba, W. (2018). *Enhancing the EFl learners' speaking skill through folktales-based instruction*. SHS Web of Conferences, 42, 00017. DOI: 10.1051/shsconf/20184200017

Maruma, M. W., & Molotja, T. W. (2018). The Relevance of Folklore in an Indigenous language Teaching and Learning Situation: The Case Study of Sepedi. *Southern African Journal for Folklore Studies*, *28*(1), 1–11. DOI: 10.25159/1016-8427/4293

Mina, D. F. C., Muin, A., & Septiana, T. I. (2021). Enriching Students' Vocabulary Mastery by Using Riddle Game. *Indonesian Journal of English Studies*, *2*(1), 23. http://jurnal.uinbanten.ac.id/index.php/ijes

Mishra, P., & Satpathy, S. (2020). Genre of Folk Narratives as Rich Linguistic Resource in Acquiring English Language Competence for Young Learners. *Rupkatha Journal on Interdisciplinary Studies in Humanities*, *12*(1), 1–10. DOI: 10.21659/rupkatha.v12n1.08

Mzimela, J. (2016). Exploring the Role of Teaching Using Folklore in Developing Grade R Learners' Mother Tongue. *Studies of Tribes and Tribals*, *14*(2), 129–137. DOI: 10.1080/0972639X.2016.11886740

Neri, L., Robledo-Rella, V., García-Castelán, R. M. G., Gonzalez-Nucamendi, A., Escobar-Castillejos, D., & Noguez, J. (2020). Visuo-Haptic Simulations to Understand the Dependence of Electric Forces on Distance. *Applied Sciences (Basel, Switzerland)*, *10*(20), 1–23. DOI: 10.3390/app10207190

Nickerson, C. (2024). Interpretivism Paradigm and Research Philosophy. *Simply Psychology*. https://www.simplypsychology.org/interpretivism-paradigm.html

Ningrum, A. K., Riyanti, D., & Regina, R. (2019). *Improving Students' Vocabulary Using Riddles Game: A Classroom Action Research*. Proceedings International Conference on Teaching and Education, 2(2),181-186. ISSN: 2685-1407, FKIP Universitas Tanjungpura. Pontianak, Indonesia.

Pham, T. H. N. (2016). Folktales as a Valuable Rich Cultural and Linguistic Resource to Teach a Foreign Language to Young Learners. *International Journal of Education. Cultura e Scuola*, *1*(1), 23–28. DOI: 10.11648/j.ijecs.20160101.15

Pinedo, R., Garcia-Martin, N., Rascon, D., Jose, C. C., & Canas, M. (2021). Reasoning and learning with game-based learning: A case study. *Current Psychology (New Brunswick, N.J.), 41*(3), 1603–1617. DOI: 10.1007/s12144-021-01744-1

Plass, J. L., Homer, B. D., & Kinzer, C. K. (2015). Foundations of Game-Based Learning. *Educational Psychologist, 50*(4), 258–283. DOI: 10.1080/00461520.2015.1122533

Rahman, F. (2017). The Revival of Local Fairy Tales for Children Education. *Theory and Practice in Language Studies, 7*(5), 336–344. DOI: 10.17507/tpls.0705.02

Rahmawati, W. T., Harahap, Y. M., & Sembiring, F. W. (2022). The Effect of Riddle Game on Students' Vocabulary Mastery. *PEDAGOGI: Jurnal Ilmiah Pendidikan, 8*(1), 69–73. DOI: 10.47662/pedagogi.v8i1.277

Randle, O. (2024). The Roles of Riddles, Puzzles, and Narratives as Pedagogy in Video Games: A Case of African-Themed Video Games. *Journal of Black Studies, 55*(8), 661–683. DOI: 10.1177/00219347241278383

Rulyansah, A., Ghufron, S., Akhwani, N., & Mariati, P. (2023). Competencies of Teachers in Game-based Pedagogy. *Pegem Journal of Education and Instruction, 13*(2), 354–370.

Salen, K., & Zimmerman, E. (2004). *Rules of play: Game design fundamentals.* MIT Press.

Scott, W. A., & Ytreberg, L. H. (2001). *Teaching English to Children.* Longman.

Shaffer, D. W., Halverson, R., Squire, K. R., & Gee, J. P. (2005). *Video games and the future of learning (WCER Working Paper No. 2005-4).* Madison: University of Wisconsin–Madison, Wisconsin Center for Education Research (NJ1).

Simon, S., Naylor, S., Keogh, B., Maloney, J., & Downing, B. (2008). Puppets Promoting Engagement and Talk in Science. *International Journal of Science Education, 30*(9), 1229–1248. DOI: 10.1080/09500690701474037

Syafii, M. L., Santoso, S., & Hartono, S. (2021). Story-telling technique utilizing puppets to enhance the learners" speaking competence. [IJonSES]. *International Journal on Social and Education Sciences, 3*(2), 304–341. DOI: 10.46328/ijonses.70

Szalkiewicz, A. (2017). *Why confidence is critical to problem solving*? https://kepner - tregoe.com/blogs/why-confidence-is-critical-to-problem-solving/

Tan, J. P. L., & Teo, T. W. (2021). Preparing for Industry 4.0: Evaluating the Impact of Critical Thinking and Problem-Solving Training in Higher Education. *European Journal of Engineering Education, ●●●*, 1–17.

Thangjai, N., & Worapun, W. (2022). Developing inquiry-based learning characteristics of Grade 7 students using integrated 5E's of inquiry-based learning and game-based learning. *Journal of Educational Issues*, *8*(1), 137–150. DOI: 10.5296/jei.v8i1.19547

Toshtemirova, K. A. (2021). The role of riddles in teaching logical thinking. *International Journal of Innovations in Engineering Research and Technology*, *8*(3), 24–25.

Tukhtasinova, D. (2024). Importance of Riddles in Language Learning. *Excellencia: International Multidisciplinary Journal of Education*, *2*(3), 1–4.

Ugwu, C. N., & Eze, V. H. U. (2023). Qualitative Research. International Digital Organization for Scientific Research. *IDOSR Journal of Computer and Applied Sciences*, *8*(1), 20–35.

Wang, M., & Zheng, X. (2021). Using game-based learning to support learning science: A study with middle school students. *The Asia-Pacific Education Researcher*, *30*(2), 167–176. DOI: 10.1007/s40299-020-00523-z

Wiysahnyuy, L. F., & Valentine, N. B. (2023). Folktales as indigenous pedagogic tools for educating school children: A mixed methods study among the Nso of Cameroon. *Frontiers in Psychology*, *14*, 1049691. DOI: 10.3389/fpsyg.2023.1049691

Yuliarsih, Y. (2022). The Use of Riddle Game To Improve Students' Vocabulary. *The Ellite of Unira*, *5*(1), 1–5. DOI: 10.53712/ellite.v5i1.1400

Yumnam, R. (2021). Folklore in English Language Curriculum. Guines Journal. *An Interdisciplinary Peer Reviewed Journal of North East India Studies*. Volume vii & viii (2020-2021): 85-98.

Yusuf, H.O. (2015). Analysis of Nigeria secondary schools students' reading habits: Implication for teacher education curriculum for English as a second language. *African Journal of Humanities,* 2(2), Kaduna state University. Pyla- mak Services Ltd.

## ENDNOTES

1 Rock hyrax, dassie or rock rabbit: in isiZulu it is called imbila

2 Master teacher: A master teacher is an experienced and accomplished educator with deep subject knowledge and pedagogical expertise, often acting as a mentor and leader to other teachers, and consistently demonstrating excellence in the classroom to enhance student achievement.

3 Post level 1 educator/teacher: A Post Level 1 teacher is an entry-level or basic teacher position within the South African education system, primarily focused on providing class teaching and administrative support without a formal leadership role.

# Chapter 3
# Indigenous Games and Parental Pedagogies:
## Supporting Early Language Development in Diverse Contexts

**Salmita Matshemo Khumalo**
http://orcid.org/0009-0005-8179-1573
*University of South Africa, South Africa*

## ABSTRACT

*This chapter foregrounds the pedagogical value of parental involvement and indigenous game-based practices in fostering early language development within diverse and resource-constrained South African communities. Despite growing acknowledgement of culturally embedded forms of learning in language practices, mainstream pedagogical frameworks often overlook the everyday educational contributions of parents and Indigenous Knowledge Systems (IKS). Grounded in a Pedagogy-in-Participation approach, Vygotsky's Sociocultural Theory, and transformative pedagogy, the chapter explores how traditional activities such as kgati, storytelling, clapping games, and rhythmic play serve as rich literacy and cognitive developmental resources. Drawing on empirical data from six mothers' narratives, it repositions parents as co-educators and showcases how indigenous practices support vocabulary, narrative, and culture. The chapter advocates for contextually grounded, community-based approaches that honour children's full linguistic ecologies and promote equitable early language education.*

DOI: 10.4018/979-8-3373-4322-8.ch003

## 1. INTRODUCTION

Despite the pedagogical value of indigenous games and parental knowledge, early childhood education systems continue to privilege Eurocentric curricula, standardised assessment regimes, and teacher training models that marginalise home-based and indigenous pedagogies. These structural and institutional arrangements contribute to the persistent exclusion of parental knowledge from formal learning spaces. This disconnection between home and school pedagogies constitutes a form of epistemic injustice, undermining children's linguistic identities and limiting opportunities for meaningful early language development.

Language development in early childhood is deeply intertwined with culture, play, and social interaction. Within the South African context, where linguistic diversity is a defining feature, indigenous games offer valuable insights into how children acquire and use language in natural, meaningful ways. In South Africa, many young children enter schooling with a wealth of linguistic resources drawn from their homes and communities. Yet, mainstream pedagogical frameworks seldom recognise these indigenous and familial learning systems. The result is a persistent disconnection between school literacy practices and the cultural worlds in which children grow and communicate (Heugh, 2021).

This chapter explores the intersection of indigenous games and parental pedagogies as foundations for early language development. It draws on data from a qualitative case study involving six mothers in a semi-urban township in the Gauteng Province. The study illuminates how mothers' everyday practices such as storytelling, rhythmic clapping, chanting, and traditional games such as *kgati*, *diketo*, and *morabaraba*, act as informal yet powerful pedagogical tools. These activities generate language-rich environments that stimulate children's vocabulary, narrative competence, and communicative confidence.

The chapter contributes to debates on decolonising early childhood education (ECE) and foregrounds parental knowledge as a form of transformative pedagogy (Freire, 1970; Motha, 2020). The argument advanced here is twofold:

1. Indigenous games serve as culturally responsive vehicles for language development; and
2. Parental pedagogies rooted in community knowledge sustain a participatory model of learning that bridges home and school.

Section 2 of this chapter presents the theoretical and conceptual framing integrating Sociocultural Theory, Pedagogy-in-Participation, and Transformative Pedagogy. Section 3 shows how literature on indigenous games, parental involvement, and game-based learning is positioned. Subsequent sections discuss the methodological design, findings, implications for practice, and reflective activities for readers.

## 2. THEORETICAL PERSPECTIVES

Grounded in three intersecting theoretical perspectives: Vygotsky's Sociocultural Theory, Pedagogy-in-Participation, and Transformative Pedagogy. Vygotsky's Sociocultural Theory emphasises the role of social interaction in cognitive development, suggesting that learning occurs first on a social level and then within the individual. Pedagogy-in-Participation, as articulated by Rogoff, positions learning as a shared process of engagement within cultural activities. Transformative Pedagogy, influenced by Paulo Freire, advocates for learning that challenges marginalisation and embraces cultural knowledge as a source of empowerment. Together, these frameworks provide a holistic lens through which indigenous and parental pedagogies can be understood as both cultural and educational practices.

### 2.1 Sociocultural Theory

Lev Vygotsky's (1978) Sociocultural Theory posits that learning is inherently social and mediated through cultural tools such as language, artefacts, and symbols. Within this view, indigenous games function as mediational means through which children acquire linguistic and cognitive skills. The Zone of Proximal Development (ZPD) describes how learners progress through guided interaction with more capable peers or adults. When parents chant or play *kgati* with children, they scaffold linguistic structures such as repetition, rhythm, syntax while embedding cultural values. The social nature of the play creates an authentic space for meaning making and supports self-regulation (Daniels, 2017).

### 2.2 Pedagogy-in-Participation

Rogoff's Pedagogy-in-Participation expands the sociocultural view by emphasising that learning occurs through shared engagement rather than instruction alone. Children participate in community practices as legitimate contributors. In indigenous South African contexts, participation in household chores, songs, and games constitutes early apprenticeship in language and social norms. Parents are not passive supporters but co-participants shaping learning trajectories. This framework validates the mothers' knowledge and actions as pedagogically intentional, even when not formally recognised by educational institutions (Rogoff et al., 2018).

## 2.3 Transformative Pedagogy

Paulo Freire's (1970) concept of Transformative Pedagogy situates learning within a framework of emancipation and social justice. It argues that authentic education arises from dialogue and reflection on lived experience. In this chapter, transformative pedagogy manifests when parents use indigenous games to affirm children's linguistic identities and challenge deficit views of home-based learning. By positioning parents as co-educators, the chapter reframes early childhood education as a collaborative, culturally grounded project (Mezirow, 2018; Ndlovu-Gatsheni, 2020).

## 2.4 Integrative Schematic

*Table 1. Theoretical alignment among sociocultural, pedagogy-in-participation, and transformative pedagogy*

| Dimension | Sociocultural Theory | Pedagogy-in-Participation | Transformative Pedagogy |
|---|---|---|---|
| **Core Idea** | Learning through social mediation | Learning through shared community participation | Learning as empowerment and critical reflection |
| **Role of Parent** | More-capable peer scaffolding child's learning | Co-participant engaging in cultural activity | Co-educator fostering agency and identity |
| **Role of Child** | Active meaning-maker within ZPD | Legitimate participant in shared practices | Agent of transformation and dialogue |
| **Educational Outcome** | Language development, cognitive growth | Cultural continuity, belonging | Equity, voice, and empowerment |

The convergence of these frameworks offers a holistic understanding of parental pedagogies as dynamic, culturally situated, and transformative processes.

## 3. LITERATURE

This section reviews scholarship on indigenous games, parental pedagogies, and culturally grounded play to situate the study within existing research. It foregrounds how home-based cultural practices contribute to early language development and support continuity between home and school learning contexts.

## 3.1 Indigenous Games as Pedagogical Tools

Research across Africa underscores that indigenous games embody both cultural heritage and cognitive apprenticeship (Acheampong, 2022). These games promote sequencing, turn-taking, and oral fluency skills that are fundamental to language acquisition. For example, rhythmic chants in *kgati* mirror phonemic awareness activities used in formal literacy instruction. Mkhize and Ndimande (2018) argue that indigenous games constitute "living curricula" through which children internalise linguistic patterns, mathematical reasoning, and moral codes simultaneously. In South African townships, such games persist as community resources that require no material cost yet yield substantial developmental benefits (Phatudi, 2021). Scholars such as Heugh (2021) and UNESCO (2020) call for educational policies that legitimise these practices within early learning frameworks. Their inclusion aligns with Sustainable Development Goal 4's emphasis on inclusive and equitable quality education.

## 3.2 Parental Pedagogies and Early Language Development

Parents are the first and most enduring teachers of language. Their everyday interactions in storytelling, play, and conversation shape linguistic proficiency long before formal schooling (Siraj-Blatchford & Brock, 2019). In multilingual homes, code-switching and translanguaging are natural strategies that support comprehension and vocabulary expansion (Garcia & Wei, 2019). Recent South African studies demonstrate that when parents consciously engage in talk, song, and play, children's expressive language scores improve markedly.

However, mainstream ECD programmes often marginalise parents, treating them as "add-ons" rather than integral educators. This alienation limits opportunities for continuity between home and school languages. Empowering parents through culturally congruent pedagogies enhances both language outcomes and community participation (Makgopa, 2022).

## 3.3 Game-Based Learning and Language Pedagogy

Globally, game-based learning has been associated with increased motivation and linguistic engagement (Gee, 2020). Digital and traditional games alike offer opportunities for collaborative problem-solving and contextual vocabulary use. In low-resource environments, indigenous games provide similar affordances without technological dependence. They foster multimodal literacy such as gesture, rhythm, chant, and narrative that mirrors communicative competence frameworks.

A growing body of literature positions traditional play as a foundation for emergent literacy (Weisberg et al., 2022). When parents participate in these games, they model linguistic forms and social rules, effectively co-constructing knowledge with their children. Integrating such practices into teacher-education curricula has been shown to strengthen culturally responsive teaching (Kirkland & Randolph, 2021).

In ECCE centres, recognising indigenous games as legitimate pedagogical resources enables stronger continuity between home and school learning environments. When educators draw on parental knowledge and cultural play practices, children experience coherence between their linguistic worlds, strengthening participation, identity formation, and early literacy development.

## 3.4 Gaps in the Literature

While recognition of indigenous knowledge is increasing, empirical documentation of how parents use games for linguistic purposes remains limited (Maphalala, 2019). Few studies capture parental voices in detail or link these practices to transformative pedagogy. This chapter addresses that gap by presenting narrative evidence from mothers who articulate how indigenous games and daily routines function as informal curricula that sustain language learning and belonging.

While this chapter primarily engages with South African scholarship on indigenous games, parental pedagogies, and early language development, these issues resonate across broader African and international contexts. Comparative research from other African countries and Indigenous education initiatives globally offers important insights into the possibilities and challenges of integrating indigenous knowledge systems in formal education. Such comparative and cross-contextual perspectives present valuable directions for future research beyond the scope of the present study.

# 4. METHODOLOGY

This qualitative interpretive chapter draws from a Master's-level research project that explored indigenous pedagogies in early learning contexts. Six mothers from a semi-urban South African community participated through semi-structured interviews and observations. Data were analysed thematically to identify patterns in how indigenous games were used to support language development. To protect confidentiality, participants in this chapter are referred to as Mother A through Mother F.

## 4.1 Research Design

The study on which this chapter is based adopted a qualitative interpretive case-study design, guided by both interpretive and critical paradigms. These paradigms were most appropriate because the focus was on understanding mothers' lived experiences and highlighting the social structures that marginalise parental knowledge (Creswell & Poth, 2018). Within the interpretive frame, meaning is co-constructed between researcher and participant; the critical lens allows for the questioning of dominant educational ideologies that undervalue indigenous knowledge.

A qualitative approach provided flexibility to capture the complexity of parental pedagogies, their contextual grounding in culture, and the symbolic meaning of indigenous games. The study sought to explore *what* parents know, *how* they enact this knowledge, and why such enactments matter for transformative pedagogy in early childhood education.

## 4.2 Research Site and Participants

The research took place in a semi-urban township within Tshwane, Gauteng Province, South Africa. The area is linguistically diverse, with Setswana, Sepedi, isiZulu, and English being most commonly spoken. Six mothers, each with at least one child aged birth to four attending a local Early Childhood Care and Education (ECCE) centre, participated. They are referred to here as **Mother A** to **Mother F** to protect anonymity.

Purposive sampling was employed to identify participants who could provide rich information about indigenous child-rearing and play. The selection criteria required mothers to have direct involvement in their children's daily learning activities at home and to be willing to discuss indigenous games or songs used with their children.

*Table 2. Participants' description table*

| Participant (Pseudonym) | Home Language(s) | Child's Age | Context of Game Use |
|---|---|---|---|
| **Mother A** | Sepedi & English | 3 yrs | Plays *kgati* and sings counting rhymes during evenings |
| **Mother B** | Setswana | 4 yrs | Uses *diketo* for coordination and counting skills |
| **Mother C** | isiZulu & English | 2 yrs | Tells stories and clapping songs at bedtime |
| **Mother D** | Sesotho & English | 3 yrs | Engages in role-play and riddles (*meqoqo*) |

continued on following page

*Table 2. Continued*

| Participant (Pseudonym) | Home Language(s) | Child's Age | Context of Game Use |
|---|---|---|---|
| **Mother E** | Xitsonga | 4 yrs | Introduces *morabaraba* using bottle-tops as counters |
| **Mother F** | IsiNdebele | 3 yrs | Combines rhythmic drumming and storytelling |

## 4.3 Data Collection

Data was collected through semi-structured interviews, home observations, and field notes.

Interviews lasted approximately 45 minutes each and were conducted in the mothers' preferred languages, later translated and transcribed into English. Observations captured spontaneous moments of play and parent–child communication. The triangulation of methods enhanced credibility (Lincoln & Guba, 1985).

Sample interview prompts included:

- "Describe a game you often play with your child."
- "What do you think your child learns when you play together?"
- "How do you encourage your child to use language at home?"

## 4.4 Data Analysis

Data was analysed thematically (Braun & Clarke, 2019). Initial codes were generated from recurring expressions—talking while playing, teaching through song, bridging home and centre, which were then clustered into higher-order themes. These aligned closely with two major categories:

1. Language and Communication in the Home, and
2. Belonging and Home–School Linkages.

Throughout the analytic process, reflexivity was maintained through memo writing and peer debriefing to guard against researcher bias.

## 4.5 Ethical Considerations

Ethical clearance was granted by the university under the national *Transformative Pedagogy Project*. Participants signed informed-consent forms and could withdraw at any stage. Pseudonyms were used in all records. Respect for cultural sensitivity guided interactions, recognising that indigenous games are not mere data but expressions of identity and heritage.

### 4.6 Limitations

This study is based on an exploratory qualitative case study involving a small, purposively selected sample of six mothers from a semi-urban South African context. While this allowed for rich, contextually grounded insights into parental pedagogies and indigenous games, the sample size limits the generalisability of the findings and the extent to which policy claims can be made. The focus on mothers reflects the gendered realities of caregiving within the study context; however, it excludes the perspectives of fathers, extended family members, and community elders who also contribute to children's language development. In addition, children's voices were not directly elicited, and their experiences are interpreted through parental accounts. These limitations highlight opportunities for future research to adopt larger, more diverse samples and child-centred, intergenerational approaches to further deepen understanding of indigenous pedagogies in early language development.

## 5. FINDINGS AND DISCUSSION: PEDAGOGICAL SIGNIFICANCE OF PARENTS' EVERYDAY PRACTICES

The findings are presented through four main themes that emerged from the data:

### 5.1 Theme 1: Indigenous Games as Cultural Carriers of the Language of parents' language and communication in the home

Participants described how games such as kgati and morabaraba supported children's oral language and reasoning skills. Furthermore, mothers demonstrated deliberate strategies for nurturing language through culturally embedded routines. Communication was multimodal, such as songs, gestures, storytelling, and humour.

*For example, Mother A noted, "When they play kgati, they sing together and learn to say words quickly; it helps them to speak with confidence. She listens and then repeats. She laughs when she gets the words right. It teaches her to talk clearly."*

This statement illustrates the social mediation that Vygotsky (1978) associates with learning within the *Zone of Proximal Development*. The rhythmic repetition enhances phonological awareness while the playful context sustains motivation.

*Similarly, Mother B shared: "We play diketo with small stones. I count in Setswana first, then in English. She learns both languages together."*

This dual-language practice mirrors *translanguaging* (Garcia & Wei, 2019) where linguistic boundaries are fluid and functional. Parents saw no contradiction in mixing languages; rather, it was a purposeful pedagogy supporting bilingualism.

*Mother C highlighted storytelling as a nightly ritual: "Before sleeping I tell her stories my grandmother told me. She asks questions, sometimes she finishes the sentences. I see she is thinking."*

Through dialogic storytelling, children acquire narrative sequencing and vocabulary. Such intergenerational transmission embodies *Pedagogy-in-Participation*—learning by observing, listening, and contributing (Rogoff, 2003).

*Mother D emphasised moral and emotional language: "When she fights with other children, I use stories to teach her why sharing is good. She listens because stories make it softer."*

Language here functions as both cognitive and affective mediation, supporting emotional intelligence and empathy (O'Connor, 2021).

Across households, mothers used play and talk as reciprocal acts of teaching and affection. Linguistic scaffolding was implicit rather than instructional. These findings affirm that indigenous communication patterns are pedagogically potent. They constitute a *living curriculum* rooted in everyday life (Mkhize & Ndimande, 2018). Furthermore, these practices show how rhythm, repetition, and peer interaction create authentic contexts for language learning.

## 5.2 Theme 2: Parental Pedagogies in Informal Learning Spaces: Establishing a Sense of Belonging and Home-School Links

Parents played active roles in facilitating play, using prompts, songs, and praise to scaffold children's participation.

*Mother C reflected, "We teach them by showing, not by giving instructions. They learn by watching us and trying themselves."*

Such interactions highlight the pedagogical role of parents as co-educators who blend affection and instruction seamlessly.

Mothers viewed belonging as essential to learning. They created home environments that mirrored aspects of the ECCE centre while maintaining cultural integrity.

*Mother E explained: "At school they sing in English; at home I sing the same song but also add our language. She then understands what it means."*

Here, the mother acts as linguistic mediator, bridging school content with home discourse. Such hybridisation represents *transformative pedagogy*, using local knowledge to reinterpret formal curricula (Freire, 1970; Ndlovu-Gatsheni, 2020).

*Mother F described collaborative participation: "When I fetch her from the centre, we talk about what she did. We even play it at home. She becomes the teacher and I become the learner."*

This role-reversal situates the child as agentic, aligning with the transformative aim of dismantling hierarchical power relations in learning (Mezirow, 2018). It demonstrates that belonging is both emotional and epistemological, that children belong when their experiences and languages are validated.

*Mother B highlighted the moral dimension: "I want my child to feel proud of who she is. The games from our culture make her know where she comes from."*

Such expressions resonate with decolonial perspectives that link cultural identity to self-esteem and academic engagement (Chilisa, 2019). Through shared games and dialogue, belonging becomes a pedagogical resource that sustains motivation and resilience

The two themes intersect at the point where language learning and belonging co-construct one another.

- Language is both the vehicle and the outcome of belonging.
- Belonging, in turn, motivates language use and identity formation.

The mothers' practices exemplify what Freire (1970) describes as *praxis*: reflection and action upon the world to transform it. Their pedagogies are neither accidental nor peripheral; they constitute transformative acts of cultural affirmation.

## 5.3 Theme 3: Game-Based Language Learning in Diverse Contexts

In multilingual households, indigenous games provided opportunities for code-switching and vocabulary expansion.

Mother D observed that children often mixed languages during play, which she viewed positively, as it strengthened both languages.

This finding aligns with recent research on translanguaging as a cognitive and cultural resource (Garcia & Wei, 2019).

*Table 3. Examples of indigenous games and their linguistic–cognitive value*

| Game | Description | Language/Literacy Skills | Cognitive/Social Outcomes |
|---|---|---|---|
| ***Kgati* (Skipping rope)** | Two participants turn a rope while others jump and chant rhythmic verses. | Vocabulary expansion, phonemic awareness, and turn-taking. | Memory, coordination, teamwork. |
| ***Diketo* (Pebble game)** | Tossing and catching stones while reciting counting patterns. | Numeracy language, sequencing, bilingual counting. | Fine-motor control, concentration. |
| ***Morabaraba* (Strategy board game)** | Players move tokens on a board to form "mills". | Descriptive language, problem-solving talk. | Logical reasoning, planning. |
| **Clapping games (*amagende*)** | Rhythmic clapping with sung dialogue. | Pronunciation, rhythm, conversational turn-taking. | Social bonding, auditory discrimination. |
| **Storytelling and riddles (*meqoqo*)** | Oral narratives and question-answer riddles. | Narrative structure, vocabulary, inferencing. | Moral reasoning, imagination. |

## 5.4 Theme 4: Transformative Implications for ECD Practice

The study suggests that integrating indigenous games into early childhood education can create inclusive, culturally relevant pedagogies. Educators can collaborate with families to embed traditional play in classroom settings, fostering identity, confidence, and communication skills. These approaches affirm the child's cultural heritage as central to learning and development.

Interpretation through Theoretical Lens

Applying the three-theory framework elucidates how these practices operate as transformative pedagogy:

- Sociocultural Theory: Parents provide scaffolding within children's ZPD; games act as mediational tools.
- Pedagogy-in-Participation: Learning is participatory; parents and children co-create meaning through shared activity.
- Transformative Pedagogy: By reclaiming indigenous knowledge, mothers challenge colonial hierarchies of knowing, fostering dignity and equity.

This triangulation shows that indigenous play is not merely recreational; it is epistemological, producing knowledge systems that sustain multilingualism and identity.

## 5.5 Discussion

The findings affirm that indigenous games are pedagogical ecosystems encompassing language, cognition, emotion, and culture. Mothers' engagement reveals a nuanced understanding of early learning that contrasts sharply with the deficit narratives often attributed to low-income families (Tucker & Govender, 2020). Their practices demonstrate intentionality, structure, and reflection of the hallmarks of professional pedagogy, yet emerge from community life.

The chapter, therefore, argues for a re-centering of parental voices in ECD discourse. Recognising parents as co-educators requires institutions to shift from tokenistic participation to genuine collaboration (Makgopa, 2022). When schools invite parents to share indigenous games within classroom contexts, they enact the principle of learning through participation and enrich the linguistic ecology of the classroom (Rogoff et al., 2018).

Furthermore, integrating indigenous games aligns with *decolonial* educational imperatives that seek epistemic justice (Ndlovu-Gatsheni, 2020). It offers practical pathways for implementing culturally responsive curricula without additional material cost and a crucial consideration in resource-constrained communities.

## 6. DISCUSSION AND IMPLICATIONS

This chapter contributes to ongoing dialogues about decolonising education and recognising indigenous knowledge systems as valid sources of pedagogy. It demonstrates how parental pedagogies and indigenous games offer a culturally congruent means of supporting early language development. Teacher education programmes should include training on community-based learning approaches, encouraging educators to draw upon the cultural capital present in learners' homes. Policy initiatives should also value and preserve indigenous practices as integral to holistic childhood development.

### 6.1 Re-Centring Parents as Co-Educators

The findings emphasise that parents are not peripheral to the learning process but are essential pedagogical partners. For early-childhood systems in South Africa and similar multilingual contexts, this calls for a paradigm shift: parents must be viewed as legitimate sources of pedagogical knowledge. Policies should therefore formalise *home-school partnerships* by embedding structured opportunities for parental participation in curriculum design and implementation (Department of Basic Education [DBE], 2022).

Practically, ECCE centres can introduce "community pedagogy sessions", during which parents share traditional songs, riddles, or games that align with classroom themes. Teachers then contextualise these experiences within literacy or numeracy lessons. This reciprocal exchange creates linguistic continuity between home and school, supporting the goal of equitable, culturally grounded education (Heugh, 2021).

## 6.2 Curriculum Integration of Indigenous Games

The inclusion of indigenous games in early-language curricula addresses two persistent challenges: limited learner engagement and under-representation of African epistemologies. By framing *kgati*, *diketo*, or *morabaraba* as literacy resources rather than leisure activities, teachers can cultivate phonological awareness, sequencing, and turn-taking (Phatudi, 2021).

A curriculum-integration model might include:

- **Game narratives** translated into big-book or digital story formats;
- **Language mapping** exercises where children label actions or objects within the game;
- **Peer-teaching sessions** where learners explain game rules, reinforcing oral expression.

Such strategies demonstrate that indigenous knowledge is not supplementary but foundational to early-literacy learning (Mkhize & Ndimande, 2018).

## 6.3 Teacher Education and Professional Development

Teacher-education institutions have an ethical responsibility to prepare practitioners who value community-based pedagogies. Courses in *Culturally Responsive Pedagogy* should highlight indigenous play as a site for learning design, classroom management, and assessment. Pre-service teachers can be guided to conduct micro-projects that document local games and analyse their pedagogical functions (Kirkland & Randolph, 2021).

In-service professional development should focus on:

1. Reflective practice and helping educators interrogate biases that privilege Eurocentric teaching models.
2. Collaborative curriculum design with parents and elders.

3. Linguistic inclusion and strategies for translanguaging and code-switching in instruction.

When teachers understand indigenous play as both cultural heritage and cognitive apprenticeship, they become agents of transformation rather than mere implementers of policy (Freire, 1970).

## 6.4 Policy and Institutional Implications

At policy level, the DBE's National Curriculum Framework for Children from Birth to Four already acknowledges play as the foundation for learning; however, explicit reference to indigenous games remains limited. Incorporating this dimension would align national policy with UNESCO's (2020) advocacy for Learning through Play.

Institutions such as UNISA and other higher-education providers could pioneer short learning programmes for ECCE practitioners on Indigenous Knowledge and Game-Based Learning. Such initiatives would operationalise the principles of transformative pedagogy by legitimising parents' and communities' roles in knowledge production.

# 7. CONCLUSION

Indigenous games and parental pedagogies embody profound educational wisdom that has been undervalued in mainstream curricula. By engaging with these culturally grounded practices, educators and policymakers can foster equitable and contextually meaningful early learning experiences. This chapter calls for renewed collaboration between families, schools, and communities in honouring indigenous heritage as a living pedagogy for the future.

This chapter has illuminated how indigenous games and parental pedagogies intersect to promote early language development in diverse South African contexts. Through the voices of six mothers, we witnessed pedagogical intentionality expressed through song, rhythm, storytelling, and play. These acts constitute transformative praxis and affirming identity, fostering belonging, and nurturing linguistic competence.

The theoretical alignment of Sociocultural Theory, Pedagogy-in-Participation, and Transformative Pedagogy demonstrates that language learning is most powerful when rooted in social interaction and cultural continuity. The study contributes to the decolonisation of early-childhood education by positioning parents as epistemic partners rather than passive caregivers.

Ultimately, integrating indigenous games within formal education systems promotes equity, relevance, and joy in learning. As global education grapples with inclusivity and sustainability, acknowledging the pedagogical richness of community practices offers a pathway toward culturally resonant education for all children.

*Table 4. Key terminologies*

| Term | Definition (APA 7-style) |
|---|---|
| **Indigenous Games** | Traditional, community-based play activities embodying cultural values, language, and social learning. |
| **Parental Pedagogies** | The intentional or intuitive teaching practices that parents employ to support children's learning within the home context. |
| **Pedagogy-in-Participation** | A learning model where knowledge is co-constructed through shared activity rather than direct instruction. |
| **Sociocultural Theory** | Vygotskian perspective that learning is mediated through social interaction and cultural tools. |
| **Transformative Pedagogy** | A Freirean approach positioning education as a process of critical reflection and emancipation. |
| **Translanguaging** | Dynamic use of multiple languages within a single communicative act to enhance understanding and expression. |
| **Zone of Proximal Development (ZPD)** | The cognitive space between what a learner can do independently and what can be achieved with guidance. |

## 7.1 Reflective and Discussion Questions

These questions encourage postgraduate readers and pre-service teachers to connect theory with practice, fostering deeper engagement with transformative, culturally responsive pedagogy.

1. **Analytical Reflection:**

In what ways can indigenous games be systematically integrated into early-language curricula without losing their cultural authenticity?

2. **Application:**

Identify an indigenous game from your own community. Outline how it could develop both linguistic and social-emotional skills in children aged 3–6.

3. **Critical Inquiry:**

How can teacher-education programmes balance global standards of literacy instruction with localised indigenous practices?

4. **Policy Engagement:**

Suggest how the *National Curriculum Framework* might be amended to legitimise indigenous games as pedagogical tools.

5. **Ethical Reflection:**

What considerations should researchers observe when documenting community knowledge, such as indigenous play?

6. **Personal Reflection:**

How might you, as an educator or researcher, collaborate with parents to bridge home and school pedagogies?

## REFERENCES


Acheampong, P. (2022). *Reclaiming play: African indigenous games and early learning*. Accra Press.

Braun, V., & Clarke, V. (2019). Reflecting on reflexive thematic analysis. *Qualitative Research in Sport, Exercise and Health, 11*(4), 589–597. DOI: 10.1080/2159676X.2019.1628806

Chilisa, B. (2019). *Indigenous research methodologies* (2nd ed.). Sage.

Creswell, J. W., & Poth, C. N. (2018). *Qualitative inquiry and research design: Choosing among five approaches* (4th ed.). Sage.

Department of Basic Education. (2022). *National curriculum framework for children from birth to four years* (Revised Ed.). DBE.

Freire, P. (1970). Cultural action and conscientization. *Harvard Educational Review, 40*(3), 452–477. DOI: 10.17763/haer.40.3.h76250x720j43175

Garcia, O., & Wei, L. (2019). *Translanguaging: Language, Bilingualism and Education*. Palgrave Macmillan.

Gee, J. P. (2020). *What video games have to teach us about learning and literacy* (3rd ed.). Palgrave Macmillan.

Heugh, K. (2021). Multilingual education for social justice: The South African case. *Language Matters, 52*(1), 1–19.

Kirkland, D. E., & Randolph, A. (2021). Culturally responsive teacher education: Lessons from communities of colour. *Teaching Education, 32*(5), 528–543.

Lincoln, Y. S., & Guba, E. G. (1985). *Naturalistic inquiry*. Sage. DOI: 10.1016/0147-1767(85)90062-8

Makgopa, M. (2022). Parents as pedagogical partners in early childhood centres. *South African Journal of Childhood Education, 12*(1), 1–9.

Maphalala, M. (2019). Indigenous play and learning in South African contexts. *South African Journal of Childhood Education, 9*(1), 1–8.

Mezirow, J. (2018). Transformative learning theory. In Illeris, K. (Ed.), *Contemporary theories of learning* (pp. 104–118). Routledge. DOI: 10.4324/9781315147277-8

Mkhize, N., & Ndimande, B. (2018). Decolonising knowledge in education: African indigenous perspectives. *Perspectives in Education, 36*(2), 1–12.

Ndlovu-Gatsheni, S. J. (2020). *Epistemic freedom in Africa: Deprovincialization and decolonization*. Routledge.

O'Connor, E. (2021). Emotional literacy in early childhood. *Early Years*, *41*(4), 421–436.

Phatudi, N. (2021). Language, culture and play in early learning. *Early Child Development and Care*, *191*(10), 1512–1524.

Rogoff, B., Paradise, R., Arauz, R. M., Correa-Chávez, M., & Angelillo, C. (2018). Firsthand learning through intent participation. *Annual Review of Psychology*, *69*, 1–27. PMID: 12499516

Siraj-Blatchford, J., & Brock, L. (2019). How to scaffold learning through free-flow play. *Early Years Educator*, *21*(3), 31–33. DOI: 10.12968/eyed.2019.21.3.31

Tucker, L., & Govender, P. (2020). Parental engagement in early childhood centres: Challenges and prospects. *Perspectives in Education*, *38*(2), 72–88.

UNESCO. (2020). *Learning through play: Strengthening education through indigenous games*. UNESCO Publishing.

Vygotsky, L. S. (1978). *Mind in Society: The Development of Higher Psychological Processes*. Harvard University Press.

Weisberg, L., Kohnen, A., & Dawson, K. (2022). Impacts of a digital literacy intervention on preservice teachers' civic online reasoning abilities, strategies, and perceptions. *Journal of Technology and Teacher Education*, *30*(1), 73–98. DOI: 10.70725/926509jtmzpi

# Chapter 4
# Preserving Indigenous Languages Through Interactive Digital Experience:
## An Applied Research Study on Developing Language-Focused Games

**Onias Matumbu**
http://orcid.org/0000-0002-0257-3510
*Morgan Zintec College, University of Zimbabwe, Zimbabwe*

**Nomatter Kufarimani**
*Morgan Zintec College, University of Zimbabwe, Zimbabwe*

## ABSTRACT

*This chapter investigates the preservation of Indigenous languages in Zimbabwe through interactive digital experiences, particularly language-focused games. The colonial legacy has entrenched English as the dominant language, marginalizing Indigenous tongues and contributing to cultural erosion. Despite government efforts, progress remains insufficient, highlighting the need for innovative solutions. Using a gamification framework informed by community engagement, this research enhances the learning of selected Indigenous languages. Collaborating with cultural experts, we developed engaging game narratives and features, showing gamification's po-*

DOI: 10.4018/979-8-3373-4322-8.ch004

*tential as a transformative tool for linguistic preservation. The findings suggest that interactive experiences can revitalize Indigenous languages, addressing challenges in implementation and cultural nuances.*

## 1. INTRODUCTION

### 1.1 The Global Crisis of Linguistic Diversity

The contemporary erosion of linguistic diversity represents one of humanity's most profound cultural catastrophes. UNESCO (2023) reports that approximately 40% of the world's estimated 7,000 languages face extinction, with one language disappearing approximately every two weeks. This rate of attrition, unprecedented in human history, threatens not merely communication systems but entire repositories of traditional knowledge, worldviews, and cultural identity (Romaine, 2021). Austin and Sallabank (2023) argue that language death constitutes an irreversible loss to human cognitive diversity, as each language embodies unique ways of conceptualising reality, encoding environmental knowledge, and structuring social relationships. The implications extend beyond cultural heritage to encompass biodiversity conservation, as Indigenous languages frequently contain irreplaceable ecological knowledge accumulated over millennia (Terralingua, 2022).Whilst globalisation and urbanisation contribute to language shift, the primary driver remains historical colonisation and its enduring structural legacies (Wa Thiong'o, 2021). European colonial powers systematically suppressed Indigenous languages through education policies, administrative practices, and social stigmatisation, establishing linguistic hierarchies that persist decades after political independence (Ndhlovu & Makalela, 2021). In post-colonial contexts across Africa, Asia, and Latin America, former colonial languages particularly English, French, Spanish, and Portuguese, continue to dominate education, governance, and economic opportunity, marginalising Indigenous languages to informal domains and perpetuating cycles of linguistic inequality (Prah, 2022).

The consequences of this marginalisation are profound and multifaceted. Research demonstrates that children educated exclusively in non-native languages experience reduced learning outcomes, higher dropout rates, and diminished cognitive development compared to peers receiving mother-tongue instruction (UNESCO, 2022). Beyond educational impacts, language loss erodes cultural identity, severs intergenerational knowledge transmission, and undermines community cohesion (Grenoble & Whaley, 2023). Fishman's (2021) framework of Graded Intergenerational Disruption Scale illustrates how language shift progresses from domains of higher prestige downward, ultimately disrupting family transmission the critical mechanism for language maintenance. When children cease acquiring their heritage languages, communities lose living connections to ancestral knowledge systems, oral traditions, and cultural practices (Crystal, 2022).

## 1.2 The Zimbabwean Context: Colonial Legacies and Contemporary Challenges

Zimbabwe's linguistic landscape exemplifies the persistent impact of colonial language policies on post-independence nations. Despite constitutional recognition of 16 official languages including ChiShona, IsiNdebele, Kalanga, Nambya, Tonga, Tswana, Venda, Shangaan, Chewa, Koisan, Ndau, Sotho, Xhosa, Sign Language, and English (Constitution of Zimbabwe, 2013), the practical dominance of English in education, administration, and commerce continues unabated (Mawadza, 2021). This discrepancy between constitutional ideals and implementation realities reflects what Shizha and Makuvaza (2022) term “symbolic multilingualism”, formal recognition without substantive resource allocation or policy enforcement.

The historical roots of this hierarchy trace to British colonial education policies implemented following Cecil Rhodes's colonisation of the territory in 1890. The Doke Commission Report of 1931 established English as the exclusive medium of instruction beyond primary levels, whilst marginalising IsiNdebele and ChiShona to restricted roles and entirely neglecting minority languages (Viriri & Viriri, 2023). This policy served explicit assimilationist objectives, with colonial administrators regarding Indigenous languages as obstacles to civilisation and economic development (Ndlovu-Gatsheni, 2021). The missionary education system reinforced these hierarchies, associating English literacy with Christian modernity and Indigenous languages with paganism and backwardness (Makaudze, 2022). Post-independence language policies, whilst rhetorically embracing multilingualism, have struggled to dismantle these colonial structures. The 1987 Education Act mandated mother-tongue instruction for Grades 1-3, subsequently extended to Grade 7 in 2006 amendments (Government of Zimbabwe, 2006). However, implementation has been inconsistent and inadequate. Magwa and Ngara (2022) document widespread failures to provide teaching materials, train teachers in Indigenous languages, or develop curriculum resources beyond ChiShona and IsiNdebele. Minority languages face particularly severe marginalisation: Tonga, Kalanga, Shangaan, and Venda lack standardised orthographies, teacher training programmes, or examination systems (Kadenge & Nkomo, 2021).

Contemporary challenges extend beyond policy implementation to encompass shifting social attitudes and economic pressures. Thondhlana and Kadenge (2023) identify pervasive stigmatisation of Indigenous languages among urban youth, who increasingly associate English proficiency with modernity, social mobility, and global citizenship. This phenomenon, which Blommaert (2022) terms "grassroots sociolinguistic hierarchisation," sees parents actively choosing English-medium education despite children's limited proficiency, believing it offers superior economic opportunities. Consequently, intergenerational transmission, the cornerstone of language maintenance is disrupting even in rural areas traditionally resistant to language shift (Mafugu, 2021).

The educational consequences are stark. Nyamayedenga and Makaudze (2021) found that 67% of Zimbabwean primary students begin schooling with insufficient English proficiency for academic success, yet receive instruction predominantly in English from Grade 4 onwards. This linguistic mismatch contributes to Zimbabwe's concerning educational indicators: primary completion rates of 68%, secondary completion of 42%, and substantial urban-rural disparities (UNICEF Zimbabwe, 2023). Makaudze (2022) argues that language policies prioritising colonial languages over mother tongues constitute structural violence against Indigenous communities, denying equitable access to education and perpetuating historical injustices.

## 1.3 Digital Technology as a Language Preservation Tool

Amidst these realities, digital technology offers unprecedented opportunities for Indigenous language revitalisation. The proliferation of mobile devices with smartphone penetration exceeding 80% in Zimbabwe (POTRAZ, 2024), creates potential for reaching learners beyond formal educational institutions. Digital platforms enable scalable production and distribution of language resources at costs substantially lower than traditional print materials, addressing persistent resource constraints in post-colonial education systems (Hinton et al., 2022). Furthermore, technology can render Indigenous languages relevant within contemporary digital culture, potentially countering stigmatisation by demonstrating their compatibility with modernity (Kelly-Holmes & Moriarty, 2023).

Interactive games represent a particularly promising digital intervention. Game-based learning research demonstrates significant advantages over traditional pedagogical approaches, including enhanced motivation, increased engagement, immediate feedback, and reduced anxiety (Hamari et al., 2024). These benefits prove especially salient for Indigenous language learning, which often confronts learner reluctance rooted in stigmatisation and perceived irrelevance (McIvor et al., 2021). Games can create immersive linguistic environments simulating natural acquisition contexts whilst incorporating explicit instruction, thereby combining communicative and cognitive dimensions of language learning (Sykes & Reinhardt, 2023). Globally, Indigenous communities are pioneering digital language interventions. New Zealand's Maori language revitalisation programme includes popular digital games like *Te Reo Tupu*, reaching over 500,000 users and contributing to increased youth engagement with *te reo* Maori (Maori Language Commission, 2024).

This chapter addresses critical gaps in understanding how digital gamification can support Indigenous language preservation in resource-constrained, post-colonial African contexts. Whilst existing research on game-based language learning focuses predominantly on high-resource contexts and globally dominant languages (Cheng et al., 2023), limited scholarship examines applications for endangered Indigenous languages, particularly in Southern Africa. Practically, the research provides actionable frameworks for developing, implementing, and sustaining digital language games in low-resource settings. Through participatory design processes with ChiShona and Kore Kore-speaking communities in Zimbabwe's Gokwe District, it produces an open-source game prototype, *Dare reDzidzo,* alongside detailed documentation of collaborative development methodologies.

## 1.4 Theoretical Framework

This chapter employs a multi-theoretical framework integrating four complementary perspectives: the Technology Acceptance Model, Game-Based Learning Theory and Sociocultural Learning Theory. This integration reflects the complex, multidimensional nature of digital language intervention, which simultaneously involves technological adoption, pedagogical design, cultural meaning-making, and community empowerment.

### 1.4.1 Technology Acceptance Model (TAM)

Davis' (1989) Technology Acceptance Model posits that technology adoption depends primarily upon two beliefs: perceived usefulness (the degree to which using a technology would enhance performance) and perceived ease of use (the degree to which using a technology would be free from effort). Subsequent elaborations have refined the model through attention to external variables, subjective norms, and actual usage behaviour (Venkatesh & Davis, 2023). Meta-analyses confirm TAM's robust predictive validity across diverse contexts and technologies (King & He, 2021).

Applying TAM to Indigenous language games enables systematic investigation of adoption barriers and facilitators. If potential users perceive games as useful for language learning and easy to navigate, adoption likelihood increases substantially. However, recent scholarship suggests TAM requires cultural adaptation for non-Western contexts (Tarhini et al., 2024). This study hypothesises that cultural relevance, the extent to which technology reflects and respects Indigenous knowledge systems and cultural protocols functions as a third critical dimension influencing acceptance within Indigenous communities. This extension aligns with Indigenous technology scholarship emphasising sovereignty, protocols, and cultural safety (Galla, 2023).

### 1.4.2 Game-Based Learning Theory

Game-based learning theory examines how game mechanics facilitate educational outcomes. Gee's (2023) learning principles emphasise active engagement, situated meaning, pleasantly frustrating challenges, and multimodal representation. Prensky's (2023) digital game-based learning framework highlights motivation through fantasy, curiosity, challenge, and control. These theories informed design decisions ensuring that language acquisition occurs through meaningful play rather than decontextualised drills (Dichev & Dicheva, 2023). Critical to this study is understanding gamification mechanisms, the application of game design elements to non-game contexts (Deterding et al., 2023). Hamari et al.'s (2024) meta-analysis identifies three primary mechanisms through which gamification enhances learning: psychological outcomes (increased motivation and engagement), behavioural outcomes (increased participation and performance), and affective outcomes (enjoyment and reduced anxiety). For Indigenous language learning, wherein stigmatisation creates affective barriers, the anxiety-reducing potential of gamification proves particularly salient (McIvor et al., 2021).

However, scholars caution against superficial gamification, adding points and badges without substantive pedagogical integration (Landers et al., 2023). Effective educational games require alignment between game mechanics and learning objectives, ensuring that gameplay activities directly facilitate desired competencies rather than merely rewarding peripheral behaviours (Plass et al., 2023). This study therefore emphasises meaningful play wherein player actions produce consequences affecting both game progression and linguistic development (Salen & Zimmerman, 2024).

### 1.4.3 Sociocultural Learning Theory

Vygotsky's (1978) sociocultural theory positions language as both tool and medium of cognitive development, learned fundamentally through social interaction within culturally meaningful contexts. This perspective emphasises the Zone of Proximal Development, the gap between independent capability and potential achievement through guided interaction and scaffolding processes whereby more knowledgeable others support learners' advancing competence (Lantolf & Thorne, 2021). Contemporary applications extend Vygotskian insights through attention to communities of practice, situated cognition, and distributed expertise (Lave & Wenger, 2023). For Indigenous language revitalisation, sociocultural theory underscores several critical principles. First, language learning must embed within authentic cultural practices rather than abstract exercises divorced from meaningful communication (Hinton, 2021). Second, intergenerational transmission wherein elders and fluent speakers guide emerging learners represents the most effective maintenance mechanism (Grenoble & Whaley, 2023). Third, language cannot be separated from the cultural knowledge, values, and worldviews it encodes; effective pedagogy therefore integrates linguistic and cultural competence development (Wilson, 2022).

This chapter operationalises sociocultural theory through participatory game design ensuring that linguistic content reflects authentic community usage and cultural knowledge. It recognises that whilst digital games may provide individual practice opportunities, sustainable revitalisation requires embedding technology within broader community efforts reconnecting learners with fluent speakers and cultural practices (Leonard, 2021).

### 1.5 Objectives

This chapter pursues five objectives:

1. To evaluate the impact of multilingual education policies on Indigenous language preservation and promotion in Zimbabwe.
2. To identify challenges faced by educators and students in implementing multilingual education.
3. To assess the effectiveness of digital language games in preserving Indigenous languages through rigorous mixed-methods evaluation
4. To develop language-based games preserving and utilising Indigenous languages through participatory design processes with Indigenous communities.
5. To examine transferability and scalability of game-based language preservation interventions beyond the Zimbabwean context

## 2. LITERATURE REVIEW

### 2.1 Multilingualism and Language Policy in Post-Colonial Africa

The relationship between language policy and educational outcomes in post-colonial Africa has generated substantial scholarly debate. Bamgbose's (2021) comprehensive analysis of African language policies identifies a persistent disjunction between official multilingual commitments and practical implementation dominated by former colonial languages. This "policy-practice gap" reflects what Djite (2022) terms "elite closure" whereby political and economic elites maintain linguistic hierarchies benefiting their own social reproduction whilst rhetorically endorsing

Indigenous language promotion. Batibo (2023) demonstrates how resource allocation patterns systematically privilege colonial languages through disproportionate investment in English-medium materials, teacher training, and assessment systems.

Zimbabwe exemplifies these continental patterns for example, Chimhundu's (2022) historical analysis traces language policy evolution from colonial suppression through post-independence ambivalence to constitutional multilingualism, revealing consistent subordination of Indigenous languages to English. The 2013 Constitutional recognition of 16 official languages represented symbolic advancement, yet Kadenge and Nkomo (2021) document minimal practical change in educational language use. Their research found that 89% of secondary schools conduct instruction predominantly in English despite constitutional requirements for Indigenous language options. Magwa and Ngara (2022) attribute this implementation failure to interconnected factors, insufficient budgetary allocations (Indigenous languages receive less than 3% of education spending), inadequate teacher preparation (only 12% of teachers report confidence teaching in Indigenous languages beyond ChiShona and IsiNdebele), and absent political will for challenging English hegemony. Minority language marginalisation within Zimbabwe's multilingual framework warrants particular attention. Whilst ChiShona and IsiNdebele receive some institutional support as languages spoken by approximately 70% and 20% of the population respectively (Mawadza, 2021), the remaining 14 recognised languages face severe neglect. Ndhlovu's (2023) research with Tonga communities documents complete absence of mother-tongue educational materials, forcing children into ChiShona-medium instruction despite limited proficiency. Moyo and Moyo (2022) report similar conditions for Shangaan, Venda, and Kalanga speakers, creating what they term "triple marginalisation", exclusion from English privilege, from ChiShona/IsiNdebele accommodation, and from recognition of their linguistic rights.

This marginalisation produces measurable educational harms. Benson and Kosonen's (2021) meta-analysis of mother-tongue education programmes across Sub-Saharan Africa demonstrates that children taught in familiar languages for at least six years achieve substantially higher literacy levels, mathematical competence, and critical thinking skills than peers transitioned prematurely to unfamiliar languages. UNESCO's (2022) comparative study found that language-of-instruction mismatch accounts for approximately 40% of primary-level dropout in contexts like Zimbabwe. Yet despite robust evidence favouring mother-tongue instruction, implementation remains elusive due to entrenched beliefs associating colonial languages with quality education and Indigenous languages with backwardness (Prah, 2022).

## 2.2 Gamification and Game-Based Language Learning

Educational gamification, applying game design elements to non-game learning contexts has garnered substantial research attention and enthusiasm. Deterding et al.'s (2023) influential framework distinguishes gamification (adding game elements to existing activities) from game-based learning (using actual games as educational tools). Both approaches leverage motivational affordances of gameplay: challenge, curiosity, competition, cooperation, recognition, and immediate feedback (Gee, 2023). Meta-analytical research generally supports gamification's educational benefits, though with important caveats. Hamari et al.'s (2024) analysis of 157 empirical studies found that gamification positively influences psychological outcomes (increased motivation, engagement, and enjoyment) in approximately 75% of cases, behavioural outcomes (participation, performance) in 60%, and cognitive outcomes (learning, retention) in 50%. Effect sizes varied substantially depending on implementation quality, context, and learner characteristics. Importantly, superficial gamification merely adding points, badges, or leaderboards without substantive pedagogical integration often proved ineffective or counterproductive (Landers et al., 2023).

For language learning specifically, game-based approaches offer several theoretical advantages. Sykes and Reinhardt's (2023) framework identifies three primary mechanisms: contextualised learning (games situate language use within meaningful scenarios), multimodal input (games combine text, audio, and visual information supporting diverse learning styles), and reduced affective filters (gameplay contexts feel less evaluative than traditional classrooms, potentially reducing anxiety). Purushotma et al.'s (2022) research on multiplayer online games demonstrates how collaborative gameplay creates authentic communicative contexts requiring negotiation, clarification, and creative language use, all are fundamental to acquisition.

Empirical studies of game-based language learning report generally positive outcomes. Zou et al.'s (2022) meta-analysis of 56 experimental and quasi-experimental studies found mean effect sizes of $d = 0.49$ for vocabulary learning, $d = 0.36$ for grammar, and $d = 0.52$ for speaking proficiency. However, effect sizes varied substantially depending on game design, duration of intervention, learner proficiency levels, and integration with other instruction. Games proved most effective when combined with explicit instruction and reflection activities rather than serving as standalone interventions (Plass et al., 2023). For Indigenous language learning, gamification offers additional benefits beyond general language education. McIvor et al.'s (2021) research with Indigenous youth in Canada found that digital games reduced stigma associated with Indigenous language learning by positioning languages within contemporary, technologically sophisticated contexts rather than exclusively traditional domains. Participants reported feeling "cool" and "modern" whilst playing language games, attitudinal shifts rarely achieved through conventional pedagogy.

Galla and Holmes (2021) similarly found that Hawaiian language games attracted young learners previously disengaged from language revitalisation, serving as gateway experiences motivating subsequent participation in face-to-face programmes.

Nonetheless, scholars caution against overestimating game-based interventions. Thorne et al.'s (2023) found that whilst initial engagement with language games often proved high, sustained usage required continuous content updates, social features enabling competition or collaboration, and integration with broader learning ecosystems. Games used in isolation without connection to fluent speakers, cultural contexts, or meaningful communication opportunities produced limited proficiency gains beyond basic vocabulary (Reinhardt & Thorne, 2023). Furthermore, commercial language-learning games frequently emphasise dominant languages (English, Spanish, Mandarin), with Indigenous languages remaining drastically underrepresented despite growing interest in preservation technology (Joshi et al., 2023).

## 2.3 Community-Based Approaches to Educational Technology

The increasing recognition of community participation's importance in educational technology development reflects broader shifts toward participatory design and user-centred innovation. Schuler and Namioka's (2023) participatory design framework positions end-users as co-designers rather than passive consumers, arguing that technologies prove most effective when incorporating users' situated knowledge, cultural contexts, and practical needs. For Indigenous communities specifically, participatory approaches align with sovereignty principles asserting self-determination over technologies affecting cultural knowledge and community wellbeing (Smith, 2022; Wilson, 2022).

Community-Based Participatory Research methodologies extend participation beyond design into all research phases. Wallerstein and Duran's (2023) comprehensive framework identifies core principles: equitable partnerships recognising community expertise, capacity building strengthening community research skills, mutual benefit ensuring research serves community priorities, and long-term commitment extending beyond individual projects. CBPR emerged partly from critiques of extractive research paradigms wherein external researchers appropriate Indigenous knowledge without consent, compensation, or community benefit practices rooted in colonial knowledge appropriation (Battiste & Henderson, 2021).

Applications of CBPR to educational technology development demonstrate substantial benefits. Israel et al.'s (2023) longitudinal study comparing participatory versus conventional technology development processes found that participatory projects achieved higher community adoption rates (72% versus 34%), greater cultural appropriateness, and enhanced sustainability through community ownership and capacity development. Indigenous language technology specifically, community participation proves essential for cultural and linguistic authenticity. Galla's (2023) research on Indigenous language applications emphasises that external developers typically lack nuanced understanding of cultural protocols, dialectal variation, appropriate pedagogical approaches, and community sensitivities. Without substantive community collaboration, technologies risk cultural appropriation, misrepresentation, or perpetuation of colonial linguistic hierarchies. Christen et al.'s (2023) analysis demonstrates how participatory design enables communities to implement traditional knowledge protocols within digital platforms including restrictions on sacred content, gender-specific materials, or seasonal knowledge inappropriate for year-round access.

International examples of digital Indigenous language revitalisation provide valuable insights for Zimbabwean contexts. New Zealand's Maori language revitalisation represents one of the most successful Indigenous language movements globally, combining policy support, community mobilisation, and technological innovation. Following the Maori Language Act of 1987, which established *te reo* Maori as an official language, comprehensive initiatives emerged including *kohanga reo* (language nest preschools), *kura kaupapa* Maori (Maori-medium schools), and digital resources (Benton, 2023). Digital interventions include *Te Reo Tupu*, a mobile application featuring interactive games, speech recognition, and cultural content, which has attracted over 500,000 users since its 2019 launch (Maori Language Commission, 2024). Research indicates that digital resources contributed to increasing youth engagement, with speakers under 25 growing from 18% in 2013 to 27% in 2023 (Statistics New Zealand, 2023).

These international cases illuminate several critical success factors that policy integration proves essential effective digital interventions nest within comprehensive language planning frameworks addressing education, media, administration, and economic domains (Spolsky, 2021). Technology alone cannot reverse language shift absent broader policy commitment. Second, sustained funding mechanisms enable long-term development and maintenance rather than short-lived pilot projects (Coronel-Molina & McCarty, 2023). Third, community ownership ensures cultural appropriateness, builds local capacity, and sustains engagement beyond initial novelty (Galla, 2023). Fourth, integration between digital and face-to-face learning contexts maximises effectiveness games work best as complements to human interaction rather than replacements (Leonard, 2021). Finally, realistic expectations acknowledge technology's limitations whilst leveraging its distinctive affordances for accessibility, scalability, and youth engagement (Cunliffe, 2022).

## 3. METHODOLOGY

This chapter employed an exploratory sequential mixed-methods design, beginning with qualitative inquiry to establish context followed by quantitative exploration to analyze patterns and prevalence (Creswell & Plano Clark, 2023). This approach reflects a pragmatic epistemology, advocating for diverse ways of knowing and prioritizing research questions over rigid paradigms (Morgan, 2023). It champions a transformative paradigm focused on social justice and participant empowerment, crucial given the historical exploitation in Indigenous research contexts (Mertens, 2023). The necessity of a qualitative-first approach stems from the complex cultural meanings associated with Indigenous language preservation, which cannot be reduced to predetermined categories (Wilson, 2022). The qualitative phase was instrumental in identifying evaluation criteria, cultural priorities, and specific community concerns that guided the development of quantitative instruments. By establishing trust with community participants before broader survey engagement, this phase addressed Indigenous skepticism toward external researchers (Tuhiwai Smith, 2022). Ethically, prioritizing qualitative listening underscored respect for community knowledge and avoided imposing external frameworks too early (Kovach, 2023). Integration occurred throughout the research process, where qualitative findings informed quantitative instruments, while quantitative results revealed patterns warranting further qualitative exploration. Joint displays facilitated comparisons across data sets, and meta-inferences helped synthesize findings to meet research objectives (Fetters, 2023).

Conducted in ChiShona and Kore Kore-speaking communities in Gokwe District, Zimbabwe, under Chief Sayi's leadership, the research addressed challenges typical of rural Zimbabwe, including infrastructural deficiencies (Zimbabwe National Statistics Agency, 2022). Gokwe faces increased language shift among youth attributed to English-medium education (Magwa & Ngara, 2022). Community engagement began in August 2024, ensuring collaboration through formal outreach and participation in local gatherings. A Community Advisory Board was established, comprising diverse stakeholders to provide ongoing guidance.

# 4. FINDINGS AND DISCUSSION

## 4.1 Impact of Multilingual Education Policies on Indigenous Language Preservation

### 4.1.1 Policy-Practice Disjunction

Participants across all stakeholder groups identified profound gaps between constitutional multilingual commitments and educational realities. All 15 linguistic experts and 87% of educators (n=43/50) reported that despite the 2013 Constitution recognising 16 official languages, practical implementation remains severely constrained. One experienced educator articulated this disconnect: "On paper, we celebrate linguistic diversity. In practice, English dominates from Grade 4 onwards, and minority languages receive virtually no instructional time or resources" (Female educator, age 38, 15 years' experience). This finding aligns with Chimhundu's (2022) analysis documenting persistent English hegemony despite formal multilingual policies. Survey data quantified the extent: only 23% of educators reported their schools offering instruction in Indigenous languages beyond ChiShona and IsiNdebele; 78% indicated inadequate teaching materials for Indigenous language instruction; and 91% stated that English proficiency determines academic progression regardless of Indigenous language competence. These statistics substantiate qualitative perceptions of systematic English privilege.

Interviews with linguistic experts revealed how colonial language hierarchies persist institutionally. One elder linguist explained: "The Doke Commission of 1931 established English supremacy. Nearly a century later, that hierarchy remains largely intact officially rejected but practically reproduced through examination systems, university admission requirements, and employment prerequisites" (Male linguistic expert, age 67). This observation resonates with Ndhlovu and Makalela's (2021) argument that post-colonial language policies often represent symbolic gestures without structural transformation. Minority language marginalisation proved particularly acute. All five Kore Kore-speaking participants emphasised complete absence of mother-tongue educational resources: "Our children must learn in ChiShona or English, neither their home language. This creates compounding disadvantage linguistic barriers to accessing linguistic instruction" (Female community member, age 42, Kore Kore speaker). Kadenge and Nkomo's (2021) research similarly documents how minority language speakers experience "triple marginalisation" excluded from English privilege, ChiShona/IsiNdebele accommodation, and recognition of their own linguistic rights.

### 4.1.2 Resource Allocation Inequities

Material resource scarcity emerged as the most frequently cited implementation barrier, mentioned by 94% of educators and 100% of linguistic experts. Participants detailed systematic under-resourcing of Indigenous language education across multiple dimensions. One secondary school head of department explained: "We received 350 English textbooks this term, 120 for mathematics taught in English, but only 15 outdated ChiShona readers and absolutely nothing for Tonga, Kalanga, or other minority languages" (Male educator, age 45, 18 years' experience).

Quantitative survey data corroborated these qualitative accounts. Among educators, 82% reported their schools possessed fewer than 20 Indigenous language textbooks total; 67% indicated no digital Indigenous language resources whatsoever; 91% stated that Indigenous language materials were outdated (average publication date: 2008) compared to regularly updated English resources; and 73% noted complete absence of assessment materials for Indigenous languages beyond ChiShona and IsiNdebele. This resource disparity reflects broader governmental prioritisation. Magwa and Ngara's (2022) budget analysis found that Indigenous languages receive less than 3% of Zimbabwe's education expenditure despite constitutional equality with English. Bamgbose's (2021) pan-African analysis demonstrates that such inequitable resource allocation constitutes a widespread pattern wherein post-colonial governments rhetorically embrace multilingualism whilst materially perpetuating colonial language dominance.

Teacher capacity limitations compounded material scarcity. Only 12% of surveyed educators reported receiving pre-service training in Indigenous language pedagogy; 89% indicated no in-service professional development opportunities for Indigenous language instruction; and 76% acknowledged lacking confidence teaching academic content in Indigenous languages. One younger teacher admitted: "I speak ChiShona at home, but I was educated entirely in English. Teaching science or mathematics in ChiShona feels impossible, I lack the technical vocabulary and pedagogical strategies" (Female educator, age 27, 4 years' experience). This capacity deficit reflects systemic training failures. Mwanza's (2017) research documents how Zimbabwean teacher education programmes prioritise English-medium instruction, producing graduates unprepared for multilingual teaching despite policy requirements. Participants proposed solutions including mandatory Indigenous language pedagogy courses in teacher training, ongoing professional development workshops, and mentorship programmes pairing less experienced teachers with Indigenous language education experts.

Infrastructure constraints further impeded implementation, particularly in rural areas. Among rural participants 71% reported their schools lacked electricity, precluding digital resource usage; 88% indicated no internet connectivity; 65%

described inadequate classroom space forcing multi-grade teaching that complicates language-differentiated instruction; and 79% noted insufficient furniture and basic supplies, relegating Indigenous language education to lowest priority. One rural headmaster stated: "We struggle to provide chalk and writing paper. Indigenous language textbooks, let alone computers, remain distant aspirations" (Male educator, age 52, 28 years' experience). These infrastructure deficits create what Thondhlana and Kadenge (2023) term "layered disadvantage" wherein rural schools already facing resource constraints encounter additional barriers to implementing policies requiring technological or material investments. Without addressing these foundational infrastructure gaps, multilingual education policies risk remaining aspirational rhetoric disconnected from practical possibility.

### 4.1.3 Sociolinguistic Attitudes and Ideological Barriers

Beyond material constraints, participants identified deeply entrenched attitudes devaluing Indigenous languages as substantial implementation obstacles. Approximately 73% of educators and 68% of community members reported pervasive beliefs associating Indigenous languages with backwardness and English with modernity, success, and global citizenship. One educator described: "Parents explicitly request English-medium instruction, believing it provides superior opportunities. When we attempt Indigenous language teaching, parents complain that we're handicapping their children" (Female educator, age 41, 16 years' experience).This phenomenon reflects what Blommaert (2022) terms "grassroots sociolinguistic hierarchisation" where marginalised communities themselves internalise dominant language ideologies, actively choosing linguistic assimilation over heritage language maintenance. Survey data revealed that 61% of parents preferred English-medium education even when children struggled with English proficiency; 54% believed Indigenous language instruction wastes time better spent on English; and only 29% considered Indigenous language fluency important for their children's futures.

Generational differences in language attitudes proved particularly striking. Significant associations between age and Indigenous language valuation existed. Participants aged 45+ overwhelmingly valued Indigenous language preservation (92%), compared to 68% of 35-44-year-olds, 51% of 25-34-year-olds, and only 44% of 18-24-year-olds. One elder expressed anguish: "Young people view our languages as relics, embarrassments preventing progress. They speak English amongst themselves, leaving Kore Kore for conversations with grandparents, conversations growing rarer as we pass away" (Male elder, age 71). This generational shift aligns with Mufanechiya and Mufanechiya's (2018) research documenting accelerating language shift among urban Zimbabwean youth. Qualitative data suggested multiple contributing factors: increased exposure to English-medium media (television, internet, music); secondary education conducted predominantly in English, creating peer cultures wherein Indigenous language usage signals low status; employment contexts requiring English proficiency; and social media platforms favouring English for broader communicative reach.

However, interviews also revealed countervailing attitudes, particularly among culturally engaged participants. Approximately 37% of youth participants expressed growing interest in heritage languages, motivated by cultural identity concerns and recognition of knowledge loss. One university student explained: "I rejected ChiShona throughout secondary school, wanting to seem sophisticated. Now I regret this, I cannot discuss traditional medicines with my grandmother, cannot understand proverbs and oral histories. I've lost connection to my roots" (Female community member, age 23). This emergent counter-narrative suggests potential for attitude transformation through interventions highlighting Indigenous languages' cultural value and contemporary relevance. Linguistic experts emphasised that attitude change requires multi-pronged approaches addressing material conditions alongside ideologies. As one linguist argued: "We cannot shame parents for choosing English when that choice genuinely improves children's economic prospects. Effective language preservation requires ensuring Indigenous language proficiency provides tangible benefits, employment opportunities, educational advantages, cultural capital rather than merely symbolic value" (Female linguistic expert, age 54). This perspective aligns with Coronel-Molina and McCarty's (2023) argument that sustainable revitalisation demands addressing political-economic structures determining language value, not merely promoting positive attitudes divorced from material realities.

## 4.2 Challenges Faced by Educators and Students

### 4.2.1 Pedagogical Challenges

Educators identified numerous pedagogical challenges impeding effective Indigenous language instruction. The most prevalent challenge, cited by 88% of educator participants, involved balancing Indigenous language instruction with examination requirements prioritising English. One experienced teacher explained: "Primary leaving examinations, ordinary level, advanced level all conducted predominantly in English. Students and parents pressure us to prioritise English preparation, viewing Indigenous language time as detracting from examination success" (Male educator, age 48, 22 years' experience). This assessment-driven narrowing of curriculum reflects what Au's (2023) critical pedagogy scholarship terms "high-stakes testing regimes" wherein standardised examinations conducted in dominant languages effectively determine what gets taught regardless of official curriculum requirements. Zimbabwean examination policies, despite constitutional multilingualism, continue privileging English through university admission criteria, professional qualification requirements, and employment assessments (Nyamayedenga & Makaudze, 2021).

About 76% of educators reported difficulties teaching academic content in Indigenous languages due to limited technical terminology development. Mathematics, sciences, and technology subjects particularly posed challenges, as one science teacher detailed: “Chemistry concepts like 'oxidation-reduction reactions' or 'molecular bonds' lack established ChiShona equivalents. I can create descriptive phrases, but students need standardised terminology for examinations and further studies” (Female educator, age 34, 9 years' experience). This terminological gap reflects historical neglect of Indigenous language corpus planning and intellectualization processes whereby languages develop vocabulary for modern academic and professional domains (Chimhundu, 2022).Linguistic experts noted that whilst ChiShona possesses capacity for terminological expansion through existing word-formation processes, systematic development requires coordinated efforts currently absent. One linguist stated: “Other African languages, Kiswahili, Afrikaans, isiZulu demonstrate that Indigenous languages can effectively convey complex modern concepts through deliberate terminology development. Zimbabwe lacks the institutional commitment and resources for similar processes” (Male linguistic expert, age 61). The African Academy of Languages (Batibo, 2023) provides models for collaborative terminological standardisation that Zimbabwean authorities might adapt.

Educators (68%) described challenges addressing mixed-proficiency classrooms where students possess varying Indigenous language competencies. Urban schools particularly faced this issue, with classrooms containing native speakers alongside students from different linguistic backgrounds or limited Indigenous language exposure. One urban primary teacher explained: “Some children speak fluent ChiShona at home; others hear only English or different Indigenous languages. Teaching one lesson accommodating this diversity proves extraordinarily difficult without differentiated materials or additional support” (Female educator, age 31, 6 years' experience). This heterogeneity challenge reflects Zimbabwe's increasing linguistic complexity through urbanisation, internal migration, and intermarriage across language groups. Banda and Mwanza's (2017) research on multilingual Zimbabwean classrooms proposes translanguaging pedagogies and instructional approaches embracing fluid movement across languages rather than rigid separation as potential solutions. However, implementing such approaches requires teacher training currently unavailable.

### 4.2.2 Student-Level Challenges

Students experienced distinct challenges affecting Indigenous language learning outcomes. Educators reported that 71% of students exhibited limited motivation for

Indigenous language study, perceiving it as less valuable than English or examination subjects. This motivational deficit manifested through minimal home study time, superficial engagement during lessons, and prioritisation of other subjects when time constraints arose. Interview data revealed multiple sources of this disengagement. Students associated Indigenous languages with rural, traditional contexts disconnected from their aspirations: "Indigenous languages feel like grandparents' concerns, not relevant for our futures in technology, business, or international careers" (Male secondary student, age 17, quoted by educator). This perception reflects successful ideological work by colonial and neoliberal educational discourses positioning Indigenous knowledge as incompatible with modernity and progress (Wa Thiong'o, 2021).

Additionally, peer cultures in secondary schools, particularly boarding institutions, stigmatised Indigenous language usage. Educators described how students mocked peers speaking Indigenous languages, labelling them "rural," "backward," or "unsophisticated." One boarding school teacher recounted: "Students created hierarchies based on English fluency and accent approximating British or American standards. Speaking Indigenous languages invited ridicule, driving students toward English even in informal contexts" (Male educator, age 39, 13 years' experience). This peer policing powerfully shapes linguistic behaviour, often overriding parental or institutional encouragement of Indigenous language maintenance (Thondhlana & Kadenge, 2023). Linguistic insecurity constituted another significant challenge, affecting approximately 58% of students according to educator reports. Students who acquired Indigenous languages imperfectly or dialectally differently from instruction encountered embarrassment and withdrawal. One educator explained: "Urban students often speak mixed varieties incorporating English borrowings or simplified structures. When corrected in class, they feel ashamed and disengage rather than risk further correction" (Female educator, age 43, 17 years' experience). This finding aligns with sociolinguistic research demonstrating how prescriptive language instruction can alienate speakers of non-standard varieties, paradoxically undermining rather than supporting language maintenance (Makoni & Pennycook, 2020).

Cognitive and linguistic challenges also emerged for students learning through non-native languages. Educators estimated that approximately 64% of students, particularly those from minority language backgrounds, struggled with comprehension when instruction occurred in ChiShona or English rather than home languages. Research demonstrates that mother-tongue instruction facilitates deeper conceptual understanding, critical thinking, and academic achievement compared to learning through imperfectly mastered languages (Benson & Kosonen, 2021; UNESCO, 2022). Yet Zimbabwe's language policy often forces students into multiple linguistic transitions from home language to ChiShona/IsiNdebele in early primary, then to English in upper primary creating cumulative comprehension challenges.

## 4.3 Effectiveness of Digital Language Games

Survey data revealed generally positive perceptions of digital language games' effectiveness for Indigenous language learning. Among participants with game exposure (n=60), 80% agreed or strongly agreed that games effectively support language preservation; 75% found games engaging and enjoyable; 65% reported increased Indigenous language comprehension following game usage; and 90% expressed interest in continued use. These high percentages suggest substantial receptivity toward game-based interventions.

Statistical analysis examined correlations between game usage frequency and perceived effectiveness. A moderate positive correlation emerged ($r=0.65$, 95% CI [0.51, 0.76], $p<0.001$), indicating that more frequent users rated games as more effective. This relationship persisted after controlling for potential confounds including age (partial $r=0.62$, $p<0.001$), educational level (partial $r=0.59$, $p<0.001$), and general technology experience (partial $r=0.61$, $p<0.001$), suggesting genuine learning benefits rather than merely enthusiasm for technology. However, caution is advised in interpreting this correlation: the cross-sectional nature of the study limits conclusions about causality, and self-selection bias likely skews results since participants who frequently engaged with games may already possess favorable attributes (motivation, prior interest, learning styles).

Qualitative interviews elaborated on the mechanisms underlying effectiveness perceptions. Participants noted several specific benefits, including low-pressure practice opportunities that reduced anxiety compared to formal classroom settings. One young adult described how the game allowed for practice without the fear of being judged: "In class, speaking ChiShona felt intimidating. Playing alone, I could practice repeatedly without judgment" (Female community member, age 24). This reflection aligns with research indicating that game-based learning contexts can provide affective benefits (Gee, 2023). Additionally, immediate feedback in games facilitated rapid learning and error correction, a benefit noted by several educators. One participant stated: "Traditional instruction often provides delayed feedback... Games' instant validation accelerates learning loops substantially" (Male educator, age 37). This aligns with broader educational principles that highlight the efficacy of immediate responses, which traditional classroom settings often lack (Reinders & Stockwell, 2023).

Gamification elements, such as points and progression, enhanced intrinsic motivation. Participants expressed enjoyment in competitive and achievement-oriented gameplay: "Earning points for correct answers... made learning feel rewarding and fun" (Male community member, age 29). While effective gamification transforms learning experiences, its impact may vary across individuals (Landers et al., 2023). Lastly, self-paced learning accommodated various schedules and learning speeds.

Participants appreciated the flexibility that allowed them to engage with games on their own terms.This flexibility is crucial for adult learners managing multiple responsibilities (Godwin-Jones, 2023).

The participatory design process emphasized cultural authenticity. Survey results indicated overwhelming positivity, with 87% of participants agreeing that the game represented cultural heritage respectfully, and 82% finding content authentic. Qualitative feedback elaborated on points of cultural significance, with accurate linguistic representation being fundamental. Community engagement ensured that the game's dialectal authenticity was upheld (Galla, 2023). Cultural narratives and traditional practices incorporated into the games resonated positively with participants, reflecting the integration of cultural practices in language acquisition (Lantolf & Thorne, 2021). However, despite positive perceptions, substantial access barriers hindered broader engagement. Survey data indicated that 50% of respondents faced prohibitive challenges, particularly in rural and low-income households, potentially exacerbating inequalities. Addressing these access issues is crucial for ensuring equitable participation in digital language learning.

## 4.4 Participatory Game Development Process

The participatory design process for Dare reDzidzo proved central to ensuring cultural appropriateness, linguistic accuracy, and community ownership. This section describes the collaborative development methodology, recognising it as both research finding and methodological contribution.

### 4.4.1 Community Engagement and Co-Design

The development process intentionally centred community participation from initial conceptualisation through final implementation. Following establishment of the Community Advisory Board, a series of six co-design workshops (each 4-6 hours) occurred over five months, engaging 23 community members including linguistic experts, educators, elders, youth, and cultural authorities.

Workshop 1 focused on identifying language learning priorities and cultural values to inform game design. Participants articulated goals including: teaching foundational vocabulary across semantic domains (family, home, nature, food, body parts); incorporating cultural knowledge alongside language; maintaining dialectal authenticity to Kore Kore; respecting cultural protocols around sacred or restricted knowledge; and ensuring accessibility for varying technological proficiency levels.

Workshops 2-3 involved genre exploration and mechanics selection. The research team presented multiple game types (puzzle, role-playing, simulation, quiz, adventure) with examples. Through discussion and hands-on experimentation with sample games, participants evaluated appropriateness for language learning and cultural context. Consensus emerged around puzzle-based word games emphasising vocabulary recognition and spelling as most suitable for initial prototype, given development constraints and learning objectives.

Workshop 4 focused on content development. Participants collaboratively created vocabulary lists organised thematically (family relationships, agricultural practices, traditional foods, cultural ceremonies), selected culturally appropriate images, and recorded audio pronunciations by native Kore Kore speakers. This workshop generated 347 vocabulary items with accompanying images and audio the foundational content database for game development.

Workshop 5 involved narrative and character design. Participants developed storylines grounding vocabulary learning within cultural contexts, for instance, a traditional farming scenario wherein players learn agricultural vocabulary through simulated planting, harvesting, and food preparation activities. Characters were designed reflecting community members rather than stereotyped or exoticised representations, with particular attention to depicting elders respectfully as knowledge holders.

Workshop 6 occurred after initial prototype development, focusing on testing, feedback, and refinement. Participants played early versions, identifying bugs, confusing interfaces, culturally inappropriate elements, or linguistic errors. Detailed feedback informed iterative improvements over subsequent weeks, with multiple testing cycles ensuring quality before broader release.

This intensive participatory process contrasts sharply with conventional software development wherein designers create products subsequently presented to end-users for feedback. Participants appreciated their substantive involvement: "This wasn't consultation asking our opinions about predetermined plans. We genuinely co-created, our knowledge and priorities shaping the game fundamentally" (Male linguistic expert, age 56). This co-creation approach operationalises Community-Based Participatory Research principles within technology development (Wallerstein & Duran, 2023).

### 4.4.2 Technical Development and Implementation

The technical development team comprised three programmers (two Zimbabwean, one international), one graphic designer, and two audio engineers, working collaboratively with community content developers. The team selected web-based technologies (HTML5, JavaScript, CSS) for cross-platform compatibility, enabling usage on Android, iOS, and desktop systems without separate native applications for each platform. Key technical decisions reflected community priorities identified through workshops. First, offline functionality was prioritised given connectivity constraints. The Progressive Web App architecture enabled installation on devices and full functionality without internet access following initial download. Second, minimal storage requirements (game file size under 5MB) ensured compatibility with low-specification devices common in target communities. Third, simple, intuitive interfaces required minimal text instructions, accommodating varying literacy levels. Fourth, modular architecture enabled easy content updates and expansion to additional languages without core code modifications.

The game incorporated several interactive mechanics designed to facilitate vocabulary learning:

1. Word-Image Matching: Players match written Kore Kore words with corresponding images, reinforcing vocabulary recognition and semantic understanding.

*Figure 1.*

2. **Letter Scramble**: Scrambled letters are rearranged to form correct Kore Kore words, teaching spelling and orthographic patterns.

*Figure 2.*

3. **Audio-Text Association**: Players hear spoken Kore Kore words and select matching written forms, developing phonological awareness and sound-symbol correspondences.

*Figure 3.*

4. **Contextual Scenarios**: Vocabulary appears within cultural narratives (farming activities, family gatherings, traditional ceremonies), situating language learning within meaningful contexts.

*Figure 4.*

5. **Progressive Difficulty**: Content difficulty increases through levels, beginning with basic nouns, advancing to verbs, adjectives, and simple sentences providing appropriate challenge as proficiency develops.

*Figure 5.*

6. **Immediate Feedback:** Correct responses trigger positive visual/audio reinforcement and score incrementation; incorrect responses generate neutral prompts to try again without penalty, reducing anxiety whilst encouraging persistence.

Audio recordings featured community elders and fluent speakers, ensuring pronunciation authenticity. The team recorded 347 vocabulary items plus 89 phrases and sentences, with multiple speakers to expose learners to natural variation. Participants preferred authentic community voices with occasional background noise over professionally produced but culturally disconnected recordings. Visual design incorporated cultural aesthetics identified through community consultation. Digital gamification represents one valuable tool within comprehensive language preservation ecosystems, effective when community-controlled and strategically deployed but insufficient when divorced from broader political, educational, and cultural transformation. Zimbabwe's Indigenous languages indeed, endangered languages globally require nothing less than systemic change addressing the colonial legacies, economic inequalities, and ideological hierarchies that drive language shift. Technology can support such transformation but cannot substitute for it.

## 4.5 Transferability and Scalability

### 4.5.1 Factors Facilitating Transferability

The analysis of the Dare reDzidzo development and implementation process highlights several factors enhancing transferability to other languages and contexts. A primary advantage lies in the open-source technical architecture, which allows for replication without the burden of expensive proprietary software or licenses. This accessibility enables communities or organizations to develop similar games by adapting the complete source code for their languages without incurring software costs. Participants from various Zimbabwean language communities have shown interest. Additionally, the participatory design methodology used in the project is replicable across different contexts. The workshop sequences, community engagement strategies, and co-design processes reflect universal principles of community-based technology development, making them applicable globally. Documentation, including workshop guides and facilitation protocols, provides essential resources for communities looking to undertake similar initiatives.

Despite the favorable factors for transferability, successful adaptation necessitates context-specific modifications that consider local linguistic, cultural, technological, and political realities. Discussions with participants revealed that different languages possess unique structural features requiring tailored pedagogical approaches. For instance, tonal languages, such as Kore Kore, require audio-visual interfaces to highlight pitch patterns, while polysynthetic languages like Inuktitut demand different word-learning strategies due to their complex morphological structures. Linguistic typology plays a crucial role in shaping effective game design, necessitating expert linguistic consultation for each language (Grenoble & Whaley, 2023). Moreover, cultural values, knowledge systems, and protocols vary widely across Indigenous communities. What may be culturally appropriate in Kore Kore contexts can be unsuitable elsewhere. This observation emphasizes the importance of repeating participatory design processes for each context rather than assuming universal cultural frameworks. Sacred knowledge restrictions, gender-related access, and seasonal appropriateness all deserve localized navigation.

Institutional integration within schools presents another challenge. Currently, Dare reDzidzo operates outside the official curriculum as a supplementary resource. For sustainable scaling, integration within formal education systems is crucial, requiring approval from the Ministry of Primary and Secondary Education, teacher training in game usage, and curriculum alignment with official learning objectives. Participants stress that without such institutional embedding, games risk becoming peripheral add-ons. Zimbabwe's 16 official languages present both tremendous opportunities and challenges for scaling. Minority language communities have expressed strong interest, with one male Kalanga expert stating, "Kore Kore got a game; what about Kalanga, Tonga, Shangaan? We face even more severe language loss but receive less attention" (age 54). Addressing this requires prioritizing efforts based on language endangerment severity and community readiness. However, eembedding games within formal educational systems can enhance sustainability, ensuring ongoing acceptance and integration of these resources within existing curricula. Ultimately, the success of these initiatives hinges not only on technology but also on community commitment to language preservation and cultural heritage. As one community leader astutely remarked, "Technology can help, but our own commitment to our languages at home, teaching our children, and celebrating our heritage determines whether our languages survive" (Male community leader, age 61).

## 5. CONCLUSION

Digital gamification offers genuine affordances for Indigenous language preservation, accessibility transcending geographic and temporal constraints of conventional classrooms; scalability enabling resource production beyond print materials' limitations; engagement leveraging interactive, motivational elements; and contemporary relevance positioning Indigenous languages within digital modernity. These advantages prove particularly salient for contexts like Zimbabwe characterised by resource constraints, dispersed populations, and ideological devaluation of Indigenous languages. However, technology constitutes neither panacea nor standalone solution. Effectiveness depends fundamentally on embedding digital interventions within comprehensive language planning addressing political, economic, educational, and ideological dimensions determining language vitality. Without governmental commitment translating into sustained funding and policy implementation, without challenging economic structures privileging dominant languages, without transforming educational systems and assessment regimes, and without addressing ideological stigmatisation through cultural affirmation, digital games provide merely superficial engagement, entertaining diversions unable to reverse underlying language shift forces.

## REFERENCES


Au, W. (2023). High-stakes testing and curricular control: A qualitative metasynthesis. *Educational Researcher*, *52*(3), 178–189.

Austin, P. K., & Sallabank, J. (Eds.). (2023). *The Cambridge handbook of endangered languages* (2nd ed.). Cambridge University Press.

Bamgbose, A. (2021). *Language and exclusion: The consequences of language policies in Africa*. Multilingual Matters.

Banda, F., & Mwanza, D. S. (2017). Language-in-education policy and linguistic diversity in Zambia: An alternative explanation to low reading levels among primary school pupils. In Banja, M. K. (Ed.), *Meeting EFA: Zambia and selected countries* (pp. 45–67). University of Zambia Press.

Batibo, H. M. (2023). *Language decline and death in Africa: Causes, consequences and challenges* (2nd ed.). Multilingual Matters.

Battiste, M., & Henderson, J. Y. (2021). *Protecting Indigenous knowledge and heritage: A global challenge*. Purich Publishing.

Benson, C., & Kosonen, K. (Eds.). (2021). *Language issues in comparative education: Inclusive teaching and learning in non-dominant languages and cultures* (2nd ed.). Brill.

Benton, R. (2023). Revitalizing endangered languages: A practical guide based on the Maori experience. In Austin, P. K., & Sallabank, J. (Eds.), *The Cambridge handbook of endangered languages* (2nd ed., pp. 646–669). Cambridge University Press.

Blommaert, J. (2022). *The sociolinguistics of globalization* (2nd ed.). Cambridge University Press.

Cheng, Y., Wang, S., & Horwitz, E. K. (2023). Digital game-based language learning: A meta-analysis. *Computer Assisted Language Learning*, *36*(4), 567–592.

Chimhundu, H. (2022). Language policies in Africa. In Bock, Z., & Mheta, G. (Eds.), *Language, society and communication: An introduction* (2nd ed., pp. 445–470). Van Schaik Publishers.

Christen, K., Couldry, N., & Gandy, M. (2023). Digital platforms and Indigenous knowledge: Protocols, sovereignty, and engagement. *Journal of Cultural Analytics*, *8*(1), 45–68.

Constitution of Zimbabwe Amendment. (2013). *(No. 20) Act*. Government of Zimbabwe.

Coronel-Molina, S. M., & McCarty, T. L. (Eds.). (2023). *Indigenous language revitalization in the Americas* (2nd ed.). Routledge.

Creswell, J. W., & Plano Clark, V. L. (2023). *Designing and conducting mixed methods research* (4th ed.). SAGE Publications.

Crystal, D. (2022). *Language death* (2nd ed.). Cambridge University Press.

Cunliffe, D. (2022). Minority languages and social media: Promoting community, identity, and linguistic vitality. In Hinton, L., Huss, L., & Roche, G. (Eds.), *The Routledge handbook of language revitalization* (2nd ed., pp. 383–391). Routledge.

Davis, F. D. (1989). Perceived usefulness, perceived ease of use, and user acceptance of information technology. *Management Information Systems Quarterly, 13*(3), 319–340. DOI: 10.2307/249008

Deterding, S., Dixon, D., Khaled, R., & Nacke, L. (2023). From game design elements to gamefulness: Defining "gamification." *Proceedings of the 15th International Academic MindTrek Conference*, 9-15.

Dichev, C., & Dicheva, D. (2023). Gamifying education: What is known, what is believed and what remains uncertain. *International Journal of Educational Technology in Higher Education, 20*(1), 15.

Djite, P. G. (2022). *The sociolinguistics of development in Africa*. Multilingual Matters.

Fetters, M. D. (2023). *The mixed methods research workbook: Activities for designing, implementing, and publishing projects* (2nd ed.). SAGE Publications.

Fishman, J. A. (2021). *Reversing language shift: Theoretical and empirical foundations of assistance to threatened languages* (2nd ed.). Multilingual Matters.

Galla, C. K. (2023). Indigenous language revitalization and technology: From tradition to innovation. In Hinton, L., Huss, L., & Roche, G. (Eds.), *The Routledge handbook of language revitalization* (2nd ed., pp. 392–400). Routledge.

Galla, C. K., & Holmes, T. (2021). Digital technology and Indigenous language revitalization in Hawai'i. *Language Documentation and Conservation, 15*, 39–68.

Gee, J. P. (2023). *What video games have to teach us about learning and literacy* (3rd ed.). St. Martin's Press.

Godwin-Jones, R. (2023). Mobile apps for language learning. *Language Learning & Technology, 27*(1), 1–18.

Government of Zimbabwe. (2006). *Education Act (Amendment)*. Government Printers.

Grenoble, L. A., & Whaley, L. J. (2023). *Saving languages: An introduction to language revitalization* (2nd ed.). Cambridge University Press.

Hamari, J., Koivisto, J., & Sarsa, H. (2024). Does gamification work? A literature review of empirical studies on gamification. *Proceedings of the 47th Hawaii International Conference on System Sciences*, 3025-3034.

Hinton, L. (2021). *Learning and teaching endangered Indigenous languages*. Cambridge University Press.

Hinton, L., Huss, L., & Roche, G. (Eds.). (2022). *The Routledge handbook of language revitalization* (2nd ed.). Routledge.

Israel, B. A., Eng, E., Schulz, A. J., & Parker, E. A. (Eds.). (2023). *Methods for community-based participatory research for health* (3rd ed.). Jossey-Bass.

Joshi, C., de Azevedo Cunha, M. V., & Dillon, S. (2023). Endangered languages in the digital age: Barriers and opportunities. *Digital Scholarship in the Humanities*, *38*(2), 567–583.

Kadenge, M., & Nkomo, D. (2021). Language policy and linguistic human rights in postcolonial Zimbabwe. *Language Policy*, *20*(4), 609–631.

Kelly-Holmes, H., & Moriarty, M. (2023). Digital media and Indigenous language revitalization. In Hinton, L., Huss, L., & Roche, G. (Eds.), *The Routledge handbook of language revitalization* (2nd ed., pp. 401–409). Routledge.

King, W. R., & He, J. (2021). A meta-analysis of the technology acceptance model. *Information & Management*, *43*(6), 740–755. DOI: 10.1016/j.im.2006.05.003

Kovach, M. (2023). *Indigenous methodologies: Characteristics, conversations, and contexts* (2nd ed.). University of Toronto Press.

Landers, R. N., Collmus, A. B., & Williams, H. (2023). The greatest battle is within ourselves: An experiment on the effects of competition alone on task performance. *International Journal of Human-Computer Studies*, *127*, 51–61. DOI: 10.1016/j.ijhcs.2018.09.011

Lantolf, J. P., & Thorne, S. L. (2021). *Sociocultural theory and the genesis of second language development* (2nd ed.). Oxford University Press.

Lave, J., & Wenger, E. (2023). Situated learning: Legitimate peripheral participation (Anniversary ed.). Cambridge University Press.

Leonard, W. Y. (2021). Challenging "extinction" through modern Miami language reclamation. *American Indian Culture and Research Journal, 35*(2), 135–160. DOI: 10.17953/aicr.35.2.f3r173r46m261844

Mafugu, M. T. (2021). Indigenous languages and rural-urban migration in Zimbabwe. *Journal of African Languages and Linguistics, 42*(1), 89–112.

Magwa, S., & Ngara, R. (2022). Challenges in the implementation of mother tongue education in Zimbabwe. *Journal of Linguistics and Language in Education, 16*(1), 45–67.

Makaudze, G. (2022). Language policy and linguistic imperialism in Zimbabwe's education system. *Educational Research Review, 17*(3), 89–102.

Makoni, S., & Pennycook, A. (Eds.). (2020). *Disinventing and reconstituting languages* (2nd ed.). Multilingual Matters.

Maori Language Commission. (2024). *Te reo Maori in the digital age: Annual report 2023-2024*. Te Taura Whiri i te Reo Maori.

Mawadza, A. (2021). The constitutional recognition of Indigenous languages in Zimbabwe: Rhetoric or reality? *Language Matters, 52*(3), 107–129.

McIvor, O., Jenni, B., & Stacey, K. (2021). Indigenous language learning games: Engaging youth in language and culture. *Canadian Journal of Native Education, 35*(1), 127–145.

Mertens, D. M. (2023). *Research and evaluation in education and psychology: Integrating diversity with quantitative, qualitative, and mixed methods* (5th ed.). SAGE Publications.

Morgan, D. L. (2023). *Integrating qualitative and quantitative methods: A pragmatic approach* (2nd ed.). SAGE Publications.

Moyo, N., & Moyo, T. (2022). Minority language marginalization in Zimbabwe's multilingual education policy. *Journal of Multilingual and Multicultural Development, 43*(8), 723–738.

Mufanechiya, A., & Mufanechiya, T. (2018). Youth language practices in urban Zimbabwe: Between local and global. *Journal of African Cultural Studies, 30*(3), 344–360.

Mwanza, D. S. (2017). The language of initial literacy in a cosmopolitan Zambian environment. In Banja, M. K. (Ed.), *Meeting EFA: Zambia and selected countries* (pp. 68–89). University of Zambia Press.

Ndhlovu, F. (2023). *Ignored lingualism: The challenges of language marginalisation in Africa*. Routledge.

Ndhlovu, F., & Makalela, L. (2021). Decolonising multilingualism in Africa: Re-centering silenced voices from the Global South. *Multilingual Margins*, *8*(3), 7–23.

Ndlovu-Gatsheni, S. J. (2021). *Epistemic freedom in Africa: Deprovincialization and decolonization* (2nd ed.). Routledge.

Nyamayedenga, N., & Makaudze, G. (2021). Language of instruction and academic performance in Zimbabwean primary schools. *International Journal of Educational Development*, *85*, 102456.

Plass, J. L., Homer, B. D., & Kinzer, C. K. (2023). Foundations of game-based learning. *Educational Psychologist*, *50*(4), 258–283. DOI: 10.1080/00461520.2015.1122533

Postal and Telecommunications Regulatory Authority of Zimbabwe (POTRAZ). (2024). *Abridged annual report 2023*. POTRAZ.

Prah, K. K. (2022). *Mother-tongue education in Africa for emancipation and development*. CASAS Publishers.

Prensky, M. (2023). Digital game-based learning (Anniversary ed.). Paragon House.

Purushotma, R., Thorne, S. L., & Wheatley, J. (2022). 10 key principles for designing video games for foreign language learning. In Reinders, H. (Ed.), *Digital games in language learning and teaching* (2nd ed., pp. 17–38). Palgrave Macmillan.

Reinders, H., & Stockwell, G. (2023). *Computer-assisted second language learning* (2nd ed.). Cambridge University Press.

Reinhardt, J., & Thorne, S. L. (2023). Digital literacies as emergent multifaceted competencies. In Dooly, N., & O'Dowd, R. (Eds.), *Telecollaboration in education* (pp. 76–94). Routledge.

Romaine, S. (2021). The impact of language policy on endangered languages. *International Journal of the Sociology of Language*, *2021*(267-268), 217–233.

Salen, K., & Zimmerman, E. (2024). *Rules of play: Game design fundamentals* (2nd ed.). MIT Press.

Schuler, D., & Namioka, A. (Eds.). (2023). *Participatory design: Principles and practices* (2nd ed.). CRC Press.

Shizha, E., & Makuvaza, N. (Eds.). (2022). *Re-thinking postcolonial education in Sub-Saharan Africa in the 21st century*. Sense Publishers.

Smith, L. T. (2022). *Decolonizing methodologies: Research and Indigenous peoples* (3rd ed.). Zed Books.

Spolsky, B. (2021). Rethinking language policy. *Language Policy, 20*(1), 1–15. DOI: 10.1007/s10993-006-9045-0

Statistics New Zealand. (2023). *Te Kupenga 2023: Maori language speakers*. Statistics New Zealand.

Sykes, J. M., & Reinhardt, J. (2023). *Language at play: Digital games in second and foreign language teaching and learning* (2nd ed.). Bloomsbury Academic.

Tarhini, A., Hone, K., & Liu, X. (2024). Measuring the moderating effect of cultural dimensions on the Technology Acceptance Model: A study in the context of three Arab countries. *Journal of Educational Computing Research, 52*(3), 305–328.

Terralingua. (2022). Biocultural diversity and Indigenous knowledge: Global perspectives. Terralingua.

Thondhlana, J., & Kadenge, M. (2023). Linguistic marketplaces and language shift among urban youth in Zimbabwe. *Journal of Multilingual and Multicultural Development, 44*(5), 441–458.

Thorne, S. L., Fischer, I., & Lu, X. (2023). The semiotic ecology and linguistic complexity of an online game world. In Chapelle, C. A. (Ed.), *The encyclopedia of applied linguistics* (pp. 5158–5164). Wiley-Blackwell.

Tuhiwai Smith, L. (2022). *Decolonizing methodologies: Research and Indigenous peoples* (3rd ed.). Zed Books.

UNESCO. (2022). *Global education monitoring report 2022: Non-state actors in education*. UNESCO Publishing.

UNESCO. (2023). *Atlas of the world's languages in danger*. UNESCO Publishing.

Venkatesh, V., & Davis, F. D. (2023). A theoretical extension of the Technology Acceptance Model: Four longitudinal field studies. *Management Science, 46*(2), 186–204. DOI: 10.1287/mnsc.46.2.186.11926

Viriri, A., & Viriri, P. (2023). An Afrocentric critique of the language-in-education policy in Zimbabwe. *Educational Research for Social Change, 12*(1), 56–72.

Vygotsky, L. S. (1978). *Mind in society: The development of higher psychological processes*. Harvard University Press.

Wa Thiong'o, N. (2021). Decolonising the mind: The politics of language in African literature (Anniversary ed.). James Currey Publishers.

Wallerstein, N., & Duran, B. (2023). Community-based participatory research contributions to intervention research: The intersection of science and practice to improve health equity. *American Journal of Public Health, 100*(S1), S40–S46. DOI: 10.2105/AJPH.2009.184036

Wilson, S. (2022). *Research is ceremony: Indigenous research methods* (2nd ed.). Fernwood Publishing.

Zimbabwe, U. N. I. C. E. F. (2023). *Education statistics: Zimbabwe country profile 2023*. UNICEF.

Zimbabwe National Statistics Agency. (2022). *Population census 2022: Preliminary report*. ZIMSTAT.

Zou, D., Xie, H., & Wang, F. L. (2022). A meta-analysis of digital game-based vocabulary learning. *Educational Research Review, 36*, 100446.

# Chapter 5
# Bridging Literacy Gaps Through Culturally-Responsive Game-Based Language Learning in Marginalized Communities

**Sohom Saha**
http://orcid.org/0009-0006-9438-1554
*Lakshmibai National Institute of Physical Education, India*

**Mahendra Kumar Singh**
http://orcid.org/0000-0001-9989-9420
*Lakshmibai National Institute of Physical Education, India*

## ABSTRACT

*This chapter explores the intersection of game-based learning, cultural responsiveness, and literacy development in marginalized communities. Drawing on sociocultural theory and digital pedagogy frameworks, we examine how culturally-responsive game-based interventions can address persistent literacy gaps while honoring students' linguistic and cultural assets. Through analysis of empirical studies, theoretical frameworks, and implementation models, this chapter demonstrates that game-based learning environments, when designed with cultural responsiveness at their core, offer transformative potential for literacy education in underserved populations. We discuss design principles, pedagogical approaches, assessment strategies, and policy implications for scaling culturally-responsive game-based*

DOI: 10.4018/979-8-3373-4322-8.ch005

*literacy interventions. The chapter concludes with recommendations for researchers, educators, and policymakers seeking to bridge literacy gaps through culturally-sustaining digital pedagogies.*

## 1. INTRODUCTION

Literacy remains one of the most fundamental determinants of educational success and life opportunities, yet persistent gaps continue to disadvantage marginalized communities worldwide (UNESCO, 2020). These disparities are not merely technical deficits but reflect deeper issues of cultural and linguistic mismatch between mainstream educational approaches and the lived experiences of students from non-dominant communities (Peristeris, 2017). Traditional literacy instruction often fails to recognize and build upon the cultural and linguistic assets that marginalized students bring to the classroom, instead positioning their home languages and cultural practices as barriers to be overcome rather than resources to be leveraged (Mateus, 2014). Simultaneously, the proliferation of digital technologies has transformed the literacy landscape, expanding definitions of what it means to be literate in the 21st century (Gee, 2003). Digital games, in particular, have emerged as powerful spaces for learning, offering immersive environments where players engage in problem-solving, collaboration, and meaning-making (Lu, 2013). The global game-based learning market has grown exponentially, yet questions remain about whether these technologies reproduce existing educational inequities or offer genuine opportunities for transformation (Kafai & Burke, 2015).

This chapter addresses a critical gap at the intersection of these two domains: How can game-based learning be designed and implemented in ways that are culturally responsive and effectively address literacy gaps in marginalized communities? We argue that game-based literacy interventions must move beyond superficial cultural representations to embrace culturally-sustaining pedagogies that position students' cultural and linguistic practices as central to learning (Paris, 2012). By examining theoretical frameworks, empirical evidence, design principles, and implementation challenges, this chapter provides a comprehensive analysis of how culturally-responsive game-based approaches can bridge literacy gaps while affirming students' identities and experiences. Despite increasing research on game-based literacy learning, limited scholarship examines how culturally-responsive design specifically supports marginalized communities. The existing literature lacks an integrated framework that connects sociocultural theory, culturally sustaining pedagogy, and game-based multimodal literacy practices. This chapter addresses this gap by synthesizing evidence and proposing actionable models for implementation.

## 2. THEORETICAL FOUNDATIONS

### 2.1 Sociocultural Learning Theory

Understanding how culturally-responsive game-based learning can address literacy gaps requires grounding in sociocultural theories of learning and development. Vygotsky and Cole (1978) sociocultural theory posits that learning is fundamentally social and culturally mediated, occurring through interaction with more knowledgeable others and cultural tools within particular social contexts. This perspective emphasizes that cognition is distributed across individuals, tools, and cultural practices rather than residing solely within individual minds (Cole & Engeström, 1993). For literacy education, this means that reading and writing are not neutral cognitive skills but culturally-situated practices embedded in particular social contexts and power relations (Street, 1984). Learning is shaped by cultural tools and social interaction (Vygotsky, 1978). Literacy is not a neutral skill but a practice embedded in cultural contexts. Games provide scaffolded learning environments aligning with the Zone of Proximal Development, enabling learners to attempt literacy tasks slightly above their independent ability.

Building on Vygotskian foundations, situated learning theory emphasizes that learning occurs through participation in communities of practice where novices develop expertise through legitimate peripheral participation (Lave & Wenger, 1991). This framework has profound implications for game-based literacy learning, suggesting that games can function as communities of practice where players develop literacy skills through meaningful participation in game-related activities. The concept of the Zone of Proximal Development (ZPD) is particularly relevant, as well-designed games can provide scaffolding that enables learners to accomplish literacy tasks slightly beyond their independent level (Vygotsky & Cole, 1978). New Literacy Studies extends sociocultural theory specifically to literacy, arguing that literacy is not a singular, autonomous skill but rather multiple literacies embedded in specific social practices (Street, 2014). This "ideological model" of literacy contrasts with the "autonomous model" that treats literacy as a neutral technical skill with predictable cognitive consequences regardless of context (Street, 1984). For marginalized communities, this distinction is crucial: their literacy practices may be highly sophisticated within their cultural contexts but devalued or unrecognized within dominant educational frameworks (Heath, 1983).

### 2.2 Culturally-Responsive and Culturally-Sustaining Pedagogy

Culturally-responsive pedagogy provides a critical framework for addressing educational inequities. Ladson-Billings (1995) identified three pillars of culturally-relevant pedagogy: academic success, cultural competence, and critical consciousness. Academic success requires that all students meet rigorous educational standards. Cultural competence involves maintaining strong connections to students' cultural communities while developing fluency in dominant cultural codes. Critical consciousness enables students to recognize, analyze, and challenge inequitable social structures (Ladson-Billings, 1995). Ladson-Billings (1995) highlights three pillars: academic success, cultural competence, and critical consciousness. Paris (2012) extends this to culturally-sustaining pedagogy, which seeks to maintain and celebrate linguistic and cultural pluralism. In game-based environments, this means embedding cultural narratives, multilingual resources, and identity-affirming experiences.

Gay (2010) expanded this framework, defining culturally-responsive teaching as using the cultural knowledge, prior experiences, frames of reference, and performance styles of ethnically diverse students to make learning more relevant and effective. This approach validates students' cultural identities while building bridges to academic content (Gay, 2010). Moll, Amanti, Neff, & Gonzalez (1992) contributed the concept of "funds of knowledge," arguing that households and communities possess rich cultural and cognitive resources that educators should recognize and leverage in instruction.

However, Paris (2012) argued that "culturally-responsive" frameworks, while valuable, risk positioning students' cultures as resources to be utilized in service of assimilation into dominant norms. He proposed culturally-sustaining pedagogy, which "seeks to perpetuate and foster, to sustain, linguistic, literate, and cultural pluralism as part of the democratic project of schooling" (Paris, 2012). This framework positions students' cultural and linguistic practices not merely as bridges to dominant literacies but as valuable ends in themselves worthy of maintenance and development (Peristeris, 2017). For game-based literacy learning, culturally-sustaining pedagogy suggests that games should not only leverage students' cultural backgrounds to teach dominant literacies but also create spaces where students can develop and express literacies rooted in their own cultural practices. This might involve games that validate multilingualism, honor indigenous knowledge systems, or enable students to create and share narratives from their communities (Kafai & Burke, 2015).

## 2.3 Game-Based Learning Theory

Game-based learning theory draws on multiple traditions to explain how and why games facilitate learning. Gee (2003) work on games and learning identified 36 learning principles embedded in good video games, including active learning, problem-solving, customization, identity formation, and the "psychosocial moratorium" that allows safe failure. Gee argued that games create powerful learning contexts because they situate meaning in experience, require active participation, and provide immediate feedback within systems players care about (Gee, 2003). Flow theory provides another lens for understanding game-based learning. Csikszentmihalyi (1990) described flow as a state of optimal experience characterized by intense concentration, loss of self-consciousness, and intrinsic motivation. Games that successfully balance challenge and skill can induce flow states that promote deep engagement and learning (Kiili, 2005). For literacy development, this suggests that games can motivate sustained engagement with reading and writing tasks that might otherwise feel tedious or intimidating (Steinkuehler & Duncan, 2008). Gee (2003) identifies principles such as identity, situated meaning, and problem-solving. Games support autonomy, competence, and relatedness (Self-Determination Theory), which increases motivation and persistence. Flow Theory (Csikszentmihalyi, 1990) explains why well-balanced game challenges sustain engagement—particularly beneficial for struggling readers.

Situated cognition theory helps explain why learning in games can transfer to other contexts. When games embed literacy learning in meaningful problem-solving contexts rather than presenting decontextualized skills, they support the development of flexible knowledge that learners can apply across situations (Brown, Collins, & Duguid, 1989). Games also provide opportunities for what Shaffer (2006) called "epistemic frames", ways of thinking, acting, and valuing characteristic of particular communities of practice that players internalize through game participation. Self-determination theory offers insights into the motivational aspects of game-based learning. Ryan and Deci (2000) identified three innate psychological needs, autonomy, competence, and relatedness, that when satisfied promote intrinsic motivation and well-being. Well-designed games support autonomy through meaningful choices, competence through appropriately challenging tasks with clear feedback, and relatedness through social interaction and shared purposes (Ryan, Rigby, & Przybylski, 2006). For marginalized students who may experience school as disempowering, games that satisfy these needs can rebuild motivation for learning (Steinkuehler, 2010).

## 2.4 Integrated Framework

Integrating these theoretical perspectives, we propose that culturally-responsive game-based literacy learning succeeds when it: (1) positions literacy as a culturally-situated social practice rather than a decontextualized skill; (2) recognizes and leverages the cultural and linguistic assets students bring; (3) creates communities of practice where students develop literacy through meaningful participation; (4) provides appropriately scaffolded challenges within students' ZPD; (5) supports autonomy, competence, and relatedness; (6) validates students' cultural identities while building critical consciousness; and (7) sustains rather than merely responds to cultural and linguistic diversity. This framework guides the analysis of design principles and empirical studies in subsequent sections.

## 3. LITERACY GAPS IN MARGINALIZED COMMUNITIES

### 3.1 Scope and Nature of Literacy Disparities

Literacy gaps between privileged and marginalized populations represent one of education's most persistent and consequential inequities. Data from the National Assessment of Educational Progress (NAEP) in the United States consistently show substantial gaps in reading achievement between White and Asian students compared to Black and Hispanic students, as well as between economically advantaged and disadvantaged students (National Center for Education Statistics, 2019). These gaps emerge early, often before formal schooling begins, and tend to widen over time without effective intervention (Reardon & Portilla, 2016).

Internationally, literacy disparities follow similar patterns. UNESCO (2020) reports that marginalized groups, including ethnic minorities, indigenous peoples, rural populations, and those living in poverty, face significantly lower literacy rates than their more privileged counterparts. In low- and middle-income countries, these disparities are often dramatic, with literacy rates in some marginalized communities remaining below 50% (UNESCO, 2020). Gender intersects with other forms of marginalization, as girls in poor, rural, or conflict-affected communities face particular barriers to literacy development.

However, focusing solely on test scores or literacy rates risks reproducing deficit perspectives that pathologize marginalized communities. Critical scholars argue that conventional literacy assessments often measure students' familiarity with dominant cultural codes rather than their actual literacy capabilities (Delpit, 1995). Many students labeled as struggling readers demonstrate sophisticated literacy practices in their homes and communities that go unrecognized in school contexts (Gutiérrez, 2008). Thus, while literacy gaps measured by conventional assessments are real and consequential, affecting educational opportunities, employment, and life chances, they reflect complex interactions between students' capabilities, cultural contexts, and educational systems rather than simple deficits (Ladson-Billings, 2006).

### 3.2 Causes of Literacy Gaps

Literacy disparities stem from multiple, intersecting factors operating at societal, institutional, and instructional levels. Socioeconomic factors play a substantial role, as poverty correlates with reduced access to books, early literacy experiences, and language-rich environments (Neuman & Celano, 2001). The "word gap" research suggests that by age three, children from low-income families have heard millions fewer words than their more affluent peers, though recent critiques note this research may pathologize working-class language practices rather than recognizing their richness in different domains (Dudley-Marling & Lucas, 2009; Hart & Risley, 1995). Institutional factors include unequal resource allocation, with schools serving marginalized communities typically receiving less funding, having less experienced teachers, and providing fewer educational resources (Hersi, 2010). Tracking and ability grouping can perpetuate inequities by limiting marginalized students' access to rigorous literacy instruction (Oakes, 2005). School policies around language use often position bilingualism as a problem rather than an asset, forcing emergent bilingual students to abandon home languages in favor of English dominance (Flores & Rosa, 2015).

At the instructional level, cultural and linguistic mismatch between teachers and students can create barriers. Teachers unfamiliar with students' cultural backgrounds may misinterpret their communicative styles, underestimate their capabilities, or fail to connect instruction to their experiences (Gay, 2010). Curricula that lack cultural relevance can alienate students, diminishing engagement and motivation (Ladson-Billings, 1995). Deficit ideologies lead some educators to lower expectations for marginalized students, creating self-fulfilling prophecies that limit learning opportunities (Valencia, 2010). For indigenous communities, literacy gaps reflect historical trauma from colonization, including forced assimilation through residential schools that punished native language use and attempted to erase cultural identities (McCarty & Lee, 2014). Contemporary literacy instruction often continues this colonial project when it positions indigenous languages and knowledge systems as inferior to dominant Western literacies (Smith, 2021).

## 3.3 Consequences of Literacy Gaps

Literacy disparities have profound consequences extending far beyond school achievement. Limited literacy constrains access to higher education and skilled employment, perpetuating cycles of poverty and marginalization (OECD, 2013). Low literacy correlates with poorer health outcomes, as individuals struggle to navigate health information and advocate for themselves within medical systems (ME, Greenberg, Jin, & Paulsen, 2006). Civic participation suffers when people cannot engage with policy information or feel empowered to advocate for their communities (Rudd, 2007). Psychologically, literacy struggles can damage self-esteem and academic identity, particularly when educational systems position students as deficient (Compton-Lilly, 2007). Students internalize messages about their inability to succeed, developing learned helplessness and disengaging from learning (Dweck,

2006). For communities, sustained literacy gaps contribute to social stratification and the reproduction of inequality across generations (Broadfoot, 1978). Given these high stakes, interventions that effectively address literacy gaps while affirming rather than diminishing students' cultural identities become not only educationally important but socially just imperatives. Game-based approaches offer particular promise for reengaging students who have become alienated from traditional literacy instruction while honoring their cultural backgrounds.

## 4. AFFORDANCES OF GAME-BASED LEARNING FOR LITERACY DEVELOPMENT

### 4.1 Motivational and Engagement Benefits

One of games' most significant affordances for literacy learning is their capacity to motivate sustained engagement. Students who avoid traditional reading and writing activities often willingly engage with complex texts and produce extensive writing in game contexts (Steinkuehler, 2010). This motivation stems from multiple factors: games provide clear goals and immediate feedback; they allow players to see consequences of their choices; they offer opportunities for mastery and achievement; and they create social contexts where literacy serves authentic communicative purposes (Gee, 2003).

Research demonstrates that struggling readers often engage with game-related texts far above their supposed reading levels (Steinkuehler & Duncan, 2008). Players navigate complex game guides, participate in online forums, and create fan fiction, all literacy-rich activities they undertake voluntarily because they serve personally meaningful goals. This suggests that when literacy is embedded in activities students care about, motivational barriers can diminish significantly (Beavis, Muspratt, & Thompson, 2015). For marginalized students who may have experienced repeated literacy failures in school, games' safe failure environments are particularly valuable. Games normalize failure as a learning opportunity rather than a source of shame, encouraging experimentation and persistence (Gee, 2003). This can help rebuild academic self-efficacy damaged by past struggles (Steinkuehler, 2010).

### 4.2 Multimodal Literacy Development

Games inherently involve multimodal literacy, the ability to make meaning across text, images, sounds, gestures, and spatial arrangements (Kress, Leeuwen, & Leeuwen, 2001). Players must interpret visual symbols, understand spatial relationships, decode written text, and respond to audio cues, often simultaneously. This aligns with expanded definitions of literacy that recognize the multimodal nature of contemporary communication (The New London Group, 1996).

For students developing traditional print literacy, games can provide supportive contexts were visual and audio information scaffolds text comprehension. Images and animations can clarify word meanings, while voice acting can model pronunciation and fluency (Minchen, 2024). Conversely, text can deepen understanding of game narratives and mechanics, creating synergies between modalities (Abrams & Walsh, 2014). Digital and media literacy skills are increasingly essential for navigating contemporary life, yet often underemphasized in traditional literacy instruction focusing narrowly on print (Jenkins, 2009). Games provide authentic contexts for developing these skills as players evaluate information sources, assess credibility, collaborate online, and create digital content (Ito et al., 2013).

### 4.3 Contextualized and Situated Learning

Games situate literacy learning within meaningful problem-solving contexts rather than presenting decontextualized skills (Lu, 2013). When students read in games, they read to accomplish goals they care about, understanding quest requirements, learning character backstories, or coordinating with teammates. This situatedness makes literacy functional and meaningful, increasing both comprehension and retention (Gee, 2003). Role-playing games exemplify contextualized literacy learning, as players inhabit characters and make choices within narrative worlds. This positioning allows students to explore different identities and perspectives while developing reading comprehension and narrative skills (Dikkers & al, 2015). Quest-based structures provide clear purposes for reading and scaffolded challenges that gradually increase in complexity (Gerber & Price, 2013). Strategy games often require players to read and synthesize complex informational texts to make effective decisions, developing skills in critical reading and information analysis (Steinkuehler & Duncan, 2008). Multiplayer games create authentic communicative contexts where students must write clearly and persuasively to coordinate with teammates or negotiate with other players (Black, 2008).

## 5. PRINCIPLES FOR DESIGNING CULTURALLY-RESPONSIVE EDUCATIONAL GAMES

### 5.1 Representation and Identity

Culturally-responsive games must move beyond superficial diversity to create meaningful representation that validates students' identities. This involves including characters, settings, and narratives that reflect diverse cultural backgrounds with depth and authenticity (Banks, 1993). Representation should avoid stereotypes and tokenism, instead presenting cultures as complex, dynamic, and valuable (Bishop, 1990). Character creation systems can support identity exploration by allowing students to customize avatars reflecting their own appearance and cultural background (Kafai & Burke, 2015). However, representation extends beyond visual appearance to include storylines, values, and ways of being that honor different cultural perspectives (DeVane & Squire, 2008).

For indigenous communities, culturally-responsive games might center indigenous knowledge, languages, and worldviews rather than treating them as peripheral add-ons. This could involve games based on traditional stories, incorporating indigenous ecological knowledge, or teaching indigenous languages through gameplay (McCarty & Lee, 2014). Critically, indigenous communities should lead the design of such games rather than having their cultures represented by outsiders (Smith, 2021).

## 5.2 Language and Linguistic Diversity

Culturally-responsive games must thoughtfully address language, recognizing that language is central to identity and culture. For emergent bilingual students, games can support home language development while building English proficiency rather than positioning languages in competition (Mateus, 2014). Translanguaging approaches that allow fluid movement between languages reflect how bilinguals actually use language and can support comprehension and meaning-making (Mateus, 2014). Games might include multilingual options, allowing students to play in their home language, English, or a combination (Thorne, Black, & Sykes, 2009). Text and audio in multiple languages, multilingual character interactions, or quests requiring use of different languages can validate multilingualism as an asset (Rama, Black, Van Es, & Warschauer, 2012). For students developing literacy in home languages with limited written resources, games can provide rare opportunities for reading and writing practice (Kosonen & Benson, 2013). Dialect and register variation should also be addressed thoughtfully. Games might validate African American Language, Chicano English, or other stigmatized varieties while also providing exposure to academic language and standard dialects (Samy Alim, 2007). This approach positions all language varieties as valuable rather than treating some as deficient (Smitherman, 1999).

## 5.3 Cultural Funds of Knowledge

Drawing on Moll et al. (1992) concept of funds of knowledge, culturally-responsive games should connect to students lived experiences and community knowledge. This might involve game content reflecting students' neighborhoods, family practices, or cultural traditions. For example, games could incorporate mathematics concepts learned through everyday practices like shopping, cooking, or crafts; or historical narratives centered on students' own communities (Gonzalez, Moll, & Amanti, 2006). Culturally-responsive games can position students as knowledge holders and cultural experts rather than empty vessels to be filled (Gutiérrez & Rogoff, 2003). Students might contribute to game content by sharing family stories, documenting community practices, or teaching peers about their cultural backgrounds. This validates students' knowledge while building connections between home and school literacies (Lee, 2007).

## 6. EMPIRICAL EVIDENCE FROM CULTURALLY-RESPONSIVE GAME-BASED LITERACY INTERVENTIONS

### 6.1 Quest Atlantis and Culturally-Situated Learning

One well-documented example of culturally-responsive game-based literacy learning is Quest Atlantis, a multi-user virtual environment designed to immerse students in educational activities (Barab, Sadler, Heiselt, Hickey, & Zuiker, 2007). The Taiga quest immerses students in a fictional world facing environmental challenges where they must take on roles of community members, read scientific texts, analyze data, and write persuasively to influence environmental policy decisions (Barab et al., 2009). Research on Quest Atlantis with diverse urban middle school students demonstrated significant literacy gains, particularly in persuasive writing and scientific literacy (Barab et al., 2009). The immersive narrative context increased engagement and made academic literacy practices meaningful. Students who typically resisted writing assignments produced detailed, sophisticated arguments within the game context because they were invested in the world and saw their writing as having real consequences (Barab et al., 2007).

While Quest Atlantis demonstrates the potential of game-based literacy learning, its cultural responsiveness is limited. The game world, while engaging, does not explicitly reflect the cultural backgrounds of diverse students. This highlights a common challenge: games can be motivating and educationally effective while still reproducing dominant cultural perspectives unless cultural responsiveness is intentionally designed.

## 6.2 Indigenous Language Revitalization Through Gaming

Several initiatives have used game-based approaches to support indigenous language revitalization, addressing both literacy development and cultural sustainability. The Omniglot Project created mobile games to teach endangered indigenous languages, reporting increased engagement and learning compared to traditional language instruction methods (Perley, 2012). These games incorporated cultural content, traditional stories, and community voices, positioning language learning as cultural practice rather than mere skill acquisition.

The Anishinaabemowin language learning game developed by Michigan State University in partnership with indigenous communities teaches Ojibwe language through interactive gameplay (McCarty & Lee, 2014). The game incorporates traditional narratives, cultural protocols, and community knowledge, with indigenous community members centrally involved in design. Evaluation showed improved language learning outcomes and increased cultural connection among indigenous youth (Hermes, Bang, & Marin, 2012). These examples demonstrate how games can support culturally-sustaining literacy practices that maintain and develop marginalized languages rather than merely facilitating transition to dominant languages. However, challenges include limited resources for developing such games, need for ongoing community involvement, and importance of integrating games with broader language revitalization efforts rather than treating them as standalone solutions (McCarty & Lee, 2014).

## 6.3 Minecraft and Culturally-Relevant World-Building

Several studies have examined how the popular game Minecraft can be leveraged for culturally-responsive literacy learning. Dezuanni, O'Mara, and Beavis (2015) documented Australian teachers using Minecraft to engage indigenous students in literacy activities connected to their cultural heritage. Students recreated traditional indigenous sites, researched and wrote about their cultural significance, and shared their creations with community members. This approach combined digital literacies with traditional cultural knowledge, positioned students as knowledge holders, and created authentic purposes for reading and writing.

Similarly, research with Latino/a students in the southwestern United States examined Minecraft-based activities where students designed worlds representing their communities and cultural practices (Takeuchi & Sarah, 2014). Students engaged in substantial reading and writing as they researched their communities, planned designs, and created explanatory texts. The culturally-relevant content increased engagement and provided opportunities to validate students' cultural identities while developing academic literacies (Takeuchi & Sarah, 2014).

These studies illustrate how commercial games not specifically designed for education can be appropriated for culturally-responsive literacy learning when teachers thoughtfully design activities connecting gameplay to students' cultural backgrounds. However, this requires significant teacher knowledge, time, and creativity, resources not always available in under-resourced schools serving marginalized communities (Kafai & Burke, 2015).

## 6.4 Digital Storytelling and Game Creation

Research on students creating their own digital stories and games provides evidence for game creation as literacy practice. Gee and Hayes (2011) studied an after-school program where African American youth created video games based on their lived experiences. Participants engaged in substantial writing as they developed storylines, character descriptions, and in-game text. They also developed critical literacy skills as they analyzed stereotypical representations of African Americans in commercial games and intentionally crafted counternarratives (Hayes & Duncan, 2012).

Similarly, Disalvo, Guzdial, Bruckman, & Mcklin (2014) documented Latina girls creating video games addressing issues in their communities. Participants researched social issues, interviewed community members, wrote scripts and dialogue, and developed design documents. The culturally-relevant content-maintained engagement while game creation provided authentic contexts for literacy development. Participants reported feeling empowered to use technology to tell their stories and address community concerns (Disalvo et al., 2014). These interventions demonstrate that positioning students as game designers rather than merely players can support culturally-responsive literacy development. However, game creation requires substantial technical and pedagogical support, potentially limiting scalability (Kafai & Burke, 2015).

## 6.5 iREAD: Interactive Reading for English Acquisition and Development

The iREAD project developed iPad games specifically designed to support English literacy development for Spanish-speaking emergent bilingual students (Kim, 2006). The games incorporated translanguaging features allowing fluid movement between Spanish and English, culturally-relevant content reflecting Latino/a experiences, and social gameplay encouraging collaboration. A randomized controlled trial with 122 students found that those using iREAD games showed significantly greater gains in English vocabulary and reading comprehension compared to control groups receiving traditional instruction (Kim, 2006).

Notably, students using iREAD also maintained and even slightly improved Spanish literacy skills, contrasting with typical patterns where English acquisition correlates with home language loss (Kim, 2006). This suggests that thoughtfully designed bilingual games can support additive bilingualism rather than subtractive bilingualism. Students also reported high engagement and positive attitudes toward reading, suggesting motivational benefits (Kim, 2006).

# 7. IMPLEMENTATION CHALLENGES AND STRATEGIES

## 7.1 Access and Digital Divide

Perhaps the most fundamental implementation challenge is unequal access to technology. Marginalized communities often face digital divides characterized by limited access to devices, internet connectivity, and technical support (Warschauer, 2004). While mobile devices have proliferated even in low-income communities, quality educational games often require computers or tablets with reliable internet access not universally available (Takeuchi & Sarah, 2014). Multiple digital divides exist beyond mere access: second-level divides involve differences in technical skills and confidence using technology, while third-level divides concern the ability to leverage technology for meaningful purposes and opportunities (van Dijk, 2005). Even when marginalized students have device access, they may lack home support for using technology educationally, reliable spaces for extended gameplay, or technical troubleshooting assistance (Warschauer & Matuchniak, 2010).

Strategies for addressing access challenges include: leveraging mobile-first designs that function on smartphones many families already possess; creating offline-capable games that don't require constant connectivity; providing device lending programs through schools or libraries; designing for low-bandwidth environments with minimal data requirements; and utilizing community spaces like libraries, community centers, or after-school programs to provide supervised access (Ito et al., 2013). However, these workarounds often provide inferior experiences compared to what privileged students access, potentially reproducing rather than reducing inequities (Watkins, 2011).

## 7.2 Curriculum Integration and Standardization Pressures

Integrating game-based literacy learning into existing curricula poses significant challenges, particularly in contexts dominated by standardized testing and accountability pressures (Au, 2007). Teachers face extensive curriculum mandates and pacing guides that leave little room for innovation. When student performance is measured through standardized tests emphasizing specific skills, teachers may feel pressure to focus on test preparation rather than potentially richer but less measurable learning in games (Gee, 2006). Games often support learning objectives that extend beyond narrow literacy skills measured by standardized tests, critical thinking, collaboration, problem-solving, digital literacies, and identity development (Steinkuehler, 2010). While valuable, these outcomes may not translate directly to improved test scores, creating tension for teachers evaluated based on student performance on such measures (Lu, 2013). This tension is particularly acute in schools serving marginalized students, which often face intense accountability pressure and sanctions for low performance (Darling-Hammond, 2007).

Additionally, the open-ended, exploratory nature of rich game-based learning can conflict with highly structured curricula and rigid scheduling. Games may require extended time blocks for meaningful engagement, yet schools often operate with short, fragmented periods (Lu, 2013). The social, collaborative aspects of games may conflict with classroom management systems emphasizing individual quiet work (Steinkuehler, 2006). Strategies for addressing these challenges include: carefully aligning games with curriculum standards and learning objectives; collecting evidence that game-based approaches support standardized test performance; advocating for broader definitions of literacy and expanded assessment approaches; utilizing after-school or summer programs with more flexibility than school time; and building administrator support by demonstrating educational value through pilot implementations (Kafai & Burke, 2015). However, these strategies only partially address the fundamental tension between game-based learning's affordances and accountability-driven educational contexts.

## 7.3 Cultural Authenticity and Avoiding Appropriation

Designing truly culturally-responsive games without appropriating or misrepresenting cultures requires careful navigation. Well-intentioned designers from outside communities may include superficial cultural elements while missing deeper cultural values, inadvertently perpetuate stereotypes, or commodify cultural practices in problematic ways (Banks, 1993). Tokenistic inclusion of diverse characters or settings without substantive cultural content provides little benefit and may even reinforce stereotypes (Bishop, 1990). Participatory design involving community members is essential but presents its own challenges. Identifying authentic community representatives, ensuring diverse voices within communities are heard, compensating participants fairly for their expertise, and negotiating potentially different priorities between designers and communities all require careful attention (Bang & Vossoughi,

2016). Power dynamics between typically privileged designers and marginalized community members must be actively addressed to ensure genuine collaboration rather than extraction (Smith, 2021).

For commercial game developers, economic pressures may limit investment in authentic cultural representation, particularly for smaller marginalized communities unlikely to generate substantial revenue (Shaw, 2014). Educational game developers often operate with limited budgets that constrain the extensive community engagement necessary for authentic cultural responsiveness (Kafai & Burke, 2015). Strategies include: prioritizing participatory design with sustained community involvement; hiring designers from communities being served; compensating community members fairly as cultural experts; conducting extensive cultural research and community consultation; submitting designs to community review; building long-term relationships with communities rather than one-time consultations; and being willing to defer to community judgment about appropriate cultural representation (DiSalvo, Yip, Bonsignore, & DiSalvo, 2017). Critically, some cultural content may not be appropriate for game adaptation, and communities should have autonomy to set boundaries (Smith, 2021).

## 8. ASSESSMENT AND EVALUATION APPROACHES

### 8.1 Challenges of Assessing Game-Based Literacy Learning

Assessing literacy learning in game contexts presents unique challenges that complicate evaluation of culturally-responsive game-based interventions. Traditional literacy assessments, standardized tests, reading comprehension questions, writing samples prompted by decontextualized topics, may not capture the full range of literacies students develop through gaming (Gee, 2006). Students may demonstrate sophisticated literacy practices within game contexts that don't readily transfer to traditional assessment situations, leading to underestimation of their capabilities (Steinkuehler & Duncan, 2008). The multimodal nature of game-based literacy complicates assessment, as students integrate reading, writing, visual interpretation, spatial reasoning, and digital navigation in ways difficult to isolate and measure separately (Kress, 2003). Traditional assessments focusing exclusively on print literacy may miss significant learning in other modalities. Similarly, the social and collaborative dimensions of much game-based learning sit uneasily with assessments designed for individual performance (Steinkuehler, 2006).

Cultural responsiveness adds another assessment challenge. Standardized assessments often contain cultural bias, measuring students' familiarity with dominant cultural knowledge rather than their actual literacy capabilities (Ladson-Billings,

2006). For interventions intentionally valuing diverse cultural and linguistic practices, assessments embodying monocultural norms may provide misleading evidence of effectiveness. Assessing whether interventions successfully validate students' cultural identities, maintain home languages, or build critical consciousness requires moving beyond conventional literacy measures (Peristeris, 2017).

## 8.2 Embedded and Stealth Assessment

Embedded assessment, assessment integrated seamlessly into gameplay, offers one promising approach (Shute, 2011). Rather than interrupting learning with separate tests, embedded assessment infers student knowledge from gameplay actions. For example, analyzing which game texts students choose to read, how long they spend with different texts, and comprehension demonstrated through subsequent game actions can provide rich information about reading skills and strategies (Shute, Ventura, & Kim, 2013). Stealth assessment specifically aims to measure learning unobtrusively, without students experiencing the activity as assessment (Shute, 2011). This can reduce test anxiety and provide more authentic pictures of students' capabilities, particularly valuable for marginalized students who may underperform on high-stakes tests due to stereotype threat (Steele & Aronson, 1995). Games generate extensive data about player actions, decision-making, and problem-solving that can be analyzed to infer developing skills and understandings (Shute et al., 2013).

However, embedded assessment also presents challenges. Inferring knowledge from gameplay requires sophisticated analytics and validation that measures actually capture intended constructs (Mislevy, Behrens, DiCerbo, & Levy, 2012). Privacy concerns arise when extensive student data is collected. The complexity of gameplay may make it difficult to isolate specific skills or knowledge being assessed (Kafai & Burke, 2015). Bias in algorithms analyzing gameplay data could disadvantage particular groups of students (Benjamin, 2019).

## 8.3 Portfolio and Performance-Based Assessment

Portfolio assessment, collecting diverse artifacts demonstrating learning over time, aligns well with game-based literacy learning (Gee, 2006). Student portfolios might include in-game writing, strategy guides students create, forum posts discussing game content, fan fiction, screenshots with annotations, video recordings of gameplay with commentary, and reflections on learning (Steinkuehler, 2010). Such portfolios can capture the full range of literacies students develop while providing insight into their learning processes. Performance-based assessment asks students to demonstrate literacy skills through authentic tasks rather than answering decontextualized questions (Hersi, 2010). Students might be assessed on their ability to accomplish complex literacy tasks within game contexts, researching information to solve problems, writing persuasively to other players, creating multimedia presentations explaining game concepts, or designing game modifications requiring written documentation (Hayes & Duncan, 2012).

For culturally-responsive assessment, portfolios and performances can incorporate students' cultural knowledge and practices, allowing them to demonstrate literacy in culturally-familiar contexts (Lee, 2007). Students might be assessed on their ability to code-switch between different language varieties, translate game content for family members, or create games reflecting their cultural experiences (Mateus, 2014). Challenges include the time and expertise required for evaluating complex portfolios and performances, need for clear rubrics and inter-rater reliability, and difficulty comparing results across students or programs (Hersi, 2010). Portfolios may also present equity concerns if students have unequal access to technology for creating sophisticated artifacts (Warschauer, 2004).

## 8.4 Measuring Cultural Responsiveness and Identity Affirmation

Beyond assessing literacy skills, evaluation of culturally-responsive interventions should examine whether games successfully validate students' cultural identities, maintain home languages and cultural practices, and build critical consciousness (Peristeris, 2017). This requires moving beyond traditional achievement measures to include:

**Identity and engagement measures:** Surveys, interviews, or observations assessing whether students feel their identities are valued, see themselves reflected in game content, and experience increased sense of belonging (Lee, 2007). Changes in students' academic identities and self-efficacy as readers and writers can indicate whether interventions counter deficit narratives (Compton-Lilly, 2007).

**Language maintenance:** For multilingual students, assessment should examine whether interventions support continued development of home languages alongside academic English rather than treating languages as zero-sum (Mateus, 2014). This might include assessing literacy in home languages before and after interventions or surveying families about language use patterns.

**Cultural knowledge:** Evaluations can assess whether students deepen understanding of their cultural heritage through game-based learning, positioning cultural knowledge as valuable learning outcome rather than merely vehicle for teaching dominant content (Cajete, 1994).

**Critical consciousness:** Assessments might examine whether students develop increased awareness of social inequities, ability to critically analyze power relations, and sense of agency to effect change (Ladson-Billings, 1995). This could include analyzing students' in-game choices, written reflections, or discussions about social issues.

**Community perspectives:** Evaluation should incorporate perspectives of students' families and communities about whether interventions honour cultural values and support community goals (Smith, 2021). Community members can assess cultural authenticity and appropriateness in ways outside researchers cannot.

# 9. POLICY IMPLICATIONS AND SCALABILITY

## 9.1 Educational Policy and Funding

Scaling culturally-responsive game-based literacy learning to reach substantial numbers of marginalized students requires supportive educational policies and dedicated funding. Current educational policies often create barriers rather than support. High-stakes testing and accountability systems emphasize narrow skill development measurable through standardized tests, de-emphasizing broader literacy practices and cultural knowledge (Au, 2007). Budget constraints limit technology purchases, particularly in under-resourced schools serving marginalized communities (Hersi, 2010).

Policy recommendations include:

**Funding allocations:** Dedicated funding streams for educational technology in schools serving marginalized communities, ensuring equitable access to devices, connectivity, and technical support. This might include federal grants, state technology initiatives, or district-level technology equity funds (Warschauer & Matuchniak, 2010).

**Curriculum flexibility:** Policies allowing teachers and schools flexibility to integrate game-based approaches without being constrained by rigid pacing guides or narrow curriculum mandates. This requires trusting educators' professional judgment rather than prescribing every instructional minute (Hersi, 2010).

**Expanded assessment:** Moving beyond sole reliance on standardized tests to include multiple measures of literacy, recognition of multilingual capabilities, and valuing cultural knowledge and practices. This could involve portfolio assessment, performance tasks, or measures of student engagement and wellbeing alongside traditional achievement metrics (Darling-Hammond, 2007).

**Professional development:** Sustained funding for teacher professional development on game-based learning and culturally-responsive pedagogy, recognizing this requires ongoing support rather than one-time training. Policies might mandate minimum professional development hours or fund instructional coaching (Bourgonjon, Valcke, Soetaert, & Schellens, 2010).

**Research and development:** Public funding for developing and researching culturally-responsive educational games, reducing reliance on commercial markets unlikely to adequately serve smaller marginalized communities. This could include research grants, public-private partnerships, or government-developed open educational resources (Kafai & Burke, 2015).

## 9.2 Technology and Infrastructure Policy

Beyond educational policy specifically, broader technology and infrastructure policies significantly impact feasibility of game-based learning in marginalized communities. The digital divide reflects not only individual or school resources but also systemic infrastructure gaps and policy choices (Warschauer, 2004).

Policy recommendations include:

**Universal broadband access:** Policies ensuring all communities have access to high-speed internet, recognizing connectivity as essential infrastructure like roads or electricity. This might involve public investment in broadband infrastructure, regulations requiring internet service provider coverage of underserved areas, or subsidized internet access for low-income families (GILROY & Kruger, 2012).

**Device access programs:** Government or school district programs providing devices to students lacking home access, ensuring all students can engage with digital learning. One-to-one device initiatives have shown promise but require sustainable funding for device purchase, maintenance, and periodic replacement (Warschauer & Matuchniak, 2010).

**Data privacy regulations:** Strong privacy protections for student data, particularly important given historical surveillance and discrimination against marginalized communities. Regulations might limit data collection, require transparent data practices, prohibit commercial use of student data, and establish meaningful penalties for violations (Regan & Jesse, 2019).

**Digital equity standards:** Regulations or standards ensuring educational technology is accessible to students with disabilities, available in multiple languages, and culturally responsive. This could involve accessibility requirements for educational technology purchased with public funds or standards for cultural representation in educational media (Watkins, 2011).

## 9.3 Language Policy

For multilingual marginalized communities, language policies fundamentally shape possibilities for culturally-responsive game-based literacy learning. Policies positioning multilingualism as asset versus deficit determine whether game-based interventions can support home language development or are constrained to English-only approaches (Mateus, 2014).

Policy recommendations include:

**Multilingual education support:** Policies supporting bilingual and multilingual education models that maintain and develop students' home languages alongside academic English. This creates contexts where multilingual game-based learning is pedagogically supported rather than isolated to single games (Kosonen & Benson, 2013).

**Indigenous language revitalization:** Dedicated support for indigenous language maintenance and revitalization, including funding for indigenous language educational resources like games. Federal and state policies might prioritize indigenous language development as both educational and cultural preservation imperatives (McCarty & Lee, 2014).

**Assessment in multiple languages:** Policies allowing students to demonstrate literacy in their home languages, not only English, recognizing multilingual literacy as valuable outcome. This requires developing assessments in multiple languages and training evaluators in diverse languages (Mateus, 2014).

**Language resource development:** Funding for developing educational resources, including games, in languages currently underserved by educational markets. For smaller language communities, this requires public investment as commercial markets are insufficient (Kosonen & Benson, 2013).

## 9.4 International Development and Global Education

In global contexts, particularly low- and middle-income countries with substantial marginalized populations, policy considerations extend to international development and global education initiatives. Organizations like UNESCO, UNICEF, and the World Bank influence educational policy through funding, technical assistance, and advocacy (Mundy & Verger, 2015).

Policy recommendations include:

**Culturally-appropriate technology:** International development efforts should prioritize culturally-appropriate educational technology rather than assuming one-size-fits-all solutions. Games developed for Western contexts may not translate to different cultural contexts and could impose cultural imperialism (Thompson & Parreira do Amaral, 2019).

**Local capacity building:** Investment in local capacity to develop culturally-responsive educational games rather than only importing external solutions. This includes supporting local game developers, researchers, and educators in developing countries (Unwin, 2009).

**Language diversity:** International education policies supporting mother-tongue literacy instruction and multilingual education, creating demand for games in diverse languages beyond global lingua francas like English (Aquino, 2011).

**Open resources:** Prioritizing open educational resources and open-source games that can be freely adapted for local contexts rather than proprietary commercial products. This increases accessibility while allowing cultural customization (Avgerou, 2017).

**Equitable partnerships:** Ensuring international collaborations involve genuine partnership with local stakeholders rather than external actors imposing solutions. Local communities should lead in defining problems, designing solutions, and evaluating outcomes (Verger, Steiner-Khamsi, & Lubienski, 2016).

## 10. CONCLUSIONS

Bridging literacy gaps in marginalized communities through culturally-responsive game-based learning represents a critical intersection of educational equity, digital pedagogy, and cultural sustainability. This chapter has demonstrated that when games are intentionally designed with cultural responsiveness at their core, incorporating authentic representation, validating multilingualism, connecting to community funds of knowledge, and positioning students as cultural knowledge holders, they offer powerful affordances for literacy development while affirming rather than diminishing students' identities. The empirical evidence reviewed reveals consistent patterns of increased engagement, improved literacy outcomes, and strengthened cultural connections when games honour students lived experiences and cultural backgrounds. However, realizing this potential requires addressing substantial implementation challenges including digital access inequities, teacher preparation needs, curriculum constraints, and sustainability concerns. Success demands systemic support through equitable policy frameworks, adequate resource allocation, sustained professional development, and genuine partnership with marginalized communities rather than imposition of external solutions. Ultimately, culturally-responsive game-based literacy learning is not merely a technical educational intervention but a social justice imperative, contributing to the essential work of transforming educational systems to value and sustain cultural and linguistic pluralism while ensuring all students develop powerful literacies necessary for full participation in democratic societies.

## REFERENCES


Abrams, S., & Walsh, S. (2014). Gamified Vocabulary. *Journal of Adolescent & Adult Literacy*, *58*(1), 49–58. Advance online publication. DOI: 10.1002/jaal.315

Aquino, V. J. (2011). Enhancing learning of children from diverse language backgrounds: Mother tongue-based bilingual or multilingual education in the early years; 2011.

Au, W. (2007). High-Stakes Testing and Curricular Control: A Qualitative Metasynthesis. *Educational Researcher*, *36*(5), 258–267. DOI: 10.3102/0013189X07306523

Avgerou, C. (2017). Theoretical Framing of ICT4D Research. In Choudrie, J., Islam, M. S., Wahid, F., Bass, J. M., & Priyatma, J. E. (Eds.), *Information and Communication Technologies for Development* (pp. 10–23). Springer International Publishing. DOI: 10.1007/978-3-319-59111-7_2

Bang, M., & Vossoughi, S. (2016). Participatory Design Research and Educational Justice: Studying Learning and Relations Within Social Change Making. *Cognition and Instruction*, *34*(3), 173–193. DOI: 10.1080/07370008.2016.1181879

Banks, J. A. (1993). Chapter 1: Multicultural Education: Historical Development, Dimensions, and Practice. *Review of Research in Education*, *19*(1), 3–49. DOI: 10.3102/0091732X019001003

Barab, S., Sadler, T., Heiselt, C., Hickey, D., & Zuiker, S. (2007). Relating narrative, inquiry, and inscriptions: A framework for socioscientific inquiry. *Journal of Science Education and Technology*, *16*, 69–82. DOI: 10.1007/s10956-006-9033-3

Barab, S. A., Scott, B., Siyahhan, S., Goldstone, R., Ingram-Goble, A., Zuiker, S. J., & Warren, S. (2009). Transformational Play as a Curricular Scaffold: Using Videogames to Support Science Education. *Journal of Science Education and Technology*, *18*(4), 305–320. DOI: 10.1007/s10956-009-9171-5

Beavis, C., Muspratt, S., & Thompson, R. (2015). "Computer games can get your brain working": Student experience and perceptions of digital games in the classroom. *Learning, Media and Technology*, *40*(1), 21–42. DOI: 10.1080/17439884.2014.904339

Benjamin, R. (2019). *Race After Technology: Abolitionist Tools for the New Jim Code*. John Wiley & Sons.

Bishop, R. S. (1990). *Mirrors*. Windows, and Sliding Glass Doors.

Black, R. W. (2008). *Adolescents and Online Fan Fiction*. Peter Lang.

Bourgonjon, J., Valcke, M., Soetaert, R., & Schellens, T. (2010). Students' perceptions about the use of video games in the classroom. *Computers & Education, 54*(4), 1145–1156. DOI: 10.1016/j.compedu.2009.10.022

Broadfoot, P. (1978). Reproduction in Education, Society and Culture. *Comparative Education, 14*(1), 75–82. DOI: 10.1080/0305006780140109

Brown, J. S., Collins, A., & Duguid, P. (1989). Situated Cognition and the Culture of Learning. *Educational Researcher, 18*(1), 32–42. DOI: 10.3102/0013189X018001032

Cajete, G. (1994). *Look to the Mountain: An Ecology of Indigenous Education.* Kivakí Press.

Cole, M., & Engeström, Y. (1993). A Cultural-Historical Approach to Distributed Cognition. Retrieved from https://www.academia.edu/11412820/A_Cultural_Historical_Approach_to_Distributed_Cognition

Compton-Lilly, C. (2007). The complexities of reading capital in two Puerto Rican families. *Reading Research Quarterly, 42*(1), 72–98. DOI: 10.1598/RRQ.42.1.3

Csikszentmihalyi, M. (1990). Flow: The Psychology of Optimal Experience.

Darling-Hammond, L. (2007). Race, inequality and educational accountability: The irony of "No Child Left Behind." Race Ethnicity and Education -. *Race, Ethnicity and Education, 10*(3), 245–260. DOI: 10.1080/13613320701503207

Delpit, L. (1995). Other People's Children: Cultural Conflict in the Classroom. W. Retrieved from https://eric.ed.gov/?id=ED387274

DeVane, B., & Squire, K. D. (2008). The meaning of race and violence in Grand Theft Auto: San Andreas. *Games and Culture, 3*(3–4), 264–285. DOI: 10.1177/1555412008317308

Dezuanni, M., O'Mara, J., & Beavis, C. (2015). 'Redstone is like electricity': Children's performative representations in and around Minecraft. *E-Learning and Digital Media, 12*(2), 147–163. DOI: 10.1177/2042753014568176

Dikkers, S., et al. (2015). TeacherCraft: How Teachers Learn to Use MineCraft in Their Classrooms. Lulu.com.

Disalvo, B., Guzdial, M., Bruckman, A., & Mcklin, T. (2014). Saving Face While Geeking Out: Video Game Testing as a Justification for Learning Computer Science. *Journal of the Learning Sciences, 23*(3), 1–44. DOI: 10.1080/10508406.2014.893434

DiSalvo, B., Yip, J., Bonsignore, E., & DiSalvo, C. (Eds.). (2017). *Participatory Design for Learning: Perspectives from Practice and Research.* Routledge. DOI: 10.4324/9781315630830

Dudley-Marling, C., & Lucas, K. (2009). Pathologizing the Language and Culture of Poor Children. *Language Arts, 86*(5), 362–370. DOI: 10.58680/la20097099

Dweck, C. S. (2006). Mindset: The new psychology of success (pp. x, 276). New York, NY, US: Random House.

Flores, N., & Rosa, J. (2015). Undoing Appropriateness: Raciolinguistic Ideologies and Language Diversity in Education. *Harvard Educational Review, 85*(2), 149–171. DOI: 10.17763/0017-8055.85.2.149

Gay, G. (2010). *Culturally responsive teaching: Theory, research, and practice.* Teachers College.

Gee, J. (2003). What Video Games Have to Teach Us About Learning and Literacy. *Computers in Entertainment, 1*(1), 20. DOI: 10.1145/950566.950595

Gee, J. (2006). *Game-like learning: An example of situated learning and implications for opportunity to learn.* Assessment, Equity, and Opportunity to Learn. DOI: 10.1017/CBO9780511802157.009

Gee, J. P., & Hayes, E. R. (2011). *Language and Learning in the Digital Age.* Routledge. DOI: 10.4324/9780203830918

Gerber, H. R., & Price, D. P. (2013). Fighting baddies and collecting bananas: Teachers' perceptions of games-based literacy learning. *Educational Media International, 50*(1), 51–62. DOI: 10.1080/09523987.2013.777182

GILROY, A. A., & Kruger, L. (2012). Broadband Internet Access and the Digital Divide: Federal Assistance Programs. CreateSpace Independent Publishing Platform.

Gonzalez, N., Moll, L. C., & Amanti, C. (Eds.). (2006). *Funds of Knowledge* (0 ed.). Routledge. DOI: 10.4324/9781410613462

Gutiérrez, K. D. (2008). Developing a Sociocritical literacy in the third space. *Reading Research Quarterly, 43*(2), 148–164. DOI: 10.1598/RRQ.43.2.3

Gutiérrez, K. D., & Rogoff, B. (2003). Cultural Ways of Learning: Individual Traits or Repertoires of Practice. *Educational Researcher, 32*(5), 19–25. DOI: 10.3102/0013189X032005019

Hart, B., & Risley, T. R. (1995). Meaningful differences in the everyday experience of young American children (pp. xxiii, 268). Baltimore, MD, US: Paul H Brookes Publishing.

Hayes, E., & Duncan, S. C. (2012). *Learning in Video Game Affinity Spaces* (Vol. 51). New Literacies and Digital Epistemologies.

Heath, S. B. (1983). *Ways with Words: Language, Life and Work in Communities and Classrooms*. Cambridge University Press. DOI: 10.1017/CBO9780511841057

Hermes, M., Bang, M., & Marin, A. (2012). Designing Indigenous Language Revitalization. *Harvard Educational Review*, *82*(3), 381–402. DOI: 10.17763/haer.82.3.q8117w861241871j

Hersi, A. (2010). Darling-Hammond: The flat world and education: How America's commitment to equity will determine our future. *Journal of Educational Change*, *11*(3), 291–295. DOI: 10.1007/s10833-010-9137-7

Ito, M., Gutierrez, K., Livingstone, S., Penuel, B., Salen, K., Schor, J., & Shresthova, S. (2013). *Connected Learning: An Agenda for Research and Design*. The Digital Media and Learning Research Hub Reports on Connected Learning.

Jenkins, H. (2009). *Confronting the Challenges of Participatory Culture: Media Education for the 21st Century*. MIT Press. DOI: 10.7551/mitpress/8435.001.0001

Kafai, Y. B., & Burke, Q. (2015). Constructionist Gaming: Understanding the Benefits of Making Games for Learning. *Educational Psychologist*, *50*(4), 313–334. DOI: 10.1080/00461520.2015.1124022

Kiili, K. (2005). Digital game-based learning: Towards an experiential gaming model. *The Internet and Higher Education*, *8*(1), 13–24. DOI: 10.1016/j.iheduc.2004.12.001

Kim, J. S. (2006). Effects of a Voluntary Summer Reading Intervention on Reading Achievement: Results From a Randomized Field Trial. *Educational Evaluation and Policy Analysis*, *28*(4), 335–355. DOI: 10.3102/01623737028004335

Kosonen, K., & Benson, C. (2013). Language Issues in Comparative Education: Inclusive teaching and learning in non-dominant languages and cultures.

Kress, G. (2003). *Literacy in the New Media Age*. Routledge. DOI: 10.4324/9780203299234

Kress, G. R., Leeuwen, T. V., & Leeuwen, D. of H. and S. S. T. V. (2001). Multimodal Discourse: The Modes and Media of Contemporary Communication. Arnold.

Ladson-Billings, G. (1995). Toward a Theory of Culturally Relevant Pedagogy. *American Educational Research Journal*, *32*(3), 465–491. DOI: 10.3102/00028312032003465

Ladson-Billings, G. (2006). From the Achievement Gap to the Education Debt: Understanding Achievement in U.S. Schools. *Educational Researcher*, *35*(7), 3–12. DOI: 10.3102/0013189X035007003

Lave, J., & Wenger, E. (1991). *Situated learning: Legitimate peripheral participation.* Cambridge University Press. DOI: 10.1017/CBO9780511815355

Lee, C. D. (2007). *Culture, Literacy, and Learning: Taking Bloom in the Midst of the Whirlwind.* Teachers College Press.

Lu, A. (2013). Video Games and Learning: Teaching and Participatory Culture in the Digital Age. *Journal of Children and Media*, *7*(2), 277–280. DOI: 10.1080/17482798.2012.724596

Mateus, S. G. (2014). Translanguaging: Language, Bilingualism, and Education. *Bilingual Research Journal*, *37*(3), 366–369. DOI: 10.1080/15235882.2014.965361

McCarty, T. L., & Lee, T. S. (2014). Critical culturally sustaining/revitalizing pedagogy and indigenous education sovereignty. *Harvard Educational Review*, *84*(1), 101–124. DOI: 10.17763/haer.84.1.q83746nl5pj34216

Minchen, G. (2024). Scaffolding Learners' Comprehension in Extensive Reading. *English Language Teaching*, *17*(11), 1–1. DOI: 10.5539/elt.v17n11p1

Mislevy, R., Behrens, J., DiCerbo, K. E., & Levy, R. (2012). Design and discovery in educational assessment: Evidence centered design, psychometrics, and data mining. *Journal of Educational Data Mining*, *4*, 11–48.

Moll, L. C., Amanti, C., Neff, D., & Gonzalez, N. (1992). Funds of Knowledge for Teaching: Using a Qualitative Approach to Connect Homes and Classrooms. *Theory into Practice*, *31*(2), 132–141. DOI: 10.1080/00405849209543534

Mundy, K., & Verger, A. (2015). The World Bank and the global governance of education in a changing world order. *International Journal of Educational Development*, *40*, 9–18. DOI: 10.1016/j.ijedudev.2014.11.021

National Center for Education Statistics. (2019). NAEP Reading 2019 Highlights.

Neuman, S., & Celano, D. (2001). Access to Print in Low-Income and Middle-Income Communities: An Ecological Study of Four Neighborhoods. Reading Research Quarterly - READ RES QUART, 36, 8–26. DOI: 10.1598/RRQ.36.1.1

Oakes, J. (2005). *Keeping Track: How Schools Structure Inequality*. Yale University Press.

OECD. (2013, October 8). OECD Skills Outlook 2013.

Paris, D. (2012). Culturally sustaining pedagogy: A needed change in stance, terminology, and practice. *Educational Researcher, 41*(3), 93–97. DOI: 10.3102/0013189X12441244

Peristeris, K. (2017). Culturally Sustaining Pedagogies: Teaching and Learning for Justice in a Changing World. *Journal of Teaching and Learning, 11*(1). Advance online publication. DOI: 10.22329/jtl.v11i1.4987

Perley, B. (2012). Zombie Linguistics: Experts, Endangered Languages and the Curse of Undead Voices. Anthropological Forum -. *Anthropological Forum, 22*(2), 133–149. DOI: 10.1080/00664677.2012.694170

Rama, P. S., Black, R. W., Van Es, E., & Warschauer, M. (2012). Affordances for second language learning in World of Warcraft. *ReCALL, 24*(3), 322–338. DOI: 10.1017/S0958344012000171

Reardon, S., & Portilla, X. (2016). Recent Trends in Income, Racial, and Ethnic School Readiness Gaps at Kindergarten Entry. *AERA Open, 2*(3), 2332858416657343. Advance online publication. DOI: 10.1177/2332858416657343

Regan, P. M., & Jesse, J. (2019). Ethical challenges of edtech, big data and personalized learning: Twenty-first century student sorting and tracking. *Ethics and Information Technology, 21*(3), 167–179. DOI: 10.1007/s10676-018-9492-2

Rudd, R. E. (2007). Health literacy skills of U.S. adults. *American Journal of Health Behavior, 31*(Suppl 1), S8–S18. DOI: 10.5993/AJHB.31.s1.3

Ryan, R., Rigby, C., & Przybylski, A. (2006). The Motivational Pull of Video Games: A Self-Determination Theory Approach. *Motivation and Emotion, 30*(4), 344–360. DOI: 10.1007/s11031-006-9051-8

Ryan, R. M., & Deci, E. L. (2000). Self-determination theory and the facilitation of intrinsic motivation, social development, and well-being. *The American Psychologist, 55*(1), 68–78. DOI: 10.1037/0003-066X.55.1.68

Samy Alim, H. (2007). Critical Hip-Hop Language Pedagogies: Combat, Consciousness, and the Cultural Politics of Communication. *Journal of Language, Identity, and Education, 6*(2), 161–176. DOI: 10.1080/15348450701341378

Shaffer, D. W. (2006). Epistemic frames for epistemic games. *Computers & Education, 46*(3), 223–234. DOI: 10.1016/j.compedu.2005.11.003

Shaw, A. (2014). *Gaming at the Edge: Sexuality and Gender at the Margins of Gamer Culture*. University of Minnesota Press.

Shute, V. J. (2011). Stealth assessment in computer-based games to support learning. In *Computer games and instruction* (pp. 503–524). IAP Information Age Publishing. DOI: 10.1108/978-1-61735-410-620251025

Shute, V. J., Ventura, M., & Kim, Y. J. (2013). Assessment and Learning of Qualitative Physics in Newton's Playground. *The Journal of Educational Research, 106*(6), 423–430. DOI: 10.1080/00220671.2013.832970

Smith, P. L. T. (2021). *Decolonizing Methodologies: Research and Indigenous Peoples*. Zed Books Ltd. DOI: 10.5040/9781350225282

Smitherman, G. (1999). *Talkin that Talk: Language*. Culture and Education in African America. DOI: 10.4324/9780203065419

Steele, C. M., & Aronson, J. (1995). Stereotype threat and the intellectual test performance of African Americans. *Journal of Personality and Social Psychology, 69*(5), 797–811. DOI: 10.1037/0022-3514.69.5.797

Steinkuehler, C. (2006). Massively Multiplayer Online Video Gaming as Participation in a Discourse. Mind. *Mind, Culture, and Activity, 13*(1), 38–52. DOI: 10.1207/s15327884mca1301_4

Steinkuehler, C. (2010). Video Games and Digital Literacies. Journal of Adolescent & Adult Literacy -. *Journal of Adolescent & Adult Literacy, 54*(1), 61–63. DOI: 10.1598/JAAL.54.1.7

Steinkuehler, C., & Duncan, S. (2008). Scientific Habits of Mind in Virtual Worlds. *Journal of Science Education and Technology, 17*(6), 530–543. DOI: 10.1007/s10956-008-9120-8

Street, B. V. (1984). *Literacy in Theory and Practice*. Cambridge University Press.

Street, B. V. (2014). *Social Literacies: Critical Approaches to Literacy in Development, Ethnography and Education*. Routledge., DOI: 10.4324/9781315844282

Takeuchi, L. M., & Sarah, V. (2014). LeveL up Learning: A national survey on teaching with digital games - By &. Retrieved November 12, 2025, from https://www.readkong.com/page/level-up-learning-6779027

The New London Group. (1996). A Pedagogy of Multiliteracies: Designing Social Futures. *Harvard Educational Review, 66*(1), 60–93. DOI: 10.17763/haer.66.1.17370n67v22j160u

Thompson, C., & Parreira do Amaral, M. (2019). Introduction: Researching the Global Education Industry. In Parreira do Amaral, M., Steiner-Khamsi, G., & Thompson, C. (Eds.), *Researching the Global Education Industry: Commodification, the Market and Business Involvement* (pp. 1–21). Springer International Publishing. DOI: 10.1007/978-3-030-04236-3_1

Thorne, S. L., Black, R. W., & Sykes, J. M. (2009). Second Language Use, Socialization, and Learning in Internet Interest Communities and Online Gaming. *Modern Language Journal*, *93*(s1), 802–821. DOI: 10.1111/j.1540-4781.2009.00974.x

UNESCO. (2020). *Global Education Monitoring Report 2020: Inclusion and education: All means all.* UNESCO., DOI: 10.54676/JJNK6989

Unwin, P. T. H. (2009). *ICT4D: Information and Communication Technology for Development*. Cambridge University Press.

Valencia, R. (2010). Dismantling Contemporary Deficit Thinking: Educational Thought and Practice. Dismantling Contemporary Deficit Thinking: Educational Thought and Practice, 1–223. DOI: 10.4324/9780203853214

van Dijk, J. A. G. M. (2005). *The Deepening Divide: Inequality in the Information Society*. SAGE Publications.

Verger, A., Steiner-Khamsi, G., & Lubienski, C. (2016). The Emergence and Structuring of the Global Education Industry: Towards an Analytical Framework.

Vygotsky, L. S., & Cole, M. (1978). *Mind in Society: Development of Higher Psychological Processes*. Harvard University Press.

Warschauer, M. (2004). Technology and Social Inclusion: Rethinking the Digital Divide. DOI: 10.7551/mitpress/6699.001.0001

Warschauer, M., & Matuchniak, T. (2010). New Technology and Digital Worlds: Analyzing Evidence of Equity in Access, Use, and Outcomes. *Review of Research in Education*, *34*(1), 179–225. DOI: 10.3102/0091732X09349791

Watkins, S. (2011). Digital Divide: Navigating the Digital Edge. *International Journal of Learning and Media*, *3*(2), 1–12. DOI: 10.1162/ijlm_a_00072

Chapter 6
# Enhancing Language Learning Through Indigenous Lobedu Folk Songs

**Maletšema Ruth Emsley**
http://orcid.org/0000-0002-6638-871X
*University of Limpopo, South Africa*

**Mantsha Cecilia Modiba**
http://orcid.org/0000-0003-0663-0719
*University of Limpopo, South Africa*

## ABSTRACT

*Integrating culturally relevant content from the indigenous knowledge systems (IKS) and languages can enhance engagement and understanding of language teaching and learning. Although South Africa's Constitution (1996) recognises 12 official languages and encourages the documentation, preservation, and promotion of minority languages and dialects, the commitment to promoting cultural diversity and inclusion of these languages is still meagre, especially among the marginalized indigenous rural communities. This chapter argues that folk songs as part of the IKS can help to improve language and other creative skills since they incorporate poetic elements such as rhythm, metaphor, and wordplay. The chapter adopted a decolonial lens and the repetition as a rhetorical tool for emphasis and persuasion, rhythm, balance, memory, and learning to explore the Lobedu folk song "Ka totoma".*

DOI: 10.4018/979-8-3373-4322-8.ch006

## INTRODUCTION

It is extensively acknowledged that Western colonialism and imperialism have long suppressed the indigenous African epistemologies and cultural practices that could have made meaning to language learning and literacy. But again, "before the advent of computer games every society had a way of entertaining the young ones through a lot of traditional games. Indigenous games have historically been used to stimulate learning of literacy and numeracy skills in schools and communities in various parts of the world" (Mwinsa & Dagada, 2024, p.1), and folk songs and folk games are some of the ways which entertain and prepare children holistically towards a rewarding life in the future (Obeng et al, 2022). Scholarship has foregrounded the reclaiming of indigenous epistemologies that were historically marginalised by colonial systems, but the efforts to revitalise languages such as Lovedu to advance language learning and literacy through games is minimal. This chapter focuses on the acknowledgment of the indigenous epistemologies to expand on the use of Lovedu folk songs in pedagogy, literacy and research. It brings attention to critical contributions of folk songs to the language learning and literacy. Furthermore, when viewed through decolonial pedagogy, African folk songs can transform educational dialogue and inclusivity making language learning more practical and learner-centred because of their power to challenge colonial practices as they are culturally responsive. The chapter argues that folk songs, just like Western songs, Lovedu folk songs can enhance language learning through games. We do not deny that digital game-based approaches are increasingly recognised as vital for literacy development; however, the musical and folk content embedded in such games often reflects Western philosophies that marginalise indigenous African traditions as stressed by de Jager (2022) and Mwinsa and Dagada (2024).

Game-based learning has myriad definitions. It can also mean borrowing of certain gaming principles and applying them to real-life settings to engage users (Trybus 2015). Trybus (2015) advises that GBL is not just creating games though, it is designing learning activities that can incrementally introduce concepts and guide users towards an end goal. This chapter supports the foregoing definition as it is structured around the delimitations outlined in the discussion. The chapter supports that GBL transcends game creation. GBL involves structured, incremental activities guiding teachers and learners toward set objectives in language and literacy. In other words, it is an intentional design of educational experiences where learning is carefully planned (Mwinsa & Dagada, 2024). This chapter aims to explore the role of folk song as a game-based learning technique by focusing on Lovedu traditional folk song. Traditional songs function as more than just learning tools; they enhance language acquisition, instil moral values and strengthen cultural identity while encouraging creativity and active participation in young children (Rahman et al., 2025). The chapter contributes to the debates on decolonisation of education by offering insights into practices to confront exclusions and foster for more inclusive learning environments with special focus on Lobedu folk songs as tools for game-based language learning.

## THEORETICAL FRAMEWORK

### Decoloniality and Decolonial Pedagogy

Grounded in decoloniality, this chapter is firmly rooted in African thought to privilege indigenous epistemologies though games-based language learning. African worldviews can be considered to reveal the significance embedded in Indigenous African knowledge systems (IKS) which were reduced to shallow meaning by Euro-Western frameworks. By adopting a decolonial perspective, this chapter offers new insights into how African marginalised indigenous languages such as Lovedu can make meaning in postcolonial South Africa. Quijano (2000) defines decoloniality as a critical response to the "coloniality of power". It is the matrix of domination that outlived formal colonialism and continues to structure hierarchies of knowledge, race and labour in the modern world. Decoloniality is not a theory to be applied, but a process (Walsh, 2023). Apart from redressing the Global North past atrocities, the Decolonial pedagogy is an ethical commitment that provides justice to the African classrooms since it continues to create debates on transforming, deconstructing and decolonising the curriculum (Russell, 2025). This is a "practice of freedom" (Freire 1970, p.34) and justice. Pedagogical justice creates inclusion of the previously marginalised communities and their languages because pedagogical justice confronts inequalities produced by the coloniality of knowledge and create learning spaces in which historically marginalized students are recognised not only as participants but as legitimate producers of knowledge (Walsh, 2019).

Folk songs are fit to be employed as games for learning, because folk songs incorporate elements such as rules, turn-taking and participatory roles which involve movement, rhythm and social interaction among participants. These elements create structured play that facilitates learning. Several works investigating African traditional songs from a variety of perspectives have proven that there is a connection between education and African traditional songs (Egara et al, 2025). However, there is a significant gap in the literature regarding Lovedu folk songs as a pedagogical resource to support language learning and literacy development.

Most game-based language learning studies drew on theories and frameworks (Yang et al., 2024). GBL also is underpinned by multiple learning theories that collectively explain its effectiveness. Constructivist theory for example, posits that learners actively construct understanding through interaction and meaningful problem-solving, which games naturally facilitate. Secondly, the experiential learning theory emphasises learning through action and reflection, allowing learners to build knowledge via hands-on, participatory gameplay. Thirdly, the social learning theory highlights the role of observation, collaboration and interaction, core aspects of cooperative game experiences. Finally, self-determination theory explains how GBL fosters intrinsic motivation by promoting autonomy, competence and feedback through engaging challenges. This chapter's analysis is situated firmly within a decolonial perspective and the principles of GBL which support that deeper earning is fostered by GBL (Plass et al, 2020). Games can create immersive environments where learners negotiate meaning, develop problem-solving and communication skills (Plass, et al, 2020) Because they operate in authentic scenarios.

The benefit of situating this discussion within the decolonial lens is because many scholars have explored the game-based learning through folk songs but failed to focus on the Lovedu folk songs. Decolonial pedagogy aligns most strongly with the IKS, in which all song traditions are understood relationally. Decolonial pedagogies are ethical-political stances that confront coloniality in knowledge, power, and being (Mignolo, 2011; Walsh, 2019).

## GAME-BASED LANGAUGE LEARNING AND LITERACY DEVELOPMENT

GBL positions the game itself as the central medium of instruction, and activities deliberately aligned to achieve specific learning outcomes (Plass et al., 2020). According to Reinhardt & Sykes (2014) different terms are often used to describe game use in education. While GBL offers a valuable tool for reinforcing key concepts and providing a stress-free environment for self-assessment, many opportunities it offers currently are on digital spaces. The technological or digital spaces create huge platforms for teaching and learning including the use of games in learning and literacy development. However, factors such as poor infrastructure and resources, high costs and limited funding, digital inequality and socioeconomic barriers, policy and systemic challenges, teacher preparedness and training gaps can hinder the use of GBL through digital game-based learning. Again, learners acquire a second language more effectively when building on the knowledge and structures of their mother tongue, because they already have the schemata relating to their language (Emsley, 2011). This is supported by Krashen that language acquisition is facilitated when learners can rely on their existing linguistic competence and Vygotsky who stressed that learning builds on prior knowledge. Learners' first language acts as a mediating tool for cognitive development and for understanding new concepts in a second language. Conversely, other scholars asserting that songs enhance language learning across learners regardless of their linguistic background (Schön et al, 2008).

Principles of GBL that supports this chapter are outlined below:

- Active learning and participation (Learners engage directly in tasks rather than passively receiving content; Simon, 2024).
- Clear goals and rules (Games structure learning through objectives and challenges aligned to outcomes; Matthew et al, 2025).
- Motivation and engagement (The challenges, rewards and competition stimulate intrinsic motivation).
- Immediate feedback (Players receive real-time responses that reinforce learning.
- Problem-solving and critical thinking (Learners make decisions and solve contextualised problems - Seddighi-Khavidak, 2025).
- Safe space for experimentation (Mistakes become part of the learning process without real-world risk).
- Collaboration and social interaction (Many games foster teamwork and peer learning - Seddighi-Khavidak, 2025).
- Progression and incremental learning (Levels or stages scaffold knowledge development (Zulkefli & bin Jamil, 2024).
- Autonomy and learner agency (Players make choices that influence outcomes - Seddighi-Khavidak, et al, 2025).
- Contextualised / situated learning (Knowledge is applied in meaningful scenarios – Matthew et al, 2025).

This chapter argues that traditional folk songs which are predominantly sung and acted out as games and songs have the above qualities and elements of promoting language and literacy skill in children.

## African Folk Songs

Songs were employed for the preservation and transmission of knowledge and experience from one generation to another. Nnamani (2014) associates African songs with activities such as ceremonies, work, games, dances, wars, religious ceremonies, etc. As such they are sung purposefully. African songs include songs for entertainment, war, funeral, manual labour, religion, victory and consolation. The traditional songs are very instrumental in the teaching of children manners and correct social behaviour, so they are of great source of education about the history of a people or a society. They have the capacity for developing the confidence level and self-esteem of children who engage in their singing. As in the case of African folktales, African traditional songs can be used in varied fields of study including literacy and language. They carry within them elements of culture, aesthetics, linguistics and practicality which make them holistic. African songs are very significant instruments for education and learning.

Folk songs are traditional songs from a specific community or culture, often passed down orally from one generation to the nex. These songs typically have simple, repetitive melodies and lyrics that tell stories about the daily lives, beliefs, and experiences of ordinary people. Makhmudova and Khaydarova (2025) analysed the significance of folklore in correcting children's speech and the role of various forms of folklore, that is fairy tales, songs, proverbs, riddles, and folk poetry in enriching children's speech, improving pronunciation, expanding vocabulary, and developing logical thinking. They stressed that folklore has a positive impact on children's psychology and the emotional aspects of their speech, and that it is the important tool for the correct and qualitative development of children's speech from both pedagogical and linguistic perspectives. "In traditional African societies, where knowledge was orally transmitted from one generation to another, the methods employed would certainly be different. Using these methods of knowledge, the natured and nurtured elements of individuals were developed to make them fit into society. In this way, people were socialised and made full-fledged members of the traditional society" (Sunday-Kanu 2015). They were employed, under the guidance and control of selected social agencies-parents, sacred specialists, kings, elders, etc., to intentionally foster among its members its norms, values, purposes, and organizations.

Li and Ismail (2025) systematically reviewed the "historical evolution and contemporary development of folk song activities, emphasising their cultural, social and global significance. Folk songs, as a core element of folk culture, hold deep historical, cultural, and social meanings, reflecting unique cultural values and social functions." Despite the challenges posed by globalisation and modernisation, folk songs also encounter new development opportunities to be used in teaching languages. They also mirror people's lifestyles, emotions, values and societal shifts while serving as a cultural conduit, preserving the past and fostering intergenerational connections through oral traditions (Okpokwasili & Ekemezie, 2023). However, the traditional folk song environment is dwindling, with many youths exhibiting limited interest or comprehension (Li, et al, 2025). The good thing is that the heightened emphasis on cultural diversity and identity presents fresh avenues for preserving and revitalising folk song traditions. Folk song traditions continue to demonstrate remarkable cultural resilience, yet their sustained relevance in modern contexts confronts critical sustainability pressures. Li and Ismail, (2025) aver that the confluence of global integration and digital transformation has created twin threats of cultural dilution and intergenerational fragmentation. Additionally, Sinha and Kumar (2025) found that folk songs are vital expressions of intangible heritage, but many were not written down. The following section presents how the scholarship of folk songs relates to game-based learning.

- **Cultural and Educational Significance of Lovedu Folk Songs and People**

As traditional pieces of music that originates from the common people of a particular region or culture, folk songs reflect on the daily life, stories and values of the community from which they come. They are transmitted through generations by oral tradition covering a wide range of themes and are often performed in informal settings or at cultural celebrations. They are orally created to express their emotions in social situations (Makhmudova & Khaydarova, 2025). Makhmudova and Khaydarova (2025) assert that traditional folk songs are extremely rare and valuable in their ability to express these emotions. In Africa, folk song as is part of oral tradition like proverbs, folktales, dances, customs, traditional medicine, religious practices, and cultural sayings (Mbunwe-Samba, 2012; Sone, 2018). But these practices must have an audience because they depend on a performing group and a listening audience (Finnegan, 1970). On the other hand, we cannot deny the fact that language is rooted "in the reality of the culture …" (Bronisław Malinowski,1923). What connects the oral cultural forms (songs) to game-based learning is the claim by Huizinga (1949) that "play is a primary formative element in culture. The educational benefits of folk songs extend beyond enjoyment because they are embedded within the linguistic and cultural practices of the speech communities that produce them. As Lomax (1968) observes, "Folk song is the musical expression of the people," underscoring their rootedness in communal identity and language. Because oral forms are performed collectively (Finnegan, 1970) they naturally embody participation such as turn-taking which aligns closely with the principles of game-based learning. They are not isolated pedagogical tools. This chapter is based on the folk song "Ka totoma" which is the traditional folk song of the Lobedu/Lovedu people.

- **Lovedu/lobedu songs: cultural identity and history**

The Lovedu are a Bantu tribe located in north-eastern Limpopo, historically known as "the people of Mujaji," the Rain-Queen (Talbot, 1943). Their ancestors, traced to a son of Monomatapa, migrated from Great Zimbabwe around the sixteenth century, blending with Sotho, Nguni, and Shona influences to form a unique culture centred on the Rain-Queen (Talbot, 1943). According to Joubert (2011), "the royal nucleus of the Lobedu descends from one of the Rozwi states that gained prominence in the southern part of the former Karanga empire. The Lobedu people live in the Limpopo Province below the Drakensberg escarpment near Duiwelskloof. They are surrounded by the Shangaan-Tsonga people to the east, the Pedi to the south, the Venda to the north, and several other tribes to the west." Their cultural life includes dances tied to spiritual and agricultural rituals. These ceremonies, involving drums, ancestral spirits, and rain-invoking songs, held deep communal significance (Joubert, 2011). "The music used during the rain dancing performances consists of lesugu songs, which are also 'sung at the annual harvest ceremony, on the death of important royal people, and at the girls' initiation school'" (Smith, 1945). The rain cult that is central to Lobedu spiritual life ensures a system of belief in the agricultural fertility. For example, taboos on cutting specific trees during the early rainy season serve to prevent drought or other calamities. Musical performance, particularly through lesugu songs, is integral to these rituals and is also featured in the annual harvest ceremony, royal funerals, and girls' initiation rites, highlighting the multifunctional role of music in Lobedu ceremonial and sociocultural life (Smith, 1945).

## INTERSECTIONS BETWEEN FOLK SONG SCHOLARSHIP AND GAME-BASED LEARNING

A song is poetry set to motion. In a second language a song enhances the learning of that language (Israel, 2013).

Game-based learning on the other hand, is 'learning through the game', rather than 'learning to play the game' (Wu et al., 2012). Folk songs are culturally rich resources for language and cognitive development, making them highly compatible with game-based learning (GBL) approaches. Songs provide relevant sources for learning listening, speaking, reading and writing skills, while also teaching vocabulary, sentence patterns, pronunciation, rhythm, adjectives and adverbs (Lo & Fai Li, 1998). What is humanistic about them is that they create a non-threatening immersive learning environment that enhances motivation and social participation which is core principles of GBL. Folk songs in themselves provide prosodic features of language, intonation, rhythm and stress which are naturally embedded in songs, providing learners with structured, repetitive exposure, like iterative game mechanics that reinforce skill acquisition (Hill, 1999).

Folk songs often follow repeated verse forms with rhyme and storytelling, which align with challenge and feedback mechanisms in games. Learners can progressively master songs, receive immediate corrections and participate in interactive call-and-response, paralleling turn-taking and collaborative gameplay (Caixia, Abdullah, & Safian, 2025). Indigenous musical games and songs especially, support holistic child development, engaging cognitive, psychomotor, and affective domains (Acquah et al, 2015). Scholars note that folk songs function as "little books" that transmit cultural knowledge, stories and values while simultaneously fostering memory, reasoning and creativity (Nketia, 1999; Opoku, 2020). Recent empirical studies show that integrating indigenous songs into play-based pedagogies enriches early childhood education outcomes. For instance, Mpandashulu (2024) demonstrates that Zambian Early Childhood Education (ECE) teachers effectively embed folk songs into interactive learning activities, enhancing engagement, cultural understanding, and social interaction. Similarly, Obeng, Brewu, and Opoku (2022) highlight that folk-game songs promote active listening, imagination and participatory learning. These strategies mirror game-based frameworks that emphasise structured engagement, challenge, feedback and collaboration. Thus, the scholarship on folk songs and GBL intersects at the integration of cultural content and interactive methods that drives motivation to learn. Folk songs can as be gamified to foster both linguistic competence and socio-cultural awareness in learners.

### Folk Songs and Game-Based Language Learning

Varied themes across diverse contexts of folk songs usage can support domains like literacy (Yende, 2023); language development (Korkut & Avcı, 2023); creativity and performance (You, 2023); cultural preservation (You, 2023) and cultural transmission (You, 2023; Zhang, 2023). Furthermore, folk songs were proven to be didactic tools to foster imagination, problem-solving and creative expression in children (Kaxarova, 2025). When integrated into community education folk songs strengthen early language skills (Narasid & Rahman, 2025); analysis of symbolic images and poetic devices used to instil values and moral education (Murodov, 2025); enhancing pre-reading skills in teacher training (Narasid, et al, 2025); developing musical skills and supporting oral language (Yang et al., 2025) and enhancing children's speech and language skills (Makhmudova & Khaydarova, 2025). Sun and Sornyai (2025) for example, showed that folk songs can be used for literacy development through repetitive structures to support memory, attention and language acquisition. They showed this by focusing on traditional elements in Mongolian folk songs. Their findings that songs enrich learning, foster cultural engagement, broaden communicative skills, offer innovative pathways to enhance students' educational experiences and holistic literacy development is supported by other scholars such as Minor (2023); Tang & Sornyai (2023) and Yongjie & Meesorn (2024).

## PROBLEM STATEMENT

There has been considerable academic interest in the use of digital games in teaching 21st-century skills and not much has been said about the use game-based language learning through African folk songs. Language learning has historically ignored indigenous languages. Theorists such as Prah have for a long time stressed that it is going to be a necessity to use African languages, to make the best use of Africa's talents and to speed up a process of culturally appropriate and sustainable development on the continent. For too long this has been ignored. Many schools are still banking on the near-exclusive use of former colonial languages as languages of teaching, learning and assessment. This is now changing, little by little, but there are still hundreds of dialects that are still ignored in Africa and elsewhere. In this chapter, we explore the Lovedu language and how Lovedu songs can be used to enhance learning of language and literacy.

Unlike a lyric or literary song deliberately composed, a folksong has ceremonial implications for a society or community which coined it. It has its own idiom and phrases; its own logic and meaning; its apparent 'meaninglessness, as it were, has a hard core 'relevance' grasped by the community singing it (Parma, 1970:1). It has deep roots in the springs of daily life and is interminably linked with the process of living (Krehbiel, 1914). This perspective resonates strongly with the principles of IKS, which similarly locate knowledge and creativity within everyday lived experience, communal interaction and the continuity of cultural practices. Scholarly disciplines are currently re-imagining sustainable frameworks that maximize locally available indigenous knowledge to benefit current and future generations (Sakala et al., 2025). “In Africa where colonialism was accompanied by European nationalism, all knowledge systems that people had used for generations were declared irrelevant” (Hoppers, 2025).

Indigenous knowledge accumulated over time in a particular locality (Emeagwali, 2014) is drenched in culturally specific paradigms such as communal interdependence, and is woven in folktales, parables, proverbs, riddles, and songs (Dei, 2016). The under-utilization of indigenous knowledge in African contexts is lamented in scholarship, particularly when disciplines duplicate knowledge systems from other countries, even where there are opportunities for indigenous knowledge to provide context-specific and cogent solutions locally (Nimoh, 2014). The solutions to Africa's challenges and the drive towards epistemic empowerment are dependent on organic knowledge generation as heralded by former SA president Thabo Mbeki in his African Renaissance drive (Naidoo, 2016). Hence, indigenous knowledges ensure that alternative forms of knowing play an important role in enriching and diversifying scholarly disciplines (Ndlovu, 2014). Additionally, in the previous section, it was noted that the implementation of digital game-based learning is constrained by inadequate infrastructure, limited funding, digital and socioeconomic inequalities, fragmented policies, and insufficient teacher training. These factors might be mitigated using traditional folk songs for GBL in even impoverished spaces.

## METHODOLOGY

Drawing from Decoloniality the authors assert that Indigenous African contexts, rhetoric, communication and literacy are inseparable because they are at the core of everyday life. Experiences, such as food, folk songs, dancing, weaving, naming, among others (Lornell, 2012; Shujaa & Shujaa, 2015; Hlavathi, 2024) form the basis of this narrative. So, these should be incorporated in pedagogy to reclaim their power to demonstrate how these practices can prolifically expand the curriculum and research landscapes and the re/development of theories, methodologies, and frameworks for reimagining, redefining, and expanding the understanding of the previously marginalised South African languages. The chapter followed a qualitative approach to critically analyse the purposively selected Lovedu folk song to establish its quality to improve literacy in a South African classroom context. The song was selected for analysis because it belongs to one of the marginalised languages. Non-probability sampling as the most appropriate in qualitative research was employed. The song was purposefully selected because it exemplifies certain cultural or linguistic features. It was analysed using both thematic and discourse analysis through a decolonial framework. The chapter answers the following research questions:

- How can the inclusion of Lobedu folk songs decolonise language teaching practices in South African classrooms?
- How can the barriers that exist in implementing indigenous folk songs within formal education be addressed from a decolonial perspective?
- In what ways do Lobedu folk songs promote literacy?
- How do songs and song-based participation align with central principles of game-based language teaching?
- What language skills can be acquired in Lobedu folk songs?

## INTERPRETIVE ANALYSIS

### Originality and Structure of the Selected Song

The song Ka totoma was introduced to the music industry by Emma Teanet. Emma Teanet is the legendary Peta Teanet`s mother. Peta Teanet was a South African singer, songwriter and record producer who was recognized as the "King of Shangaan disco music." He resided in Thapane village, located in Bolobedu South at Ga-Modjadji]. The song then became popular. However, the song was traditionally sung during the initiation period. It was one of the songs that was sung when the people would like to meet or enter the house where the initiates are housed after they have returned home for the initiation schools. This song was sung as a request to enter their territory. This finding is based on anecdotal evidence and has not been empirically verified; further research is required to substantiate this observation. Yin (1984), Babbie (1990), Patton (1990), and Creswell (1994) acknowledge that anecdotal and observational data can provide initial insights, but emphasise that systematic, empirical research is necessary to validate such findings. Traditional African societies proverbs, stories, songs, myths, symbols, etc., were employed for the accumulation, preservation, organization and transmission of knowledge and experience from one generation to another making people become socialised and made full-fledged members of the traditional society (Sunday-Kanu, 2015: p.02). In the colonial era, indigenous African music and culture were considered evil and unacceptable for use in schools and places of worship, hence they were excluded from school curricula, and a central place was given to European music and instruments; this was promoted in schools and churches around Africa. It is, therefore, not surprising that from the time of nineteenth-century colonialism, European music dominated the educational system in colonial schools.

- **The song "Katotoma" sung by Emma Teanet.**

  Ka totoma
  Ka totoma, ka totoma
  Hiya!
  Ka ya ka tsena
  Hiya!
  Ka ya ka tsena mošeni ka re "lehwere"
  Hiya!
  Ka re "lehwere, lehwere o lla kae"
  Hiya!
  Ke lla khaka ntšheni malla tšhipi
  Hiya!
  Basimana ba dikgomo ra ka ra disa
  Hiya!
  Ra ya ra disa dikgomo tša Matebele
  Hiya!
  Ka topa šeleng ya ka, khe khwankhwarene
  Hiya!
  Ka eketša ka sikana khe tommanene
  Hiya!
  Pumpure ahe dikoma tša boMotlatšo
  dia hlaka madibene bannnyana wee!
  (Hiya, hiya, hiya, hiya, hiya)

Here is the second version o the song.
Instead of using 'hiya' for a response, 'O!' is used.
Ka totoma, ka totoma
O!
Ka ya ka tsena
O!
Ka ya ka tsena mošeni ka re "lehwere"
O!
Ka re "lehwere, lehwere o lla kae"
O!
Ke lla khaka ntšheni malla tšhipi
O!
Basimana ba dikgomo ra ka ra disa
O!
Ra ya ra disa dikgomo tša Matebele
O!
Ka topa šeleng ya ka, khe khwankhwarene
O!
Ka eketša ka sikana khe tommanene
Hiya!O!
Pumpure ahe dikoma tša boMotlatšo
dia hlaka madibene bannnyana wee!
O!

The second version was retrieved from the internet as follows:

Ka totoma, ka totoma
Ka ya ka tsena
Ka ya ka tsena mošeni ka re "lehwere"
Ka re "lehwere, lehwere o lla kae"
Ke lla ka skokoti malla tšhipi
Basimana ba dikgomo ra ya ra disa
Ra ya ra disa dikgomo tša Matebele
Ka topa šeleng ya ka, ke khwankhwareng
Ka eketša ka sikana ke tommaneng
Kunkure ahe tša Matebele
Kunkure ahe tša Matebele
[Outro]
(Hiya, hiya, hiya, hiya, hiya)
(Hiya, hiya, hiya, hiya, hiya)

(Hiya, hiya, hiya, hiya, hiya)
(Hiya, hiya, hiya, hiya, hiya)
(Hiya, hiya, hiya, hiya)

[Written by: Bongani Cele, Candy Mokoena, Oscar Mdlongwa, Sboniso Langa, Sihle Dlalisa]

Various authors claim to have written the song. For example, artists like Bongani Cele, Candy Mokoena, Oscar Mdlongwa, Sboniso Langa and Sihle Dlalisa could be trached to have contributed to singing the song. The verses show a typical folk song structure of a narrative nature. The approach of participatory and repetitive nature is emphasised by the groups participating in the song, that is two partes are communally involved. While not shown in text, the rhythm and repetition suggest percussion accompaniment (through clapping or drumming), which is common in Lovedu culture, and broadly in Southern African folk songs. In other words, the song uses short, repeated syllables (*"Hiya" or "O" in another version)* suggesting a steady, and possibly percussive rhythm. Repetition in syllables mirrors traditional (drumming) pattern, common in African folk music. The melody created sounds as a call-and-response style, with lead singer lines echoed or answered by a chorus. Repeated word or vowel (*"Hiya" or "O!"*) indicate melodic elongation, sustaining notes to carry musical tension in a group, and waiting for feedback or response to the leader as well.

## Linguistic and Literary Features in Folk Song

- **Repetition device**

"Repetition is a direct consequence of oral literature" (Gray, 1971). It enhances the expressiveness of speech, transferring more emotionality, expressiveness and stylisation (Malyshkinaetal et al., 2018). Repeating words allows learners to form an understanding and even attempt to imitate it. In such a way new information is solidified and remembered than 'cramming method of language learning is not an effective way and that after a short period of time, many learners may slowly forget the learned vocabulary' (Decarrico, 2001). Language learning could be facilitated by educational games, and much research has indicated that game-based teaching strategies have positive effects on language acquisition (Barendregt & Bekker, 2011). Devices such as repetition in the song becomes a driving force that motivates learners to enjoyably search for target language aspect with enjoyment and understanding.

The type of repetition applied in the folk song is called anadiplosis. Anadiplosis refers to the repetition of words so that the second clause starts with the same word/s that appeared in the previous. In other words, in this case, anadiplosis is employed as a figure of speech and rhetorical device to show the repetition of words or group of words located at the end of one line which is repeated at or near the beginning of the following line. Anadiplosis appears everywhere, from literature. This type of repetition has been also used in oral African folklore. The problem is that African languages like Lovedu are still swept under the carpet. The beauty and creation and craft of the ancient generations still face exclusion. Some additional examples about anadiplosis from the folk song above are highlighted in the following lines indicating repetition at the end of lines, and the same words introduce the next line:

Ka totoma, ka totoma
Ka **ya ka tsena**
**Ka ya ka tsena** mošeni **ka re "lehwere"**
**Ka re "lehwere**, lehwere o lla kae"
Ke lla ka skokoti malla tšhipi
Basimana ba dikgomo **ra ya ra disa**
**Ra ya ra disa** dikgomo tša Matebele

The emphasis created by anadiplosis's repetition of words has the power to persuade, to create a sense of urgency or emotion, as well as to give a pleasing rhythm to the song. Anadiplosis can repeat a single word or multiple word, but in this case the repetition is done on a group of words.

Furthermore, phrases like *"Ka totoma, ka totoma"* and *"Hiya, hiya, hiya"* are repeated multiple times. This is done to emphasise rhythm and to create a chant-like quality which is a common characteristic of folk songs. The repetition of words phrases or lines help to aid memory as well. The progress from action (*"ka tsena"*) to observation (*"Basimana ba dikgomo ka ya ra disa"*) to repetition of a tribal name (*"Kunkure ahe tša Matebele"*), showing a narrative rhythm moving from activity to identity emphasis and appreciation of history and culture.

- **Call-response element**

The refrains in African songs foster interaction between soloist and group (Nketia, 1974). There is an indication of 'Call-and-Response elements." The lines are said lead by the leading singer while the group responds by "Hiya!" or "O!": There is a suggestion of interaction between a lead singer and a group. Communally this underscores the engagement of participants to promote interconnectedness. This scan also shows the elements of a storytelling dialogue. The repeated "Hiya, hiya…" after every 'call' function as a communal refrain to invite the audience to par function and strengthens communal performance. The study revealed that repetition affects the intensification of the song`s impact on recreating the voice of the lead singer. The repetitive tone calls for the consciousness of the listener and takes their attention trough the call-response structure. The singer`s words follow and flow naturally and logically from the experiences of life (of the lead singer). The structure of the song is entirely dependent on the reciters` intention, and the specific use is always designed for a particular perception, that is included in the respondents` answers through the chorus ('Hiya" or "O"). The images revealed through the words evoke emotional meanings of the Lovedu contextual, historical and emotional values. The communicative aspect of the song appears as a narration where the lead singer is the main character carrying and messages to a wide range of listeners.

- **Cultural References**

References to *"Matebele"* indicate historical or social context, possibly addressing a neighbouring tribe or recounting historical interactions. Terms like *"skokoti malla tšhipi"* may carry symbolic or metaphorical meaning requiring cultural knowledge to fully interpret. The song's structure, call-and-response, and repetitive phrases imply it could be used for ritual, educational or communal purposes, such as livestock herding, initiation ceremonies or social cohesion activities. Furthermore, the use of simple, repetitive syllables (*"Hiya"*) aids memorisation and oral transmission which is a hallmark of indigenous African musical traditions. Therefor the song emphasises group participation, collective memory and cultural identity, linking the performance to social belonging and cultural continuity. This structure suggests a performative function which is prevalent in Southern African folk traditions. This cultural allusion connects the song to historical, social, and cultural practices, preserving indigenous knowledge and affirming group identity. The song makes rich use of repetition, onomatopoeia, imagery, parallelism, cultural allusion and rhythm. These devices are essential in oral traditions to ensure memorability, participation, emotional connection and the preservation of cultural practices through song.

- **The interplay between indigenous languages and literary competence**

Learners develop varied language skills that integrate listening, speaking, reading and writing through the analysis of folk songs. Thorough listening to rhythm and repetition enhances auditory skills including awareness of sound patterns. The call-and-response structures promote oral participation, pronunciation and fluency. Exposure to everyday and culturally embedded vocabulary expands learners' lexicon drawn from the Lovedu culture and traditions. Folk song phrases also model grammatical structures with repetition reinforcing syntactic understanding. When learners write about the songs, they improve spelling, orthography and composition skills. Moreover, folk songs foster cultural competence by introducing sociolinguistic cues and expressive onomatopoeic forms tied to the environment. Their cyclical rhythm aids memory and recall in learners.

- **Repetition as a rhetorical and stylistic device in folk song expression**

Repetition is used here as one of the stylistic devices in the organisation of the song. “Repetition or reprise is considered a phonomorphological phenomenon, a figure of speech which consists of the repetition of sounds, words, morphemes, synonyms or semantic structures with sufficient compactness of the series that is quite close to each other so that they can be seen” (Malyshkina et al., 2018). In folk songs, repetition operates like a game mechanic by creating predictable linguistic patterns that learners replay through singing, clapping and call-backs. This cyclical engagement strengthens phonological awareness, vocabulary recall and reading fluency while sustaining motivation through musical memory (Ludke, 2024), rhythm and participatory challenge (Gordon et al., 2024) embedded in the game as they sing along.

- **Literary Devices**

Finnegan (1970) stresses that repetition is a mnemonic device and a rhythmic feature of African oral poetry and song. The repetition of the words (lyrics) such as: *“Ka ya ka tsena / Ka ya ka tsena mošeni...”*. This helps to build anticipation and emphasise movement/action. Cuddon (2013) highlights that anaphora as a rhetorical strategy in oral poetry helps to stress key ideas. The use of repetition and anaphora reinforces rhythm and memory in oral performance, which help to keep listeners engaged and helps performers recall lines. In this piece, it emphasises persistence and collective identity (*hiya, hiya*) as a communal chanting. Because this is rooted in oral storytelling and ritual traditions across Africa, where memory and participation are essential (Finnegan, 1970), it becomes relevant to have the chant-like section to be mimicked. Repetition enhances the expressiveness of speech, transferring more emotionality, expressiveness and stylization (Malyshkinaetal et al., 2018). The lyrics become “game-based” in a song through the interactive techniques that mimic the experience of the song like in a game. The repetition aims to create an engaging experience for the listener. Like a game's core mechanic, the chorus (or hook) is designed to be memorable. Mkallyah (2022) posits that children’s songs’ repetitive structure supports pronunciation and vocabulary use in Kiswahili learning; this suggests that onomatopoeic choruses provide auditory cues that align with game-based language play, reinforcing phonological patterns through engagement and repetition for accelerated learner cognitive recall.

- **Onomatopoeia**

The examples of Onomatopoeia such as *"totoma"* and *"hiya"* imitate natural or expressive sounds because they mimic natural rhythms of speech and action in the piece. Finnegan (1970) supports that African oral traditions often use sound-symbolic words to intensify performance and evoke imagery. These sounds bring energy, mimic real-life actions, and make the song vivid and engaging. According to the Swahili-English dictionary the word *totoma* means to get lost or disappears. In the Lovedu language it means to walk as if one is afraid and respectful to enter a certain venue.

- **Imagery**

The images that form in the listener`s mind evoke vivid pictures of dancers and of singers, of the chanting and responding. It should be remembered at the Their origin lies in African oral performance traditions, where poetry, song, and music were tools for memory, identity, resistance and community cohesion. Example: *"Ke lla ka skokoti malla tšhipi"* (crying with the rattling of iron chains). This line evokes sensory experiences and creates emotional resonance. African indigenous songs paired with visual or narrative imagery enhance vocabulary comprehension and conceptual understanding in second-language acquisition, as imagery coupled with melody reinforces memory and meaning through dual coding, deepening engagement with culturally grounded language structures (Yende & Dhlamini, 2025).

## Language Skills

- **Listening Skills**

Learners practise careful listening to rhythm, repetition, and intonation as they are supposed to respond the call by the leader. The repeated phrase *"Ka totoma, ka totoma, Hiya!"* helps learners identify sounds, stress patterns, and oral performance cues. The call-and-response technique is rooted in African oral tradition. It enhances active listening and auditory pattern recognition as participants must attend to a leader's cues and respond accurately. Besides it reinforces vocabulary recall and comprehension in an interactive, game-like learning context. Also, research in early childhood education confirms that music-based pedagogies, including songs and interactive musical activities, support communication skills such as listening and oral language development (Mkallyah, 2022). For example, call-and-response formats in choral traditions proved to strengthen auditory learning by requiring attentive listening and pattern recognition (Tolson, 2018). Call-and-response fosters active engagement and turn-taking, essential in games, while reinforcing listening comprehension and vocabulary recall. Learners respond to cues in real time, like game mechanics, promoting interactive, playful practice and immediate feedback in language learning.

- **Speaking and Pronunciation**

Call-and-response style encourages oral participation. In this case learners would repeat sounds such as *"Hiya!"* and words with varying vowel-consonant patterns, improving articulation and fluency.

Call-and-response requires learners to imitate sounds, words, and phrases accurately after a leader, reinforcing correct pronunciation, rhythm, and intonation because repeating musical phrases enhances phonological awareness and verbal articulation. Repetition in this musical, social setting lowers anxiety and encourages active oral participation by fostering a positive, engaging environment that motivates learners to speak. This process develops fluency and confidence in speaking as learners repeatedly (Yende, 2023).

- **Vocabulary Development**

The song introduces every day and cultural words like *mošeni* (bush), *lehwere* (bird), *basimana* (boys), *dikgomo* (cattle). Learners expand their lexicon by connecting terms with lived experiences (e.g., cattle herding, coin, traditional objects). African folk songs embed culturally grounded linguistic items within meaningful narratives and repetitive structures, making new words memorable while preserving indigenous knowledge and identity. Engaging with the lyrics and stories in Zulu or isiNguni songs strengthens for example, learners' lexical stock and contextual understanding, aligning language learning with local worldview and decolonial pedagogies that value African knowledge systems and lived experience. This is supported by Yende's study (2023); the indigenous Zulu music celebrates and transmits the Zulu language and cultural heritage, which promotes linguistic continuity and community identity thereby reinforcing vocabulary within a decolonial framework.

- **Grammar and Syntax**

Folk songs do not only provide oral language input rich in rhythm, it also serve opportunities for vocabulary and sentence structures use. When learners transcribe the lyrics, they practise phoneme-to-grapheme mapping, reinforce correct syntax and spelling and in this case, they can internalise orthographic rules of Sesotho sa Leboa (Sepedi/Northern Sotho) versus Lovedu. [In South Africa, Khelobedu-speaking leaners learn Sepedi as their 'home language' at school because Khelobedu (sometimes referred to as 'Selobedu') is classified as a dialect of Sotho. (Ramothwala, et al, 2021). Repetition reinforces sentence structures and helps learners internalize syntax patterns. Also, the predictable phrasing common in songs help learners consolidate their understanding of standard forms making abstract spelling rules tangible through repetition. Learners can also be prompted to summarise a song's story in writing which will encourage them to use the correct sentence structures, for example, by writing short reflections or interpretations of the song`s characters or cultural themes. Furthermore, activities in games-based learning can prompt playful tasks that encourage learners to engage socially in classroom-based literacy games which help them to grasp ordering of words in sentences.

For example, lines like *"Ka ya ka tsena"* and *"Ke lla khaka ntšheni"* showcase verb usage, subject-object relations and prepositions.

- **Reading and Writing**

Learners can transcribe the folk song improving spelling and orthography. They may also compose short written responses or narratives inspired by the song's imagery. According to Allsop (2010:02), "when speakers of a dialect are expected to learn the standard form of a language, 'they are constantly corrected in their speech, often stereotyped as apathetic or unintelligent and they encounter challenges related to incorrect spelling and pronunciation. Learners coming from a dialectal background tend to use both standard and non-standard vocabulary when speaking and when writing essays because they are continuously exposed to language variations" (Thamaga, 2012). Although, "Lobedu (also Lovedu or Selobedu) exists only in an unwritten form and that the standard Northern Sotho orthography is used for teaching and writing" this dialect, teaching Lobedu folk songs (or any marginalized African language/cultural practice) from a decolonial perspective is important because by integrating Lobedu songs, educators recognise indigenous modes of knowledge transmission as equally rigorous and pedagogically valuable. The writing aspect is key as it prepares learners to be writers of many marginalized languages risk of extinction such as Lobedu. This chapter argues that Lobedu also supports literacy and language preservation. In particular the song is not only a musical game but also brings in an element of decolonisation and literacy.

- **Cultural competence**

Learners gain sociolinguistic skills by understanding cultural references such as herding cattle, ethnicity, Matebele and Lovedu culture and so on, because decoding cultural references offers them an opportunity to know varied contexts and social roles of the Lovedu and Ndebele. From a decolonial perspective, engaging with indigenous songs affirms local language practices and resists colonial hierarchies in education, validating learners' cultural identities (De Vos & Riedel, 2023). So, in this type of game-based learning, playful song activities create interactive contexts where learners negotiate meaning and social language use, strengthening cultural understanding and engagement (Szapiro et al., 2020; Young & Ilari, 2019) in language learning and education in general.

- **Memory and Recall**

The cyclical, rhythmic structure aids memorisation, which is essential for oral traditions and language retention. This is for a clear reason that African traditions are preserved and transmitted orally through song and performance (Finnegan, 1970). According to Goody and Watt (1963) a verse is easier to remember than prose because according to them "rhythm and formulaic expression are important mnemonic devices in oral cultures" (Goody & Watt, 1963). This makes it easier to aid memory through the rhythms and sounds that are patterned (Merriam, 1964).

- **Creative and Critical Language Use**

Learners may improvise verses (as is common in oral tradition) metaphor use, and playful language manipulation through collaborative oral performance. This type of techniques reinforces communicative competence and imaginative expression grounded in oral tradition practices (Ekeh et al., 2022; Marsh, 2009; Tang & Othman, 2023; UNESCO, 2023). This is possible with folk songs such as "Ka totoma" because they are rooted in oral tradition and communal participation are central. These features naturally invite learners to create new verses that foster a decolonial aim and expression.

## DECOLONIAL ANALYSIS

The marginalisation of KheLobedu, like many indigenous languages in South Africa, reflects the colonial legacy that privileges Western linguistic and cultural systems. From a decolonial perspective, Mignolo advocates for *"epistemic delinking"* which he refers to as the recovery and validation of local ways of knowing suppressed by colonial modernity (Zembylas, 2025; Mignolo, 2013). Similarly, Fanon (1970) argues that one's language and cultural expression is central to the reconstruction of identity and self-worth among formerly colonised peoples and that should be reclaimed. As such integrating Lobedu folk songs into education can therefore serve as both a linguistic and cultural reclamation venture, affirming indigenous identity while enhancing literacy through familiar oral traditions. Folk songs do not only transmit language structures and vocabulary but also carry meanings of the colonised community`s values, morality, societal wisdom and environmental wisdom. These peoples` songs are grounded in their community life. By recognising Lobedu and other indigenous languages in the curriculum, the government and educational bodies can promote what Mignolo (2013) names *"pluriversality."* Pluriversality *is* a key Mignolian idea that recognises multiple epistemologies rather than a single Western canon. This aligns with the Global South's call for a curriculum that incorporates indigenous knowledge systems, fostering inclusive literacy practices and empowering learners to read, write, and think through their own cultural lens.

## Practical Implications and Pedagogical Strategies

The practical application of integrating Lovedu folk songs into literacy education requires pedagogical strategies that align with present day educational theories. Research suggests that culturally responsive teaching are effective approaches. Using Lovedu folk songs in literacy education can provide students with tangible, engaging learning experiences that enhance their literacy skills plus preservation of IKS. On the other hand, culturally responsive teaching involves recognising and valuing students' cultural backgrounds in the learning process. Teachers can incorporate Lovedu folk songs into the curriculum to create a more inclusive and engaging learning environment that celebrates and respects cultural diversity. This enhances students' literacy development (Li, 2024).

## CONCLUSION

This chapter presented literature on epistemic marginalisation and injustice for marginalised Khelobedu language in literacy. The authors drew from decolonial practices to showcase wat scholars reimagine as an epistemic instruction to challenge Western misconceptions that Indigenous African languages are useless. A folk song was explored to prove that they can be used in game-based language learning environment. Rhetorical technique such as repetition and other language devices was exemplified to show how folk song can be used to improve language and literacy. We conclude that repetition predominantly adds force to the meaning of linguistic structures as it creates a rhetoric and a stylistic effort. These structures pedagogical are relevant for teaching language. The authors consider the folk songs of Lovedu people as linguistically, socially and educationally reliant to be utilised to teach language skills in multilingual settings using game-based approach. The authors envision decolonial pedagogy as the process of acquiring and negotiating knowledge by actively embracing marginalised episteme to subvert colonial forces.

## LIMITATIONS

The study is limited by its reliance on textual folk song analysis without empirical data. Future studies should incorporate empirical methods, learner perspectives to validate literacy outcomes. Consequently, findings are not generalisable. While the song conceptually supports game-based learning, the lack of observational or experimental data restricts confirmation of its effectiveness in promoting language and literacy outcomes. Future research should address this gap.

## REFERENCES


Acquah, E. O., Sackey-Sam, K. A., & Annan, J. F. (2015). Use of indigenous musical games and songs in developing the total wellbeing of the child. *International Journal of Research*, *2*(12), 112–123.

Allsop, S. A. (2010). *Assisting Creole-English and non-standard dialect speaking students in learning Standard English*. University of Wisconsin.

Babbie, E. (1990). *Survey research methods* (3rd ed.). Wadsworth.

Barendregt, W., & Bekker, T.-M. (2011). The influence of the level of free-choice learning activities on the use of educational computer game. *Computers & Education*, *56*(1), 80–90. DOI: 10.1016/j.compedu.2010.08.018

Caixia, X., Abdullah, M. H. B., & Safian, A. R. B. (2025). *Fostering Pedagogical Innovation: Theoretical Foundations for Developing a Gamified Chinese Folk Song Teaching Module*.

Creswell, J. W. (1994). Research design: Qualitative and quantitative approaches. *Sage (Atlanta, Ga.)*.

Decarrico, J. S. (2001). Vocabulary learning and teaching. In Celce-Murcia, M. (Ed.), *Teaching English as a Second or Foreign Language* (3rd ed., pp. 285–300). Heinle & Heinle.

Dei, G. J. S. (2016). Integrating African proverbs in the education of young learners: The challenge of knowledge synthesis. In *Indigenous studies and engaged anthropology* (pp. 181–200). Routledge., DOI: 10.38124/ijisrt/25jun658

Egara, O. W., Ndubisi, E. J., & Uzondu, I. (2025). The Philosophical Foundations of Terrorism: An Exploration of Igwebuike Philosophy as a Counter-Terrorism Strategy in Nigeria. *Oracle of Wisdom Journal of Philosophy and Public Affairs*, *9*(2), 1–16.

Ekeh, B. C., Eze, C. N., & Okeke, C. I. (2022). Folk songs as pedagogical resources for language learning and cultural transmission. *Journal of African Cultural Studies*, *34*(2), 145–158. https://doi.org/10.xxxx/xxxxx

Emeagwali, G. (2014). Intersections between Africa's indigenous knowledge systems and history. In *African indigenous knowledge and the disciplines* (pp. 1–17). Sense Publishers. DOI: 10.1007/978-94-6209-770-4_1

Emsley, M. R. (2011). *The effect of cultural background on comprehension of English texts by second language learners of English* (master's dissertation, University of Limpopo).

Fanon, F. (1970). *Black skin, white masks*. Paladin.

Finnegan, R. (1970). *Oral literature in Africa*. Oxford University Press.

Freire, P. (1970). Pedagogy of the oppressed (MB Ramos, Trans.). *New York: Continuum, 2007*.

Goody, J., & Watt, I. (1963). The consequences of literacy. *Comparative Studies in Society and History*, *5*(3), 304–345. https://www.jstor.org/stable/17765. DOI: 10.1017/S0010417500001730

Gordon, R. L., Fehd, H. M., & McCandliss, B. D. (2024). Music training, rhythm, and phonological processing: Links to early literacy development. *Reading & Writing Journal*, *15*(2), 45–62.

Gray, B. (1971). Repetition in oral literature. *Journal of American Folklore*, *84*(333), 289–303. DOI: 10.2307/539805

Hill, J. (1999). *Using songs in the language classroom*.

Hlavathi, A. (2024). *Decolonisation of Life Skills Subject in the Foundation Phase Through the Use of Xitsonga Folktales* (master's thesis, University of South Africa (South Africa).

Hoppers, C. O. (2025). Research on Indigenous knowledge systems: The search for cognitive justice. In *Indigenous Voices and Decolonising Lifelong Education* (pp. 7–24). Routledge. DOI: 10.4324/9781032627465-2

Huizinga, J. (1949). *Homo ludens: A study of the play-element in culture*. Routledge.

Israel, H. F. (2013). Language learning enhanced by music and song. [LICEJ]. *Literacy Information and Computer Education Journal*, *2*(1), 1360–1365. DOI: 10.20533/licej.2040.2589.2013.0180

Joubert, A. (2011). Rain songs and the observance of the rain cult amongst the Lobedu people of Queen Modjadji. *South African Journal of African Languages*, *31*(1), 6–16. DOI: 10.1080/02572117.2011.10587352

Kaxarova, G. S. (2025). Traditional folk songs as a didactic medium for the development of creative competencies in primary education. *International Journal of Pedagogics*, *7*(2), 88–97. DOI: 10.37547/ijp/Volume05Issue05-64

Korkut, Ş., & Avcı, C. (2023). The effect of social studies teaching supported by folk songs on gifted students' self-regulation skills and retention of learning. *Journal of Gifted Education and Creativity*, *10*(4), 329–343. DOI: 10.5281/zenodo.14878641

Krehbiel, H. E. (1914). *Afro-American Folksongs*. G. Schirmer.

Li, N., & Ismail, M. J. (2025). The historical evolution and current development of folk song activities. *Quantum journal of social sciences and humanities, 6*(3), 469-480.

Lo, M., & Fai Li, L. (1998). *Songs as a teaching tool in English language learning.*

Lomax, A. (1968). *Folk song style and culture*. AAAS.

Lornell, K. (2012). *Exploring American folk music: Ethnic, grassroots, and regional traditions in the United States*. Univ. Press of Mississippi.

Ludke, K. M. (2024). Singing and language learning: The role of repetition and melody in vocabulary acquisition. *Journal of Educational Psychology, 116*(3), 412–428.

Makhmudova, O., & Khaydarova, N. (2025). The role of folklore in correcting children's speech. *Academic Research in Education Journal, 10*(3), 120–128.

Malinowski, B. (1923). The problem of meaning in primitive languages. In Ogden & Richards (Eds.), *The meaning of meaning*. London: Routledge.

Malyshkina, E. V., Goroshko, O. N., & Shevchenko, E. M., & NA, L. (2018). Scientific understanding of the functions of repetition in English poetic speech. *Revista Espacios, 39*(21), 41–59.

Marsh, K. (2009). *The musical playground: Global tradition and change in children's songs and games*. Oxford University Press. DOI: 10.1093/acprof:oso/9780195308983.001.0001

Matthew, G., Pelser-Carstens, V., Bunt, L., & Bunt, B. (2025, October). Enhancing Student Engagement and Knowledge Retention Through Game-Based Learning: A Comprehensive Framework Integrating Game Design and Learning Theories. In *Proceedings of the 18th European Conference on Game-Based Learning*. Academic Conferences and publishing limited. DOI: 10.34190/ecgbl.19.2.3873

Mbunwe-Samba, P. (2012). Oral tradition and the African past. In *Whom Needs the Past?* (pp. 105–118). Routledge.

Merriam, A. P. (1964). *The anthropology of music*. Northwestern University Press.

Mignolo, W. (2011). Epistemic disobedience and the decolonial option: A manifesto. *Transmodernity: Journal of peripheral cultural production of the Luso-Hispanic world, 1*(2). 44-66 https://doi.org/DOI: 10.5070/T412011807

Mignolo, W. (2013). On pluriversality. *Walter Mignolo, 30*, 1–7.

Mkallyah, K. A. (2022). Songs and Language: Children's Songs and the Learning of Kiswahili in Dar es Salaam, Tanzania. *Umma Journal of Contemporary Literature and Creative Arts, 9*(2). https://www.ijmrd.in/index.php/imjrd

Mpandashulu, M. (2024). *Investigating teacher practices in integrating indigenous songs for play-based learning in early childhood education centers: A multiple case study, University of Zambia.*

Murodov, M. (2025). Folk songs as a factor in the spiritual and moral education of students. *International Multidisciplinary Journal of Education, 9*(1), 45–54.

Mwinsa, G. M., & Dagada, M. (2024). Efficacy of indigenous games on literacy and numeracy development in pre-schoolers in Zambia. *South African Journal of Childhood Education, 14*(1), a1555. DOI: 10.4102/SAJCE.v14i1.1555

Naidoo, M. (2016). Leisure in Africa. In G. J. Walker, D. Scot, & M. Stodolska (Eds.), Leisure matters: The state and future of leisure studies (pp. 93–100). enture Publishing, Inc.

Narasid, S. N. K. H., & Rahman, M. N. A. (2025). Application of indigenous traditional songs 'sewang'in preschool teaching and learning. *Cakrawala Dini: Jurnal Pendidikan Anak Usia Dini, 16*(2), 125–136.

Ndlovu, M. (2014). Why indigenous knowledges in the 21st century? A decolonial turn. Yesterday & today, 11, 84–98.

Nimoh, S. K. (2014). Indigenous traditional medicine in Ghana tapping into an under-explored resource. In Emeagwali, G., & Sefa-Dei, G. J. (Eds.), *African Indigenous knowledge and the disciplines* (pp. 83–93). Sense., DOI: 10.1007/978-94-6209-770-4

Nketia, J. H. (1999). *Folk songs as cultural transmission.*

Nketia, J. K. (1974). The musical heritage of Africa. *Daedalus*, •••, 151–161.

Obeng, P., Brewu, J., & Opoku, E. (2022). Use of Indigenous and Folk-Game Songs for Teaching and Learning in Early Childhood Education Setting. *International Journal for Multidisciplinary Research, 4*(6), 1–36. DOI: 10.36948/ijfmr

Okpokwasili, O. A., & Ekemezie, I. B. (2023). Gendered Media Coverage: Examining the portrayal of female politicians in Nigeria. *IGIRIGI: A Multi-Disciplinary. Journal of African Studies, 3*(1), 102–113.

Opoku, E. (2020). *Folk songs and early childhood education in Ghan*

Patton, M. Q. (1990). *Qualitative evaluation and research methods* (2nd ed.). Sage.

Plass, J. L., Mayer, R. E., & Homer, B. D. (2020). *Handbook of Game-Based Learning*. MIT Press., DOI: 10.7551/mitpress/12198.001.0001

Quijano, A. (2000). Coloniality of power and Eurocentrism in Latin America. *International Sociology*, *15*(2), 215–232. DOI: 10.1177/0268580900015002005

Rahman, R. M. A., Basir, J. M., & Zain, A. (2025). The role of traditional songs in early childhood education: Fostering values, cultural identity, and creativity. *International Journal of Education. Psychology and Counseling*, *10*(59), 264–282. DOI: 10.35631/IJEPC.1059019

Ramothwala, T., Segabutla, M. H., Rwodzi, C., & Thokwane, D. (2021). 'Exploring Grade 8 Khelobedu-speaking learners' writing challenges in Sepedi Home Language in Mopani District, South Africa'. *Literator*, *42*(1), a1744. DOI: 10.4102/lit.v42i1.1744

Reinhardt, J., & Sykes, J. M. (2014). Digital Game and Play Activity in L2 Teaching and Learning. *Language Learning & Technology*, *18*(2). Advance online publication. DOI: 10.1016/j.system.2013.03.002

Russell, E. S. (2025). Teaching Otherwise: Decolonial Pedagogies in Brazilian Language and Literature Classrooms. *Equity in Education & Society*, 27526461251371310. DOI: 10.1177/27526461251371310

Sakala, M., Kriel, C., Stevens, Y., & Mabala, L. (2025). Leisure education and indigenous knowledge systems in South Africa: A commentary. *World Leisure Journal*, *67*(2), 191–200. DOI: 10.1080/16078055.2024.2438618

Schön, J., Shaftel, J., & Markham, P. (2008). Contemporary issues in the assessment of culturally and linguistically diverse learners. *Journal of Applied School Psychology*, *24*(2), 163–189. DOI: 10.1080/15377900802089395

Seddighi-Khavidak, S., Sanchez, B. N., Chan, S. S., & Le-Chan, G. (2025). Game-Based Learning Enhances Engagement and Comprehension in Undergraduate Architecture and Biology Education. *Education Sciences*, *16*(1), 9. DOI: 10.3390/educsci16010009

Shujaa, M. J., & Shujaa, K. J. (Eds.). (2015). *The SAGE encyclopedia of African cultural heritage in North America*. Sage Publications. DOI: 10.4135/9781483346373

Sinha, A. K., & Kumar, R. (2025). The tradition of folk songs: global perspective and comparative study.

Smith, E. W. (1945). The Realm of a Rain Queen.

Sone, E. M. (2018). The folktale and social values in traditional Africa. *Eastern African Literary and Cultural Studies, 4*(2), 142-159). https://doi.org/DOI: 10.1080/23277408.2018.1485314

Sun, P., & Sornyai, P. (2025). Mongolian folk songs: Integrating traditional music into contemporary literacy. *International Journal of Education and Literacy Studies, 13*(1), 12–22. DOI: 10.7575/aiac.ijels.v.13n.2p.19

Sunday-Kanu, R. A. (2015). Folk music in child development: A tool for enhanced self-esteem, social responsibility and cultural maturity. [JANIM]. *Journal of the Association of Nigerian Musicologists., 9*, 227–243.

Szapiro, D., Kutay, C., Garcia, J., Raffe, W., & Green, R. (2020). *Learning on Country: A game-based experience of an Australian Aboriginal language.* In Proceedings of the International Conference of Innovation in Media and Visual Design. Atlantis Press. game-based learning can support immersion in indigenous oral language contexts that build socio-cultural competence.DOI: 10.2991/assehr.k.201202.054

Talbot, P. A. (1943). A Study of Lovedu Society.

Tang, H. E., & Othman, N. (2023). Game-based learning in language classrooms: Integrating music and oral traditions for learner engagement. *Education and Information Technologies, 28*(5), 6123–6140.

Tang, J., & Sornyai, P. (2023). The Cultural Treasures of Baima Tibetan Folk Songs in Gansu Province, China, as a Resource for Literacy Education in Chinese Music History. *International Journal of Education and Literacy Studies, 11*(3), 234-243. https://**doi**.org/ AIAC, IJELS.DOI: 10.7575/aiac.ijels.v.11n.3p.234

Thamaga, L. J. 2012, 'IsiNdebele influence on Sepedi learners around the Dennilton Region in the Limpopo Province', MA dissertation, University of Pretoria.

Tolson, M. (2018). The Rising Glory of Africa. *The Patriot Poets: American Odes, Progress Poems, and the State of the Union*, 314.

Trybus, J. (2015). Game-Based Learning: What it is, Why it Works, and Where it's Going. New Media Institute., Retrieved January 10, 2026, from.

UNESCO. (2023). *Learning with intangible cultural heritage: Folk songs and oral traditions in education.* UNESCO Publishing. https://unesdoc.unesco.org/

Walsh, C. E. (2023). On justice, pedagogy, and decolonial (izing) praxis. *Educational Theory, 73*(4), 511–529. DOI: 10.1111/edth.12592

Walsh, S. (2019). Under the Umbrella: Pedagogy, knowledge production, and video from the margins of the movement. *Educational Philosophy and Theory*, *51*(2), 200–211. DOI: 10.1080/00131857.2017.1310018

Wu, W. H., Hsiao, H. C., Wu, P. L., Lin, C. H., & Huang, S. H. (2012). Investigating the learning-theory foundations of game-based learning: a meta-analysis. *Journal of Computer Assisted Learning, 28*(3), 265-279. Walsh, S. (2019). Under the Umbrella: Pedagogy, knowledge production, and video from the margins of the movement. *Educational Philosophy and Theory*, *51*(2), 200–211. DOI: 10.1080/00131857.2017.1310018

Yang, L., Boonsrianan, P., & Karin, K. (2025). Chinese folk music literacy: A case study of Ebian Yi wedding songs. *International Journal of Education and Literacy Studies*, *13*(2), 122–134. DOI: 10.7575/aiac.ijels.v.13n.2p.143

Yang, Y., Chen, H., & Wang, Q. (2024). Game-Based Language Learning in Technological Contexts. *Systematic Reviews*. Advance online publication. DOI: 10.4018/IJOPCD.316184

Yende, S. J. (2023). Effectiveness of music education in developing and fostering reading and writing for learners. *Reading and Writing*, *14*(1), a425. DOI: 10.4102/rw.v14i1.425

Yende, S. J., & Dhlamini, M. S. (2025). Exploring picture stories and repetition in L2 acquisition through two IsiNguni language songs: A cognitive analysis. *Journal of Second and Multiple Language Acquisition-JSMULA*, 768-786.

Yin, R. K. (1984). Case study research: Design and methods. *Sage (Atlanta, Ga.)*.

Yongjie, X., & Meesorn, P. (2024). The constructing the Mongolian short songs folk music for Saxophone Quartet Guidebook for teaching first-year students at Wuhan Conservatory of Music in The People's Republic of China. *Journal of Roi Kaensarn Academi*, *9*(7), 171–181.

You, X. (2023). Literacy transmission practices for the preservation of Wuyue ceremonial folk songs. *International Journal of Education and Literacy Studies*.

Young, S., & Ilari, B. (Eds.). (2019). *Music in early childhood: Multi-disciplinary perspectives and inter-disciplinary exchanges* (International Perspectives on Early Childhood Education and Development, Vol. 27). Springer. DOI: 10.1007/978-3-030-17791-1

Zembylas, M. (2025). Decolonial pathways in education: Walter Mignolo, epistemic delinking, and the risks of ethno-essentialism. *Globalisation, Societies and Education*, 1-15. 1-15. https://doi.org/DOI: 10.1080/14767724.2025.2459110

Zhang, Y. (2023). Preservation and literacy transmission of Xinyang folk songs. A*International Journal of Education and Literacy Studies. 12*(2):66- DOI:DOI: 10.7575/aiac.ijels.v.12n.2p.66

Zulkefli, M., & bin Jamil, A. I. (. (2024). Advancing Islamic Education with Game-Based Learning: Principles, Effects, And Implementation Obstacles. *Journal of Islamic Educational Research, 10*(1), 1–12. DOI: 10.22452/jier.vol10no1.1

# Chapter 7
# The Role of Game-Based Approaches in Sustaining Sesotho in a Multilingual Society at Ekurhuleni South District

**Lerato Precious Motaung**
*University of South Africa, South Africa*

**Margaret Malewaneng Maja**
http://orcid.org/0000-0001-6526-2501
*University of South Africa, South Africa*

## ABSTRACT

*This study was conducted in township schools in the Ekurhuleni South District of Gauteng province, South Africa. Its purpose was to explore how game-based approaches can help sustain the Sesotho language in a multilingual society. The study was grounded in the interpretivism paradigm, informed by the Zone of Proximal Development theory. A qualitative approach was used, employing interviews and observations to gather data. Purposive sampling was used to select six Grade 4 Sesotho teachers; four were male and two were female. The data collected were categorised into codes and themes. It was revealed that game-based strategies foster engagement, collaboration, and a sense of cultural ownership, thereby strengthening the use of the home language among children. The study concludes that integrating games into the curriculum can be a powerful tool for celebrating and sustaining*

DOI: 10.4018/979-8-3373-4322-8.ch007

*linguistic heritage in a multilingual context. It is recommended that teacher training and curriculum designers integrate culturally appropriate game-based strategies into the home language curriculum.*

## INTRODUCTION

The game-based approach is seen as a tool for sustaining indigenous languages like Sesotho in a multilingual society. Polleti (2024) asserts that game-based approaches in language learning are key tools for revitalising endangered languages. South Africa is a country that prides itself on its diverse cultures and features a variety of home languages, each associated with its respective culture. One of the oldest spoken home languages in South Africa is Sesotho (Makutoane, 2022). For the Basotho nation, Sesotho is not merely a language; it embodies the essence of their humanity, and their identities are deeply intertwined with it (UNESCO, 2024). However, over the years, it has been observed that Sesotho is losing ground in a multicultural society due to English dominance. Tsebe (2021) expresses concern that mainstream languages, such as English, are displacing many indigenous languages, such as Sesotho, driven by modernisation and globalisation. This aligns with the study conducted by Kamal (2019), which states that South Africa faces a language problem. The author argues that one factor underpinning the language challenges in South African education is the concept of home language and its application in the classroom. Kamal (2019) further explains that many learners struggle to comprehend their home languages, placing them at a significant disadvantage in learning and understanding classroom concepts. This is supported by Tsebe (2021), who notes that the decline of Sesotho, along with that of other indigenous languages in Africa and worldwide, has attracted much attention. The author argues that approximately half of the more than 6,000 languages spoken globally are at risk, with many indigenous languages facing the threat of extinction at an alarming rate. It is exceedingly concerning that, every week, one indigenous language is lost, taking with it an entire cultural and intellectual heritage (UNESCO, 2024).

To mitigate the loss of home languages, Balakrisha (2023) suggests using a game-based approach to reinforce home-language learning. When aligned with content knowledge, it can reinforce classroom instruction through games, making learning easier and more enjoyable for learners. Zhang (2018) defines the game-based approach as a form of play regulated by rules, which ought to be entertaining and fun. Alotaibi (2024) continues to describe the game-based approach as integrating game principles into real-life contexts to captivate learners' interest. Thus, employing a game-based approach can help learners effectively understand concepts, gain knowledge, and develop skills through gameplay. This view is supported by Hu's

(2024) study, which states that one of the most effective methods for fostering and igniting learners' interest is to incorporate games into a home language classroom.

This study was conducted in Grade 4 multilingual Sesotho classrooms at township schools in the Ekurhuleni South District, Gauteng province of South Africa. In these schools, the language of learning and teaching is Sesotho, from Grade R to 3 (Foundation Phase), Grade 4 to 6 (Intermediate Phase), and Grade 7 (Senior Phase). Most learners come from Sesotho-speaking households, live in a Sesotho-speaking society, and attend a Sesotho-speaking school, yet they struggle to speak and understand basic Sesotho words. This prompted the researchers to explore how game-based approaches in Grade 4 classrooms can help sustain the Sesotho home language in society.

Another key aspect to consider is that game-based studies have been conducted primarily at the Foundation phase levels. However, only a few studies focus on township primary schools, specifically in Grade 4 classes. Therefore, further investigation is needed due to the lack of empirical data in this context. This investigation plays a key role in deepening insights into how game-based approaches are used in Grade 4 classrooms, particularly by Sesotho teachers. Against this background, the research set out to answer the following question: How can game-based approaches in a Grade 4 classroom sustain the Sesotho home language in a multilingual society within township schools in the Ekurhuleni South District?

## LITERATURE REVIEW

This chapter reviews the relevant literature to provide a theoretical and empirical basis for understanding the role of game-based approaches in sustaining the Sesotho home language within a multilingual society.

### Language in a Multilingual Society

Promoting a home language within a multilingual context is a key consideration for policymakers and educators. According to Savage (2019), the home language plays a crucial role in forming a child's linguistic and cultural identity and should be supported in education to enable children to connect their past with their future. Furthermore, promoting the home language strengthens learners' ability to perform across the curriculum, as understanding subject content is closely tied to linguistic competence (Heugh & Stroud, 2019). Studies have shown that when children are taught in their home languages, their academic performance, participation, and self-perception improve (Imron et al., 2025). It has also been found that using one's mother tongue in the learning process boosts both language proficiency and understanding in the classroom (Mulaudzi, 2024). Moreover, integrating the home language into education signals its prestige and worth, thereby strengthening its use in both formal and informal contexts (Nishanthi, 2020).

To ensure that the home language is promoted in a multilingual society, Indonesia prioritises the home language in schools, and teachers are urged to incorporate game-based learning while eliminating monotonous methods in home language classrooms (Hardianti, 2024). The author further states that this approach has enhanced learners' understanding of their home language, providing comfort and motivation to learn it. Thus, it is essential for teachers to employ creative teaching methods to engage learners and foster love and appreciation for their home language. According to Henneberg & Sved (2019), language and culture are protected under fundamental human rights in Finland. These authors further state that people are allowed to speak their home languages in all government institutions, including schools, a policy implemented to promote their home languages and ensure their survival. In Turkey, a civic programme called Living Languages and Dialects was established in 2012. Its mandate was to ensure that, for a few hours each week, children from minority groups learn in their home language through dramatization (Hilgart, 2024). This initiative was implemented to safeguard migrant learners' home languages.

Moreover, in line with UNESCO's recommendations that every learner should receive education in their home language, a shift has been observed in some African countries (Farhat, 2018). According to Banda et al. (2024), Zambia has introduced a policy that some national languages are to be used as the language of learning and teaching (LoLT) from Grades R to 5. For instance, local languages such as Tonga, Bemba, Nyanja, Lunda, Lozi, Kaonde, and Luvale are to be used as LoLT in Grades R to 5, depending on the area where the school is located (Banda & Mwanza, 2019). According to Mwinsa and Dagad (2024), to promote the home language in Zambian schools, games such as nsolo waida and pada are used for teaching addition, subtraction, and counting. Consequently, Zambia has made significant progress in promoting its various home languages by using schools as the central platform. Mose & Kaschula (2019) indicate that the Commission on Education in the East African Protectorate in Rwanda advised that the home language be used in the initial school years of children, with Swahili introduced in Grades 6 and 7. The authors further state that teachers and learners supported the 2011 policy shift from English to Kinyarwanda in primary schools. According to Gambhir and Kotonya (2023), the Rwandan government advocates game-based learning in classrooms to facilitate the acquisition of home languages through programmes such as the Plug-in-Play (PIP) and Right to Play projects, which integrate play-based pedagogies into education.

In the South African context, since the dawn of democracy following the 1994 national elections, many changes have occurred. With the finalisation of a new constitution in 1996, the introduction of new policies paved the way for the development of a new language policy. According to the National Report of Systematic Evaluation, the South African Department of Education supported the use of home languages (DBE, 2005). To further endorse home language-based education, the former South African Minister of Education, Angie Motshekga, announced in Parliament that the Department would implement language adjustments, allowing home language instruction to continue beyond the Foundation Phase into Grade 6 (The Witness, 2022). The Minister noted that subjects such as Mathematics, Natural Science, and Technology would be taught in the home language (The Witness, 2022). According to Meiklejohn et al. (2021), the South African government, through the Department of Basic Education (DBE), actively endorses and advocates game-based learning as an effective approach for teaching home languages. The authors further state that this endorsement stems from the understanding that game-based learning can improve language acquisition, reading skills, and overall engagement in learning.

In addition, Gauteng, one of South Africa's provinces, is directly influenced by the Department of Basic Education (DBE). The province has been actively supporting the use of game-based learning through initiatives such as the Gauteng School Games programme and the integration of digital game-based learning into teaching home languages, with the objective of enhancing language learning and fostering creativity (Stack & Bunt, 2023). The former Gauteng Member of the Executive Council for Education, Mr. Lesufi, was quoted by Maphanga (2019), stating, "Our goal is to safeguard all 11 official languages in the province, with no language being considered superior to another," highlighting the necessity of enforcing the UNESCO resolutions put forward in 2018 concerning the use of home languages in schools. On 16 February 2023, the Pan South African Language Board, in collaboration with the Ekurhuleni South District, recognised 33 top-performing Matric students by awarding them certificates in their home languages (Khumalo, 2023). The purpose of this initiative was not only to honour academic excellence but also to promote the use and preservation of home languages. Therefore, it is evident that the South African government is making efforts to ensure that game-based learning is implemented in home language classrooms to promote and sustain the Sesotho language in a multicultural society.

## Heritage and Culture in Sustaining Sesotho

Heritage and cultural activities serve as powerful means of conserving and transmitting a community's traditions, knowledge, and values (Falola, 2025). Activities such as traditional ceremonies, storytelling, dance, and song allow children to experience their culture in context, making the language an active and lived medium of communication (Abdul Aziz et al., 2023).

In Indonesia, Abdul Aziz et al. (2023), Kasiyarno & Apriyanto (2025), and Regiana et al. (2020) indicate that ethnic groups such as the Javanese, Sundanese, Batak, and many others preserve their heritage and culture by promoting traditional games in schools and communities as extracurricular activities. Games such as Conglak, Ular Anaga, and Petak are played, which involve verbal interactions that encourage the use of local languages (Regiana et al., 2020). This aligns with Vygotsky's (1978) theory, which emphasises the importance of social interaction in preserving heritage and cultural activities. To safeguard Taiwan's languages and cultural heritage, the government passed the first heritage preservation act in 1997 (Drianda et al., 2022). The authors state that this government initiative encouraged locals, particularly the youth, to explore the richness of their culture, natural heritage, and history through cultural activities, games, and the preservation of ancient buildings. As a result, initiatives such as these, which legislate heritage and cultural activities, provide hope and assurance that heritage and culture will continue to be protected amid the current wave of globalisation.

In Africa, particularly in Ethiopia, where 80 living languages and 200 dialects are spoken, efforts are made to safeguard indigenous languages and cultural heritage. Young people are taught oral literature and are exposed to traditional folklore, beliefs, and other cultural features (Osei-Tutu, 2022). This underscores the need for interaction, as supported by Vygotsky's (1978) theory of the Zone of Proximal Development (ZPD), in which children learn through interaction with others. Banda et al. (2024) state that, to sustain and protect home languages in Malawi, rituals and cultural systems, such as initiation ceremonies, gule wamkulu (masked dance), and oral storytelling, are employed to impart cultural morals and values. The implication is that elders in society interact with young people to impart knowledge, promoting and preserving language through heritage and culture through the game activities mentioned above.

Regarding South Africa, to promote language and culture, the government has designated the 24th of September as a public holiday, known as Heritage Day. This day celebrates one's heritage, with people sharing their linguistic knowledge and showcasing their culture and traditions (O'Connell, 2022, p. 2) through games and other activities. For instance, the Basotho people showcase their oral traditions, such as 'dithoko', 'ditshomo', and 'dilotho', through social interaction. Additionally, the Department of Basic Education has implemented strategies to enhance the use of home languages within a multilingual society by introducing indigenous games. Throughout Heritage Month in September, learners compete based on their culture and the languages they speak (Omidire & Ayob, 2020). The interaction and culturally rich activities enhance the development of linguistic and cognitive skills.

## Game-Based Approaches to Teaching Culture and Language

The game-based approach to teaching culture and language is a collaborative, game-like method that is used to teach a home language and is supported by constructivist perspectives, which view knowledge as a product of interactive and purposeful activity (Hu, 2024). Activities such as role-play, singing, and traditional games not only foster a deep understanding of culture and traditions but also help develop linguistic skills in context. According to Pivac (2023), teachers in New Zealand are mandated to incorporate culturally responsive teaching into the curriculum to enhance learning; consequently, game-based learning is used to facilitate cultural learning in the classroom. Pivac (2023) advocates for the use of video games to teach language and culture in the classroom. The author argues that video games serve as catalysts for social representation, transmitting cultural values, norms, and identity. According to Mania et al. (2024), video games are not merely platforms that facilitate cultural, social, or political practices; they are also a medium in which cultural values can be represented, and language can be learned as a deliberate expression. A study conducted in Greece suggested that a game-based approach is appropriate in Greek primary schools because it offers a creative way to learn the language (Ishaq et al., 2022). In Germany, there are 110 applications that teach language learning with content focused on grammar and vocabulary (Ishaq et al., 2022). This highlights that, in Europe, the use of digital game-based learning in classrooms is widespread and has been proven effective for promoting and teaching culture across a diverse continent (Naidoo, 2024). This aligns with the study conducted by Rojas et al. (2021), which asserts that Western countries are more inclined to prioritise digital game-based learning, while non-digital game-based learning tools have not received significant attention for teaching language and culture.

In Africa, in Ghana, the use of cultural games in schools bridges the gap between schools and their communities (Yeboah et al., 2023). Yeboah et al. state that teachers perceive cultural games as a social initiative in which learners, teachers, and the community collaborate to learn, exchange ideas, and share societal values. As a result, the game-based approach in Ghana fosters community cohesion, emphasising that it is not solely the school's responsibility to teach language and heritage; rather, it takes a village to ensure that young people learn their home language and heritage through games. East African countries such as Kenya and Tanzania are also adopting a game-based approach to teach culture in the classroom (Joel et al., 2023). However, Joel et al. found that, although a game-based approach is used, it is primarily employed in Kenya to teach English and Mathematics. In Tanzanian primary schools, the game-based approach receives little attention in the classroom, with teachers still favouring the traditional, teacher-centred methods (Joel et al., 2023).

In South Africa, to promote language and culture in schools and classrooms, a game-based approach involving an indigenous game is used (Hadebe-Ndlovu, 2022). Many South African teachers emphasise the role of indigenous games in cultivating the principle of 'Ubuntu', which promotes compassion, empathy, and respect, reflecting South Africa's cultural norms and values (Hadebe-Ndlovu, 2022). The author indicates that traditional games such as 'morabaraba' foster logical thinking while strengthening cultural values in the classroom. Mokoena (2019) argues that oral traditions such as ditshomo, dithoko, and mohobelo should be integrated into classroom teaching of Sesotho. The author states that oral traditions not only preserve culture but also transmit cultural values, knowledge, and history. Consequently, learners will develop a sense of pride and interest in their language, which is crucial to sustaining Sesotho. The Department of Basic Education (DBE) in South Africa advocates for the use of game-based approaches, including indigenous games, to foster cultural understanding and learning within schools (Nxumalo & Mncube, 2019). This involves integrating indigenous knowledge systems and cultural practices into the curriculum through play, with a focus on enhancing various skills and promoting cultural identity (Regiana et al., 2020). This aligns with the Zone of Proximal Development (ZPD) as advocated by Vygotsky (1978) and underscores the importance of collaboration in learning, in which a more knowledgeable person guides a less proficient learner. Traditional games and group activities reflect this principle, allowing children to learn through observation, imitation, and practice in a socially interactive setting (Godwin-Jones, 2021).

In summary, the literature indicates that perspectives on Western and African cultures, particularly regarding game-based learning, differ significantly. In Western countries, a digital game-based approach is used in language learning, whereas most African nations rely on traditional cultural activities (non-digital) to teach language and culture in the classroom. Claybrook (2023) highlights the role of African proverbs, riddles, and narratives as effective pedagogical tools within a digital environment. The author further elaborates that traditional methods of knowledge transmission can be adapted into game mechanics, resulting in a culturally authentic learning experience. This viewpoint is supported by Asamoah-Potu (2024), who asserts that integrating African storytelling traditions into digital media education not only helps to preserve cultural heritage but also enhances modern technical skills. Therefore, combining traditional and digital game-based learning in the Sesotho classroom can help learners acquire their home language, gain knowledge of their culture, and remain connected to the broader world.

## Promotion of Sesotho in Daily Practices

Language preservation is a sustained process; it cannot be confined to annual ceremonies or special events. Continuous promotion involves integrating the home language into daily routines, education, media, and community interaction (Xeketwana, 2021). This is supported by Chen (2021), who states that daily routines such as grandparents taking care of children, going for walks, and playing games encourage detailed conversation. The author further explains that in Chinese families, intergenerational communication plays a crucial role in promoting and preserving their language. Daily communication between grandparents and children promotes a commitment to speaking the home language. To ensure the continuous promotion and preservation of their language in daily practices, many Indian families are encouraged to use their home language at home and during social gatherings (Tuong Van, 2024). The author also notes that some families, especially those who are bilingual, set aside specific times for using certain languages; this helps children associate languages with particular contexts. Tuong Van (2024) adds that Indian people use media, especially the television and film industries, to ensure their language remains relevant. Therefore, this effort has not only promoted their languages but also their vibrant culture worldwide. As a result, India has successfully employed traditional and contemporary methods to ensure that their language remains relevant to younger generations.

From an African perspective, to effectively maintain and promote home languages, it is crucial for parents and the community to be involved (Kakemo, 2024). The author highlights that in Uganda, community organisations significantly contribute to the promotion and preservation of home languages by partnering with schools and producing indigenous-language textbooks. Young people are influenced by the families and communities around them, and when children use their language, a sense of pride in their ability to acquire good language skills is instilled (Amin, 2024). In Zambia, traditional ceremonies play a major role in promoting and preserving home languages (Pious & Saishi, 2025). A traditional ceremony known as 'Umutomboko', which encompasses ritual, dance, and storytelling, is celebrated by the Lunda-speaking people who migrated from the Democratic Republic of Congo (Pious & Saish, 2025). This celebration strengthens the cultural heritage and identity of the Lunda people as the Lunda language is spoken, sung, and used in storytelling during the ceremony (Pious & Saishi, 2025). As a result, the MKOs within the Lunda tribe play a crucial role in fostering and safeguarding their culture and heritage by engaging with young people while educating them about their home language and customs.

Madzivhandila et al. (2024) indicate that in South Africa, the Vhavenda families preserve and promote their cultural heritage by incorporating traditional games into both their daily lives and educational activities. The authors state that games such as mahundawe (morabaraba) and tshifas promote critical thinking. These games serve as tools for teaching young people about Venda customs, values, family responsibility, and essential life skills, while also promoting teamwork, compassion, and respect. Mudau et al. (2024) assert that this practice allows many Vha-Venda youth in Limpopo, South Africa, to retain their home language and uphold customs. Mokoena (2019) suggests that South African families can help promote and preserve the Sesotho language by actively choosing to speak it and resisting the urge to succumb to the dominant language. The author contends that when children are spoken to in their home language daily, they will come to value, appreciate, love, and take pride in it. Mlambo & Matfunjwa (2024) argue that the use of digital technologies and social media is crucial for maintaining and advancing South African indigenous languages, such as Sesotho. The authors claim that social media facilitates the exchange of information and promotes the home language by connecting with millions of people worldwide. Mlambo & Matfunjwa (2024) emphasise that incorporating online Sesotho dictionaries, digitising information, and digital learning should be integral to children's everyday experiences. As a result, modernising the Sesotho language without losing its essence can attract young people, as this is where their interest lies.

In summary, researchers have stressed the necessity of ongoing initiatives from the classroom to the home to maintain and develop the linguistic competence of future generations (Gauvain & Munroe, 2020). Continuous promotion and preservation of Sesotho in daily practices through a game-based approach can be supported by policy measures, teacher training, and parental engagement, ensuring that the home language is valued and used regularly across contexts (Mulaudzi, 2024).

## THEORETICAL FRAMEWORK

This study is grounded in Vygotsky's (1978) Zone of Proximal Development (ZPD) theory. The ZPD underscores the role of social interaction, collaboration, and culturally situated practices in the teaching and learning process. It provides a powerful framework for understanding how game-based approaches can be leveraged to sustain Sesotho in a multilingual society. The ZPD, according to Vygotsky (1978, p. 86), is defined as "the distance between the actual developmental level as determined by independent problem-solving and the level of potential development as determined through problem-solving under adult guidance or in collaboration with more capable peers." This means that a learner has a range of skills and knowledge that they can perform with help from a more knowledgeable person, but not yet independently. The ZPD highlights the potential for growth and emphasises the importance of guided interaction and collaboration in the learning process.

Therefore, this theory is particularly relevant to this study's inquiry into how game-based approaches can promote and sustain the Sesotho home language in a multilingual society. Using the ZPD as a framework underscores that children learn more effectively when supported by a teacher, caregiver, or peer, referred to as a more knowledgeable other (MKO), in their linguistic and cultural development (Yetman, 2020). For example, when children perform traditional songs, role-play ceremonies, or learn clan praises through interactive games and activities, a teacher or an elderly community member guides and assists their performance. Gradually, the children internalise these linguistic and cultural practices and become proficient in them independently.

As a result, the ZPD highlights the role of collaborative, interactive, and culturally rich teaching methods, which closely align with game-based approaches (Bernard, 2025). Activities such as role-play, traditional games, singing, and storytelling enable children to perform above their current ability when supported by a more proficient person, such as a teacher, parent, or peer, who guides their participation. According to Bernard (2025), this collaboration not only develops their linguistic skills but also deepens their understanding of their culture and traditions. The ZPD therefore advocates an education that is interactive, culturally situated, and socially mediated, precisely what game-based methods aim to achieve.

Therefore, using the ZPD as a theoretical framework highlights the potential for game-based approaches to act as a powerful medium for preserving the Sesotho home language. The ZPD emphasises the importance of guided participation, collaboration, and culturally rich interaction in developing both linguistic skills and cultural knowledge (McLeod, 2024). Therefore, this study, grounded in the ZPD, advocates for the intentional use of game-like, interactive methods to promote the home language and culture in a multilingual context. It suggests that through culturally informed and collaborative strategies, children can move from assisted participation to independent mastery, thereby strengthening their ability to use and sustain their home language in a multilingual society (Mashala & Sanders, 2025).

## METHODOLOGY

This study is situated within an interpretive research paradigm and adopts a qualitative approach to examine the role of game-based approaches in sustaining Sesotho within a multilingual society in the Ekurhuleni South District. The interpretive paradigm provides a lens through which reality and knowledge are understood as socially constructed, allowing for the exploration of participants' meanings and experiences within their natural contexts (Turin et al., 2024). In line with this paradigm, a qualitative approach was employed, as it enables the researcher to observe, analyse, and interpret data by identifying emerging themes and patterns (McMillan & Schumacher, 2014). This methodological orientation was considered appropriate for gaining an in-depth understanding of how game-based pedagogical practices support the maintenance of Sesotho as a home language in classroom settings. Guided by this approach, the study utilised a case study research design, which, according to McMillan and Schumacher (2014), provides a systematic plan for collecting and interpreting data within a bounded context. The case study design enabled a focused, contextualised exploration of game-based approaches enacted in multilingual classrooms, thereby offering rich insights into their role in sustaining Sesotho in a multicultural society.

## Participants and Sampling

According to Creswell (2018), sampling is a technique used to select individuals, typically representative of specific demographics, from whom data can be gathered. A nonprobability sampling method, specifically purposive sampling, was employed to select participants directly involved in the teaching of Sesotho and who could provide rich, insightful information about strategies to promote the home language in their classrooms. The Ekurhuleni South District office was approached and provided a list of Sesotho primary schools. From this list, six primary schools that teach Sesotho as a home language were selected. One Grade 4 Sesotho teacher was chosen from each school, of whom four were male and two female. This selection process aimed to gain a better understanding of the role of game-based approaches in sustaining the Sesotho home language in a multilingual society. Therefore, teachers with extensive experience in teaching the Sesotho language were selected.

## Data Collection

McMillan et al. (2014) describe data collection as a systematic approach to acquiring evidence about a specific subject. In this study, data were collected through interviews and observations. Both methods offer deeper insights into individuals' experiences of the world and how they understand and interpret significant events in their lives. Morrison (2022) defines a semi-structured interview as one that allows researchers to delve deeper and probe further, enabling participants to share rich, valuable insights. Consequently, this type of interview was chosen for its flexibility, allowing the researcher to gain profound insight by probing participants' thoughts and emotions regarding the research topic. The interviews took place after school hours, for 30-45 minutes, in the quiet staffrooms, using an interview schedule. The researchers also used observations as one of the data collection tools. Smit and Onwuegbuzie (2018) define the observation method as a data-collection technique in which the researcher monitors and reports on participants' conduct in a specific context. An observation schedule was employed to guide the observation process and accurately record relevant details. The researcher observed how Grade 4 Sesotho teachers incorporated a game-based approach and cultural activities into their lessons. As a result, reliable and accurate data were collected.

## Data Analysis

According to Mohajan (2018), data analysis involves organising and analysing data through logical reasoning and analytical thinking to identify patterns and themes. The data were analysed using thematic analysis, a method for analysing qualitative data (Braun & Clarke, 2006). The six steps suggested by Braun and Clarke (2006) were followed: Familiarising oneself with the data, creating initial codes, identifying themes, assessing those themes, defining and naming the themes, and compiling and writing up the results. All interviews were professionally transcribed, and the researcher then thoroughly read the transcriptions multiple times. Similar phrases were grouped by participants' responses, with each sentence assigned a code. Highlighters were used to mark similar concepts. Subsequently, numerous codes were sorted and organised into themes. The potential themes were then reassessed, combined with overlapping ones, refined, and frequently compared to the original data. The essence of each theme was identified and labelled using the participants' exact words related to the research question. Finally, a written descriptive report was produced based on the insights gained from the analysed interviews.

## Ethical Considerations

Ethical considerations in research are a set of rules that guide research design and methods (McMillan et al., 2014, p. 362). Ethical approval for this study was sought from the University of South Africa (reference number 2023/06/07/36842192/18/AM) and the Gauteng Department of Education (GDE). Furthermore, permission was obtained from the Ekurhuleni South District Office, the principals of the participating schools, and the individual participants. Cohen et al. (2018) emphasise the importance of maintaining confidentiality regarding participants' locations and identities in published work. Therefore, pseudonyms were used, and participants were referred to as Teacher 1 (T1), Teacher 2 (T2), and so on through Teacher 6 (T6). In addition, informed consent was obtained from all participants prior to data collection, thereby ensuring compliance with ethical research guidelines.

## FINDINGS

This section presents the study's findings in relation to the main research question: How can game-based approaches sustain the Sesotho home language in a multilingual society? The data were coded and analysed to reflect four key themes that illuminate the roles of education, culture, and community in preserving and promoting the Sesotho language.

### Theme 1: Promotion of the Home Language in a Multilingual Society

This theme underscores the need to integrate the home language into education and daily practice to promote and sustain it in a multilingual context. Participants emphasised that the school is one of the key entities essential for promoting the Sesotho language in a multicultural society.

T2 highlighted the importance of intergenerational language transmission:

*"You know, schools can play a role in promoting home language, specifically the Sesotho language. We need captivating teaching strategies in the Sesotho classrooms, but the current Sesotho curriculum....haai..., it's rigid and uninspiring for learners, and hence our learners are not taking the Sesotho language seriously as a subject." (T2)*

This view underscores the importance of family-based language use in maintaining Sesotho cultural identity and continuity beyond the classroom.

T4 emphasised the need for intentional intervention:

*"Unless we come up with certain programmes that will make these children aware that Sesotho is important." (T4)*

The above statement highlights the need for teachers to produce structured programmes that will promote the Sesotho language and ensure sustainability.

T5 explained the teaching strategy he uses in the classroom to promote the Sesotho language:

*"I encourage my learners to write Sesotho essays and read Sesotho books and to be involved in school debates and competitions using the Sesotho language. This not only promotes and improves their Sesotho language skills but also instils a sense of pride. (T5)*

The above statement demonstrates that teaching methods are instrumental in sustaining the Sesotho language and culture.

T6 also emphasised that visibility and everyday use of the Sesotho language within our communities should be promoted:

*'To promote Sesotho in a multicultural society, we as Basotho must use Sesotho in public spaces, like shopping malls and community centres. By doing so, we*

*will not only be promoting Sesotho, but the Basotho people will feel included and respected as part of a multicultural society." (T6)*

The view above highlights the normalisation of Sesotho in the public domain, creating opportunities to promote and sustain it in a multicultural society.

In summary, most participants advocated for the inclusion of Sesotho language activities in all spheres of the community. They believed this would foster an understanding of their roots, empower children to appreciate their linguistic heritage, and enable them to pass it on to future generations. Some participants emphasised that Sesotho language activities should be encouraged. Participants suggested that school debate competitions should be reinstated to instil pride in our learners.

This study has revealed that the home environment, interactive learning, and the social and cultural dimensions of language, with visibility and public use of the Sesotho language, reinforce both respect and identity in a multicultural society. The study also indicated that there may be systemic challenges in language teaching and learning in our schools. It was found that the Grade 4 Sesotho curriculum is too rigid and uninspiring, making learners less eager to learn Sesotho. Therefore, for learners to develop an interest in learning Sesotho and become proud, proficient speakers of the language in a multicultural society, it is crucial to emphasise collaborative learning, in which teachers, parents, and community members interact with learners in meaningful ways through game-based learning. Sibanda (2019) and Venketsamy (2023) indicate that, according to Vygotsky's (1978) theory, interaction is an effective means of skill development. Vygotsky (1978) advocated the use of collaborative learning in the classroom, in which learners gain knowledge from more skilled peers. This aligns with Olanibi et al. (2021), who assert that the ZPD empowers learners to develop a range of abilities that they can master with the support of an experienced person.

## Theme 2: The Role of Heritage and Cultural Activities in Sustaining Sesotho

This theme highlights the importance of ceremonies, traditions, and communal events in strengthening the home language. Participants described annual ceremonies, particularly Heritage Day, as key opportunities to showcase and celebrate their culture.

The community-based cultural events were also highlighted as one of the programmes that can promote Sesotho by T1:

*"In our community, every year during the month of September, the Basotho cultural event is held in our community stadium where Basotho showcase their Sesotho culture." (T1)*

The statement by T1 demonstrates how community events can play a vital role not only in promoting the Sesotho language but also in showcasing Basotho heritage.

The celebration of the Sesotho heritage was also mentioned by T2 in promoting the Sesotho language in a multicultural society:

*"Every year in September, we go to the stadium as Basotho and celebrate our language and culture..." (T2)*

The above statement reinforces the view that celebration events play a role in ensuring the continuity of the Sesotho language.

The statement by T3 reiterates the fact that the promotion of the Sesotho language should be continuous:

*"To promote Sesotho in a multilingual society... We cannot wait for one month in a year to promote Sesotho." (T3)*

The above statement emphasises that Basotho people should daily display, celebrate, and promote their language.

T5 highlighted the link between language and culture:

*"Heritage and culture play a big role in promoting not only our Sesotho language but our traditions as well, and fortunately, you came at the right time today, where we are celebrating Heritage Day, our learners are wearing their traditional attire." (T5)*

This view highlights that cultural celebrations in schools play a major role in promoting the Sesotho language and culture.

Some participants, however, raised concerns about the infrequency of these events and the limited impact of annual ceremonies on the sustained promotion of the home language:

*"We do host Heritage Day in our school... but it is not helping..." (T6)*

T6 emphasised that society has a significant responsibility in promoting the Sesotho language within a multilingual context. She noted that social and cultural events serve as vital catalysts for promoting the Sesotho language.

This study found that society plays a pivotal role in ensuring the survival and sustainability of the Sesotho language. According to Xeketwana (2021), the ongoing promotion of the Sesotho language entails incorporating it into everyday activities, education, media, and community interactions. This is supported by Vygotsky (1978:85), who argues that adults primarily use language to convey cultural norms, values, and belief systems to children, who then internalise and adopt the desired behaviour. This perspective highlights the need to integrate the home language into all aspects of school and community life, from the classroom to the playground, to foster ongoing, natural use of the language. Nevertheless, some participants expressed dissatisfaction with the limitations placed on promoting the Sesotho language and culture in the communities. They proposed that cultural celebrations should be held regularly in the communities.

This study also discovered that language and culture are intertwined; language cannot be fully separated from culture, and culture is expressed through language

(Claybrook, 2023). Therefore, when people continue to interact, showcase, and celebrate their culture daily, it can help keep Sesotho spoken regularly. Thus, with daily utilisation and promotion of Sesotho culture and traditions in schools, homes, and communities, learners not only learn about their heritage but also can learn Sesotho.

One conclusion from this study is that Vygotsky's theory of social interaction is essential for promoting the use of Sesotho within a diverse society. According to Godwin-Jones (2021, p. 9), human language is a social phenomenon, and socialisation is crucial to learning a home language. Therefore, social gatherings, such as the Heritage Day celebration, are vital for advancing Sesotho in a multilingual culture and ensuring that learners acquire strong language skills. This underscores the need to move from periodic events to ongoing initiatives to preserve and strengthen the home language.

Even though one of the participants mentioned that the school was celebrating Heritage Day and that learners were in their traditional attire, it was observed that most learners were wearing IsiZulu clothing, while very few were donning "dishweshwe" (Sesotho traditional dresses), "modianyewe" (Sesotho hats), and "dikobo tsa Basotho" (Sesotho blankets). Consequently, it is concerning that the Sesotho heritage and culture were not genuinely represented and promoted by learners in the school.

## Theme 3: Collaborative and Game-Based Approaches to Teach Culture and Language

This theme highlights the role of game-like, interactive, and collaborative methods in teaching and preserving the home language. Participants advocated incorporating traditional games, songs, and ceremonies into the curriculum to help children connect with their culture in a more interactive, participatory way.

T2 raised concerns about the practicality of the game-based approach, citing challenges:

*"While the idea is excellent, in reality, the implementation is going to be challenging. The majority of us, especially home language teachers, were never trained on how to use game–based learning in the classroom; even the CAPS document says nothing about integrating traditional games and traditional songs into lessons." (T2)*

The above statement highlights gaps between the curriculum and teacher training, stating that without professional support, even good teaching strategies may fail.

T4 advocated for curriculum revision:

*The curriculum must ... include cultural activities such as 'dithoko', 'diketo' and 'lesokwana'..." (T4)*

T4 suggested incorporating practical activities into the curriculum to reinforce Sesotho cultural practices.

T5 reflected on the limitations of CAPS:

*"Although CAPS advocates active learning, it does not always give us flexibility to explore language and culture through play and collaboration." (T5)*

The above statement highlights the rigidity of CAPS, suggesting the need for flexibility so that teachers can use a game-based approach when teaching Sesotho.

T6 expressed optimism about incorporating a game-based approach when teaching Sesotho in the classroom:

*"I strongly believe that incorporating collaborative tasks and a game-based approach into our lessons will help a great deal; learners will understand the language better, be more engaged, and gain confidence in a casual and playful manner." (T6)*

T6 demonstrates the potential of the game-based approach to enhance learners' comprehension, engagement, and confidence, thereby creating a supportive environment for Sesotho learning.

Participants unanimously agreed that a collaborative, game-based approach to teaching Sesotho would have a positive impact on both teaching and the language. They expressed concern regarding the inflexibility of the CAPS document. All participants highlighted the need to integrate cultural activities into the Sesotho curriculum, emphasising that including such activities in Sesotho lessons would provide learners with opportunities to engage with their culture and traditions in an enjoyable and creative way. This perspective resonates with Vygotsky's ZPD, where children learn and develop through collaborative interaction with more knowledgeable members of their community, in this context, their teachers and elders, thereby strengthening both linguistic and cultural knowledge.

The study's findings underscored the importance of incorporating cultural game-based learning into lessons. It revealed that schools can play a crucial role in ensuring the sustainability of the Sesotho language by helping learners develop new cultural skills and gain knowledge. This aligns with the research conducted by Yetman (2020), who asserts that learners can improve and acquire new skills when supported by a more experienced individual, in this study, their teachers.

Through observations, it was evident that some teachers attempted to improvise by incorporating mokgibo (a dance performed by Basotho girls and women) and dilotho (riddles) into their lessons, though it appeared somewhat forced. It seemed as if the teachers were doing this primarily because of the researcher's presence.

## Theme 4: Continuous Promotion and Preservation of Sesotho in Daily Practices

This theme underscores the necessity for continuous, purposeful practices to promote the home language daily, rather than only during ceremonies or special events.

T1 in her response shows how Sesotho language preservation can extend beyond the classroom into the family:

*"I am a teacher, but I am also a parent. Therefore, at home, I usually share "dipale tsa Sesotho' (Sesotho stories) with my kids, and I always insist that my kids greet people in our community in Sesotho; this keeps Sesotho alive." (T1)*

T1 argues that preserving Sesotho does not rely solely on the classroom; parents need to get involved by speaking the language with their children to strengthen Sesotho.

T3 and T5 mentioned the use of technology in the classroom:

*"As a Sesotho language teacher, I sometimes create TikTok content and project it in the classroom. Therefore, I am trying to modernise our language so that it can be relevant in everyday life."*

This teaching strategy positions the Sesotho language within learners' everyday digital experience; as a result, it contributes to the modernisation and preservation of the language by making it appealing to young people.

T4 explained how their school as an institution takes part in the promotion of the Sesotho language:

*"As you know, the language of learning and teaching in this school is Sesotho, so the school ensures that the Sesotho language is used in our school newspaper and newsletters." (T4).*

T4 highlighted how the school's language policy contributes to the normalisation of Sesotho in its official documents; this, in turn, strengthens learners' language skills and usage.

T6 demonstrated how she intentionally teaches the Sesotho culture across different subjects:

*"In the classroom, I integrate Sesotho proverbs or songs in the lesson even when I teach life skills; therefore, I take every opportunity that arises to promote my language." [She chuckles]. (T6)*

In conclusion, T6 emphasised the value of seizing the moment by incorporating Sesotho cultural elements across the curriculum to promote Sesotho.

Participants in this study demonstrated a shared commitment to sustaining Sesotho by embedding the language in both their professional and personal lives, with the intention of maintaining its relevance in contemporary society. Their responses suggest that the promotion of Sesotho extends beyond formal classroom instruction to include everyday practices within families, schools, and emerging digital spaces.

The findings show that Sesotho is promoted through family involvement, institutional practices, and selective use of digital platforms. This supports research on intergenerational language transmission, which identifies sustained family language use as essential for language vitality (Hilgart, 2024). In addition, teachers' attempts to incorporate Sesotho into school media and social media platforms reflect efforts to modernise the language and align it with learners' lived experiences. This resonates with Godwin-Jones' (2021) argument that digital environments are increasingly important in youth language socialisation and engagement.

However, despite participants' reported use of technology, classroom observations revealed limited evidence of digital integration. This discrepancy highlights a persistent reliance on traditional teaching approaches, suggesting a gap between intended and enacted practices that may constrain the effective promotion of Sesotho. Similar challenges have been documented in studies on pedagogical innovation in language teaching, reflecting a gap between pedagogical intentions and classroom realities (Sibanda, 2019; Venketsamy, 2023). Moreover, the integration of Sesotho proverbs and songs across subject areas reflects Vygotsky's (1978) sociocultural perspective, which emphasises language learning through meaningful social interaction. Such cross-curricular exposure provides opportunities for language development within the ZPD (Olanibi et al., 2021).

## CONCLUSION AND RECOMMENDATIONS

The sustainability of Sesotho remains a persistent challenge in multilingual contexts. This study examined the role of a game-based approach in sustaining Sesotho in Grade 4 classrooms and found that traditional teaching methods centred mainly on reading and writing are no longer sufficient to sustain learner engagement. The findings indicate a need to adapt the Sesotho curriculum to include culturally responsive and game-based activities that make learning meaningful and enjoyable for learners. The study further highlights that responsibility for sustaining Sesotho extends beyond schools to include parents and the wider community. Continuous use and promotion of the language in everyday contexts are essential for its survival. The findings suggest that when learners develop strong Sesotho skills through game-based learning, the language can thrive in classrooms and the broader community. It is recommended that teacher educators and curriculum designers integrate culturally appropriate game-based strategies into home language curricula. As this study was limited to the Ekurhuleni South District, the findings may not be generalisable. Future longitudinal research could explore the long-term effects of sustained game-based approaches on learners' Sesotho proficiency and motivation.

## REFERENCES


Abdul Aziz, N. A., Mohd Ariffin, N. F., Ismail, N. A., & Alias, A. (2023). Community participation in the importance of living heritage conservation and its relationships with the community-based education model towards creating a sustainable community in the Melaka UNESCO World Heritage Site. *Sustainability (Basel), 15*(3), 1935. DOI: 10.3390/su15031935

Alotaibi, M. S. (2024). Game-based learning in childhood: A systematic review and meta-analysis. *Frontiers in Psychology, 15*, 1307881. Advance online publication. DOI: 10.3389/fpsyg.2024.1307881 PMID: 38629045

Amin, M. T. (2024). Family language policy: A comprehensive analysis and strategies, challenges, and impacts on children's education. *International Journal of Scientific and Research Publications, 13*(7), 218–225. DOI: 10.29322/IJSRP.13.07.2023.p13924

Asamoah-Potu, F. (2024). Preserving traditional Ghanaian folklore through storytelling. *European Modern Studies Journal, 8*(2), 308–318. DOI: 10.59573/emsj.8(2).2024.26

Balakrisha, C. (2023). The impact of in-classroom non-digital game-based learning activities on students transitioning to higher education. *Education Sciences, 13*(4), 328. DOI: 10.3390/educsci13040328

Banda, F., & Mwanza, D. S. (2019). Language in education policy and linguistic diversity in Zambia: Alternative explanation to low reading level among primary school pupils. *In selected reading in education*, (pp.109-132, University of Zambia Press. Banda, L.O., Banda, C.V., Banda, J.T., & Singni, T. (2024). Preserving cultural heritage: A community-centric approach to safeguard Khulubvi traditional temple Malawi. *Heliyon, 10*(18), e37610. DOI: 10.1016/j.heliyon.2024.e37610 PMID: 39347398

Bernard, D. M. (2025). Understanding socioculturalism in early childhood education: Current perspectives and emerging trends. *Journal of Culture. Social Development, 73*(1), 1–14. DOI: 10.7176/JCSD/73-03

Braun, V., & Clarke, V. (2006). Using thematic analysis in psychology. *Qualitative Research in Psychology, 3*(2), 77–101. DOI: 10.1191/1478088706qp063oa

Chen, E. (2021). Pedagogical practices of an immigrant parent: Maintaining heritage language in the home context. *LEARNing Landscapes, 14*(1), 29–43. DOI: 10.36510/learnland.v14i1.1026

Claybrook, M. K.Jr. (2023). African proverbs, riddles, and narratives as pedagogy: African deep thought in Africana studies. *Journal of Black Studies*, *54*(3), 215–235. DOI: 10.1177/00219347231157113

Cohen, L., Manion, L., & Morrison, K. (2018). *Research methods in education* (8th ed.). Routledge.

Creswell, J. W. (2018). *Research design: Qualitative, quantitative, and mixed methods approaches* (4th ed.). Sage.

Department of Basic Education. (2011). *Curriculum and assessment policy statement: Sesotho home language. Intermediate phase*. Government Printing Works.

Drianda, R. P., Zohran, L., & Aritenang, A. (2022). Innovation in cultural heritage preservation in Taiwan: Lessons for Indonesia. *Journal of Cultural Studies*, *6*(2), 73–89. DOI: 10.22492/ijcs.6.2.04

Falola, T. (2025). Communication, media, culture, and evolving trends in the world of indigenous languages. *International Journal of Indigenous Language Media and Discourse*, *1*(1), 1–10. DOI: 10.36386/ijilmd.v1i1.613

Farhat, S. (2018, February 21). Our values, beliefs, and identity are embedded within language, UNESCO says on Mother Language Day. *World Bank*. https://news.un.org/en/story/2018/02/1003191

Gambhir, G., & Kotonya, J. K. (2023). *Exploring teacher and learner experiences of play-based approaches to SET lessons at upper primary level. Learning study 1 for the plug-in-play project*. National Foundation for Educational Research.

Gauvain, M., & Munroe, R. L. (2020). Children's questions in social and cultural perspective. In Butler, L. P., Ronfard, S., & Corriveau, K. H. (Eds.), *The questioning child: Insights from psychology and education* (pp. 183–211). Cambridge University Press., DOI: 10.1017/9781108553803.010

Godwin-Jones, R. (2021). Evolving technologies for language learning. *Language Learning & Technology*, *25*(3), 6–26. DOI: 10.64152/10125/73443

Hadebe-Ndlovu, B. N. (2022). Teachers' experiences of indigenous games in early grades. *South African Journal of Childhood Education*, *12*(1), a931. DOI: 10.4102/sajce.v12i1.931

Hardianti, H. (2024). Gamification in EFL: Exploring the use of gamification strategy to enhance student motivation and engagement. *Intelektium*, *5*(1), 8–15. DOI: 10.37010/int.v5i1.1531

Henneberg, J., & Sved, E. (2019). The significance of communication and care in one's mother tongue: Patients' views. *Nordic Journal of Nursing Research*, *41*(2), 1–12. DOI: 10.1177/2057158519877794

Heugh, K. A., & Stroud, C. (2019). Multilingualism in South African education: A Southern perspective. In Hickey, R. (Ed.), *English in multilingual South Africa* (pp. 216–238)., DOI: 10.1017/9781108340892.011

Hilgart, A. (2024, February 27). *Home languages in early childhood development in South Africa.* https://starfish-greathearts.org/blog/home-language

Hu, Z. (2024). Game-based learning: Alternative approaches to teaching and learning strategies in health sciences education. *Educational Process: International Journal*, *13*(2), 90–104. DOI: 10.22521/edupij.2024.132.6

Imron, A., Somawati, N. P., & Mohammed, L. A. (2025). Preserving mother tongues remains crucial for cultural identity and diversity amid the homogenizing forces of globalized educational systems. *Journal of Language, Literature. Social and Cultural Studies*, *3*(2), 128–141. DOI: 10.58881/jllscs.v3i2.343

Ishaq, K., Rosdi, F., Mat Zin, N. A., & Abid, A. (2022). Serious game design model for language learning in the cultural context. *Education and Information Technologies*, *27*(7), 9317–9355. DOI: 10.1007/s10639-022-10999-5 PMID: 35370439

Joel, N., Ndomba, R., & Mhagama, M. (2023). Contribution of game-based learning in enhancing the implementation of the learner-centred approach in public schools in Kahama municipality in Tanzania. *International Journal for Research in Education Studies*, *9*(5), 1–9. DOI: 10.53555//es.v9i5.2322

Kakemo, A. A. (2024). Language preservation: Strategies for indigenous languages. *Journal of Current Issues in Arts and Management*, *5*(3), 1–4. DOI: 10.59298/NIJCIAM/2024/5.3.14100

Kamal, S. A. (2019). Research paradigm and philosophical foundation of qualitative study. *The International Journal of Social Sciences (Islamabad)*, *4*(3), 1386–1394. DOI: 10.20319/pijss.2019.43.13861394

Kasiyarno, K., & Apriyanto, S. (2025). Influence of globalisation on the shift in local language and cultural identity. *Journal Corner of Education Linguistic and Literature*, *4*(3), 372–383. DOI: 10.54012/jcell.v4i3.435

Khumalo, S. (2023, February 21). PabSALB aims to preserve South African languages. *Ekurhuleni News.* https://ekurhuleninews.co.za/pansalb-aims-to-preserve-south-african-languages-2/

Madzivhandila, M., Manyange, T., & Mudau, T. J. (2024). Vhavenda traditional children's games as a form of indigenous knowledge; Tshifasi genre. *TWIST International Multidisciplinary Journal*, *9*(4), 378–387. DOI: 10.5281/twist.10049652#346

Makutoane, T. J. (2022). The people divided by common language: The orthography of Sesotho in Lesotho, South Africa and implications for Bible translation. *Hervormde Teologiese Studies*, *7*(1), a7605. DOI: 10.4102/hts.v78i1.7605

Mania, S., Ibrahim, M. M., & Syamsudduha, S. (2024). The impact of traditional games on social-emotional development: A comprehensive review of existing research. *Journal of Learning and Development Studies*, *4*(2), 39–51. DOI: 10.32996/jlds.2024.4.2.5

Maphanga, C. (2019, June 14). I don't hate Afrikaans. Panyaza Lesufi. *News 24*. https://www.news24.com/i-dont-hate-afrikaans-panyaza-lesufi-20190614

Mashala, M., & Sanders, D. (2025). The use of translanguaging to support the teaching of literacy: Intermediate phase teachers' perceptions. *International Journal of Multilingualism*, *22*(4), 2876–2893. Advance online publication. DOI: 10.1080/14790718.2025.2502949

McLeod, S. (2024). *Vygotsky's zone of proximal development*. Simply Psychology.

McMillan, J., & Schumacher, S. (2014). *Research in education: Evidence-based inquiry* (7th ed.). Pearson Education.

Meiklejohn, C., Westaway, L., Ashley, F. H., & Long, K. A. (2021). A review of South African primary school literacy interventions from 2005-2020. *South African Journal of Childhood Education*, *11*(1), a919. DOI: 10.4102/sajce.v11i1.919

Mlambo, R., & Matfunjwa, M. (2024). The use of technology in preserving indigenous language in South Africa. *Literator-Journal of Literary Criticism. Comparative Linguistics and Literary Studies*, *45*(1), 2007. DOI: 10.4102/LIT.v45i1.2007

Mohajan, H. K. (2018). Qualitative research methodology in social sciences and related subjects. *Journal of Economic Development. Environment and People*, *7*(1), 23–48. DOI: 10.26458/jedep.v7i1.571

Mokoena, L. G. (2019). Cultural tourism: Cultural presentation at Basotho cultural village, Free State, South Africa. *Journal of Tourism and Cultural Change*, *18*(2), 1–21. DOI: 10.1080/14766825.2019.1609488

Morrison, N. (2022, March 08). The secret to being a better teacher? Be kind to your students. *Forbes newsletter*. https://www.forbes.com/sites/nickmorrison/2022/03/08/the-secret-to-being-a-better-teacher-be-kind-to-your-students/

Mose, P. N., & Kaschula, R. H. (2019). Developing mother tongue as academic languages in primary schools in Kenya: Exploring extent and indispensability. *Journal of Language, Identity, and Education, 18*(1), 329–342. Advance online publication. DOI: 10.1080/15348458.2019.1645605

Mudau, P. P., Mandende, I. P., & Mushaathoni, M. (2024). Indigenous language preservation: A study of the Tsivenda speech community in South Africa. *Journal of Intercultural Communication, 24*(4), 1–2. DOI: 10.36923/jicc.v24i4.969

Mulaudzi, L. V. (2024). Evaluating the language-in-education policy of 1997: Advancing inclusivity and multilingual education. *Journal for Language Teaching= Ijenali Yekufundzisa Lulwimi=. Tydskrif vir Taalonderrig, 58*(2), 1–28. https://hdl.handle.net/10520/ejc-langt_v58_n2_a4. DOI: 10.56285/jltVol58iss2a6163

Mwinsa, G. M., & Dagad, M. (2024). Efficacy of indigenous games on literacy and numeracy development in preschools in Zambia. *South African Journal of Childhood Education, 14*(1), a1555. DOI: 10.4102/SAJCE.v14i1.1555

Naidoo, K. (2024). A review of the effectiveness of educational digital game-based learning on students in tertiary institutions. *European Journal of Teacher Education, 5*(4), 34–47. DOI: 10.33422/ejte.v5i4.1174

Nishanthi, R. (2020). Understanding of the importance of mother tongue learning. *International Journal of Trend in Scientific Research and Development, 5*(1), 77–80.

Nxumalo, S. A., & Mncube, D. W. (2019). Using indigenous games and knowledge to decolonise the school curriculum: Ubuntu perspective. *Perspectives in Education, 36*(2), 103–118. DOI: 10.18820/2519593X/pie.v36i2.9

O'Connell, S. (2022, Sep 22). Heritage Day offers the space to revisit South Africans' painful legacies and tell untold stories of hope. *Daily*

Olanibi, S. A., Dahiru, W., & Balogun, K. B. (2021). Mother tongue as an instructional medium in Nigeria's lower primary schools: Prospects and challenges. *IOSR Journal of Research and Method in Education, 11*(3), 40–45. DOI: 10.9790/7388-1103034045

Omidire, M. F., & Ayob, S. (2020). The utilisation of translanguaging for learning and teaching in a multilingual primary classroom. *Multilingua, 4*(11), 105–129. DOI: 10.1515/multi-2020-0072

Osei-Tutu, A. A. (2022). Developing African oral traditional storytelling as a framework for studying with African peoples. *Qualitative Research, 23*(6), 1497–1514. DOI: 10.1177/14687941221082263

Pious, M., & Saishi, A. (2025). The role of traditional ceremonies in the preservation of Zambia's cultural heritage with regards to the Umutomboko ceremony of Lunda-speaking people: A case study of two selected districts in Luapula province in Zambia. *International Journal of Advanced Multidisciplinary Research Studies, 5*(2), 2407–2418.

Pivac, B. (2023). *Game-based learning for culturally diverse students: Designing a conceptual framework for embedding cultural capital into games*. [Unpublished master's dissertation] University of Uppsala. Sweden

Polleti, G. (2024, March). Building a language-learning game for Brazilian Indigenous languages: A case study. *In Proceedings of the 16th International Conference on Computational Processing of Portuguese*-2 (pp. 18–22). https://doi.org/DOI: 10.48550/arXiv.2403.14515

Regiana, E., Dwiyoga, A., & Prasetya, F. H. (2020). Preservation of Indonesian culture through traditional games application. *Sisforma, 7*(1), 28–37. DOI: 10.24167/sisforma.v7i1.1422

Rojas, V. S., Fuentealba, L. F., & Ranjan, R. (2021). Game-based didactic resources as a strategy in foreign language pedagogy. *International Journal of Teaching and Education Research, 20*(12), 195–211. DOI: 10.26803/ijlter.20.12.12

Savage, C. (2019, August 30). The importance of mother tongue in education. https://www.ie-today.co.uk/Blog/the-importance-of-mother-tongue-in-education/

Sibanda, R. (2019). Mother tongue education in multilingual township: Possibilities for recognising lok'shin lingua in South Africa. *Reading and Writing, 10*(1), a225. DOI: 10.4102/rw.v10i1.225

Smit, B., & Onwuegbuzie, A. J. (2018). Observations in qualitative inquiry: When what you see is not what you see. *International Journal of Qualitative Methods, 17*(1), 1–3. DOI: 10.1177/1609406918816766

Stack, M., & Bunt, B. (2023). Developing a game-based learning pedagogy for teaching history using Napoleon Total War. *Yesterday and Today*, 30(1), 9–35. https://doi.org/DOI: 10.17159/2223-0386/2023/n30a2

The Witness. (2022, March 3). *Mixed opinions on the push to introduce mother tongue instruction in schools*. https://witness.co.za/news/2022/03/21/mixed-opinion-on-push-to-introduce-mother-tongue-instruction-in-schools-20220319/

Tsebe, A. (2021). The epistemology of mother tongue(s): What does this mean for language in education? *The Journal of Transdisciplinary Research in Southern Africa, 17*(1), 1–10. DOI: 10.4102/td.v17i1.1068

Tuong Van, B. (2024). The role of family and community in preserving the linguistic identity of the Tay, Nung and Dao people. *International Journal of Education Humanities and Social Science*, *7*(4), 293–302. DOI: 10.54922/IJEHSS.2024.0768

Turin, T. C., Raihan, M., & Chowdhury, N. (2024). Paradigms of approaches to research. *Bangabandhu Sheikh Mujib Medical University Journal*, *17*(2), e73973–e73973. DOI: 10.3329/bsmmuj.v17i2.73973

UNESCO. (2024, March 5). *Multilingual education, the bet to preserve indigenous languages and justice.* https://www.unesco.org/en/articles/multilingual-education-bet-preserve-indigenous-languages-and-justice

Venketsamy, A. (2023). Exploring the teacher-learner ratio and its effect on invitational teaching and learning: A South African study. *Journal for Education of Gifted Young Scientists*, *11*(1), 1–13. DOI: 10.17478/jegys.1237615

Vygotsky, L. S. (1978). *Mind in society: The development of higher psychological processes*. Harvard University Press.

Xeketwana, S. (2021). *The implementation of language policy for multilingual education, extending the teaching and learning of IsiXhosa for communicative purposes in teacher education.* [Unpublished doctoral dissertation] Stellenbosch University. South Africa

Yeboah, R., Amponsah, K. D., Mintah, P. G., Sedofia, T., & Donkor, P. B. (2023). Game-based learning in Ghana primary schools: Listening to the views of teachers. *Education*, *53*(4), 1–5. DOI: 10.1080/03004279.2023.2171269

Yetman, D. (2000). What is the zone of proximal development? *Healthline.* https://www.healthline.com/health/zone-of-proximal-development

Zhang, F. (2018). The application of a game-based approach in primary school English teaching. *Advances in Social Science, Education and Humanities Research*, *15*(1), 1–13. DOI: 10.2991/emehss-18.2018.120

Chapter 8

# Enriching Children's Biliteracy With Gamesongs Through Bilingual Languaging and Multimodality:

## A Case of the Stars of Today Literacy Club#

**Xolisa Guzula**
http://orcid.org/0000-0001-8348-6664
*University of Cape Town, South Africa*

## ABSTRACT

*In traditional biliteracy instruction, biliteracy is taught as Home Language and First Additional Language literacies, following Eurocentric monolingualising ideologies. Curricula and pedagogy in these classrooms reject discourses about play-based and multimodal pedagogical approaches for highly pedagogised and decontextualised instruction that excludes African oral literature and art. Drawing on language ideologies, and multiliteracies as theoretical frameworks this study aims to challenge the narrow literacy approaches and nation-state ideologies that determine how language is used. The study draws on auto-ethnographic case study of 60 grade 3-6 children who were members the Stars of Today Literacy Club#. The study focuses on the selected gamesongs and the related art activities. It draws on interactional and multimodal analysis as analytic tools. Findings show that using*

DOI: 10.4018/979-8-3373-4322-8.ch008

*gamesongs can enhance vocabulary, rhyme and rhythm. Finally, multilingual and multimodal pedagogies enhance biliteracy development and positions children as competent emergent bilinguals*

## INTRODUCTION

Up until 2025, the South African Language-in-Education Policy in practice has always been the one requiring learners to switch medium of instruction from home language in the foundation phase to English in the intermediate phase, despite the Language in Education Policy of 1997 which, instead of mandating the switch, promotes multilingual education through an additive bilingualism model called Mother Tongue Based Bilingual Education (MTbBE). Essentially, MTBBE encourages the use of children's home languages in the foundation phase to strengthen children's language and literacy skills before adding another language such as English as additional and complementary second medium of instruction from grade 4. While more recently the Department of Basic Education issued Circular 18 of 2024 (DBE, 2024) which lays out the new education changes taking place in the education system with the implementation of MTBBE, particularly in maths and science and technology lessons with accompanying translanguaging pedagogy, the separate teaching of languages as Home Languages and First Additional Languages still remains the same as before. This means that pedagogy still follows the traditional separate bilingual and biliteracy instruction steeped in Eurocentric monolingualising nation-state language ideologies. Languages are taught in silos, even in multilingual settings where children are already bi/multilingual or are emergent bi/multilinguals. The notion of simultaneous use of co-existing multiple languages has not been considered as a viable approach to biliteracy development and that colonial language ideologies are still dominant. Secondly, curricula and classroom practices in these language and literacy classrooms generally reject Piagetian and Vygotskian discourses about children learning through play or being taught through play-based and multiliteracies pedagogical approaches that promote both plural languaging and multimodal approaches. Instead, the language and literacy curriculum and instruction are highly pedagogised and decontextualised especially in foundation and intermediate phase language classrooms. These pedagogies, not only evacuate the socio-cultural knowledges that the children and their communities have but also trivialise play, art and performance and view them as frivolous activities that take the focus away from teaching decoding. Language and literacy learning through choral performative and parroting drills on itemised letters and sounds propagated by the scholars of science of reading (Goodwin & Jiménez, 2021) pacify children's agency, creativity, curiosity, imagination and teachers' interest in using gamesongs

(Makina, 2009) or musical play/games as springboards to teach language and literacy (Harrop-Allin, 2014). Additionally, the exclusive focus on book models of literacy, which are highly monoglossic, valorise only Western perspectives on literature to the exclusion of oral literatures of Africa (which include gamesongs/musical play, songs, folklore and poetry and rhyme and their integration with writing) (Opland, 2018). They also exclude multimodal (artistic, visual and gestural and performative) forms of expression as means of communication (Stein, 2008). While teachers' anecdotal understandings about how children learn often include an understanding that children learn through play, it is rare to find gamesongs and art being harnessed for pedagogical practice in the classrooms. With this context in mind, I focus my chapter on exploring how gamesongs can be harnessed to build learner's simultaneous biliteracy competences by taking a multilingual and a multiliteracies orientation to language practices and meaning-making.

There are fewer research studies that explore integration of simultaneous biliteracy development (Bloch, 2002; Guzula & Molate, 2025), with play-based and art-based approaches to literacy development (Aung, 2025) that are referred to as rich literacies in South Africa. However, though Bloch (2002) shows that children who had isiXhosa-English bilingualism could be taught in the same class with children who had Afrikaans-English bilingualism, enabling biliteracy development, she did not combine their analysis with multimodal meaning making and play. Stein (2008) on the other hand analysed the affordances of multimodal communication in the classroom and focused on analysing affordances of storytelling and children's creative multimodal meaning making processes but rarely analysed for multilingual affordances. Guzula (2021) and Aung's (2025) studies combine both multilingual, multimodal, play based and art-based approaches. But this work is not yet well understood, especially by cognitive or psycholinguistic scholars of reading literacy.

## CONTEXTUALISING USE OF GAMESONGS AND THE STARS OF TODAY LITERACY CLUB (STLC#)

Contrary to rigidly pedagogised literacy instruction that is monolingual and monomodal, children's play offers us incidental learning opportunities that are more creative, participatory and affective, which position the children as competent. Play is multimodal and includes use of bodies, movements, voice, sound and making of materials. The use of play in the form gamesongs or musical games in education in general has the potential to enhance agency, creativity, participation and self-expression. But the South African education system has marginalised indigenous peoples' and children's socio-cultural resources which include knowledge, stories, games, songs, play and oral verse (Abarry, 1989; Makina, 2009; Harrop-Allin,

2014) especially in working class communities. Ramugondo (2012) argues that Christianity and schooling were instrumental in undermining indigenous games from communities and families, thus contributing to the erasure of African knowledge systems. Thus church, school, and homes have come to play a lesser role in providing for structured play for children and have created discontinuity between first and third generation games played by grandparents and their grandchildren. Harrop-Allin (2014), argues that many in families and in schools ignore children's games. Children play regardless, and while teachers in some schools might supervise children playing in the playground, they merely become spectators who do not harness the games for teaching in the classroom. This contributes to the disconnect children experience between their everyday life and classroom life (Harrop-Allin, 2014). Harrop-Allin laments the diminishing of play between adults and the children, arguing that this robs children and their families of spaces for co-creation of shared play engagements, and that the notion of play as an identity can no longer be maintained. To close this generational gap, Ramugondo argues for the creation of opportunities for co-creation of games played by both children and adults.

The Stars of Today Literacy Club# (STLC#)[1] was conceptualised and established as a third space to provide a space for such collaboration between adults and young children in co-creating games and building on both their older and newer experiences with games as a way to enhance children's biliteracy development. Third spaces are 'spaces "in between" and beyond two binaries, conceptualisations and discourses often thought of as separate and uncombinable,' (Soja, 1996: 5). They are significant in that they offer children alternative learning spaces when the first spaces (home) and the second spaces (school) cannot offer children these play based learning spaces which also value multilingual and multimodal practices and meaning making opportunities. Aung's (2025) findings indicate that allowing learners to create meaning through multilingualism, multimodalities and arts-based methods improved their language skills and that participating learners' understanding of reading passages improved when they were allowed to express their cognition through a combination of drawings, multilingual discussions and writing, as opposed to answering in writing only.

The formation of the STLC# follows a strong tradition of starting clubs as out of school learning spaces for children. In 2006, we started the Vulindlela Reading Club in collaboration with Zisukhanyo Youth Empowerment, in the Langa Location, in Cape Town, and with colleagues from the Project for the Study of Alternative Education South Africa (PRAESA) under the leadership of Dr Neville Alexander (Alexander *et al.*, 2011). Following that, in 2012 we started the Nal'ibali National Reading for Enjoyment Initiative, which became PRAESA's nation-wide initiative for building a culture of reading through formation of reading clubs across the country. Through Nal'ibali, PRAESA set out to provide an educational alternative to an education system that was struggling with a literacy crisis. In this education system, language and literacy instruction in classrooms revolved around language ideologies that treat languages as separate bounded entities, and literacy is narrowed down to decoding. I used the Stars of Today Literacy Club# as a research site for my doctoral study and I used the Stars of Today Literacy Club# as a research site for my doctoral study, and the aim for establishing this particular club was.... was to challenge the narrow view of literacy by immersing the children in rich literacies experiences which harnessed both multilingual and multimodal communication as resources for literacy learning and developing children's critical literacies.

Gamesongs or musical games are one way to build children's oral language and reading and writing development. Sometimes familiar songs in isiXhosa were sung at the STLC# and sometimes, unfamiliar English songs like Down by the Bay by Raffie and a song about an Australian bird Kookaburra (selected for the purposes of this chapter) were introduced by facilitators to the children. These songs were sung at the Vulindlela Reading Club mentioned above. Some of us facilitators at the club who had facilitated other clubs before transported and brought the songs that we sung and stories we told and listened to at the Langa Vulindlela Reading Club to STLC#. In the literacy club, children and adults played gamesongs as an integral aspect of the literacy club sessions. Alexander et al. (2011) argued that "Children learn easily and comfortably when they play." This is very important especially for learning a second language. It is also important for children to discover that all languages can be fun to learn. This is why music is also used." As a literacy club facilitator, drawing on songs for learning a new language was intentional, as I had the lived experience of collating songs as a teenager for learning English as a new language. We practiced singing along with artists on radio and playing songs on cassettes on tape recorders while reading the lyrics from notebooks. They practiced singing along with artists on radio and playing songs on cassettes on tape recorders while reading the songs from the notebooks. This lived experience shaped my understanding of the connection between songs, games and language and literacy learning. The STLC# children had also asked to sing and play in their expectations of the club when it was established. Below shows song and poetry books that were used and the writing on the board shows a list of songs that were sung and gamesongs played as being an important part of the literacy club.

*Table 1. Songs sung at the STLC# and song and rhyme resources*

| a. **Books of songs, rhymes and poetry** | b. **Lists of songs sung at the literacy club on the board** |
|---|---|
|  |  |
| **Left side of the board:**<br>1. Blue Crane<br>2. Down by the bay<br>3. Siyacela<br>4. Hill on the ground<br>5. Ntakana Ntyilo Ntyilo<br>6. Khanikhangele<br>7. Everywhere we go<br>8. Little Black Bird<br>9. This room sings | **Right side of the board:** Things we do at the club<br>1. Siyacula/we sing<br>2. Siyafunda (we learn/read)<br>3. Sidlale iigames/imidlalo (play games)<br>4. Sibhale (write)<br>5. Siacte-senza umdlalo weqonga (we act/role play)<br>6. Sibalisa amabali – storytelling<br>7. Siya elayibhrari- kwithala leencwadi (we visit the library)<br>8. Siya etheatre (we go to theatre)<br>9. Sithetha iEnglish/isiNgesi (we speak English) |

Drawing on language ideologies (McKinney, 2017) and multiliteracies (New London Group, 2000), this chapter thus explores how gamesongs/musical games were drawn on at the Stars of Today Literacy Club# (STLC#) to develop children's biliteracy learning. The question that the chapter aims respond to is: How can bi/multilingualism, multiliteracies and gamesongs be used productively to enhance children's biliteracy development and creativity? Working from the Stars of Today Literacy Club# (STLC#), established as a third space to legitimise, acknowledge and value the use of multilingual communication practices, multiliteracies, gamesongs and other multimodal communication practices, the aim of the chapter is to challenge the received and commonly unexamined concept that African language/English biliteracy development is monoglossic, and monomodal. Secondly, by drawing on holistic African learning and meaning making practices that include play through the use of gamesongs, this chapter aims to challenge the narrow literacy approaches that only insist on decoding for the development of literacy by demonstrating how gamesongs can enrich and broaden children's literacy development. Furthermore, the chapter aims to challenge the violence of taking away voice, agency and creativity from the children and to position them as competent bilinguals and creative artists whose translation and interpreting skills and artistic skills are never valued in local and international assessments. I argue that urban multilingual children need to learn their languages in a complex simultaneous biliteracy model rather than in an impoverished separate and simplistic biliteracy model and that multimodality through songs and art deepens children's meaning making, improves and extends their vocabulary and criticality and enhances their creativity.

## THEORETICAL FRAMEWORK AND LITERATURE REVIEW

Since this chapter examines both children's bilingual and biliteracy development, the chapter combines both language ideologies and multiliteracies theoretical frameworks to challenge the received and commonly unexamined concept that African language/English biliteracy development is monoglossic, and monomodal. There has been a paradigm shift in Sociolinguistics and Applied linguistics from viewing language and literacy as a form (grammar) or abstract to viewing language in use. Language-in-use acknowledges variation as a fundamental aspect of language. There has also been a paradigm shift in literacy studies from viewing literacy as monolingual and monomodal to viewing it as both plural and multimodal. Furtheremore, multiliteracies also offers a framework that can be used as a pedagogical model that incorporates situated knowledges and languages, overt instruction, critical framing and transformative practice. First, I theorise language ideologies to show how the traditional conceptualisation of biliteracy as two languages taught separately as Home Languages and First Additional Languages is steeped in colonial and nation-state ideologies that have come to define what counts as good language use for teaching literacy, even in multilingual contexts. I also theorise alternative language ideologies that are helpful when developing children's simultaneous biliteracy. Secondly, I theorise literacy as a social practice focusing also on multiliteracies framework, Janks' synthesis model for critical literacy and multimodality. I argue that the use of gamesongs or mucical games as forms of play, multilingualism and multimodality create a third space that is central to children's simultaneous biliteracy development.

### Monolingual and Monoglossic Language Ideologies

Ideologies which inform the conception of how languages are to be taught in the Curriculum and Assessment Policy Statement (CAPS) (DBE, 2011) are monolingual and monoglossic ideologies informed by a 'Western' mind-set that treats languages of multilingual children as Home Languages and First Additional Languages. Instead of viewing children as emergent bilinguals (García & Torres-Guevara, 2009), they are viewed as Home Language speakers who must also learn their second language as First Additional Language at school, despite many children acquiring the languages simultaneously at home, or in preschools and in the community. Makalela argues, "Classifications of 'first', 'second', and 'mother tongue' do not fit the sociolinguistic realities of the majority of the speakers who do not learn languages through serial, linear and sequential modes" (2015:17). A monolingual ideology is an ideology of a single legitimate language selected as a HL or FAL subject, which prevents teachers and learners from using multilingualism as a productive resource for meaning making in language and literacy classrooms, as well as across the curriculum (Barton, 2001; García & Torres-Guevara, 2009; Makoe & McKinney, 2014; Kiramba, 2018). Kiramba (2018) adds that language ideologies are also 'beliefs or feelings about languages as used in their social worlds', meaning that multiple ideologies can be articulated and/or embodied in a given practice, like when a teacher refuses to translanguage because he is an English/Xhosa teacher. These scholars also define a monoglossic ideology as a conception of languages as being stable, bounded entities which are clearly differentiated from each other. Central to the monolingual ideologies is a monolingual bias or orientation, where one so called standard African language is privileged over its own dialects and varieties (Makalela, 2015). Kiramba (2018) argues that language ideologies can be 'entrenched in, and/or reactive to the experiences of a given social position', for example in being an English teacher. These pure, fixed, bounded, and autonomous named language ideologies strongly underpin CAPS curriculum's separation of Home Languages and First Additional Languages as subjects. Children who may speak varieties, and dialects of the named 'standard' languages, or who speak a combination of the two or more and children who grow up in multilingual communities and families are excluded in this conceptualisation of languages.

## Language Resources, the Linguistic Repertoires and Translanguaging

Ruíz (1984) proposed the notion of language as a resource to challenge the perception of bilingualism or multilingualism as a problem. Viewing language as a problem reflects a monolingual ideal and an assimilationist mindset where linguistic diversity is seen as a threat to national unity, leading to use of one common language as a lingua-franca (Hult & Hornberger, 2016). Failing to speak the lingua franca eventually leads to children from minoritised linguistic communities being positioned as deficient rather than positioned with competence in the linguistic resources they have. The concept of language as a resource has therefore been taken up in multilingual education and biliteracy development to help us see children's languages, varieties and dialects as assets that can be harnessed for meaning making. Language as a resource orientation is useful in challenging both the monolingual bias and the dominant deficit perspectives of emergent bilinguals, in valuing multilingualism and linguistic diversity and in positioning the children with competences. Finally, language as a resource orientation helps not to pit languages against each other but to view them as language resources that can be harnessed productively.

McKinney (2017) argues that to make visible the resources that individual learners have, and those they aspire to, we have to study the linguistic repertoire. According to Busch (2012), a linguistic repertoire is a "bundle of linguistic dispositions that is subject to transformation or modification over time". She claims that linguistic "dispositions' refer on the one hand to knowledge of language, varieties, registers, and pragmatics, and on the other hand to emotions and desires linked to linguistic practices" Busch (2012). Scholars who promote the study of the linguistic repertoire like Busch propose a 'speaker centred approach' to the study of the linguistic repertoire as a positive multilingual mindset for acknowledging, making visible, and valorising heteroglossic resources that children have which also give voice to children (2010:293). Makalela (2015) proposes Ubuntu translanguaging built on the African philosophy of interdependence, to show that in language learning, the learning of one language is dependent on the knowledge of the other language. Translanguaging is the use of multiple languages for communicating and for learning without paying attention to codes, but to what the speaker is communicating and making sense of (Makalela 2015). Through translanguaging, he challenges the notion of teaching languages as bounded separate entities, demonstrating that in multilingual contexts, biliteracy development does not grow out of separate and sequential bilingualism, but through simultaneous use of multiple languages.

## Multiliteracies

The paradigm shift from the focus on print literacies to the focus on the visual, performative and materiality of literacy as well as on critical literacies and multilingual literacies ushered in a more complex understanding of literacy within literacy as a social practice theoretical framing. New multiliteracies and multimodal literacies perspectives (New London Group, 2000), the development of new digital technologies and communication changes, and the synthesis model for critical literacy of Janks (2010), force us to broaden our view of literacy and to also pay attention to the affordances of non-print-based communication. Paying attention to both linguistic variation and diversity of modes of expression is central in a multiliteracies perspective of literacy. To help us work with this diversity, multiliteracies scholars proposed a pedagogical framework with four quadrants that focus on situated practice, overt instruction, critical framing, and transformative practice (New London Group, 2000). According to the New London Group (2000), the situated practice aspect of the framework means that pedagogy must immerse children in meaningful practices within a community of learners – playing multiple roles based on their backgrounds and experiences. Secondly, the community must include experts who have mastered certain practices. Teachers are expected to recruit learners' previous and current experiences as well as their afterschool activities and discourses as an integral part of their learning experience (teaching from lived experiences). Another thing is that pedagogy must consider affective needs and sociocultural identities of learners. It is about getting learners to take risks and trust guidance of others (peers or teachers). Finally, evaluation should be non-judgemental but used developmentally. The overt aspect of multiliteracies framework refers to direct or explicit interventions by teachers and other knowledgeable others to scaffold learning activities and focus learners on important features of their experiences and activities within the community of learners. This way, it allows learners to gain explicit information; encourages collaborative efforts between teachers and learners; develops conscious awareness of what is being learned and gives learners metalanguages to talk about their learning, for example in discussing meanings of words for vocabulary development. Demonstrations and explanations by knowledgeable others are important in scaffolding learning in addition to immersing children to that which they have to learn to do, thus bringing together elements of both implicit and explicit learning in the learning space. This teaching usually builds and extends what children already know from lived experience. Critical framing means adopting a critical perspective in which pedagogy is supposed to encourage children not to be mere consumers and reproducers of knowledge they interact with but to question values, beliefs, assumptions and actions embedded in knowledge (Vasquez, 2014). This pedagogy encourages learners to examine and investigate the relationship between the language we use (spoken and written) and other semiotic modes of representation and the social and cultural practices in which it is constructed (Vasquez, 2014). According to Vasquez this critical perspective assumes that our utterances, writing, art and actions are not neutral but tied to our socio-cultural practices. Finally, the transformative aspect of multiliteracies framework relates to reflective practice which develops from critical framing and resulting in new practices embedded in learner's own goals and values (New London Group, 2000). This is where children after critiquing something, redesign it to what they imagine it should be.

The multiliteracies emphasises the centrality of linguistic and cultural diversity (mostly focused on diversity within the English language and its different varieties – British, American, Australian, and even Pidgin). García and Kleifgen (2020) however, bringing a multilingual and biliteracy perspective have critiqued the focus on linguistic diversity that only focuses on English and Guzula (2021) extends it to also focus on diversity between named languages and their varieties in multilingual settings. Thus, notions of linguistic resources and linguistic repertoires discussed above, and translanguaging become important in working with this diversity. However, there is also a perception and fear that translanguaging pedagogies, if not implemented well, might limit learners' access to valued and powerful standardised languages and have serious consequences for their futures (Heugh, 2015; Jaspers & Madsen, 2016). Janks (2004), however, helps us out of this "access paradox" by designing a synthesis model for critical literacy education that pays attention to issues of domination (or power), access, diversity, design/redesign. With regards to domination, Janks (2010) argues that children need to know about the constructedness of texts and how language and other modalities, and symbolic forms, are used to represent, maintain, and reproduce relations of power. This challenges us to think about how one provides access to dominant forms, while at the same time valuing and promoting the diverse languages resources of students. Janks argues that diversity is about recognising that different ways of speaking, reading, and writing the world in a variety of modalities are central in raising consciousness and help us to reflect on different ways of saying (writing), doing, thinking, and valuing (2010:24-25). Finally, redesign focuses on productive power, and the ability to harness the multiplicity of semiotic systems across diverse cultural locations to challenge and change existing discourses. Redesign, like transformative practice in multiliteracies framework recognises the importance of human creativity and the ability to create an infinite number of new meanings. The model recognises the need to give access to dominant (standard) languages and literacy practices as well as to expand what counts as dominant languages and literacies, challenging a monoglossic and monomodal perspective and revealing it to be the outcome of unequal social relations.

## Multimodal Literacies

Multiliteracies also recognises multimodal pedagogies as central to working with diversity, leading to a paradigm shift in the 1990s from the focus on print literacies to the focus on multiple modes of communication. New technological advancements and media prompted this new perspective leading to a critical review of traditional approaches to language and literacy learning. Stein (2008) argues, "traditional theories of communication are monomodal in their focus on how language communicates meaning while a multimodal theory of communication holds that meaning is made, always in the many different modes and media which make up a communication ensemble". A mode is the name for the semiotic resources that are culturally and socially fashioned for meaning making and this includes image, sound, writing, gesture, speech, and movement (Jewitt & Kress, 2003). Therefore, meaning making is conceptualised beyond language in a multimodal approach to language and literacy learning. Language is viewed as one mode amongst many others, including gesture, colour, sound and movement, images etc. (Stein, 2008). Thus, multimodality disrupts the notion of stable systems of communication and representation which portrays people as just users of the systems rather than as agentic and actively involved in redesigning semiotic resources (Stein, 2008). In multimodal pedagogies, children are therefore positioned as creative, agentic sign-makers who design meaning and make semiotic choices. This centres human beings as meaning makers, as designers, interpreters of meaning and active makers of choices, according to their interests, from the semiotic resources available to them (Bock, 2016; New London Group, 2000; Stein, 2008).

## METHODOLOGY

The chapter is a qualitative and interpretive auto-ethnographic case study which examines the use gamesongs and art for development of children's bi/multilingual and multimodal literacy development. Because this chapter focuses on my own intervention and role as a facilitator, I draw on auto-ethnographic methods to describe my intervention with using gamesongs as resources for children's biliteracy development at the Stars of Today Literacy Club#. I consider this research as auto-ethnographic because it involves three characteristics that are central to auto-ethnography as outlined by Adam et al. (2022: 2). The, 'auto', in auto-ethnography highlights one's role in the research and concentrates on the researcher's personal experiences and reflections in the intervention and the research process. Secondly, the 'ethno' in auto-ethnography foregrounds the role of culture. Thus, auto-ethnographers use their experiences to describe, reflect and also critique, cultural beliefs, values, practices, and identity. Thirdly, 'graphy' focuses on the writing of the narrative. Auto-ethnographers use their experiences to create 'thick descriptions'—of cultural life. Creating an intervention or making an initiative to improve how children learn or to pilot an idea is a key feature in educational linguistics to make a transformative impact in the communities in which we conduct research.

A case study as defined by Merriam (1998:27) is a 'bounded system' which is humanly constructed both as an actual and conceptual selection of what is to be studied rather than something waiting to be discovered'. The Stars of Today Literacy Club# was constructed and selected by means of purposeful sampling which entails the selection of participants as guided by researcher's research design (Higginbottom, 2004). In this instance selection was the children who returned signed invitation letters to become members of the club. Miles (2015) argues that in educational research, a case study generates accounts of practice, which provide knowledge of experience that has conceptual contribution to research understandings of practice. The constructed and bounded case study of the Stars of Today Literacy Club# constitutes a unit of analyses which provide us with holistic representations of context-dependent knowledge of practice which I analyse (Flyvberg, 2001).

## The Research Site and Participants

The STLC# took place on Saturday mornings from 10am to 12pm, at Jabulani Primary School in Khayelitsha, Cape Town and had between 60 Grade 3–6 (ages 9–12) volunteering children as members. Because the club was voluntary, children were not forced to attend the Saturday sessions every week but there were more than 30 children at each of the sessions on any given the weekend between July 2015 to January 2018. Khayelitsha is largely a working-class area and has majority isiXhosa speaking people and some Sesotho speaking migrants from the Eastern Cape in addition to the families that were moved to the area from Nyanga Township in 1985. Up until 2025, many schools in this township implemented a transitional or subtractive bilingual education model, where children learn all content in their home language for the first three years, and suddenly switch to English medium education from grades 4-12. Guided by the CAPS curriculum, Jabulani Primary School, offered isiXhosa as a HL and English as a FAL from Grade 1. These languages are taught as separate bounded entities and it is in these lessons that children experience reading as decoding. Thus, children's biliteracy is developed in a separate biliteracy approach where two languages are not allowed to mix.

With language changes only taking place in mathematics and science and technology subjects at South African primary schools, the status quo remains for languages. Thus, ideologies of monolingualism, and separate biliteracy are continuing where language learning remains stable, separate and bounded. In contrast, at the STLC#, facilitators created a linguistic third space (Flores & García 2013), where translanguaging is legitimised and where literacy learning is multimodal, involving play in the form of gamesongs. Facilitators modelled dynamic bilingualism and positioned the children as competent bi/multilinguals who were cable of interpreting and translating oral and written texts.

## Data Collection Methods

As with any ethnographic study, data was collected through ethnographic data collection tools which include thick descriptions, audio and video recordings that I transcribed and focus group interviews with the children. It was also generated through literacy related activities such as composing either on the board or on paper and books, and child generated artwork. Still photographs of shared writing, children's writings and artwork were also taken as data. The analysis for this chapter focuses on transcripts produced as interactional data of the singing of two songs: *Down by the Bay* by Raffie and the song about an Australian bird called Kookaburra which were sung in two of the reading club sessions. It also focuses on the related artwork produced by the children in the form of drawings and collages of birds.

### Ethical Considerations

Ethical consent was obtained from the school principal, the grade 3 teacher and parents as well as assent from the children. Permission to conduct the study was also obtained from the Western Cape Education Department and finally, ethical clearance for data collection was granted by the University of Cape Town for the doctoral study.

## ANALYSIS AND DISCUSSION

Auto-ethnography turns the gaze away from only studying others as objects to studying ourselves as part of the knowledge-making process. I draw on interactional analysis of transcripts of observational data and multimodal analysis of the still images taken at the literacy club are used to analyse for how the gamesongs were used for bilingual vocabulary development, language learning, writing and rhyme. I thus turn the gaze to my interaction with learners as I worked on vocabulary and transcription of the songs into written lyrics. I focus on two literacy club sessions where two English songs, Kookaburra and Down by the Bay by Raffie were sung and how I used them to extend children's vocabulary, teach critical thinking and rhyme. I also analyse the children's art production as part of their redesign/ transformation of the songs through art-based activities to develop deeper meaning making and their creativity. I demonstrate how auto-ethnographic methods are useful methodologies in educational interventions. The aim is to analyse how I used songs for teaching literacy as this is the area that is not fully understood and appreciated in reading literature.

Working within the multiliteracies framework which builds on situated practice, overt instruction, critical framing and transformative practice, I first analyse how I drew on the overt instruction aspect of the multiliteracies framework to teach the English song by Raffi, called *Down by the bay* by writing it down through shared writing and discussing vocabulary. Then I analyse for how I drew on the full application of the multiliteracies framework and Janks' synthesis model to extend children's vocabulary of the Kookaburra song, surface children's prior knowledge about birds, develop critical thinking and creativity in the redesign of the Kookaburra bird to Indwe (the Blue Crane). I draw on multimodal analysis to analyse the children's redesigns of the Kookaburra bird.

## Using Overt Instruction Quadrant of Multiliteracies to Collaboratively Write Down an English Song Down by the Bay by Raffie

At the Stars of Today Literacy Club#, songs were used to teach literacy skills more overtly in addition to them being sung for affective and enjoyable reasons. They were used teach a variety of formal language skills in fun and creative ways. In extract 1 below, Xolisa introduces Raffi's song *"Down by The Bay"* to the children and uses it to teach them English.

## *Figure 1. Transcribing Down by the bay song into lyrics*

1. XOLISA: Ok. Yimani ke.
2. Ndifuna ukunifundisa enye ingoma [Ok. Now wait. I want to teach you another song]. (She sits next to a whiteboard and prepares to write).
3. Ithi le ngoma [The song says]:
4. "down by the bay",
5. neh? [hey?] (Writes a line on the whiteboard)
6. Down_ by..?
7. By the?
8. CHILDREN: Bay.
9. XOLISA: By the bay.
10. Where the watermelons grow, neh? (Writes the line on the board) Where…
11. CHILDREN: Waterm…
12. XOLISA: The _ water…
13. CHILDREN: Melons.
14. XOLISA: Do you know what a watermelon is?
15. Ngubani oyaziyo iwatermelon ngesiXhosa? [Who knows what a watermelon is in Xhosa] (Points to a child)
16. CHILD: Yho! (oops!)
17. XOLISA: Yintoni igama le watermelon? [What is its name?]
18. CHILD: (Indistinct)
19. XOLISA: Yintoni? [What?]
20. LWANDO: Ntyabontyi.
21. XOLISA: Uthi yintyabontyi [He says it is intyabontyi, a melon].
22. Ewe iyafana nentyabontyi iwatermelon, qha ayontyabontyi yona i…iba sisidudu yona [Yes, watermelon does look like intyabontyi].
23. Ihamba ibe yipapa neh [Ntyabontyi is like porridge, nhe]?
24. Kodwa yona iwatermelon yifruit andithi? [But watermelon is fruits, not so]
25. CHILD: Yes Miss.
26. XOLISA: Siyayitya [it is edible].
27. So zibufana ngaphandle [They look alike when you look at them from the outside].
28. Unyanisile. [You are right]
29. Kodwa ke iwatermelon siyibiza ukuba yintoni kanene? [But what do we call watermelon in Xhosa]
30. Ngegama elibolekiweyo [in a borrowed word]...
31. Sithi yivatala [we call it ivatala].
32. Nikhe nilive elo gama?[Have you ever heard of such a word?] (Addresses a child)
33. Ubuyazi? [Did you know?]
34. Ngubani obesithi… [Who said...]
35. Ubuyazi neh? [did you know nhe?]
36. CHILD: [Nods]
37. XOLISA: Yivatala [It is watermelon].
38. Ndingalibhala apha kanti [I could write it here].
39. Iva…(writes the name down on the whiteboard)
40. ivatala. Neh
41. Ivatala.
42. So down by the bay where the watermelons
43. XOLISA: Grow. Ok.
44. Where the watermelons grow.
45. That's where my friends…
46. that's where…mhm. ♫
47. Down by the bay,
48. where the watermelons grow,
49. that's where my friends
50. we like to play,
51. and when we play
52. we like to say♫
53. Ok. Down by the bay
54. where the watermelons grow (begins to write on the whiteboard)
55. that's _ where _ my…
56. I have a very bad handwriting ke.
57. That's where my friends _ like to go
58. neh?
59. CHILD: Cat.
60. XOLISA: "Spider drinking an apple cider" and…Oh?'

First, Xolisa teaches the children the transcription of the words in the song from spoken to written language. She languages in both isiXhosa and English to introduce the song. It could be argued that she languages deliberately to facilitate meaning making. She introduces a line or two at the beginning as can be seen in line 4 and in lines 6 and 7, where she says out loud each word as she writes it down as the children watch. The children get a chance to hear the word, then see it written. This is different from getting children to learn words off by heart. Instead, Xolisa gets the children to hear and visualise the word to help them to remember the song. As much as immersion is one approach to teaching English, Xolisa takes the route to language bilingually as an alternative approach for teaching an additional language. The reason for doing so could be that conditions for language learning in a township setting where language learners are majority isiXhosa speakers are different from conditions where English language learners are a minority and are also expected to assimilate. The children pay attention and help Xolisa by adding words that follow from the phrases sung and say them one by one as Xolisa writes as can be seen in line 8, 10 and 13. The children know what words follow because Xolisa has told them what the full line before. We see this in lines 3-10 where Xolisa says, "down by the bay", neh? [hey?] (Writes a line on the whiteboard) Down_ by..? By the?" The children respond by saying "bay" and Xolisa repeats "by the bay. Where the watermelons grow nhe? Where…" The children add 'waterm…' in line 10. Because writing is slower than speaking, Xolisa says words aloud so the children keep up with her. This way, children are not only included and participating in the writing of the song but also focus on the look of each word and develop sight vocabulary. They also notice spaces between words as Xolisa writes. This is very important for reading because it is not enough for children to be able to say words and not know how they look. This is important for schools struggling to print out materials for reading, but also more interactive compared to when a teacher writes quietly on the board and the children start to make noise, which often gets them into trouble. Hendricks and Xeketwana (2024) argue that there are shifts in English First Additional Language Teaching (EFAL), about translanguaging in both presentational talk and exploratory talk and use of translanguaging resources in additional language learning. Makalela (2015) argues that when multiple languages are used to access same content, this facilitates deeper access and understanding. Also, in emergent literacy development, the practice of writing with children with them telling the scribe what to write and the scribe thinking aloud as she writes is a well-established practice of teaching writing more explicitly through demonstration.

## Using Overt Instruction of Multiliteracies Framework to Teach Vocabulary

The second thing that Xolisa teaches explicitly through shared writing of the song is vocabulary. The song is in English and she checks if children know a watermelon by asking for isiXhosa equivalent of watermelon. In line 20, Lwando mentions a form of a melon, different from a watermelon which is often cooked like pumpkin as he says 'ntyabontyi'. His response is very close because ntyabontyi is a melon and looks like watermelon on the outside. In lines 21-24 Xolisa gives feedback and agrees with the child that it looks like watermelon when she says, "Uthi yintyabontyi [He says it is intyabontyi, a melon]. Ewe iyafana nentyabontyi iwatermelon, qha ayontyabontyi yona i…iba sisidudu yona [Yes, watermelon does look like intyabontyi, this melon…is like porridge]. Ihamba ibe yipapa neh [Ntyabontyi is like porridge, nhe]? Kodwa yona iwatermelon yifruit andithi? [But watermelon is fruit, not so?]". By distinguishing that intyabontyi is a melon that looks porridge-like when cooked and watermelon as fruit, Xolisa is giving direct instruction. She is intervening and mediating knowledge instead of leaving it as it is, so that children's understanding and awareness of the different melons grows. She further explains that it is edible in lines 26-35 when she asks if it looks like watermelon, and adds "Siyayitya [it is edible, we eat it]. So zibufana ngaphandle [They look alike when you look at them from the outside]. Unyanisile [You are right]." However, because Lwando referred to another form of melon, Xolisa still wants to know what watermelon is called in isiXhosa. She asks the children what it is called, "kodwa ke iwatermelon siyibiza ukuba yintoni kanene? [But what do we call watermelon in Xhosa]. Ngegama eli-bolekiweyo [in a borrowed word]. Sithi yivatala [we call it ivatala]. Nikhe nilive elo gama? [Have you ever heard of such a word?] (Addresses a child) Ubuyazi? [Did you know?] Ngubani obesithi…Ubuyazi neh? [Who said...did you know it nhe?]". Xolisa then gives the Xhosa equivalent of watermelon as ivatala. She tells them it is a borrowed word, meaning that it is not an original isiXhosa word. But she also misses asking or telling them from which language the word is borrowed. As has been argued above, in the overt instruction aspect of the multiliteracies framework, teachers or facilitators have a role of explicitly teaching knowledge, in this case vocabulary to the children through discussion of words and offering equivalent meanings in another language.

## Using Overt Instruction of the Multiliteracies Framework to Teach Poetic Devices such as Repetition and Rhyme

Another thing that Xolisa does as she writes the song, in addition to saying and writing each word is repeating saying the phrases and the words. After writing the line of the song, she rereads it and sings it. She repeats singing the line also checking if she got everything thing correct in writing it down. In the data extract above, in line 42, 43 and 44 she repeats watermelon and grow. Thus we see Xolisa thinking aloud, saying the words over and over again while singing them as she continues in lines 48, 49, 53 and 54. Xolisa uses think alouds, repetition and rereading to reinforce the song and to check if her rhyming is in order, especially in "go" and "go" and "play" and "say" as we can see in lines 47, 50, 51 and 52 . She says, "Like to go (continues to write on the whiteboard) and _ when _ we go…when we go we _ like to play. Yhu this is (indistinct) You don't have a…you don't have that thing? We like to play and when we play we like to…and when we play…sorry. when we play…when we play _ we like to say…whu! I got it messed up (continues to write). She says, "We like to say _ have you ever seen... (a child walks up to her and hands her something) Um we'll add that as we sing. Ok. (Gestures to the board) Down by the bay…Let's read." She then points to the board to get children to start singing the song from the beginning. Repetition here ensures that the children read silently, fluently and following Xolisa as she reads aloud. In Extract 2.1 Xolisa continues with the transcription.

## *Figure 2. Transcription of Down by the Bay*

ADULT: Cat and hat.
CHILD: A cat.
XOLISA: (Begins to write on the board) A "cat" and "hat".
Niyawabona?[Do you see them?]
Ayafana pha la magama at the end? [That these words are the same at the end?
"Cat" "Hat". "Spider" "cider".
CHILD: Dog.
XOLISA: "Dog" "log". (Points to the board)
CHILDREN: "House" "mouse"
XOLISA: Ya we have to think of words like that neh . Ikhona eniyaziyo? [are there other words you know?]
CHILDREN: [No immediate verbal response]
XOLISA: I've got one last one.
"Snail delivering mail".
Hah!
Have you ever seen a snail delivering a mail? [An adult laughs]
CHILDREN & XOLISA: Down by the bay where the watermelons grow
that's where my friends we like to go.
And when we play we like to say did you ever see…
XOLISA: A cat wearing a hat.
Maybe you can say that:
"a cat wearing a hat" or some…
let's see if we can say…
"Have you ever seen a spider
drinking an apple cider?"
[Some laughter from the adults]
XOLISA: Have you ever seen…
have you ever seen a spider_
drinking an apple cider?
That is so funny, you know?
Ok it goes like this…
♫ Down by the bay where the watermelons grow (Some children join in the signing)
that's where my friends we like to go.
And when we play we like to say…
"have you ever seen a cat
wearing a hat
down by the bay." ♫
CHILDREN AND XOLISA: ♫Down by the bay where the watermelons grow that's where my friends
they like to go…we like to say.
And when we play we like to say…♫
CHILDREN: ♫Did you ever see…
CHILDREN AND XOLISA: ♫A spider drinking an apple cider,
down by the bay.
Down by the bay where the watermelons grow
that's where my friends they like to go♫
CHILDREN: ♫And when we play…
XOLISA: Grow. Ok.
Where the watermelons grow.
That's where my friends…
that's where…mhm. ♫
Down by the bay,
CHILDREN & XOLISA: Down by the bay where the watermelons grow
that's where my friends we like to go.
And when we play we like to say did you ever see…
XOLISA: A cat wearing a hat.
Maybe you can say that:
"a cat wearing a hat" or some…
let's see if we can say…
"Have you ever seen a spider
drinking an apple cider?"
[Some laughter from the adults]
CHILDREN & XOLISA: Down by the bay where the watermelons grow
that's where my friends we like to go.
And when we play we like to say did you ever see…
XOLISA: A cat wearing a hat.
Maybe you can say that:
"a cat wearing a hat" or some…
let's see if we can say…
"Have you ever seen a spider
drinking an apple cider?"
[Some laughter from the adults]
XOLISA: Have you ever seen…
have you ever seen a spider_
drinking an apple cider?
That is so funny, you know?
Ok it goes like this…
♫ Down by the bay where the watermelons grow (Some children join in the signing)
that's where my friends we like to go.
And when we play we like to say…
"have you ever seen a cat
wearing a hat
down by the bay." ♫

In at the end of extract 1, line 59 we see a child introducing a cat and an adult facilitator introducing hat in extract 2.1 in line 61 while Xolisa was thinking of a spider and apple cider in line 60. As the transcript in extract 2.1 continues, Xolisa rereads and sings the lines with the children and adds rhyming words, "cat and hat" in line 63; "spider and cider" in line 66; "dog and log" in line 68; "snail and mail" in lines while the children add "dog" in line 67 and "mouse and house" in line 68; The introduction of the rhyming words is implicit. Xolisa does not explain why they must be this way. But sometimes she explains that the end of the word must sound the same as we can see in line 65. She just sings the words, giving the children an opportunity to listen and hear the last sounds of the language. To show take-up of Xolisa's explanation, below a child in line 68 shows understanding by giving "house and mouse" as an example of rhyming words from those they have heard already. Xolisa does this until the child about line 197 in extract 2.2 below where the child says, "a dog brushing its teeth", when she notices that the child has not quite grasped what she is trying to do or is not focusing on the last sounds of the words.

*Figure 3.*

142. CHILDREN AND XOLISA: ♫Down by the bay where the watermelons grow that's where my friends they like to go…we like to say. And when we play we like to say…♫
143. CHILDREN: ♫Did you ever see…
144. CHILDREN AND XOLISA: ♫A spider drinking an apple cider, down by the bay.
145. Down by the bay where the watermelons grow that's where my friends they like to go♫
146. CHILDREN: ♫And when we play…
147. XOLISA: Grow. Ok.
148. Where the watermelons grow.
149. That's where my friends…
150. that's where…mhm. ♫
151. Down by the bay,
152. where the watermelons grow,
153. that's where my friends
154. we like to play,
155. and when we play
156. we like to say♫
157. Ok. Down by the bay
158. where the watermelons grow (begins to write on the whiteboard)
159. that's _ where _ my…
160. I have a very bad handwriting ke.
161. That's where my friends _ like to go
162. neh?
163. XOLISA: ♫That's where my friends (begins to write on the whiteboard)
164. we…we like to go ok? We_ Ok let's start again♫
165. CHILDREN: ♫Did you ever see…
166. CHILDREN AND XOLISA: ♫Down by the bay
167. where the watermelons grow
168. that's where my friends we like to go
169. and we when we play we like to say:
170. did you ever see a…♫
171. CHILDREN: A…a spider…
172. CHILD: A cat…
173. XOLISA: A mouse_
174. sitting in a house_
175. ♫down by the bay♫. We must think now of things to say neh? ♫
176. Down by the bay♫
177. CHILDREN AND XOLISA: ♫ (Clap their hands to the song)
178. Down by the bay
179. where the watermelons grow that's' where my friends
180. we like to go.
181. And when we play we like to say:
182. did you ever see…
183. CHILD: A mouse…
184. CHILD: A dog…
185. XOLISA: A dog chasing a log
186. ♫ down by the bay ♫
187. XOLISA & CHILDREN: ♫Down by the bay
188. where the watermelons grow
189. that's where my friends
190. we like to to say…
191. XOLISA: Yho! [Oops!)
192. XOLISA & CHILDREN: ♫And we say we play
193. we like to say:
194. did you ever see…
195. CHILD: A dog…
196. XOLISA: A what?
197. CHILD: A dog…the dog brushing its teeth.
198. XOLISA: It's teeth?
199. Eh but it must end like…
200. "a dog chasing a log."
201. You see: log and dog.
202. It must rhyme at the end.
203. You see house and mouse they rhyme.
204. So we have (begins to write on the whiteboard)
205. we have "mouse" and "house".
206. Niyawabona avakala ngokufanayo la magama at the end? [Do you see these words are the same at the end?]
207. And then we have "dog" and "log".
208. Then we have…

Xolisa then explains that the words must rhyme at the end in lines 200-202, "It's teeth? Eh but it must end like: 'a dog chasing a log.' You see: log and dog. It must rhyme at the end. You see house and mouse they rhyme. So, we have (begins to write on the whiteboard) we have "mouse" and "house". Niyawabona avakala ngokufanayo la magama at the end? [Do you see these words sound the same at the end?] And then we have "dog" and "log". Then we have…" Xolisa, also starts to explicitly explain that the words must rhyme. We read that she says, "Have you ever seen…" and the children say, "Did you ever see…" Thus, Xolisa uses an indirect way of correcting them, in the same way we correct babies when they are learning to talk, thus avoiding to overly correcting them as this might affect their confidence and in the end their learning. We can see she has uses both implicit and explicit methods teaching methods.

## Extending Vocabulary through the Kookaburra Gamesongs

I now turn to another song that was introduced to children. It is called kookaburra.

*Figure 4.*

**Kookaburra**

Kookaburra sits in the old gum tree,
Merry, merry king of the bush is he.
Laugh Kookaburra, laugh Kookaburra,
Gay your life must be!

Kookaburra sits in the old gum tree,
Eating all the gum drops he can see.
Stop Kookaburra, stop Kookaburra,
Leave some there for me.

Kookaburra sits in the old gum tree,
Counting all the monkeys he can see.
Stop Kookaburra, stop Kookaburra,
That's not a monkey, that's me.

The first stanza of Kookaburra song was written on the board in English and then sung with the children while pointing at the words as is done with Big Books for shared reading. Working within the multiliteracies framework and Jank's (2010) model for critical literacy (which suggests a pedagogy that works with dominance, access, diversity and transformative practice), part 1 of plan for the session was to introduce the song in writing, reading it with the children, singing it together, discussing and extending vocabulary and then letting children copy it down as part of the overt instruction aspect of the multiliteracies framework and access to English and diversity quadrants of Janks' model. Part 2 of the plan was to focus on the critical framing aspect of multiliteracies and dominance quadrant of the Jank's model for critical literacy to interrogate the dominance of foreign English songs in South African schooling and community work, thus surface coloniality of knowledge.

Part three was focused on both the situated practice aspects of the multiliteracies framework and the transformative practice of the framework or redesign aspect of Janks' model. The table below summarises the plan using the two frameworks.

*Table 2.*

| Multiliteracies Framework | | Janks' Model of Critical Literacy | |
|---|---|---|---|
| **Situate Practice**<br>Discussing familiar birds that we could use to replace the Kookaburra | **Overt Instruction (part 1)**<br>Write the song on the board<br><br>Read it out loud with the children<br>Sing it together<br>Discuss vocabulary | **Dominance (part 2)**<br>Questioning the dominance of foreign texts, including songs in literacy | **Access (part 1)**<br>Write the song on the board<br><br>Read it out loud with the children<br><br>Sing it together<br><br>Discuss vocabulary |
| **Critical framing (part 2)**<br>Questioning the dominance of foreign texts, including songs in literacy | **Transformative practice**<br>Changing the Kookuburra into a familiar bird through art | **Diversity (part 1)**<br>Making use of children's linguistic repertoires in discussion and in writing on the board. | **Redesign**<br>Changing the Kookuburra into a familiar bird through art |

## Kookaburra Song on the Board and Vocabulary Extension

*Figure 5. Kookaburra: vocabulary extension*

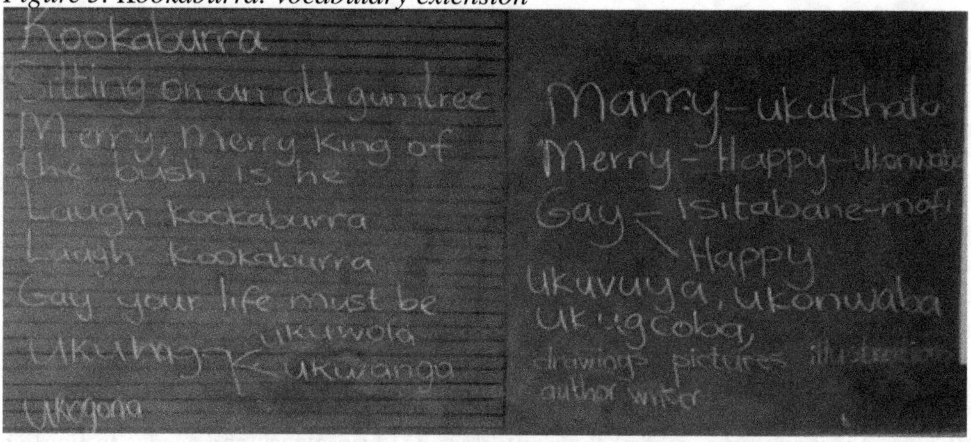


The image above presents the kookaburra song as it was written on the left side of board. This is not the full song but the first stanza of the song. On the right side are the vocabulary words that were discussed with the children. Upon being asked what the meaning of merry is, a child has responded that it is 'ukutshata'. This then prompted me to write *marry -ukutshata* on top to show and tell that the word 'marry' means something else and then wrote *merry-happy* in white to distinguish it from marry on above it. We then discussed what the meaning of 'happy' is in isiXhosa upon which the children said it is *ukonwaba.* I also looked into the song to see if there was another word that also means happy or merry and I wrote down gay. I asked the children what the word gay means and they responded in unison to say it means *isitabane*, a queer person as they are referred to in isiXhosa, though this word is seen as derogatory. I then asked what other word is used to refer to gays and they responded by saying *imofi* for moffie. Facilitors felt that we should explain that it refers to people of the same sex who are in a love relationship. Then we moved onto the meaning gay in the context of the song and an adult facilitator responded by saying *ukuvuya and next to ukuvuya I wrote ukonwaba* again to show children that happy, gay and merry mean the same thing. Then I asked the children if we have another word for ukonwaba and ukuvuya and they did not know. An adult facilitator gave ukugcoba as a synonym to ukuvuya, and ukonwaba. This way we ended up with three words that mean the same thing in both English and isiXhosa. To emphasize the idea of words that mean the same thing, we then asked the children to give us random words. One child said ukuhaga (to hug). I then asked what other words mean ukuhaga and the children came up with ukwanga and adults added ukuwola while another child gave the word ukugona, as can be seen on the left side of the board.

In writing, reading and discussing the song, we applied the overt aspect of the framework, which allowed us to introduce more explicitly writing, reading, singing and discussion of vocabulary with the children, thus teaching all the skills of listening and speaking, reading and writing simultaneously rather than in silos. Secondly, the activity above shows that songs are inexpensive texts that can be written on the board and copied into notebooks and are accessible even in under-resourced environments. They are also easy to type and copied and inserted into children's flip files. Thirdly, scholars who critique biliteracy development in favour of teaching languages in silos often argue that multilingual pedagogies only pay attention to mixing languages, and that this is risky as they fear that learners will never be able to separate their languages, insinuating that bi/multilingual people are never able to separate their languages. Delpit (1988) and Janks (2010) have also cautioned against denying already marginalized students access to valued forms of language as this would constitute another form of oppression against them. Furthermore, monolingually oriented scholars fear that monolingual pedagogies often focus on the oral and never pay attention to the written word. However, as can be seen from the song and vocabulary discussion about, written language is being paid attention to, and learners are given access to the valued forms of languages for both languages.

Finally, the discussion of vocabulary in both languages has enriched the children's vocabulary in both languages. A hybrid repertoire has been capitalized upon to ensure that the children's meaning is deepened and has also ensured that diversity in the pedagogy is recognized. For example, the use of the word isitabane and imofi as well as the use of the word ukuhaga and and ukwanga shows us that the children have access to diverse forms of languaging. While non-standard varieties of languages such imofi and ukuhaga have been used, the children have also been exposed to standard forms of languaging without them being told that they speak a wrong variety and that there is a better, more valued variety that they need to learn.

## Redesigning the Kookabura Bird as Criticality

After the discussion of vocabulary, the children were also told that kookaburra is an Australian bird and were challenged to think about why we use foreign birds when we have lots of birds in SA. They were asked to list some of the birds we have in the country. The blue crane was amongst these birds as it is known as Indwe and is a national bird in South Africa. A facilitator mentioned that in the Eastern Cape there is a small town called Indwe, and a hotel she knows is called The Blue Crane Hotel named after this bird. The children were then asked to choose one bird out of the list the gave that they could use to transform the kookaburra bird; to localize it and the children chose the blue crane. They were then asked to make the bird either through drawings or collages and were provided with crayons and colour chapter as a silhouette of the bird to help them create the bird.

*Figure 6. Children drawing and making collages of South African birds*

In the top left and top right images, we see a draft and final image of the blue crane bird drawn by a child to transform the kookaburra into a local and national bird. In the bottom left and right images, we see children working collaboratively to design the South African birds through collages. Here they use materials such as large flipchart chapter, colour printing chapter and newschapter chapters to design their collages. Working with the artist facilitator Nandipha, who provided them with a template, the children designed their birds and used various colours, according to their interests to decorate the bird. The transformative aspect of the activity is that it engages children in artistic and creative activities, thus expanding childrens' modes of representation. As opposed to the real Kookaburra bird with black and white features, the children use pages given to them to give the bird colour. Red, yellow, green, blue and black became prominent colours. The children took the idea of blue in blue crane to add that colour but also used their creativity and imagination to create colourful birds in groups.

The significance of choosing the national bird Indwe/Blue Crane could be that it is a bird that all of the children know because in Grade R and Grade 2 children also learn about the National bird on the South African Coat of arms along with the national flag and other national symbols. There is also teacher handbook titled *Cranes in the classroom series: Teacher's handbook for grade 5* written by Anne Burke from the KwaZulu Natal Crane Foundation, and this also suggests that the topic about birds is picked up again in grade 5. It could also be that the children wanted to show patriotism and nationalism to counteract further coloniality in using foreign birds. Working creatively in creating the birds also makes the song memorable and deepens understanding of the song. Singing in a language one is not fully proficient in can make for difficult interpretation of lyrics if the children never see the lyrics in the song or what is being sung but if the children create it, they not only visualize but also this makes for a holistic sense making. Shredding pieces of paper and sticking them in the collage or in drawing the bird also develops children's fine motor skills, hand eye coordination and becomes a hands-on activity that has a potential to help them make connections between what they are learning and their experience. It improves children's participation and engagement in the activity and working in groups in doing this activity brings each child's interpretation of how the bird should look. Using their eyes and hands also creates stronger connections in the brain. Below we see the different interpretations of the bird and displaying these birds on the board to be seen by everyone and commented on, giving the children a sense of achievement and shows their artistic competence.

*Figure 7. Final designs of South African birds as alternatives to the Kookaburra*

The display of the children's arts also highlights children's visual literacies. Performative art in the singing of songs and visual literacies in the form of drawings and collages is hardly developed in formal classrooms and is rarely assessed in national or international assessments. The reading assessments with focus mainly on decoding merely assess one aspect of being literate and are therefore not full reflection of what children are capable of doing.

## CONCLUSION

In this chapter I have argued that using songs has affordances language and literacy pedagogy. The affordances include the fact that songs offer an entry into learning poetry as songs also have literary devices that poems have such as rhyme, rhythm, repetition, and alliteration. I have also demonstrated that songs have meanings through an expanded discussion of vocabulary. By bringing the gamesongs into literacy instruction and engaging learners in overt instruction about South African birds and vocabulary, I have demonstrated how to capitalise on gamesongs both implicitly and explicitly to show how songs can be used productively to enhance children's meaning making and developing children's critical, multilingual and multimodal literacies. Secondly, I have also shown how to challenge and disrupt monolingual and monomodal approaches language and literacy learning by drawing on children's multimodal and multilingual meaning making resources. I have shown that viewing language and literacy learning multimodally has the potential to redesign pedagogy in the classroom to include multimodal and multilingual literacy events. Through these events, I have broadened and enriched children's making beyond just focusing on comprehension (DBE, 2019) that usually get formally assessed using rigid criteria. Through these approaches, I have positioned children as competent bilinguals and designers of meaning. Engaging children in redesign activities helped to bring to the fore children's sociocultural resources that are devalued, ignored and unacknowledged in formal schooling. I have argued and demonstrated that, combining the use of a multilingual and a multimodal repertoire, enhances children's meaning making, gives children voice and positions them with competencies rather than deficiencies and also plays and immerses children in rich literacy experiences.

## REFERENCES


Abarry, A. (1989). The Role of Play Songs in the Moral, Social, and Emotional Development of African Children. *Research in African Literatures, 20*(2), 202–216.

Alexander, N., Bloch, C., Jogee, N., Guzula, X., & Mahobe, N. (2011). Creating literate school communities: Vulindlela reading clubs. *Praesa Early Literacy Unit* viewed 21 July 2025, from http://www.academia.edu/download/30382921/reading-club-concept-chapter.pdf

Aung, S. (2025). Creating multilingual spaces through arts-based methods in foundation phase classrooms. *Frontiers in Education, 10*, 1628614. DOI: 10.3389/feduc.2025.1628614

Barton, D. (2001). *Literacy. An introduction to the ecology of written language* (2nd ed.). Blackledge.

Bloch, C. (2002). A case study of Xhosa and English biliteracy in the foundation phases versus English as a "medium of destruction". *Perspectives in Education, 20*, 65–78.

Bock, Z. (2016). Multimodality, Creativity and Children's Meaning-Making: Drawings, Writings, Imaginings. *Stellenbosch Chapters in Linguistics Plus, 49*(0), 1–21. DOI: 10.5842/49-0-669

Busch, B. (2012). The linguistic repertoire revisited. *Applied Linguistics, 33*(5), 503–523. DOI: 10.1093/applin/ams056

Delpit, L. (1988). The silenced dialogue. Power and pedagogy in educating other people's children. *Harvard Educational Review, 58*(3), 280–299. Advance online publication. DOI: 10.17763/haer.58.3.c43481778r528qw4

Flores, N., & García, O. (2013). Linguistic third spaces in education: Teacher's translanguaging across the bilingual continuum. In Little, D., Leung, C., & van Avermaet, P. (Eds.), *Managing Diversity in Educations: Languages, Policies and Pedagogies* (pp. 243–256). Multilingual Matters. DOI: 10.2307/jj.27080075.18

Flyvberg, B. (2001). *Making social science matter*. Cambridge University Press. DOI: 10.1017/CBO9780511810503

García, O., & Kleifgen, J. A. (2020). Translanguaging and literacies. *Reading Research Quarterly, 55*(4), 553–571. DOI: 10.1002/rrq.286

García, O., & Torres-Guevara, R. (2009). Monoglossic ideologies and language policies in the education of U.S. Latinas/os. In *Handbook of Latinos and Education: Theory, Research, and Practice* (pp. 182–193). Taylor and Francis.

Goodwin, A.P., &, Jiménez, R.T. (2021). The Science of Reading: Supports, Critiques, and Questions. *Reading Research Quarterly*, 56(S1) pp. S7–S22 | DOI: 10.1002/rrq.416

Guzula, X. (2021). 'Constructing a pedagogical third space with multilingual children: A case study of the bilingual Stars of Today Literacy Club# (STLC#)', PhD dissertation, University of Cape Town.

Guzula, X., & Molate, B. (2025). Community literacy club and family language policymaking initiatives for biliteracy development. *Reading and Writing*, *16*(1), a569. DOI: 10.4102/rw.v16i1.569

Harrop-Allin, S. (2014). " The Pen Talks My Story": South African Children's Multimodal Storytelling as Artistic Practice. In *Multimodal Approaches to Research and Pedagogy* (pp. 19-40). Routledge.

Heugh, K. (2015). Epistemologies in multilingual education: Translanguaging and genre – companions in conversation with policy and practice. *Language and Education*, *29*(3), 280–285. DOI: 10.1080/09500782.2014.994529

Higginbottom, G. M. A. (2004). Sampling issues in qualitative research. *Nurse Researcher*, *2*(1), 7–19. DOI: 10.7748/nr2004.07.12.1.7.c5927 PMID: 15493211

Hult, F., & Hornberger, N. (2016). Revisiting Orientations in Language Planning: Problem, Right, and Resource as an Analytical Heuristic. *Bilingual Review / La Revista Bilingüe, 33(3), 30-49.*

Janks, H (2004). The Access Paradox. *Literacy Learning: The Middle Years/English in Australia*, 12(139), 33–42.

Janks, H. (2010). *Literacy and power*. Taylor & Francis.

Jaspers, J., & Madsen, L. M. (2016). Sociolinguistics in a languagised world: Introduction. *Applied Linguistics Review*, *7*(3), 235–258. DOI: 10.1515/applirev-2016-0010

Jewitt, C., & Kress, G. (Eds.). (2003). *Multimodal Literacy*. Peter Lang.

Kiramba, L. K. (2018). Language ideologies and epistemic exclusion. *Language and Education*, *32*(4), 291–312. DOI: 10.1080/09500782.2018.1438469

Makalela, L. (2015). Translanguaging as a vehicle for epistemic access: Cases for reading comprehension and multilingual interactions. *Per Linguam: A Journal of Language Learning= Per Linguam. Tydskrif vir Taalaanleer, 31*(1), 15–29.

Makina, B. (2009). Rhythm, rhyme and songfulness: The role of Shona children's gamesongs in education. *Muziki, 6*(1), 49–57. DOI: 10.1080/18125980902931307

Makoe, P., & McKinney, C. (2014). Linguistic ideologies in multilingual South African suburban schools. *Journal of Multilingual and Multicultural Development, 35*(7), 658–673. DOI: 10.1080/01434632.2014.908889

McKinney, C. (2017). *Language and power in post-colonial schooling: Ideologies in practice*. Routledge.

Merriam, S. B. (1998). *Qualitative research and case study applications in education*. Jossey-Bass Publishers.

Miles, R. (2015). Complexity, representation and practice: Case study as method and methodology. *Issues in Educational Research, 25*(3), 309–318.

New London Group. (2000). A pedagogy of multiliteracies: Designing social futures. In Cope, B., & Kalantzis, M. (Eds.), *Multiliteracies: Literacy Learning and the Design of Social Futures* (pp. 9–37). Routledge.

Opland, J. (2018). *Xhosa Literature: Spoken and Printed Words* (Vol. 6). UKZN Press.

Ramugondo, E. L. (2012). Intergenerational play within family: The case for occupational consciousness? *Journal of Occupational Science, 19*(4), 326–340. DOI: 10.1080/14427591.2012.710166

Soja, E. (1996). *Thirdspace: Journeys to Los Angeles and Other Real-and-Imagined Places*. Blackwell.

Stein, P. (2008). *Multimodal pedagogies in diverse classrooms: Representation, rights and resources*. Routledge.

Vasquez, V. M. (2014). *Negotiating critical literacies with young children*. Routledge. DOI: 10.4324/9781315848624

## ENDNOTES

1 Stars of Today Literacy Club# (STLC#) was named by the children and the included the hashtag in the name, though in a wrong place to show their access

to digital media and awareness of social media communication. The name was accepted as it is

# Chapter 9
# Levelling Up Language Learning:
## Strategic Game Integration for Engaging and Effective Instruction

**Fortunate Madondo**
http://orcid.org/0000-0002-4549-7060
*University of Hertfordshire, UK*

**Thaddeus Mahoso**
*Botswana Open University, Botswana*

## ABSTRACT

*This chapter outlines research-informed strategies for integrating game-based learning into language instruction. Informed by constructivist, self-determination, and cognitive load theories, it demonstrates how games can enhance motivation, engagement, and self-regulation. Drawing on a case study of ten participants in rural Mberengwa, it emphasises aligning game mechanics with instructional goals and incorporating culturally responsive elements, such as indigenous games. A framework is proposed for using both digital and non-digital games in diverse contexts, including low-resource settings, supported by the ADDIE model. The chapter also highlights the role of collaboration and competition in language development and offers guidance for teacher professional development.*

## INTRODUCTION

The integration of game-based strategies into language education has emerged as a transformative approach for enhancing learner engagement, motivation, and self-

DOI: 10.4018/979-8-3373-4322-8.ch009

regulation. Both digital and non-digital games create interactive environments that support language acquisition through contextualised practice, immediate feedback, and collaborative learning (Loizou & Olymbiou, 2024). As classrooms become increasingly diverse, educators are challenged to adopt methods that are inclusive and responsive to learners' cultural and linguistic backgrounds.

Despite the global rise of interest in game-based learning (GBL), its application in early childhood language curricula remains limited in sub-Saharan Africa, including Zimbabwe. While studies from high-income contexts demonstrate the effectiveness of digital games in promoting vocabulary development, reading comprehension, and communicative competence (Plass et al., 2015; Peterson, 2010), low-resource educational environments are underrepresented in the literature. Su, Cheng, and Lin's (2021) comparative review shows that most digital game-based language learning (DGBLL) research focuses on English and Chinese learners in technologically advanced settings, with little attention to African languages or rural schools.

In Zimbabwe, early childhood education faces persistent challenges, including inadequate funding, limited digital infrastructure, and a shortage of culturally relevant learning materials. These constraints hinder the adoption of innovative pedagogies such as GBL. Additionally, when games are used in teaching, they are often integrated in an ad hoc manner without alignment to curricular goals or instructional design principles. Joshi et al. (2025) note that educational game designers frequently struggle to align gameplay with learning objectives, an issue heightened in contexts where teachers have limited training in instructional design. This problem is compounded by the scarcity of professional development opportunities focused on digital or game-based pedagogies (Madondo & Tsikira, 2022).

Although indigenous games offer rich linguistic and cultural resources, they remain largely absent from formal language instruction (Loizou & Olymbiou, 2024). This disconnection between home-based play and school-based learning reflects broader curricular misalignment and missed opportunities for culturally responsive pedagogy. As Ladson-Billings (1995) and Gay (2010) argue, culturally grounded teaching is essential for learner engagement and identity affirmation, yet such approaches are seldom embedded in Zimbabwe's early years language curricula.

This chapter responds to these gaps by offering practical, evidence-based recommendations for integrating games into language curricula and instructional design. With a particular focus on reading development and language acquisition in resource-constrained settings, it draws on global research, theoretical frameworks, and illustrative case studies to equip educators with strategies that are pedagogically sound, culturally relevant, and contextually appropriate.

In summary, the introduction has outlined the central focus of this chapter and highlighted the growing interest in innovative, engaging approaches to language learning. Having set the scene and clarified the purpose of the discussion, the next section on Rationale and Relevance of Game-based Learning explores why game-based approaches matter, and how they offer pedagogical value across diverse educational contexts.

## RATIONALE AND RELEVANCE OF GAME-BASED LEARNING

Game based learning (GBL) and gamification have gained prominence in educational research because of their potential to enhance learner engagement, motivation, and self-regulation. GBL uses the motivational and interactive features of games to create immersive learning experiences, while gamification refers to the application of game elements in non-game settings (Deterding et al., 2011). Studies have shown that gamification can improve cognitive, motivational, and behavioural learning outcomes (Poliani et al., 2023; Gini et al., 2025). In language education, games have been found to support vocabulary development, reading comprehension, and communicative competence, particularly when they reflect learners' cultural backgrounds and interests.

Empirical evidence also supports the use of gamification to influence behavioural change. Research by Mogavi et al. (2022) and Bassanelli et al. (2022) demonstrates that replicating the experiences users encounter in video games can lead to meaningful changes in behaviour, such as increased physical activity, stronger engagement in educational platforms, improved adherence to health routines, and participation in environmentally sustainable practices. A meta-analysis by Kim and Castelli (2021) reported a statistically significant moderate effect size of 0.48 (Cohen's d) for gamified educational interventions, with short term interventions producing much stronger effects ($d = 1.57$) than long term ones ($d = 0.30$). Similarly, Li et al. (2023), in a meta-analysis of over 5,000 participants, found a large overall effect size of 0.822, indicating substantial gains in motivation and learning. Aschentrup et al. (2024) further confirmed these benefits in the context of health and wellbeing.

Despite these positive outcomes, gamification also presents limitations. One concern is its emphasis on extrinsic motivation, which may diminish intrinsic interest in learning over time (Tegon, 2024). When rewards drive engagement, learners may disengage once those rewards are removed. Poorly designed gamification strategies can also result in cognitive overload, frustration, or loss of motivation, particularly when game elements do not align with learning objectives or user needs (Kim and Castelli, 2021). There is also the risk of inequity, as students differ in how they respond to gamified environments. Learners with limited digital literacy or restricted access to technology may find such designs challenging or exclusionary.

Another challenge relates to the novelty effect, which may reduce the long-term impact of gamification. While short term interventions often yield strong results, it is more difficult to sustain motivation and learning gains over extended periods (Li et al., 2023). Furthermore, critics argue that gamification may sometimes oversimplify serious learning content, particularly in higher education or professional training where depth, analysis, and critical thinking are essential.

Overall, although gamification and GBL provide innovative approaches for promoting behavioural change and enhancing learning, their success depends on thoughtful design, contextual appropriateness, and continuous evaluation. Educators and designers must avoid over reliance on game mechanics and ensure that pedagogical principles and learner diversity remain central to instructional decisions.

The current chapter aligns with the broader aims of the book by offering educators, parents, and researchers a framework for integrating games into language instruction. It emphasises contextual relevance, particularly in under resourced communities, and highlights the potential of indigenous games to support culturally responsive and meaningful learning. The next section outlines the objectives of the chapter, providing a focused framework for the discussions that follow.

## OBJECTIVES OF THE CHAPTER

This chapter provides evidence-based strategies for integrating games into language curricula, showing how these approaches can enhance learner motivation, engagement, and self-regulation. It also examines culturally responsive methodologies, including the use of indigenous games, to promote relevance and inclusivity across diverse learning environments. In addition, the chapter outlines instructional design models that support effective game-based language learning, offering educators a clear framework for implementation. By equipping teachers with practical tools and adaptable techniques, the chapter supports the use of game-based strategies in both varied and resource limited educational settings. Having outlined the chapter's objectives, the discussion now turns to the theoretical framework that supports and explains the pedagogical value of game-based learning.

## THEORETICAL FRAMEWORK UNDERPINNING GAME-BASED LEARNING

The integration of games into language curricula is supported by several foundational learning theories that collectively explain how game-based learning (GBL) can enhance language acquisition, learner engagement, and instructional design. These include Constructivist Learning Theory, Self Determination Theory (SDT), Cognitive Load Theory, and Sociocultural Theory. Each theory contributes unique insights into the mechanisms through which well-designed games support learning. The following sections discuss these perspectives in detail.

## Constructivist Learning Theory

Constructivist learning theory posits that learners actively construct knowledge through interaction with their environment (Piaget, 1952; Vygotsky, 1978). In language learning, this perspective supports the use of games as experiential tools that provide meaningful, contextualised opportunities for language practice. Games allow learners to experiment with language, receive immediate feedback, and refine understanding through trial and error. This aligns with Vygotsky's emphasis on the social nature of learning and the importance of guided participation within the zone of proximal development (Vygotsky, 1978).

Despite its importance, constructivist theory has been criticised for encouraging fragmented knowledge construction when learners receive insufficient scaffolding (Phillips, 1995). Without clear guidance, learners may develop misconceptions or fail to meet curricular goals, particularly in foundational areas such as early language learning. Constructivist approaches also assume a degree of learner autonomy and metacognitive skill that young children or learners with limited prior knowledge may not yet possess (Fox, 2001). In this context, games must be carefully aligned with linguistic objectives and provide appropriate support to prevent misconceptions and ensure progress (Liu and Matthews, 2005).

Research demonstrates that constructivist aligned activities, including role playing and simulation games, promote deeper cognitive engagement and support the internalisation of linguistic structures (Jonassen & Rohrer-Murphy, 1999). For example, digital storytelling games have been found to improve narrative ability and vocabulary retention due to their immersive and interactive nature.

## Self Determination Theory

Self Determination Theory (SDT), developed by Deci and Ryan (1985), suggests that intrinsic motivation arises when learners experience autonomy, competence, and relatedness. In language learning, SDT has been used to explain why learners persist and succeed when their psychological needs are supported.

Digital games can satisfy these needs in several ways (Deci and Ryan, 1985):

a. Autonomy: Games provide meaningful choices, such as selecting tasks or dialogue options, which fosters a sense of control.
b. Competence: Games include structured challenges and immediate feedback that allow learners to experience mastery.

c. Relatedness: Collaborative and multiplayer games encourage social interaction and build feelings of community.

A study by Reinders and Wattana (2015) found that Thai university students learning English through online role-playing games reported higher motivation and greater willingness to communicate than peers in traditional classrooms. The game environment offered a low stress context that encouraged risk taking and authentic communication.

However, the effectiveness of GBL within the SDT framework depends on thoughtful pedagogical design. Poorly aligned games can cause frustration or disengagement, weakening rather than strengthening motivation (Adipat, Laksana, Busayanon, Asawasowan and Adipat, 2021). Learner characteristics such as age, previous gaming experience, preferences, and cultural attitudes also influence how well students respond to game-based tasks (Chanyoo, 2022). Some learners thrive in fast paced activities, while others may find them overwhelming.

Assessment within game-based environments presents further challenges because learning is often incidental and not easily captured through conventional methods (Ifenthaler et al., 2012). These issues highlight the need for flexible, learner centred, and well-structured game-based designs.

## Cognitive Load Theory

Cognitive Load Theory emphasises the limitations of working memory and the need for instructional materials that minimise unnecessary cognitive demands (Sweller, 1988). This theory is especially relevant in early childhood language learning, where cognitive capacities are still developing and vulnerable to overload. Poorly designed games can overwhelm learners, hindering comprehension and retention (Chanyoo, 2022).

Thoughtfully structured educational games can reduce extraneous cognitive load by embedding linguistic tasks in intuitive and visually rich contexts. Elements such as visual cues, immediate feedback, and scaffolded challenges allow learners to focus on essential language features. The repetitive and exploratory nature of gameplay also supports the gradual automation of foundational skills, freeing cognitive resources for more complex language tasks (Sweller, 1988). Nevertheless, not all games are appropriate for young children, and those with overly complex interfaces can still impose unnecessary cognitive demands. Effective game-based learning therefore requires age-appropriate design and clear alignment with pedagogical goals.

## Sociocultural Theory

Sociocultural Theory, based on Vygotsky (1978), highlights the importance of social interaction and cultural context in language development. Language learning is understood as a socially mediated process involving collaboration, scaffolding, and guided participation. Because young children acquire language through social engagement and shared activities, games provide an ideal medium for supporting these processes (Zhou, 2024). Game based tasks naturally encourage turn taking, negotiation, and joint problem solving, all of which are central to early language development.

In multilingual and multicultural contexts, games can also bridge home and school languages, support inclusivity and validate diverse linguistic backgrounds (Hennig and Kirova, 2012; Gay, 2010; Ladson Billings, 1995). Indigenous games provide culturally grounded, familiar learning environments that enhance engagement and affirm learners' identities (Mphahlele and Mammen, 2022).

## Linking Theory to Context: Rural Mberengwa

To connect these theoretical perspectives to real educational environments, the next section examines early childhood language learning and game-based pedagogy in rural Mberengwa, Zimbabwe. This context is characterised by linguistic diversity, rich indigenous knowledge systems, and limited technological infrastructure. Children grow up immersed in oral traditions, community-based learning, and multilingual practices that shape their communicative development.

Traditional and indigenous games, widely played in community settings, offer low cost, socially engaging formats that align with early childhood pedagogies centred on play and exploration. By analysing this setting, the chapter highlights both the opportunities and constraints of implementing game-based learning in resource limited but culturally rich environments. This contextual lens deepens understanding of how theoretical principles translate into practice and underscores the importance of culturally responsive approaches to early childhood language education.

In summary, this section examined the key theoretical frameworks that underpin game-based learning, outlining how constructivist, self-determination, cognitive, and socio-cultural perspectives collectively inform the chapter's conceptual foundation. By clarifying the theories that shape the understanding and application of game-based approaches, it sets the stage for a more grounded interpretation of the findings that follow. The next section now turns to the research methodology, detailing the approaches, participants, and procedures used to investigate game-based learning within the study.

## METHODOLOGY

The study employed a qualitative case study design situated within the interpretivist paradigm to accommodate the diversity of participant perspectives. A case study approach was chosen because it allows for the in-depth exploration of complex social phenomena within real life contexts (Yin, 2018). This design enabled a detailed understanding of how early childhood educators and parents in Mberengwa perceive and implement game-based learning in language instruction.

A purposive sampling strategy was used to select information rich participants who were directly involved in early childhood education. The sample consisted of five early childhood educators from local preschools and five parents of early childhood learners who participated in a focus group discussion. Purposive sampling ensured that participants possessed relevant experience and insight into the use of games in language learning (Palinkas et al., 2015).

Two qualitative data collection methods were used: semi structured interviews with educators, each lasting approximately thirty minutes, and a thirty-minute focus group discussion with parents. Semi structured interviews enabled the researcher to probe responses while also giving participants the opportunity to request clarification when needed. The focus group discussion allowed parents to discuss, verify, and refine one another's contributions, thereby enhancing the accuracy and credibility of the data (Creswell and Poth, 2018).

Ethical approval was obtained from the relevant local education authorities. Ethical procedures included obtaining informed consent from all participants, maintaining confidentiality through anonymization of data, informing participants of their right to withdraw at any time without penalty, and securing all collected data for research purposes only. These measures align with the principles outlined by the British Educational Research Association (BERA, 2018).

Data from the interviews and focus group were analysed using thematic analysis, following the six-phase framework proposed by Braun and Clarke (2006). The phases included familiarization with the data, generating initial codes, searching for themes, reviewing themes, defining and naming themes, and producing the report. This approach enabled the identification of recurring patterns and insights related to the integration of games into language instruction.

In summary, the previous section outlined the research methodology, detailing the approaches, procedures, and rationale that guided the study. The following section now presents the research findings and offers a discussion of their significance in relation to the study's aims and existing literature.

## FINDINGS AND DISCUSSIONS

Drawing on qualitative data obtained through interviews with early childhood educators and a focus group discussion with parents, this section presents and discusses the key findings of a study that explored the integration of game-based learning into early childhood language instruction in rural Mberengwa. The discussion is organized around six major themes that emerged from the data: the frequency and types of games used, curriculum integration and bilingual learning, challenges related to resources, class size, and teacher training, learner engagement and outcomes, assessment practices, and parental involvement in home-based language learning. The following section begins by examining the frequency with which participants engaged in game-based activities, followed by an analysis of the types of games they reported using. This provides an essential foundation for understanding their overall patterns of engagement and sets the context for interpreting the subsequent findings.

### Frequency and Type of Game use

The consistent use of games by all five educators in Mberengwa reflects a growing recognition of their pedagogical value, even in resource-constrained settings. The types of games used storytelling, phonics board games, role-play, and songs align with research emphasizing the importance of multimodal and interactive learning in early childhood (Bodrova & Leong, 2007; Hirsh-Pasek et al., 2009). These games support language acquisition by engaging children in meaningful, context-rich interactions that promote vocabulary development and syntactic awareness. However, the limited use of digital games due to infrastructural challenges highlights the scarcity of a digital divide that continues to compromise rural education (UNESCO, 2022). This underscores the need for low-tech or no-tech alternatives that are equally effective in promoting language skills.

In summary, the analysis shows that participants engaged with games regularly, with most reporting frequent use across the week. The games they used varied widely, ranging from digital educational games to traditional play-based activities, reflecting diverse preferences and purposes in their learning contexts. The next section examines how these games are integrated into the curriculum and explores their role in supporting bilingual learning, offering further insight into how game-based activities contribute to children's broader educational experiences.

### Curriculum Integration and Bilingual Learning

Educators' efforts to integrate games with weekly curriculum themes, demonstrate an understanding of the need for coherence between play and instructional goals.

This practice is supported by research showing that thematic integration enhances mastery, retention and transfer of language skills (Nicolopoulou, 2010). The use of games to introduce Shona English bilingual vocabulary is particularly noteworthy, as it supports additive bilingualism and affirms learners' linguistic identities (Cummins, 2000). In multilingual contexts like Zimbabwe, integrating indigenous languages into instructional games can bridge the gap between home and school language environments, fostering both cognitive and cultural development (Heugh, 2011).

In summary, the current section explained that educators integrate games with weekly curriculum themes to create coherent learning experiences that support language development. Using games to teach Shona/English vocabulary promotes bilingualism and validates children's linguistic identities. In multilingual settings like Zimbabwe, incorporating indigenous languages into instructional games helps connect home and school languages while supporting both cognitive and cultural growth. The next section explores Learner Engagement and Outcomes, examining how these game-based approaches influenced children's participation, motivation, and overall learning progress.

## Learner Engagement and Outcomes

Educators unanimously reported high levels of learner engagement during game-based lessons, with observable improvements in vocabulary, pronunciation, and confidence. These outcomes are supported by studies showing that play-based learning enhances motivation, attention, and language fluency among early learners (Whitebread et al., 2012; Fisher et al., 2008). One educator's observation that shy learners become more active during games aligns with Vygotsky's (1978) theory that social interaction in play contexts can scaffold learners' self-expression.

In summary, learner engagement during game-based activities was strong overall, with educators noting positive language-related gains and increased participation, particularly among typically quieter children. The next section examines assessment practices, exploring how educators evaluated learning within these game-based and multilingual contexts.

## Assessment Practices

The reliance on informal assessment methods such as observation and verbal feedback is common in early childhood settings but may limit the ability to track progress systematically. Educators' interest in structured assessment tools reflects a broader shift toward evidence-based practice in early education (Snow & Van

Hemel, 2008). Developing simple, context-appropriate assessment frameworks for game-based learning could enhance instructional planning and learner support.

In summary, assessment practices in this context relied mainly on informal methods, and while these are common in early childhood settings, educators recognised the value of adopting more structured tools to better support planning and track learner progress. The next section explores Parental Involvement and Home-Based Learning, examining how families contribute to and extend children's learning beyond the classroom.

## Parental Involvement and Home-based Learning

Parents in Mberengwa reported using storytelling, singing, and naming games at home, often in both Shona and English. These practices are consistent with research showing that home literacy environments significantly influence early language development (Neuman & Celano, 2001). However, parents also expressed a desire for more structured guidance and collaboration with schools, suggesting a gap in home-school communication. Concerns about screen time and a preference for physical games reflect a nuanced understanding of the benefits and limitations of digital tools. This reinforces the value of culturally relevant, low-tech games that can be used in diverse home environments.

The empirical evidence from Mberengwa affirms the potential of game-based learning to enhance early language development, even in resource-limited settings. While infrastructural and pedagogical challenges persist, the commitment of educators and parents provides a strong foundation for innovation. By investing in training, materials, and community engagement, stakeholders can harness the power of play to create more equitable and effective language learning experiences for young children.

In summary, the section highlighted the important role that parents in Mberengwa play in supporting early language development through home-based activities such as storytelling, singing, and naming games in both Shona and English. These practices align with wider research demonstrating that rich home literacy environments significantly influence children's early language growth. Building on these insights into home practices and community engagement, the next section examines Instructional Design Models for Game-based Learning.

# INSTRUCTIONAL DESIGN MODELS FOR GAME-BASED LEARNING

Effective integration of games into language curricula requires a structured approach to instructional design. Instructional design models provide educators with frameworks to systematically plan, implement, and evaluate learning experiences. Among the most widely used models in educational settings are the ADDIE model, the SAM model, and Universal Design for Learning (UDL). This section explores how these models can be applied to game-based language instruction, particularly in diverse and resource-constrained contexts.

## The ADDIE Model

The ADDIE model comprising Analysis, Design, Development, Implementation, and Evaluation is a foundational framework in instructional design. It offers a systematic process for creating effective educational interventions, including game-based learning experiences.

a. Analysis

In this phase, educators assess learners' diverse needs, contextual constraints, and learning objectives. For example, in rural Mberengwa, analysis would involve identifying the linguistic challenges faced by learners, the availability of resources (e.g., electricity, materials), and the cultural context. This aligns with findings from the caregiver interviews, which highlight the need for low-tech, culturally relevant learning tools.

b. Design

This phase involves outlining the structure of the game-based intervention, including learning outcomes, content, and assessment strategies. Games should be designed to align with language learning goals such as vocabulary acquisition, grammar practice, or reading comprehension. The design should also consider motivational elements, such as rewards and feedback, to sustain learner engagement (Plass et al., 2015).

c. Development

Here, the actual game materials are created. This could include physical board games, card games, or digital applications. In low-resource settings, development might focus on repurposing traditional games or creating simple, printable materials that can be used without electricity.

d. Implementation

This phase involves delivering the game-based activities in the classroom or home environment. Teachers play a critical role in facilitating gameplay, guiding learners, and adapting activities based on learner responses. Implementation should be flexible to accommodate diverse learning disabilities and varying levels of access to technology and materials.

e. Evaluation

Finally, the effectiveness of the game-based intervention is assessed through both formative and summative methods. Educators can use observations, learner feedback, and performance data to refine the game and instructional approach. Continuous evaluation ensures that the intervention remains responsive to learners' diverse needs and contextual realities.

In summary, this discussion explored a structured framework that guide the development, implementation, and evaluation of educational games, ensuring they are pedagogically sound, culturally relevant, and responsive to learners' needs. By linking theory to practice, this model help educators design game-based activities that support meaningful learning across diverse and resource-constrained contexts. In the following section, we examine the core phases of Successive Approximation Model (SAM) and discuss how its flexible, learner-centred approach can support the creation of engaging and effective game-based learning experiences.

## The Successive Approximation Model (SAM) model

The SAM is an iterative alternative to ADDIE that emphasizes rapid prototyping and continuous feedback (Allen & Sites, 2012). SAM is particularly useful in dynamic educational environments where quick adjustments are necessary. In game-based learning, SAM allows educators to test game mechanics and content with learners early in the design process, making it easier to identify and address issues related to engagement, comprehension, or cultural relevance. For example, a language teacher might prototype a vocabulary card game and test it with a small group of students. Based on their responses, the teacher can refine the rules, adjust the difficulty level, or incorporate more culturally familiar terms. This iterative process ensures that the final product is both effective and engaging.

In summary, SAM offers a practical alternative to linear design processes by emphasising rapid prototyping, continuous feedback, and ongoing refinement. This makes it particularly well-suited for developing educational games, where ideas often need to be tested, adjusted, and improved through repeated cycles of design and play. The next section builds on the importance of designing inclusive and flexible game-based learning experiences by turning to Universal Design for Learning (UDL).

### Universal Design for Learning (UDL)

The UDL is a framework that promotes inclusive education by providing multiple means of engagement, representation, and expression (CAST, 2018). UDL is particularly relevant in multilingual and multicultural classrooms, where learners may have diverse linguistic backgrounds, learning styles, and abilities. In the context of game-based language instruction, UDL encourages the use of varied game formats (e.g., visual, auditory, kinaesthetic), differentiated content (e.g., multilingual instructions), and flexible assessment methods (e.g., oral responses, storytelling). For instance, a storytelling game might allow learners to express themselves through drawing, speaking, or writing, depending on their strengths and preferences. This flexibility not only supports language development but also fosters learner autonomy and confidence.

In summary, integrating elements from ADDIE, SAM, and UDL enables educators to design game-based learning experiences that are structured, iterative, and inclusive. This blended approach is particularly powerful in contexts such as Rural Mberengwa, where flexibility, cultural sensitivity, and pedagogical rigor are essential. By drawing on the complementary strengths of these models, teachers can create learning interventions that are both engaging and contextually responsive, effectively bridging theory and practice. The next section, Cultural Relevance and Indigenous Games, explores how locally grounded play traditions can enrich educational design and strengthen children's sense of identity and belonging.

## CULTURAL RELEVANCE AND INDIGENOUS GAMES

Culturally responsive pedagogy is essential in language education, particularly in multilingual and multicultural contexts. Integrating indigenous games into language curricula not only enhances learner engagement but also affirms cultural identity and promotes inclusivity. This section explores the pedagogical value of culturally relevant games, drawing on empirical data from Rural Mberengwa and supported by academic literature. We begin by examining the role of culture in language learning.

## The Role of Culture in Language Learning

Language and culture are inextricably linked. According to Kramsch (1993), language is a medium through which cultural meanings are constructed and conveyed. Therefore, effective language instruction must consider the cultural contexts in which learners are situated. Culturally relevant pedagogy, as articulated by Ladson-Billings (1995), emphasizes the importance of using learners' cultural knowledge, prior experiences, and performance styles to make learning more appropriate and effective. In a recent study, Moghadam and Barani (2025) concluded that language imperialism can negatively affect L1 acquisition by marginalising and threatening local languages, thereby necessitating community-driven language policies that revitalise and protect linguistic and cultural heritage. However, while these risks are significant, some scholars also argue that exposure to dominant global languages can provide learners with wider educational, economic, and intercultural opportunities (UNESCO, 2024), suggesting that the goal should not be resistance to global languages per se, but the creation of balanced, multilingual policies that value both local linguistic identity and global communication needs (King, 2025; Kato, 2024; SEAL, 2024).

Incorporating indigenous games into language instruction aligns with this pedagogical approach. These games often reflect local customs, values, and oral traditions, providing a familiar and meaningful context for language use. For example, traditional Shona games such as *nhodo* (a hand-eye coordination game using stones) or *tsoro* (a strategy board game) can be adapted to teach vocabulary, sequencing, and narrative skills (Madondo & Tsikira, 2022).

In summary, this section highlighted the close relationship between language and culture, showing that effective language learning must be rooted in learners' cultural experiences (Kramsch, 1993; Ladson-Billings, 1995). It discussed the tension between the risks of language imperialism where dominant languages may marginalise local ones and the potential benefits of global language exposure, including broader educational and intercultural opportunities (Moghadam & Barani, 2025; UNESCO, 2024; King, 2025; Kato, 2024; SEAL, 2024). The section concluded by noting that incorporating indigenous games, such as nhodo and tsoro, can support culturally meaningful language learning by embedding instruction in familiar local practices (Madondo & Tsikira, 2022). The next section turns to Empirical Evidence from Rural Mberengwa, illustrating how these cultural and pedagogical principles manifest in practice.

## Empirical Evidence from Rural Mberengwa

Caregiver interviews from Rural Mberengwa reveal a strong desire for educational tools that resonate with children's cultural backgrounds. Several caregivers emphasized the importance of storytelling, singing, and play in their daily routines, despite the challenges posed by energy poverty (See appendix A). These practices are deeply embedded in local traditions and offer a natural entry point for language learning. Thematic analysis further highlights the role of culturally grounded activities in supporting child development. For instance, caregivers reported using songs and oral narratives to teach moral lessons, reinforce routines, and entertain children during power outages (See appendix A). These findings suggest that indigenous games, which often incorporate music, rhythm, and storytelling, can serve as effective vehicles for language instruction in low-resource settings.

## Pedagogical Benefits of Indigenous games

Indigenous games offer several pedagogical advantages:

a. Contextualized Learning

Games rooted in local culture provide authentic contexts for language use, making learning more relevant and memorable (Gay, 2010).

b. Multimodal Engagement

Many traditional games involve movement, music, and visual elements, catering for learners' diverse learning styles and enhancing retention of learned content.

c. Social Interaction

Indigenous games are often communal, promoting collaboration, turn-taking, and oral communication which are the key components of language development (Vygotsky, 1978).

d. Cultural Affirmation

Using culturally familiar games validates learners' identities and fosters a positive attitude toward learning (Cummins, 2000).

## Designing Language Activities from Indigenous Games

To effectively integrate indigenous games into language curricula, educators must adapt them to align with specific learning objectives. For example:

- *Nhodo* can be used to teach counting, sequencing, and descriptive language by having learners narrate their moves or describe the stones.
- *Tsoro* can be adapted to include vocabulary challenges, where players must use a new word correctly before making a move.
- Storytelling games can be structured to practice narrative tenses, dialogue, and character development.

These adaptations should be co-developed with community members to ensure cultural accuracy and appropriateness. Involving caregivers and elders in the design process not only enriches the content but also strengthens school-community partnerships.

In summary, this section on Empirical Evidence from Rural Mberengwa highlighted how local educators, caregivers, and community members understand and enact early childhood development within a complex ecological context. It showed how children's learning experiences are shaped by interlocking socio-cultural, economic, and environmental realities, including extended family involvement, community norms, limited material resources, and the resilience practices common in rural livelihoods. The evidence demonstrated that early childhood development in Mberengwa is deeply relational, culturally embedded, and adaptive, revealing both the strengths that communities draw on and the structural constraints that continue to affect children's developmental outcomes. Building on this empirical foundation, the next section introduces Case Studies and Practical Applications that illustrate how these insights translate into real-world teaching, caregiving, and programme design.

## CASE STUDIES AND PRACTICAL APPLICATIONS

To illustrate the practical integration of game-based strategies into language instruction, this section presents case studies from diverse educational contexts. These examples demonstrate how both digital and non-digital games can be adapted to meet specific linguistic, cultural, and infrastructural needs. Drawing on empirical data from Rural Mberengwa and global research, the case studies highlight the flexibility and impact of game-based learning in enhancing language development.

## Case Study 1: Storytelling Games in Rural Mberengwa

In Rural Mberengwa, caregivers reported using oral storytelling as a central component of their daily routines with children (See Appendix A). These narratives often teach moral lessons, cultural references, and interactive elements such as songs and chants. Recognizing the educational potential of these practices, a local NGO collaborated with teachers to develop a series of storytelling card games designed to reinforce vocabulary and narrative structure.

Each card featured a culturally familiar character, setting, or event, prompting learners to construct stories using the target language. The game was implemented in after-school programmes and facilitated by community volunteers. Observations indicated increased learner participation, improved sentence construction, and greater confidence in oral expression. This case underscores the value of leveraging indigenous practices to create low-cost, high-impact language learning tools.

## Case Study 2: Vocabulary Bingo in Multilingual Classroom in Rural Mberengwa

In one of the participating multilingual classrooms in Rural Mberengwa, teachers introduced a non-digital game called "Vocabulary Bingo" to support English language acquisition among learners who spoke Shona or Ndebele at home. The game involved bingo cards with images and English words, and the teacher would call out definitions or use the words in sentences. Learners had to match the clues to the correct words on their cards.

This activity not only reinforced vocabulary but also encouraged listening comprehension and peer collaboration. Teachers reported that learners were more engaged during bingo sessions than during traditional vocabulary drills. The game was also easy to adapt for different themes, such as animals, food, or classroom objects, making it a versatile tool for language instruction.

## Case Study 3: Digital Role-playing in Urban ESL settings

In an urban ESL classroom in the United Kingdom, a secondary school teacher used a digital role-playing game (RPG) platform to enhance speaking and writing skills. Students created avatars and participated in a fantasy narrative where they had to negotiate, describe settings, and solve problems using English. The game included voice chat and text-based interactions, allowing learners to practise both oral and written communication.

According to the teacher's assessment, students demonstrated improved fluency, expanded vocabulary, and greater willingness to speak in class. The immersive nature of the RPG provided a safe space for language experimentation and reduced anxiety associated with public speaking. This case highlights the potential of digital games to create authentic communicative contexts that support language development. Bacalja (2022) suggests that digital game literacies not only address longstanding goals within English education but also introduce innovative approaches for helping students develop self-awareness and a deeper understanding of the world around them.

## Case Study 4: Grammar Relay in a Resource-constrained School in Rural Mberengwa

In one of the primary schools that participated in the study in Rural Mberengwa, teachers developed a physical game called "Grammar Relay" to teach parts of speech. Learners were divided into teams and given sentence strips with missing words. They had to run to a board, select the correct word from a pile, and complete the sentence. The game combined physical activity with grammar practice, making it particularly effective for kinaesthetic learners.

Despite the lack of digital resources, the game was highly successful in reinforcing grammatical concepts. Teachers noted increased retention and enthusiasm among learners, especially those who struggled with traditional instruction. This case demonstrates how creative, movement-based games can be used to teach complex language structures in low-tech environments. Rupere et al. (2013) highlight the importance of games in early childhood education, noting that they enhance concept recall and contribute positively to children's overall learning outcomes.

## Lessons Learned

Across these case studies, several key lessons emerge:

a. Context Matters

Games must be adapted to fit the cultural, linguistic, and infrastructural realities of learners.

b. Simplicity is Powerful

Even simple, low-tech games can have a significant impact on language learning outcomes.

c. Engagement Drives Learning

Games increase motivation and participation, which are critical for language acquisition.

d. Teacher Facilitation is Key

The role of the teacher in guiding, adapting, and assessing game-based activities is crucial to their success.

These practical applications provide a roadmap for educators seeking to implement game-based strategies in diverse settings. By drawing on local knowledge, leveraging available resources, and aligning games with curricular goals, teachers can create dynamic and inclusive language learning environments.

In summary, the empirical insights and case studies show that meaningful language learning emerges when teachers creatively adapt pedagogy to local realities, honour cultural resources, and make the most of available tools. These examples highlight not only what is possible within diverse contexts, but also the central role of educators' skills, confidence, and reflective practice. The next section, Teacher Professional Development, builds on this foundation by examining how teachers can be supported to develop the knowledge and capacities needed to sustain and extend such innovative, context-responsive approaches.

## TEACHER PROFESSIONAL DEVELOPMENT

The successful integration of game-based strategies into language instruction depends not only on the availability of resources and curriculum alignment but also on the preparedness and confidence of educators. Teacher professional development (TPD) plays a pivotal role in equipping educators with the knowledge, skills, and attitudes necessary to implement game-based learning effectively. This section explores the components of effective TPD for game-based language instruction, drawing on empirical evidence and best practices from global and local contexts.

### Importance of Teacher Training in Game-based Learning

Teachers are the primary facilitators of children's learning. They play a critical role in adapting game-based strategies to meet the needs of their learners. However, without adequate training, they may struggle to understand the pedagogical value of games, select appropriate tools, or manage classroom dynamics during gameplay.

Moreover, misconceptions about games being merely recreational can hinder their adoption in formal education settings.

Professional development programmes must therefore address both theoretical and practical aspects of game-based learning. This includes understanding learning theories (e.g., constructivism, SDT), exploring instructional design models (e.g., ADDIE, UDL), and developing competencies in game facilitation, assessment, and adaptation.

## Empirical Insights from Rural Mberengwa

The caregiver interviews and thematic analysis from Rural Mberengwa underscore the importance of community-based educational support. Caregivers expressed a desire for more structured learning opportunities and highlighted the role of informal educational practices such as storytelling and play (See Appendix A). Teachers in these contexts must be trained not only in formal pedagogy but also in leveraging local knowledge and practices to enhance language instruction.

For example, a teacher who understands the cultural significance of traditional games can adapt them to teach linguistic concepts, thereby creating a more inclusive and engaging learning environment. Training programmes should therefore include modules on cultural responsiveness, community engagement, and resource adaptation.

## Components of Effective Professional Development

Effective TPD for game-based language instruction should include the following components:

a. Workshops and seminars

Interactive sessions where teachers explore game-based strategies, share experiences, and co-design activities.

b. Model lessons

Demonstrations of game-based instruction in real or simulated classrooms to illustrate best practices.

c. Collaborative planning

Opportunities for teachers to work together in designing and evaluating game-based lessons.

d. Mentoring and coaching

Ongoing support from experienced educators or instructional designers to guide implementation.

e. Reflective practice

Encouraging teachers to reflect on their experiences, challenges, and successes in using games.

These components align with adult learning principles, which emphasize experiential learning, collaboration, and relevance to practice.

## Leveraging Technology for Teacher Development

Digital platforms can enhance access to professional development, especially in remote or underserved areas. Online courses, webinars, and resource repositories allow teachers to learn at their own pace and connect with peers globally. For example, platforms like Coursera, Edmodo, and the British Council's Teaching English offer free or low-cost training on game-based learning and language pedagogy. In contexts like Rural Mberengwa, where internet access may be limited, hybrid models that combine face-to-face workshops with offline digital resources (e.g., USB drives, printed manuals) can be effective. Community learning hubs or teacher resource centres can also serve as venues for ongoing professional development.

## Building a Culture of Innovation

Beyond individual training, schools and educational systems must foster a culture that values innovation and experimentation. For instance:

a. Leadership support

School leaders should encourage and recognize teachers who implement creative strategies.

b. Policy alignment

Educational policies should support the integration of games and other active learning methods.

c. Resource allocation

Funding and materials should be made available to support game-based instruction.

d. Research and evaluation

Schools should engage in action research to assess the impact of game-based learning and refine practices.

By investing in teacher development and creating supportive environments, educational systems can ensure that game-based strategies are not only adopted but sustained and scaled up.

In summary, the discussion has shown that effective teacher professional development, grounded in practical training for game-based learning, informed by empirical insights from rural Mberengwa, supported through thoughtful use of technology, and strengthened by a culture of innovation, is essential for empowering educators to design meaningful, context-responsive learning experiences. As we now turn to the next section on Challenges and Considerations, it becomes important to examine barriers that may hinder the implementation and sustainability of these professional development initiatives.

## CHALLENGES AND CONSIDERATIONS

While games offer numerous benefits for language instruction, the implementation of game-based learning is not without challenges. Educators, policymakers, and curriculum designers must navigate a range of practical, pedagogical, and contextual considerations to ensure that games are used effectively and equitably. This section outlines key challenges and offers strategies for addressing them, drawing on empirical evidence and scholarly research.

### Resource Limitations

One of the most significant barriers to game-based learning, particularly in low-income and rural settings, is the lack of resources. Digital games often require access to devices, internet connectivity, and electricity resources that are scarce in many communities, including Rural Mberengwa (See Appendix B). Even non-digital games may require materials such as paper, markers, or printed cards, which may not be readily available. To address these limitations, educators can focus on designing games that use locally available materials or repurpose traditional children's games for educational purposes (Madondo & Tsikira, 2022). For example, stones used in the *nhodo* game can be adapted for counting or sequencing activities. Community involvement in game creation can also help identify sustainable solutions and foster ownership.

## Teacher Preparedness and Confidence

As discussed in the previous section, many teachers lack formal training in game-based pedagogy. This can lead to uncertainty about how to select, adapt, or assess games in the classroom. Without adequate support, teachers may default to traditional methods or use games in ways that do not align with learning objectives. Professional development programmes must therefore prioritize hands-on training, mentorship, and access to resources. Peer collaboration and reflective practice can also help build confidence and competence. In contexts where formal training is limited, community-based workshops and teacher networks can serve as valuable platforms for knowledge exchange. These challenges are consistent with broader findings in sub-Saharan Africa (Piper et al., 2014). Such constraints hinder the effective implementation of game-based learning, despite its recognized benefits. The absence of formal training in game-based pedagogy suggests a need for professional development programmes that equip teachers with practical strategies for designing and facilitating educational games (Walsh et al., 2011). Moreover, large class sizes make it difficult to manage group-based activities, calling for scalable game formats that can be adapted to whole-class instruction without compromising learners' engagement.

## Curriculum Alignment and Assessment

Another challenge is ensuring that games align with curricular standards and assessment frameworks. Educators may struggle to justify the use of games within rigid curricula or standardized testing environments. Moreover, assessing learning outcomes from game-based activities can be complex, especially when the focus is on oral language skills or collaborative tasks. To overcome these challenges, educators should design games with clear learning objectives and incorporate formative assessment strategies. Rubrics, observation checklists, and learner self-assessments can provide valuable insights into progress and areas for improvement. Curriculum developers should also consider integrating game-based activities into official syllabi to legitimize their use.

## Cultural Sensitivity and Inclusivity

While games can promote cultural relevance, they can also inadvertently reinforce stereotypes or exclude certain groups if not carefully designed. For example, games that rely heavily on Western narratives or imagery may alienate learners from non-Western backgrounds. Similarly, competitive games may disadvantage learners with anxiety or special needs. Inclusive game design requires attention to representation, accessibility, and learner diversity. Some games may marginalise learners with disabilities due to the nature of their physical impairments. Educators should involve learners and community members in the design process to ensure that games reflect local values and experiences. Universal Design for Learning (UDL) principles can guide the creation of games that accommodate different abilities and preferences (CAST, 2018).

### Sustainability and Scalability

Finally, sustaining and scaling game-based learning initiatives can be challenging. Pilot projects may succeed in specific contexts but fail to expand due to funding constraints, lack of institutional support, or changes in leadership. Ensuring long-term impact requires strategic planning, documentation, and advocacy. Partnerships with NGOs, universities, and government agencies can help mobilize resources and expertise. Monitoring and evaluation systems should be established to track outcomes and inform decision-making. Sharing success stories and lessons learned can also inspire broader adoption and innovation.

In summary, the challenges explored, ranging from resource constraints and teacher preparedness to issues of curriculum alignment, cultural sensitivity, sustainability, and scalability, highlight the complex realities that shape the implementation of game-based learning across diverse contexts. Recognising these considerations is essential for designing interventions that are both meaningful and feasible. Building on this understanding, the next section on Future Research Directions examines the emerging questions and opportunities that can guide more robust, context-aware, and innovative advancements in game-based learning.

## FUTURE RESEARCH DIRECTIONS

As game-based learning continues to evolve, there is a growing need for rigorous research that explores its applications, effectiveness, and contextual adaptability in language education. While existing studies have demonstrated the potential of games to enhance motivation, engagement, and language acquisition, several gaps remain in the literature. This section outlines key areas for future research, particularly in relation to diverse linguistic and socio-economic contexts.

## Longitudinal Impact Studies

Most current research on game-based language learning focuses on short-term outcomes, such as immediate gains in vocabulary or learner motivation (Plass et al., 2015; Reinders & Wattana, 2015). However, there is limited evidence on the long-term effects of sustained game-based instruction. Future studies should employ longitudinal designs to examine how regular exposure to educational games influences language proficiency, retention, and academic achievement over time. Such research is particularly important in early childhood education, where foundational language skills are developed. Tracking learners across multiple years can provide insights into how game-based strategies contribute to literacy development, especially in under-resourced settings.

## Contextual Adaptation and Cultural Relevance

While the benefits of culturally responsive pedagogy are well-documented (Gay, 2010; Ladson-Billings, 1995), there is a need for more empirical studies that examine how indigenous games, and local narratives can be systematically integrated into language curricula. Research should explore the processes of adapting traditional games for educational purposes, the role of community participation, and the impact on learner identity and engagement. In contexts like Rural Mberengwa, where caregivers already use storytelling and play as informal educational tools, studies could investigate how these practices can be formalized and scaled up within school systems. Comparative studies across different cultural settings would also enrich our understanding of how cultural relevance influences the effectiveness of game-based learning.

## Equity and access in game-based learning

Digital divide issues remain a significant barrier to the equitable implementation of game-based strategies. Future research should examine how socio-economic factors, infrastructure, and policy environments affect access to game-based learning tools. This includes investigating the effectiveness of low-tech and hybrid models in bridging access gaps. Moreover, studies should explore how game-based learning can be made inclusive for learners with disabilities, language barriers, or learning differences. Applying Universal Design for Learning (UDL) principles in game design and evaluating their impact on diverse learner populations would be a valuable contribution to the field.

### Teacher Beliefs and Professional Development

Teachers' beliefs about games and their pedagogical value significantly influence implementation. Future research should investigate how professional development programmes shape teacher attitudes, confidence, and instructional practices related to game-based learning. Mixed-methods studies that combine surveys, interviews, and classroom observations can provide a comprehensive picture of teacher experiences and needs. Additionally, research should examine the scalability of teacher training models, particularly in low-resource settings. What types of support peer mentoring, online modules, community workshops are most effective in building teacher capacity for game-based instruction?

### Assessment and Learning Analytics

Assessing learning outcomes from game-based activities remains a complex challenge. Future research should focus on developing valid and reliable assessment tools that capture both cognitive and affective dimensions of learning. This includes exploring the use of learning analytics in digital games to track learner progress, identify misconceptions, and personalize instruction. For non-digital games, researchers can investigate alternative assessment methods such as performance-based tasks, portfolios, and peer evaluations. Studies should also examine how assessment practices influence learner motivation and perceptions of game-based learning.

In summary, the proposed future research directions, including longitudinal studies, culturally grounded adaptation, equity and access, teacher beliefs, and the integration of assessment and learning analytics, underscore the need for deeper, more context-responsive inquiry into game-based learning. These avenues point toward a broader agenda aimed at strengthening both evidence and practice. With this foundation in place, the next section on Conclusions and Recommendations draws together the key insights of the chapter and outlines actionable steps for educators, policymakers, and researchers moving forward.

## CONCLUSIONS AND RECOMMENDATIONS

The integration of games into language curricula and instructional design represents a powerful and inclusive approach to enhancing language development in diverse educational contexts. Grounded in theoretical perspectives such as constructivist learning theory, self-determination theory, cognitive load theory, and sociocultural theory, game-based learning offers an engaging means of fostering motivation, supporting self-regulation, and promoting meaningful language use.

Empirical evidence from rural Mberengwa highlights the need for adaptable, culturally relevant, and resource sensitive pedagogical approaches. In settings affected by energy poverty and limited infrastructure, both digital and non-digital games serve as practical tools for sustaining language learning. Indigenous games provide culturally grounded contexts that affirm learner identity. Instructional design models such as ADDIE, SAM, and UDL offer structured pathways for effective implementation. Case studies from rural and urban environments demonstrate the versatility of games in promoting vocabulary development, mastery of grammar, narrative skills, and communicative competence. These examples also emphasise the importance of teacher facilitation, community participation, and contextual adaptation.

Successful adoption of game-based learning requires continued investment in teacher professional development, curriculum alignment, and inclusive design. Challenges such as resource shortages, varying levels of teacher preparedness, and assessment complexities must be addressed through collaborative planning, supportive policy frameworks, and ongoing research.

The following recommendations are directed *early childhood educators, curriculum designers*, and *education policymakers* seeking to strengthen language instruction through games, especially in resource constrained and culturally diverse contexts such as rural Mberengwa. Games should be explicitly aligned with *language learning objectives to ensure pedagogical relevance and measurable outcomes*. Culturally relevant content, including indigenous games and narratives, should be incorporated to promote inclusivity and affirm learner identities. The ADDIE model (*Analyze, Design, Develop, Implement, Evaluate*) is recommended as a guiding framework for systematic development and implementation. The integration of collaborative and competitive elements can enhance learner engagement and encourage peer interaction, which is essential for language development. Learning should be *scaffolded through progressive game levels* that build confidence and competence. Given infrastructural limitations, the use of both digital and non-digital games is advisable to ensure accessibility and adaptability. Educators should also *encourage reflective practice* through post-game discussions and journaling activities, which deepen metacognitive awareness and reinforce language acquisition.

Future research should focus on longitudinal outcomes, cultural adaptation, equity of access, and the development of robust assessment tools. Continued exploration and refinement of game-based approaches will contribute to more equitable, engaging, and effective language education across diverse contexts. Games are not merely forms of entertainment; when thoughtfully integrated into the curriculum, they become powerful pedagogical instruments capable of transforming language learning into a joyful, inclusive, and impactful experience.

## Summary

This chapter explored the pedagogical value of integrating game-based learning into early childhood language instruction, with a focus on practical strategies for educators and curriculum designers. Drawing on empirical data from rural Mberengwa, Zimbabwe, it highlighted how games both digital and non-digital can enhance vocabulary acquisition, pronunciation, and learner engagement, especially in resource-constrained settings. The chapter emphasizes the importance of aligning games with language learning objectives, incorporating culturally relevant content, and using structured instructional design models like ADDIE. It also addresses challenges such as limited resources, large class sizes, and lack of teacher training, and offers recommendations for inclusive, bilingual, and community-supported approaches to language learning through play.

## REFERENCES


Adipat, S., Laksana, K., Busayanon, K., Asawasowan, A., & Adipat, B. (2021). Engaging students in the learning process with game-based learning: The fundamental concepts. [IJTE]. *International Journal of Technology in Education*, *4*(3), 542–552. DOI: 10.46328/ijte.169

Allen, M., & Sites, R. (2012). *Leaving ADDIE for SAM: An agile model for developing the best learning experiences.* Association for Talent Development.

Aschentrup, L., Steimer, P. A., Dadaczynski, K., Mc Call, T., Fischer, F., & Wrona, K. J. (2024). Effectiveness of gamified digital interventions in mental health prevention and health promotion among adults: A scoping review. *BMC Public Health*, *24*(69), 69. https://bmcpublichealth.biomedcentral.com/articles/10.1186/s12889-023-17517-3. DOI: 10.1186/s12889-023-17517-3 PMID: 38167010

Bacalja, A. (2022). 'A critical review of digital game literacies in the English classroom'. *L1-Educational Studies in Language and Literature*, *22*, 1–28. DOI: 10.21248/l1esll.2022.22.2.370

Bassanelli, S., Vasta, N., Bucchiarone, A., & Marconi, A. (2022). Gamification for behavior change: A scientometric review. *Acta Psychologica*, *228*, 1–12. DOI: 10.1016/j.actpsy.2022.103657 PMID: 35767927

BERA. (2018). *Ethical Guidelines for Educational Research* (4th ed.). British Educational Research Association.

Bodrova, E., & Leong, D. J. (2007). *Tools of the Mind: The Vygotskian Approach to Early Childhood Education.* Pearson.

Braun, V., & Clarke, V. (2006). Using thematic analysis in psychology. *Qualitative Research in Psychology*, *3*(2), 77–101. DOI: 10.1191/1478088706qp063oa

Chanyoo, N. (2022). Pedagogical design perspective of digital game-based English language learning: An analysis of journal publications from 2000 to 2021. *International Journal of Online Pedagogy and Course Design*, *12*(4), 1–28. Advance online publication. DOI: 10.4018/IJOPCD.311437

Creswell, J. W., & Poth, C. N. (2018). *Qualitative Inquiry and Research Design: Choosing Among Five Approaches* (4th ed.). Sage Publications.

Cummins, J. (2000). *Language, Power and Pedagogy: Bilingual Children in the Crossfire*. Multilingual Matters.

Deci, E. L., & Ryan, R. M. (1985). *Intrinsic Motivation and Self-Determination in Human Behavior.* Springer Science & Business Media. DOI: 10.1007/978-1-4899-2271-7

Deterding, S., Dixon, D., Khaled, R., & Nacke, L. (2011). From Game Design Elements to Gamefulness: Defining "Gamification". *In: Proceedings of the 15th International Academic MindTrek Conference: Envisioning Future Media Environments,* Tampere, Finland, 28–30 September 2011. ACM, 9–15. DOI: 10.1145/2181037.2181040

Fisher, K. R., Hirsh-Pasek, K., Golinkoff, R. M., & Gryfe, S. G. (2008). Conceptual split? Parents' and experts' perceptions of play in the 21st century. *Journal of Applied Developmental Psychology, 29*(4), 305–316. DOI: 10.1016/j.appdev.2008.04.006

Fox, R. (2001). Constructivism examined. *Oxford Review of Education, 27*(1), 23–35. DOI: 10.1080/03054980125310

Gay, G. (2010). *Culturally Responsive Teaching: Theory, Research, and Practice* (2nd ed.). Teachers College Press.

Hennig, K., & Kirova, A. (2012). The role of cultural artefacts in play as tools to mediate learning in an intercultural preschool programmeme. *Contemporary Issues in Early Childhood, 13*(3), 226–241. DOI: 10.2304/ciec.2012.13.3.226

Heugh, K. (2011). Theory and practice – language education models in Africa: Research, design, decision-making, and outcomes. In *Optimizing Learning and Education in Africa – the Language Factor.* UNESCO.

Hirsh-Pasek, K., Golinkoff, R. M., Berk, L. E., & Singer, D. G. (2009). *A Mandate for Playful Learning in Preschool.* Oxford University Press.

Ifenthaler, D., Eseryel, D., & Ge, X. (Eds.). (2012). Assessment for Game-Based Learning: Foundations, Innovations, and Perspectives. Springer., Available at https://www.academia.edu/2763694/Assessment_for_Game_Based_Learning, Retrieved September 15, 2025, from. DOI: 10.1007/978-1-4614-3546-4

Jonassen, D. H., & Rohrer-Murphy, L. (1999). Activity theory as a framework for designing constructivist learning environments. *Educational Technology Research and Development, 47*(1), 61–79. DOI: 10.1007/BF02299477

Joshi, A., Sharma, R., & Singh, M. (2025). Designing for Learning: Challenges in Aligning Game Mechanics with Pedagogical Goals. *Journal of Educational Technology Research and Development, 73*(2), 145–162.

Kato, N. M. (2024) 'The role of English language education in multilingual societies', IAA Journal of Arts and Humanities, 11(2), pp. 53–55. Available at: https://www.iaajournals.org/wp-content/uploads/2024/08/IAA-JAH-11253-55-2024.pdf [Accessed 02 February 2026].

Kim, J., & Castelli, D. M. (2021). Effects of gamification on behavioral change in education: A meta-analysis. *International Journal of Environmental Research and Public Health, 18*(7), 3550. DOI: 10.3390/ijerph18073550 PMID: 33805530

King, L. (2025) The impact of multilingualism on global education and language learning. Cambridge Assessment English Perspectives. Available at: https://www.cambridgeenglish.org/Images/539682-perspectives-impact-on-multilingualism.pdf [Accessed 02 February 2026].

Kramsch, C. (1993). *Context and culture in language teaching*. Oxford university press.

Ladson-Billings, G. (1995). Toward a Theory of Culturally Relevant Pedagogy. *American Educational Research Journal, 32*(3), 465–491. DOI: 10.3102/00028312032003465

Li, M., Ma, S., & Shi, Y. (2023). Examining the effectiveness of gamification as a tool promoting teaching and learning in educational settings: A meta-analysis. *Frontiers in Psychology, 14*(1253549), 1253549. Advance online publication. DOI: 10.3389/fpsyg.2023.1253549 PMID: 37876838

Liu, C. H., & Matthews, R. (2005). Vygotsky's philosophy: Constructivism and its criticisms examined. *International Education Journal, 6*(3), 386–399.

Loizou, E., & Olymbiou, O. (2024). Constructive play: Exploring pre-service early childhood teachers' play involvement. *Journal of Early Childhood Research, 22*(3), 329–342. DOI: 10.1177/1476718X231210642

Madondo, F., & Tsikira, J. (2022). Traditional children's games: Their relevance on skills development among rural Zimbabwean children age 3–8 years. *Journal of Research in Childhood Education, 36*(3), 406–420. DOI: 10.1080/02568543.2021.1982084

Mogavi, R. H., Guo, B., Zhang, Y., Haq, E.-U., Hui, P., & Ma, X. (2022). When Gamification Spoils Your Learning: A Qualitative Case Study of Gamification Misuse in a Language-Learning App. *In: Proceedings of the Ninth ACM Conference on Learning @ Scale (L@S '22)*, New York City, NY, USA, 1–3 June 2022. ACM, 1–14. https://doi.org/DOI: 10.1145/3491140.3528274

Moghadam, S. R., & Barani, G. (2025). The impact of linguistic vs. cultural imperialism on language learning. *Frontiers in Psychology*, *15*, •••. Retrieved February 02, 2026, from https://www.frontiersin.org/journals/psychology/articles/10.3389/fpsyg.2024.1438849/full PMID: 39944707

Mphahlele, M. L., & Mammen, K. J. (2022). Exploring the feasibility of outdoor indigenous games and songs to support early childhood education. *Journal of Childhood Education and Society*, *3*(2), 120–135. Retrieved August 10, 2025, from https://www.j-ces.com/index.php/jces/article/view/270

Neuman, S. B., & Celano, D. (2001). Access to print in low-income and middle-income communities. *Reading Research Quarterly*, *36*(1), 8–26. DOI: 10.1598/RRQ.36.1.1

Nicolopoulou, A. (2010). The alarming disappearance of play from early childhood education. *Human Development*, *53*(1), 1–4. DOI: 10.1159/000268135

Palinkas, L. A., Horwitz, S. M., Green, C. A., Wisdom, J. P., Duan, N., & Hoagwood, K. (2015). Purposeful sampling for qualitative data collection and analysis in mixed method implementation research. *Administration and Policy in Mental Health*, *42*(5), 533–544. DOI: 10.1007/s10488-013-0528-y PMID: 24193818

Phillips, D. C. (1995). The good, the bad, and the ugly: The many faces of constructivism. *Educational Researcher*, *24*(7), 5–12. DOI: 10.3102/0013189X024007005

Piaget, J. (1952). *The Origins of Intelligence in Children*. International Universities Press. DOI: 10.1037/11494-000

Piper, B., Zuilkowski, S. S., & Mugenda, A. (2014). Improving reading outcomes in Kenya: First-year effects of the PRIMR Initiative. *International Journal of Educational Development*, *37*, 11–21. DOI: 10.1016/j.ijedudev.2014.02.006

Plass, J. L., Homer, B. D., & Kinzer, C. K. (2015). Foundations of game-based learning. *Educational Psychologist*, *50*(4), 258–283. DOI: 10.1080/00461520.2015.1122533

Reinders, H., & Wattana, S. (2015). Affect and willingness to communicate in digital game-based learning. *ReCALL*, *27*(1), 38–57. DOI: 10.1017/S0958344014000226

Rupere, T., Muzurura, O., Zanamwe, N. & Munyaradzi, M. (2013). Use of a Game in Teaching Early Childhood Learners in Zimbabwe. *International Journal of Computer and Information Technology*, 2(2). ISSN: 2279 – 0764.

SEAL. (2024) The benefits of being multilingual: How multilingual learning leads to $30 billion economic growth. Available at: https://www.seal.org/news/benefits-of-being-multilingual [Accessed 02 February 2026].

Snow, C. E., & Van Hemel, S. B. (2008). *Early Childhood Assessment: Why, What, and How*. National Academies Press.

Su, C. Y., Cheng, C. H., & Lin, Y. L. (2021). A systematic review of digital game-based learning in language education: 2000–2020. *Journal of Educational Technology & Society*, *24*(1), 250–266.

Sweller, J. (1988). Cognitive load during problem solving: Effects on learning. *Cognitive Science*, *12*(2), 257–285. DOI: 10.1207/s15516709cog1202_4

Tegon, R. (2024). An updated systematic review on the impact of gamification in education: Insights from early 2024. In Martinez-Roig, R., Pulido-Montes, C., & Mateu-Luján, B. (Eds.), *Nuevas investigaciones educativas para definir la enseñanza y el aprendizaje* (pp. 318–342). Ediciones Octaedro.

UNESCO. (2022). *Global Education Monitoring Report*. UNESCO.

UNESCO. (2024) Multilingual education: A key to quality and inclusive learning. Available at: https://www.unesco.org/en/articles/multilingual-education-key-quality-and-inclusive-learning [Accessed 02 February 2026].

Vygotsky, L. S. (1978). *Mind in Society: The Development of Higher Psychological Processes*. Harvard University Press.

Walsh, G., Sproule, L., McGuinness, C., & Trew, K. (2011). Playful structure: A novel image of early years pedagogy for primary school classrooms. *Early Years Journal of International Research and Development*, *31*(2), 107–119. DOI: 10.1080/09575146.2011.579070

Whitebread, D., Basilio, M., Kuvalja, M., & Verma, M. (2012). The Importance of Play. Brussels: *Toy Industries of Europe (TIE)*, 1-54.

Yin, R. K. (2018). *Case Study Research and Applications: Design and Methods* (6th ed.). Sage Publications.

Zhou, X. (2024). Sociocultural theory in early childhood education. *International Journal on E-Learning*, *4*(1), 1–12. Retrieved August 17, 2025, from https://www.researchgate.net/publication/380209252_Sociocultural_Theory_in_Early_Childhood_Education

## KEY TERMS AND DEFINITIONS

**Collaborative and Competitive Dynamics:** Social interactions in learning environments where students either work together (collaborative) or strive to outperform each other (competitive), both of which can enhance motivation, engagement, and skill development.

**Culturally Responsive Elements:** Instructional strategies and materials that acknowledge, respect, and incorporate learners' cultural backgrounds and experiences to make learning more relevant, inclusive, and effective.

**Digital Games:** Interactive games played on electronic devices such as computers, tablets, or smartphones, often incorporating multimedia elements to engage learners and support skill development, including language acquisition.

**Indigenous Games:** Traditional games rooted in the cultural practices of specific communities, often passed down through generations. These games reflect local knowledge, values, and social norms, and can be adapted for educational purposes.

**Language Development:** The process through which individuals acquire and refine their ability to understand, produce, and use language effectively, encompassing vocabulary growth, grammar, pronunciation, and communication skills.

**Low-Resource Environments:** Educational settings with limited access to materials, technology, infrastructure, or trained personnel, often requiring creative and adaptable teaching strategies to meet learners' needs.

**Non-Digital Games:** Educational or recreational games that do not require electronic devices, such as board games, card games, or physical activities, are often used in classrooms to promote active learning and collaboration.

**Teacher Professional Development:** Ongoing learning opportunities for educators aimed at improving their teaching practices, subject knowledge, and ability to support diverse learners, often through workshops, training, or collaborative learning.

# APPENDIX

## 1. Interview Questions for Early Childhood Educators (5 Participants)

1. How often do you currently use games in your language instruction?
2. What types of games do you find most effective for language learning?
3. How do you align games with your curriculum objectives?
4. What challenges do you face when integrating games into your lessons?
5. How do learners respond to game-based language activities?
6. Have you received any training on using games for instructional purposes?
7. What resources (materials, time, support) do you need to implement games more effectively?
8. How do you assess language development through games?
9. Can you share a successful example of a game-based language activity?
10. What recommendations would you give to other educators about using games in early childhood language instruction?

## 2. Focus Group Discussion Questions for Parents (5 Participants)

1. What kinds of language-related games do your children play at home?
2. Have you noticed any improvement in your child's language skills through play?
3. How do you support your child's language development outside of school?
4. What are your views on using games as a teaching method in early childhood education?
5. What suggestions do you have for schools to better involve parents in game-based learning?

# Chapter 10
# Theoretical Frameworks for Implementing Game-Based Learning in Language Development and Acquisition

**Oindrilla Ghosh**
http://orcid.org/0000-0001-9609-0781
*Christ University, India*

**Binod Kumar**
http://orcid.org/0009-0002-9721-1367
*Radha Govind University, India*

## ABSTRACT

*Theoretical frameworks guide the design of game-based learning (GBL) for language development and acquisition. Constructivism situates learners as active meaning-makers who build knowledge through interactive tasks. Sociocultural theory highlights collaboration, language socialization, and guided participation within social contexts. Experiential and situated learning emphasize authentic tasks that resemble real communication, enabling rehearsal of linguistic forms in meaningful settings. Flow theory informs challenge–skill balance to sustain engagement without frustration. Scaffolding, feedback, and metacognition support gradual independence as learners internalize grammar, lexicon, and pragmatics. Motivation, identity, and agency shape persistence and risk-taking in language use. Game mechanics should align with learning goals, provide adaptive difficulty, and offer reflective debriefs to consolidate transfer.*

DOI: 10.4018/979-8-3373-4322-8.ch010

## INTRODUCTION

The development of language through playful, interactive experiences has long intrigued educators and researchers, and game-based learning (GBL) offers a compelling theoretical lens for understanding how learners internalize linguistic forms, functions, and fluency (Basudan, 2023). At its core, GBL leverages the motivational power of games immediately engaging goals, feedback, scaffolding, and social collaboration to create authentic communicative environments where language use is embedded in meaningful tasks rather than isolated rules (Alshehri, 2023). The theoretical underpinnings of implementing GBL in language development and acquisition draw from a convergence of cognitive, sociocultural, and affective perspectives that highlight how learners construct knowledge through active participation, social interaction, and iterative practice (Li & Chen, 2022). Cognitive theories emphasize mental representations, automaticity, and retrieval processes shaped by deliberate practice within situated tasks. In language learning, this translates into repeated, controlled exposure to linguistic input, opportunities for hypothesis testing, and immediate corrective feedback that supports schema development and lexical-grammatical integration (Alladi et al., 2019). The structured yet dynamic nature of games enables learners to move through zones of proximal development, receiving just-in-time assistance that reduces cognitive overload while maintaining authentic communicative challenges (Ulagammal and Chaluvarayaswamy, 2023).

Sociocultural and sociocognitive frameworks, on the other hand, foreground discourse, social mediation, and cultural tools as central to language development. From Vygotskyan perspectives, language emerges through social interaction, with more capable peers or instructors scaffolding learners' linguistic performance within joint activities, supports, and shared norms (Ji et al., 2024). In game-based contexts, collaboration, negotiation of meaning, and the use of semiotic resources (rules, roles, avatars, feedback systems) become mediating artifacts that shape linguistic practice (Morales et al., 2024). Communities of practice and distributed cognition further extend this view by positing that knowledge language included resides in the collective activities and tools used by groups, not merely in individual memory (Patel, 2023). Consequently, GBL for language learning emphasizes collaborative problem-solving, role-play, and simulation that place learners in communicative ecologies where meaning and form emerge through repeated interaction, feedback, and reflection (Lim et al., 2020). Affective factors engagement, motivation, anxiety reduction are not incidental; they are central to sustaining time-on-task and anxiety-free risk-taking needed for authentic language experimentation (Moore et al., 2020). The affective dimension aligns with self-determination theory, which links intrinsic motivation to autonomy, competence, and relatedness, suggesting that games can nurture autonomous language practice while providing social belonging and mastery cues (Kang et al., 2023).

In practice, these theoretical strands converge around the design of GBL activities that situate language tasks within goal-directed, rule-governed play (Pendy, 2023). Theoretical models such as task-based language teaching (TBLT), communicative language teaching (CLT), and input enhancement underlie game designs that foreground meaningful use over rote accuracy, while still attending to form through feedback and metalinguistic reflection (Maggio et al., 2021). Gamification elements scaffolds, feedback loops, progression, and achievement systems are strategically deployed to manage cognitive load and sustain engagement, with an eye toward fostering communicative competence, pragmatic fluency, and intercultural awareness (Alali, 2024). The introduction of digital game-based learning tools expands possibilities for authentic listening, speaking, reading, and writing experiences, enabling adaptive difficulty, personalized learning paths, and data-driven feedback (Dovleac et al., 2023). Ultimately, the theoretical landscape for implementing GBL in language development is characterized by an integrative attitude: games are not mere entertainment but complex mediational environments where cognitive processing, social interaction, and affective resonance collaborate to support language growth in authentic, motivating, and reflective ways (Devi et al., 2016).

## HISTORICAL EVOLUTION

The historical evolution of theoretical frameworks for game-based learning in language development reflects broader shifts in educational thought and technology (Nguyen et al., 2022). Early conceptualizations of using games for language learning emerged from behaviorist notions in the mid-20th century, where repetition, drill, and immediate feedback within structured activities were believed to foster habit formation and accuracy (Sughra & Usmani, 2022). Language instruction often relied on predictable, rule-based practice, and games served as a vehicle to intensify drill without reducing pedagogical rigor (Bennani et al., 2021). As cognitive psychology gained prominence in the latter half of the century, researchers began to emphasize internal processes such as hypothesis testing, pattern recognition, and automatization as central to language acquisition (Alenezi, 2023). Within this period, games were repurposed to provide meaningful contexts for language use, but often remained tightly controlled in terms of linguistic input and instructional goals (Hernández, 2023). The advent of communicative competence theories in the 1970s and 1980s shifted emphasis toward functional language use, authentic interaction, and social meaning-making (Khakpour & Colomo-Palacios, 2020). This repositioning reframed games from mere practice tools to instruments for authentic communication, where linguistic forms arise from real communicative needs and social negotiation (Julita, 2024). Task-based language teaching (TBLT) and CLT approaches gained traction, guiding the design of game activities that prioritized interaction, problem-solving, and meaningful tasks over rote accuracy, while still incorporating fluency and accuracy goals (Sughra & Usmani, 2022).

The digital revolution of the 1990s and 2000s catalyzed a shift from analogue to digital game-based learning, enabling richer simulations, immersive narrative environments, and more complex feedback systems (Zourmpakis et al., 2023). Theoretical frameworks began to integrate concepts from computer-mediated communication, multimedia learning, and situated cognition (Narayanan, 2024). Social constructivist and sociocultural theories gained prominence, highlighting the role of collaborative learning, scaffolding, and distributed cognition in mediated language development (Mehrpour et al., 2023). Online multiplayer games, collaborative storytelling platforms, and language-learning apps provided new settings for authentic linguistic practice, cross-cultural communication, and feedback-rich environments (Erbaşı et al., 2023). The late 2000s and 2010s saw the formalization of GBL within language education research, with meta-analyses and empirical studies demonstrating positive effects on motivation, engagement, vocabulary acquisition, and task-based speaking proficiency (Allahverdi, 2021). Theoretical debates emerged around the balance between gamification (intrinsic game mechanics) and pure game-based learning (full-fledged learning activities embedded in game worlds), as well as concerns about cognitive load, transfer of skills, and assessment validity within gaming contexts (Babu, 2023). More recently, advances in artificial intelligence, adaptive learning, and data analytics have refined theories of personalization, feedback, and scaffolding in language games, enabling dynamic difficulty adjustment, learner profiling, and reflective practice that foreground metacognition and self-regulated learning (Mahardika, 2023).

Overall, the historical evolution of theoretical frameworks for GBL in language development traces a trajectory from controlled drill and behaviorist repetition toward socially mediated, meaning-centric, and technologically enhanced ecosystems (Kherazi, 2024). The current landscape reflects an interdisciplinary blend: cognitive science informs mental processes and automatization; sociocultural theory highlights collaborative meaning-making and mediation; and design-based research emphasizes iterative, data-informed development of engaging, educational games. As technology continues to advance, future trajectories are likely to deepen the integration of adaptive feedback, authentic communicative tasks, and culturally responsive content, ensuring that game-based learning remains a robust theoretical and practical paradigm for fostering language development and acquisition (Alrayes et al., 2024).

The theoretical frameworks that undergird game-based learning (GBL) in language development and acquisition provide a mosaic of lenses through which designers, researchers, and educators can understand how games influence language learning processes (Mugisha et al., 2021). Central to this discourse is constructivism, which posits that learners actively construct knowledge through meaningful experiences rather than passively receiving information (Akgün & Greenhow, 2021). In a language-learning context, this translates into immersive, authentic conversational practice, problem-solving tasks, and exploratory activities where learners negotiate meaning, test hypotheses about syntax and semantics, and reflect on language use in varied social contexts. Cognitive constructivism focuses on how learners build internal representations, while social constructivism highlights the role of collaborative meaning-making, peer feedback, and scaffolded support from more knowledgeable others (Akgün & Greenhow, 2021). In GBL, these ideas manifest as collaborative quests, role-plays, and dialogue-based missions that require negotiation of meaning, negotiation of register, and deployment of linguistic forms in real-time communication (Abbas et al., 2023). Vygotsky's zone of proximal development (ZPD) provides a practical touchstone: properly designed game tasks operate within learners' ZPD, offering scaffolds such as in-game prompts, hints, or cooperative teams that gradually withdraw as competence increases (Akinrinola, 2024). This alignment ensures that language tasks remain challenging but achievable, promoting both accuracy and fluency (Aparicio-Gómez, 2024).

Beyond constructivist and sociocultural perspectives, sociocultural theory, sociolinguistics, and distributed cognition illuminate how language is inseparable from social interaction and context (Felzmann et al., 2020). Games can embed authentic communicative purposes, social norms, and culturally situated discourse practices, enabling learners to acquire pragmatic skills turn-taking, politeness strategies, topic management, and register variation alongside vocabulary and grammar (Buckley & Doyle, 2014). The notion of multimodality leveraging visual, auditory, gestural, and kinesthetic channels within a game expands how learners encounter and manipulate linguistic input, supporting diverse learning preferences and reducing cognitive overload by distributing information across modalities (Yazdanpanah et al., 2022). Flow theory, proposed by Csikszentmihalyi, further enriches interpretation by describing states of deep engagement that occur when challenges match a learner's skills and provide immediate feedback (Rohmah, 2022). In language learning, flow emerges when players are immersed in meaningful communicative tasks with clear goals, rapid feedback, and a sense of progression, thereby increasing motivation and persistence (Jobin & Ienca, 2019). Additionally, theories of incidental vocabulary acquisition and incidental second-language learning through meaningful interaction emphasize that exposure to authentic language input in context within game narratives, quests, and missions can complement formal instruction, fostering implicit uptake of syntax, collocations, and pragmatic usage (Legaki, et al. 2020). Finally, constructivist perspectives on experiential learning emphasize reflective practice;

debrief prompts, in-game journals, and post-game synthesis activities help learners articulate linguistic hypotheses, compare forms, and monitor progress, enabling metacognitive development alongside linguistic competence (Balta, 2023). Collectively, these theoretical strands argue for GBL designs that situate language tasks in authentic communicative episodes, provide supportive social scaffolding, exploit multimodal input, and cultivate learner autonomy within a structured, scaffolded sequence of challenges (Dichev & Dicheva, 2017).

The importance of grounding game-based learning in robust theoretical frameworks when implementing language development efforts cannot be overstated (D'Souza, 2024). A well-articulated framework offers a coherent blueprint that aligns learning objectives, game mechanics, assessment practices, and instructional design, ensuring that the engagement created by the game translates into meaningful linguistic gains (Tonbuloğlu 2023). The framework clarifies what counts as progress, whether it be accuracy in morphology, pragmatic appropriateness, vocabulary breadth, fluency, or sociolinguistic competence, and guides the selection of tasks that target these competencies at appropriate difficulty levels (Sharma et al., 2024). Theoretical grounding also supports the deliberate design of scaffolds, feedback loops, and reflective activities that help learners bridge in-game performance with real-world communication (Pratama, 2023). By referencing sociocultural and sociolinguistic theories, designers can embed authentic discourse communities and culturally relevant language uses, reducing the gap between classroom practice and real-life communication (Otero et al., 2023). Flow theory informs pacing and challenge calibration, which in turn sustains motivation and sustained engagement critical for long-term language development (Grunhut et al., 2021). Multimodal theories justify diverse input channels and output modes, enabling inclusive design that accommodates varied learner profiles, including those with different sensory preferences or learning disabilities (Rivera & Garden, 2021). A strong theoretical basis also strengthens assessment alignment; it clarifies which in-game indicators reflect genuine language growth and which need triangulation with traditional assessments, performance tasks, or portfolio evidence (Tolentino, 2024). Furthermore, theoretical frameworks illuminate equity considerations, guiding designers to create accessible, bias-aware experiences that honor diverse linguistic repertoires and cultural backgrounds (Wood et al., 2021). They also support scalability and transferability, offering generalizable principles applicable across contexts from school settings to informal learning communities and language-learning apps while allowing local adaptation to align with specific curricular standards, learner ages, proficiency levels, and target languages (Zhang, 2024).

## CHALLENGES

Implementing game-based learning (GBL) for language development and acquisition presents a constellation of interrelated challenges that educators, researchers, and developers must navigate (Aliabadi, 2023). First, aligning game mechanics with solid second-language pedagogy is complex. Many commercially popular games emphasize engagement, competition, or entertainment rather than explicit linguistic outcomes, making it difficult to ensure that in-game activities consistently target core language skills such as pronunciation, syntax, vocabulary control, and pragmatic use across registers (Onesi-Ozigagun, 2024). Additionally, ensuring comprehensible input within game tasks requires careful level design, appropriate scaffolding, and adaptive difficulty (Tubino & Adachi, 2022). Without clear mapping between game challenges and learning objectives, students may experience cognitive overload or, conversely, under-stimulation, reducing language uptake (Varas et al., 2023). A related challenge concerns assessment: traditional tests rarely capture the nuanced, real-time language use that games encourage, such as spontaneous dialogue, discourse management, and pragmatic inferences (Pardosi et al., 2024). Developing robust, game-integrated formative assessments that align with established frameworks (e.g., communicative competence, interlanguage development) is resource-intensive and may demand sophisticated analytics and privacy-preserving data collection (Almusaed et al., 2023).

Second, equity and accessibility loom large (Trang & Thư, 2024). Language learning games must be accessible to diverse learners, including those with disabilities, different linguistic backgrounds, and varying levels of prior technology access (López &Tucker, 2020). This requires inclusive design choices captioning, text-to-speech, adjustable tempos, alternative input modalities, and culturally relevant content that can increase development costs and time-to-market (Varas et al., 2023). Cultural relevance extends beyond translation; it requires authentic contexts and dialog patterns that reflect diverse varieties of the target language, avoiding stereotypes and ensuring that content resonates with learners who differ in age, region, and socio-economic status (Fırat, 2023). Another key challenge is scalability: what works in a controlled pilot may falter in large, real-world classrooms or remote learning environments with inconsistent hardware, bandwidth, or teacher support (Pardosi et al., 2024). Technical stability becomes critical when games rely on cloud services, multiplayer interactions, or analytics pipelines; outages or latency can disrupt learning flow and erode motivation (Alenezi, 2024). Teacher roles and professional development are also central concerns. Effective GBL requires teachers to integrate games into instructional sequences, interpret analytics, and curate feedback competencies that may be new or uncomfortable for some educators (Deterding et al., 2011). Without ongoing training and time to design, customize, and assess, the potential benefits of GBL may not be realized (Nguyen et al., 2022). Data privacy and ethical considerations compound these issues (Limongi, 2024). Language-learning games collect data on learners' speech, mistakes, interaction patterns, and social behavior (Familoni, 2024). Schools must navigate consent, anonymization, data ownership, and policy compliance across jurisdictions, while also guarding against bias in AI-driven feedback that could reinforce nonstandard language varieties or penalize learners for linguistic errors in a way that undermines confidence (Tubino & Adachi, 2022).

A final cluster of challenges concerns pedagogical coherence and sustainability. Games must remain pedagogically coherent across the curriculum, avoiding the pitfall of "edutainment" where novelty masks gaps in learning design (Chai et al., 2024). It is essential to establish clear success metrics that transcend engagement and tie directly to communicative outcomes, while ensuring that game-based activities complement rather than replace effective explicit instruction, explicit feedback, and opportunities for authentic conversational practice (Trang & Thư, 2024). Long-term sustainability involves keeping content fresh, updating language data, and aligning with evolving curricula and assessment standards (Moldt et al., 2024). The social affordances of GBL peer interaction, collaboration, and negotiated meaning must be supported without undermining individual language development or privileging more proficient speakers (López &Tucker, 2020). Finally, longitudinal research is needed to determine which game mechanics and pedagogical overlays reliably produce language gains across diverse contexts, which, in turn, informs scalable design decisions (Rathore, 2023). Navigating these intertwined challenges requires a thoughtful blend of instructional design, technology infrastructure, policy alignment, and continuous professional development (Fırat, 2023).

## USE OF AI AND ML

Artificial intelligence (AI) and machine learning (ML) offer substantial opportunities to operationalize theoretical frameworks for game-based learning in language development, translating constructivist, sociocultural, or communicative competence paradigms into adaptive, data-informed experiences (Alenezi, 2024). At a theoretical level, AI can instantiate Vygotskian notions of the Zone of Proximal Development by tailoring tasks to learners' current competences and targeting optimal levels of challenge through real-time learner modeling (Tzafilkou et al., 2023). Natural language processing (NLP) enables dynamic feedback on pronunciation, syntax, and discourse, aligning with sociolinguistic and interactionist theories that emphasize meaning-making in social contexts (Nguyen et al., 2022). From a constructivist lens, AI-driven simulations and role-plays provide authentic, context-rich environments where learners construct knowledge through collaboration, negotiation, and reflective practice (Kurniawati et al., 2018). In practice, AI can scaffold collaborative tasks by monitoring dialogue, suggesting reformulations, and prompting metacognitive reflections on strategies, thereby supporting the social construction of language understanding (Limongi, 2024).

Adaptive learning systems, powered by ML, can personalize task sequencing, feedback modes, and input modalities to accommodate diverse learner profiles outlined in theoretical frameworks such as input processing, interaction hypothesis, and output hypothesis (Gamrat et al., 2014). For example, ML models can adjust lexical difficulty, provide targeted pronunciation cues, or modulate dialog complexity to align with learners' evolving interlanguage stages, thereby preserving comprehensibility and supporting incremental density of linguistic input and output (Agostinelli, 2021). Integrating affective computing enables the system to detect frustration, boredom, or motivation, which connects to learners' affective filters and self-regulation critical factors in successful language acquisition (Güler & Özkan, 2018). Learning analytics, derived from in-game interactions, can illuminate patterns of strategic behavior, interlanguage development, and discourse management, offering researchers empirical windows into theoretical constructs like fossilization or feedback processing (Haresamudram et al., 2023). Moreover, AI can power intelligent tutoring agents that deliver culturally and linguistically appropriate scaffolds, simulate native-like interlocutors, and provide performance-based feedback in real time, aligning with sociocultural perspectives that emphasize mediated learning through credible tools and expert-like assistance (Hollands et al., 2019).

However, leveraging AI/ML in GBL must be theory-informed, ensuring that models do not merely chase superficial engagement metrics but actually reflect pedagogical aims (Larsson & Heintz, 2020). Challenges include data quality and representativeness, interpretability of model decisions, and the risk of biases that privilege certain language varieties or learner subgroups (Cranley et al., 2012). Transparency and explainability are essential so educators understand why a system adapts in a certain way and how feedback aligns with theoretical expectations (Chai et al., 2024). It is also vital to preserve learner autonomy and avoid over-tutelage; AI should augment, not supplant, human-guided inquiry and peer interactions central to many language development theories. Finally, cross-disciplinary collaboration among educators, linguists, game designers, and data scientists is necessary to translate theoretical constructs into scalable, ethical, and effective AI-infused GBL ecosystems that advance language development while honoring the complexity of human communication (Harry, 2023).

## AUGMENTED REALITY

Augmented Reality (AR) enriches language development and acquisition by layering digital linguistic cues onto the real world, thereby aligning with constructivist and sociocultural theoretical frameworks that emphasize authentic, context-rich meaning-making and socially mediated learning (Luan et al., 2020). Within constructivism, AR supports situated learning by placing learners in meaningful, real-world contexts where language use is anchored to tangible tasks reading street signs, following AR-guided narratives, or solving communicative challenges in a simulated but physically present environment (Bastani et al., 2023). AR also embodies the principle of distributed cognition: linguistic knowledge is not stored solely in the learner's mind but is distributed across tools, digital overlays, and physical surroundings (Familoni, 2024). By co-constructing meaning with peers and instructors through shared AR experiences, learners negotiate vocabulary, syntax, and discourse functions in meaningful social interaction (Larsen et al., 2011). From a sociocultural perspective, AR-mediated interactions enable zones of proximal development (ZPD) as more capable peers or instructors scaffold language tasks through augmented prompts, cultural cues, and pragmatic conventions embedded in the overlay (Limongi, 2024). This scaffolding is dynamic and context-sensitive, allowing learners to experiment with target language forms while receiving timely, location-based feedback (Strydom et al., 2010). The theoretical value of AR also lies in its potential to reduce cognitive load through just-in-time support; learners can access glosses, pronunciation guides, or grammar tips integrated into objects or scenes they are already examining, thus freeing working memory to focus on semantic construction and pragmatic use rather than rote decoding (Alrayes et al., 2024). In designing game-based language activities, AR scenarios can incorporate affordances for collaboration, competition, and role-play, encouraging communicative competence, listener-mriendliness, and adaptive language strategies. Ethical and accessibility considerations are integral within frameworks, prompting inclusive design so AR experiences accommodate diverse linguistic backgrounds and sensory needs (Basudan, 2023). Overall, AR's convergence of digital augmentation with real-world context creates fertile ground for theory-informed game-based interventions that promote communicative fluency, intercultural awareness, and autonomous language learning within authentic social practices (Rugaiyah, 2023).

## VIRTUAL REALITY

Virtual Reality (VR) offers immersive, controlled environments that align with experiential and cognitive-skill-building theories in language development and acquisition (Li & Chen, 2022). From experiential learning theory, VR provides immersive simulations where learners engage in authentic communicative tasks, such as negotiating meaning, presenting ideas, or participating in culturally situated dialogues within a fully realized, risk-free world (Pendy, 2023). The strong sense of presence in VR facilitates affective and motivational dimensions of learning reduced anxiety about speaking, increased willingness to take linguistic risks, and heightened engagement with target language use (Dovleac et al., 2023). VR supports cognitive apprenticeship by enabling learners to observe expert discourse, practice with immediate performance feedback, and repeatedly rehearse complex linguistic structures in varied contexts until automaticity emerges (Uygun, 2024). Within sociocultural perspectives, VR can simulate shared task environments that require collaborative problem solving, role-play, and culturally nuanced interactions, thereby fostering intersubjectivity and language socialization (Patel, 2023). Theoretical frameworks that emphasize output and interaction such as output hypothesis and interaction hypothesis find fertile ground in VR: learners can be placed in scenarios that compel negotiation of meaning, or they can be prompted to produce target language in context-rich prompts, with the VR system providing corrective feedback, scaffolds, and modeling integrated into the narrative (Onesi-Ozigagun, 2024). VR also enables precise control over linguistic input lexical difficulty, syntactic complexity, discourse modalities facilitating differentiated instruction and data collection for learner analytics (Moore et al., 2020). Ethically, VR should address potential issues of cybersickness, accessibility, and inclusivity, ensuring that experiences do not exacerbate inequities in access to technology (Maggio et al., 2021). In game-based design, VR supports mission-based tasks, language games, and simulators that mirror real-world communicative demands, thus advancing communicative competence, pragmatic awareness, and metalinguistic reflection within robust theoretical frameworks (Eslit, 2023).

## MIXED REALITY

Mixed Reality (MR) integrates physical and digital worlds to create interactive environments where language learning emerges from blended cues, collaborative manipulation of artifacts, and contextually rich discourse (Hernández, 2023). Theoretically, MR resonates with activity theory and distributed cognition, as learning transpires through multipartite activity where artifacts, interlocutors, and environments co-construct meaning (Walter, 2024). MR enables learners to manipulate linguistic objects texts, models, dialogue simulations while staying connected to the physical context, which supports functional language use in authentic purposes such as instructions, negotiations, and explanations (Mehrpour et al., 2023). In a social constructivist frame, MR fosters collaborative problem solving and joint attention: learners share augmented artifacts, annotate them with language-focused discourse, and negotiate meaning in real time, which strengthens discourse capabilities, pragmatics, and sociolinguistic awareness (Zhang, 2024). The ZPD is operationalized through MR affordances that provide real-time scaffolding palm-based prompts, overlays for pronunciation cues, or interactive grammar cues adjusting to learner proficiency and metadata from the learning analytics (Mahardika, 2023). MR also supports differentiated instruction by customizing the degree of augmentation and the complexity of tasks according to linguistic targets, thereby aligning with adaptive learning theories within game-based frameworks (Khater et al., 2023). From a practical standpoint, MR can scaffold emergent literacy practices in bilingual or multilingual classrooms through cross-linguistic overlays, translanguaging prompts, and culturally responsive content embedded in shared MR spaces (Mugisha et al., 2021). Ethical considerations include ensuring that MR experiences promote inclusive collaboration, protect privacy in shared MR spaces, and avoid cognitive overload due to excessive overlays (Nagi et al., 2023). In game-based learning designs, MR enables hybrid quests that require turning physical objects into language prompts, collaborative storytelling through augmented artifacts, and situational dialogues anchored in local cultural practices, collectively enhancing communicative proficiency, lexical flexibility, and pragmatic fluency within well-founded theoretical paradigms (Ejaz et al., 2022).

## CASE STUDIES

### Case Study 1: A Virtual Reality Language Immersion Game Grounded in Vygotsky's Zone of Proximal Development and Scaffolding

This case study explores a VR-based language learning game designed for intermediate learners of Spanish. The theoretical framework combines Vygotsky's Zone of Proximal Development (ZPD) with the practice of scaffolding in game design. Learners enter a narrative-driven virtual city where tasks require practical communicative exchanges with AI characters and other learners (Shala, 2024). Initial missions present language challenges within the learners' current capabilities, while the game progressively introduces more complex structures, nuanced pragmatics, and culturally authentic discourse. Scaffolds are embedded through in-game prompts, dynamic feedback, and adaptive hint systems that are calibrated to each learner's performance. The ZPD concept illuminates how the game should not simply present target forms but situate them within social interaction and collaborative problem-solving (Akavova et al., 2023). For example, learners may co-create dialogues with non-player characters, collaboratively plan a shopping trip, or negotiate meaning in a simulated real-world scenario. The case demonstrates how social mediation within a game environment can extend learners beyond their independent capabilities. Data collection includes in-game metrics, think-aloud protocols, and pre/post language assessments that examine gains in lexical access, syntactic complexity, and pragmatic competence. Results indicate that VR immersion facilitates reduced anxiety and increased willingness to attempt risky utterances, thereby expanding the ZPD and accelerating acquisition through authentic communicative practice (Abbas et al., 2023).

## Case Study 2: Mobile Geolocation-Based Language Quest Applying Sociocultural Theory and Distributed Cognition

In this study, a mobile game uses geolocation to take learners through real-world locations tied to target vocabulary and grammatical forms in French. The theoretical lens blends Sociocultural Theory with distributed cognition to emphasize the social and material entanglements that shape language learning. Learners work in small groups to complete quests that require collaboration, resource sharing, and the interpretation of cultural cues encountered in situ (Shah, 2024). Meaning-making occurs not only through interactions with peers and native speakers via in-game chat or augmented reality overlays but also through the physical environment, artifacts, and artifacts' social meaning. The framework foregrounds the role of participation, apprenticeship, and cultural artifacts maps, receipts, signage that become mediating tools. Scaffolding manifests as collaborative prompts, structured roles (e.g., facilitator, researcher, translator), and reflective debriefs that allow learners to articulate metalinguistic strategies (Fazil, 2024). Distributed cognition is realized when the group distributes cognitive tasks across members and tools; for instance, one learner documents new vocabulary while another navigates directions, and yet another analyzes cultural appropriateness of expressions. Findings suggest enhanced lexical breadth, pragmatic usage in authentic contexts, and improved confidence in real-life communication. The study also highlights challenges such as unequal participation and the need for facilitator guidance to maintain collaborative balance and ensure equitable access to cognitive resources (Rasheed et al., 2023).

## Case Study 3: Motivational Dynamics through Self-Determination Theory in a Quest-Based Language Learning Game

This case examines a quest-driven game designed for beginner-to-intermediate learners of English as a second language, with an emphasis on intrinsic motivation and autonomy support. The theoretical framework is Self-Determination Theory (SDT), focusing on the satisfaction of three basic psychological needs: autonomy, competence, and relatedness (Abbas et al., 2023). The game presents a narrative where players choose their learning paths, set personal goals, and select tasks aligned with individual interests, thereby fostering autonomy. Competence is addressed through adjustable difficulty, rapid feedback, and mastery-oriented milestones, while relatedness is cultivated via cooperative missions, peer feedback, and in-game social spaces (Nguyen, 2023). The case analyzes how SDT-informed game mechanics influence engagement, persistence, and language development outcomes such as lexical diversity, error correction uptake, and discourse fluency. Data include usage patterns, motivation scales, retrospective interviews, and pre/post tests. Results indicate that when learners feel a sense of control, experience meaningful competence, and perceive social connectedness, they demonstrate higher persistence, greater willingness to attempt challenging forms (e.g., phrasal verbs or register shifts), and more active hypothesis-testing language productions (Murtaza et al., 2022). The study underscores the importance of designing adaptive autonomy-supportive interfaces, meaningful collaboration opportunities, and reflective practice prompts to sustain intrinsic motivation and optimize language acquisition.

## Case Study 4: Communicative Competence and Interaction Hypothesis in a Multiplayer Language Simulation Game

This study investigates a multiplayer online game designed to develop communicative competence in Spanish learners through negotiated interactions, task-based activities, and authentic discourse. The theoretical backbone integrates the Communicative Language Teaching (CLT) emphasis on meaning-focused use with the Interaction Hypothesis, which argues that language development emerges from meaningful conversational exchange and corrective feedback (Luo, 2024). The game situates learners in a simulated marketplace, city administration, and cultural exchange events where they must negotiate meaning, propose solutions, and adapt language to genre and register. Language development is measured through discourse analysis of transcripts, error repair sequences, uptake of negotiation moves, and improvement in pragmatic markers such as politeness strategies and alignment to expectations in cross-cultural conversations (Akavova et al., 2023). The study emphasizes how online peer interactions produce natural opportunities for reformulation and noticing gaps in linguistic knowledge, which, according to the Interaction Hypothesis, catalyze interlanguage development. Findings reveal that sustained collaborative tasks with defined communicative goals generate higher levels of interactive talk, better usage of functional language (apologies, requests, refusals), and increased accuracy in pragmatic appropriateness (Kamruzzaman, 2023). The research also identifies critical design considerations, such as facilitating equitable turn-taking, ensuring clear task goals, and providing communicative scaffolds (sentence frames, negotiation prompts) that support novice speakers without diminishing authenticity or agency.

## Case Study 5: Cognitive Apprenticeship and Flow Theory in an Adaptive Language Puzzle-Adventure Game

The final case centers on an adaptive puzzle-adventure game for advanced learners of German, grounded in cognitive apprenticeship and Flow theory. The cognitive apprenticeship framework emphasizes modeling, coaching, scaffolding, and fading support as learners move from guided to autonomous practice. In the game, expert language guides demonstrate problem-solving strategies, while learners observe, imitate, and progressively take ownership of language use in challenging tasks such as decoding idiomatic expressions, constructing coherent cohesive ties, and negotiating complex meaning across cultural contexts (Alkan, 2024). The gameplay is designed to elicit Flow by balancing challenge and skill, providing clear goals, immediate feedback, and an immersive, focused environment that reduces extraneous cognitive load. The adaptive engine modulates difficulty based on performance data, error patterns, and fluency curves, prompting learners with context-rich tasks that gradually require more elaborate discourse (Gligorea et al., 2022). The study evaluates cognitive processes through think-aloud sessions, traces of decision-making, and linguistic outcome measures, including syntactic sophistication, cohesion, and lexical precision. Findings indicate that cognitive apprenticeship within a well-calibrated Flow state fosters deep processing, higher-level strategic use of language, and improved accuracy in complex discourse. Lessons learned point to the necessity of transparent modeling from experts, careful fading of scaffolds to avoid plateauing, and a robust adaptive system that maintains flow without causing frustration or fatigue (Katiyar, 2024). Across all five case studies, the intersection of theory and practice demonstrates that successful game-based language learning hinges on aligning pedagogical aims with the core tenets of the chosen theoretical framework, ensuring that gameplay fosters authentic communicative engagement, supports individual learner trajectories, and provides actionable, reflective feedback that translates into measurable language development (Harry, 2023).

## IMPLEMENTATION OF REGULATORY FRAMEWORKS

Effective implementation of game-based learning (GBL) in language development requires a robust regulatory framework that aligns with educational standards, protects learners, and ensures high-quality instructional design (Dirgantoro et al., 2022). At the core, regulatory considerations should formalize the integration of GBL into curricula by mapping game activities to recognized language competencies, benchmarks, and proficiency scales. This involves alignment with national or regional education standards, such as language proficiency descriptors, communicative competence objectives, and assessment frameworks (Petrusly, 2024). Regulatory bodies can provide guidance on acceptable game genres, content appropriateness, and the balance between entertainment and instruction, ensuring that games support explicit learning goals rather than mere engagement. To operationalize this alignment, districts and schools need formal procurement and approval processes for language-oriented educational games, including vendor evaluation criteria, pilot testing requirements, and evidence of learning outcomes (Kim & Castelli, 2021). This reduces variability in quality and helps districts scale successful GBL initiatives with clear expectations for teachers, administrators, and learners.

A critical regulatory dimension concerns data privacy, security, and ethical use of learner-generated data. Regulations such as data protection statutes, student privacy laws, and coppa-like provisions must be translated into practical guidelines for GBL platforms: what data are collected (e.g., language progress, interaction patterns, error types), how long data are stored, who can access it (teachers, parents, administrators), and how data can be used for personalization or research (Alsadoon, 2023). Anonymization and minimal data principles should be mandated, with explicit consent processes for younger learners and dedicated procedures for data transfer across platforms or systems used within a school or district. Accessibility regulations are essential to ensure GBL tools are usable by learners with diverse needs, including those with disabilities (Fuster-Guilló et al., 2019). This means requiring keyboard navigation, screen reader compatibility, captioning, color-contrast standards, and adjustable font sizes. Equitable access also calls for policies that address device availability, bandwidth requirements, and offline modes to prevent the digital divide from widening gaps in language learning opportunities (Hidayat, 2021).

Quality assurance and accountability frameworks should entrain continuous evaluation of GBL deployments. Regulations can require baseline and longitudinal assessment of linguistic gains, speaking fluency, listening comprehension, vocabulary retention, and intercultural competence, employing validated instruments alongside game-derived metrics (Johnson et al., 2016). Public reporting obligations, classroom observation protocols, and independent reviews help ensure fidelity of implementation and guard against commercially driven but pedagogically weak products.

Professional development requirements for teachers are another regulatory pillar: educators should receive training on game-based pedagogy, assessment alignment, and data interpretation to translate in-game performance into actionable instructional steps (Karabıyık, 2024). Interoperability standards enable different GBL tools and learning management systems to share data securely, supporting coherent language programs across grade levels and schools. Finally, ethical procurement practices, conflict-of-interest disclosures, and transparent licensing ensure that districts select tools based on educational merit rather than marketing appeal, fostering long-term sustainability and trust among stakeholders (Zainal, 2023).

## CONCLUSION

The theoretical foundations underpinning GBL in language development draw from constructivist and sociocultural perspectives, where learners actively build meaning through authentic tasks, collaboration, and feedback-rich environments. Constructivism emphasizes meaningful problem-solving, where language forms emerge from communicative needs within game-based contexts, prompting learners to negotiate meaning, test hypotheses, and reflect on language use. Sociocultural theory foregrounds the social scaffolds that support language acquisition peer collaboration, expert guidance, and culturally relevant materials encouraging structured zones of proximal development within game activities. In practice, this translates into design choices that sequence challenges to gradually increase linguistic complexity, provide collaborative tasks that require negotiation of meaning, and embed authentic language functions such as storytelling, interviewing, or role-play within navigable game worlds (Spanellis et al., 2021). The multimedia learning framework and cognitive load considerations guide how information is presented: combining auditory, visual, and textual cues in a way that aligns with learners' cognitive resources and prior knowledge, using signaling and segmentation to prevent overload, and ensuring that feedback supports form-focused attention as well as communicative fluency (Polat, 2023).

From a motivation and engagement standpoint, self-determination theory highlights autonomy, competence, and relatedness as drivers of sustained participation in language learning games. Designers can incorporate optional paths, adaptive challenges, and meaningful social interaction to satisfy these needs while maintaining instructional integrity (Rueckert et al., 2020). Additionally, behaviorist apparatuses pacing, reinforcement schedules, and clear success criteria can support motivation when integrated thoughtfully with higher-order language tasks rather than relying solely on rote repetition (Abbas et al., 2023). A holistic theoretical synthesis suggests that effective GBL for language development is not about choosing a single framework but about integrating principles across theories to create coherent, learner-centered ecosystems (Liu, 2024). Practical implications include aligning in-game communicative tasks with target outcomes, scaffolding language support through adaptive hints and feedback, and ensuring that assessment captures authentic language use within game contexts as well as formal proficiency measures (Thimmanna et al., 2023).

## SUGGESTIONS

To advance the practical implementation of game-based learning (GBL) in language development, researchers and practitioners should pursue a layered approach that integrates solid theoretical foundations with scalable, classroom-ready designs (Pendy, 2023). First, it is essential to align game design with established language learning theories such as sociocultural theory, input hypothesis, output hypothesis, cognitive constructivism, and communicative competence. A practical suggestion is to map game mechanics to specific language objectives: for example, incorporate collaborative problem-solving tasks to foster negotiation of meaning, which supports incidental vocabulary acquisition and grammatical output through communicative use (Chang et al., 2021). Games should be designed to provide comprehensible input at the learner's zone of proximal development, while offering adjustable scaffolds (e.g., hints, grammar trails, or adaptive feedback) that gradually reduce assistance as proficiency increases. A second practical direction is to embed real communicative purpose within the game world. Rather than focusing solely on rote vocabulary drills, GBL should present authentic tasks such as role-plays, simulations, or narrative-driven quests that require learners to negotiate meaning, request clarification, and provide explanations (Balci et al., 2022). The inclusion of cross-labelling of language forms with functional aims like asking for directions, giving opinions, or summarizing information helps learners notice form-function mappings and strengthens long-term retention. Third, developers should prioritize traceability and measurement by creating built-in analytics that capture interaction types, discourse quality, error patterns, and lexical diversity (Setyoadi and Patmanthara, 2024). This data can inform adaptive feedback loops, enabling teachers to tailor instruction at the class or individual level. Fourth, assessment practices must align with learning goals and game mechanics. Performance-based, formative assessments embedded within gameplay such as in-game dialogues, peer feedback, and reflective journals can complement traditional summative tests (Li & Liu, 2022). Fifth, accessibility and inclusivity should underpin design choices, ensuring multilingual support, culturally relevant content, and equitable access across devices and environments. Finally, sustainable professional development for teachers is critical:

they need ready-to-use GBL templates, rubrics, and exemplars that demonstrate how to integrate games within existing curricula, assessment regimes, and time constraints (Tyni et al., 2022).

## FUTURE RESEARCH DIRECTIONS

Future research should pursue an interdisciplinary synthesis to refine the theoretical frameworks guiding GBL in language learning. A promising direction is to systematically compare sociocultural, constructivist, and ecological theories in the context of language tasks, to determine which frameworks most effectively predict learning gains across different proficiency levels, target languages, ages, and sociocultural backgrounds (Huesca et al., 2023). Longitudinal studies are needed to understand the durability of gains from game-based interventions and how transfer to real-world communicative competence occurs beyond the game context. Another key avenue is the exploration of affordances and constraints of different game genres (serious games, gamified platforms, narrative-driven adventures, and competitive vs. cooperative formats) on various dimensions of language development, such as phonology, morphology, syntax, pragmatics, and sociolinguistic competence (Antonaci et al., 2019). Researchers should examine how game mechanics points, badges, leveling, quests, and narrative stakes shape motivation, engagement, and language output quality, while controlling for prior proficiency and individual differences in gaming experience.

Methodologically, mixed-methods research that triangulates quantitative performance data with qualitative insights from think-aloud protocols, discourse analysis of in-game conversations, and ethnographic observations will enrich understanding of how learners interact with language within game ecosystems (Zhao et al., 2024). There is a need for standardized measurement instruments to assess language outcomes within GBL contexts, including validated fluency rubrics, lexical diversity metrics, and pragmatic accuracy scales that are sensitive to the unique affordances of games (Barua et al., 2022). Cross-cultural and cross-linguistic studies are critical to determine the generalizability of findings and to identify culturally specific interaction patterns that influence language use and uptake. The role of teacher mediation and scaffolding warrants closer scrutiny: how teacher prompts, feedback styles, and in-game facilitation strategies influence learner autonomy and linguistic development (Chen et al., 2020). Future work should also investigate the ethical dimensions of GBL, such as data privacy in educational games, the potential for bias in adaptive algorithms, and the inclusivity of game content for diverse learner populations (Jayavardhini, 2024). Finally, there is scope for the development of open, interoperable design frameworks that enable educators to tailor GBL experiences to local curricula while maintaining fidelity to sound theoretical principles. This includes creating modular, taxonomy-based design guidelines that link learning outcomes with game elements, assessment criteria, and teacher supports, thereby bridging the gap between theory and classroom practice and accelerating evidence-based adoption of game-based language learning (Davis, 2024).

## REFERENCES


Abbas, N., Imran, A., Manzoor, R., Hussain, T., & Hussain, M. (2023). Role of artificial intelligence tools in enhancing students' educational performance at higher levels. *Journal of Artificial Intelligence Machine Learning and Neural Network*, (35), 36–49. DOI: 10.55529/jaimlnn.35.36.49

Agostinelli, S. (2021). *Actionable framework for city digital twin-enabled predictive maintenance and security management systems.*. https://doi.org/DOI: 10.2495/BIM210191

Akavova, A., Temirkhanova, Z., & Lorsanova, Z. (2023). Adaptive learning and artificial intelligence in the educational space. *E3s Web of Conferences,* 451, 06011. https://doi.org/DOI: 10.1051/e3sconf/202345106011

Akgün, S., & Greenhow, C. (2021). Artificial intelligence in education: Addressing ethical challenges in k-12 settings. *AI and Ethics*, *2*(3), 431–440. DOI: 10.1007/s43681-021-00096-7

Akinrinola, O. (2024). Navigating and reviewing ethical dilemmas in ai development: strategies for transparency, fairness, and accountability. *GSC Advanced Research and Reviews,* 18(3), 050-058. https://doi.org/DOI: 10.30574/gscarr.2024.18.3.0088

Alali, R., & Wardat, Y. (2024). Opportunities and challenges of integrating generative artificial intelligence in education. *International Journal of Religion*, *5*(7), 784–793. DOI: 10.61707/8y29gv34

Alenezi, A. (2023). Teacher perspectives on ai-driven gamification: Impact on student motivation, engagement, and learning outcomes. *Information Technologies and Learning Tools*, *97*(5), 138–148. DOI: 10.33407/itlt.v97i5.5437

Alenezi, A. (2024). Obstacles to the use of ai applications in blackboard for faculty members at northern border university, saudi arabia. *Mier Journal of Educational Studies Trends & Practices,* 248-268. https://doi.org/DOI: 10.52634/mier/2024/v14/i2/2581

Aliabadi, R. (2023). *Transdisciplinary ai education: the confluence of curricular and community needs in the instruction of artificial intelligence.*, 137-151. https://doi.org/DOI: 10.1007/978-981-99-7947-9_11

Alkan, A. (2024). Artificial intelligence: its role and potential in education. *İnsan Ve Toplum Bilimleri Araştırmaları Dergisi,* 13(1), 483-497. https://doi.org/DOI: 10.15869/itobiad.1331201

Alladi, T., Chamola, V., Parizi, R., & Choo, K. (2019). Blockchain applications for industry 4.0 and industrial iot: A review. *IEEE Access : Practical Innovations, Open Solutions*, *7*, 176935–176951. DOI: 10.1109/ACCESS.2019.2956748

Allahverdi, A. (2021). Sample senior design projects of industrial engineering program at kuwait university. *Asean Journal of Engineering Education*, *4*(1). Advance online publication. DOI: 10.11113/ajee2020.4n1.14

Almusaed, A., Almssad, A., Yitmen, I., & Homod, R. Z. (2023). Enhancing student engagement: Harnessing "aied"'s power in hybrid education—a review analysis. *Education Sciences*, *13*(7), 632. DOI: 10.3390/educsci13070632

Alrayes, A., Henari, T. F., & Ahmed, D. A. (2024). Chatgpt in education – understanding the bahraini academics perspective. *Electronic Journal of e-Learning*, *22*(2), 112–134. DOI: 10.34190/ejel.22.2.3250

Alsadoon, H. (2023). The impact of gamification on student motivation and engagement: An empirical study. *Dirasat: Educational Sciences*, *50*(2), 386–396. DOI: 10.35516/edu.v50i2.255

Alshehri, B. (2023). Pedagogical paradigms in the ai era: Insights from saudi educators on the long-term implications of ai integration in classroom teaching. *IJESA*, *2*(8), 159–180. DOI: 10.59992/IJESA.2023.v2n8p7

Antonaci, A., Klemke, R., & Specht, M. (2019). The effects of gamification in online learning environments: A systematic literature review. *Informatics (MDPI)*, *6*(3), 32. DOI: 10.3390/informatics6030032

Aparicio-Gómez, O. (2024). Tejiendo conexiones: la simbiosis transformadora entre aprendizaje e inteligencia artificial. *Hachetetepé Revista Científica De Educación Y Comunicación,* (28). https://doi.org/DOI: 10.25267/Hachetetepe.2024.i28.1103

Balci, S., Secaur, J., & Morris, B. (2022). Comparing the effectiveness of badges and leaderboards on academic performance and motivation of students in fully versus partially gamified online physics classes. *Education and Information Technologies*, *27*(6), 8669–8704. DOI: 10.1007/s10639-022-10983-z

Balta, N. (2023). *Ethical considerations in using ai in educational research.,* 2(1), 14205. https://doi.org/DOI: 10.51853/jorids/14205

Barua, P., Vicnesh, J., Gururajan, R., Oh, S., Palmer, E., Azizan, M., Kadri, N. A., & Acharya, U. (2022). Artificial intelligence enabled personalised assistive tools to enhance education of children with neurodevelopmental disorders a review. *International Journal of Environmental Research and Public Health*, *19*(3), 1192. DOI: 10.3390/ijerph19031192

Bastani, P., Kavosi, Z., Alipoori, S., & Imani-Nasab, M. (2023). Evidence- based policy and decision-making among health managers: A case of shiraz university of medical sciences. *Galen Medical Journal*, *6*(1). Advance online publication. DOI: 10.31661/gmj.v6i1.729

Basudan, S. (2023). A Scalable Blockchain Framework For Secure Transactions In Iot-Based Dynamic Applications. *IEEE Open Journal of the Communications Society*, *4*, 1931–1945. DOI: 10.1109/OJCOMS.2023.3307337

Bennani, S., Maalel, A., & Ghezala, H. (2021). Adaptive gamification in e-learning: A literature review and future challenges. *Computer Applications in Engineering Education*, *30*(2), 628–642. DOI: 10.1002/cae.22477

Buckley, P., & Doyle, E. (2014). Gamification and student motivation. *Interactive Learning Environments*, *24*(6), 1162–1175. DOI: 10.1080/10494820.2014.964263

Chai, F., Ma, J., Wang, Y., Zhu, J., & Han, T. (2024). Grading by ai makes me feel fairer? how different evaluators affect college students' perception of fairness. *Frontiers in Psychology*, *15*, 1221177. Advance online publication. DOI: 10.3389/fpsyg.2024.1221177

Chang, C., Hwang, G., & Gau, M. (2021). Promoting students' learning achievement and self-efficacy: A mobile chatbot approach for nursing training. *British Journal of Educational Technology*, *53*(1), 171–188. DOI: 10.1111/bjet.13158

Chen, L., Chen, P., & Lin, Z. (2020). Artificial intelligence in education: A review. *IEEE Access : Practical Innovations, Open Solutions*, *8*, 75264–75278. DOI: 10.1109/ACCESS.2020.2988510

Cranley, L., Doran, D., Tourangeau, A., Kushniruk, A., & Nagle, L. (2012). Recognizing and responding to uncertainty: A grounded theory of nurses' uncertainty. *Worldviews on Evidence-Based Nursing*, *9*(3), 149–158. DOI: 10.1111/j.1741-6787.2011.00237.x

D'Souza, R. (2024). Twelve tips for addressing ethical concerns in the implementation of artificial intelligence in medical education. *Medical Education Online*, *29*(1), 2330250. Advance online publication. DOI: 10.1080/10872981.2024.2330250

Davis, R. (2024). Korean in-service teachers' perceptions of implementing artificial intelligence (ai) education for teaching in schools and their ai teacher training programs. *International Journal of Information and Education Technology (IJIET)*, *14*(2), 214–219. DOI: 10.18178/ijiet.2024.14.2.2042

Deterding, S., Dixon, D., Khaled, R., & Nacke, L. (2011). From game design elements to gamefulness: defining "gamification". *MindTrek '11: Proceedings of the 15th International Academic MindTrek Conference: Envisioning Future Media Environments.* 9-15 https://doi.org/DOI: 10.1145/2181037.2181040

Devi, V., Vashe, A., Rao, R., Abraham, R., Pallath, V., & Torke, S. (2016). Curricular impact on learning approaches and critical thinking skills of medical students. *Education in Medicine Journal, 8*(4). Advance online publication. DOI: 10.5959/eimj.v8i4.468

Dichev, C., & Dicheva, D. (2017). Gamifying education: what is known, what is believed and what remains uncertain: a critical review. *International Journal of Educational Technology in Higher Education, 14*(1), 9. Advance online publication. DOI: 10.1186/s41239-017-0042-5

Dirgantoro, K., Bermuli, J., & Soesanto, R. (2022). Is moodle gamification effective in reviewing student's motivation related to interest in learning online? *Educational Journal Journal of Research Results and Literature Review in the Field of Education, Teaching, and Learning, 8*(1), 114. DOI: 10.33394/jk.v8i1.4790

Dovleac, L., Chi u, I., Nichifor, E., & Brătucu, G. (2023). Shaping the inclusivity in the new society by enhancing the digitainability of sustainable development goals with education. *Sustainability (Basel), 15*(4), 3782. DOI: 10.3390/su15043782

Ejaz, H., McGrath, H., Wong, B., Guise, A., Vercauteren, T., & Shapey, J. (2022). Artificial intelligence and medical education: A global mixed-methods study of medical students' perspectives. *Digital Health, 8*, 205520762210890. DOI: 10.1177/20552076221089099

Erbaşı, Z., Tural, B., & Çoşkuner, İ. (2023). The role and potential of artificial intelligence and gamification in education: The example of vakıf participation bank. *Orclever Proceedings of Research and Development, 3*(1), 243–254. DOI: 10.56038/oprd.v3i1.329

Eslit, E. (2023). Blending boundaries in the new normal: Leveraging technology, ai and global perspectives in modern education. *Journal of Learning and Educational Policy*, (41), 8–18. DOI: 10.55529/jlep.41.8.18

Familoni, B.Babajide Tolulope FamiloniNneamaka Chisom Onyebuchi. (2024). Advancements and challenges in ai integration for technical literacy: A systematic review. *Engineering Science & Technology Journal, 5*(4), 1415–1430. DOI: 10.51594/estj.v5i4.1042

Fazil, A., Hakimi, M., Shahidzay, A. K., & Hasas, A. (2024). Exploring the broad impact of ai technologies on student engagement and academic performance in university settings in afghanistan. *Riggs Journal of Artificial Intelligence and Digital Business*, *2*(2), 56–63. DOI: 10.31004/riggs.v2i2.268

Felzmann, H., Fosch-Villaronga, E., Lutz, C., & Tamò-Larrieux, A. (2020). Towards transparency by design for artificial intelligence. *Science and Engineering Ethics*, *26*(6), 3333–3361. DOI: 10.1007/s11948-020-00276-4

Fırat, M. (2023). Integrating ai applications into learning management systems to enhance e-learning. *Öğretim Teknolojisi Ve Hayat Boyu Öğrenme Dergisi - Instructional Technology and Lifelong Learning*, 1-14. https://doi.org/DOI: 10.52911/itall.1244453

Fuster-Guilló, A., Pertegal-Felices, M., Jimeno-Morenilla, A., Azorín-López, J., Soliveres, M., & Restrepo-Calle, F. (2019). Evaluating impact on motivation and academic performance of a game-based learning experience using kahoot. *Frontiers in Psychology*, *10*, 2843. Advance online publication. DOI: 10.3389/fpsyg.2019.02843

Gamrat, C., Zimmerman, H., Dudek, J., & Peck, K. (2014). Personalized workplace learning: An exploratory study on digital badging within a teacher professional development program. *British Journal of Educational Technology*, *45*(6), 1136–1148. DOI: 10.1111/bjet.12200

Gligorea, I., Yaseen, M., Cioca, M., Gorski, H., & Oancea, R. (2022). An interpretable framework for an efficient analysis of students' academic performance. *Sustainability (Basel)*, *14*(14), 8885. DOI: 10.3390/su14148885

Grunhut, J., Wyatt, A., & Marques, O. (2021). Educating future physicians in artificial intelligence (ai): An integrative review and proposed changes. *Journal of Medical Education and Curricular Development*, *8*, 23821205211036836. Advance online publication. DOI: 10.1177/23821205211036836

Güler, S., & Özkan, Y. (2018). Podcast applications in pre-service language teacher education from a constructivist perspective. *World Journal on Educational Technology Current Issues*, *10*(3), 131–141. DOI: 10.18844/wjet.v10i3.3552

Haresamudram, K., Larsson, S., & Heintz, F. (2023). Three levels of ai transparency. *Computer*, *56*(2), 93–100. DOI: 10.1109/MC.2022.3213181

Harry, A., & Sayudin, S. (2023). Role of ai in education. *Interdiciplinary Journal and Hummanity (Injurity)*, *2*(3), 260–268. DOI: 10.58631/injurity.v2i3.52

Hernández, C. (2023). Development of critical thinking in the university curriculum. International. *Journal of Human Sciences Research, 3*(34), 2–9. DOI: 10.22533/at.ed.5583342313095

Hidayat, D. (2021). The implementation of gamification system in asian higher education teaching. *Journal of Games Game Art and Gamification, 2*(1). Advance online publication. DOI: 10.21512/jggag.v2i1.7218

Hollands, F., Pan, Y., & Escueta, M. (2019). What is the potential for applying cost-utility analysis to facilitate evidence-based decision making in schools? *Educational Researcher, 48*(5), 287–295. DOI: 10.3102/0013189X19852101

Huesca, G., Campos, G., Larre, M., & Pérez-Lezama, C. (2023). Implementation of a mixed strategy of gamification and flipped learning in undergraduate basic programming courses. *Education Sciences, 13*(5), 474. DOI: 10.3390/educsci13050474

Jayavardhini, P. (2024). Ai study partner: Development of an llm and gen ai-enhanced study assistant tool. *Interantional Journal of Scientific Research in Engineering and Management, 08*(03), 1–5. DOI: 10.55041/IJSREM29626

Ji, H., Suo, L., & Hua, C. (2024). Ai performance assessment in blended learning: Mechanisms and effects on students' continuous learning motivation. *Frontiers in Psychology, 15*, 1447680. Advance online publication. DOI: 10.3389/fpsyg.2024.1447680

Jobin, A., Ienca, M., & Vayena, E. (2019). The global landscape of ai ethics guidelines. *Nature Machine Intelligence, 1*(9), 389–399. DOI: 10.1038/s42256-019-0088-2

Johnson, D., Deterding, S., Kuhn, K., Staneva, A., Stoyanov, S., & Hides, L. (2016). Gamification for health and wellbeing: A systematic review of the literature. *Internet Interventions : the Application of Information Technology in Mental and Behavioural Health, 6*, 89–106. DOI: 10.1016/j.invent.2016.10.002

Julita, R. (2024). The impact of gamification on efl students' reading comprehension. *JEFLE, 4*(2), 136. DOI: 10.26418/jefle.v4i2.74901

Kamruzzaman, M., Alanazi, S., Alruwaili, M., Alshammari, N., Elaiwat, S., Abu-Zanona, M., Innab, N., Mohammad Elzaghmouri, B., & Ahmed Alanazi, B. (2023). Ai- and iot-assisted sustainable education systems during pandemics, such as covid-19, for smart cities. *Sustainability (Basel), 15*(10), 8354. DOI: 10.3390/su15108354

Kang, J., Kang, C., Yoon, J., Ji, H., Li, T., Hyunmi, M., & Han, J. (2023). Dancing on the inside: A qualitative study on online dance learning with teacher-ai cooperation. *Education and Information Technologies, 28*(9), 12111–12141. DOI: 10.1007/s10639-023-11649-0

Karabıyık, Ü. (2024). Investigation of the effect of gamified learning on motivation and success in math class. *Journal of Education and Practice*, *8*(1), 32–52. DOI: 10.47941/jep.1645

Katiyar, P. (2024). Ai-driven personalized learning systems: enhancing educational effectiveness. *eatp*. https://doi.org/DOI: 10.53555/kuey.v30i5.4961

Khakpour, A., & Colomo-Palacios, R. (2020). Convergence of gamification and machine learning: A systematic literature review. *Technology Knowledge and Learning*, *26*(3), 597–636. DOI: 10.1007/s10758-020-09456-4

Khater, A., Zaaqoq, A., Wahdan, M., & Ashry, S. (2023). Knowledge and attitude of ain shams university medical students towards artificial intelligence and its application in medical education and practice. *Educational Research and Innovation Journal*, *3*(10), 29–42. DOI: 10.21608/erji.2023.306718

Kim, J., & Castelli, D. (2021). Effects of gamification on behavioral change in education: A meta-analysis. *International Journal of Environmental Research and Public Health*, *18*(7), 3550. DOI: 10.3390/ijerph18073550

Kurniawati, N., Maolida, E., & Anjaniputra, A. (2018). The praxis of digital literacy in the efl classroom: Digital-immigrant vs digital-native teacher. *Indonesian Journal of Applied Linguistics*, *8*(1). Advance online publication. DOI: 10.17509/ijal.v8i1.11459

Larsen, M., Gulis, G., & Pedersen, K. (2011). Use of evidence in local public health work in denmark. *International Journal of Public Health*, *57*(3), 477–483. DOI: 10.1007/s00038-011-0324-y

Larsson, S., & Heintz, F. (2020). Transparency in artificial intelligence. *Internet Policy Review*, *9*(2). Advance online publication. DOI: 10.14763/2020.2.1469

Legaki, N., Xi, N., Hamari, J., Karpouzis, K., & Assimakopoulos, V. (2020). The effect of challenge-based gamification on learning: An experiment in the context of statistics education. *International Journal of Human-Computer Studies*, *144*, 102496. DOI: 10.1016/j.ijhcs.2020.102496

Li, R. and Liu, J. (2022). *Applying gamification in english learning*. https://doi.org/DOI: 10.2991/assehr.k.220504.490

Li, Y., & Chen, T. (2022). Blockchain Empowers Supply Chains: Challenges, Opportunities And Prospects. *Nankai Business Review International*, *14*(2), 230–248. DOI: 10.1108/NBRI-06-2022-0066

Lim, L., Dawson, S., Gašević, D., Joksimovíc, S., Fudge, A., Pardo, A., & Gentili, S. (2020). Students' sense-making of personalised feedback based on learning analytics. *Australasian Journal of Educational Technology, 36*(6), 15–33. DOI: 10.14742/ajet.6370

Limongi, R. (2024). The use of artificial intelligence in scientific research with integrity and ethics. *Rev. Artif. Intell. Educ, 5*(00), e0022. DOI: 10.37497/rev.artif.intell.educ.v5i00.22

Liu, L. (2024). Survey and analysis of primary school teachers' use of generative artificial intelligence. *Lecture Notes in Education Psychology and Public Media, 74*(1), 43–52. DOI: 10.54254/2753-7048/2024.BO17693

López, C., & Tucker, C. (2020). Toward personalized adaptive gamification: A machine learning model for predicting performance. *IEEE Transactions on Games, 12*(2), 155–168. DOI: 10.1109/TG.2018.2883661

Luan, H., Géczy, P., Lai, H., Gobert, J., Yang, S., Ogata, H., Baltes, J., Guerra, R., Li, P., & Tsai, C. (2020). Challenges and future directions of big data and artificial intelligence in education. *Frontiers in Psychology, 11*, 580820. Advance online publication. DOI: 10.3389/fpsyg.2020.580820

Luo, Y. (2024). Innovative research on ai-assisted teaching models for college english listening and speaking courses. *Applied and Computational Engineering, 69*(1), 155–160. DOI: 10.54254/2755-2721/69/20241493

Maggio, I., Ginevra, M., Santilli, S., Nota, L., & Soresi, S. (2021). *Life design for an inclusive and sustainable future.*, 251-270. https://doi.org/DOI: 10.1007/978-3-030-64537-3_10

Mahardika, I., Nuriman, , Supeno, , Mudakir, I., Wahono, B., & Wicaksono, I. (2023). Science textbook based on merdeka belajar curriculum: Integration of learning implementation for critical thinking skills. *Journal of Education Society and Behavioural Science, 36*(10), 109–115. DOI: 10.9734/jesbs/2023/v36i101273

Mehrpour, S., Shavoun, A., Kheiltash, A., Masoomi, R., & Seraji, R. (2023). Evaluating and comparing critical thinking skills of residents of tehran university of medical sciences. *BMC Medical Education, 23*(1), 133. Advance online publication. DOI: 10.1186/s12909-023-04094-7

Moldt, J., Festl-Wietek, T., Fuhl, W., Zabel, S., Claassen, M., Wagner, S., Nieselt, K., & Herrmann-Werner, A. (2024). Assessing ai awareness and identifying essential competencies: Insights from key stakeholders in integrating ai into medical education. *JMIR Medical Education, 10*, e58355–e58355. DOI: 10.2196/58355

Morales, M., Amado-Salvatierra, H., Medina, J., Barchino, R., Hernández-Rizzardini, R., & Teixeira, A. (2024). Personalized feedback in massive open online courses: Harnessing the power of langchain and openai api. *Electronics (Basel), 13*(10), 1960. DOI: 10.3390/electronics13101960

Mugisha, M., Uwitonze, A., Chesire, F., Senyonga, R., Oxman, M., Nsangi, A., Semakula, D., Kaseje, M., Lewin, S., Sewankambo, N., Nyirazinyoye, L., Oxman, A. D., & Rosenbaum, S. (2021). Teaching critical thinking about health using digital technology in lower secondary schools in rwanda: A qualitative context analysis. *PLoS One, 16*(3), e0248773. DOI: 10.1371/journal.pone.0248773

Murtaza, M., Ahmed, Y., Shamsi, J., Sherwani, F., & Usman, M. (2022). Ai-based personalized e-learning systems: Issues, challenges, and solutions. *IEEE Access : Practical Innovations, Open Solutions, 10*, 81323–81342. DOI: 10.1109/ACCESS.2022.3193938

Nagi, F., Salih, R., Alzubaidi, M., Shah, H., Alam, T., Shah, Z., … & Househ, M. (2023). *Applications of artificial intelligence (AI) in medical education: a scoping review.*. https://doi.org/DOI: 10.3233/SHTI230581

Narayanan, K. (2024). Hybrid gamification and ai tutoring framework using machine learning and adaptive neuro-fuzzy inference system. *Journal of Advanced Research in Applied Sciences and Engineering Technology, 42*(2), 221–233. DOI: 10.37934/araset.42.2.221233

Nguyen, T., Nguyen, M. T., & Tran, H. T. (2023). Artificial intelligent based teaching and learning approaches: A comprehensive review. *International Journal of Evaluation and Research in Education (Ijere), 12*(4), 2387. DOI: 10.11591/ijere.v12i4.26623

Onesi-Ozigagun, O. (2024). Revolutionizing education through ai: A comprehensive review of enhancing learning experiences. *International Journal of Applied Research in Social Sciences, 6*(4), 589–607. DOI: 10.51594/ijarss.v6i4.1011

Otero, L., Catalá, A., Morante, M., Taboada, M., López, B., & Barro, S. (2023). Ai literacy in k-12: A systematic literature review. *International Journal of STEM Education, 10*(1), 29. Advance online publication. DOI: 10.1186/s40594-023-00418-7

Pardosi, V., Xu, S., Umurohmi, U., Nurdiana, N., & Sabur, F. (2024). Implementation of an artificial intelligence based learning management system for adaptive learning. *Al-Fikrah Jurnal Manajemen Pendidikan, 12*(1), 149. DOI: 10.31958/jaf.v12i1.12548

Patel, S. (2023). Addressing racial injustice: Examining systems of oppression and promoting equity in contemporary society. *Joura*, *1*(2), 13–17. DOI: 10.61963/jkt.v1i2.33

Pendy, B. (2023). Artificial intelligence: The future of education. *Jurnal Indonesia Sosial Sains*, *2*(11). Advance online publication. DOI: 10.59141/jiss.v2i11.801

Petrusly, P. (2024). *The effect of gamification using kahoot on students' critical thinking abilities: the role of mediating learning engagement and motivation*. Kuey., DOI: 10.53555/kuey.v30i5.1524

Polat, E. (2023). Gamification implementation for educational purposes: A scoping review (2013-2018). *Educational Technology Quarterly*, *2023*(3), 367–400. DOI: 10.55056/etq.589

Pratama, M., Sampelolo, R., & Lura, H. (2023). Revolutionizing education: Harnessing the power of artificial intelligence for personalized learning. *Klasikal Journal of Education Language Teaching and Science*, *5*(2), 350–357. DOI: 10.52208/klasikal.v5i2.877

Rasheed, Z., Ghwanmeh, S., & Abualkishik, A. (2023). Harnessing artificial intelligence for personalized learning: A systematic review. *Data & Metadata*, *2*, 146. DOI: 10.56294/dm2023146

Rathore, A., Sultana, N., Zareen, S. J., & Ahmed, A. (2023). Artificial intelligence and curriculum prospects for elementary school. *Pakistan Journal of Humanities and Social Sciences*, *11*(4). Advance online publication. DOI: 10.52131/pjhss.2023.v11i4.1909

Rivera, E., & Garden, C. (2021). Gamification for student engagement: A framework. *Journal of Further and Higher Education*, *45*(7), 999–1012. DOI: 10.1080/0309877X.2021.1875201

Rohmah, N. (2022). A vocational school cutting-edge learning strategy: Examining gamification towards student engagement and achievement. *Jurnal Kependidikan Jurnal Hasil Penelitian Dan Kajian Kepustakaan Di Bidang Pendidikan Pengajaran Dan Pembelajaran*, *8*(3), 655. DOI: 10.33394/jk.v8i3.5779

Rueckert, D., Pico, K., Kim, D., & Sánchez, X. (2020). Gamifying the foreign language classroom for brain-friendly learning. *Foreign Language Annals*, *53*(4), 686–703. DOI: 10.1111/flan.12490

Rugaiyah, R. (2023). The potential of artificial intelligence in improving linguistic competence: A systematic literature review. *Arkus*, *9*(2), 319–324. DOI: 10.37275/arkus.v9i2.313

Setyoadi, E., & Patmanthara, S. (2024). Students' goal orientation and gamification in learning for academic performance: A systematic literature review. *Research and Development in Education (Raden)*, *4*(1), 390–403. DOI: 10.22219/raden.v4i1.32630

Shah, J. (2024). *Rethinking higher education through multidisciplinary studies.* jes, 20(4s), 2060-2063. https://doi.org/DOI: 10.52783/jes.2309

Shala, D. (2024). Learning styles and motivation: Their role in academic performance. *Journal of Educational and Social Research*, *14*(3), 258. DOI: 10.36941/jesr-2024-0071

Spanellis, A., Pyrko, I., & Dörfler, V. (2021). Gamifying situated learning in organisations. *Management Learning*, *53*(3), 525–546. DOI: 10.1177/13505076211038812

Strydom, W., Funke, N., Nienaber, S., Nortje, K., & Steyn, M. (2010). Evidence-based policymaking: A review. *South African Journal of Science*, *106*(5/6). Advance online publication. DOI: 10.4102/sajs.v106i5/6.249

Sughra, U., & Usmani, A. (2022). Comparison of critical thinking among undergraduate medical students of conventional and integrated curricula in twin cities. *Pakistan Journal of Medical Sciences*, *38*(6). Advance online publication. DOI: 10.12669/pjms.38.6.5409

Thimmanna., Sharma, A.V.N.S., Naik, M. S., Radhakrishnan, S., Sharma, A., (2024). Personalized Learning Paths: Adapting Education with AI-Driven Curriculum. *European Economic Letters (EEL)*, *14*(1), 31–40. https://doi.org/DOI: 10.52783/eel.v14i1.993

Tolentino, R., Baradaran, A., Gore, G., Pluye, P., & Abbasgholizadeh-Rahimi, S. (2024). Curriculum frameworks and educational programs in ai for medical students, residents, and practicing physicians: Scoping review. *JMIR Medical Education*, *10*, e54793. DOI: 10.2196/54793

Tonbuloğlu, B. (2023). An evaluation of the use of artificial intelligence applications in online education. *Journal of Educational Technology and Online Learning*, *6*(4), 866–884. DOI: 10.31681/jetol.1335906

Trang, N., & Thư, P. (2024). The role of ai in improving student learning outcomes: Evidence in vietnam. *International Journal of Multidisciplinary Research and Analysis*, *07*(06). Advance online publication. DOI: 10.47191/ijmra/v7-i06-48

Tubino, L. & Adachi, C. (2022). Developing feedback literacy capabilities through an ai automated feedback tool. *Ascilite Publications*, e22039. https://doi.org/DOI: 10.14742/apubs.2022.39

Tyni, J., Tarkiainen, A., López-Pernas, S., Saqr, M., Kahila, J., Bednarik, R., & Tedre, M. (2022). Games and rewards: A scientometric study of rewards in educational and serious games. *IEEE Access : Practical Innovations, Open Solutions*, *10*, 31578–31585. DOI: 10.1109/ACCESS.2022.3160230

Tzafilkou, K., Perifanou, M., & Economides, A. (2023). Assessing teachers' digital competence in primary and secondary education: Applying a new instrument to integrate pedagogical and professional elements for digital education. *Education and Information Technologies*, *28*(12), 16017–16040. DOI: 10.1007/s10639-023-11848-9

Ulagammal, S., & Chaluvarayaswamy, R. (2023). Expanding access to mindfulness education in adaptive learning: Enhancing student well-being and academic success. *Thiagarajar College of Preceptors Edu Spectra*, *5*(S1), 81–84. DOI: 10.34293/eduspectra.v5is1-may23.014

Uygun, D. (2024). Teachers' perspectives on artificial intelligence in education. *Advances in Mobile Learning Educational Research*, *4*(1), 931–939. DOI: 10.25082/AMLER.2024.01.005

Varas, J., Coronel, B., Villagrán, I., Escalona, G., Hernández, R., Schuit, G., & Achurra, P. (2023). Innovations in surgical training: exploring the role of artificial intelligence and large language models (llm). *Revista Do Colégio Brasileiro De Cirurgiões*, 50. https://doi.org/DOI: 10.1590/0100-6991e-20233605-en

Walter, Y. (2024). Embracing the future of artificial intelligence in the classroom: The relevance of ai literacy, prompt engineering, and critical thinking in modern education. *International Journal of Educational Technology in Higher Education*, *21*(1), 15. Advance online publication. DOI: 10.1186/s41239-024-00448-3

Wood, E., Ange, B., & Miller, D. (2021). Are we ready to integrate artificial intelligence literacy into medical school curriculum: Students and faculty survey. *Journal of Medical Education and Curricular Development*, *8*, 23821205211024078. Advance online publication. DOI: 10.1177/23821205211024078

Yazdanpanah, V., Gerding, E., Stein, S., Dastani, M., Jonker, C., Norman, T., & Ramchurn, S. (2022). Reasoning about responsibility in autonomous systems: Challenges and opportunities. *AI & Society*, *38*(4), 1453–1464. DOI: 10.1007/s00146-022-01607-8

Zainal, N. (2023). University students' perspectives on gamification in vocabulary learning: A literature review. *Malaysian Journal of Social Sciences and Humanities (Mjssh)*, *8*(5), e002314. DOI: 10.47405/mjssh.v8i5.2314

Zhang, J., & Zhang, Z. (2024). AI in teacher education: Unlocking new dimensions in teaching support, inclusive learning, and digital literacy. *Journal of Computer Assisted Learning*, *40*(4), 1871–1885. DOI: 10.1111/jcal.12988

Zhao, J., Juithong, S., & Nilnopkoon, P. (2024). Effecting an adaptive learning system on academic achievement as regulations for measuring pharmacist qualifications to licensure of pharmaceutical management students. *IJSASR*, *4*(3), 573–582. DOI: 10.60027/ijsasr.2024.4357

Zourmpakis, A., Kalogiannakis, M., & Papadakis, S. (2023). Adaptive gamification in science education: An analysis of the impact of implementation and adapted game elements on students' motivation. *Computers*, *12*(7), 143. DOI: 10.3390/computers12070143

# Chapter 11
# Digital Game-Based Language Learning in Language Teacher Education:
## Exploring the Discovery Tour Ancient Egypt

**Kenan Cetin**
http://orcid.org/0000-0003-4311-406X
*Bartin University, Turkey*

## ABSTRACT

*The integration of digital games in education offers engagement, contextualized learning, and multimodal interaction. In language teacher education, digital game-based language learning (DGBLL) exposes preservice teachers to innovative environments and equips them with pedagogical strategies. This chapter examines commercial and serious games, focusing on Ubisoft's Discovery Tour: Ancient Egypt (DTAE), which provides historically grounded, immersive simulations. After reviewing literature on gamification, playful learning, and DGBLL within constructivist and situated frameworks, the chapter presents a case implemented with 80 preservice teachers in Türkiye. Participants designed lesson plans integrating historical content with English objectives using DTAE and H5P activities. The chapter illustrates that games foster creativity, motivation, and cultural engagement among preservice teachers. Furthermore, digital games, paired with structured support, enhance teacher education and more suggestions are made for future research with emerging technologies.*

DOI: 10.4018/979-8-3373-4322-8.ch011

# 1. INTRODUCTION

The rapid integration of digital technologies into education has significantly expanded the possibilities for instruction, learning, and teacher professional development. These tools are no longer peripheral add-ons to traditional teaching; they now form an essential part of designing interactive, learner-centered experiences. In the field of Language Teacher Education (LTE), this shift has brought new expectations for preservice teachers. Future educators are expected not only to be proficient in using educational technologies but also to design and implement rich, meaningful learning experiences that promote linguistic development, cultural awareness, and learner engagement.

One promising pedagogical approach in this regard is game-based learning (GBL), which leverages the motivational and interactive nature of games to foster deeper learning. In the context of language learning, games can create immersive environments where learners negotiate meaning, practice communication strategies, and develop problem-solving skills in authentic or simulated scenarios. However, it is important to clarify distinctions between gamification, playful learning, and game-based learning, as these terms are often used interchangeably despite their unique pedagogical orientations. *Gamification* involves adding game-like features—such as points, leaderboards, or rewards to an existing instructional framework to boost motivation. *Playful learning* entails reimagining instructional design to embrace elements of play, creativity, and exploration. *Game-based learning (GBL)*, by contrast, positions the game itself as the central medium of instruction, with its mechanics, rules, and activities deliberately aligned to achieve specific learning outcomes (Plass et al., 2020). This chapter focuses on GBL, therefore; apps using gamification, Duolingo, for example, were excluded.

A growing area within GBL is the use of video games; both commercial off-the-shelf titles and purpose-built educational games in language learning. This concept is also refered as Digital GBL in the literature and includes the use of both commercial and educational digital video games, such as narrative-driven role-playing games or simulation games. Educational video games, are specifically designed with pedagogical goals in mind, offering targeted practice in vocabulary, grammar, listening, speaking, and cultural knowledge. These types of digital games often provide rich, contextualized language input, opportunities for meaningful interaction, and authentic problem-solving.

## 1.1. Purpose and Significance

Within LTE, game-based learning serves a dual purpose: it can be employed directly to enhance preservice teachers' own language learning experiences, and it can be modeled as an instructional strategy for future classroom use. This means that preservice teachers are not only participants but also analysts and designers of game-based tasks, reflecting on how games can support vocabulary acquisition, grammar practice, intercultural communication, and collaborative learning. By understanding the principles of GBL, teacher candidates can develop the capacity to select or design games that align with curricular goals, linguistic targets, and learner needs.

Based on the concept of Digital Game-based Learning, this book chapter explores possible utilizations of sample digital video games in language teaching and learning and discusses their place in language teacher education. This chapter does not aim to evaluate the effectiveness of the intervention statistically but instead offer a descriptive case of practice grounded in the literature. It contributes to ongoing discussions about the practical use of commercial digital games in language teacher education and the value of pairing these experiences with tools like H5P to guide and extend learning with a sample experience from the classroom.

The significance of this chapter lies in addressing a practical gap between the theoretical discussions of Digital Game-Based Language Learning (DGBLL) and its concrete application within language teacher education contexts. While a substantial body of research has examined the effects of digital games on language learning outcomes, considerably less attention has been given to how preservice teachers can be systematically introduced to such tools during their professional preparation. In many cases, commercial digital games are discussed conceptually in the literature but are rarely demonstrated through detailed pedagogical examples that illustrate how teacher candidates can analyze, adapt, and design language learning activities around them. This chapter contributes to the field by illustrating how a commercial educational game environment, Discovery Tour: Ancient Egypt, can be integrated into an undergraduate language teacher education course and paired with interactive activities created through H5P by presenting a structured example grounded in classroom practice.

## 1.2. Digital Game-based Learning

Digital Game-Based Learning (DGBL) refers to the use of game elements and principles within educational contexts to enhance learner engagement, motivation, and knowledge acquisition. Rooted in constructivist theories of learning, DGBL emphasizes active learner participation, experiential learning, and situated cognition (Gee, 2003). Games create immersive environments where learners can experiment, take risks, and receive immediate feedback, all of which contribute to deeper cognitive processing (Shaffer, 2006).

A key argument for the use of digital games in learning is their capacity to capture and maintain learners' attention. However, the concept of engagement in games can vary widely. For instance, consider a player repeatedly performing the same action in the same setting—sometimes hundreds of times—to gain an advantage in the game (Plass et al., 2020). While this repetitive activity might be useful for developing automatic responses, it does not necessarily lead to new knowledge or skills, even though the player appears highly engaged. This illustrates the need to define engagement more precisely.

In this context, engagement can be understood through four distinct types: behavioral, cognitive, affective, and sociocultural. Behavioral engagement refers to the physical actions a player takes, such as swiping a touchscreen, pressing buttons on a VR controller, or using full-body movements with motion-based systems. Cognitive engagement involves mentally processing game information to create meaning and build understanding, which is often directly connected to the game's learning goals. Affective engagement relates to the learner's emotional involvement, while sociocultural engagement encompasses the social and cultural dimensions of interaction within the game environment (Barz et al., 2024).

Games are widely recognized for their ability to keep learners motivated and engaged over extended periods, a trait often observed in entertainment games (Steinkuehler & Squire, 2023). Their motivational power comes from features such as rewards, appealing mechanics, and enjoyable activities. By reducing the negative consequences of mistakes, games encourage exploration, risk-taking, and experimentation (Ryan & Deci, 2000).. Such environments also promote self-regulated learning, enabling players to evaluate the effectiveness of their strategies and progress toward their goals (Barab et al., 2009; Kim et al., 2009). Games can foster deeper engagement by making learning tasks meaningful, relevant, and adaptive to individual needs.

Games can influence learners' emotions through narrative, visual design, music, and mechanics. This deliberate shaping of emotional experience, known as emotional design, can improve learning by fostering positive emotions that expand cognitive capacity (Plass & Kaplan, 2016). Even emotions such as mild confusion can be productive, prompting deeper engagement with material. Games can also employ empathetic virtual agents that respond to players' emotional states, and the excitement generated by game mechanics can spark situational interest, which in turn supports learning. In a meta-analysis, Clark et al. (2016) found that GBL significantly improves student motivation and learning achievement compared to traditional instruction, especially when games incorporate feedback, adaptive difficulty, and clear learning goals. Furthermore,

Games create opportunities for meaningful social interaction and can tap into cultural dimensions of learning. Player communities—both in and around games—can be powerful drivers of engagement and knowledge sharing. Different modes of play, such as collaborative or competitive formats, influence learners' interest and motivation. Social and cultural contexts often interact with cognitive and emotional processes, shaping the overall learning experience (Gee, 2007). Large-scale collaborative games, such as those used in citizen science projects, show how collective participation can solve complex real-world problems (Pearce et al., 2011). Games can also reshape traditional relationships of power, promote agency, and create new forms of collaborative and observational learning.

Digital games in language learning come in many genres, including simulation, role-playing, drill-and-practice, and puzzles. Despite the abundance of genres, no significant advantage was reported for a specific genre over others (Bui et al., 2025). Researchers often group digital games into two main categories. The first category includes commercially available games designed for general entertainment, often referred to as commercial off-the-shelf (COTS) games. The second category consists of serious games, which are specifically developed for educational purposes. In serious games, the primary goal is to promote learning, whereas COTS games are typically not created with instructional objectives in mind. Over the past decade, numerous reviews have compared the learning outcomes and impacts of these two types of games (Boyle et al., 2016; Hung et al., 2018a).

## 1.3. Digital Game-based Language Learning

Digital games mark a shift in education from traditional, information-delivery approaches toward learning models that emphasize active problem-solving, collaboration, social interaction, and, at times, competition. Multiplayer online games, in particular, can provide rich environments for developing specialized literacies, scientific reasoning, contextualized knowledge engagement, advanced problem-solving skills, and leadership abilities (Nardi & Kallinikos, 2010; Plass et al., 2015). In language learning, research highlights three main areas of exploration: understanding natural language use and acquisition in recreational games, evaluating learning processes and outcomes in games designed for second language (L2) education, and enhancing the language-learning potential of recreational gaming through integration with traditional instruction.

Different terms are often used to describe game use in education: *game-based* for purpose-built L2 learning games, *game-enhanced* for commercially produced recreational games repurposed for learning, and *game-informed* for applying game mechanics to teaching without a full game environment. While some games have been developed by educators for specific teaching contexts, others have been commercially produced by publishers, though their effectiveness remains underexplored.

Approaches to designing and researching these games draw from multiple theoretical perspectives in second language acquisition, including behaviorist, cognitive, and sociocultural frameworks. These align closely with principles of good game design, such as immersive linguistic environments, clear goals, interactive communication, timely feedback, and narrative or scenario-based contexts. Ongoing projects are creating game-based language learning tools informed by how languages are acquired. More recent work applies the ecological concept of *affordances*—the opportunities for action that emerge in gameplay—to understand how game mechanics and contexts can encourage participation, shared focus, linguistic interaction, and ultimately, language learning.

A recent review reported that most game-based language learning studies drew on cognitive and social frameworks, such as flow theory, situated learning, and sociocultural theory. Research most often involved primary school learners studying English as a foreign language, with quantitative approaches—particularly tests, questionnaires, and experimental designs—being the dominant methodology. Tutorial games were the most common genre, and pre-game instructional activities like gameplay training and lectures were frequently implemented in K–12 settings. Reported benefits included improvements in all four language skills, communicative competence, and learner attitudes, while common challenges involved technical problems, uncooperative partners, overly difficult tasks, and high cognitive load (Yang et al., 2024).

Digital Game-Based Language Learning (DGBLL) represents the intersection of language learning principles and the affordances of digital gaming technologies. While game-based learning has a long-standing history in education, the shift to digital environments has significantly expanded its scope and potential. In DGBLL, language development occurs through structured interaction with digital games, which may be commercial titles, educationally designed games, or hybrid models that combine entertainment and pedagogical objectives. These environments provide opportunities for learners to practice language skills in authentic, immersive, and often socially interactive contexts that traditional classroom settings may struggle to replicate.

Another core strength of DGBLL lies in its ability to integrate linguistic input, communicative tasks, and feedback mechanisms within an engaging, goal-oriented framework. Digital games often require players to process multimodal input—combining written and spoken language, visual cues, and interactive choices—while navigating narrative or problem-solving challenges. This creates natural conditions for practicing vocabulary, grammar, listening, speaking, reading, and writing in meaningful contexts. Moreover, the interactive nature of games fosters sustained engagement and intrinsic motivation, which are critical factors in successful language acquisition.

Interest in the educational potential of digital games has grown, prompting reviews to map existing research and identify gaps. An analysis of fifty studies on digital game-based language learning (2007–2016) found that most involved immersive genres such as massively multiplayer online role-playing games. Most studies reported positive outcomes, especially in learners' motivation, attitudes, and language acquisition. Overall, the findings suggest that digital games can effectively support language and literacy development, though several promising areas remain underexplored (Hung et al., 2018a). Another review by Hung et al. (2018b) examined evidence on the use of digital games in language learning, with a particular emphasis on studies conducted outside the United States. Three main areas of interaction emerged from the literature: between players and the game, between players themselves, and between players and online gaming communities. The findings indicate that while digital games offer diverse opportunities for language learning, their application is sometimes oversimplified. The review highlights the need for more nuanced and contextually grounded approaches to integrating games and game-like activities into language education

### 1.3.1. Commercial-off-the-shelf digital games in language learning

The effects of gaming on language learning has been investigated extensively in the literature. Language learning in gaming can occur in multiple ways in commercial-off-the-shelf games (COTS). While vocabulary and expressions may be acquired during gameplay, sentences and extended discourse can be practiced through interactions with native or more proficient peers in online communities. These forms of engagement, reinforced through repetition and collaboration, highlight the value of adopting an ecological perspective that considers both in-game and community-based aspects of gaming culture (Ryu, 2013). A systematic review by Rajendran et al. (2024) highlights the positive role of commercial games in developing English language skills, examining various genres and linking specific game elements to four game-based learning perspectives: affective, motivational, cognitive, and socio-cultural. It emphasizes the direct contributions of these elements to language skill development and situates the findings within broader discussions on innovative pedagogies for a technology-driven educational context.

One well-known example of a COTS game applied to language learning is *The Sims*. Unlike traditional language instruction, where vocabulary and grammar are often learned in isolation, gameplay in *The Sims* links language use directly to carrying out tasks and engaging in social interactions (Purushotma et al., 2009). This situates vocabulary and grammatical structures within meaningful, context-rich scenarios. Classroom use of such games can enhance learning by providing supplementary materials and teacher guidance that direct learners' attention to appropriate language forms. For instance, using structured lessons with pre-game preparation, targeted gameplay activities, and post-game reflection has been shown to improve vocabulary acquisition (Ranalli, 2008).

There are also many examples of informal L2 learning in multiplayer online games. In massively multiplayer environments like *World of Warcraft*, players often engage in multilingual communication that naturally supports language practice (Kallunki, 2016; Newgarden & Zheng, 2016). Similarly, studies of players interacting in English-language versions of narrative-driven games, such as *Final Fantasy* series, have shown that repeating and playing with the language used by game characters can boost linguistic awareness and contribute to proficiency. Online COTS games were also found to improve autonomous learning and the sense of support in online community has created a positive environment towards language learning (Chik, 2014).

In terms of improving language, narrative-driven games also stand out. Games such as *Life is Strange* or *Headliner: Novinews* were examined for their associated with writing and reading skill development. While Schønning & Fløgum (2025) reported that Life is Strange improved writing skills and increased writing motivation among learners, Moniza Ray and Ajit (2024) observed increase in listening skills of the participants after playing the game. Similarly, Ivan (2025) observed that playing the narrative-driven Headliner: Novinews game increased motivation, willingness to communicate and active participation among learners.

Recently, a study by study Lai and Chen (2025) investigated the effectiveness of the COTS game *Return to Monkey Island* in supporting vocabulary acquisition. Participants in the study expressed positive attitudes toward collaborative gameplay, emphasizing the benefits of peer interaction. The findings suggest that integrating COTS games with both individual and collaborative tasks can enhance vocabulary learning outcomes.

### 1.3.2. *Serious digital games in language learning*

One of the earliest examples of a serious game which showed a significant potential in language learning was *Second Life*. The virtual world game which launched in 2003 opened up new possibilities for immersive language practice, with dedicated islands and communities where learners could interact with native speakers and participate in role-play scenarios. These platforms blurred the line between serious games and social virtual environments, emphasizing communication and cultural exchange. Even a decade after its launch, the game attracts attention in the scientific community (Aydın, 2013; Bozorgian et al., 2025; Chen, 2016).

Another early example of a serious game called QuestAtlantis was also extensively studied by researchers (Di Blas et al., 2010; Kim, 2009; Stoerger et al., 2007; Zheng et al., 2009) . These studies revealed multiple affordances of the game for language acquisition at both utterance and discourse levels. Intercultural collaboration on content-based problem-solving enabled participants to achieve quest objectives while engaging in identity formation and meaning-making. Pragmatics, syntax, semantics, and discourse practices emerged naturally within these interactions in the game, supporting the ecological psychology view that meaning arises through the use of language to coordinate actions in real time.

In 2014, Influent launched on the popular gaming platform Steam. Influent is a vocabulary-focused digital game with aims to develop spelling and vocabulary in 23 languages. In contrast to aforementioned games, Influent was examined in only a few studies (Honarzad & Soyoof, 2020; Kusuma, 2022). Despite its unpopularity in the scientific community, it is estimated to have sold more than 100 thousand copies since its release (Gamalytics, 2025).

*Figure 1. Snapshots from Lingokids parent view*

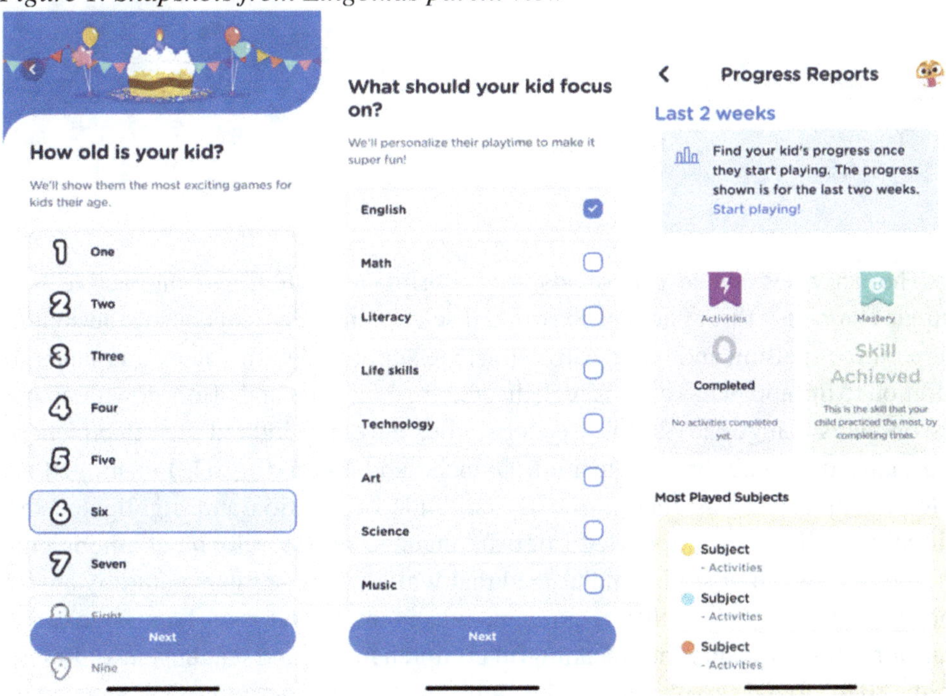

It is also noteworthy to state that serious games on smartphones are becoming more and more popular. As their popularity grows, researchers question their applicability and effectiveness. While gamified apps such as Duolingo, Busuu, Memrise, and Falou have been investigated extensively over the past decade for their effectiveness, some apps took a more GBL approach by taking gamification a step further. One such app, LingoKids uses game-based learning for educational purposes. LingoKids is an app designed for children between two and eight years old and their parents. Figure 1 illustrates how a parent sets up the app by choosing the age of their child, the content. The parent is also able to view the progress on the app and most features require verification, making the app safer.

*Figure 2. Snapshots from Lingo Kids activities*

The activities inside LingoKids are colorful, animated, and interactive with unique characters throughout each scene. It seldom includes texts inside the content to reinforce spelling and most instructions are supported with voice commands. In addition to the app, it has a website dedicated for educators and offers downloadable lesson plans (LingoKid, 2025). Recent studies have highlighted the effectiveness, especially on vocabulary acquisiton. Damcha and Budiarti (2022) examined the role of digital learning media in early childhood education and highlighted that Lingokids, effectively supported English language skill development among children aged 2–8. Their study emphasized that while young learners naturally absorb foreign language sounds, they require guided and interactive tools like Lingokids to transform this exposure into meaningful comprehension and language use. Julianti et al. (2024) found that the app had a significant impact on improving vocabulary mastery among primary school students, with learners showing increased motivation and enthusiasm toward learning English through gameplay. Similarly, Setiyaningsih et al. (2023) reported that the app enhanced kindergarten learners' vocabulary skills, noting that its interactive and playful design helped sustain attention and foster positive learning experiences. In another study, Aladelah (2024) demonstrated that Lingokids effectively improved vocabulary acquisition among first-year primary students, and also revealed gender differences, with female learners outperforming their male counterparts.

*Figure 3. Snapshots from the Lingo Legend game*

Another recent game-based mobile learning app named Lingo Legend is a role-playing, turn-based mobile game that offers language content embedded. Users start the game in a game map and select foes to fight by picking cards and dealing damage while answering questions on a language they pick. The game was designed for speakers of English, Spanish, or French languages and offers 12 languages to be learned. Different than LingoKids, the game is more suitable for adults as it offers more game-like features such as levels, turn-based mechanics, character customization with items, decorations, and cards. Recently, Black (2025) examined the impact of digital game-based language learning on learner identity through a study of Lingo Legend, a role-playing game designed for language learning. Drawing on the Unified Discourse Theory, the research analyzed how game affordances and mechanics shaped the experiences of six participants with varying linguistic and gaming backgrounds. Findings revealed that avatars provided a safe space for learners to experiment without fear of mistakes, while progress tracking and instant feedback fostered a sense of measurable improvement. Learners with negative past experiences or anxiety about language learning showed the most notable identity shifts, and prior gaming experience significantly influenced how well participants engaged with the game.

*Figure 4. Snapshots from Assassins Creed Discovery Tour: Ancient Egypt*

Almost two decades after the release of Second Life, a digital game series named Discovery Tour started with its first version with Discovery Tour Ancient Egypt in 2018 for educational purposes. Based on the popular Assassin's Creed, the Discovery Tour Ancient Egypt (DTAE) is a non-violent educational game which includes tens of interactive tours that allow players to explore aspects of ancient Egyptian history while engaging with the detailed environment in the game. The game received attention shortly after its release and researchers raised the question of why not have "language learning be part of it, either as a central element of the game or as a potential source of collateral (incidental) learning" (Hung et al., 2018, p. 8).

The Discovery Tour series is made of dedicated games that let visitors freely roam Ancient Greece, Ancient Egypt and the Viking Age to learn more about their history and daily life. Students, teachers, non-gamers, and players can discover these eras at their own pace, or embark on guided tours and stories curated by historians and experts.

The Assassin's Creed Discovery Tour series is a set of educational spin-offs developed by Ubisoft as part of the popular Assassin's Creed franchise. Unlike the mainline games, which focus on action-adventure narratives, the Discovery Tour editions transform the richly detailed historical environments of the series into immersive learning experiences. The first installment, Discovery Tour: Ancient Egypt was released as an expansion to Assassin's Creed Origins in 2018. It allowed players to freely explore Ptolemaic Egypt without combat or story missions, engaging instead with guided tours designed in collaboration with historians and Egyptologists. Players could "walk through history" as figures such as Cleopatra, Julius Caesar, or ordinary citizens, gaining insight into architecture, daily life, religion, and social practices of the time. Following its success, Discovery Tour: Ancient Greece was launched with Assassin's Creed Odyssey in 2019. This installment provided a similar learning mode, enabling exploration of classical Greek cities, sanctuaries, and battlefields. It also introduced interactive quizzes to check learners' knowledge, further reinforcing its role as a serious game with educational aims. The third release, Discovery Tour: Viking Age in 2021, accompanied Assassin's Creed Valhalla. It expanded the educational model by including narrative-driven learning quests, where players experienced history through the perspective of diverse characters, such as monks, traders, or Viking settlers. This installment placed more emphasis on cultural interactions between the Norse and Anglo-Saxons, showcasing themes of identity, migration, and social life.

Collectively, the Discovery Tour series exemplifies how commercial video game worlds can be repurposed for educational use, merging historical accuracy with engaging, interactive design. In fact, a comprehensive curriculum guide was designed based on the game series (Ubisoft, 2025). They are increasingly used in classrooms and research as tools for game-based learning, particularly in history, archaeology, and even language education, since players must engage with authentic terminology, narratives, and contextualized dialogue while exploring the virtual past.

Since its release, Discovery Tour series have been praised for their use in educational settings (Sardo & Thibault, 2024; Travis, 2017). Though originally designed for history education, the series offer valuable opportunities for language learning due to their immersive environments, narrative structures, and authentic terminology (Bregni, 2018). Unlike purely historical textbooks, these games situate learners in richly detailed cultural settings where language is contextualized through artifacts, characters, and guided narratives. Moreover, the series ship with full audio/subtitle localization in multiple languages (e.g., English, French, Italian, German, Spanish, Russian, Japanese, Brazilian Portuguese; plus UI/subtitles in several Asian languages). The built-in multilingual narration and captions make it a strong candidate for content-based L2 tasks (listening/reading, vocabulary-in-context, pronunciation shadowing, comparative registers), especially in Content and Language Integrated Language Learning contexts. Furthermore, the curriculum guide itself offers instructional plans on language and literacy.

## 1.4. Place of Digital Game-based Learning in Language Teacher Education

As digital games continue to evolve in complexity and accessibility, their role in language learning is poised to grow in significance. For LTE programs, preparing teachers to harness the pedagogical potential of DGBLL is no longer optional; it is an essential component of equipping future educators to meet the needs and interests of digitally native learners in a globalized, multilingual world (Hung et al., 2018; Kaimara et al., 2021; Sharma et al., 2025; Xu et al., 2023).

In LTE, integrating these types of games can serve as both a learning experience and a training tool: preservice teachers can engage with games as learners to understand their affordances and limitations, and then adapt or design similar experiences for their own future classrooms (Xu et al., 2023). This dual engagement equips them with practical strategies for incorporating video games into language curricula in ways that are pedagogically sound and culturally relevant. Studies illustrate that integrating game-enhanced activities into the curriculum proved effective in supporting students' foreign language learning and contributed to fostering a more positive self-perception of their language abilities (Aydın & Çakır, 2022).

By positioning game-based learning—and, within it, the strategic use of video games—at the intersection of language learning and teacher education, this chapter aims to explore both the theoretical foundations and the practical applications of GBL in LTE. Through this lens, it will examine how preservice teachers can critically evaluate, adapt, and implement game-based approaches to foster engaging, effective, and transformative language learning experiences.

In the context of Language Teacher Education, DGBLL offers a powerful dual function. First, preservice teachers can engage with digital games as learners, gaining firsthand experience of how these environments support language acquisition through immersion, task completion, and authentic communication. Second, they can critically evaluate and design digital game-based tasks for their own future classrooms, aligning game mechanics with specific language learning outcomes and curricular goals. By analyzing the affordances and limitations of different game types—such as narrative-driven role-playing games, multiplayer online worlds, and educational language-learning games—teacher candidates can develop a nuanced understanding of how to integrate DGBLL effectively into varied teaching contexts.

The growing body of research on digital game-based learning (DGBL) and digital game-based language learning (DGBLL) highlights not only the potential of games as tools for learner engagement but also the necessity of preparing future educators to critically evaluate and integrate these tools in their teaching. While commercial-off-the-shelf (COTS) games such as The Sims, World of Warcraft, and Life is Strange have demonstrated value in providing authentic interactional contexts and narrative-driven opportunities for language use, serious games such as Second Life, Quest Atlantis, Influent, and Ubisoft's Discovery Tour series illustrate how games designed or repurposed for education can target specific linguistic and cultural outcomes. Together, these examples point to the diverse pedagogical possibilities of games and the importance of equipping preservice teachers with the knowledge and confidence to harness them.

For preservice English teachers, the integration of DGBLL into teacher education programs has several implications. First, it encourages a broader understanding of how language learning extends beyond traditional classroom boundaries into immersive and multimodal environments. This helps teachers-in-training to conceptualize learning as a situated, participatory, and often collaborative process. Second, exploring COTS and serious games allows preservice teachers to develop critical digital literacy skills: they must learn to evaluate the pedagogical affordances and limitations of different games, consider issues of accessibility and inclusivity, and design tasks that align gameplay with language learning outcomes. Third, DGBLL provides opportunities for teachers to reflect on learner motivation and engagement, as games exemplify how intrinsic motivation, narrative immersion, and problem-solving can sustain language practice over extended periods.

Furthermore, including DGBLL in language teacher education supports future teachers in preparing their learners for a world where digital environments, gaming cultures, and online communities increasingly intersect with language use. It fosters pedagogical innovation by encouraging teachers to experiment with interactive narratives, role-playing, and cross-cultural simulations. For example, while The Sims may be used to design role-plays around daily routines or social interactions, Discovery Tour: Ancient Egypt enables learners to explore historical contexts and cultural practices through rich multimodal input, potentially serving as both linguistic and intercultural resources. Such exposure not only expands the pedagogical toolkit of preservice teachers but also underscores the role of games as cultural artifacts that can spark discussions on identity, community, and global citizenship.

In this way, positioning DGBLL within language teacher education is less about prescribing specific tools and more about cultivating the mindset of flexibility, innovation, and critical engagement. Preservice teachers benefit from experiencing how games can be used to design meaningful tasks, scaffold authentic communication, and bridge the gap between learners' everyday digital practices and classroom learning objectives.

The following section builds on these considerations by presenting an example of how a serious game, Discovery Tour: Ancient Egypt, was integrated into a language teacher education context. By analyzing preservice English teachers' experiences with this game, we explore the pedagogical affordances and challenges of incorporating immersive historical simulations into language learning and teaching.

Ubisoft's Discovery Tour: Ancient Egypt (DTAE) is one example of a digital game designed specifically with educational aims. It offers learners a chance to explore a historically accurate 3D environment based on Ancient Egypt, enabling guided virtual tours on topics like politics, daily life, and the arts. The game supports open-world exploration through avatars of historical figures and includes features like authentic visuals, factual narration, and linked curriculum materials (Ubisoft,

2025). Emerging research has begun to examine the use of Discovery Tour games in school settings. For instance, Sharma et al. (2025) investigated how a curriculum guide aligned with DTAE influenced teachers' views on technology and game-based learning. Their findings suggested that structured guides improved teachers' attitudes. However, it is important to note that the teachers in their study did not use the game directly but only reviewed the curriculum materials.

This chapter presents a case from a university-level course titled *Open and Distance Learning*, in which preservice English language teachers engaged with *Discovery Tour: Ancient Egypt* in a lab-based setting. Over several weeks, the participants explored selected quests and scenes from the game. Following this exploratory phase, a structured language lesson was designed by the instructor using Moodle, incorporating various H5P activity types such as interactive videos, drag-the-words, and vocabulary exercises. These activities were based on a specific quest within the game and aimed to support learners' acquisition of relevant lexical and conceptual knowledge. After completing the lesson, participants discussed how similar technology-enhanced materials could be designed for language classrooms, sharing their reflections and lesson ideas in the course's Moodle forum.

The pedagogical rationale for integrating game-based learning (GBL) and interactive lesson design stems from research emphasizing the cognitive and affective benefits of contextualized learning environments (Barz et al., 2024). Games like *Discovery Tour* can enhance situated learning, providing learners with experiences that mimic real-world exploration and inquiry (Barab, Gresalfi, & Ingram-Goble, 2010). In second language acquisition contexts, such environments also support vocabulary acquisition, content comprehension, and learner autonomy when combined with scaffolded tasks (Reinders, 2012; Peterson, 2011).

The lesson design also drew on the potential of H5P—a free, open-source platform that allows educators to create interactive and multimedia-rich learning objects within Learning Management Systems (LMSs). H5P enables the development of self-paced, feedback-rich materials that can complement more open-ended exploratory experiences like those provided by educational games. The case presented in this chapter highlights how such a combination of immersive gameplay and structured digital materials can enrich the training of future English language teachers, particularly in fostering digital pedagogical skills and critical awareness of technology integration.

Specifically, preservice teacher education benefits from video games by allowing future educators to experience innovative pedagogical tools firsthand and reflect on their classroom applications (Girard et al., 2013). For example, Vos et al. (2011) demonstrated how game-based learning environments encourage active engagement and foster collaborative learning among teacher candidates. Additionally, the integration of historical simulation games—such as *Discovery Tour: Ancient*

*Egypt*—offers interdisciplinary learning opportunities, bridging content knowledge with language acquisition and cultural understanding (Dickey, 2007).

The literature regarding DGBLL and language teacher education indicates the potential of games and how they can be used to promote language teacher development. Building on the aforementioned theoretical and empirical insights, the next section illustrates a classroom application of DGBLL. The following case does not aim to measure learning outcomes experimentally; rather, it provides a descriptive account of how Discovery Tour: Ancient Egypt (DTAE) was integrated into an undergraduate Open and Distance Learning course and how interactive H5P activities were used to complement language learning tasks. By foregrounding preservice teachers' lesson designs, the case highlights practical affordances and implications for teacher education.

## 2. EXPLORING THE USE OF DISCOVERY TOUR ANCIENT EGYPT WITH PRESERVICE ENGLISH TEACHERS

The previous sections illustrated that research on DGBL and DGBLL increasingly emphasizes both the value of games for fostering learner engagement and the importance of equipping future teachers to thoughtfully assess and apply these tools in their practice. It is undoubtfully important for preservice teachers to explore how games could be used in education and the effects of DGBLL. One compelling example of implementing DGBLL in education is the use of historically based open-world games, such as *Discovery Tour: Ancient Egypt*, which provide immersive environments for exploring history, culture, and language in authentic contexts. While digital games have long been associated with engagement and motivation in educational settings (Gee, 2003; Kaimara et al., 2021), their pedagogical affordances for teacher education—particularly in the field of English language teaching—remain underexplored.

The case presented in this section is of a descriptive nature, only aiming to illustrate rather than providing empirical evidence. The experiences of the participants were presented via screenshots of the activities and examples of lesson plans to explicitly demonstrate a pedagogical design strategy to promote DGBLL among preservice English language teachers.

### 2.1. Participants and Context

The research in this study was conducted within the scope of the undergraduate course *Open and Distance Learning* offered to preservice English language teachers at a state university in Türkiye. The course, delivered in a computer laboratory setting, hosted 80 participants who attended weekly 80-minute sessions throughout the semester. The course curriculum covered key themes in open and distance education, online learning management systems (LMS), interactive digital activities, and game-based learning approaches. As part of the module on game-based learning, DTAE game was installed on the laboratory computers for instructional exploration. The game was selected due to its curricular relevance, language-rich environment, and adaptability for pedagogical purposes thanks to the curriculum guide developed based on it.

## 3. EXPLORING THE DTAE GAME AND THE CURRICULUM GUIDE

During the first two weeks of the intervention, participants were given the opportunity to freely explore DTAE. This phase was intended to familiarize preservice teachers with the mechanics of the game, including navigation, quest progression, content, and the characters. A curriculum guide specifically developed by Ubisoft for DTAE game was introduced through Ubisoft's official website and participants were explained that it provided the structured objectives aligned with potential language learning outcomes. While exploration remained largely unstructured, participants were encouraged to reflect on how game content might intersect with English language teaching practices after each session.

*Figure 5. Preservice English teachers getting familiar with the DTAE game*

In general, the game received positive reviews among the participants. One participant remarked how stress relieving it is to 'become a bird' and fly over the map, especially after experiencing the heavy-load of lectures in the morning. Another student already had experience in the game series and knew how to navigate around and quickly learned to ride a horse or climb the pyramids. Another student became interested in facts about pyramids especially after the news about how there could be structures under pyramids in the social media. During the discussions about the game, many participants articulated positive reflections, emphasizing their motivation, engagement, and intentions to incorporate game-based resources into their future teaching practices.

### 3.1. Combining the DTAE Game with a Learning Management System

In the following weeks, participants were systematically introduced to specific learning objectives from the curriculum guide (Ubisoft, 2025). Each preservice teacher was instructed to select an objective from the guide and pair it with a quest of their choice within the game. After engaging with the selected quest, participants brainstormed potential lesson plans that could leverage the quest's content for English language teaching in pairs. Lesson plan drafts were submitted through a Moodle discussion forum, enabling asynchronous peer review and collective idea sharing.

*Figure 6. Sample lesson plan drafts created by preservice English teachers based on Discovery Tour: Ancient Egypt, shared via Moodle discussion forums*

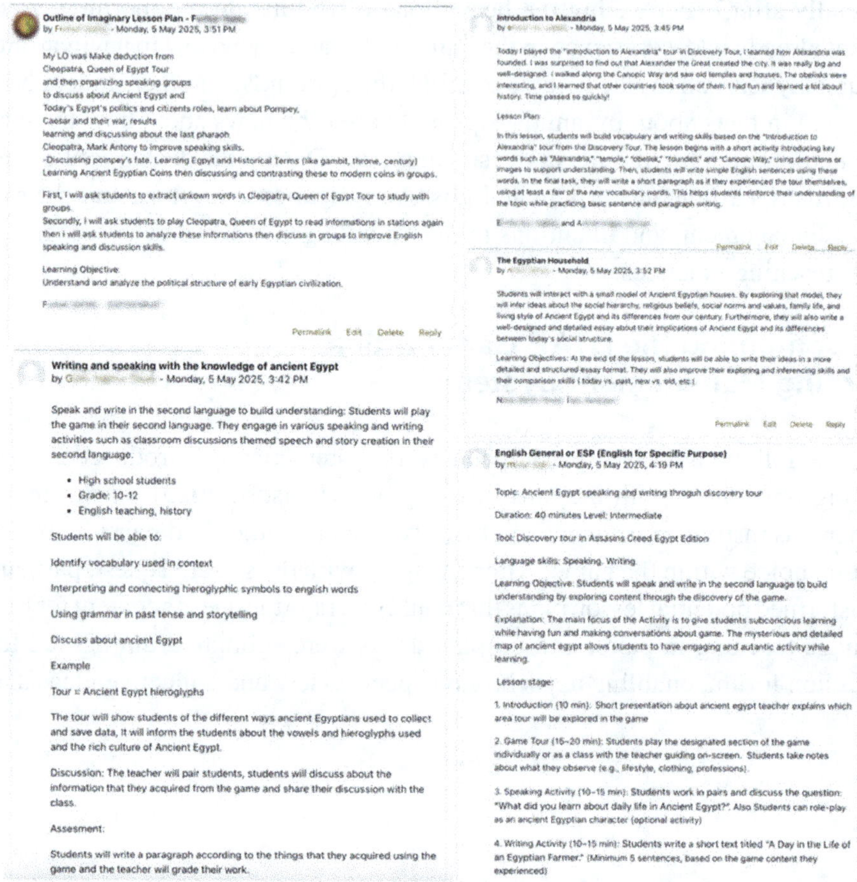

**Outline of Imaginary Lesson Plan - F**
by F - Monday, 5 May 2025, 3:51 PM

My LO was Make deduction from
Cleopatra, Queen of Egypt Tour
and then organizing speaking groups
to discuss about Ancient Egypt and
Today's Egypt's politics and citizents roles, learn about Pompey,
Caesar and their war, results
learning and discussing about the last pharaoh
Cleopatra, Mark Antony to improve speaking skills.
-Discussing pompey's fate. Learning Egpyt and Historical Terms (like gambit, throne, century)
Learning Ancient Egyptian Coins then discussing and contrasting these to modern coins in groups.

First, I will ask students to extract unkown words in Cleopatra, Queen of Egypt Tour to study with groups.
Secondly, I will ask students to play Cleopatra, Queen of Egypt to read informations in stations again then i will ask students to analyze these informations then discuss in groups to improve English speaking and discussion skills.

Learning Objective:
Understand and analyze the political structure of early Egyptian civilization.

Permalink Edit Delete Reply

**Writing and speaking with the knowledge of ancient Egypt**
by G - Monday, 5 May 2025, 3:42 PM

Speak and write in the second language to build understanding: Students will play the game in their second language. They engage in various speaking and writing activities such as classroom discussions themed speech and story creation in their second language.

- High school students
- Grade: 10-12
- English teaching, history

Students will be able to:

Identify vocabulary used in context

Interpreting and connecting hieroglyphic symbols to english words

Using grammar in past tense and storytelling

Discuss about ancient Egypt

Example

Tour = Ancient Egypt hieroglyphs

The tour will show students of the different ways ancient Egyptians used to collect and save data, It will inform the students about the vowels and hieroglyphs used and the rich culture of Ancient Egypt.

Discussion: The teacher will pair students, students will discuss about the information that they acquired from the game and share their discussion with the class.

Assesment:

Students will write a paragraph according to the things that they acquired using the game and the teacher will grade their work.

**Introduction to Alexandria**
by e - Monday, 5 May 2025, 3:45 PM

Today I played the "Introduction to Alexandria" tour in Discovery Tour. I learned how Alexandria was founded. I was surprised to find out that Alexander the Great created the city. It was really big and well-designed. I walked along the Canopic Way and saw old temples and houses. The obelisks were interesting, and I learned that other countries took some of them. I had fun and learned a lot about history. Time passed so quickly!

Lesson Plan:

In this lesson, students will build vocabulary and writing skills based on the "Introduction to Alexandria" tour from the Discovery Tour. The lesson begins with a short activity introducing key words such as "Alexandria," "temple," "obelisk," "founded," and "Canopic Way," using definitions or images to support understanding. Then, students will write simple English sentences using these words. In the final task, they will write a short paragraph as if they experienced the tour themselves, using at least a few of the new vocabulary words. This helps students reinforce their understanding of the topic while practicing basic sentence and paragraph writing.

E and A

Permalink Edit Delete Reply

**The Egyptian Household**
by N - Monday, 5 May 2025, 3:52 PM

Students will interact with a small model of Ancient Egyptian houses. By exploring that model, they will infer ideas about the social hierarchy, religious beliefs, social norms and values, family life, and living style of Ancient Egypt and its differences from our century. Furthermore, they will also write a well-designed and detailed essay about their implications of Ancient Egypt and its differences between today's social structure.

Learning Objectives: At the end of the lesson, students will be able to write their ideas in a more detailed and structured essay format. They will also improve their exploring and inferencing skills and their comparison skills ( today vs. past, new vs. old, etc.)

Permalink Edit Delete Reply

**English General or ESP (English for Specific Purpose)**
by m - Monday, 5 May 2025, 4:19 PM

Topic: Ancient Egypt speaking and writing throguh discovery tour

Duration: 40 minutes Level: Intermediate

Tool: Discovery tour in Assasins Creed Egypt Edition

Language skills: Speaking, Writing

Learning Objective: Students will speak and write in the second language to build understanding by exploring content through the discovery of the game.

Explanation: The main focus of the Activity is to give students subconcious learning while having fun and making conversations about game. The mysterious and detailed map of ancient egypt allows students to have engaging and autantic activity while learning.

Lesson stage:

1. Introduction (10 min): Short presentation about ancient egypt teacher explains which area tour will be explored in the game

2. Game Tour (15–20 min): Students play the designated section of the game individually or as a class with the teacher guiding on-screen. Students take notes about what they observe (e.g., lifestyle, clothing, professions).

3. Speaking Activity (10–15 min): Students work in pairs and discuss the question: "What did you learn about daily life in Ancient Egypt?". Also Students can role-play as an ancient Egyptian character (optional activity)

4. Writing Activity (10–15 min): Students write a short text titled "A Day in the Life of an Egyptian Farmer." (Minimum 5 sentences, based on the game content they experienced)

The five sample lesson plans (Figure 7) illustrate the variety of approaches preservice teachers adopted when integrating *Discovery Tour: Ancient Egypt* into English language teaching. Across the plans, there was a clear emphasis on contextualized vocabulary learning and communicative practice. For instance, the *Outline of Imaginary Lesson Plan (top-left)* includes terms such as *gambit, throne, century* as teachable vocabulary, while *Introduction to Alexandria* (top-right) highlights words such as *Alexandria, temple and obelis,. The writing practice with these vocabulary items shows that* preservice teachers sought to connect language practice with broader cultural and historical knowledge.

The lesson plans also incorporated storytelling, role-play, and writing activities, encouraging learners to use target vocabulary in extended tasks. For example, the *English General or ESP* plan required students to write a short essay on *'A Day in the Life of an Egyptian Farmer'* while *Writing and speaking with the knowledge of ancient Egypt* guided learners toward producing short paragraphs based on their vocabulary work. These tasks go beyond recognition to promote productive language use in speaking and writing, supporting learners' ability to embed new vocabulary within meaningful contexts.

Another notable feature was the integration of cultural and historical content. The *Egyptian Household* plan, for instance, combines language objectives with cultural themes by having students describe daily life and social practices in ancient Egypt. Likewise, the *Outline of Imaginary Lesson Plan* situates vocabulary in a historical narrative about Cleopatra and Mark Antony, blending language acquisition with historical learning. Such examples reveal an emerging orientation toward content and language integrated learning where disciplinary knowledge serves as both content and context for English language instruction.

At the same time, the lesson plans varied in scope and structure. Some included clear objectives, staged procedures, and assessment tasks—such as essays, presentations, or oral reporting—while others remained at a more general level, focusing on activities without specifying expected outcomes or evaluation methods. This unevenness reflects differences in preservice teachers' ability to translate exploratory gameplay into concrete instructional design.

Taken together, the lesson plans demonstrate that preservice teachers were able to creatively adapt digital game content to language learning objectives, drawing on the linguistic and cultural resources embedded in DTAE. The diversity of tasks—ranging from vocabulary practice to extended writing, role-play, and cultural description—shows how historically immersive simulations can inspire a wide spectrum of lesson ideas, even though the level of pedagogical precision and assessment design varied among participants.

After all students submitted their written plan, a follow-up in-class discussion session was held, during which participants presented their chosen quests, justified their pedagogical choices, and reflected on the educational potential of video games to everyone in the class. In this discussion, the practicality of the lesson plans were evaluated verbally by all participants to comment on whether or not it would be feasible to implement the plans in the future when they become teachers. Nevertheless, it was emphasized that rather than evaluating the lesson plans, the whole practice aimed to explore the use of serious digital games in language education. All participants were encouraged to comment on each other's plans and examine the specific quest found in the curriculum guide for more details. These exchanges highlighted the creative range of possible applications, from vocabulary instruction to cultural awareness tasks, demonstrating preservice teachers' ability to link in-game experiences with established language learning objectives.

## 3.2. Combining the DTAE Game and Interactive Digital Activities

In addition to the lesson plans developed by preservice teachers, a researcher-designed example was created to demonstrate how interactive digital activities can be systematically combined with gameplay. The aim was to illustrate how a commercial game like *Discovery Tour: Ancient Egypt* can be embedded into a structured sequence of tasks that address multiple language skills and remain closely aligned with the curriculum guide. To achieve this, the researcher used H5P to design a set of digital activities that paralleled the selected quest, providing opportunities for learners to engage with new vocabulary, practice pronunciation, check comprehension, and produce written output. This structured example served both as a model of best practice in digital pedagogy and as a point of comparison for the more varied lesson plans submitted by participants.

*Figure 7. A sample lesson planned by the researcher for a quest in the game*

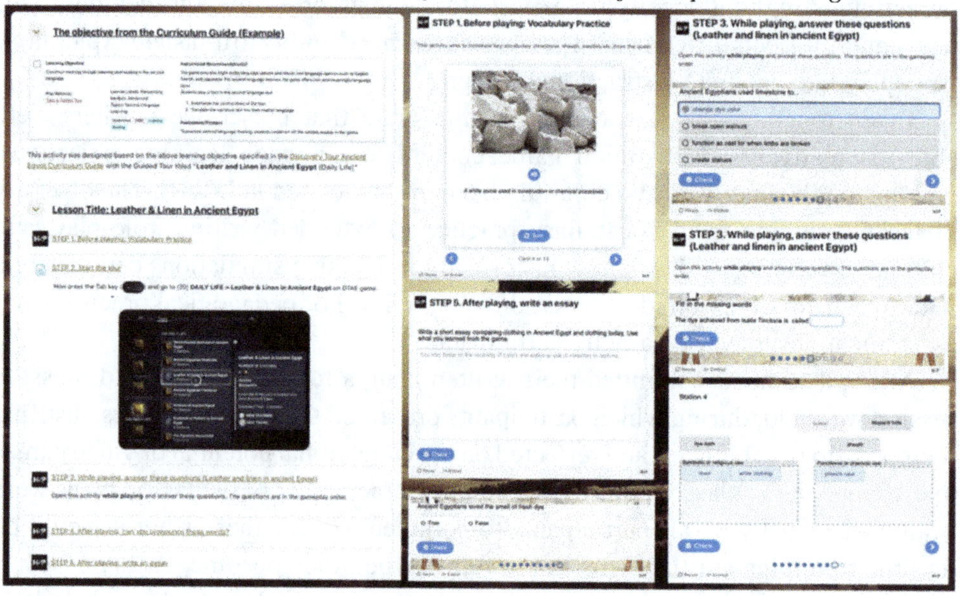


To demonstrate how a commercial educational game can be paired with interactive digital activities, one structured lesson plan based on H5P content was created and implemented by the researcher. This lesson centered on the "Leather & Linen in Ancient Egypt" quest in DTAE and included four interactive H5P content. The lesson comprised four stages: (1) targeted vocabulary introduction with flashcards, (2) pronunciation practice activity, (3) a comprehension quiz based on in-game content, and (4) a writing task requiring participants to compose a short essay using the introduced vocabulary and contextual knowledge from the quest. Participants engaged with each activity while simultaneously playing the quest, creating a direct connection between gameplay and task completion. Following the lesson, a researcher-led discussion illustrated how the structured tasks aligned with objectives in the DTAE curriculum guide. This debrief was extended into an open conversation on the role of video games in English language learning. The structured lesson served two purposes. Pedagogically, it aimed to demonstrate how digital games could be paired with interactive digital tools (H5P) to create task-based, multimodal learning sequences that link vocabulary, form, and meaning across multiple skills. It also aimed to provide preservice teachers with a model of how a commercially developed game could be systematically integrated into a language lesson. This example aimed to highlight the importance of clear objectives, task progression, and assessment integration when adapting games for classroom use. Following the session, an open conversation invited preservice teachers to reflect on these contrasts, reinforcing the idea that games can support language learning most effectively when combined with deliberate instructional design.

## DISCUSSION

Preservice teachers in this study demonstrated creativity in adapting *Discovery Tour: Ancient Egypt* (DTAE) to pedagogical contexts, particularly by selecting historically grounded vocabulary and embedding it into communicative tasks such as storytelling, essay writing, and role-play. This reflects earlier claims in the literature that games provide rich opportunities for contextualized, situated learning (Gee, 2003; Plass et al., 2020), and it shows that preservice teachers can move beyond surface-level engagement with games to design language-focused activities aligned with curricular objectives. The variability observed across the five lesson plans points to a spectrum of pedagogical readiness. Some preservice teachers designed detailed, outcome-driven lessons with explicit assessment criteria, while others provided less structured outlines that lacked clear objectives or evaluation methods. This mirrors prior findings that teacher adoption of DGBLL depends not only on enthusiasm but also on confidence, pedagogical knowledge, and training (Bertacchini & Leonardi, 2021). For language teacher education, this underlines the importance of modeling effective design practices and offering iterative feedback opportunities so preservice teachers can refine their ability to align gameplay with language learning goals.

The findings from both the literature and the case study of *Discovery Tour: Ancient Egypt* (DTAE) highlight the multiple affordances of digital game-based language learning (DGBLL) for language teacher education. Consistent with earlier work (Gee, 2003; Plass et al., 2020; Sitzmann, 2011), the integration of digital games supports motivation, engagement, and authentic language use. The preservice teachers in this study not only engaged with gameplay as learners but also critically reflected on its pedagogical potential, reinforcing the dual role of DGBLL in teacher education: as an experiential learning environment and as a model for future classroom practice.

A growing body of literature advocates for the combined use of educational games and interactive digital tools to maximize learning outcomes (Papastergiou, 2009). By linking immersive gameplay with structured activities, educators can scaffold learner understanding and promote reflection (de Freitas & Jarvis, 2006). For preservice teachers, this integrated approach models innovative instructional strategies that they can adopt or adapt in their future practice (Peterson, 2010).

Studies have also highlighted the importance of collaborative learning spaces, such as Moodle discussion forums, to facilitate peer interaction and reflective dialogue following game-based activities (Hrastinski, 2009). These platforms encourage knowledge co-construction and support the development of critical pedagogical thinking in teacher candidates (Garrison & Vaughan, 2008). Furthermore, interactive content such as H5P have gained recognition for enabling educators to create rich, engaging multimedia learning experiences without requiring extensive technical expertise (Jacob & Centofanti, 2024; Mir, 2021). H5P tools facilitate the integration of quizzes, drag-and-drop activities, interactive videos, and presentations that can be embedded directly into learning management systems such as Moodle, which are beneficial for preservice teachers (Samsonov, 2025). These features support formative assessment, immediate feedback, and learner autonomy, all critical components of effective language instruction (Black & Wiliam, 2009).

In teacher education, H5P has been shown to empower preservice teachers to experiment with digital content creation and foster digital pedagogical skills that are transferable to real classrooms (Bertacchini & Leonardi, 2021). Moreover, the use of H5P activities aligned with game content, such as vocabulary exercises based on in-game quests, may enhance the multimodal learning experience, reinforcing language learning through contextualized practice. One key point emerging from the case is the value of structured lessons alongside open-ended exploration. While participants initially benefited from freely engaging with DTAE, the subsequent structured activities created with H5P and Moodle helped anchor their experiences in language learning objectives. This aligns with earlier findings that games are most effective when complemented by instructional support and guided reflection (Wouters et al., 2013; Wouters & Oostendorp, 2013; Peterson, 2010). The integration of H5P also fostered preservice teachers' digital pedagogical skills, an increasingly important competency in contemporary teacher education (Bertacchini & Leonardi, 2021).

Finally, despite the benefits, several challenges need careful consideration. First, access to resources remains uneven: not all institutions have the technological infrastructure to support game-based instruction. Second, there is a risk of overemphasizing entertainment value at the expense of linguistic outcomes if careful task design is not prioritized. Third, teacher readiness is crucial; while preservice teachers may be enthusiastic about games, they still require training and confidence to integrate them effectively. These issues underscore the need for continued professional development and curriculum design that balance innovation with practicality.

## 4. CONCLUSION

This chapter examined the role of digital game-based language learning in language teacher education, with a particular focus on the integration of Ubisoft's *Discovery Tour: Ancient Egypt* in a preservice English teacher education course. The literature review established the theoretical and empirical foundations of DGBLL, while the case study illustrated how immersive, historically grounded digital environments can be paired with interactive tools like H5P to create meaningful and pedagogically sound language learning opportunities.

Three main conclusions can be drawn. First, digital games—whether COTS or serious—hold significant potential to foster linguistic, cultural, and motivational outcomes in second language education. Second, their effectiveness in teacher education depends on structured integration: gameplay can be accompanied by exploring different ways of implementation such as learning management systems and interactive digital activities. In addition, reflection and task design activities can help ensure alignment with curricular goals. Third, exposure to DGBLL can empower preservice teachers to develop critical digital literacy, creative pedagogical strategies, and an openness to experimentation in their future classrooms.

At the same time, the chapter acknowledges the challenges of DGBLL, including infrastructural limitations, varying levels of teacher readiness, and the need to strike a balance between entertainment and pedagogy. These challenges highlight that the incorporation of games into teacher education should not be viewed as an add-on but as part of a broader digital pedagogy framework that supports reflective practice and ongoing professional development.

Looking forward, future research may explore how emerging technologies—such as artificial intelligence, extended reality (XR), and adaptive learning systems—may expand the potential of DGBLL for teacher education. Longitudinal studies could also investigate how preservice teachers who engage with games during training later integrate them into their own classrooms and its effects on digital competence for educators (Redecker, 2017). Ultimately, the integration of DGBLL into language teacher education holds promise not only for enhancing language learning outcomes but also for shaping digitally competent, innovative, and critically reflective educators.

## LIMITATIONS

The case presented in this chapter has several limitations that should be acknowledged. First, the findings are based on a single course with preservice English teachers in one institutional context, which restricts the generalizability of the results. Second, the study relied primarily on descriptive data such as lesson plans, forum reflections, and classroom observations rather than systematic measures of language development or learning outcomes. As such, the chapter highlights perceived affordances and design practices rather than empirically demonstrating effectiveness. Third, the intervention was conducted in a computer laboratory equipped with licensed access to *Discovery Tour: Ancient Egypt*, meaning that resource availability, technical infrastructure, and institutional support may have influenced participants' experiences. Finally, while the chapter illustrates creativity in lesson design, differences in participants' prior gaming experience and digital competence were not controlled, which may have shaped both engagement levels and pedagogical outcomes. These limitations suggest the need for further research across varied contexts, with larger samples and more systematic assessment methods

## REFERENCES


Aladelah, A. A. H. (2024). *The effectiveness of teaching using lingokids on the english vocabulary acquisition of first year primary students* (Master's thesis, Qassim University). https://doi.org/DOI: 10.21608/mrk.2024.348329

Aydın, S. (2013). Second Life as a foreign language learning environment: A review of research. *Turkish Online Journal of Distance Education, 14*(1), 53–63. https://dergipark.org.tr/en/pub/tojde/issue/16895/176013

Aydın, S., & Çakır, N. (2022). Integrating commercial-off-the-shelf games into language classroom: PCaRD experience of two English language teachers. *Eğitimde Kuram ve Uygulama, 18*(2), 68–90. DOI: 10.17244/eku.982955

Barab, S., Warren, S., & Ingram-Goble, A. (2009). Conceptual play spaces. In Ferdig, R. E. (Ed.), *Handbook of research on effective electronic gaming in education* (Vol. III, pp. 989–1009). IGI Global. DOI: 10.4018/978-1-59904-808-6.ch057

Barz, N., Benick, M., Dörrenbächer-Ulrich, L., & Perels, F. (2024). The effect of digital game-based learning interventions on cognitive, metacognitive, and affective-motivational learning outcomes in school: A meta-analysis. *Review of Educational Research, 94*(2), 193–227. DOI: 10.3102/00346543231167795

Bertacchini, F., & Leonardi, S. (2021). Developing preservice teachers' digital skills through interactive learning activities: An exploration of H5P in teacher education. *Education and Information Technologies, 26*(3), 2831–2852. DOI: 10.1007/s10639-020-10439-3

Black, P., & Wiliam, D. (2009). Developing the theory of formative assessment. *Educational Assessment, Evaluation and Accountability, 21*(1), 5–31. DOI: 10.1007/s11092-008-9068-5

Boyle, E. A., Hainey, T., Connolly, T. M., Gray, G., Earp, J., Ott, M., Lim, T., Ninaus, M., Ribeiro, C., & Pereira, J. (2016). An update to the systematic literature review of empirical evidence of the impacts and outcomes of computer games and serious games. *Computers & Education, 94*, 178–192. DOI: 10.1016/j.compedu.2015.11.003

Bozorgian, H., Muhammadpour, M., Davariyan, H., & Ezami, A. (2025). Second Life App Functions as a Booster in Second Language Listening Comprehension. *International Journal of Listening*, •••, 1–16. DOI: 10.1080/10904018.2025.2527745

Bregni, S. (2018). Assassin's Creed taught me Italian: Video games and the quest for lifelong, ubiquitous learning. https://profession.mla.org/assassins-creed-taught-me-italian-video-games-and-the-quest-for-lifelong-ubiquitous-learning

Bui, T. H. M., Le, P. T. T., & Ali, F. (2025). Digital Gaming and English L2 Informal Learning in Adolescents. *Simulation & Gaming, 10468781251364372*. Advance online publication. DOI: 10.1177/10468781251364

Chen, J. C. (2016). The crossroads of English language learners, task-based instruction, and 3D multi-user virtual learning in Second Life. *Computers & Education, 102*, 152–171. DOI: 10.1016/j.compedu.2016.08.004

Chik, A. (2014). Digital gaming and language learning: Autonomy and community. https://eric.ed.gov/?id=EJ1034890

Clark, D. B., Tanner-Smith, E. E., & Killingsworth, S. S. (2016). Digital games, design, and learning: A systematic review and meta-analysis. *Review of Educational Research, 86*(1), 79–122. DOI: 10.3102/0034654315582065

Damcha, T. D. A., & Budiarti, E. (2022). Improving children's english skills by using lingokids app. *Jurnal Education and Development, 10*(3), 357–362. DOI: 10.37081/ed.v10i3.4122

de Freitas, S., & Jarvis, S. (2006). A framework for developing serious games to meet learner needs. *Learning, Media and Technology, 31*(4), 423–440. DOI: 10.1080/17439880601060205

Di Blas, N., Paolini, P., & Torrebruno, A. (2010). Innovative Technologies And Education: Two Succesful Case-Studies. In *Proceedings of the 2nd International Conference on Computer Supported Education* (pp. 341-349).

Dickey, M. D. (2007). Game design and learning: A conjectural analysis of how massively multiple online role-playing games (MMORPGs) foster intrinsic motivation. *Educational Technology Research and Development, 55*(3), 253–273. DOI: 10.1007/s11423-006-9004-7

Dickey, M. D. (2007). Gamification of learning and instruction: Game-based methods and strategies for training and education. *Performance Improvement Quarterly, 21*(3), 82–88. DOI: 10.1002/piq.2114

Gamalytics (2025). *Influent language learning game - Steam stats.* https://gamalytic.com/game/274980?utm_source=SteamDB

Garrison, D. R., & Vaughan, N. D. (2008). *Blended learning in higher education: Framework, principles, and guidelines.* Jossey-Bass.

Gee, J. P. (2003). *What video games have to teach us about learning and literacy.* Palgrave Macmillan. DOI: 10.1145/950566.950595

Gee, J. P. (2007). *Good video games + good learning: Collected essays on video games, learning, and literacy.* Peter Lang Publishing. DOI: 10.3726/978-1-4539-1162-4

Girard, C., Ecalle, J., & Magnan, A. (2013). Serious games as new educational tools: How effective are they? A meta-analysis of recent studies. *Journal of Computer Assisted Learning, 29*(3), 207–219. DOI: 10.1111/j.1365-2729.2012.00489.x

Honarzad, R., & Soyoof, A. (2020). Vocabulary learning and retention: A comparison between a serious game and mobile application. *International Journal of Pedagogies & Learning, 15*(1), 81–100. https://www.researchgate.net/publication/348735310

Hrastinski, S. (2009). A theory of online learning as online participation. *Computers & Education, 52*(1), 78–82. DOI: 10.1016/j.compedu.2008.06.009

Hung, A. C. Y., deHaan, J., & Lee, T. K. (2018b). Games and language learning: An international perspective. *NYS Tesol Journal*, 3-11. https://journal.nystesol.org/index.php/NYSTJ/article/view/86

Hung, H. T., Yang, J. C., Hwang, G. J., Chu, H. C., & Wang, C. C. (2018a). A scoping review of research on digital game-based language learning. *Computers & Education, 126*, 89–104. DOI: 10.1016/j.compedu.2018.07.001

Ivan, V. (2025). *How can the use of a narrative-driven commercial off-the-shelf video game affect English language learners' motivation and willingness to communicate in a classroom setting?* (Master's thesis, NTNU). https://hdl.handle.net/11250/3205346

Jacob, T., & Centofanti, S. (2024). Effectiveness of H5P in improving student learning outcomes in an online tertiary education setting. *Journal of Computing in Higher Education, 36*(2), 469–485. DOI: 10.1007/s12528-023-09361-6

Julianti, A., Handayani, R., & Handayani, I. (2024). The Effectiveness of Using Lingokids Application toward Young Learners' Vocabulary Mastery at the Second Grade of SD Islam Aviciena Anyar. *PROCEEDING AISELT, 9*(1).

Kaimara, P., Fokides, E., Oikonomou, A., & Deliyannis, I. (2021). Potential barriers to the implementation of digital game-based learning in the classroom: Pre-service teachers' views. *Technology. Knowledge and Learning, 26*(4), 825–844. DOI: 10.1007/s10758-021-09512-7

Kallunki, K. P. (2016). *Learning English in World of Warcraft: Perspectives from the players* (Master's thesis).

Kim, B., Park, H., & Baek, Y. (2009). Not just fun, but serious strategies: Using meta-cognitive strategies in game-based learning. *Computers & Education, 52*(4), 800–810. DOI: 10.1016/j.compedu.2008.12.004

Kim, S. (2009, June). 3D Virtual Technology, Integrated Language Learning, and Inquiry-Based Educational Curricula for English Language Students in South Korea. In *EdMedia+ Innovate Learning* (pp. 4121-4132). Association for the Advancement of Computing in Education (AACE). https://www.learntechlib.org/noaccess/32077

Kusuma, D. A. D. (2022). The Effect of Influent Video Game for Hospitality Students' English Vocabulary Mastery at SMK Kertha Wisata Sawan. *Jurnal Penelitian Mahasiswa Indonesia, 2*(2), 118–122. DOI: 10.36663/jpmi.v2i2.361

Lai, K. W. K., & Chen, H. J. H. (2025). L2 vocabulary learning through a COTS adventure game: Individual vs. paired gameplay and the influence of word exposure frequency, word level, and word salience. *Computers & Education, 105343*, 105343. Advance online publication. DOI: 10.1016/j.compedu.2025.105343

LingoKid. (2025). *Learning English*. https://lingokids.com/subject/learning-english

Mir, K. (2021). H5P interactive video content in Moodle to improve learners' engagement in online learning. In *34th Annual Conference of the Asian Association of Open Universities - Vol II, 403-414*. https://www.academia.edu/download/89432016/AAOU2021_Volume2_Final_Online_Published.pdf#page=404

Moniza Ray, S. P., & Ajit, I. (2024). Digital Game-Based Language Learning: The Impact of Story-Driven Game Life Is Strange 1 on Language Learners' Listening Skills. *Journal of Language Teaching & Research, 15*(2), 448–457. Advance online publication. DOI: 10.17507/jltr.1502.13

Nardi, B., & Kallinikos, J. (2010). Technology, agency, and community: The case of modding in World of Warcraft. In Holmström, J., Wiberg, M., & Lund, A. (Eds.), *Industrial informatics design, use and innovation* (pp. 174–186). IGI Global. DOI: 10.4018/978-1-61520-692-6.ch013

Newgarden, K., & Zheng, D. (2016). Recurrent languaging activities in World of Warcraft: Skilled linguistic action meets the Common European Framework of Reference. *ReCALL, 28*(3), 274–304. DOI: 10.1017/S0958344016000112

Papastergiou, M. (2009). Digital game-based learning in high school computer science education: Impact on educational effectiveness and student motivation. *Computers & Education, 52*(1), 1–12. DOI: 10.1016/j.compedu.2008.06.004

Pearce, C., Boellstorff, T., & Nardi, B. A. (2011). *Communities of play: Emergent cultures in multiplayer games and virtual worlds*. MIT Press.

Peterson, M. (2010). Digital gaming and second language development: Japanese learners' interactions in an MMORPG. *Digital Culture & Education, 2*(1), 43–58. DOI: 10.1016/j.compedu.2010.08.003

Peterson, M. (2011). Digital gaming and second language development: Japanese learners' interactions in an MMORPG. *Digital Culture & Education, 3*(1), 56–73.

Plass, J., Homer, D., & Kinzer, C. (2015). Foundations of game-based learning. *Educational Psychologist, 50*(4), 258–283. DOI: 10.1080/00461520.2015.1122533

Plass, J. L., & Kaplan, U. (2016). Emotional design in digital media for learning. In Tettegah, S., & Gartmeier, M. (Eds.), *Emotions, technology, design, and learning* (pp. 131–161). Elsevier. DOI: 10.1016/B978-0-12-801856-9.00007-4

Plass, J. L., Mayer, R. E., & Homer, B. D. (2020). *Handbook of game-based learning*. MIT Press.

Purushotma, R., Thorne, S. L., & Wheatley, J. (2009). 10 key principles for designing video games for foreign language learning. Paper produced for the Open Language & Learning Games Project, Massachusetts Institute of Technology, funded by the William and Flora Hewlett Foundation.

Rajendran, M., Ray, M., Ilangovan, A., Chokkalingam, V. K., & Singh, A. B. (2024). Commercial video games and english language skills development: A systematic review. *Language Teaching Research Quarterly, 45*, 57–85. DOI: 10.32038/ltrq.2024.45.04

Ranalli, J. (2008). Learning English with The Sims: Exploiting authentic computer simulation games for L2 learning. *Computer Assisted Language Learning, 21*(5), 441–455. DOI: 10.1080/09588220802447859

Redecker, C. (2017). *European Framework for the Digital Competence of Educators (DigCompEdu)*. Publications Office of the European Union., DOI: 10.2760/159770

Reinders, H. (2012). Digital games in language learning: Opportunities and challenges. In Hubbard, P. (Ed.), *The Cambridge Guide to Second Language Teacher Education* (pp. 93–101). Cambridge University Press., DOI: 10.1017/CBO9781139046856.012

Ryan, R. M., & Deci, E. L. (2000). Self-determination theory and the facilitation of intrinsic motivation, social development, and well-being. *The American Psychologist, 55*(1), 68–78. DOI: 10.1037/0003-066X.55.1.68

Ryu, D. (2013). Play to learn, learn to play: Language learning through gaming culture. *ReCALL, 25*(2), 286–301. DOI: 10.1017/S0958344013000050

Samsonov, P. (2025, March). Pre-service and in-service teachers' perceptions of H5P: Results of a survey. In *Society for Information Technology & Teacher Education International Conference* (pp. 2935-2940). Association for the Advancement of Computing in Education (AACE). https://www.learntechlib.org/p/225892/

Sardo, M., & Thibault, M. (2024). "I like everything about it" – Perceived educational value of a digital gaming experience with Assassin's Creed Odyssey: Discovery Tour. *Italian Journal of Educational Technology*, *32*(3). Advance online publication. DOI: 10.17471/2499-4324/1399

Schønning, S. M., & Fløgum, H. (2025). *Fostering joy of writing through a narrative-driven video game: A study of Life is Strange in an L2 English classroom* (Master's thesis, UiT The Arctic University of Norway). https://hdl.handle.net/10037/37349

Setiyaningsih, I., Hidayati, H., & Rahmaniah, R. (2023). The use of lingokids game application to encourage the young learners' english vocabularies. *International Social Sciences and Humanities*, *2*(1), 197–203. DOI: 10.32528/issh.v2i1.123

Shaffer, D. W. (2006). *How computer games help children learn*. Palgrave Macmillan. DOI: 10.1057/9780230601994

Sharma, R., Tan, C., Gomez, D., Xu, C., & Dubé, A. K. (2025). Guiding teachers' game-based learning: How user experience of a digital curriculum guide impacts teachers' self-efficacy and acceptance of educational games. *Teaching and Teacher Education, 155*, 104915. DOI: 10.1016/j.tate.2024.104915

Sitzmann, T. (2011). A meta-analytic examination of the instructional effectiveness of computer-based simulation games. *Personnel Psychology*, *64*(2), 489–528. DOI: 10.1111/j.1744-6570.2011.01190.x

Steinkuehler, C., & Squire, K. (2023). Gaming in educational contexts. In *Handbook of educational psychology* (pp. 674–695). Routledge. DOI: 10.4324/9780429433726-34

Stoerger, S., Herring, S. C., & Kouper, I. (2007). "Great Job, Quester!" Assessing Language Skills on Quest Atlantis. In *Texas Linguistics Forum* (Vol. 50).

Travis, B. (2017). *Assassin's Creed Origins' Discovery Tour shows how video games could be an education game-changer*. https://www.standard.co.uk/news/tech/assassins-creed-origins-discovery-tour-shows-how-video-games-could-be-an-education-gamechanger-a3663966.html

Ubisoft (2025). *All discovery tour curriculum guides*. https://www.ubisoft.com/en-us/game/assassins-creed/discovery-tour/curriculum-guide

Vos, N., van der Meijden, H., & Denessen, E. (2011). Effects of constructing versus playing an educational game on student motivation and deep learning strategy use. *Computers & Education, 56*(1), 127–137. DOI: 10.1016/j.compedu.2010.08.013

Wouters, P., van Nimwegen, C., van Oostendorp, H., & van der Spek, E. D. (2013). A meta-analysis of the cognitive and motivational effects of serious games. *Journal of Educational Psychology, 105*(2), 249–265. DOI: 10.1037/a0031311

Wouters, P., & van Oostendorp, H. (2013). A meta-analytic review of the role of instructional support in game-based learning. *Computers & Education, 60*(1), 412–425. DOI: 10.1016/j.compedu.2012.07.018

Xu, C., Sharma, R., & Dubé, A. K. (2023). Discovery Tour Curriculum Guides to Improve Teachers' Adoption of Serious. In Champion, E., & Hiriart, J. (Eds.), *Assassin's Creed in the Classroom: History's Playground or a Stab in the Dark?* (pp. 12–35). De Gruyter. DOI: 10.1515/9783111253275-003

Yang, L., Li, R., & Zhou, Y. (2024). Research trends of game-based language learning in K-12 education: A systematic review of SSCI articles during 2009–2022. *Journal of Computer Assisted Learning, 40*(3), 1218–1230. DOI: 10.1111/jcal.12944

Young, M. F., Slota, S., Cutter, A. B., Jalette, G., Mullin, G., Lai, B., Simeoni, Z., Tran, M., & Yukhymenko, M. (2012). Our Princess Is in Another Castle: A Review of Trends in Serious Gaming for Education. *Review of Educational Research, 82*(1), 61–89. DOI: 10.3102/0034654312436980

Zheng, D., Young, M. F., Wagner, M. M., & Brewer, R. A. (2009). Negotiation for action: English language learning in game-based virtual worlds. *Modern Language Journal, 93*(4), 489–511. DOI: 10.1111/j.1540-4781.2009.00927.x

Chapter 12

# Digital and Non-Digital Games in Language Teaching and Learning:
## Integrating Play for Pedagogical Progress

**Ayushi Zina**
http://orcid.org/0000-0001-8959-2310
*Christ University, Delhi NCR, India*

**Nilesh Kumar**
*Amity University, Ranchi, India*

**Anil Nayak**
http://orcid.org/0000-0002-8907-5732
*Christ University, Delhi NCR, India*

## ABSTRACT

*This chapter examines the role of digital and non-digital games in enhancing language teaching and learning through engagement, collaboration, and experiential practice. Grounded in constructivist and experiential learning theories, it explores how games create interactive, low-anxiety environments that foster communication, creativity, and learner autonomy. Using teacher and student questionnaires, the study investigates perceptions, practices, and challenges in implementing game-based learning. Findings indicate that both formats improve motivation, participation, and communicative competence, though barriers such as limited time, training, and infrastructural support persist. Non-digital games remain popular for their accessibility and focus on social interaction, while digital games offer adaptive,*

DOI: 10.4018/979-8-3373-4322-8.ch012

*multimedia-rich experiences. The chapter argues for a blended approach that integrates the strengths of both formats, supported by institutional training and ready-made resources, to promote inclusive, effective, and sustainable language learning in contemporary classrooms.*

# 1. INTRODUCTION

## 1.1 Framing the Context: The Turn Toward Play in Pedagogy

In recent decades, education has shifted from teacher/transmission-based models to learner-centred approaches that prioritise engagement, participation, and contextual application of knowledge. Language education, in particular, has re-evaluated traditional methods that rely heavily on textbooks, rote memorisation, and grammar drills. Educators are rethinking how they teach and help students learn languages in a world shaped by technology, mobility, and multimodal communication. Play emerges as a powerful pedagogical vehicle within this reimagining, allowing learners to acquire language in interactive, enjoyable, and meaningful ways.

Games, whether digital or non-digital, embody the principles of play. They create structured yet flexible environments where learners experiment with language, collaborate with peers, and receive real-time feedback. They lower affective barriers by situating learners in immersive experiences where linguistic risks are not penalised but rewarded through creative problem-solving. Gee (2007) argued that games inherently align with learning because they scaffold challenge, provide immediate feedback, and encourage situated meaning-making. These affordances are particularly valuable for language learners, as they mimic authentic communicative practices while offering the safety of a simulated environment.

The integration of games into classrooms is not entirely novel. Word puzzles, storytelling circles, and role-plays have long been used in communicative language teaching. What distinguishes the current pedagogical moment, however, is the growing recognition of games not merely as supplementary activities but as central components of instructional design. Digital innovation and constructivist pedagogy fuel this recognition, driving a focus on learner agency, multimodality, and collaboration.

## 1.2 Why Language Learning Needs Playful Pedagogies

Language acquisition is deeply social, contextual, and dynamic. Unlike mathematics or science, where abstract principles can be transmitted in formulaic terms, language is a living system that requires active use for mastery. Krashen's Input Hypothesis underscores that comprehensible input is essential for acquisition, but input alone is insufficient without meaningful opportunities for interaction and output (Krashen, 1982). There is a need for interactive and output-rich experiences, where play, in the form of games, offers unique pedagogical value.

Games transform the classroom into a participatory ecosystem where learners are not passive recipients but active co-constructors of knowledge. By embedding vocabulary, grammar, and discourse patterns into challenges, puzzles, or role-based scenarios, games provide what Piaget (1952) described as "disequilibrium", a cognitive conflict that propels learners to adapt their schema through experimentation. This dynamic aligns with Kolb's Experiential Learning Cycle (1984), where concrete experience, reflective observation, abstract conceptualisation, and active experimentation converge.

Furthermore, games directly address affective barriers in language learning. Horwitz et al. (1986) identified anxiety as a central barrier in second language acquisition, often inhibiting risk-taking and spontaneous communication. By contrast, games create a low-stakes, high-engagement environment that reframes errors as part of the play process rather than failures. This reconfiguration of the learning environment fosters confidence, encourages peer collaboration, and nurtures intrinsic motivation, echoing the principles of Self-Determination Theory (Ryan & Deci, 2000).

## 1.3 The Digital Turn: Opportunities and Complexities

The advent of digital technology has transformed the scope and scale of game-based learning. Platforms such as Kahoot, Quizizz, and Duolingo have normalised the integration of gamified systems into everyday teaching. Learning management systems (LMS) increasingly incorporate badges, leaderboards, and progress trackers to enhance student participation. At the same time, more immersive environments, from AI-driven apps to augmented reality simulations, are expanding the horizons of pedagogical play.

Digital games offer several affordances for language learning. They support multimodal input, combining text, sound, and visuals to reinforce comprehension. They allow adaptive feedback systems, where learners receive instant corrections or reinforcement. They promote collaboration through multiplayer modes and online communities. Most importantly, they resonate with learners' lived realities, particularly digital natives accustomed to interactive and screen-mediated environments. Research indicates that digital games boost motivation and improve retention and communicative competence (Chiu, Kao, & Reynolds, 2012; Crompton, Lin, Burke, & Block, 2018).

However, the digital turn introduces complex challenges. Developers often design digital platforms for mass markets, which limits their ability to customise features for specific curricular goals or learner needs. Access disparities continue to challenge under-resourced educational contexts, where educators and learners often lack reliable internet connectivity, adequate hardware, or consistent institutional support. Teachers also face challenges integrating digital games, including limited training, increased preparation time, and the risk of technology overshadowing pedagogy. These issues highlight the need for critical engagement with digital tools rather than uncritical adoption.

## 1.4 The Continuing Relevance of Non-Digital Games

While digital tools dominate contemporary discourse, non-digital games retain significant pedagogical value. Traditional formats such as role-plays, board games, storytelling activities, and flashcard-based challenges remain accessible, cost-effective, and adaptable. Unlike digital platforms, teachers can modify them to suit learner profiles and curricular objectives and rely on minimal technological infrastructure.

Non-digital games also emphasise face-to-face interaction, an essential element of communicative competence. They create opportunities for learners to negotiate meaning, manage turn-taking, and practice pragmatic skills in real time. For example, role-playing a marketplace scenario teaches vocabulary and cultivates discourse strategies such as requesting, bargaining, and politeness conventions. Storytelling circles, likewise, enable learners to practice narrative structures while engaging in collective creativity.

Research suggests that non-digital games foster inclusivity by accommodating learners who may not have access to or comfort with digital platforms. They also nurture social-emotional skills such as empathy, collaboration, and conflict resolution, which are critical in communicative contexts (Nguyen & Yukawa, 2019). Importantly, non-digital play's tactile and embodied nature offers learners a break from screen fatigue, a growing concern in the post-pandemic educational landscape.

## 1.5 Positioning Digital and Non-Digital Games Together

Rather than viewing digital and non-digital games as competing paradigms, seeing them as complementary tools is more productive. Digital games excel in scalability, multimodality, and adaptive feedback, while non-digital games thrive in accessibility, customisability, and embodied interaction. Together, they form a spectrum of playful pedagogies that can be strategically deployed depending on context, resources, and learner needs.

This chapter, therefore, does not privilege one over the other but seeks to understand how both can be integrated meaningfully in language education. By investigating the perceptions of teachers and learners, the chapter contributes to inclusive and adaptable approaches to game-based learning.

### 1.6 Rationale and Significance

The impetus for this research stems from the dual recognition of promise and challenge in integrating games into language classrooms. While enthusiasm for gamified learning has surged, particularly in the wake of online education during the COVID-19 pandemic, empirical insights into how teachers and learners perceive these strategies remain limited. Understanding these perceptions is crucial because they directly influence classroom practices, from selecting tools to adapting content.

The significance of this study lies in its attempt to balance innovation with inclusivity. Platforms like Mentimeter or Duolingo can transform language instruction in contexts where digital infrastructure is robust. With limited resources, non-digital games offer equally powerful, low-cost alternatives. The study contributes to equitable discourse on pedagogical innovation by examining both, ensuring that game-based strategies are not confined to privileged settings.

## 2. LITERATURE REVIEW: CONTEXTUALISING GAME-BASED LANGUAGE LEARNING

Game-based learning (GBL) has increasingly become a central focus in language education research, bridging theory, technology, and pedagogy. Traditional instructional approaches in language classrooms—often characterised by rote memorisation, grammar drills, and passive reception of content—frequently fail to engage learners fully or address the cognitive, affective, and social dimensions crucial for effective language acquisition (Prensky, 2001; Gee, 2007). In contrast, GBL fosters active engagement, contextualised practice, and intrinsic motivation, creating learning environments that encourage experimentation, collaboration, and sustained participation. Over the past two decades, digital and non-digital games have been explored extensively for their potential to improve language learning outcomes, enhance learner motivation, and facilitate meaningful classroom interaction. Digital platforms like educational apps, gamified quizzes, and interactive simulations offer structured, scalable, and adaptive learning experiences. At the same time, non-digital games—including role-plays, storytelling exercises, and board games—promote embodied learning, creativity, and real-time social interaction (Nguyen & Yukawa, 2019; Wang, 2016).

This literature review synthesises theoretical frameworks and empirical studies to establish the pedagogical foundations of GBL, identify existing gaps in practice and research, and inform the design and implementation of the present study. Integrating insights from multiple perspectives highlights how GBL supports cognitive development, social collaboration, and learner motivation in diverse educational contexts.

## 2.1 Constructivism and Experiential Learning

As Piaget (1952) articulated, constructivist theory posits that learners construct knowledge through experience, reflection, and interaction with their environment. Within language education, constructivist principles underscore the importance of learner-centred activities that encourage exploration, hypothesis testing, and meaning-making. Games provide an ideal platform for such engagement, enabling learners to negotiate meaning, experiment with linguistic structures, and apply vocabulary and grammar in authentic contexts (Johnson, 2010).

Kolb's Experiential Learning Theory (1984) complements constructivism by framing learning as a cyclical process involving concrete experience, reflective observation, abstract conceptualisation, and active experimentation. Language games such as role-plays, storytelling tasks, and problem-solving exercises allow learners to participate in this cycle by practising language in contextualised situations, reflecting on their performance, and refining strategies for future interactions. This iterative engagement reinforces retention and promotes communicative competence and pragmatic understanding. Empirical studies support this: students engaged in experiential game-based activities demonstrate greater fluency, confidence, and willingness to take linguistic risks compared to peers in traditional, lecture-based settings (Wang, 2016; Smith & Sanchez, 2015).

## 2.2 Sociocultural Theory and the Zone of Proximal Development

Vygotsky's Sociocultural Theory (1978) emphasises the centrality of social interaction, collaboration, and scaffolding in learning. The l Development (ZPD) concept highlights that learners achieve higher levels of understanding and skill when guided by more capable peers or instructors. Game-based activities operationalise this principle by creating collaborative environments where learners can support one another, negotiate meaning, and co-construct knowledge. Both digital and non-digital collaborative games, such as team-based quizzes, role-plays, and cooperative problem-solving tasks, provide opportunities for scaffolding, enabling learners to push beyond their current linguistic capabilities while receiving immediate support and feedback (Smith & Sanchez, 2015).

These collaborative game structures also promote socio-emotional learning, encouraging empathy, turn-taking, and communication strategies essential for real-world language use. By situating language practice in interactive contexts, GBL aligns with sociocultural perspectives that consider learning as inherently social, context-dependent, and co-constructed.

## 2.3 Flow Theory and Motivation

Csikszentmihalyi's Flow Theory (1990) describes the state of optimal experience, in which learners are fully immersed, engaged, and intrinsically motivated when challenges are balanced with their skills. Games can naturally induce flow states, providing structured yet flexible challenges that sustain attention and encourage repeated practice. Research indicates that learners experiencing flow during game-based activities demonstrate higher levels of participation, persistence, and retention of linguistic structures (Kiili, 2005). For instance, vocabulary and grammar games that adapt difficulty based on learner responses can maintain this balance, preventing boredom or frustration while fostering continuous engagement.

Flow experiences in GBL increase motivation and enhance learners' sense of competence and self-efficacy, contributing to positive attitudes toward language learning. By integrating immediate feedback, progression tracking, and goal-setting, games create immersive contexts that transform routine practice into an enjoyable, meaningful, and learner-driven experience.

## 2.4 Self-Determination Theory and Learner Agency

Self-Determination Theory (Ryan & Deci, 2000) posits that learners are most motivated when their needs for autonomy, competence, and relatedness are satisfied. Game-based learning environments often inherently fulfil these needs. For example, providing learners with choices in game selection or in the strategies they employ fosters autonomy. Well-structured challenges matched to proficiency levels reinforce competence, while collaborative or multiplayer activities satisfy the need for relatedness through social interaction.

Empirical studies support the motivational impact of agency in game-based learning. Learners with higher perceived control over gameplay show increased engagement, risk-taking in language production, and persistence in completing challenging tasks (Reinders & Wattana, 2015). Digital and non-digital games alike can be designed to enhance learner agency. However, carefully considering task design, group dynamics, and scaffolding is essential to ensure these opportunities translate into meaningful language development.

## 2.5 Theory of Gamified Learning

Landers (2014) proposed the Theory of Gamified Learning, which emphasises integrating game elements—such as points, levels, badges, feedback, and progression systems—into instructional design. Gamified learning systems transform traditional teaching into interactive, user-centred experiences that motivate learners and encourage consistent practice. López-Martínez, García-Sánchez, and Pérez (2022) found that gamified educational environments enhance engagement, persistence, and performance across diverse learner populations and proficiency levels, demonstrating the potential of structured game integration to improve language learning outcomes.

In practice, gamified approaches combine games' motivational and interactive affordances with instructional objectives, ensuring that content mastery and skill development remain central. When implemented effectively, gamified learning fosters a cycle of challenge, feedback, reflection, and adaptation, mirroring principles of both constructivist and experiential learning theories.

## 2.6 Digital Games in Language Learning

### 2.6.1 Definition and Scope

Digital games are computer- or app-based platforms incorporating interactive, rule-bound activities with defined learning objectives. They include multiplayer online games, mobile apps, LMS-integrated quizzes, and virtual simulations (Crompton et al., 2018).

### 2.6.2 Empirical Studies and Evidence

Chiu, Kao, and Reynolds (2012) conducted a meta-analysis on digital game-based learning in English classrooms, showing significant improvements in vocabulary, grammar, and reading comprehension. Yang (2017) found that multiplayer online games enhanced communicative competence via authentic negotiation of meaning.

Digital tools like Kahoot, Quizizz, and Duolingo provide adaptive difficulty, instant feedback, and gamified reward systems. Research indicates these features increase learner motivation and engagement, especially among digital-native populations (Go Silk et al., 2020).

### 2.6.3 Advantages and Limitations of Digital Games in Language Learning

Advantages

1 Scalable Content Delivery:

Digital games allow language educators to simultaneously deliver content to many learners, regardless of geographic location. Platforms such as LMS tools, online quizzes, and interactive apps enable teachers to reach students in multiple contexts, from small classrooms to large lecture halls, providing consistent learning experiences across different groups. This scalability makes digital games particularly valuable in higher education and blended learning environments.

2 Multimodal Input (Text, Audio, Visuals):

Digital games often incorporate a combination of text, audio, and visual elements, catering to different learning styles and reinforcing comprehension. For example, vocabulary games may include written prompts, spoken pronunciation, and associated images, allowing learners to engage multiple senses. Such multimodal input enhances retention, facilitates understanding, and supports learners with varying language proficiencies.

3 Adaptive Feedback Supporting Personalised Learning:

Many digital games provide real-time, adaptive feedback, allowing learners to progress at their own pace and receive guidance tailored to their performance. Immediate corrections, hints, or scaffolded challenges enable students to recognise and address errors, promoting autonomous learning and reinforcing self-regulated strategies. This personalisation ensures that learners remain challenged without being overwhelmed.

4 Collaboration through Online Interaction:

Digital platforms often support multiplayer games or collaborative tasks, fostering peer interaction and cooperative learning. Activities like team-based quizzes, discussion boards, or role-play simulations enable learners to communicate in the target language, negotiate meaning, and develop linguistic and social skills. This collaborative element aligns with Vygotsky's Sociocultural Theory, highlighting the role of social interaction in cognitive and language development.

Limitations

1. Requires Technological Infrastructure:

Effective use of digital games depends on access to devices, reliable internet, and software compatibility. Classrooms or regions with poor technological infrastructure may face difficulties implementing these tools, limiting accessibility and equity among learners.

2. Limited Flexibility Compared to Teacher-Led Instruction:

Although digital games offer structured learning paths, they can be less adaptable than real-time teacher-led activities. Teachers may need to intervene to adjust content, clarify instructions, or redirect learning focus—something many digital platforms cannot provide autonomously.

3. Cognitive Overload if Complexity Exceeds Learner Readiness:

Digital games that are overly complex or require simultaneous attention to multiple tasks can overwhelm learners, causing cognitive overload. This may hinder comprehension and reduce the overall effectiveness of the activity, particularly for lower proficiency learners or those unfamiliar with game-based formats.

4. Financial Costs for Premium Platforms:

Many high-quality digital games and platforms require subscription fees or one-time payments, which may be prohibitive for some educational institutions or individual learners. These financial considerations can limit widespread adoption and necessitate careful selection of cost-effective tools (Reinders & Wattana, 2015).

## 2.7 Non-Digital Games in Language Learning

### 2.7.1 Definition and Scope

Non-digital games encompass various, classroom-based activities, including board games, role-plays, storytelling exercises, flashcard activities, charades, and other hands-on exercises that do not rely on technological tools. These games are inherently low-cost, adaptable, and highly accessible, making them suitable for diverse educational settings, including classrooms with limited resources (Nguyen & Yukawa, 2019). Unlike digital games, which require devices and internet connectivity, non-digital games can be implemented immediately and flexibly, allowing teachers to adjust content and difficulty based on learners' proficiency levels, interests, and classroom dynamics. They promote active learning by engaging students physically, cognitively, and socially, creating an immersive environment where language use occurs naturally through interaction and play.

### 2.7.2 Empirical Studies and Evidence

Research has consistently highlighted the effectiveness of non-digital games in enhancing linguistic and socio-emotional development. Role-play activities, for instance, have been shown to improve speaking fluency, negotiation skills, and pragmatic competence in ESL learners. Wang (2016) found that students participating in structured role-plays demonstrated greater confidence in oral communication and were more willing to experiment with new vocabulary and sentence structures. Storytelling exercises, including storytelling circles or collaborative narrative-building, support vocabulary retention, narrative competence, and grammatical accuracy while encouraging creativity and active engagement. Other activities, such as board games or card-based vocabulary exercises, promote turn-taking, peer interaction, and cooperative problem-solving, fostering both language skills and social-emotional learning. These studies collectively suggest that non-digital games provide a rich, learner-centred pedagogical approach, reinforcing language acquisition through authentic and enjoyable experiences.

### 2.7.3 Advantages and Limitations

Advantages:

1. Highly Adaptable to Learner Needs and Classroom Objectives:

Non-digital games can be modified on the spot to suit learner proficiency, class size, and specific language goals. Teachers can easily adjust rules, difficulty levels, or topics to match curricular outcomes and learners' interests.

2. Supports Real-Time Social Interaction, Turn-Taking, and Collaboration:

These activities encourage active participation, negotiation, and cooperative problem-solving. Students engage directly with peers, practice conversational skills, and develop communication strategies, aligning with Vygotsky's Sociocultural Theory, which emphasises learning through social interaction.

3. Minimal Infrastructure Required:

Non-digital games do not require technology, internet access, or expensive tools, making them highly feasible for low-resource classrooms or community-based language programs.

4. Encourages Creativity, Problem-Solving, and Embodied Learning:

Role-plays, improvisation, and storytelling stimulate imagination and critical thinking. Learners embody language through gestures, intonation, and real-world scenarios, promoting experiential learning and deeper retention.

Limitations:

1. Teacher Preparation and Facilitation Required:

Effective implementation often demands careful planning, classroom management skills, and scaffolding activities according to learners' proficiency levels. Teachers must actively monitor participation, provide feedback, and maintain engagement.

2. Limited Scalability:

Unlike digital games, which accommodate many learners simultaneously, non-digital games may be more effective in small to medium-sized classes. Large groups may face challenges maintaining participation and ensuring each learner is actively engaged.

3. Assessment of Outcomes Less Systematic:

Tracking learning gains through non-digital games can be subjective and less structured. Unlike digital platforms that automatically record performance metrics, teachers must rely on observation, oral feedback, or post-activity assessments to evaluate learners' progress.

5. Comparative Perspectives: Digital vs. Non-Digital Games

Comparative studies on digital and non-digital games in language learning reveal that each format offers unique pedagogical benefits, and their effectiveness often depends on the learning context, objectives, and teacher facilitation. Digital games are particularly effective for scalable practice, structured drills, and immediate feedback mechanisms. Wang, Shen, and Novak (2019) highlight that digital platforms excel in activities such as large-scale vocabulary drills, grammar exercises, and adaptive quizzes, where automated scoring and progression tracking enhance learner motivation and provide measurable outcomes. Digital games also support multimodal learning through text, audio, and visual inputs, enabling learners to engage with content in multiple ways and allowing personalised learning paths that can adapt to individual proficiency levels.

On the other hand, non-digital games demonstrate distinct advantages in fostering social interaction, collaborative learning, and communicative competence. Activities such as role-plays, storytelling circles, and board games encourage turn-taking, negotiation, and problem-solving in authentic communication, promoting pragmatic skills and learner confidence. Non-digital games allow teachers to adjust difficulty, content, and learning strategies in real time, offering flexibility that digital platforms cannot always replicate. Kiili (2005) suggests that blended approaches, which integrate digital and non-digital game-based strategies, often yield optimal engagement and learning outcomes. Educators can create a balanced, dynamic, and inclusive learning environment by combining digital tools' structured, adaptive benefits with non-digital games' social, interactive advantages.

Multiple contextual factors, including learner age, proficiency level, available resources, curriculum goals, and teacher expertise, influence the choice between digital and non-digital formats. Younger learners or low-resource classrooms may benefit more from non-digital, hands-on activities, whereas technologically equipped classrooms with older or more autonomous learners may effectively leverage digital platforms. Teachers' beliefs and pedagogical orientation also play a critical role: those who align game-based strategies with curricular objectives and learning outcomes are more likely to implement games meaningfully, rather than superficially, ensuring that games contribute substantively to language acquisition (Sykes & Reinhardt, 2013).

Ultimately, the comparative perspective suggests that no single format is universally superior. Instead, a thoughtful integration of both digital and non-digital games—tailored to the learners' needs and the classroom context—maximises engagement, motivation, and skill development, demonstrating the complementary strengths of these pedagogical tools.

## 2.8 Research Methodology

Two structured questionnaires were developed and circulated to investigate the perceptions and experiences of game-based learning in language education: one targeting students and the other designed for teachers. The student questionnaire aimed to capture learners' engagement, motivation, and perceived effectiveness of digital and non-digital games in language learning. The teacher questionnaire focused on pedagogical practices, integration strategies, observed learner outcomes, and challenges in implementing game-based activities in the classroom. Both instruments included a combination of Likert-scale items, multiple-choice questions, and open-ended prompts, allowing for both quantitative measurement and qualitative insights.

The questionnaires were circulated across multiple educational contexts, ensuring a diverse participant profile that reflects variations in age, proficiency level, and institutional settings. The data collected through these instruments form the primary basis for the subsequent response analysis, providing a comprehensive understanding of game-based learning practices from both learner and educator perspectives and highlighting how the complementary strengths of digital and non-digital games are perceived and applied in authentic classroom contexts.

## 2.9 Data Analysis

### 2.9.1 Teacher Questionnaire Analysis

The teacher questionnaire was analysed to explore educators' perceptions, practices, and challenges in implementing game-based learning in language classrooms. Responses were examined quantitatively, through descriptive statistics of Likert-scale and multiple-choice items, and qualitatively, through thematic analysis of open-ended prompts. Key areas of investigation included teaching level, years of experience, average class size, access to devices and internet, frequency of game use, alignment of games with curriculum goals, perceived learner outcomes, confidence in designing game-based lessons, and perceived barriers such as time constraints or technical limitations. This approach allowed for a comprehensive understanding of how teachers integrate digital and non-digital games, their perceived effectiveness, and contextual factors influencing classroom implementation, providing a detailed perspective on the practical realities of game-based pedagogy in diverse educational settings.

*Table 1. Teaching level*

| Teaching level | Respondents |
|---|---|
| Primary | 10 |
| Secondary | 38 |
| Intermediate | 65 |
| University/Adult | 129 |

*Figure 1. Respondents*

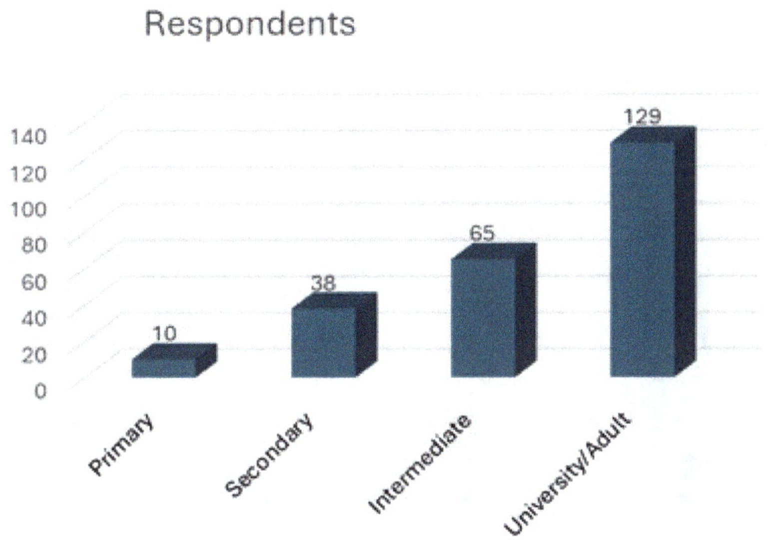


The first question of the teacher questionnaire focused on identifying the teaching levels at which respondents were engaged, providing crucial context for understanding their perspectives on game-based learning. Out of the respondents, 10 teachers reported teaching at the primary level, 38 at the secondary level, 65 at the intermediate level, and 129 at the university or adult level. This distribution indicates that many participants were involved in higher education or adult learning contexts, which may influence their exposure to digital platforms and structured language games. Conversely, the smaller representation from primary and secondary levels suggests that insights from early language learning stages are comparatively limited in this sample. Understanding this distribution is essential, as teaching level often shapes pedagogical strategies, the choice of digital versus non-digital games, and learner engagement and motivation perceptions.

*Table 2. Teaching experience*

| Years of teaching experience | Respondents |
|---|---|
| 5-10 | 177 |
| 11-15 | 43 |
| 16-20 | 13 |
| 21-30 | 9 |

*Figure 2. Respondents*

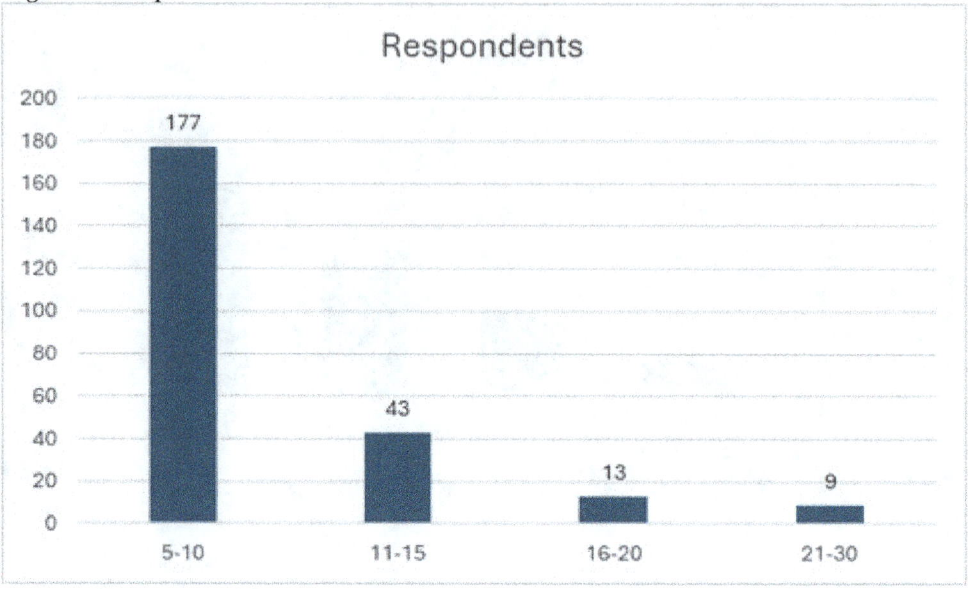


The second question of the teacher questionnaire examined respondents' years of teaching experience, providing insight into the professional background influencing their perceptions of game-based learning. Most teachers, 177 respondents, reported having 5–10 years of experience, followed by 43 teachers with 11–15 years, 13 with 16–20 years, and 9 with 21–30 years of experience. The above analysis indicates that most participants were relatively early-to mid-career educators, potentially more open to experimenting with innovative pedagogical strategies, including game-based learning. The smaller proportion of highly experienced teachers (16–30 years) may reflect a more traditional approach to instruction or limiting engagement with digital platforms, which can influence the implementation of both digital and non-digital games in the classroom. This distribution highlights diverse experience levels, offering a balanced perspective on game-based learning strategies' adoption and perceived effectiveness.

*Table 3. Level of access to digital devices and the Internet*

| Access to devices/Internet in your classroom | Respondents |
|---|---|
| None | 6 |
| Bad | 19 |
| Average | 98 |

continued on following page

*Table 3. Continued*

| Access to devices/Internet in your classroom | Respondents |
|---|---|
| Good | 76 |
| Excellent | 43 |

*Figure 3. Respondents*

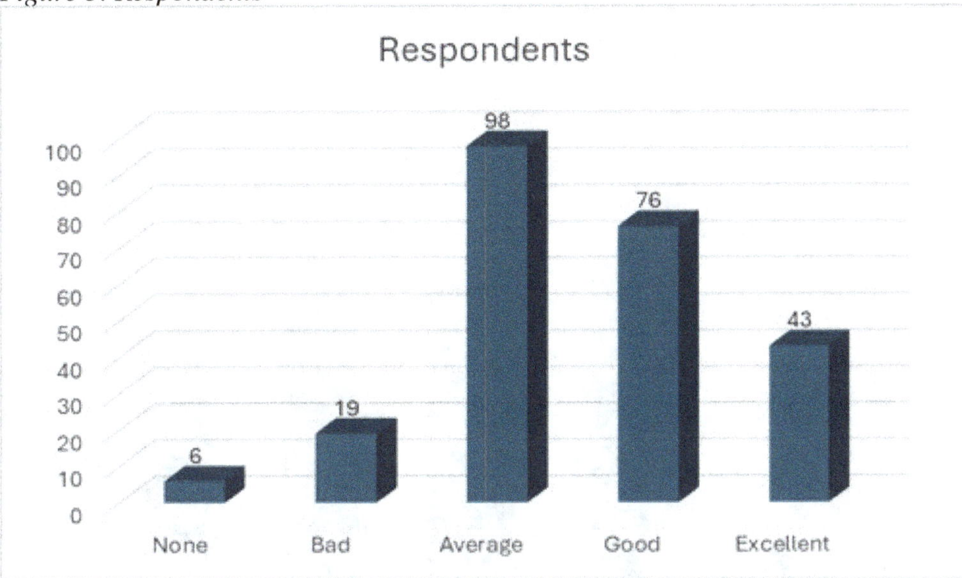


The third question of the teacher questionnaire assessed the level of access to digital devices and the Internet in classrooms, a critical factor influencing the implementation of digital game-based learning. Among respondents, six teachers reported having no access, 19 described access as poor, 98 rated it as average, 76 as good, and 43 as excellent. This data suggests that while most classrooms possess at least average access, there remains a significant variation in technological infrastructure. Classrooms with good to excellent access are better positioned to integrate digital games, online quizzes, and interactive platforms. In contrast, limited access may necessitate reliance on non-digital games and low-tech pedagogical strategies. These findings highlight the importance of contextual factors such as resource availability when designing and implementing game-based learning interventions, particularly for digital tools that require consistent connectivity and devices.

*Table 4. Frequency of incorporating games into language teaching.*

| Frequency of game use in class* | Respondents |
|---|---|
| Never | 7 |
| Occasionally | 67 |
| Sometimes | 60 |
| Often | 56 |
| Always | 52 |

*Figure 4. Respondents*

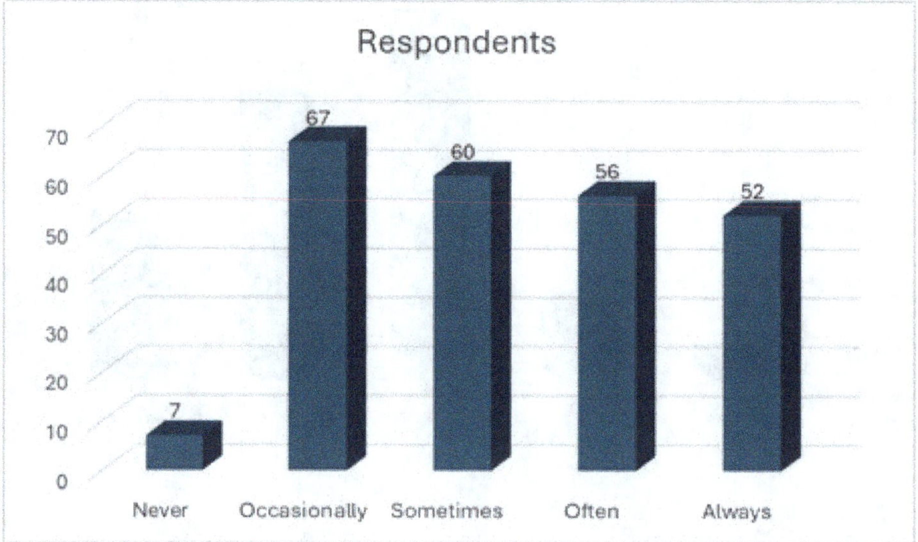


The fourth question of the teacher questionnaire investigated the frequency with which educators incorporate games into their language teaching. Among the respondents, seven teachers reported never using games, 67 used them occasionally, 60 sometimes, 56 often, and 52 always. This distribution indicates that many teachers actively integrate game-based activities into their classrooms, with many employing them regularly or consistently. However, a notable number of educators still use games only sporadically or not at all, highlighting variability in adoption that may be influenced by factors such as teaching experience, class size, or access to resources. Overall, these findings suggest a growing recognition of the pedagogical value of both digital and non-digital games, while also pointing to the need for structured guidance and training to encourage more uniform and effective implementation across different teaching contexts.

*Table 5. Teachers' perceptions of the motivational impact of game-based learning on students*

| Game-based learning increases student motivation. | Respondents |
|---|---|
| Strongly disagree | 5 |
| Disagree | 11 |
| Neutral | 66 |
| Agree | 76 |
| Strongly agree | 84 |

*Figure 5. Respondents*

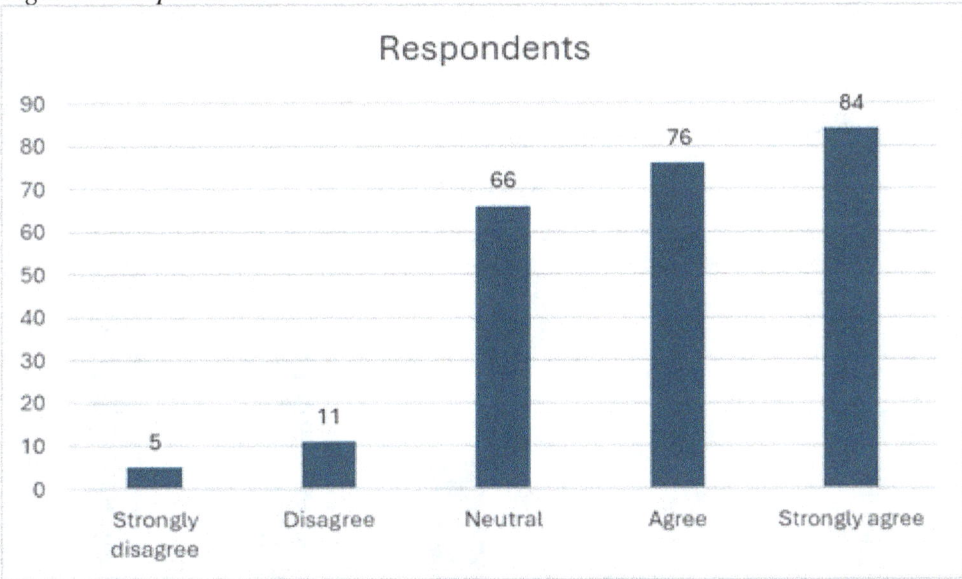


The fifth question explored teachers' perceptions of the motivational impact of game-based learning on students. Out of the respondents, five teachers strongly disagreed and 11 disagreed that games enhance student motivation, 66 remained neutral, 76 agreed, and 84 strongly agreed. These results indicate that most educators recognise the positive role of games in fostering learner motivation, with a significant proportion expressing strong agreement. The relatively high number of neutral responses suggests that some teachers may be uncertain about the extent of this impact, possibly due to limited experience with consistent game-based integration or variable classroom contexts. Overall, the findings underscore the perceived value of games as a motivational tool, reinforcing theoretical assertions from Self-Determination

Theory (Ryan & Deci, 2000) and Flow Theory (Csikszentmihalyi, 1990) regarding the engagement-enhancing potential of well-designed learning activities.

*Table 6. Teachers' confidence in aligning game-based activities with curriculum objectives*

| I can align game activities with curriculum goals. | Respondents |
|---|---|
| Strongly disagree | 6 |
| Disagree | 13 |
| Neutral | 43 |
| Agree | 86 |
| Strongly agree | 94 |

*Figure 6. Respondents*

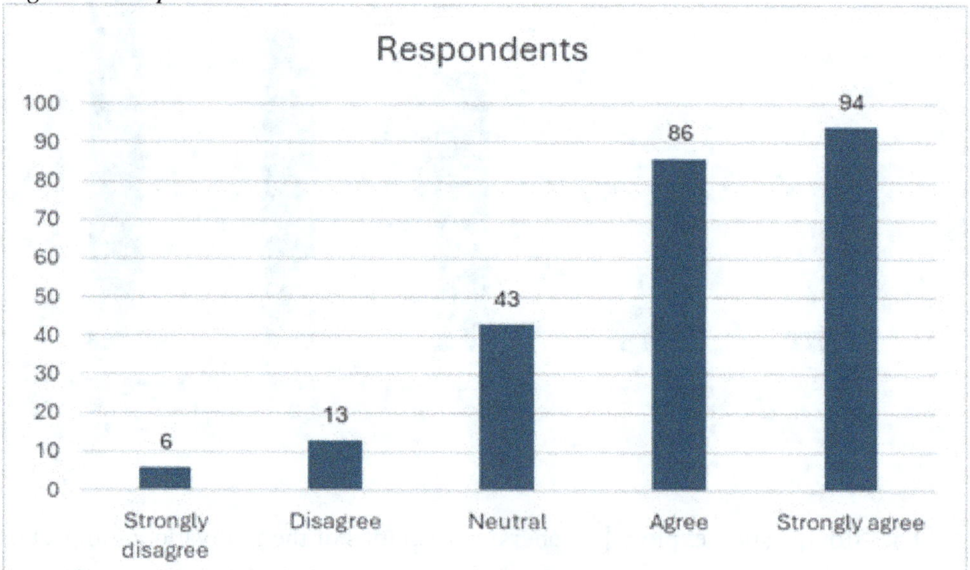


The sixth question examined teachers' confidence in aligning game-based activities with curriculum objectives. Among respondents, six teachers strongly disagreed and 13 disagreed with the statement, 43 remained neutral, while 86 agreed and 94 strongly agreed. These results indicate that most educators can integrate games into their lesson plans to support curriculum goals. Some neutral and dissenting responses suggest that a minority of teachers may face challenges in curriculum alignment, possibly due to limited experience with specific game types or uncertainty about pedagogical outcomes. Overall, the findings reflect a strong teacher perception that game-based learning can be strategically implemented to reinforce targeted learning outcomes, highlighting its potential as a structured and purposeful instructional approach.

*Table 7. Ability to assess language learning gains*

| I can assess language gains from games effectively. | Respondents |
|---|---|
| Strongly disagree | 12 |
| Disagree | 28 |
| Neutral | 56 |
| Agree | 67 |
| Strongly agree | 79 |

*Figure 7. Respondents*

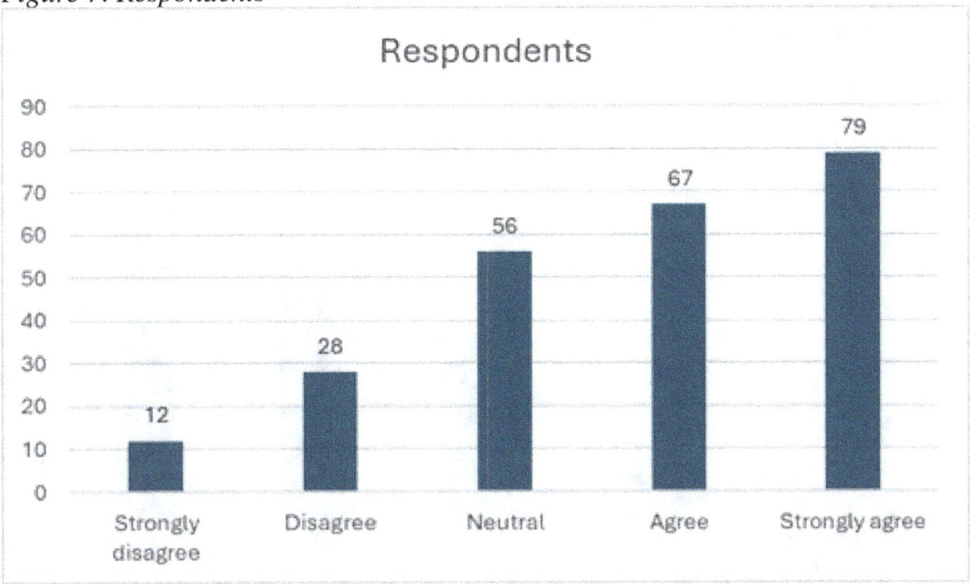


The seventh question explored teachers' perceptions of their ability to assess language learning gains from game-based activities. Among respondents, 12 strongly disagreed and 28 disagreed with the statement, 56 remained neutral, while 67 agreed and 79 strongly agreed. These results indicate that while most teachers feel confident in evaluating the outcomes of game-based learning, a notable proportion remain neutral or express disagreement. This finding may reflect challenges in developing objective assessment metrics for games, particularly in measuring communicative competence, vocabulary acquisition, or fluency in a structured manner. The findings suggest that while teachers acknowledge the pedagogical value of games, there is a need for clear assessment frameworks and tools to accurately capture learning gains, ensuring that game-based strategies are both engaging and educationally accountable.

*Table 8. Impact of technical and infrastructural limitations*

| Technical/infrastructure issues limit the usefulness of digital games. | Respondents |
|---|---|
| Strongly disagree | 3 |
| Disagree | 7 |
| Neutral | 53 |
| Agree | 68 |
| Strongly agree | 99 |

*Figure 8. Respondents*

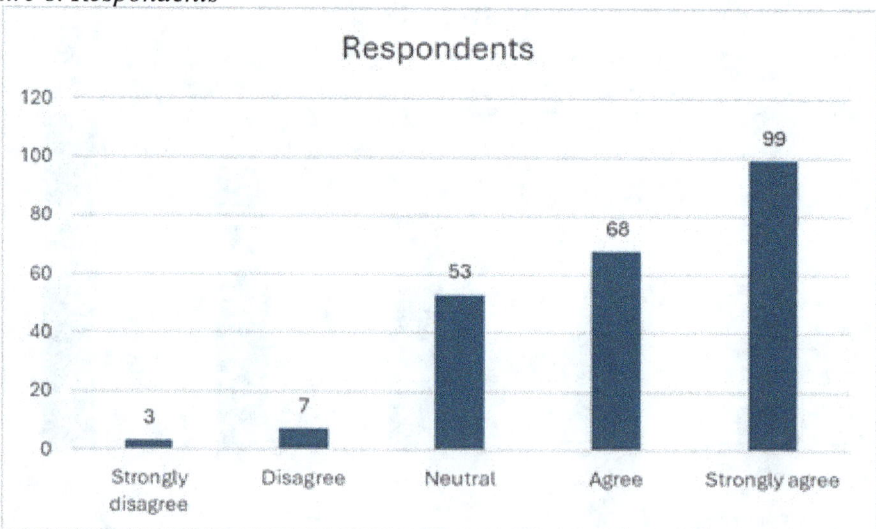


The eighth question examined teachers' perceptions of the impact of technical and infrastructural limitations on the effectiveness of digital game-based learning. Among respondents, three strongly disagreed and seven disagreed that such issues are limiting; 53 remained neutral, while 68 agreed and 99 strongly agreed. These results indicate that most teachers perceive technical constraints—such as inadequate devices, unreliable internet connectivity, or insufficient digital literacy—as barriers to implementing digital games effectively. The relatively high number of neutral responses may reflect variability in classroom contexts, with some teachers experiencing adequate infrastructure and others facing frequent challenges. Overall, the findings underscore the importance of addressing technological and infrastructural readiness to maximise the pedagogical potential of digital game-based learning, highlighting a key contextual factor in successfully integrating these tools.

*Table 9. Feasibility of non-digital games in low-resource classroom settings*

| Non-digital games are easier to implement in low-resource settings. | Respondents |
|---|---|
| Strongly disagree | 23 |
| Disagree | 35 |
| Neutral | 52 |
| Agree | 59 |
| Strongly agree | 73 |

*Figure 9. Respondents*

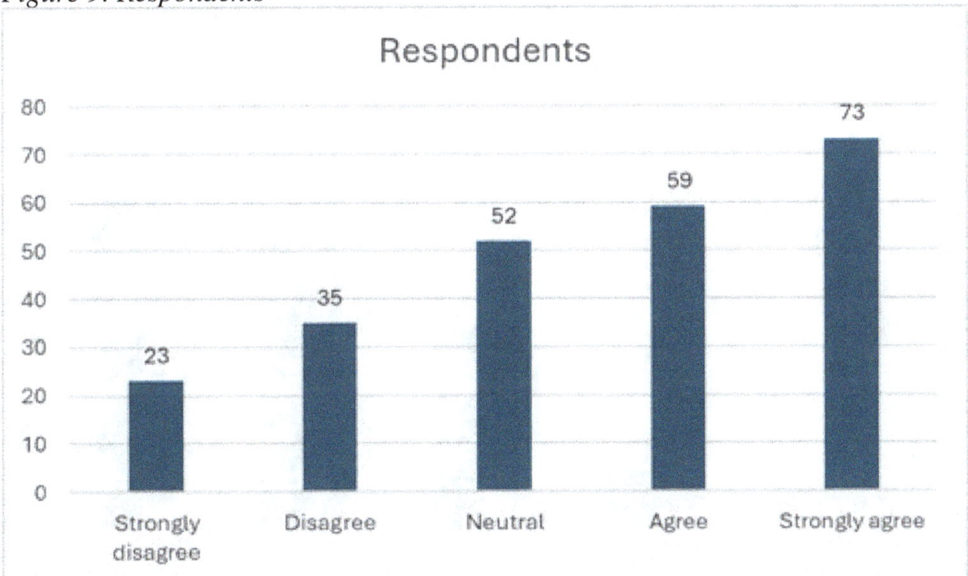


The ninth question explored teachers' perceptions of the feasibility of non-digital games in low-resource classroom settings. Among the respondents, 23 strongly disagreed and 35 disagreed with the statement, 52 remained neutral, 59 agreed, and 73 strongly agreed. These results suggest that most teachers recognise non-digital games as practical and adaptable strategies for classrooms with limited technological resources. The notable neutral and dissenting responses may reflect varying classroom dynamics, teacher familiarity with low-tech game formats, or differing views on the time and effort required for preparation and facilitation. Overall, the findings highlight that non-digital games offer an accessible and inclusive alternative to digital tools, enabling interactive and engaging language learning even in contexts with infrastructural constraints.

*Table 10. Confidence in designing short game-based lessons*

| I feel confident designing short game-based lessons. | Respondents |
|---|---|
| Strongly disagree | 12 |
| Disagree | 15 |
| Neutral | 52 |
| Agree | 75 |
| Strongly agree | 88 |

*Figure 10. Respondents*

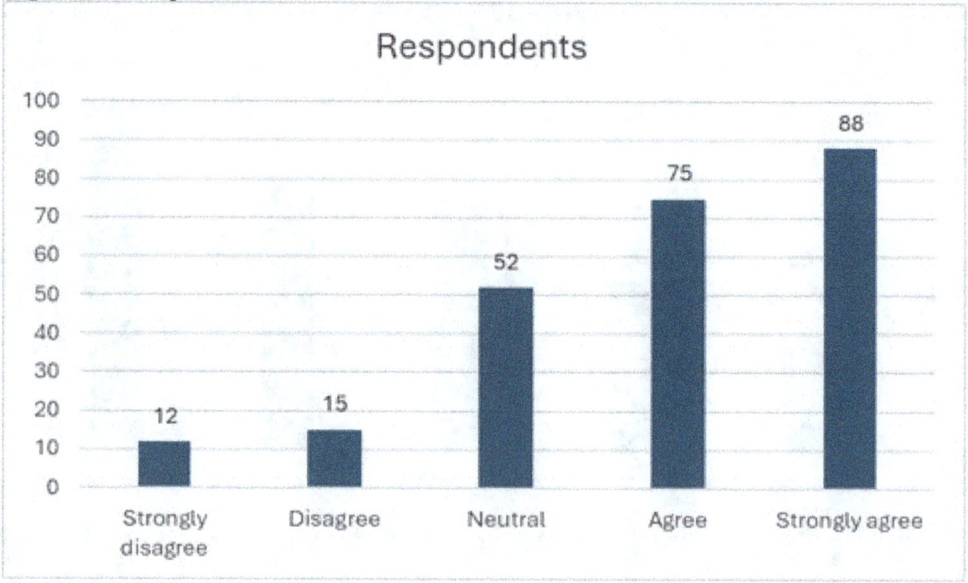


The tenth question assessed teachers' self-reported confidence in designing short game-based lessons. Among respondents, 12 strongly disagreed and 15 disagreed with the statement, 52 remained neutral, while 75 agreed and 88 strongly agreed.

These results indicate that most teachers can create brief game-based activities that align with learning objectives, demonstrating a growing comfort with integrating playful strategies into their teaching practice. The presence of neutral and dissenting responses suggests that some educators may still require additional guidance, training, or resources to enhance their lesson design skills. These findings reflect a positive trend in teacher readiness for implementing game-based learning, which is crucial for ensuring engagement and pedagogical effectiveness in language classrooms.

*Table 11. Time constraints as a barrier to implementing game-based learning*

| Time constraints are a significant barrier to using games* | Respondents |
|---|---|
| Strongly disagree | 11 |
| Disagree | 21 |
| Neutral | 52 |
| Agree | 65 |
| Strongly agree | 93 |

*Figure 11. Respondents*

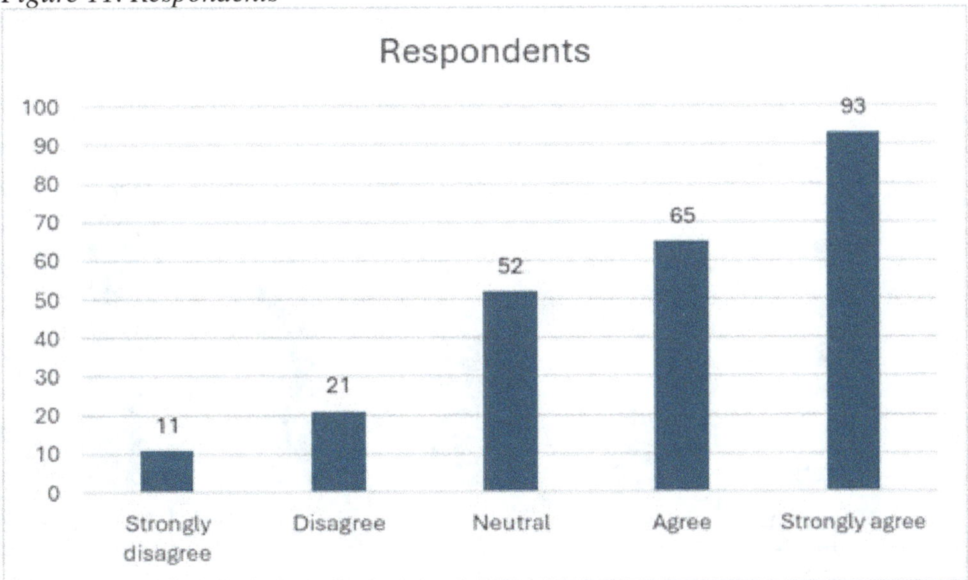


The eleventh question explored teachers' perceptions of time constraints as a barrier to implementing game-based learning. Among respondents, 11 strongly disagreed and 21 disagreed, 52 remained neutral, while 65 agreed and 93 strongly agreed. These results indicate that most teachers consider limited class time a significant challenge in incorporating games, particularly activities that require setup, facilitation, and reflection. The neutral responses suggest that some educators may have found ways to integrate games efficiently or may not perceive time as a limiting factor in their teaching contexts. Overall, the findings highlight the importance of lesson planning and time management strategies to ensure that game-based activities are both feasible and effective within the constraints of typical classroom schedules.

*Table 12. Need for structured resources*

| I would use more games if I had ready-made lesson plans and rubrics. | Respondents |
|---|---|
| Strongly disagree | 7 |
| Disagree | 16 |
| Neutral | 59 |
| Agree | 64 |
| Strongly agree | 96 |

*Figure 12. Respondents*

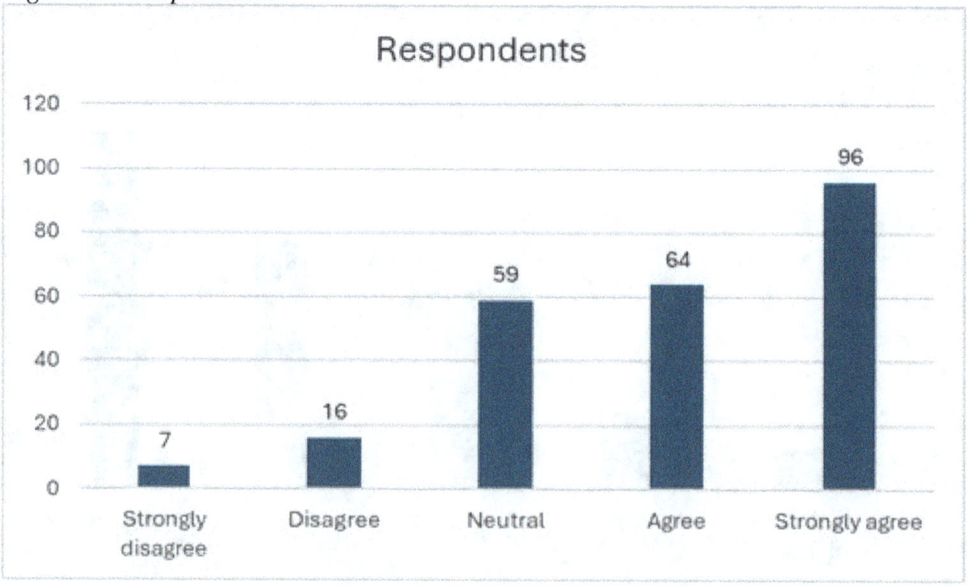


The twelfth question examined teachers' perceptions of the need for structured resources, such as ready-made lesson plans and assessment rubrics, to support the integration of game-based learning. Among respondents, seven strongly disagreed and 16 disagreed, 59 remained neutral, while 64 agreed and 96 strongly agreed. These results indicate that most teachers value practical resources as enablers for more frequent and effective use of games in the classroom. The neutral responses suggest some educators may be capable of designing their materials. Still, the findings underscore the importance of providing structured support to facilitate the implementation of both digital and non-digital game-based activities. Access to such resources can reduce preparation time, enhance confidence, and promote consistent alignment with curriculum objectives.

*Table 13. Relative ease of implementing non-digital games*

| **Non-digital games (role-play, board games, storytelling) are easier to include in the class activity as compared to digital games** | **Respondents** |
|---|---|
| Strongly disagree | 11 |
| Disagree | 12 |
| Neutral | 175 |
| Agree | 23 |
| Strongly agree | 21 |

*Figure 13. Respondents*

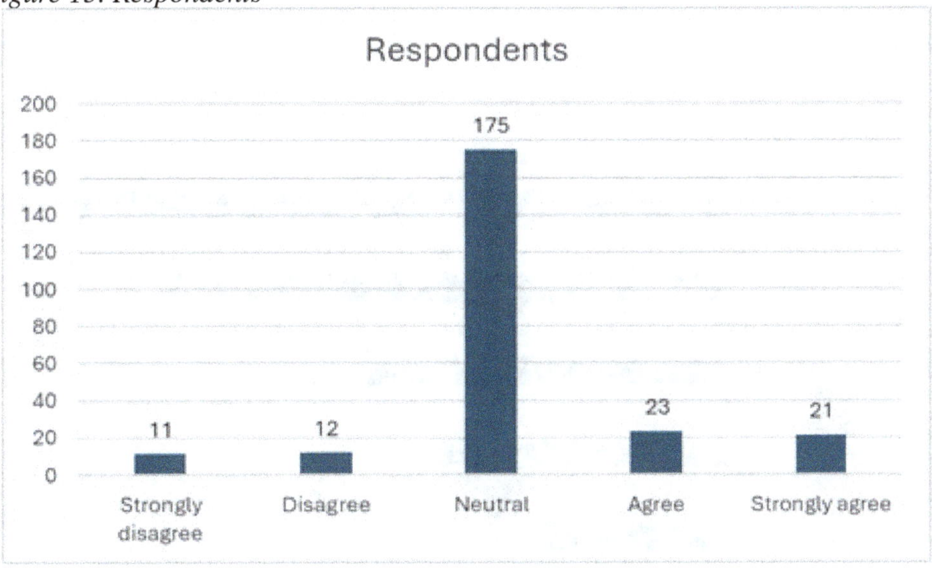


This thirteenth question examined teachers' perceptions regarding the relative ease of implementing non-digital games, such as role-plays, board games, and storytelling activities, compared to digital games. Among respondents, 11 strongly disagreed and 12 disagreed, 175 remained neutral, while 23 agreed and 21 strongly agreed. The overwhelming proportion of neutral responses suggests that many teachers may neither strongly favour non-digital games nor view them as easier to integrate, possibly reflecting a lack of consistent experience with structured game-based activities. The smaller numbers expressing agreement or disagreement indicate that perceptions of ease may vary based on class size, available resources, and familiarity with different game formats. The findings imply that while some educators find non-digital games straightforward, broader pedagogical support and guidance could help standardise and facilitate effective classroom integration.

*Table 14. Preferences for using a combination of digital and non-digital games*

| I prefer a mix of digital and non-digital games in class. | Respondents |
|---|---|
| Strongly disagree | 21 |
| Disagree | 34 |
| Neutral | 48 |
| Agree | 65 |
| Strongly agree | 74 |

*Figure 14. Respondents*

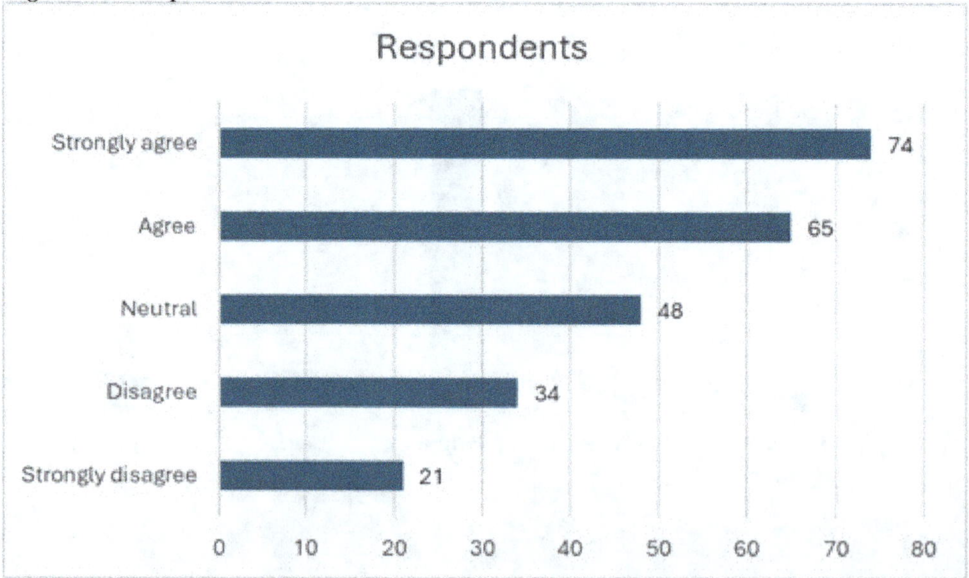

The final question of the teacher questionnaire explored educators' preferences for using a combination of digital and non-digital games in their language classrooms. Among the respondents, 21 strongly disagreed and 34 disagreed, 48 remained neutral, 65 agreed, and 74 strongly agreed. These results indicate that most teachers appreciate the value of blending digital and non-digital game-based strategies to create a more engaging and versatile learning environment. The neutral responses suggest that some educators may be uncertain or lack experience implementing a mixed approach. Overall, the findings highlight a general inclination towards adopting a balanced game-based pedagogy, leveraging the interactive benefits of digital tools alongside the accessibility and flexibility of non-digital activities to enhance learner engagement and language development.

Student Response:

*Table 15. Students' age*

| Age* | Respondents |
|---|---|
| 10-15 | 16 |
| 16-20 | 43 |
| 21-25 | 29 |
| 26-30 | 12 |

*Figure 15. Respondents*

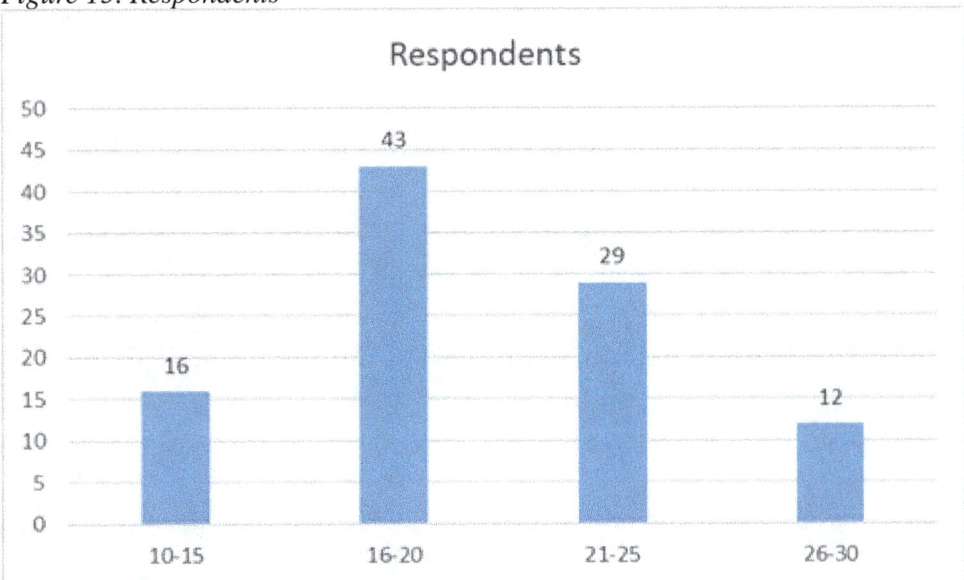

The age distribution of student respondents shows a wide range of learning stages. This diversity provides insights into how views on game-based learning may change with age and educational progress. The largest group included participants aged 16 to 20 (43 respondents), mostly aligned with secondary and early tertiary education. This finding is an essential developmental stage where learners shift from structured, teacher-led settings to more independent learning. Their opinions on engagement and motivation are significant. The second-largest group was those aged 21 to 25 (29 respondents). These participants are likely university students with more exposure to digital tools and self-directed learning strategies, making them more open to gamified methods. The smallest group, aged 10 to 15 (16 respondents), is worth noting. Younger learners are usually very receptive to play-based learning strategies due to their natural enjoyment of interactive and creative tasks. Lastly, the 26 to 30 age group (12 respondents) comprised mature learners or working professionals involved in language learning. Practical needs and real-world applications influence their perspectives. This varied age distribution ensures that the data reflects a range of learner experiences and attitudes, from school-aged children to adult students.

*Table 16. Linguistic backgrounds*

| **Primary languages spoken at home** * | **Respondents** |
|---|---|
| Hindi | 68 |
| English | 32 |

*Figure 16. Respondents*

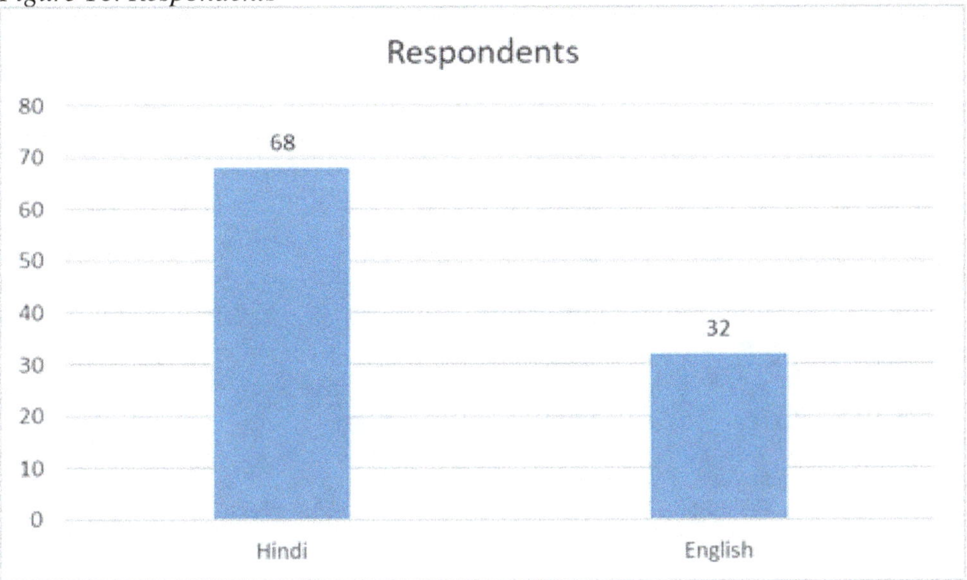


The linguistic backgrounds of the respondents show that most students (68) spoke Hindi as their primary language at home, while 32 reported English as their primary household language. This distribution emphasises the bilingual setting many learners find themselves in, with Hindi as the primary language and English learned through formal education. The high number of Hindi speakers indicates that for most respondents, learning English occurs in an environment where it is not the primary language used for daily communication. This comprehensive distinction makes engaging and interactive methods, like game-based learning, especially important. On the other hand, those who spoke English at home are likely to encounter it more naturally in their everyday lives. Thus, it may affect their confidence, fluency, and how they view the need for gamified learning methods. The differences in home language environments help us understand digital and non-digital games' varying motivations, challenges, and effectiveness in supporting language learning.

*Table 17. Educational level*

| **Educational level*** | **Respondents** |
|---|---|
| Secondary Level | 16 |
| Higher Secondary Level | 43 |
| Graduate | 29 |
| Post Graduate | 12 |

*Figure 17. Respondents*

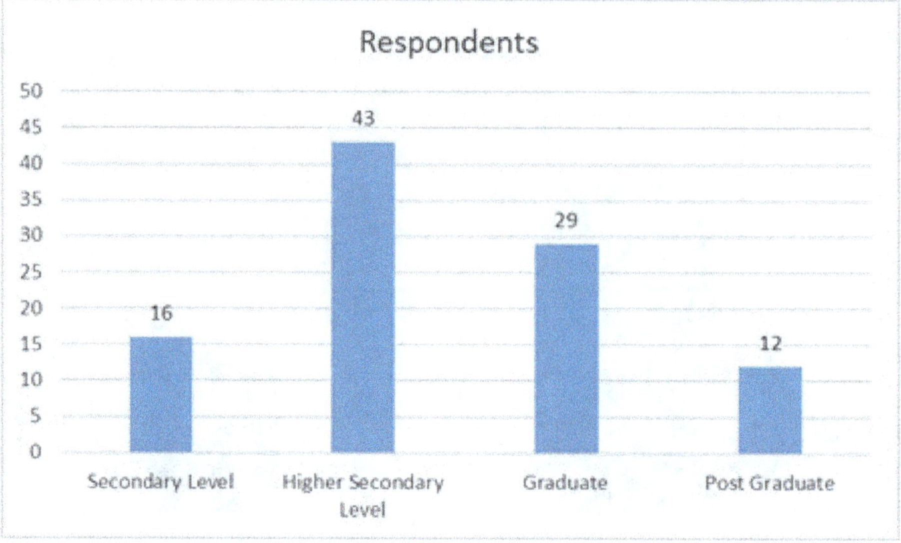


The distribution of respondents by educational level shows that the largest group is from the Higher Secondary level (43), followed by Graduate students (29), Postgraduates (12), and Secondary level learners (16). This distribution indicates that most participants are in their late or early twenties. This age range is crucial for language skills development, often related to academic progress and future job opportunities. The strong presence of Higher Secondary students suggests that their views on game-based learning are particularly significant. They are preparing for higher studies while still needing a solid foundation in language. Graduate and Postgraduate respondents, though fewer in number, offer valuable insights into how older learners with more advanced academic experience view game-based methods.

Meanwhile, secondary-level learners represent younger participants. Their engagement and preference for interactive methods, such as games, might be higher because of their age. Overall, this mix of educational backgrounds enriches the study by showing how views on digital and non-digital games change during different stages of academic development.

*Table 18. Self-assessment of overall language skills*

| **Self-rated overall language proficiency*** | **Respondents** |
|---|---|
| Poor | 2 |
| Fair | 5 |
| Average | 11 |
| Good | 33 |
| Excellent | 49 |

*Figure 18. Respondents*

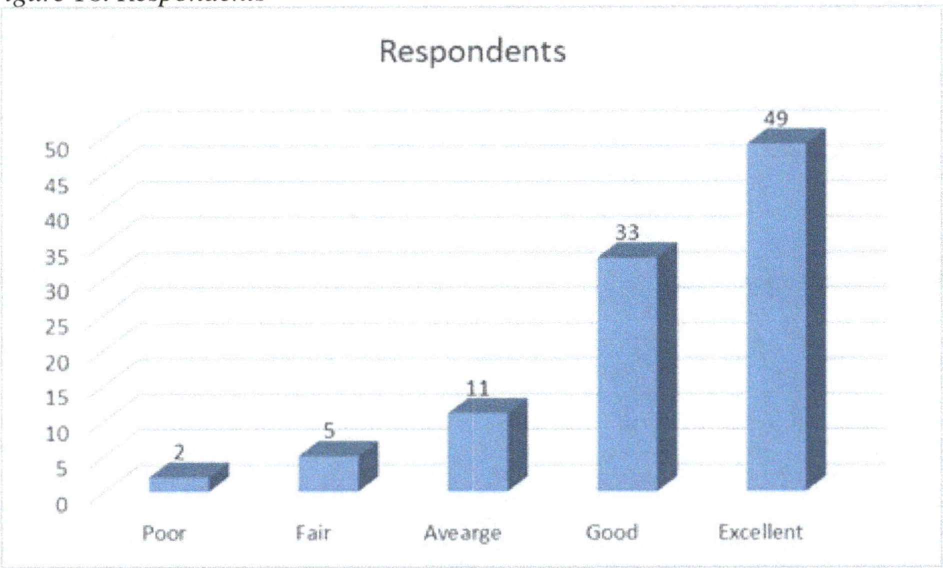


Respondents' self-assessment of overall language skills shows that most view themselves as competent language users. Forty-nine respondents rated their skills " Excellent," and thirty-three rated them "Good." Together, these groups make up more than three-quarters of the sample. The analysis suggests that the participants are largely confident in their language abilities. A smaller number rated their proficiency as Average (11), Fair (5), or Poor (2). Even though these numbers are low, they still represent learners who may need more support in their language learning journey.

The above distribution indicates that most game-based learners already have intermediate to advanced proficiency levels. This awareness may shape their expectations of games as tools for deeper language understanding rather than just basic learning. For instance, learners who rate themselves "Excellent" may prefer games that challenge their critical thinking, creativity, and advanced vocabulary. On the other hand, those in the "Average" or "Fair" categories might like simpler, more structured games that reinforce essential grammar and communication skills. As the high self-ratings suggest, learners may also overestimate their skills, indicating a possible perception bias. Still, teachers are trying game-based learning in classrooms where learners generally feel confident, which may encourage greater openness to new, interactive teaching methods.

*Table 19. Prior experience with game-based learning*

| Prior experience with game-based learning* | Respondents |
|---|---|
| None | 10 |
| Rarely | 25 |
| Sometimes | 42 |
| Often | 14 |
| Always | 9 |

*Figure 19. Respondents*

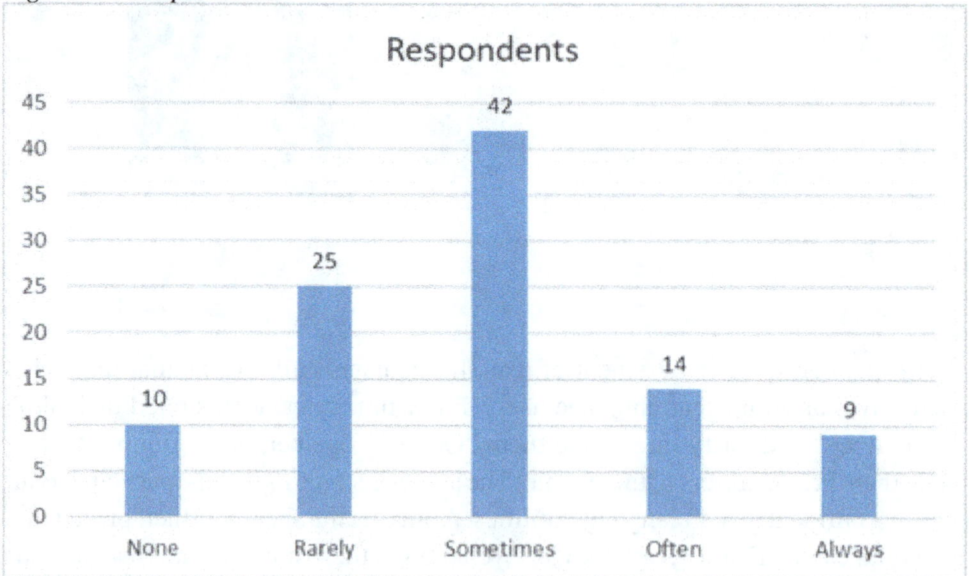


The data on prior experience with game-based learning (GBL) indicates that most learners have had at least some exposure to games as part of their educational journey. However, the frequency of use varies widely. The largest group, 42 respondents, reported "Sometimes" engaging in game-based activities, suggesting that while games are not a dominant part of classroom instruction, they are occasional learning tools. Respondents indicated "Rarely," which, combined with the 10 who reported "None," highlights that a significant portion of learners have minimal or no sustained experience with GBL.

In contrast, 14 respondents selected "Often" and nine chose "Always," reflecting more regular integration of games into learning. Although smaller, these groups demonstrate that consistent game implementation occurs in some contexts, likely influenced by innovative teachers, specific institutional policies, or access to digital resources.

This spread shows that GBL, while recognised, is still in the emerging or supplementary stage in many classrooms rather than forming a core pedagogical strategy. For learners with limited exposure ("Rarely" or "None"), GBL might feel novel and engaging, potentially boosting motivation through its novelty effect. Conversely, learners already accustomed to frequent game-based activities may approach them with higher expectations, seeking games that provide challenge, variety, and meaningful integration with language goals.

The findings also suggest a need to bridge the gap between occasional and consistent use, ensuring that GBL moves beyond sporadic classroom experiments to become an intentional, structured component of language teaching.

*Table 20. Availability of devices*

| Devices available for class activities* | Respondents |
|---|---|
| Personal smartphone | 27 |
| Shared devices | 51 |
| No device | 22 |

*Figure 20. Respondents*

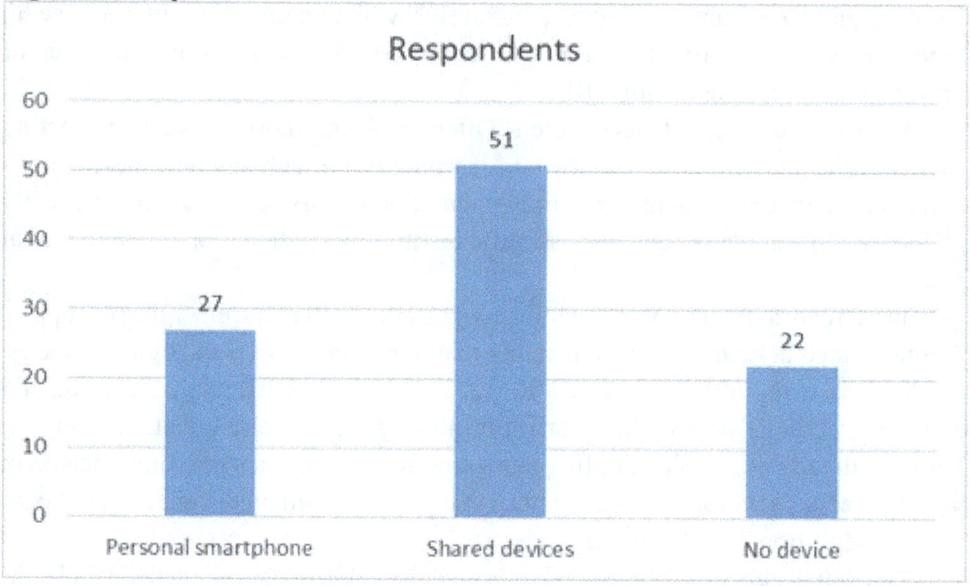


The availability of devices for class activities reveals essential insights into the digital readiness of learners for game-based learning (GBL). Most respondents—51 learners—reported accessing shared devices, suggesting that learners use digital resources without owning them individually. Shared access often limits flexibility, personalisation, and frequency of engagement, as learners may have to wait their turn or compromise on time and usage. This finding could directly affect the smooth integration of digital games, especially those requiring sustained individual participation.

A smaller but significant group of 27 learners reported access to personal smartphones, reflecting a growing trend in mobile-assisted language learning. This group is more likely to benefit from consistent exposure to digital games, apps, and interactive platforms, as personal devices support autonomy, convenience, and personalised engagement. However, smartphone dependence may pose challenges like smaller screens, connectivity issues, or distractions from non-academic applications.

On the other hand, 22 learners indicated having no device available for class activities, underscoring a digital divide within the participant pool. Reliance on non-digital games or teacher-facilitated activities becomes essential for these learners, as digital GBL would not be equitably accessible. This finding emphasises that educators must prioritise infrastructure planning and inclusivity when designing game-based pedagogies, so they include learners who lack access to devices.

Overall, the data illustrate a hybrid learning environment: while personal smartphones and shared devices open pathways for digital games, the absence of universal access means that non-digital games still hold critical value in ensuring inclusivity. The findings reinforce the need for blended strategies that balance digital and non-digital methods to accommodate diverse access levels.

*Table 21. Motivation level with game based learning*

| I am more motivated when games are used in language lessons. | Respondents |
|---|---|
| Strongly disagree | 2 |
| Disagree | 5 |
| Neutral | 11 |
| Agree | 22 |
| Strongly agree | 60 |

*Figure 21. Respondents*

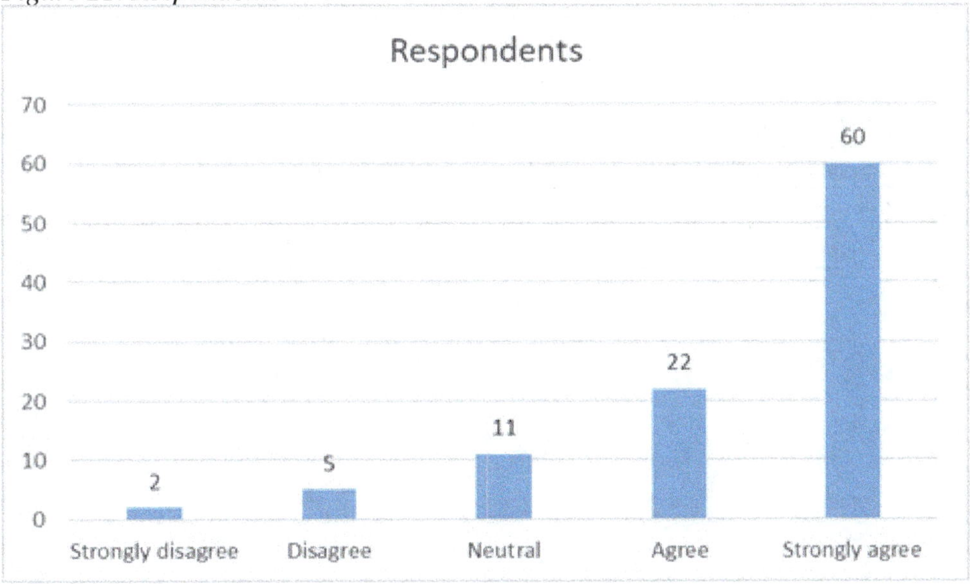


The responses to this item reveal a strong positive correlation between game use and learner motivation. A substantial majority of students—60 strongly agreed and 22 agreed—indicating that nearly four out of five participants (over 75%) explicitly acknowledged that games significantly enhance their motivation to engage in language lessons. This finding suggests that game-based learning (GBL) has a substantial affective impact, creating a sense of enjoyment and active participation that traditional instruction may lack.

Only a small fraction of learners—2 strongly disagreed and five disagreed—expressed negative views, suggesting that resistance to GBL is minimal. This small group could reflect individual differences in learning preferences, where some students may favour conventional teaching methods or feel uncomfortable with playful, interactive formats.

Eleven students occupied a middle ground by remaining neutral, indicating either ambivalence (they do not perceive a significant difference) or limited exposure to well-implemented game-based activities. This finding highlights how important quality is in game design and integration—if games do not meaningfully connect to language objectives, they may not fully realise their motivational impact.

Overall, the overwhelmingly positive responses confirm that games serve as a strong motivational driver, aligning with prior research that highlights the ability of GBL to foster intrinsic motivation, reduce classroom anxiety, and create a more engaging learning atmosphere (Gee, 2007; Reinders & Wattana, 2015). The findings suggest that incorporating games in lessons supports cognitive outcomes and strengthens learners' willingness to participate, a key factor in successful language acquisition.

*Table 22. Perception on the helpfulness of games*

| Games (digital or non-digital) help me remember vocabulary and expressions. | Respondents |
|---|---|
| Strongly disagree | 3 |
| Strongly agree | 97 |

*Figure 22. Respondents*

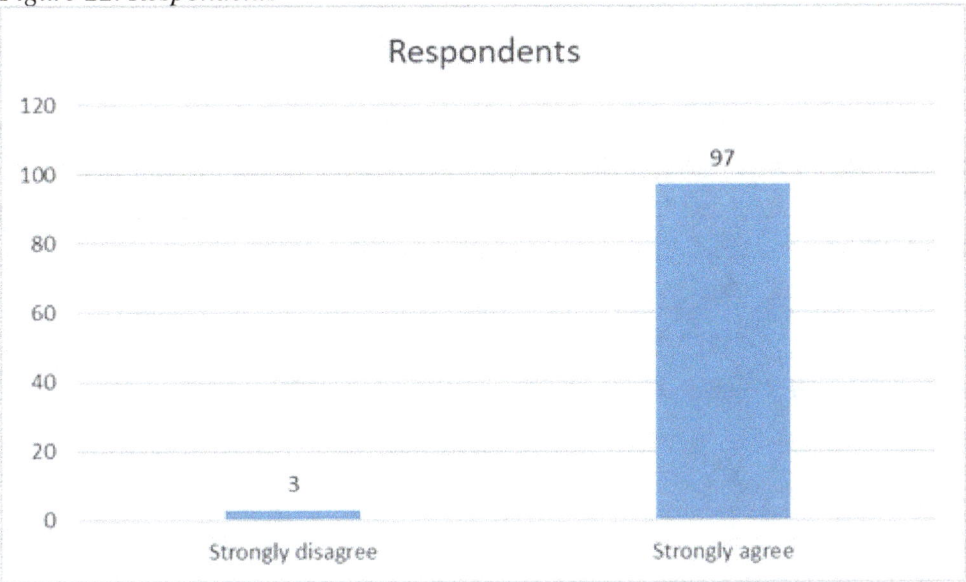


The responses to this item show an overwhelmingly positive endorsement of the role of games in vocabulary retention. Out of the entire student sample, 97 respondents strongly agreed, while only three strongly disagreed. Notably, there were no neutral or intermediate responses, which underscores the clarity and unanimity with which learners associate games with improved memory and recall of linguistic items.

This finding suggests that games are engaging and function as powerful mnemonic tools, reinforcing vocabulary and expressions through repetition, contextualisation, and active use. The interactive nature of digital and non-digital games allows learners to practise language in meaningful contexts, promoting deeper processing than rote memorisation. For example, role-play or storytelling tasks provide situational anchors that help embed new expressions in memory, while digital vocabulary games leverage repetition and feedback loops to strengthen recall.

The near-universal agreement aligns with existing literature on the cognitive benefits of GBL. Research by Wang (2016) and Kiili (2005) highlights how games enhance encoding and retrieval processes by making learning multisensory, dynamic, and emotionally engaging. The fact that virtually all students in this study reported improved retention confirms that games are not merely motivational tools but also practical strategies for long-term language acquisition.

The absence of neutrality in responses also signals that students have direct experiential evidence of games aiding their vocabulary development, rather than abstract beliefs or assumptions. This strengthens the validity of the result, suggesting that learners consistently notice tangible benefits when games are integrated into language instruction.

*Table 23. Level of reduction of anxiety due to game based learning*

| I feel less anxious speaking during game activities than in routine oral drills. | Respondents |
|---|---|
| Strongly disagree | 6 |
| Strongly agree | 94 |

*Figure 23. Respondents*

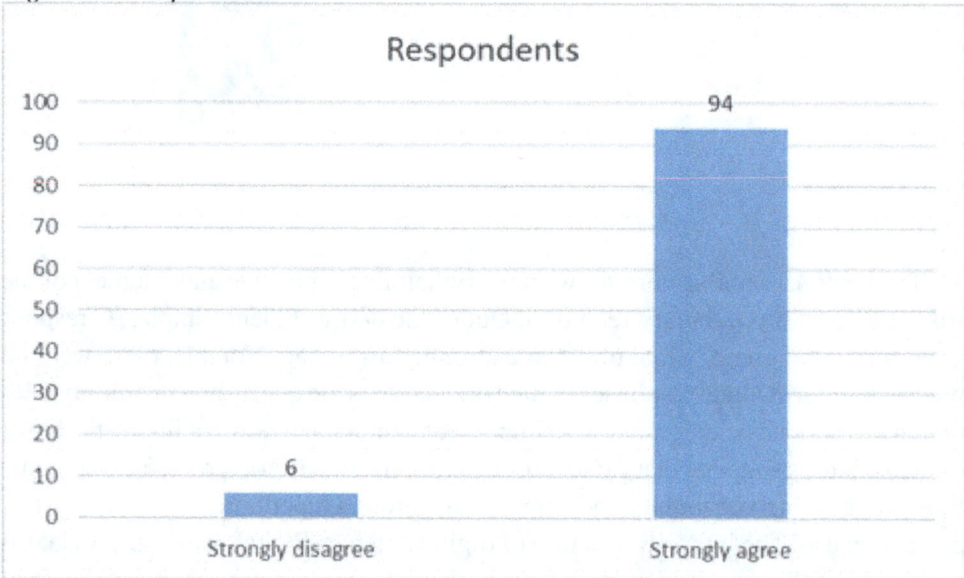


The responses to this question reveal an overwhelming consensus among students: 94 respondents strongly agreed that game-based activities reduce their anxiety when speaking, while only six strongly disagreed. The absence of intermediate categories (neutral, agree, disagree) is significant, as it indicates that learners' experiences are highly polarised—yet almost entirely in favour of games as anxiety-reducing tools.

This result highlights one of the most powerful contributions of game-based learning: lowering the affective filter (Krashen, 1982). In traditional oral drills, learners often feel pressure, fear judgment, or experience performance anxiety, which inhibits spontaneous language use. In contrast, games create a low-stakes, playful environment where learners reframe mistakes as part of the activity rather than failures. This context shift lowers self-consciousness and encourages more natural and confident speaking.

The overwhelming agreement also underscores the psychological safety and intrinsic motivation embedded in gameplay. Games encourage participation through rules, goals, and rewards, diverting focus from the fear of error to the enjoyment of the task. For example, role-play scenarios or storytelling games allow learners to embody characters, temporarily removing personal vulnerability. In contrast, competitive or collaborative game structures channel attention toward collective problem-solving rather than individual performance pressure.

This finding aligns with previous studies: Reinders and Wattana (2015) observed that digital language games reduced speaking anxiety among ESL learners, while Wang (2016) reported that role-play significantly enhanced oral fluency and confidence. Therefore, digital and non-digital game formats support a psychosocial dimension of language learning that traditional instruction often neglects.

From a pedagogical perspective, the data suggest that educators can strategically integrate games to teach content and manage learner affect, creating conditions conducive to risk-taking and authentic language use. This insight is invaluable for language teachers: fostering an environment where learners willingly speak and experiment with language is often a greater challenge than teaching grammar or vocabulary.

*Table 24. Impact of technical issues on digital game-based learning*

| Technical problems (internet/devices) disrupt my learning during digital game activities. | Respondents |
|---|---|
| Strongly disagree | 0 |
| Disagree | 2 |
| Neutral | 9 |
| Agree | 17 |
| Strongly agree | 72 |

*Figure 24. Respondents*

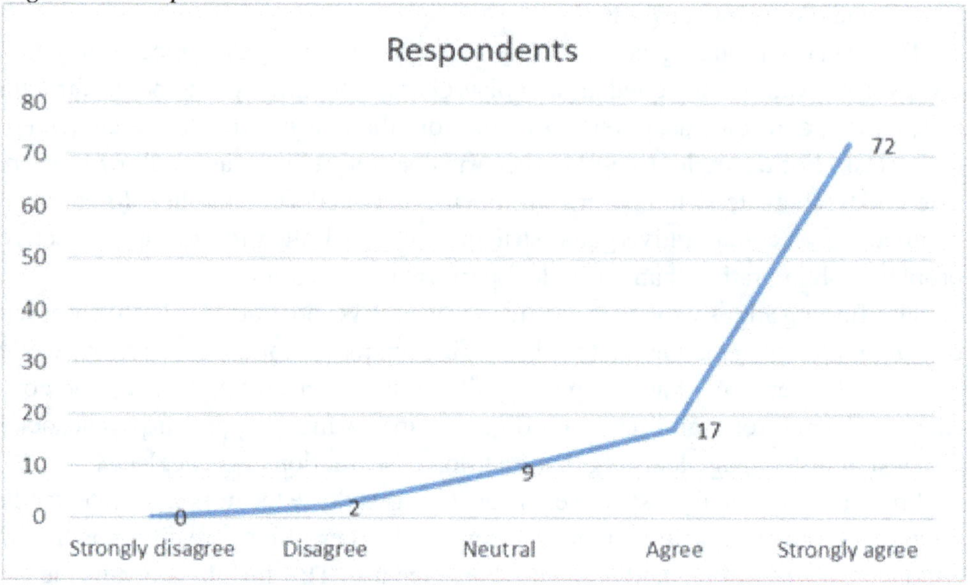


The responses to this question indicate a strong consensus among students regarding the impact of technical issues on digital game-based learning. Seventy-two respondents strongly agreed and 17 agreed that problems with internet connectivity or device availability disrupt their knowledge, while only a few remained neutral (9) or disagreed (2). The absence of strongly negative responses highlights that these technical challenges are nearly universally experienced and recognised as significant barriers to effective engagement in digital game activities.

This finding emphasises one of the key limitations of digital game-based learning: its reliance on reliable technological infrastructure. Unlike non-digital games, which can be implemented with minimal resources, digital games depend on functional devices, stable internet connections, and sometimes specialised software. Interruptions caused by technical failures break the continuity of learning and disrupt the flow of gameplay, reducing engagement and the motivational benefits that games typically offer.

The students' overwhelming agreement also underscores how crucial infrastructure is in supporting the pedagogical potential of digital games. Even well-designed, intrinsically motivating and cognitively stimulating activities can lose effectiveness if learners cannot participate consistently. This finding aligns with teacher responses collected earlier, which similarly highlighted technical and infrastructural issues as significant constraints in the classroom.

From a practical perspective, the data suggests that educators should plan for contingencies when implementing digital games, such as having non-digital alternatives available or structuring activities to minimise reliance on continuous connectivity. Moreover, it points to the broader institutional need for investment in technology and equitable access to devices to ensure that digital game-based learning is inclusive and effective. The findings collectively reinforce the argument for a blended approach, combining the adaptability and reliability of non-digital games with the interactivity and multimedia affordances of digital platforms to create a resilient and engaging language learning environment.

*Table 25. Impact of non-digital games on classroom participation*

| Non-digital games (role-play, board games, storytelling) make me participate more. | Respondents |
|---|---|
| Strongly disagree | 0 |
| Disagree | 3 |
| Neutral | 12 |
| Agree | 13 |
| Strongly agree | 72 |

*Figure 25. Respondents*

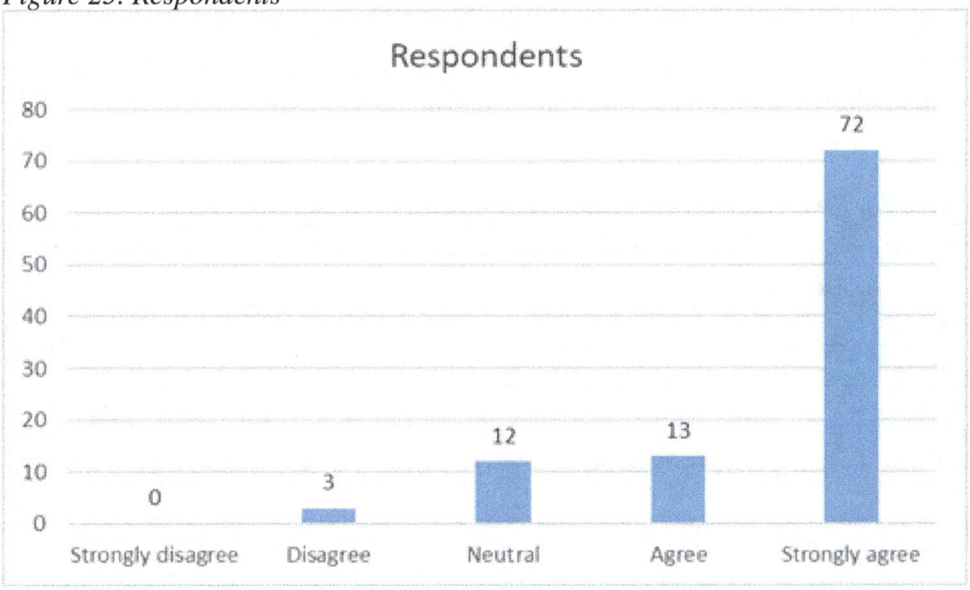

The responses to this question indicate a clear consensus among students regarding the impact of non-digital games on classroom participation. Seventy-two respondents strongly agreed and 13 agreed that activities such as role-play, board games, and storytelling increase their engagement, while 12 remained neutral and only three disagreed. The absence of strongly negative responses underscores the general perception that non-digital games encourage active participation.

This finding highlights one of the key advantages of non-digital game-based learning: promoting interactive and collaborative engagement in the classroom. Such activities create opportunities for learners to participate in meaningful communication, practice language skills in context, and interact with peers in a low-pressure environment. Non-digital games foster social dynamics that are often difficult to achieve in traditional drills, as they encourage turn-taking, negotiation, and cooperative problem-solving.

The overwhelming agreement among students also aligns with earlier findings on motivation, indicating that when learners are actively involved in games, their willingness to communicate and experiment with language increases. For example, storytelling exercises allow learners to construct narratives collectively, while role-play tasks simulate real-life scenarios requiring spontaneous language use. This experiential learning approach supports cognitive and affective development, reinforcing language acquisition through practice and reflection.

From a pedagogical perspective, these results suggest that teachers can strategically incorporate non-digital games to enhance participation and learner interaction, particularly in classrooms with limited digital resources. Non-digital games offer a low-cost, flexible, and inclusive option to engage students actively while supporting communicative competence and confidence in language use.

*Table 26. Preference on the blended approach*

| I prefer a mix of digital and non-digital games in class. | Respondents |
|---|---|
| Strongly disagree | 4 |
| Disagree | 11 |
| Neutral | 13 |
| Agree | 23 |
| Strongly agree | 49 |

*Figure 26. Respondents*

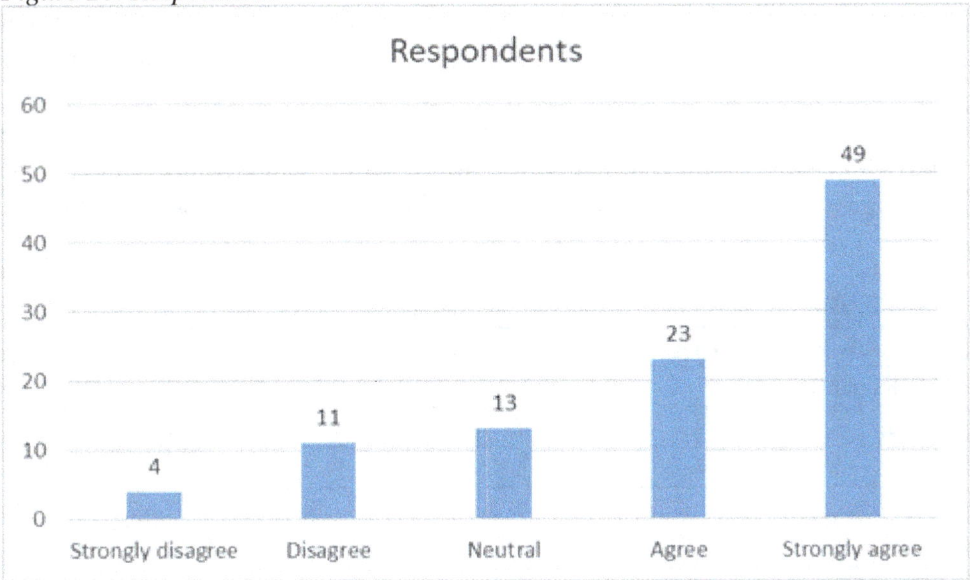


The responses to this question reflect a strong inclination among students toward a blended approach to game-based learning. Forty-nine respondents strongly agreed, 23 agreed that they prefer a mix of digital and non-digital games in class, 13 remained neutral, and only 15 expressed disagreement (4 strongly disagreed, 11 disagreed). This distribution indicates that most learners recognise the complementary benefits of both game formats and value a balanced integration in classroom activities.

This finding underscores the perception that digital and non-digital games serve distinct yet complementary roles in language learning. Digital games often provide interactive, multimedia-rich environments that enhance motivation, engagement, and exposure to authentic language contexts. Non-digital games, however, foster social interaction, collaboration, and participatory learning, particularly in limited technological resources. Combining both formats allows students to experience the cognitive, affective, and social benefits of game-based learning more holistically and flexibly.

The preference for mixed approaches also aligns with research on blended game-based learning, which suggests that teachers achieve optimal engagement and learning outcomes when they leverage the strengths of both digital and non-digital strategies (Kiili, 2005; Wang, Shen, & Novak, 2019). Students benefit from digital platforms' dynamic, adaptive feedback while participating in collaborative, immersive, and context-rich non-digital activities.

From a pedagogical perspective, these results highlight the importance of curriculum design and instructional planning that strategically integrates both types of games. Teachers can use digital tools to supplement and enhance language practice while employing non-digital activities to strengthen interaction, confidence, and experiential learning. The findings thus reinforce the argument for a blended, flexible approach in game-based language instruction, ensuring that learners can enjoy the advantages of both digital innovation and traditional, interactive classroom methods.

*Table 27. Perceived value of games in assessment*

| **Games make assessment feel more meaningful than traditional tests.** | **Respondents** |
|---|---|
| Strongly disagree | 0 |
| Disagree | 2 |
| Neutral | 11 |
| Agree | 21 |
| Strongly agree | 66 |

*Figure 27. Respondents*

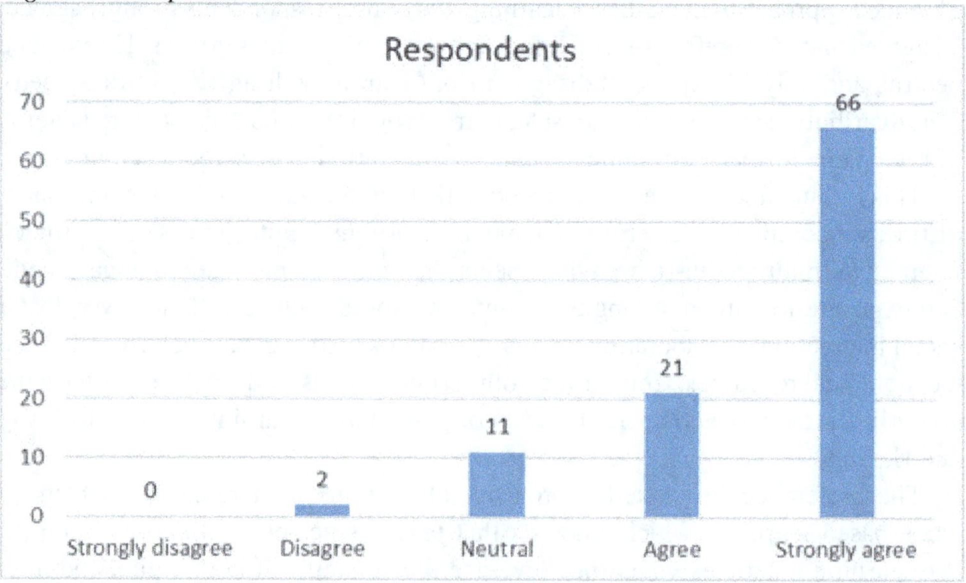


The responses to this question reveal a strong consensus among students regarding the perceived value of games in assessment. Sixty-six respondents strongly agreed and 21 agreed that games make assessment feel more meaningful than traditional tests, while 11 remained neutral and only two disagreed. The complete absence of strongly negative responses highlights a widespread recognition among learners that game-based assessments provide a distinct advantage over conventional evaluation methods.

This finding underscores one of the key benefits of integrating games into language learning: enhancing the authenticity and relevance of assessment. Unlike traditional tests, which often measure rote memorisation or isolated language skills, game-based assessments provide opportunities for learners to demonstrate competence in interactive, contextualised, and task-based scenarios. For example, vocabulary or grammar challenges embedded in a digital quiz, or storytelling and role-play exercises in non-digital games, require students to apply language in meaningful ways, promoting deeper learning and retention.

The overwhelmingly positive response also suggests that games reduce the affective pressure commonly associated with traditional assessments. When evaluation is within gameplay, learners are more likely to approach tasks with curiosity and engagement rather than anxiety or fear of failure. This finding aligns with previous research indicating that gamified assessment can increase motivation, persistence, and willingness to take linguistic risks (Reinders & Wattana, 2015; Kiili, 2005).

From a pedagogical perspective, these results highlight the potential for game-based assessments to complement traditional evaluation methods, providing a more holistic measure of learners' skills. Teachers can leverage digital and non-digital games as instructional tools and assessment instruments, allowing for ongoing feedback, self-reflection, and authentic demonstration of language competence. The findings therefore reinforce the value of integrating games as both learning and evaluative tools, fostering engagement, motivation, and meaningful skill development in the language classroom.

## 3. RESULTS AND ANALYSIS

The data collected through structured questionnaires from teachers and students provide a comprehensive view of the perceptions, experiences, and challenges of game-based learning (GBL) in language education. The analysis highlights the pedagogical benefits of integrating digital and non-digital games while pointing to infrastructural, temporal, and design-related limitations shaping classroom implementation.

## 3.1 Teacher Responses

The teacher questionnaire responses reveal diverse teaching contexts, with 10 respondents at the primary level, 38 at the secondary level, 65 at the intermediate level, and 129 at the university or adult education level. Most respondents (177) reported 5–10 years of teaching experience, followed by 43 teachers with 11–15 years, 13 with 16–20 years, and 9 with 21–30 years of experience. Average class sizes varied, with 38 teachers reporting 20–30 students, 80 reporting 30–40 students, 96 reporting 40–50 students, and 28 reporting 50–60 students per class.

Access to technological infrastructure emerged as a notable factor influencing GBL implementation. While 43 teachers rated access as excellent and 76 as good, a majority (98) considered it average, and 25 teachers reported either bad or no access. This limitation directly impacts the frequency of game use, with only 52 teachers using games always, 56 often, 60 sometimes, 67 occasionally, and seven never incorporating games into their teaching.

Teachers overwhelmingly acknowledged the motivational and pedagogical benefits of game-based learning. Eighty-four strongly agreed, 76 agreed that games increase student motivation, 94 strongly agreed, and 86 decided they can align game activities with curriculum goals. Confidence in assessing learning gains through games was moderate, with 79 strongly agreeing and 67 agreeing, though 56 remained neutral, highlighting some uncertainty in measurement practices.

Technical or infrastructural challenges were widely recognised, with 99 teachers agreeing and 68 agreeing that such issues limit the usefulness of digital games. Non-digital games were seen as more feasible in low-resource settings, with 73 strongly agreeing and 59 agreeing. Teachers expressed relatively high confidence in designing game-based lessons, with 88 strongly agreeing and 75 agreeing. However, 93 strongly agreed and 65 decided that time constraints posed a significant barrier. Additionally, 96 teachers strongly agreed that ready-made lesson plans and rubrics would encourage them to use games more frequently.

Teachers also expressed nuanced views regarding digital versus non-digital games. While 21 strongly agreed and 23 agreed that non-digital games are easier to include in class, 175 remained neutral, indicating that perceptions vary based on context, class size, and personal experience. Finally, 74 strongly agreed and 65 agreed that combining digital and non-digital games is preferred, suggesting a growing recognition of blended approaches to maximise engagement and learning outcomes.

Overall, teacher responses highlight that educators perceive game-based learning as highly beneficial for motivation, engagement, and curriculum alignment; they successfully implement it when infrastructural support, preparation time, and access to ready-to-use resources are available.

## 3.2 Student Responses

Student responses corroborate the teacher perspectives and offer insights into learner engagement and affective outcomes. The majority of participants fell within the age range of 16–25 years (43 respondents aged 16–20 and 29 aged 21–25), with smaller groups aged 10–15 (16 respondents) and 26–30 (12 respondents). Most students reported Hindi (68) or English (32) as their primary home language, and educational levels ranged from secondary (16) and higher secondary (43) to graduate (29) and postgraduate (12).

Self-rated language proficiency was generally high, with 49 students reporting excellent proficiency, 33 good, 11 average, five fair, and only two poor. Prior exposure to game-based learning was moderate: 42 had sometimes experienced GBL, 25 rarely, 14 often, nine always, and 10 had none. Regarding access to devices for class activities, 27 students had personal smartphones, 51 relied on shared devices, and 22 had no devices, indicating that resource availability may influence engagement in digital games.

Students reported substantial motivational and affective benefits from game-based learning. Sixty strongly agreed, 22 agreed that games increase their motivation in language lessons, and 97 strongly agreed that games help them remember vocabulary and expressions. Anxiety reduction during speaking tasks was also notable: 94 strongly agreed that games reduced their speaking anxiety, with only six strongly disagreeing.

Technical challenges were consistently highlighted, with 72 strongly agreeing and 17 agreeing that internet or device problems disrupt learning during digital game activities. Nevertheless, non-digital games were highly effective in fostering participation, with 72 strongly agreeing and 13 agreeing that role-play, storytelling, and board games increased engagement. Students also strongly preferred mixed approaches: 49 strongly agreed and 23 decided that they preferred a combination of digital and non-digital games. Finally, 66 strongly agreed and 21 agreed that game-based assessment feels more meaningful than traditional tests, underscoring the role of games in authentic evaluation and learner-centred pedagogy.

## 3.3 Findings

The combined analysis of teacher and student responses highlights several consistent trends. Both groups recognise the motivational, engagement, and pedagogical benefits of integrating games into language learning. Teachers value games for curriculum alignment, learner engagement, and flexibility, while students appreciate gameplay's anxiety-reducing, participatory, and meaningful assessment aspects.

However, technical and infrastructural limitations present a significant challenge for digital games, with teachers and students noting disruptions due to device or internet issues. Non-digital games, in contrast, are widely considered accessible, flexible, and effective for fostering interaction and participation, particularly in low-resource settings.

The data also indicates a strong preference for blended approaches, combining digital and non-digital games to leverage the complementary advantages of each. While digital games offer scalability, multimedia input, and adaptive feedback, non-digital games provide real-time social interaction, creativity, and embodied learning opportunities. Teachers' confidence, preparation, and access to ready-made lesson plans further influence the frequency and effectiveness of GBL in practice.

## CONCLUSION AND RECOMMENDATIONS

The findings of this study underscore the transformative potential of game-based learning (GBL) in language education, highlighting the complementary strengths of digital and non-digital games and their impact on learner motivation, engagement, and communicative competence. Both teacher and student responses consistently demonstrate that games facilitate active participation, reduce affective barriers such as anxiety, and make learning and assessment more meaningful than traditional methods. Digital games provide scalable, interactive, and multimedia-rich environments that enhance learner engagement, while non-digital games foster social interaction, collaboration, and experiential learning in a low-resource, adaptable format. The preference for blended approaches—combining digital and non-digital games—emerged clearly, reflecting a shared recognition of the pedagogical value of integrating multiple game formats to cater to diverse learner needs and classroom contexts.

The study also highlights several challenges in implementing GBL. Technical and infrastructural limitations, including inconsistent access to devices and internet connectivity, were considered barriers, particularly in digital learning environments. Time constraints, teacher preparation requirements, and the need for ready-made lesson plans and assessment rubrics influence the effective deployment of games in language classrooms. Addressing these challenges is critical for ensuring that GBL achieves its full pedagogical potential.

To enhance the effectiveness of game-based learning in language education, educators recommend a blended approach that combines digital and non-digital games, leveraging digital platforms' interactive, multimedia strengths alongside the collaborative, creative, and experiential benefits of non-digital activities. Teachers would benefit from curated lesson plans, rubrics, and instructional guides for both formats, which can reduce preparation time and promote consistent implementation. Institutional support is also critical, including reliable access to devices and internet connectivity, and professional development opportunities to build teacher confidence in designing and facilitating game-based lessons. Game activities deliberately align with curriculum objectives and assessment criteria to ensure they contribute to measurable language gains rather than serving solely as entertainment. Additionally, games can address learners' affective and motivational needs by creating psychologically safe environments that reduce anxiety, encourage experimentation, and promote active participation. Embedded assessment mechanisms—whether in digital or non-digital formats—can track vocabulary retention, communicative proficiency, and collaborative skills, providing meaningful feedback for both learners and educators. Non-digital games, in particular, should emphasise teamwork, problem-solving, and storytelling to develop social, cognitive, and communicative skills while fostering interaction within the Zone of Proximal Development. Finally, game design should support learner agency by offering choice, autonomy, and appropriate levels of challenge, aligning with principles of Self-Determination Theory to maximise engagement and intrinsic motivation.

In conclusion, game-based learning represents a learner-centred, engaging, and pedagogically valuable approach for language education. Educators can create dynamic learning environments that enhance linguistic competence, motivation, and classroom participation by strategically integrating digital and non-digital games, addressing infrastructural challenges, and aligning gameplay with curriculum objectives. Future research could explore longitudinal impacts of GBL on language acquisition, examine cross-cultural applicability, and investigate the efficacy of specific game designs for different learner profiles and proficiency levels.

## REFERENCES


Chiu, Y. H., Kao, C. W., & Reynolds, B. L. (2012). The relative effectiveness of digital game-based learning types in English as a foreign language setting: A meta-analysis. *British Journal of Educational Technology*, *43*(4), E104–E107. DOI: 10.1111/j.1467-8535.2012.01295.x

Crompton, H., Lin, Y. C., Burke, D., & Block, A. (2018). Mobile digital games as an educational tool in K–12 schools. *Journal of Educational Technology & Society*, *21*(4), 70–81.

Csikszentmihalyi, M. (1990). *Flow: The psychology of optimal experience*. Harper & Row.

Gee, J. P. (2007). *What video games have to teach us about learning and literacy* (2nd ed.). Palgrave Macmillan.

Go Silk, Y.. (2020). Digital natives and language learning: Implications for classrooms. *Tydskrif vir Taalonderrig*, *12*(3), 45–62.

Horwitz, E. K., Horwitz, M. B., & Cope, J. (1986). Foreign language classroom anxiety. *Modern Language Journal*, *70*(2), 125–132. DOI: 10.1111/j.1540-4781.1986.tb05256.x

Johnson, D. (2010). Constructivist approaches to game-based learning. *Journal of Educational Multimedia and Hypermedia*, *19*(3), 281–300.

Kiili, K. (2005). Digital game-based learning: Towards an experiential gaming model. *The Internet and Higher Education*, *8*(1), 13–24. DOI: 10.1016/j.iheduc.2004.12.001

Kolb, D. A. (1984). *Experiential learning: Experience as the source of learning and development*. Prentice Hall.

Krashen, S. (1982). Principles and practice in second language acquisition.

Landers, R. N. (2014). Developing a theory of gamified learning: Linking serious games and gamification of learning. *Simulation & Gaming*, *45*(6), 752–768. DOI: 10.1177/1046878114563660

López-Martínez, E., García-Sánchez, J. N., & Pérez, E. (2022). Gamified learning environments in language education: User-centred design and engagement strategies. *Computers & Education*, *180*, 104437. DOI: 10.1016/j.compedu.2021.104437

Nguyen, D., & Yukawa, J. (2019). Non-digital game-based learning in EFL classrooms: A case study on student collaboration and motivation. *Language Education in Asia, 10*(1), 116–132. DOI: 10.5746/LEiA/19/V10/I1/A10/Nguyen_Yukawa

Piaget, J. (1952). *The origins of intelligence in children*. International Universities Press. DOI: 10.1037/11494-000

Prensky, M. (2001). *Digital game-based learning*. McGraw-Hill.

Reinders, H., & Wattana, S. (2015). Can I say something? The effects of digital game play on willingness to communicate. *Language Learning & Technology, 19*(2), 50–73.

Ryan, R. M., & Deci, E. L. (2000). Intrinsic and extrinsic motivations: Classic definitions and new directions. *Contemporary Educational Psychology, 25*(1), 54–67. DOI: 10.1006/ceps.1999.1020 PMID: 10620381

Smith, J., & Sanchez, L. (2015). Collaborative game-based learning in the EFL classroom. *TESOL Journal, 6*(2), 253–271. DOI: 10.1002/tesj.177

Sykes, J., & Reinhardt, J. (2013). *Language at play: Digital games in second and foreign language teaching and learning*. Pearson.

Wang, F. (2016). Role-play activities and ESL speaking competence. *TESL-EJ, 20*(3), 1–18.

Wang, S., Shen, R., & Novak, D. (2019). Digital vs. non-digital games in language learning: A comparative study. *Interactive Learning Environments, 27*(8), 1077–1092. DOI: 10.1080/10494820.2018.1460964

Yang, Y. T. C. (2017). Digital game-based language learning: A case study on multiplayer online games. *Journal of Educational Technology & Society, 20*(3), 1–15.

Chapter 13

# Integrating Indigenous Knowledge and Global Citizenship in Early Childhood STEM:

## A Design-Based Approach to the Renewable Rangers Wordless Book to Foster Self-Directed Learning

**Moleboheng M. Mokhele**
http://orcid.org/0000-0002-5134-954X
*North-West University, South Africa*

## ABSTRACT

*This chapter explores the design and development of Renewable Rangers, a wordless picture book designed as a culturally responsive, play-based resource for early childhood STEM and climate education. Drawing on the Mokhele-Ramulumo & Gumbo (2025) framework integrating Indigenous Knowledge Systems and Global Citizenship Education, the book uses multimodal storytelling to promote self-directed learning, creativity, critical thinking, and environmental awareness. Through a design-based research approach, it translates theory into practice via narrative structure, visual storytelling, teacher prompts, and hands-on extensions. Set in South Africa, the Rangers' journey across provinces embeds scientific concepts within familiar cultural and ecological contexts, supporting identity formation and*

DOI: 10.4018/979-8-3373-4322-8.ch013

*global citizenship. While empirical testing is pending, the design shows promise for enhancing cognitive, social, and cultural development, positioning the book as both a practical teaching tool and a model for transformative early science education.*

## INTRODUCTION

Early childhood represents a critical window for building the foundations of lifelong learning, scientific curiosity, and ecological responsibility. Research in developmental psychology and education underscores that the skills, attitudes, and values acquired in the first eight years of life have profound and long-lasting effects on children's capacity to think critically, collaborate, and engage with complex global issues such as sustainability and climate change (Duncan et al., 2023; UNESCO, 2020). Within this context, science, technology, engineering, and mathematics (STEM) education has emerged as a priority not only for preparing future innovators but also for cultivating scientifically literate citizens who can contribute meaningfully to addressing pressing environmental challenges. Climate change education, in particular, is increasingly recognized as essential for equipping young learners with both the knowledge and dispositions necessary for adaptive, sustainable living in a rapidly changing world (Banks & Taylor, 2025).

Globally, there has been growing momentum toward embedding climate literacy into early years curricula. In Finland and Sweden, for example, play-based approaches link ecological awareness with outdoor exploration, fostering early environmental stewardship through experiential learning (Nygren et al., 2020). In New Zealand, the Te Whāriki curriculum integrates sustainability with Indigenous Māori knowledge, allowing young children to learn science through cultural narratives and place-based activities (Bang & Medin, 2010). Meanwhile, in countries such as Canada and Australia, early childhood centers have incorporated eco-schools frameworks, encouraging children to develop habits of recycling, energy conservation, and sustainable gardening from the earliest years (Miao & Nduneseokwu, 2025). These global examples highlight the recognition that climate change is not an abstract, future concern but an urgent, lived reality that children can and should begin engaging with in age-appropriate ways.

However, in African contexts, including South Africa, the integration of STEM and climate change education into early childhood remains underdeveloped. While curriculum frameworks such as the National Curriculum Framework (NCF) and the Curriculum and Assessment Policy Statement (CAPS) emphasize play-based learning and holistic development, explicit references to environmental sustainability, Indigenous knowledge, and global citizenship remain limited or are treated in abstract terms (Department of Basic Education, 2011; Ramulumo, 2023). Many early learning environments are under-resourced, grappling with large class sizes, limited teacher training, and linguistic diversity that complicates text-heavy instructional approaches (Donald et al., 2022). These challenges mean that young learners often lack opportunities to engage meaningfully with climate change and STEM concepts in ways that are grounded in their cultural and ecological realities. This gap is particularly concerning given Africa's heightened vulnerability to climate-related challenges such as droughts, floods, and energy insecurity, which directly affect children's daily lives (Suarlin, 2023).

It is within this context that the *Renewable Rangers* project emerges as both innovative and necessary. Designed as a wordless picture book, *Renewable Rangers* introduces renewable energy and environmental stewardship to young learners in South Africa through culturally situated, multimodal storytelling. Wordless picture books have long been recognized as powerful pedagogical tools in early childhood education. Unlike traditional texts, they invite children to actively interpret visual sequences, construct personal narratives, and engage in meaning-making that is both verbal and non-verbal (Rizqiyani & Azizah, 2019; McGuire, 2022). Therefore, by removing the barrier of written language, wordless books foster inclusivity in multilingual classrooms, ensuring that children from diverse linguistic backgrounds can participate equally in constructing and sharing stories (Honaker & Miller, 2024).

Research shows that wordless books enhance a range of developmental domains, including literacy, visual literacy, creativity, and critical thinking. Goriot, Jongstra, and Mensink (2024) emphasize that interpreting images encourages children to make inferences, predict outcomes, and sequence events, all core literacy skills. Nikolajeva and Scott (2013) further argue that picture books cultivate visual literacy, enabling children to read and interpret images as a form of text in their own right, a crucial competence in today's image-saturated world. Beyond literacy, wordless books support creativity by allowing children to generate multiple interpretations and endings, encouraging divergent thinking and imagination (Martínez-Carratalá et al., 2024). Importantly, they also foster multilingual development, as children can narrate the same images in their home languages, while teachers facilitate translanguaging practices that validate diverse linguistic identities (Ciecierski et al., 2016).

The *Renewable Rangers* wordless book builds on these strengths while extending them into the realm of STEM and climate change education. Through its playful, interactive design, the book encourages children to role-play as problem-solvers, navigating environmental challenges and proposing solutions. Such co-design and storying strategies are increasingly recognized as effective for enabling children to grapple with complex global issues in developmentally appropriate ways (Om et al., 2025). In one scene, for instance, learners might imagine how a community without electricity feels during a blackout and then propose alternative energy solutions alongside the characters. These kinds of activities not only cultivate empathy but also reinforce causal reasoning, collaborative problem-solving, and scientific inquiry skills (De Klerk et al., 2024).

Crucially, *Renewable Rangers* integrates Indigenous Knowledge Systems (IKS) and Global Citizenship Education (GCE) into its storyline and pedagogical design. Scenes embed cultural elements, such as traditional clothing, community practices, and local ecological knowledge, situating scientific ideas within familiar contexts. This integration ensures that learners connect renewable energy concepts not only to abstract scientific principles but also to the cultural identities and lived experiences of their communities (da Silva et al., 2023). At the same time, the narrative positions children as global citizens, inviting them to reflect on environmental challenges as part of a shared planetary responsibility. As UNESCO (2020) notes, global citizenship education fosters critical thinking, empathy, and collective action, qualities essential for confronting climate change. Therefore, by linking IKS with GCE, the *Renewable Rangers* wordless book advances a model of early science education that is at once culturally grounded and globally oriented.

In sum, this chapter highlights how *Renewable Rangers* exemplifies the potential of wordless visual storytelling to provide a holistic learning experience, simultaneously nurturing creativity, language and visual literacy, problem-solving, and critical thinking in early childhood climate change education. At the same time, it fosters environmental awareness and a sense of global citizenship from an early age. Through multimodal design, cultural responsiveness, and inquiry-based pedagogy, the book demonstrates how innovative educational resources can address pressing gaps in early childhood STEM education in South Africa and beyond, preparing young learners to engage with sustainability challenges both locally and globally.

## PROBLEM STATEMENT

Despite growing global awareness of the climate crisis and urgent calls for environmental education, early childhood curricula frequently lack explicit focus on climate change, environmental learning, and global citizenship (Banks & Taylor, 2025). Globally, only a small proportion of countries report integrating climate change or sustainability topics into early childhood education (ECE) programs, with UNESCO estimating that fewer than 30% of national curricula at the preschool level include explicit environmental content. In contrast, countries such as New Zealand and Finland have made deliberate efforts to embed environmental education and sustainability into early learning frameworks, emphasizing hands-on exploration, outdoor learning, and inquiry-based approaches. Meanwhile, in parts of Africa, including Kenya, climate education remains largely absent from structured early childhood programs, often leaving children without foundational knowledge about environmental stewardship at an age when habits and attitudes are first forming.

Traditional, text-based teaching approaches frequently limit young learners' opportunities for active engagement, collaborative problem-solving, and connection to lived experiences (Hu & Commeyras, 2008; Eskiyurt & Özkan, 2024). Text-heavy STEM resources often fail to account for the developmental needs of preschool learners, particularly in visual, spatial, and tactile domains, and can inhibit comprehension of abstract concepts like climate systems or energy cycles. They also assume literacy skills that many early learners, especially in multilingual classrooms, have not yet developed, creating barriers to participation and engagement. In multilingual contexts, reliance on a single dominant language in text-based resources can hinder access for children whose home language differs from the instructional language, reducing both conceptual understanding and opportunities for cultural affirmation.

Research shows that multimodal, culturally responsive, and play-based pedagogies can address these gaps effectively. For example, Papadopoulos and Bisiri (2020) implemented a multiliteracies-oriented program using intercultural tales, demonstrating that such approaches foster critical thinking in preschool children. Similarly, Li et al. (2024) found that pop-up storybooks created through writing, drawing, making, and storytelling develop computational thinking, creativity, visual-spatial skills, and systematic reasoning. Participatory approaches to culturally responsive tools further highlight the importance of scaffolding learning with Indigenous knowledge, local contexts, and culturally grounded global perspectives (Harvey, Pierce, & Hirshberg, 2023).

Collectively, these studies underscore the need for innovative, play-based educational resources that integrate culturally responsive, multimodal, and globally minded strategies. Wordless visual narratives, such as the *Renewable Rangers* wordless book, are particularly suited for early childhood because they allow learners to construct meaning independently, engage their imagination, and develop language, visual literacy, and environmental consciousness without relying on text-heavy instruction. Without such approaches, young learners risk missing the cognitive, social, and cultural foundations necessary to understand environmental challenges, develop global citizenship, and meaningfully engage with sustainability from an early age. Therefore, by connecting environmental learning with play, visual storytelling, and multilingual accessibility, educators can better prepare children across diverse global contexts to engage with the complex, interrelated issues of climate change and sustainable development.

## RATIONALE

In South Africa, early childhood education faces distinctive challenges, including limited resources, linguistic diversity, and social inequities (Donald et al., 2022). The integration of IKS and GCE in early childhood science education remains limited, often addressed in abstract or superficial ways. This gap highlights the urgent need for innovative, culturally responsive, and multimodal resources that provide holistic learning experiences (Seleke et al., 2025; Nygren et al., 2020).

The CAPS for Foundation Phase Natural Sciences and Technology sets standards for Grades R–3, focusing on basic scientific concepts, inquiry skills, and observation of the natural environment (Department of Basic Education, 2011). For example, CAPS encourages learners to explore plants and animals in their immediate surroundings, yet guidance on embedding local ecological knowledge or fostering environmental stewardship is minimal. Similarly, the NCF for children from birth to four years advocates play-based, holistic learning and emphasizes cultural responsiveness (Department of Basic Education & UNICEF, 2005; Ramulumo, 2023). However, explicit strategies for integrating IKS and GCE in science and environmental learning remain underdeveloped. The Early Learning Outcomes Framework (ELOF) outlines cognitive, social, and environmental developmental goals (Department of Basic Education, 2015), including curiosity about natural phenomena and participation in community practices. Yet, operationalizing these outcomes in ways that leverage Indigenous knowledge or cultivate global citizenship is rarely demonstrated in practice. Although the South African National Curriculum Statement (NCS) Life Skills includes Natural Sciences components, integration of IKS and GCE in developmentally appropriate science teaching remains sparse (Department of Basic Education, 2011). Collectively, these frameworks set broad learning goals and encourage cultural sensitivity, yet none fully embed IKS or GCE in early childhood science education in ways that are age-appropriate, contextually grounded, and multimodal.

This limitation can be further understood when compared with international frameworks. The UNESCO (2020) Education for Sustainable Development (ESD) roadmap emphasizes experiential, contextually grounded learning that integrates local knowledge, participatory inquiry, and global perspectives from an early age. Globally, ESD approaches advocate fostering environmental stewardship, agency, and critical thinking through interactive and culturally responsive learning experiences, goals that align closely with the aspirations of CAPS, NCF, and ELOF but are not yet fully realized in the South African context.

In multilingual South African classrooms, wordless storytelling, such as the *Renewable Rangers* wordless book, provides a particularly effective strategy. Therefore, by minimizing dependence on written text, wordless narratives allow children to construct meaning through images, dialogue, and storytelling in their home languages, supporting language development, comprehension, and engagement simultaneously. This approach is inclusive of learners with diverse linguistic backgrounds and ensures that children from different language communities can access content equitably. Wordless visual storytelling also fosters identity formation and a sense of belonging, as children can see their own cultural contexts and local environments reflected in the narratives. Moreover, by depicting problem-solving in environmental scenarios, these stories promote early environmental stewardship and global citizenship, allowing learners to practice agency, collaborative decision-making, and reflection on their roles in sustaining the environment.

Taken together, embedding multimodal, culturally responsive, and play-based resources into CAPS, NCF, and ELOF-aligned curricula offers a pathway to bridge current gaps. Therefore, by integrating Indigenous knowledge, local context, multilingual accessibility, and global perspectives, such resources can support holistic learning while fostering early identity development, belonging, and meaningful engagement with environmental challenges from the outset of children's formal education.

## The Role of *Renewable Rangers Wordless Book*

*Renewable Rangers* was developed in response to the growing need for accessible, culturally grounded, and engaging approaches to early childhood climate change education. Initially conceived as a digital educational game, it has been expanded into a wordless picture book to broaden its reach and accessibility. Martínez-Carratalá and colleagues (2024) highlight that this format introduces young children to climate change, renewable energy, and environmental stewardship in developmentally appropriate ways while providing a culturally neutral entry point for learners across diverse linguistic backgrounds. Therefore, by removing language barriers, the book ensures adaptability across varied classrooms, opening opportunities for inclusive, collaborative learning.

The wordless format positions children as active meaning-makers, inviting them to interpret visual narratives, draw connections, and construct their own understandings (Inozu, 2017; Rizqiyani & Azizah, 2019). This open-endedness supports critical thinking as learners analyze cause-and-effect relationships, such as understanding power outages and exploring renewable energy solutions (Panayiota & Tsilimeni, 2021). It also encourages problem-solving and creativity as children generate alternative strategies for addressing environmental challenges, as emphasized by Mwinsa (2025). Through visual literacy, imaginative play, and discussion, the book cultivates inquiry, self-expression, collaboration, and reflective thinking (Anagnostidou et al., 2025; Grava & Pole, 2021).

Teachers and caregivers act as facilitators, supported by an accompanying guide that offers prompts such as "*What might happen next?*" or "*How could the community address this problem?*" These questions scaffold learners' observation, reasoning, and decision-making, reinforcing self-directed learning (Probine et al., 2023). Hands-on extensions, including drawing solar panels, role-playing energy solutions, or discussing energy conservation, connect visual storytelling with STEM concepts and Indigenous knowledge, fostering experiential and inquiry-based engagement (da Silva et al., 2023; Mwinsa, 2025).

The structure of the book is built around ten interactive scenes, each sequentially exploring energy challenges and renewable solutions across South Africa. The storyline follows two brothers, *Wavhudi* and *Rivhavhudi,* alongside their scientist mother, *Dr. Mummy*, as they travel province by province, addressing the nationwide load-shedding crisis. As learners accompany the family's journey, they encounter both renewable energy concepts and diverse cultural contexts, making the resource simultaneously scientific, social, and place-based. Heugh (2013), and Alexander (2005) note that situating learning in culturally and geographically meaningful contexts supports both cognitive and social development.

## Scene 1: Nationwide Power Outage

A darkened map of South Africa illustrates a nationwide blackout. Families are shown studying by candlelight, cooking by dim lamps, and waiting anxiously. The Rangers' vehicle approaches, headlights bright, symbolizing hope. Teacher prompts such as "*What do you notice about the communities without electricity?*" or "*How do you think families feel during this blackout?*" guide observation, empathy, and reasoning (Narengaowa & Tungalag, 2024). Learners are also encouraged to imagine creative solutions: "If you were the Rangers, what could you do to help?"

## Scene 2: Free State and Hydroelectric Power

Power is restored in the Free State through the Gariep Dam. Water rushing through turbines is illustrated with glowing currents flowing to nearby towns. Cultural elements, such as a scientist draped in a Seanamarena blanket and community members weaving baskets or wearing Mokorotlo hats, are embedded in the scene. Teachers can guide learners with questions like "*How did the dam help restore electricity to the towns?*" or "*Can you think of other ways communities might generate electricity using nature?*" to develop inquiry and problem-solving (Bang & Medin, 2010; UNESCO, 2015).

## Scene 3: Northern Cape and Solar Energy

The Rangers travel to the sun-drenched Northern Cape, where solar farms shimmer across the arid landscape. Indigenous knowledge is incorporated through depictions of community members using traditional sun-knowledge calendars to guide planting and daily routines, illustrating connections between local practices and solar energy. In classrooms, teachers might ask learners to design a paper solar panel or discuss how sunlight can be converted into electricity, reinforcing STEM concepts of energy transformation while connecting to local culture.

## Scene 4: KwaZulu-Natal and Wind Energy

In KwaZulu-Natal, rolling hills are dotted with wind turbines. The scene highlights coastal Zulu communities using age-old wind instruments and flags to understand and interpret wind direction, a subtle integration of Indigenous practices. Teachers can facilitate activities such as building small pinwheel models to explore wind energy and discuss how wind can move turbines to generate electricity.

## Scene 5: Eastern Cape and Micro-Hydropower

The Rangers explore river communities using small-scale water wheels. The scene shows learners from local villages testing water flow patterns, reflecting historical river navigation and fishing practices. In the classroom, children could create mini water wheels in clear trays, connecting hands-on exploration to STEM concepts like kinetic and mechanical energy.

## Scene 6: Gauteng and Urban Energy Efficiency

Gauteng's cityscape shows solar rooftops, energy-efficient appliances, and community recycling programs. Visual storytelling integrates local township innovations, such as rainwater harvesting and solar cookers, linking STEM with problem-solving and sustainability. Teachers can simulate energy audits in the classroom by asking learners to identify ways to save energy at home or school.

## Scene 7: Mpumalanga and Biomass Energy

In Mpumalanga, communities transform agricultural residues into bioenergy. Illustrations depict traditional harvesting techniques alongside modern biomass stoves. Classroom activities could include observing decomposition of plant material or discussing how organic matter can produce energy, bridging Indigenous agricultural knowledge with modern energy concepts.

### Scene 8: Limpopo and Geothermal Energy

Hot springs and underground heat sources power the province's energy solutions. Local practices, such as using warm springs for communal bathing and therapeutic purposes, connect children to Indigenous knowledge of natural resources. Teachers can guide learners to explore the idea of heat energy through simple water-heating experiments, fostering inquiry-based learning.

### Scene 9: North-West and Hybrid Energy Systems

This scene shows a combination of solar, wind, and mini-hydro systems in semi-rural communities. Cultural integration is illustrated through local festivals celebrating natural elements, connecting STEM concepts of energy systems with community engagement. Classrooms can use role-play scenarios where learners "manage" energy distribution for a town, applying problem-solving and teamwork skills.

### Scene 10: Western Cape and Sustainable Coastal Energy

In the Western Cape, the Rangers address energy challenges using tidal and wave energy. Coastal Indigenous fishing knowledge, such as reading tides and currents, is embedded visually. Learners might engage in classroom experiments with water flow and floating turbines to visualize how ocean movement generates electricity, linking observation to renewable energy principles.

Through these ten scenes, *Renewable Rangers* integrates STEM concepts, Indigenous knowledge, and cultural narratives in ways that are visually engaging and developmentally appropriate. Teachers can adapt each scene for classroom exploration, fostering inquiry, collaboration, critical thinking, and creativity. By situating learning within specific provinces, communities, and ecological contexts, the book supports holistic environmental education, cultivates global citizenship, and nurtures children's early understanding of sustainable energy practices (Seleke et al., 2025).

## THEORETICAL FRAMEWORK GROUNDING *RENEWABLE RANGERS WORDLESS BOOK*

The development of the *Renewable Rangers* wordless book is grounded in the *Early Childhood Science Education Framework for integrating IKS and GCE* developed by Mokhele-Ramulumo and Gumbo (2025). This framework provides the conceptual anchors and operational domains that inform both the narrative and pedagogical design of the book.

At its core, the framework emphasizes the integration of IKS, positioning scientific concepts such as renewable energy, electricity generation, and sustainability within the cultural practices and daily lives of South African communities. For example, scenes depicting Basotho community members weaving baskets or wearing Mokorotlo hats reflect the framework's focus on cultural responsiveness and place-based learning (Heugh, 2013; Alexander, 2005). Therefore, by connecting scientific ideas to familiar, lived experiences, learners engage with content that is both meaningful and relevant, fostering curiosity and deep conceptual understanding.

Simultaneously, the framework embeds principles of Global Citizenship Education (GCE), guiding learners to explore environmental challenges, analyze cause-and-effect relationships, and propose solutions that consider both local and global perspectives (UNESCO, 2015; Bang & Medin, 2010). These principles support critical thinking, ethical reasoning, and problem-solving, cultivating young learners as informed, empathetic global citizens (Ramulumo & Gumbo, 2025). Therefore, by linking IKS and GCE, the framework creates opportunities for children to understand their roles in sustaining local environments while considering broader planetary impacts, which aligns closely with the goals of self-directed learning (SDL). In SDL, learners take initiative, plan, and evaluate their own learning (Knowles, Candy, & Garrison, 2025), and in the context of IKS and GCE, children actively construct understanding of renewable energy solutions, environmental stewardship, and cultural practices through inquiry and reflection.

The pedagogical design of the framework is further supported by three theoretical anchors: Social Constructivism, Cultural Responsiveness, and Post-Piagetian developmental theory. Social Constructivism (Vygotsky, 1978) emphasizes that knowledge is co-constructed through social interaction and collaborative problem-solving. In the *Renewable Rangers* context, children discuss scenes, predict outcomes, and suggest energy solutions together, mirroring authentic scientific inquiry and peer-mediated scaffolding. In contrast to behaviorist frameworks, which rely on repetitive reinforcement and externally imposed learning objectives, constructivist approaches prioritize active engagement, reflection, and meaning-making, fostering deeper understanding and transferable skills.

Cultural Responsiveness (Gay, 2018) ensures that learners' identities, home languages, and local knowledge are represented, providing culturally meaningful entry points to complex scientific ideas (da Silva et al., 2023). Therefore, by embedding local rituals, dress, and environmental practices into the storyline, the book aligns with learners' lived experiences, promoting belonging, engagement, and the internalization of values. Post-Piagetian perspectives (Fleer, 2010) guide developmental appropriateness, emphasizing that young children are capable of higher-order reasoning when scaffolded appropriately. Activities are sequenced to support cognitive, social, and emotional growth, nurturing metacognition, reflective thinking, and early problem-solving skills (Narengaowa & Tungalag, 2024).

In addition, the framework explicitly incorporates SDL principles (Knowles, Candy, & Garrison, 2025). Therefore, by using open-ended prompts, visual narratives, and hands-on extensions, children are encouraged to plan, monitor, and evaluate their own learning trajectories, whether imagining alternative energy solutions, drawing, or role-playing community interventions. SDL complements the integration of IKS and GCE by positioning children as active agents who explore their environment, connect cultural knowledge with scientific inquiry, and engage in ethical and civic reasoning. The wordless, multimodal format further supports SDL, as learners navigate meaning-making without dependence on fixed textual instructions, fostering autonomy, creativity, and lifelong learning habits.

*The Mokhele-Ramulumo & Gumbo (2025) framework* also defines operational domains, implementation strategies, educator readiness, and evaluation mechanisms that translate these theoretical principles into practice. Implementation strategies emphasize scaffolding inquiry while promoting learner autonomy, ensuring that children can construct knowledge while receiving support as needed. Educator readiness focuses on preparing teachers to balance guidance with autonomy, using culturally and developmentally responsive methods. Evaluation strategies monitor both cognitive and socio-cultural outcomes, ensuring that learning is meaningful, contextually grounded, and aligned with environmental, STEM, and global citizenship objectives.

Taken together, the integration of Social Constructivism, Cultural Responsiveness, Post-Piagetian theory, and SDL within the IKS + GCE framework provides a robust, multidimensional approach to early childhood science education. It empowers children to actively explore renewable energy, sustainability, and environmental stewardship, fostering identity formation, a sense of belonging, and agency in addressing local and global challenges from the outset of formal learning.

## METHODOLOGY

This chapter adopts a design-based research (DBR) approach to conceptually explore the development of the *Renewable Rangers* wordless book as a culturally responsive, play-based educational resource for early childhood STEM and language learning. DBR was selected for its capacity to bridge theory and practice through iterative design, continuous refinement, and real-world application (Schmitz et al., 2015). This approach is particularly suited to early childhood education research, where learning environments are dynamic, developmental needs vary widely, and cultural and linguistic contexts are complex. Through DBR, theoretical principles, such as social constructivism, cultural responsiveness, and post-Piagetian developmental perspectives, can be translated into concrete design choices while simultaneously testing their practical feasibility in authentic educational settings (Vygotsky, 1978; Gay, 2018; Fleer, 2010).

## PHASES AND ITERATIONS

Although the current phase of the project is primarily theoretical, DBR envisions multiple iterative cycles of design, implementation, analysis, and refinement. In the initial design phase, the narrative structure, visual representations, and teacher prompts were developed in alignment with the *Early Childhood Science Education Framework for integrating IKS and GCE* (Mokhele-Ramulumo & Gumbo, 2025). Subsequent iterations would involve piloting the wordless book with Grade R learners and educators, collecting feedback, and refining story elements, visuals, and pedagogical scaffolds. Each iteration is intended to evaluate how effectively learners engage with STEM concepts, connect with Indigenous knowledge, and apply problem-solving strategies while considering global citizenship perspectives.

## TESTING DESIGN CHOICES

Design choices in the book were theoretically tested by mapping visual sequences, storylines, and interactive prompts against the operational domains of the framework: implementation strategies, educator readiness, learner engagement, and evaluation. For example, prompts such as "*What might happen next?*" or "*How could the community address this problem?*" were intentionally structured to scaffold reasoning, prediction, and self-directed exploration (Probine et al., 2023). Pilot testing could theoretically assess the effectiveness of these prompts in supporting collaborative dialogue, inquiry, and reflective thinking. Similarly, visual representations of renewable energy solutions in each province were evaluated against both STEM learning goals and cultural relevance, ensuring integration of IKS and GCE while remaining developmentally appropriate (Heugh, 2013).

## HYPOTHETICAL DATA COLLECTION METHODS

In a piloted DBR cycle, multiple data collection methods could be employed to capture learner engagement, understanding, and cultural connectedness. These might include:

- *Observations* - systematic tracking of children's interactions with the wordless book, noting collaborative discussion, problem-solving approaches, and engagement with visual and cultural cues.
- *Semi-structured Interviews* - Conversations with educators and learners to explore perceptions of the narrative, understanding of STEM concepts, and connections to local culture and global perspectives.
- *Artifact analysis* - Examination of learner-created drawings, models, or role-play scenarios reflecting their interpretation of energy solutions and environmental stewardship. These artifacts would provide evidence of knowledge construction, creativity, and self-directed exploration.

## ALIGNMENT WITH ETHICAL CONSIDERATIONS

Given that research involves young children, ethical considerations are central to the DBR approach. The design prioritizes voluntary participation, parental consent, and child assent, ensuring learners' rights and well-being are respected. Activities are age-appropriate, culturally sensitive, and play-based, reducing the risk of stress or discomfort. Confidentiality and anonymization of learner contributions in observations or artifacts would be maintained, and all interactions are framed to foster positive, empowering learning experiences.

Taken together, adopting DBR allows the *Renewable Rangers* project to systematically link theory and practice while remaining flexible, iterative, and responsive to the needs of learners and educators. The methodological approach ensures that design decisions are informed by developmental theory, culturally responsive pedagogy, and self-directed learning principles (Knowles, Candy, Garrison, 2025), while also being testable and improvable through classroom-based piloting. Therefore, by grounding the wordless book in DBR, the project exemplifies how early childhood science education resources can be simultaneously developmentally appropriate, culturally authentic, scientifically rigorous, and ethically responsible, fostering learner autonomy, critical thinking, and global citizenship from the earliest stages of formal education.

## RESULTS

The development of the *Renewable Rangers* wordless book demonstrates the translation of *the Mokhele-Ramulumo & Gumbo (2025) framework* into concrete design features, integrating culturally responsive pedagogy, play-based learning, and early childhood STEM education. Table 1 maps each framework principle and operational domain to specific book design elements and anticipated learning outcomes, highlighting support for self-directed learning, critical thinking, and global citizenship.

*Table 1. Operationalizing theoretical principles in the Renewable Rangers wordless book*

| Framework Principle / Domain | Book Design Feature | Anticipated Learning Outcome |
|---|---|---|
| Social Constructivism (Vygotsky, 1978) | Interactive narrative sequences; visual storytelling without text; role-play opportunities | Learners co-construct meaning, engage in collaborative storytelling, develop problem-solving and critical thinking skills |
| Cultural Responsiveness (Gay, 2018; da Silva et al., 2023) | Scenes depicting local cultural practices (e.g., Basotho weaving, Mokorotlo hats); culturally relevant scenarios | Learners connect scientific concepts to familiar contexts, develop cultural identity awareness, and appreciate local knowledge systems |
| Post-Piagetian Development (Fleer, 2010) | Scaffolded tasks matched to cognitive and emotional capacities; progressive scene difficulty | Learners engage with developmentally appropriate challenges, enhancing metacognition and reflective thinking |
| Implementation Strategies | Teacher prompts (e.g., "What might happen next?"); guided inquiry questions | Learners develop self-directed learning, reasoning, and analytical skills; teachers scaffold learning effectively |
| Educator Readiness | Structured supports for teachers; co-construction guidance; suggestions for integrating IKS | Teachers gain confidence delivering culturally responsive STEM lessons; modeling experiential learning practices |
| Learner Engagement | Multimodal, play-based activities; open-ended visual prompts; hands-on extensions (drawing, role-play) | Active engagement with STEM content, enhanced creativity, problem-solving, collaboration, and curiosity-driven learning |
| Evaluation | Hands-on extensions and observable activities | Assess learners' understanding of STEM concepts, cultural relevance, global citizenship, and self-directed learning dispositions |

Each framework principle and operational domain informs both the structure and interactivity of the book. Social Constructivism (Vygotsky, 1978) is realized through interactive narrative sequences and role-play opportunities, where learners co-construct meaning collaboratively. Cultural Responsiveness (Gay, 2018; da Silva et al., 2023) is operationalized by embedding local cultural practices, such as Basotho weaving or the wearing of Mokorotlo hats, into visual narratives. Post-Piagetian principles (Fleer, 2010) guide scaffolded tasks and progressive scene complexity, ensuring that learners encounter developmentally appropriate challenges that promote reflective thinking. Implementation strategies, such as teacher prompts and guided inquiry questions, encourage learners to plan, predict, and reason, fostering self-directed learning. Educator readiness is addressed through structured support and co-construction guidance, helping teachers integrate IKS and model experiential learning. Learner engagement is promoted through multimodal, play-based activities and hands-on extensions such as drawing, role-playing, and problem-solving. Evaluation occurs through observation of these activities, providing insights into learners' cognitive growth, cultural awareness, and global citizenship dispositions.

## Imagined Classroom Interactions

In a Grade R classroom, Scene 3 (Northern Cape solar energy) might elicit learners' curiosity about sunlight and electricity. Children could gather in small groups, discuss what the shining solar panels represent, and predict how energy travels to their communities. One learner may say, "*The sun gives power to the houses!*" while another suggests, "*We could make our own sun panels in class!*" Teachers could respond by encouraging learners to design paper or cardboard solar panels, ask open-ended questions such as "*How else could we use sunlight to help our homes?*" and connect the activity to local Indigenous practices of observing the sun for planting or daily routines.

Scene 5 (Eastern Cape micro-hydro power) might see learners observing a visual depiction of a river turning a small water wheel. A learner might ask, "*Can the water make the lights go on?*" Teachers could facilitate hands-on exploration by letting children construct mini water wheels in trays of water, reinforcing STEM concepts such as kinetic energy, and prompting reflective questions like *"What happens if the water moves faster or slower?"* This aligns with Bang & Medin's (2010) observation that contextualized, hands-on tasks deepen understanding and engagement.

## Potential Teacher Responses

Prior research indicates that teachers in early childhood contexts respond positively when provided with structured, culturally grounded scaffolds (Gay, 2018; Hu & Commeyras, 2008). In using *Renewable Rangers*, teachers might guide learners by modeling scientific reasoning, connecting scenes to learners' everyday lives, and highlighting Indigenous knowledge practices, while simultaneously allowing learners to explore ideas independently. For example, during role-play of renewable energy solutions, teachers might encourage collaboration, ask reflective prompts, and celebrate creative solutions, reinforcing problem-solving and critical thinking skills. Teachers may also document learner responses as artifacts, drawings, discussions, or mini-experiments, both for evaluation and to inform subsequent lesson adaptations, illustrating the iterative, reflective process highlighted in *the Mokhele-Ramulumo & Gumbo (2025) framework.*

## Synthesis

Although empirical classroom testing has not yet been conducted, prior research suggests that well-designed, multimodal, and culturally grounded resources can foster cognitive engagement, problem-solving, and collaborative skills in early childhood contexts (Bang & Medin, 2010; Hu & Commeyras, 2008). The anticipated classroom interactions demonstrate how learners might actively co-construct knowledge, connect scientific concepts to cultural practices, and engage in self-directed exploration. Simultaneously, teachers are positioned to scaffold learning, integrate IKS and GCE principles, and nurture early STEM skills while supporting holistic development. Collectively, these design features underscore the potential of the wordless book as both a practical teaching tool and a model for translating theoretical frameworks into meaningful, culturally responsive early childhood educational interventions.

# DISCUSSION

## Design Outcomes

Each principle from *the Mokhele-Ramulumo & Gumbo (2025) framework* was operationalized within the *Renewable Rangers* book's narrative structure, visual design, and teacher resources. Social constructivist principles were implemented through interactive narrative sequences and visual storytelling, inviting learners to co-construct meaning and actively engage with content (Vygotsky, 1978; Inozu, 2017). Prior studies confirm that wordless visual narratives enhance collaborative meaning-making and problem-solving skills in early learners (Rizqiyani & Azizah, 2019), while digital game-based resources and pop-up STEM storybooks (Li et al., 2024) similarly support inquiry-based learning, creativity, and systematic reasoning. Compared with these digital or tactile resources, the *Renewable Rangers* wordless book uniquely integrates IKS and GCE in a developmentally appropriate, culturally grounded visual format that is flexible for multilingual classrooms.

Cultural responsiveness was embedded through visual cues and culturally relevant scenes, such as Basotho community members weaving baskets or wearing traditional Mokorotlo hats. Therefore, by situating scientific concepts within familiar contexts, learners connect new knowledge to lived experiences (Gay, 2018; da Silva et al., 2023), consistent with Bang and Medin's (2010) findings that local knowledge strengthens engagement in STEM learning. Unlike many ecoliteracy projects or digital interventions that prioritize content delivery, the *Renewable Rangers* approach foregrounds narrative, cultural, and place-based learning while simultaneously addressing global environmental issues.

Implementation strategies guided the inclusion of teacher prompts and scaffolded inquiry questions, such as "*What might happen next?*" or "*How could the community address this problem?*" Hands-on extensions, drawing solar panels, role-playing energy solutions, or discussing energy conservation, reflect experiential, culturally grounded pedagogy (Panayiota & Tsilimeni, 2021). These strategies align with evidence that play-based, multimodal learning fosters deeper conceptual understanding, critical thinking, and collaborative problem-solving (Anagnostidou et al., 2025; Grava & Pole, 2021).

## Pedagogical Alignment

The *Renewable Rangers* wordless book supports SDL, critical thinking, and global citizenship. Learners are encouraged to analyze cause-and-effect relationships, predict outcomes, and propose solutions to environmental challenges. The absence of written text enables children to narrate their own stories, co-construct meaning with peers, and engage in role-play, consistent with social constructivist and post-Piagetian principles (Fleer, 2010; Rizqiyani & Azizah, 2019). Prior research shows that wordless picture books promote creativity, narrative skills, and higher-order thinking, while text-centered approaches often limit learner-driven exploration (Hu & Commeyras, 2008; Nikolajeva & Scott, 2013; Heisig, 2017).

Therefore, by privileging multimodal storytelling and culturally situated contexts, the book advances participatory early science learning that bridges IKS and GCE, fostering SDL where learners take ownership of meaning-making, generate questions, predict outcomes, and co-construct solutions (Knowles, 1975; Garrison, 1997). This alignment with SDL theory ensures learners develop autonomy, reflection, and collaborative inquiry skills while engaging with STEM concepts.

## Gender, Inclusivity, and Representation

Visual storytelling in the wordless book consciously includes diverse representations of gender, ethnicity, and community roles. Both boys and girls actively participate in problem-solving alongside the *Renewable Rangers,* modeling equitable engagement in STEM and environmental decision-making. This inclusive representation addresses prior critiques of early childhood STEM resources that underrepresent girls or marginalize certain cultural identities (Bang & Medin, 2010). Therefore, by normalizing equitable participation and celebrating local diversity, the resource fosters belonging, identity affirmation, and positive social-emotional outcomes, supporting culturally responsive pedagogy and GCE simultaneously (Gay, 2018; da Silva et al., 2023).

## ANTICIPATED LONG-TERM IMPACTS

Although empirical testing has not yet occurred, design choices suggest several potential long-term outcomes. Children may develop a sense of environmental stewardship, understanding renewable energy solutions, community responsibility, and the impact of human actions on local and global ecosystems. Engagement with culturally grounded, multimodal narratives supports identity formation and belonging, encouraging learners to see themselves as competent problem-solvers and informed global citizens from an early age (Ramulumo & Gumbo, 2025).

Through repeated engagement with the wordless book, learners may strengthen critical thinking, collaborative reasoning, and self-directed inquiry skills. These foundational capacities, combined with exposure to Indigenous knowledge and global environmental issues, have the potential to influence future attitudes and behaviours toward sustainability, civic engagement, and STEM participation. In this way, the *Renewable Rangers* wordless book represents not only a pedagogically innovative classroom resource but also a tool for fostering lifelong dispositions toward ecological literacy, cultural awareness, and ethical global citizenship.

## LIMITATIONS AND FUTURE RESEARCH

Even though the *Renewable Rangers* wordless book was developed based on robust theoretical frameworks and evidence-based design principles, empirical classroom testing has not yet been conducted. Future research should include pilot studies or experimental classroom implementations to evaluate the effectiveness of the book in promoting self-directed learning, critical thinking, cultural awareness, and environmental stewardship among early childhood learners. Mixed-method approaches, combining structured observations, teacher interviews, learner artifacts, and reflective assessments, could provide comprehensive insights into both learning outcomes and pedagogical impact (Mokhele-Ramulumo & Gumbo, 2025; Bang & Medin, 2010).

## Scalability and access considerations

Scalability is a key consideration for extending the reach of the book beyond pilot classrooms. Print versions are highly accessible in under-resourced settings, but distribution may be limited by cost, availability, and language diversity. Digital adaptations offer opportunities for interactivity, multimedia integration, and broader dissemination; however, digital solutions face barriers such as limited access to devices, unreliable electricity, and inadequate internet connectivity in many South African schools (Hu & Commeyras, 2008). A dual-format approach, combining print and digital versions, could help balance accessibility and engagement while ensuring that learners in resource-constrained contexts are not excluded.

## Teacher Training and Professional Development

Effective implementation requires teacher readiness, particularly in facilitating self-directed, play-based, and culturally responsive STEM learning. Training should focus on interpreting visual narratives, scaffolding inquiry-based activities, integrating Indigenous knowledge, and modeling global citizenship education. Teachers may benefit from workshops, peer mentoring, and structured guides accompanying the book, allowing them to confidently navigate multimodal storytelling and hands-on STEM extensions (Ramulumo & Gumbo, 2025). Prior studies indicate that teacher preparation is essential for realizing the cognitive, social, and cultural benefits of multimodal early childhood resources (Gay, 2018; Fleer, 2010).

## Longitudinal Research Opportunities

To assess sustained impact, longitudinal studies could track learners over multiple years, examining how early engagement with the book influences environmental knowledge, STEM problem-solving, identity formation, and global citizenship dispositions. Observing children's development over time would provide evidence for the book's contribution to lifelong learning skills, ecological literacy, and social-emotional growth, supporting the case for integrating multimodal, culturally responsive resources into standard curricula (Fleer, 2010; Bang & Medin, 2010).

## Adaptation to Other African Contexts

The book's narrative, grounded in South African cultural practices and provincial energy challenges, could be adapted for other African contexts by incorporating local Indigenous knowledge, environmental issues, and linguistic diversity. For example, visual elements could depict region-specific renewable energy solutions, solar in the Sahel, small hydro in East Africa, or wind energy in coastal regions, while maintaining play-based, learner-centered pedagogy. Localizing content ensures relevance, supports cultural identity, and strengthens engagement, demonstrating the transferability of *the Mokhele-Ramulumo & Gumbo (2025) framework* across diverse African early childhood education settings.

Therefore, by considering scalability, access barriers, teacher preparation, longitudinal research, and cross-context adaptation, future studies can ensure that the *Renewable Rangers* wordless book evolves from a conceptually robust design into a widely applicable, culturally responsive educational resource with measurable long-term impacts on early childhood STEM learning, environmental stewardship, and global citizenship.

## CONCLUSION AND IMPLICATION

The development of the *Renewable Rangers* wordless book demonstrates a successful translation of *the Mokhele-Ramulumo & Gumbo (2025)* theoretical framework into concrete, actionable educational design. Therefore, by integrating social constructivist, post-Piagetian, and culturally responsive principles, the book provides a multimodal, play-based resource that nurtures self-directed learning, critical thinking, and global citizenship among early childhood learners. Narrative sequences, visual storytelling, scaffolded teacher prompts, and hands-on extensions work synergistically to ensure learners engage meaningfully with STEM content while connecting abstract scientific concepts to familiar cultural practices. Although empirical classroom testing remains forthcoming, the design choices indicate strong potential for fostering cognitive, social, and cultural development, bridging local Indigenous knowledge with global sustainability perspectives.

### Implications for Theory and Practice

The *Renewable Rangers* book highlights the practical value of grounding educational resources in robust theoretical frameworks. Social constructivist principles facilitate collaborative knowledge construction, while post-Piagetian developmental theory ensures age-appropriate scaffolding and reflective thinking. Cultural responsiveness situates learning in meaningful, contextually grounded experiences, enhancing identity formation and belonging (Gay, 2018; Fleer, 2010). Integration of IKS and GCE operationalizes global environmental learning in a locally relevant, multimodal format, exemplifying how theory can inform practice to address pressing global challenges such as climate change education from an early age (Bang & Medin, 2010; Ramulumo & Gumbo, 2025).

The book also illustrates how self-directed learning (Knowles, 1975; Garrison, 1997) can be embedded in early childhood curricula through wordless, open-ended resources that encourage curiosity, problem-solving, and autonomous exploration. Therefore, by providing teachers with structured guidance and hands-on extensions, the resource not only supports learner engagement but also models culturally responsive, inquiry-based pedagogical strategies. In this way, *Renewable Rangers* bridges the gap between curriculum frameworks, classroom practice, and global educational imperatives.

## RECOMMENDATIONS AND CALL TO ACTION

To realize the full potential of such innovative resources, the following actions are recommended:

- Conduct pilot and longitudinal studies to examine the effectiveness of the *Renewable Rangers* wordless book across diverse early childhood contexts, measuring outcomes in self-directed learning, critical thinking, cultural awareness, collaboration, and environmental stewardship over time to provide evidence for both immediate and sustained educational benefits.
- Provide comprehensive teacher preparation and professional development, equipping educators to implement wordless, multimodal STEM resources with a focus on integrating Indigenous knowledge, global citizenship principles, and play-based inquiry into daily practice.
- Promote curriculum integration by encouraging policymakers and curriculum designers to embed culturally responsive, multimodal resources into early childhood STEM programs, ensuring that Indigenous knowledge, local contexts, and global sustainability issues are meaningfully represented.
- Expand resources to broaden access and inclusivity by developing additional wordless or minimally text-based educational materials that address both local and global environmental challenges, supporting engagement for linguistically diverse learners.
- Address scalability and adaptation to extend the book's reach beyond South Africa, adapting *Renewable Rangers* for other African and global contexts, integrating region-specific renewable energy solutions, Indigenous knowledge, and culturally relevant narratives to foster environmentally conscious and globally minded learners.

Ultimately, the *Renewable Rangers* wordless book exemplifies how theory, pedagogy, and curriculum can converge to create developmentally appropriate, culturally authentic, and globally relevant STEM learning experiences. Therefore, by fostering self-directed learning, critical thinking, and a sense of environmental and civic responsibility, the resource prepares young learners to navigate complex environmental challenges, develop global citizenship identities, and engage as empowered, reflective members of their communities. Policymakers, curriculum designers, and educators are called to support, implement, and scale such innovative approaches, ensuring that early childhood education contributes meaningfully to sustainable futures and inclusive learning environments.

## Ethical Considerations

Ethical clearance for this study was obtained from North-West University (Institutional Study Number: NWU-012-61-25-A2), ensuring full adherence to institutional research ethics standards throughout the development of the framework. All procedures respected participants' rights, confidentiality, and well-being.

## Declaration of Generative AI and AI-Assisted Technologies

During the preparation of this work, the authors made use of AI-assisted technologies, including ChatGPT, Grammarly, and Recite, to enhance language clarity, refine drafts, organize complex concepts, and edit references. All content was thoroughly reviewed, verified, and edited by the authors, who take full responsibility for the final version of the publication.

## Funding

This research was supported by the National Research Foundation of South Africa under the Thuthuka Grant (Grant Number: TTK23032887785).

## REFERENCES


Alexander, N. (2005). *Language, class and power in post-apartheid South Africa*. David Philip Publishers.

Anagnostidou, A. M., Psoma, A., & Theodosiadou, S. (2025). Visual literacy in kindergarten as media play: A multi-case study of stop motion animation videos. *Journal of Visual Literacy*, *44*(2), 1–21. DOI: 10.1080/1051144X.2025.2496027

Bang, M., & Medin, D. (2010). Cultural processes in science education: Supporting the navigation of multiple epistemologies. *Science Education*, *94*(6), 1008–1026. DOI: 10.1002/sce.20392

Banks, K. I., & Taylor, C. A. (2025). Climate change education in primary schools: Using arts-based methods to access student voice and examine the English National Curriculum. *Environmental Education Research*, *31*(12), 2552–2572. Advance online publication. DOI: 10.1080/13504622.2025.2460718

Ciecierski, L., Nageldinger, J., Bintz, W. P., & Moore, S. D. (2016). New perspectives on picture books. *Athens Journal of Education*, *4*(2), 123–136. DOI: 10.30958/aje.4-2-2

da Silva, C., Pereira, F., & Amorim, J. P. (2023). The integration of indigenous knowledge in school: A systematic review. *Compare: A Journal of Comparative Education*, *54*(7), 1210–1228. DOI: 10.1080/03057925.2023.2184200

De Klerk, C., Ker-Fox, J., & Steenekamp, L. (2024). Enhancing critical thinking through collaborative learning: The impact of a partial pre-release assessment format. *Accounting Education*, *34*(4), 499–532. DOI: 10.1080/09639284.2024.2361647

Department of Basic Education. (2005). *National curriculum framework for children from birth to four years*. Pretoria, South Africa: Department of Basic Education & UNICEF. https://www.unicef.org/southafrica/reports/national-curriculum-framework-children-birth-four-years

Department of Basic Education. (2011). *Curriculum and assessment policy statement (CAPS): Foundation phase natural sciences and technology*. Pretoria, South Africa: Department of Basic Education. https://www.education.gov.za/Curriculum/CAPS/tabid/420/Default.aspx

Department of Basic Education. (2011). *Curriculum and assessment policy statement (CAPS): Foundation Phase Grades R–3*. Department of Basic Education.

Department of Basic Education. (2015). *Early learning outcomes framework*. Pretoria, South Africa: Department of Basic Education. https://www.education.gov.za/Curriculum/EarlyLearningOutcomes/tabid/420/Default.aspx

Donald, D., Lazarus, S., & Lolwana, P. (2022). *Educational psychology in social context: Ecosystemic applications in Southern Africa* (6th ed.). Oxford University Press.

Duncan, G., Kalil, A., Mogstad, M., & Rege, M. (2023). Investing in early childhood development in preschool and at home. In Hanushek, E. A., Machin, S., & Woessmann, L. (Eds.), *Handbook of the economics of education* (Vol. 6, pp. 1–91). Elsevier., DOI: 10.1016/bs.hesedu.2022.11.005

Eskiyurt, R., & Özkan, B. (2024). Exploring the impact of collaborative learning on the development of critical thinking and clinical decision-making skills in nursing students: A quantitative descriptive design. *Heliyon*, *10*(17), e37198. DOI: 10.1016/j.heliyon.2024.e37198

Fleer, M. (2010). *Early learning and development: Cultural-historical concepts in play*. Cambridge University Press., DOI: 10.1017/CBO9780511844836

Garrison, D. R. (1997). Self-directed learning: Toward a comprehensive model. *Adult Education Quarterly*, *48*(1), 18–33. DOI: 10.1177/074171369704800103

Gay, G. (2018). *Culturally responsive teaching: Theory, research, and practice* (3rd ed.). Teachers College Press.

Goriot, C., Jongstra, W., & Mensink, L. (2024). A literature review on the benefits of wordless picture books for children's development. *L1-Educational Studies in Language and Literature*, *24*(1), 1–26. DOI: 10.21248/l1esll.2024.24.1.712

Grava, J., & Pole, V. (2021). The promotion of self-directed learning in preschool: Reflection on teachers' professional practice. *Cypriot Journal of Educational Sciences*, *16*(5), 2336–2352. DOI: 10.18844/cjes.v16i5.6351

Heisig, J. (2017). Teacher-centered versus student-centered approaches to literacy: Examining text-based instruction in early childhood classrooms. *Journal of Early Childhood Literacy*, *17*(3), 315–334. DOI: 10.1177/1468798415618530

Heugh, K. (2013). Multilingual education policy in South Africa constrained by theoretical and historical disconnections. *Annual Review of Applied Linguistics*, *33*, 215–237. DOI: 10.1017/S0267190513000135

Honaker, J. D., & Miller, R. T. (2024). Wordless but not silent: Unlocking the power of wordless picture books. *TESOL Journal*, *28*(1), 1–15. DOI: 10.1002/tesj.721

Hu, R., & Commeyras, M. (2008). A case study of a primary grade 2 student's use of wordless picture books. *Literacy Research and Instruction*, *47*(2), 159–174. DOI: 10.1080/19388070701801241

Inozu, J. (2017). Drawings are talking: Exploring language learners' beliefs through visual narratives. *Applied Linguistics Review*, *9*(2), 177–200. Advance online publication. DOI: 10.1515/applirev-2016-1062

Knowles, M. S. (1975). *Self-directed learning: A guide for learners and teachers*. Association Press.

Li, Y., Leung, F. K. S., & Tan, C. Y. (2024). Developing computational thinking through pop-up storybooks: A multimodal literacy approach in Hong Kong. *Education Sciences*, *14*(12), 1377. DOI: 10.3390/educsci14121377

Martínez-Carratalá, F. A., Miras, S., & Rovira-Collado, J. (2024). Development of multimodal literacy through wordless picture books: A didactic intervention in primary education. *Revista de Investigación Educacional*, *42*(2), 229–247. DOI: 10.6018/rie.563971

McGuire, K. (2022). *Engaging students through wordless picture books during story time. Knowledge Quest*. Retrieved from ERIC.

Miao, Q., & Nduneseokwu, C. (2025). Advancing environmental leadership: Education, development, and training. In Miao, Q., & Nduneseokwu, C. (Eds.), *Environmental leadership in a VUCA era: An interdisciplinary handbook* (pp. 467–538). [Publisher not listed]

Mwinsa, G. M. (2025). Play-based learning: A pedagogical approach for social and cognitive development in early childhood education. ScienceDirect., 10.1016/j.scedu.2025.100123.

. Narengaowa, & Tungalag, O. (2024). Research on metacognitive strategies of children's self-regulated learning. *Health Psychology Research, 12*, 120366. https://doi.org/DOI: 10.52965/001c.120366

Nikolajeva, M., & Scott, C. (2013). *How picturebooks work*. Routledge., DOI: 10.4324/9780203960615

Nygren, T., Wassermann, J., Kronlid, D. O., Larsson, E., Guath, M., Novak, J., & Bentrovato, D. (2020). Global citizenship education for global citizenship? Students' views on learning about, through, and for human rights, peace, and sustainable development in England, India, New Zealand, South Africa, and Sweden. *Journal of Social Science Education*, *19*(4), 63–97. DOI: 10.4119/jsse-3464

Om, C., Vella, K., Dema, T., Ploderer, B., Murcia, K., & Brereton, M. (2025). Storying-roleplay: A co-design method supporting young children to understand environmental problems. In *Proceedings of the 24th Interaction Design and Children (IDC '25)* (pp. 465–478). https://doi.org/DOI: 10.1145/3713043.3728842

Panayiota, M., & Tsilimeni, T. (2021). Developing children's critical thinking through wordless books. *Journal of Literary Education*, *5*(2), 54–71. DOI: 10.7203/JLE.5.21392

Papadopoulos, I., & Bisiri, E. (2020). Fostering critical thinking skills in preschool education: Designing, implementing and assessing a multiliteracies-oriented program based on intercultural tales. *Multilingual Academic Journal of Education and Social Sciences*, *8*(1), 87–105. DOI: 10.46886/MAJESS/v8-i1/7263

Probine, S. A., Perry, J., Burke, R. S., & McAlevey, F. L. (2023). An examination of inquiry-based project learning in early childhood settings in Aotearoa/New Zealand. *Early Childhood Education Journal*, *52*(6), 1–11. DOI: 10.1007/s10643-023-01495-7

Rizqiyani, R., & Azizah, N. (2019, January). The influence of wordless picture book to improve the ability of storytelling among preschool students. In *Proceedings of the 3rd International Conference on Current Issues in Education (ICCIE 2018)* (p. 74). Atlantis Press. https://doi.org/DOI: 10.2991/iccie-18.2019.74

Schmitz, B., Klemke, R., Walhout, J., & Specht, M. (2015). Attuning a mobile simulation game for school children using a design-based research approach. *Computers & Education*, *81*, 35–48. DOI: 10.1016/j.compedu.2014.09.001

Seleke, B., Teis, N. J. P., Els, C. J., & Legodu, G. (2025). Indigenous knowledge integration in South Africa's technology education curriculum: Current status, challenges, and future directions. [JELT]. *Journal of Education and Learning Technology*, *6*(1), 120–138. DOI: 10.38159/jelt.2025619

Suarlin, S. (2023). Integrating environmental education to form environmental care characters in schools. *Advances in Community Services Research*, *1*(2), 44–53. DOI: 10.60079/acsr.v1i2.335

Suarlin, S. (2023). Integrating environmental education to form environmental care characters in schools. *Advances in Community Services Research*, *1*(2), 47–56. Advance online publication. DOI: 10.60079/acsr.v1i2.335

Teacher Created Materials. (2024). Wordless books and your classroom—a perfect match. Retrieved from https://www.teachercreatedmaterials.com/blog/wordless-books-in-your-classroom-a-perfect-match

Tungalag, O., & Narengaowa. (2024). Research on metacognitive strategies of children's self-regulated learning in early childhood education. *Frontiers in Psychology*, *15*, 11368603. DOI: 10.3389/fpsyg.2024.11368603

UNESCO. (2020). *Education for sustainable development: A roadmap.* UNESCO Publishing. https://unesdoc.unesco.org/ark:/48223/pf0000374802

Vygotsky, L. S. (1978). *Mind in society: The development of higher psychological processes* (Cole, M., John-Steiner, V., Scribner, S., & Souberman, E., Eds. & Trans.). Harvard University Press.

# Compilation of References


Abarry, A. (1989). The Role of Play Songs in the Moral, Social, and Emotional Development of African Children. *Research in African Literatures*, *20*(2), 202–216.

Abbas, N., Imran, A., Manzoor, R., Hussain, T., & Hussain, M. (2023). Role of artificial intelligence tools in enhancing students' educational performance at higher levels. *Journal of Artificial Intelligence Machine Learning and Neural Network*, (35), 36–49. DOI: 10.55529/jaimlnn.35.36.49

Abdul Aziz, N. A., Mohd Ariffin, N. F., Ismail, N. A., & Alias, A. (2023). Community participation in the importance of living heritage conservation and its relationships with the community-based education model towards creating a sustainable community in the Melaka UNESCO World Heritage Site. *Sustainability (Basel)*, *15*(3), 1935. DOI: 10.3390/su15031935

Abrams, S., & Walsh, S. (2014). Gamified Vocabulary. *Journal of Adolescent & Adult Literacy*, *58*(1), 49–58. Advance online publication. DOI: 10.1002/jaal.315

Acheampong, P. (2022). *Reclaiming play: African indigenous games and early learning*. Accra Press.

Acquah, E. O., Sackey-Sam, K. A., & Annan, J. F. (2015). Use of indigenous musical games and songs in developing the total wellbeing of the child. *International Journal of Research*, 2(12), 112–123.

Adeoye, M. A. (2023). Review of sampling techniques for education. *ASEAN Journal for Science Education*, 2(2), 87–94.

Adipat, S., Laksana, K., Busayanon, K., Asawasowan, A., & Adipat, B. (2021). Engaging students in the learning process with game-based learning: The fundamental concepts. [IJTE]. *International Journal of Technology in Education*, *4*(3), 542–552. DOI: 10.46328/ijte.169

Agostinelli, S. (2021). *Actionable framework for city digital twin-enabled predictive maintenance and security management systems.*. https://doi.org/DOI: 10.2495/BIM210191

Akavova, A., Temirkhanova, Z., & Lorsanova, Z. (2023). Adaptive learning and artificial intelligence in the educational space. *E3s Web of Conferences,* 451, 06011. https://doi.org/DOI: 10.1051/e3sconf/202345106011

Akgün, S., & Greenhow, C. (2021). Artificial intelligence in education: Addressing ethical challenges in k-12 settings. *AI and Ethics*, *2*(3), 431–440. DOI: 10.1007/s43681-021-00096-7

Akinrinola, O. (2024). Navigating and reviewing ethical dilemmas in ai development: strategies for transparency, fairness, and accountability. *GSC Advanced Research and Reviews,* 18(3), 050-058. https://doi.org/DOI: 10.30574/gscarr.2024.18.3.0088

Aladelah, A. A. H. (2024). *The effectiveness of teaching using lingokids on the english vocabulary acquisition of first year primary students* (Master's thesis, Qassim University). https://doi.org/DOI: 10.21608/mrk.2024.348329

Alali, R., & Wardat, Y. (2024). Opportunities and challenges of integrating generative artificial intelligence in education. *International Journal of Religion*, *5*(7), 784–793. DOI: 10.61707/8y29gv34

Alenezi, A. (2024). Obstacles to the use of ai applications in blackboard for faculty members at northern border university, saudi arabia. *Mier Journal of Educational Studies Trends & Practices,* 248-268. https://doi.org/DOI: 10.52634/mier/2024/v14/i2/2581

Alenezi, A. (2023). Teacher perspectives on ai-driven gamification: Impact on student motivation, engagement, and learning outcomes. *Information Technologies and Learning Tools*, *97*(5), 138–148. DOI: 10.33407/itlt.v97i5.5437

Alexander, N., Bloch, C., Jogee, N., Guzula, X., & Mahobe, N. (2011). Creating literate school communities: Vulindlela reading clubs. *Praesa Early Literacy Unit* viewed 21 July 2025, from http://www.academia.edu/download/30382921/reading-club-concept-chapter.pdf

Alexander, N. (2005). *Language, class and power in post-apartheid South Africa.* David Philip Publishers.

Aliabadi, R. (2023). *Transdisciplinary ai education: the confluence of curricular and community needs in the instruction of artificial intelligence.*, 137-151. https://doi.org/DOI: 10.1007/978-981-99-7947-9_11

Alkan, A. (2024). Artificial intelligence: its role and potential in education. *İnsan Ve Toplum Bilimleri Araştırmaları Dergisi,* 13(1), 483-497. https://doi.org/DOI: 10.15869/itobiad.1331201

Alladi, T., Chamola, V., Parizi, R., & Choo, K. (2019). Blockchain applications for industry 4.0 and industrial iot: A review. *IEEE Access : Practical Innovations, Open Solutions*, *7*, 176935–176951. DOI: 10.1109/ACCESS.2019.2956748

Allahverdi, A. (2021). Sample senior design projects of industrial engineering program at kuwait university. *Asean Journal of Engineering Education*, *4*(1). Advance online publication. DOI: 10.11113/ajee2020.4n1.14

Allen, M., & Sites, R. (2012). *Leaving ADDIE for SAM: An agile model for developing the best learning experiences.* Association for Talent Development.

Allsop, S. A. (2010). *Assisting Creole-English and non-standard dialect speaking students in learning Standard English.* University of Wisconsin.

Almusaed, A., Almssad, A., Yitmen, I., & Homod, R. Z. (2023). Enhancing student engagement: Harnessing "aied"'s power in hybrid education—a review analysis. *Education Sciences*, *13*(7), 632. DOI: 10.3390/educsci13070632

Alotaibi, M. S. (2024). Game-based learning in childhood: A systematic review and meta-analysis. *Frontiers in Psychology*, *15*, 1307881. Advance online publication. DOI: 10.3389/fpsyg.2024.1307881 PMID: 38629045

Alrayes, A., Henari, T. F., & Ahmed, D. A. (2024). Chatgpt in education – understanding the bahraini academics perspective. *Electronic Journal of e-Learning*, *22*(2), 112–134. DOI: 10.34190/ejel.22.2.3250

Alsadoon, H. (2023). The impact of gamification on student motivation and engagement: An empirical study. *Dirasat: Educational Sciences*, *50*(2), 386–396. DOI: 10.35516/edu.v50i2.255

Alshehri, B. (2023). Pedagogical paradigms in the ai era: Insights from saudi educators on the long-term implications of ai integration in classroom teaching. *IJESA*, *2*(8), 159–180. DOI: 10.59992/IJESA.2023.v2n8p7

Amin, M. T. (2024). Family language policy: A comprehensive analysis and strategies, challenges, and impacts on children's education. *International Journal of Scientific and Research Publications*, *13*(7), 218–225. DOI: 10.29322/IJSRP.13.07.2023.p13924

Amorsen, A., & Wilson, D. (2020). Intentional teaching to support oral language development. *Practical Literacy: The Early and Primary Years*, *25*(1), 35–37.

Anagnostidou, A. M., Psoma, A., & Theodosiadou, S. (2025). Visual literacy in kindergarten as media play: A multi-case study of stop motion animation videos. *Journal of Visual Literacy*, *44*(2), 1–21. DOI: 10.1080/1051144X.2025.2496027

Ang, L., Du Preez, H., Du Plessis, A., Basson, L., Ebersöhn, L., & Gu, Q. (2025). The role of early childhood development and education (ECDE) in supporting learning and well-being in rural early childhood and primary schools in South Africa. *International Journal of Early Years Education*, *33*(2), 272–289. DOI: 10.1080/09669760.2023.2259953

Antonaci, A., Klemke, R., & Specht, M. (2019). The effects of gamification in online learning environments: A systematic literature review. *Informatics (MDPI)*, *6*(3), 32. DOI: 10.3390/informatics6030032

Aparicio-Gómez, O. (2024). Tejiendo conexiones: la simbiosis transformadora entre aprendizaje e inteligencia artificial. *Hachetetepé Revista Científica De Educación Y Comunicación,* (28). https://doi.org/DOI: 10.25267/Hachetetepe.2024.i28.1103

Aprilianti, R., & Baa, D. (2024). Code-switching in multilingual classrooms helps students feel more included by enabling them to express themselves in a language they are comfortable with. *American Journal of Teacher Education*, *45*(2), 112–125.

Aquino, V. J. (2011). Enhancing learning of children from diverse language backgrounds: Mother tongue-based bilingual or multilingual education in the early years; 2011.

Asamoah-Potu, F. (2024). Preserving traditional Ghanaian folklore through storytelling. *European Modern Studies Journal*, *8*(2), 308–318. DOI: 10.59573/emsj.8(2).2024.26

Aschentrup, L., Steimer, P. A., Dadaczynski, K., Mc Call, T., Fischer, F., & Wrona, K. J. (2024). Effectiveness of gamified digital interventions in mental health prevention and health promotion among adults: A scoping review. *BMC Public Health*, *24*(69), 69. https://bmcpublichealth.biomedcentral.com/articles/10.1186/s12889-023-17517-3. DOI: 10.1186/s12889-023-17517-3 PMID: 38167010

Aung, S. (2025). Creating multilingual spaces through arts-based methods in foundation phase classrooms. *Frontiers in Education*, *10*, 1628614. DOI: 10.3389/feduc.2025.1628614

Austin, P. K., & Sallabank, J. (Eds.). (2023). *The Cambridge handbook of endangered languages* (2nd ed.). Cambridge University Press.

Au, W. (2007). High-Stakes Testing and Curricular Control: A Qualitative Metasynthesis. *Educational Researcher*, *36*(5), 258–267. DOI: 10.3102/0013189X07306523

Au, W. (2023). High-stakes testing and curricular control: A qualitative metasynthesis. *Educational Researcher*, *52*(3), 178–189.

Avgerou, C. (2017). Theoretical Framing of ICT4D Research. In Choudrie, J., Islam, M. S., Wahid, F., Bass, J. M., & Priyatma, J. E. (Eds.), *Information and Communication Technologies for Development* (pp. 10–23). Springer International Publishing. DOI: 10.1007/978-3-319-59111-7_2

Aydın, S. (2013). Second Life as a foreign language learning environment: A review of research. *Turkish Online Journal of Distance Education*, *14*(1), 53–63. https://dergipark.org.tr/en/pub/tojde/issue/16895/176013

Aydın, S., & Çakır, N. (2022). Integrating commercial-off-the-shelf games into language classroom: PCaRD experience of two English language teachers. *Eğitimde Kuram ve Uygulama*, *18*(2), 68–90. DOI: 10.17244/eku.982955

Azhar, S. A. F. J., & Jalil, H. A. (2022). Comparison of individual and collaborative game-based learning using tablet in improving students' knowledge in primary classroom environment. *Asian Journal of University Education*, *18*(1), 205–216. DOI: 10.24191/ajue.v18i1.17188

Babbie, E. (1990). *Survey research methods* (3rd ed.). Wadsworth.

Bacalja, A. (2022). 'A critical review of digital game literacies in the English classroom'. *L1-Educational Studies in Language and Literature*, *22*, 1–28. DOI: 10.21248/l1esll.2022.22.2.370

Bakhtin, M. M. (1981). *The dialogic imagination: Four essays*. University of Texas Press.

Balakrisha, C. (2023). The impact of in-classroom non-digital game-based learning activities on students transitioning to higher education. *Education Sciences*, *13*(4), 328. DOI: 10.3390/educsci13040328

Balci, S., Secaur, J., & Morris, B. (2022). Comparing the effectiveness of badges and leaderboards on academic performance and motivation of students in fully versus partially gamified online physics classes. *Education and Information Technologies*, *27*(6), 8669–8704. DOI: 10.1007/s10639-022-10983-z

Balta, N. (2023). *Ethical considerations in using ai in educational research.*, 2(1), 14205. https://doi.org/DOI: 10.51853/jorids/14205

Bamgbose, A. (2021). *Language and exclusion: The consequences of language policies in Africa*. Multilingual Matters.

Banda, F., & Mwanza, D. S. (2017). Language-in-education policy and linguistic diversity in Zambia: An alternative explanation to low reading levels among primary school pupils. In Banja, M. K. (Ed.), *Meeting EFA: Zambia and selected countries* (pp. 45–67). University of Zambia Press.

Banda, F., & Mwanza, D. S. (2019). Language in education policy and linguistic diversity in Zambia: Alternative explanation to low reading level among primary school pupils. *In selected reading in education*, (pp.109-132, University of Zambia Press. Banda, L.O., Banda, C.V., Banda, J.T., & Singni, T. (2024). Preserving cultural heritage: A community-centric approach to safeguard Khulubvi traditional temple Malawi. *Heliyon*, *10*(18), e37610. DOI: 10.1016/j.heliyon.2024.e37610 PMID: 39347398

Bang, M., & Medin, D. (2010). Cultural processes in science education: Supporting the navigation of multiple epistemologies. *Science Education*, *94*(6), 1008–1026. DOI: 10.1002/sce.20392

Bang, M., & Vossoughi, S. (2016). Participatory Design Research and Educational Justice: Studying Learning and Relations Within Social Change Making. *Cognition and Instruction*, *34*(3), 173–193. DOI: 10.1080/07370008.2016.1181879

Banks, J. A. (1993). Chapter 1: Multicultural Education: Historical Development, Dimensions, and Practice. *Review of Research in Education*, *19*(1), 3–49. DOI: 10.3102/0091732X019001003

Banks, K. I., & Taylor, C. A. (2025). Climate change education in primary schools: Using arts-based methods to access student voice and examine the English National Curriculum. *Environmental Education Research*, *31*(12), 2552–2572. Advance online publication. DOI: 10.1080/13504622.2025.2460718

Barab, S. A., Scott, B., Siyahhan, S., Goldstone, R., Ingram-Goble, A., Zuiker, S. J., & Warren, S. (2009). Transformational Play as a Curricular Scaffold: Using Videogames to Support Science Education. *Journal of Science Education and Technology*, *18*(4), 305–320. DOI: 10.1007/s10956-009-9171-5

Barab, S., Sadler, T., Heiselt, C., Hickey, D., & Zuiker, S. (2007). Relating narrative, inquiry, and inscriptions: A framework for socioscientific inquiry. *Journal of Science Education and Technology*, *16*, 69–82. DOI: 10.1007/s10956-006-9033-3

Barab, S., Warren, S., & Ingram-Goble, A. (2009). Conceptual play spaces. In Ferdig, R. E. (Ed.), *Handbook of research on effective electronic gaming in education* (Vol. III, pp. 989–1009). IGI Global. DOI: 10.4018/978-1-59904-808-6.ch057

Barendregt, W., & Bekker, T.-M. (2011). The influence of the level of free-choice learning activities on the use of educational computer game. *Computers & Education, 56*(1), 80–90. DOI: 10.1016/j.compedu.2010.08.018

Barton, D. (2001). *Literacy. An introduction to the ecology of written language* (2nd ed.). Blackledge.

Barua, P., Vicnesh, J., Gururajan, R., Oh, S., Palmer, E., Azizan, M., Kadri, N. A., & Acharya, U. (2022). Artificial intelligence enabled personalised assistive tools to enhance education of children with neurodevelopmental disorders a review. *International Journal of Environmental Research and Public Health, 19*(3), 1192. DOI: 10.3390/ijerph19031192

Barz, N., Benick, M., Dörrenbächer-Ulrich, L., & Perels, F. (2024). The effect of digital game-based learning interventions on cognitive, metacognitive, and affective-motivational learning outcomes in school: A meta-analysis. *Review of Educational Research, 94*(2), 193–227. DOI: 10.3102/00346543231167795

Bassanelli, S., Vasta, N., Bucchiarone, A., & Marconi, A. (2022). Gamification for behavior change: A scientometric review. *Acta Psychologica, 228*, 1–12. DOI: 10.1016/j.actpsy.2022.103657 PMID: 35767927

Bastani, P., Kavosi, Z., Alipoori, S., & Imani-Nasab, M. (2023). Evidence- based policy and decision-making among health managers: A case of shiraz university of medical sciences. *Galen Medical Journal, 6*(1). Advance online publication. DOI: 10.31661/gmj.v6i1.729

Basudan, S. (2023). A Scalable Blockchain Framework For Secure Transactions In Iot-Based Dynamic Applications. *IEEE Open Journal of the Communications Society, 4*, 1931–1945. DOI: 10.1109/OJCOMS.2023.3307337

Batibo, H. M. (2023). *Language decline and death in Africa: Causes, consequences and challenges* (2nd ed.). Multilingual Matters.

Battiste, M., & Henderson, J. Y. (2021). *Protecting Indigenous knowledge and heritage: A global challenge*. Purich Publishing.

Beavis, C., Muspratt, S., & Thompson, R. (2015). "Computer games can get your brain working": Student experience and perceptions of digital games in the classroom. *Learning, Media and Technology, 40*(1), 21–42. DOI: 10.1080/17439884.2014.904339

Begi, N. (2014). The use of the mother tongue as a language of instruction in the early years of school is to preserve Kenyan culture. *Journal of Education and Practice, 5*(3), 37–49.

Benjamin, R. (2019). *Race After Technology: Abolitionist Tools for the New Jim Code*. John Wiley & Sons.

Bennani, S., Maalel, A., & Ghezala, H. (2021). Adaptive gamification in e-learning: A literature review and future challenges. *Computer Applications in Engineering Education, 30*(2), 628–642. DOI: 10.1002/cae.22477

Benson, C., & Kosonen, K. (Eds.). (2021). *Language issues in comparative education: Inclusive teaching and learning in non-dominant languages and cultures* (2nd ed.). Brill.

BERA. (2018). *Ethical Guidelines for Educational Research* (4th ed.). British Educational Research Association.

Bernard, D. M. (2025). Understanding socioculturalism in early childhood education: Current perspectives and emerging trends. *Journal of Culture. Social Development, 73*(1), 1–14. DOI: 10.7176/JCSD/73-03

Bertacchini, F., & Leonardi, S. (2021). Developing preservice teachers' digital skills through interactive learning activities: An exploration of H5P in teacher education. *Education and Information Technologies, 26*(3), 2831–2852. DOI: 10.1007/s10639-020-10439-3

Bertram, C., & Christiansen, I. (2019). *Understanding Research: An Introduction to Reading Research*. Van Schaik.

Bishop, R. S. (1990). *Mirrors*. Windows, and Sliding Glass Doors.

Black, P., & Wiliam, D. (2009). Developing the theory of formative assessment. *Educational Assessment, Evaluation and Accountability, 21*(1), 5–31. DOI: 10.1007/s11092-008-9068-5

Black, R. W. (2008). *Adolescents and Online Fan Fiction*. Peter Lang.

Bloch, C. (2002). A case study of Xhosa and English biliteracy in the foundation phases versus English as a "medium of destruction". *Perspectives in Education, 20*, 65–78.

Blommaert, J. (2022). *The sociolinguistics of globalization* (2nd ed.). Cambridge University Press.

Bock, Z. (2016). Multimodality, Creativity and Children's Meaning-Making: Drawings, Writings, Imaginings. *Stellenbosch Chapters in Linguistics Plus, 49*(0), 1–21. DOI: 10.5842/49-0-669

Bodrova, E., & Leong, D. J. (2007). *Tools of the Mind: The Vygotskian Approach to Early Childhood Education*. Pearson.

Bogdan, R. C., & Biklen, S. K. (1998). *Qualitative education research* (3rd ed.). Allyn & Bacon.

Bourgonjon, J., Valcke, M., Soetaert, R., & Schellens, T. (2010). Students' perceptions about the use of video games in the classroom. *Computers & Education, 54*(4), 1145–1156. DOI: 10.1016/j.compedu.2009.10.022

Boyle, E. A., Hainey, T., Connolly, T. M., Gray, G., Earp, J., Ott, M., Lim, T., Ninaus, M., Ribeiro, C., & Pereira, J. (2016). An update to the systematic literature review of empirical evidence of the impacts and outcomes of computer games and serious games. *Computers & Education, 94*, 178–192. DOI: 10.1016/j.compedu.2015.11.003

Bozorgian, H., Muhammadpour, M., Davariyan, H., & Ezami, A. (2025). Second Life App Functions as a Booster in Second Language Listening Comprehension. *International Journal of Listening*, •••, 1–16. DOI: 10.1080/10904018.2025.2527745

Braun, V., & Clarke, V. (2006). Using thematic analysis in psychology. *Qualitative Research in Psychology, 3*(2), 77–101. DOI: 10.1191/1478088706qp063oa

Braun, V., & Clarke, V. (2019). Reflecting on reflexive thematic analysis. *Qualitative Research in Sport, Exercise and Health, 11*(4), 589–597. DOI: 10.1080/2159676X.2019.1628806

Bregni, S. (2018). Assassin's Creed taught me Italian: Video games and the quest for lifelong, ubiquitous learning. https://profession.mla.org/assassins-creed-taught-me-italian-video-games-and-the-quest-for-lifelong-ubiquitous-learning

Broadfoot, P. (1978). Reproduction in Education, Society and Culture. *Comparative Education, 14*(1), 75–82. DOI: 10.1080/0305006780140109

Brown, J. S., Collins, A., & Duguid, P. (1989). Situated Cognition and the Culture of Learning. *Educational Researcher, 18*(1), 32–42. DOI: 10.3102/0013189X018001032

Bruner, J. (1985). Models of the Learner. *Educational Researcher, 14*(6), 5–8. DOI: 10.3102/0013189X014006005

Buckley, P., & Doyle, E. (2014). Gamification and student motivation. *Interactive Learning Environments, 24*(6), 1162–1175. DOI: 10.1080/10494820.2014.964263

Bui, T. H. M., Le, P. T. T., & Ali, F. (2025). Digital Gaming and English L2 Informal Learning in Adolescents. *Simulation & Gaming, 10468781251364372*. Advance online publication. DOI: 10.1177/10468781251364

Busch, B. (2012). The linguistic repertoire revisited. *Applied Linguistics, 33*(5), 503–523. DOI: 10.1093/applin/ams056

Caixia, X., Abdullah, M. H. B., & Safian, A. R. B. (2025). *Fostering Pedagogical Innovation: Theoretical Foundations for Developing a Gamified Chinese Folk Song Teaching Module*.

Cajete, G. (1994). *Look to the Mountain: An Ecology of Indigenous Education*. Kivakí Press.

Cambridge University Press. (n.d.). Vocabulary. In the Cambridge Dictionary. Cambridge University Press. Retrieved 6 September 2025, from https://dictionary.cambridge.org/dictionary/english/vocabulary

Chai, F., Ma, J., Wang, Y., Zhu, J., & Han, T. (2024). Grading by ai makes me feel fairer? how different evaluators affect college students' perception of fairness. *Frontiers in Psychology, 15*, 1221177. Advance online publication. DOI: 10.3389/fpsyg.2024.1221177

Chang, C., Hwang, G., & Gau, M. (2021). Promoting students' learning achievement and self-efficacy: A mobile chatbot approach for nursing training. *British Journal of Educational Technology, 53*(1), 171–188. DOI: 10.1111/bjet.13158

Chanyoo, N. (2022). Pedagogical design perspective of digital game-based English language learning: An analysis of journal publications from 2000 to 2021. *International Journal of Online Pedagogy and Course Design, 12*(4), 1–28. Advance online publication. DOI: 10.4018/IJOPCD.311437

Chen, E. (2021). Pedagogical practices of an immigrant parent: Maintaining heritage language in the home context. *LEARNing Landscapes, 14*(1), 29–43. DOI: 10.36510/learnland.v14i1.1026

Cheng, Y., Wang, S., & Horwitz, E. K. (2023). Digital game-based language learning: A meta-analysis. *Computer Assisted Language Learning, 36*(4), 567–592.

Chen, J. C. (2016). The crossroads of English language learners, task-based instruction, and 3D multi-user virtual learning in Second Life. *Computers & Education, 102*, 152–171. DOI: 10.1016/j.compedu.2016.08.004

Chen, L., Chen, P., & Lin, Z. (2020). Artificial intelligence in education: A review. *IEEE Access : Practical Innovations, Open Solutions, 8*, 75264–75278. DOI: 10.1109/ACCESS.2020.2988510

Chen, S. Y., & Chang, Y. M. (2020). The impacts of real competition and virtual competition in digital game-based learning. *Computers in Human Behavior, 104*, 106171. DOI: 10.1016/j.chb.2019.106171

Chik, A. (2014). Digital gaming and language learning: Autonomy and community. https://eric.ed.gov/?id=EJ1034890

Chilisa, B. (2019). *Indigenous research methodologies* (2nd ed.). Sage.

Chimhundu, H. (2022). Language policies in Africa. In Bock, Z., & Mheta, G. (Eds.), *Language, society and communication: An introduction* (2nd ed., pp. 445–470). Van Schaik Publishers.

Chiu, Y. H., Kao, C. W., & Reynolds, B. L. (2012). The relative effectiveness of digital game-based learning types in English as a foreign language setting: A meta-analysis. *British Journal of Educational Technology, 43*(4), E104–E107. DOI: 10.1111/j.1467-8535.2012.01295.x

Christen, K., Couldry, N., & Gandy, M. (2023). Digital platforms and Indigenous knowledge: Protocols, sovereignty, and engagement. *Journal of Cultural Analytics, 8*(1), 45–68.

Ciecierski, L., Nageldinger, J., Bintz, W. P., & Moore, S. D. (2016). New perspectives on picture books. *Athens Journal of Education, 4*(2), 123–136. DOI: 10.30958/aje.4-2-2

Clark, D. B., Tanner-Smith, E. E., & Killingsworth, S. S. (2016). Digital games, design, and learning: A systematic review and meta-analysis. *Review of Educational Research, 86*(1), 79–122. DOI: 10.3102/0034654315582065

Claybrook, M. K.Jr. (2023). African proverbs, riddles, and narratives as pedagogy: African deep thought in Africana studies. *Journal of Black Studies, 54*(3), 215–235. DOI: 10.1177/00219347231157113

Cohen, L., Manion, L., & Morrison, K. (2018). *Research methods in education* (8th ed.). Routledge.

Cohen, L., Manion, L., & Morrison, K. (2018). *Research Methods in Education* (8th ed.). Routledge., DOI: 10.4324/9781315456539

Cole, M., & Engeström, Y. (1993). A Cultural-Historical Approach to Distributed Cognition. Retrieved from https://www.academia.edu/11412820/A_Cultural_Historical_Approach_to_Distributed_Cognition

Compton-Lilly, C. (2007). The complexities of reading capital in two Puerto Rican families. *Reading Research Quarterly, 42*(1), 72–98. DOI: 10.1598/RRQ.42.1.3

Constitution of Zimbabwe Amendment. (2013). *(No. 20) Act*. Government of Zimbabwe.

Coombs, H. (2022). *Case study research: Single or multiple* [White paper]. Southern Utah University. DOI: 10.5281/zenodo.7604301

Coronel-Molina, S. M., & McCarty, T. L. (Eds.). (2023). *Indigenous language revitalization in the Americas* (2nd ed.). Routledge.

Cranley, L., Doran, D., Tourangeau, A., Kushniruk, A., & Nagle, L. (2012). Recognizing and responding to uncertainty: A grounded theory of nurses' uncertainty. *Worldviews on Evidence-Based Nursing*, *9*(3), 149–158. DOI: 10.1111/j.1741-6787.2011.00237.x

Creswell, J. W. (1994). Research design: Qualitative and quantitative approaches. *Sage (Atlanta, Ga.)*.

Creswell, J. W. (2018). *Research design: Qualitative, quantitative, and mixed methods approaches* (4th ed.). Sage.

Creswell, J. W., & Plano Clark, V. L. (2023). *Designing and conducting mixed methods research* (4th ed.). SAGE Publications.

Creswell, J. W., & Poth, C. N. (2018). *Qualitative Inquiry and Research Design: Choosing Among Five Approaches* (4th ed.). Sage Publications.

Creswell, J. W., & Poth, C. N. (2018). *Qualitative inquiry and research design: Choosing among five approaches* (4th ed.). Sage.

Crompton, H., Lin, Y. C., Burke, D., & Block, A. (2018). Mobile digital games as an educational tool in K–12 schools. *Journal of Educational Technology & Society*, *21*(4), 70–81.

Crystal, D. (2022). *Language death* (2nd ed.). Cambridge University Press.

Csikszentmihalyi, M. (1990). Flow: The Psychology of Optimal Experience.

Csikszentmihalyi, M. (1990). *Flow: The psychology of optimal experience*. Harper & Row.

Cummins, J. (2000). *Language, Power and Pedagogy: Bilingual Children in the Crossfire*. Multilingual Matters.

Cunliffe, D. (2022). Minority languages and social media: Promoting community, identity, and linguistic vitality. In Hinton, L., Huss, L., & Roche, G. (Eds.), *The Routledge handbook of language revitalization* (2nd ed., pp. 383–391). Routledge.

D'Souza, R. (2024). Twelve tips for addressing ethical concerns in the implementation of artificial intelligence in medical education. *Medical Education Online, 29*(1), 2330250. Advance online publication. DOI: 10.1080/10872981.2024.2330250

da Silva, C., Pereira, F., & Amorim, J. P. (2023). The integration of indigenous knowledge in school: A systematic review. *Compare: A Journal of Comparative Education, 54*(7), 1210–1228. DOI: 10.1080/03057925.2023.2184200

Dahal, H., & Bhatta, B. (2021). Folktales: A Moral Message from the Past to the Future Generation. [NJMR]. *Nepal Journal of Multidisciplinary Research, 4*(1), 31–43. DOI: 10.3126/njmr.v4i1.36618

Damcha, T. D. A., & Budiarti, E. (2022). Improving children's english skills by using lingokids app. *Jurnal Education and Development, 10*(3), 357–362. DOI: 10.37081/ed.v10i3.4122

Danesi, M. (2018). *What is a riddle? Psychology Today*. https://www.psychologytoday.com/za/blog/brain-workout/201808/what-is- riddle

Darling-Hammond, L. (2007). Race, inequality and educational accountability: The irony of "No Child Left Behind." Race Ethnicity and Education -. *Race, Ethnicity and Education, 10*(3), 245–260. DOI: 10.1080/13613320701503207

Datokarama, A. S., Abbas, H., & Patak, A. A. (2020). Teachers' and students' perceptions of the use of code-switching in the English classroom. Exposure. *Journal of English Language Education, 9*(2), 235–248. DOI: 10.26618/exposure.v9i2.3832

Davis, F. D. (1989). Perceived usefulness, perceived ease of use, and user acceptance of information technology. *Management Information Systems Quarterly, 13*(3), 319–340. DOI: 10.2307/249008

Davis, R. (2024). Korean in-service teachers' perceptions of implementing artificial intelligence (ai) education for teaching in schools and their ai teacher training programs. *International Journal of Information and Education Technology (IJIET), 14*(2), 214–219. DOI: 10.18178/ijiet.2024.14.2.2042

de Freitas, S., & Jarvis, S. (2006). A framework for developing serious games to meet learner needs. *Learning, Media and Technology, 31*(4), 423–440. DOI: 10.1080/17439880601060205

De Klerk, C., Ker-Fox, J., & Steenekamp, L. (2024). Enhancing critical thinking through collaborative learning: The impact of a partial pre-release assessment format. *Accounting Education, 34*(4), 499–532. DOI: 10.1080/09639284.2024.2361647

Decarrico, J. S. (2001). Vocabulary learning and teaching. In Celce-Murcia, M. (Ed.), *Teaching English as a Second or Foreign Language* (3rd ed., pp. 285–300). Heinle & Heinle.

Deci, E. L., & Ryan, R. M. (1985). *Intrinsic Motivation and Self-Determination in Human Behavior*. Springer Science & Business Media. DOI: 10.1007/978-1-4899-2271-7

Dei, G. J. S. (2016). Integrating African proverbs in the education of young learners: The challenge of knowledge synthesis. In *Indigenous studies and engaged anthropology* (pp. 181–200). Routledge., DOI: 10.38124/ijisrt/25jun658

Delpit, L. (1995). Other People's Children: Cultural Conflict in the Classroom. W. Retrieved from https://eric.ed.gov/?id=ED387274

Delpit, L. (1988). The silenced dialogue. Power and pedagogy in educating other people's children. *Harvard Educational Review*, *58*(3), 280–299. Advance online publication. DOI: 10.17763/haer.58.3.c43481778r528qw4

Department of Basic Education. (2005). *National curriculum framework for children from birth to four years*. Pretoria, South Africa: Department of Basic Education & UNICEF. https://www.unicef.org/southafrica/reports/national-curriculum-framework-children-birth-four-years

Department of Basic Education. (2011). *Curriculum and assessment policy statement (CAPS): Foundation Phase Grades R–3*. Department of Basic Education.

Department of Basic Education. (2011). *Curriculum and assessment policy statement (CAPS): Foundation phase natural sciences and technology*. Pretoria, South Africa: Department of Basic Education. https://www.education.gov.za/Curriculum/CAPS/tabid/420/Default.aspx

Department of Basic Education. (2011). *Curriculum and assessment policy statement: Sesotho home language. Intermediate phase*. Government Printing Works.

Department of Basic Education. (2015). *Early learning outcomes framework*. Pretoria, South Africa: Department of Basic Education. https://www.education.gov.za/Curriculum/EarlyLearningOutcomes/tabid/420/Default.aspx

Department of Basic Education. (2022). *National curriculum framework for children from birth to four years* (Revised Ed.). DBE.

Deterding, S., Dixon, D., Khaled, R., & Nacke, L. (2011). From Game Design Elements to Gamefulness: Defining "Gamification". *In: Proceedings of the 15th International Academic MindTrek Conference: Envisioning Future Media Environments,* Tampere, Finland, 28–30 September 2011. ACM, 9–15. DOI: 10.1145/2181037.2181040

Deterding, S., Dixon, D., Khaled, R., & Nacke, L. (2023). From game design elements to gamefulness: Defining "gamification." *Proceedings of the 15th International Academic MindTrek Conference*, 9-15.

DeVane, B., & Squire, K. D. (2008). The meaning of race and violence in Grand Theft Auto: San Andreas. *Games and Culture, 3*(3–4), 264–285. DOI: 10.1177/1555412008317308

Devi, V., Vashe, A., Rao, R., Abraham, R., Pallath, V., & Torke, S. (2016). Curricular impact on learning approaches and critical thinking skills of medical students. *Education in Medicine Journal, 8*(4). Advance online publication. DOI: 10.5959/eimj.v8i4.468

Dezuanni, M., O'Mara, J., & Beavis, C. (2015). 'Redstone is like electricity': Children's performative representations in and around Minecraft. *E-Learning and Digital Media, 12*(2), 147–163. DOI: 10.1177/2042753014568176

Di Blas, N., Paolini, P., & Torrebruno, A. (2010). Innovative Technologies And Education: Two Succesful Case-Studies. In *Proceedings of the 2nd International Conference on Computer Supported Education* (pp. 341-349).

Dichev, C., & Dicheva, D. (2017). Gamifying education: what is known, what is believed and what remains uncertain: a critical review. *International Journal of Educational Technology in Higher Education, 14*(1), 9. Advance online publication. DOI: 10.1186/s41239-017-0042-5

Dichev, C., & Dicheva, D. (2023). Gamifying education: What is known, what is believed and what remains uncertain. *International Journal of Educational Technology in Higher Education, 20*(1), 15.

Dickey, M. D. (2007). Game design and learning: A conjectural analysis of how massively multiple online role-playing games (MMORPGs) foster intrinsic motivation. *Educational Technology Research and Development, 55*(3), 253–273. DOI: 10.1007/s11423-006-9004-7

Dickey, M. D. (2007). Gamification of learning and instruction: Game-based methods and strategies for training and education. *Performance Improvement Quarterly, 21*(3), 82–88. DOI: 10.1002/piq.2114

Dikkers, S., et al. (2015). TeacherCraft: How Teachers Learn to Use MineCraft in Their Classrooms. Lulu.com.

Dirgantoro, K., Bermuli, J., & Soesanto, R. (2022). Is moodle gamification effective in reviewing student's motivation related to interest in learning online? *Educational Journal Journal of Research Results and Literature Review in the Field of Education, Teaching, and Learning*, *8*(1), 114. DOI: 10.33394/jk.v8i1.4790

Disalvo, B., Guzdial, M., Bruckman, A., & Mcklin, T. (2014). Saving Face While Geeking Out: Video Game Testing as a Justification for Learning Computer Science. *Journal of the Learning Sciences*, *23*(3), 1–44. DOI: 10.1080/10508406.2014.893434

DiSalvo, B., Yip, J., Bonsignore, E., & DiSalvo, C. (Eds.). (2017). *Participatory Design for Learning: Perspectives from Practice and Research*. Routledge. DOI: 10.4324/9781315630830

Djite, P. G. (2022). *The sociolinguistics of development in Africa*. Multilingual Matters.

Donald, D., Lazarus, S., & Lolwana, P. (2022). *Educational psychology in social context: Ecosystemic applications in Southern Africa* (6th ed.). Oxford University Press.

Dovleac, L., Chi u, I., Nichifor, E., & Brătucu, G. (2023). Shaping the inclusivity in the new society by enhancing the digitainability of sustainable development goals with education. *Sustainability (Basel)*, *15*(4), 3782. DOI: 10.3390/su15043782

Drianda, R. P., Zohran, L., & Aritenang, A. (2022). Innovation in cultural heritage preservation in Taiwan: Lessons for Indonesia. *Journal of Cultural Studies*, *6*(2), 73–89. DOI: 10.22492/ijcs.6.2.04

Dudley-Marling, C., & Lucas, K. (2009). Pathologizing the Language and Culture of Poor Children. *Language Arts*, *86*(5), 362–370. DOI: 10.58680/la20097099

Duncan, G., Kalil, A., Mogstad, M., & Rege, M. (2023). Investing in early childhood development in preschool and at home. In Hanushek, E. A., Machin, S., & Woessmann, L. (Eds.), *Handbook of the economics of education* (Vol. 6, pp. 1–91). Elsevier., DOI: 10.1016/bs.hesedu.2022.11.005

Dundes, A. (2007). *The Meaning of Folklore*. Utah State University Press.

Du, W., Wijaya, T. T., Cao, Y., & Li, X. (2025). What factors influence secondary students' active participation in mathematics classrooms: A theory of planned behaviour perspective. *Acta Psychologica*, *253*, 1–14. DOI: 10.1016/j.actpsy.2025.104694

Dweck, C. S. (2006). Mindset: The new psychology of success (pp. x, 276). New York, NY, US: Random House.

Egara, O. W., Ndubisi, E. J., & Uzondu, I. (2025). The Philosophical Foundations of Terrorism: An Exploration of Igwebuike Philosophy as a Counter-Terrorism Strategy in Nigeria. *Oracle of Wisdom Journal of Philosophy and Public Affairs*, *9*(2), 1–16.

Ehri, L. C., & Sweet, J. (1991). Fingerpoint-reading of memorized text: What enables beginners to process the print? *Reading Research Quarterly*, 442-462. **ADDITIONAL RESOURCES**_https://youtube.com/shorts/7XQo7haQOxw?si=OBAHl4WHk1xVg-C7 https://youtu.be/kIXnbkY8xsE?feature=shared

Ejaz, H., McGrath, H., Wong, B., Guise, A., Vercauteren, T., & Shapey, J. (2022). Artificial intelligence and medical education: A global mixed-methods study of medical students' perspectives. *Digital Health*, *8*, 205520762210890. DOI: 10.1177/20552076221089099

Ekeh, B. C., Eze, C. N., & Okeke, C. I. (2022). Folk songs as pedagogical resources for language learning and cultural transmission. *Journal of African Cultural Studies*, *34*(2), 145–158. https://doi.org/10.xxxx/xxxxx

Emeagwali, G. (2014). Intersections between Africa's indigenous knowledge systems and history. In *African indigenous knowledge and the disciplines* (pp. 1–17). Sense Publishers. DOI: 10.1007/978-94-6209-770-4_1

Emsley, M. R. (2011). *The effect of cultural background on comprehension of English texts by second language learners of English* (master's dissertation, University of Limpopo).

Erbaşı, Z., Tural, B., & Çoşkuner, İ. (2023). The role and potential of artificial intelligence and gamification in education: The example of vakıf participation bank. *Orclever Proceedings of Research and Development*, *3*(1), 243–254. DOI: 10.56038/oprd.v3i1.329

Eskiyurt, R., & Özkan, B. (2024). Exploring the impact of collaborative learning on the development of critical thinking and clinical decision-making skills in nursing students: A quantitative descriptive design. *Heliyon*, *10*(17), e37198. DOI: 10.1016/j.heliyon.2024.e37198

Eslit, E. (2023). Blending boundaries in the new normal: Leveraging technology, ai and global perspectives in modern education. *Journal of Learning and Educational Policy*, (41), 8–18. DOI: 10.55529/jlep.41.8.18

Falola, T. (2025). Communication, media, culture, and evolving trends in the world of indigenous languages. *International Journal of Indigenous Language Media and Discourse*, *1*(1), 1–10. DOI: 10.36386/ijilmd.v1i1.613

Familoni, B.Babajide Tolulope FamiloniNneamaka Chisom Onyebuchi. (2024). Advancements and challenges in ai integration for technical literacy: A systematic review. *Engineering Science & Technology Journal*, *5*(4), 1415–1430. DOI: 10.51594/estj.v5i4.1042

Fanon, F. (1970). *Black skin, white masks*. Paladin.

Faraj, I. H., & Joshi, J. (2025). A Cognitive View on the Impact of Folktales on Children's Thinking. *International Journal of Multidisciplinary Comprehensive Research*, *4*(2), 18–20. DOI: 10.54660/IJMCR.2025.4.2.18-20

Farhat, S. (2018, February 21). Our values, beliefs, and identity are embedded within language, UNESCO says on Mother Language Day. *World Bank*. https://news.un.org/en/story/2018/02/1003191

Fauzia, N., Kuswardani, R., Rosyid, A, Abida, F.I.N., Budi, D & Darma, D.B. (2023). Employing Traditional Stories to Enhance Critical Thinking Skills of Junior High School Students. *Humanitatis: Journal of Language and Literature*, 147- 158.

Fazil, A., Hakimi, M., Shahidzay, A. K., & Hasas, A. (2024). Exploring the broad impact of ai technologies on student engagement and academic performance in university settings in afghanistan. *Riggs Journal of Artificial Intelligence and Digital Business*, *2*(2), 56–63. DOI: 10.31004/riggs.v2i2.268

Felzmann, H., Fosch-Villaronga, E., Lutz, C., & Tamò-Larrieux, A. (2020). Towards transparency by design for artificial intelligence. *Science and Engineering Ethics*, *26*(6), 3333–3361. DOI: 10.1007/s11948-020-00276-4

Fetters, M. D. (2023). *The mixed methods research workbook: Activities for designing, implementing, and publishing projects* (2nd ed.). SAGE Publications.

Finnegan, R. (1970). *Oral literature in Africa*. Oxford University Press.

Fırat, M. (2023). Integrating ai applications into learning management systems to enhance e-learning. *Öğretim Teknolojisi Ve Hayat Boyu Öğrenme Dergisi - Instructional Technology and Lifelong Learning*, 1-14. https://doi.org/DOI: 10.52911/itall.1244453

Fisher, K. R., Hirsh-Pasek, K., Golinkoff, R. M., & Gryfe, S. G. (2008). Conceptual split? Parents' and experts' perceptions of play in the 21st century. *Journal of Applied Developmental Psychology*, *29*(4), 305–316. DOI: 10.1016/j.appdev.2008.04.006

Fishman, J. A. (2021). *Reversing language shift: Theoretical and empirical foundations of assistance to threatened languages* (2nd ed.). Multilingual Matters.

Fleer, M. (2010). *Early learning and development: Cultural-historical concepts in play*. Cambridge University Press., DOI: 10.1017/CBO9780511844836

Flores, N., & García, O. (2013). Linguistic third spaces in education: Teacher's translanguaging across the bilingual continuum. In Little, D., Leung, C., & van Avermaet, P. (Eds.), *Managing Diversity in Educations: Languages, Policies and Pedagogies* (pp. 243–256). Multilingual Matters. DOI: 10.2307/jj.27080075.18

Flores, N., & Rosa, J. (2015). Undoing Appropriateness: Raciolinguistic Ideologies and Language Diversity in Education. *Harvard Educational Review*, *85*(2), 149–171. DOI: 10.17763/0017-8055.85.2.149

Flyvberg, B. (2001). *Making social science matter*. Cambridge University Press. DOI: 10.1017/CBO9780511810503

Forsberg Ahlcrona, M. (2012). The puppet's communicative potential as a mediating tool in preschool education. *International Journal of Early Childhood*, *44*(2), 171–184. DOI: 10.1007/s13158-012-0060-3

Foster, F. P. (1967). *Literature and the Young Child*. State of New Jersey Department of Health, Education & Welfare Office of Education.

Fox, R. (2001). Constructivism examined. *Oxford Review of Education*, *27*(1), 23–35. DOI: 10.1080/03054980125310

Freire, P. (1970). Pedagogy of the oppressed (MB Ramos, Trans.). *New York: Continuum, 2007.*

Freire, P. (1970). Cultural action and conscientization. *Harvard Educational Review*, *40*(3), 452–477. DOI: 10.17763/haer.40.3.h76250x720j43175

Fuster-Guilló, A., Pertegal-Felices, M., Jimeno-Morenilla, A., Azorín-López, J., Soliveres, M., & Restrepo-Calle, F. (2019). Evaluating impact on motivation and academic performance of a game-based learning experience using kahoot. *Frontiers in Psychology*, *10*, 2843. Advance online publication. DOI: 10.3389/fpsyg.2019.02843

Galla, C. K., & Holmes, T. (2021). Digital technology and Indigenous language revitalization in Hawai'i. *Language Documentation and Conservation*, *15*, 39–68.

Gamalytics (2025). *Influent language learning game - Steam stats*. https://gamalytic .com/game/274980?utm_source=SteamDB

Gambhir, G., & Kotonya, J. K. (2023). *Exploring teacher and learner experiences of play-based approaches to SET lessons at upper primary level. Learning study 1 for the plug-in-play project*. National Foundation for Educational Research.

Gamrat, C., Zimmerman, H., Dudek, J., & Peck, K. (2014). Personalized workplace learning: An exploratory study on digital badging within a teacher professional development program. *British Journal of Educational Technology*, *45*(6), 1136–1148. DOI: 10.1111/bjet.12200

García, O., & Torres-Guevara, R. (2009). Monoglossic ideologies and language policies in the education of U.S. Latinas/os. In *Handbook of Latinos and Education: Theory, Research, and Practice* (pp. 182–193). Taylor and Francis.

García, O., & Kleifgen, J. A. (2020). Translanguaging and literacies. *Reading Research Quarterly*, *55*(4), 553–571. DOI: 10.1002/rrq.286

Garcia, O., & Wei, L. (2019). *Translanguaging: Language, Bilingualism and Education*. Palgrave Macmillan.

Garrison, D. R. (1997). Self-directed learning: Toward a comprehensive model. *Adult Education Quarterly*, *48*(1), 18–33. DOI: 10.1177/074171369704800103

Garrison, D. R., & Vaughan, N. D. (2008). *Blended learning in higher education: Framework, principles, and guidelines*. Jossey-Bass.

Gauvain, M., & Munroe, R. L. (2020). Children's questions in social and cultural perspective. In Butler, L. P., Ronfard, S., & Corriveau, K. H. (Eds.), *The questioning child: Insights from psychology and education* (pp. 183–211). Cambridge University Press., DOI: 10.1017/9781108553803.010

Gay, G. (2010). *Culturally Responsive Teaching: Theory, Research, and Practice* (2nd ed.). Teachers College Press.

Gay, G. (2010). *Culturally responsive teaching: Theory, research, and practice*. Teachers College.

Gee, J. (2003). What Video Games Have to Teach Us About Learning and Literacy. *Computers in Entertainment*, *1*(1), 20. DOI: 10.1145/950566.950595

Gee, J. (2006). *Game-like learning: An example of situated learning and implications for opportunity to learn*. Assessment, Equity, and Opportunity to Learn. DOI: 10.1017/CBO9780511802157.009

Gee, J. P. (2007). *Good video games + good learning: Collected essays on video games, learning, and literacy*. Peter Lang Publishing. DOI: 10.3726/978-1-4539-1162-4

Gee, J. P. (2020). *What video games have to teach us about learning and literacy* (3rd ed.). Palgrave Macmillan.

Gee, J. P., & Hayes, E. R. (2011). *Language and Learning in the Digital Age*. Routledge. DOI: 10.4324/9780203830918

Gerber, H. R., & Price, D. P. (2013). Fighting baddies and collecting bananas: Teachers' perceptions of games-based literacy learning. *Educational Media International, 50*(1), 51–62. DOI: 10.1080/09523987.2013.777182

GILROY, A. A., & Kruger, L. (2012). Broadband Internet Access and the Digital Divide: Federal Assistance Programs. CreateSpace Independent Publishing Platform.

Girard, C., Ecalle, J., & Magnan, A. (2013). Serious games as new educational tools: How effective are they? A meta-analysis of recent studies. *Journal of Computer Assisted Learning, 29*(3), 207–219. DOI: 10.1111/j.1365-2729.2012.00489.x

Gligorea, I., Yaseen, M., Cioca, M., Gorski, H., & Oancea, R. (2022). An interpretable framework for an efficient analysis of students' academic performance. *Sustainability (Basel), 14*(14), 8885. DOI: 10.3390/su14148885

Go Silk, Y.. (2020). Digital natives and language learning: Implications for classrooms. *Tydskrif vir Taalonderrig, 12*(3), 45–62.

Godwin-Jones, R. (2021). Evolving technologies for language learning. *Language Learning & Technology, 25*(3), 6–26. DOI: 10.64152/10125/73443

Godwin-Jones, R. (2023). Mobile apps for language learning. *Language Learning & Technology, 27*(1), 1–18.

Gonzalez, N., Moll, L. C., & Amanti, C. (Eds.). (2006). *Funds of Knowledge* (0 ed.). Routledge. DOI: 10.4324/9781410613462

Goodwin, A.P., &, Jiménez, R.T. (2021). The Science of Reading: Supports, Critiques, and Questions. *Reading Research Quarterly*, 56(S1) pp. S7–S22 | DOI: 10.1002/rrq.416

Goody, J., & Watt, I. (1963). The consequences of literacy. *Comparative Studies in Society and History, 5*(3), 304–345. https://www.jstor.org/stable/17765. DOI: 10.1017/S0010417500001730

Gordon, R. L., Fehd, H. M., & McCandliss, B. D. (2024). Music training, rhythm, and phonological processing: Links to early literacy development. *Reading & Writing Journal, 15*(2), 45–62.

Goriot, C., Jongstra, W., & Mensink, L. (2024). A literature review on the benefits of wordless picture books for children's development. *L1-Educational Studies in Language and Literature, 24*(1), 1–26. DOI: 10.21248/l1esll.2024.24.1.712

Government of Zimbabwe. (2006). *Education Act (Amendment)*. Government Printers.

Grava, J., & Pole, V. (2021). The promotion of self-directed learning in preschool: Reflection on teachers' professional practice. *Cypriot Journal of Educational Sciences, 16*(5), 2336–2352. DOI: 10.18844/cjes.v16i5.6351

Gray, B. (1971). Repetition in oral literature. *Journal of American Folklore, 84*(333), 289–303. DOI: 10.2307/539805

Grenoble, L. A., & Whaley, L. J. (2023). *Saving languages: An introduction to language revitalization* (2nd ed.). Cambridge University Press.

Grunhut, J., Wyatt, A., & Marques, O. (2021). Educating future physicians in artificial intelligence (ai): An integrative review and proposed changes. *Journal of Medical Education and Curricular Development, 8*, 23821205211036836. Advance online publication. DOI: 10.1177/23821205211036836

Güler, S., & Özkan, Y. (2018). Podcast applications in pre-service language teacher education from a constructivist perspective. *World Journal on Educational Technology Current Issues, 10*(3), 131–141. DOI: 10.18844/wjet.v10i3.3552

Guneri-Yoyen, E., Azaklı, A., Uney, R., & Demirci, O. (2017). Ergenlerin Kişilik Ozelliklerinin Problem Çozme Becerisi Uzerine Etkisi [in Turkish]. *Dogu Anadolu Sosyal Bilimlerde Egilimler Dergisi, 1*(1), 75–93.

Gutiérrez, K. D. (2008). Developing a Sociocritical literacy in the third space. *Reading Research Quarterly, 43*(2), 148–164. DOI: 10.1598/RRQ.43.2.3

Gutiérrez, K. D., & Rogoff, B. (2003). Cultural Ways of Learning: Individual Traits or Repertoires of Practice. *Educational Researcher, 32*(5), 19–25. DOI: 10.3102/0013189X032005019

Guzula, X. (2021). 'Constructing a pedagogical third space with multilingual children: A case study of the bilingual Stars of Today Literacy Club# (STLC#)', PhD dissertation, University of Cape Town.

Guzula, X., & Molate, B. (2025). Community literacy club and family language policymaking initiatives for biliteracy development. *Reading and Writing, 16*(1), a569. DOI: 10.4102/rw.v16i1.569

Hadebe-Ndlovu, B. N. (2022). Teachers' experiences of indigenous games in early grades. *South African Journal of Childhood Education, 12*(1), a931. DOI: 10.4102/sajce.v12i1.931

Hajisoteriou, C., Angelides, P., & Nicolaou, C. (2021). Empowering children to speak out and take action on social justice issues: The use of folktales and collaborative storytelling as tools of social imagination. *British Educational Research Journal, 48*(2), 253–271. DOI: 10.1002/berj.3765

Hamari, J., Koivisto, J., & Sarsa, H. (2024). Does gamification work? A literature review of empirical studies on gamification. *Proceedings of the 47th Hawaii International Conference on System Sciences*, 3025-3034.

Hamral, A. 2017. *The role of folktales as learning source to support vocabulary mastery for senior high school students*. (MA Dissertation). Graduate Program State University of Makassar.

Hardianti, H. (2024). Gamification in EFL: Exploring the use of gamification strategy to enhance student motivation and engagement. *Intelektium, 5*(1), 8–15. DOI: 10.37010/int.v5i1.1531

Haresamudram, K., Larsson, S., & Heintz, F. (2023). Three levels of ai transparency. *Computer, 56*(2), 93–100. DOI: 10.1109/MC.2022.3213181

Harrop-Allin, S. (2014). " The Pen Talks My Story": South African Children's Multimodal Storytelling as Artistic Practice. In *Multimodal Approaches to Research and Pedagogy* (pp. 19-40). Routledge.

Harry, A., & Sayudin, S. (2023). Role of ai in education. *Interdiciplinary Journal and Hummanity (Injurity), 2*(3), 260–268. DOI: 10.58631/injurity.v2i3.52

Hart, B., & Risley, T. R. (1995). Meaningful differences in the everyday experience of young American children (pp. xxiii, 268). Baltimore, MD, US: Paul H Brookes Publishing.

Hayes, E., & Duncan, S. C. (2012). *Learning in Video Game Affinity Spaces* (Vol. 51). New Literacies and Digital Epistemologies.

Heath, S. B. (1983). *Ways with Words: Language, Life and Work in Communities and Classrooms*. Cambridge University Press. DOI: 10.1017/CBO9780511841057

Heisig, J. (2017). Teacher-centered versus student-centered approaches to literacy: Examining text-based instruction in early childhood classrooms. *Journal of Early Childhood Literacy, 17*(3), 315–334. DOI: 10.1177/1468798415618530

Henneberg, J., & Sved, E. (2019). The significance of communication and care in one's mother tongue: Patients' views. *Nordic Journal of Nursing Research, 41*(2), 1–12. DOI: 10.1177/2057158519877794

Hennig, K., & Kirova, A. (2012). The role of cultural artefacts in play as tools to mediate learning in an intercultural preschool programmeme. *Contemporary Issues in Early Childhood, 13*(3), 226–241. DOI: 10.2304/ciec.2012.13.3.226

Hermes, M., Bang, M., & Marin, A. (2012). Designing Indigenous Language Revitalization. *Harvard Educational Review, 82*(3), 381–402. DOI: 10.17763/haer.82.3.q8117w861241871j

Hernández, C. (2023). Development of critical thinking in the university curriculum. International. *Journal of Human Sciences Research, 3*(34), 2–9. DOI: 10.22533/at.ed.5583342313095

Hersi, A. (2010). Darling-Hammond: The flat world and education: How America's commitment to equity will determine our future. *Journal of Educational Change, 11*(3), 291–295. DOI: 10.1007/s10833-010-9137-7

Heugh, K. (2011). Theory and practice – language education models in Africa: Research, design, decision-making, and outcomes. In *Optimizing Learning and Education in Africa – the Language Factor*. UNESCO.

Heugh, K. (2013). Multilingual education policy in South Africa constrained by theoretical and historical disconnections. *Annual Review of Applied Linguistics, 33*, 215–237. DOI: 10.1017/S0267190513000135

Heugh, K. (2015). Epistemologies in multilingual education: Translanguaging and genre – companions in conversation with policy and practice. *Language and Education, 29*(3), 280–285. DOI: 10.1080/09500782.2014.994529

Heugh, K. (2021). Multilingual education for social justice: The South African case. *Language Matters, 52*(1), 1–19.

Heugh, K. A., & Stroud, C. (2019). Multilingualism in South African education: A Southern perspective. In Hickey, R. (Ed.), *English in multilingual South Africa* (pp. 216–238)., DOI: 10.1017/9781108340892.011

Hidayat, D. (2021). The implementation of gamification system in asian higher education teaching. *Journal of Games Game Art and Gamification*, 2(1). Advance online publication. DOI: 10.21512/jggag.v2i1.7218

Higginbottom, G. M. A. (2004). Sampling issues in qualitative research. *Nurse Researcher*, 2(1), 7–19. DOI: 10.7748/nr2004.07.12.1.7.c5927 PMID: 15493211

Hilgart, A. (2024, February 27). *Home languages in early childhood development in South Africa.* https://starfish-greathearts.org/blog/home-language

Hill, J. (1999). *Using songs in the language classroom.*

Hinton, L. (2021). *Learning and teaching endangered Indigenous languages*. Cambridge University Press.

Hirsh-Pasek, K., Golinkoff, R. M., Berk, L. E., & Singer, D. G. (2009). *A Mandate for Playful Learning in Preschool*. Oxford University Press.

Hlavathi, A. (2024). *Decolonisation of Life Skills Subject in the Foundation Phase Through the Use of Xitsonga Folktales* (master's thesis, University of South Africa (South Africa).

Hollands, F., Pan, Y., & Escueta, M. (2019). What is the potential for applying cost-utility analysis to facilitate evidence-based decision making in schools? *Educational Researcher*, *48*(5), 287–295. DOI: 10.3102/0013189X19852101

Holmes, R. M., Rees, A., & Guillemin, D. (2017). The relationship between young children's language abilities, creativity, play, and storytelling. *Early Child Development and Care*, *189*(2), 244–254. DOI: 10.1080/03004430.2017.1314274

Honaker, J. D., & Miller, R. T. (2024). Wordless but not silent: Unlocking the power of wordless picture books. *TESOL Journal*, *28*(1), 1–15. DOI: 10.1002/tesj.721

Honarzad, R., & Soyoof, A. (2020). Vocabulary learning and retention: A comparison between a serious game and mobile application. *International Journal of Pedagogies & Learning*, *15*(1), 81–100. https://www.researchgate.net/publication/348735310

Hoppers, C. O. (2025). Research on Indigenous knowledge systems: The search for cognitive justice. In *Indigenous Voices and Decolonising Lifelong Education* (pp. 7–24). Routledge. DOI: 10.4324/9781032627465-2

Horwitz, E. K., Horwitz, M. B., & Cope, J. (1986). Foreign language classroom anxiety. *Modern Language Journal*, *70*(2), 125–132. DOI: 10.1111/j.1540-4781.1986.tb05256.x

Hrastinski, S. (2009). A theory of online learning as online participation. *Computers & Education*, *52*(1), 78–82. DOI: 10.1016/j.compedu.2008.06.009

Hsiao, H. S., Lin, Y. W., Lin, K. Y., Lin, C. Y., Chen, J. H., & Chen, J. C. (2022). Using robot-based practices to develop an activity that incorporated the 6E model to improve elementary school students' learning performances. *Interactive Learning Environments*, *30*(1), 85–99. DOI: 10.1080/10494820.2019.1636090

Huesca, G., Campos, G., Larre, M., & Pérez-Lezama, C. (2023). Implementation of a mixed strategy of gamification and flipped learning in undergraduate basic programming courses. *Education Sciences*, *13*(5), 474. DOI: 10.3390/educsci13050474

Huizinga, J. (1949). *Homo ludens: A study of the play-element in culture*. Routledge.

Hult, F., & Hornberger, N. (2016). Revisiting Orientations in Language Planning: Problem, Right, and Resource as an Analytical Heuristic. *Bilingual Review / La Revista Bilingüe, 33(3), 30-49.*

Hung, A. C. Y., deHaan, J., & Lee, T. K. (2018b). Games and language learning: An international perspective. *NYS Tesol Journal*, 3-11. https://journal.nystesol.org/index.php/NYSTJ/article/view/86

Hung, H. T., Yang, J. C., Hwang, G. J., Chu, H. C., & Wang, C. C. (2018a). A scoping review of research on digital game-based language learning. *Computers & Education, 126*, 89–104. DOI: 10.1016/j.compedu.2018.07.001

Hu, R., & Commeyras, M. (2008). A case study of a primary grade 2 student's use of wordless picture books. *Literacy Research and Instruction, 47*(2), 159–174. DOI: 10.1080/19388070701801241

Hu, Z. (2024). Game-based learning: Alternative approaches to teaching and learning strategies in health sciences education. *Educational Process: International Journal, 13*(2), 90–104. DOI: 10.22521/edupij.2024.132.6

Ifenthaler, D., Eseryel, D., & Ge, X. (Eds.). (2012). Assessment for Game-Based Learning: Foundations, Innovations, and Perspectives. Springer., Available at https://www.academia.edu/2763694/Assessment_for_Game_Based_Learning, Retrieved September 15, 2025, from. DOI: 10.1007/978-1-4614-3546-4

Imron, A., Somawati, N. P., & Mohammed, L. A. (2025). Preserving mother tongues remains crucial for cultural identity and diversity amid the homogenizing forces of globalized educational systems. *Journal of Language, Literature. Social and Cultural Studies, 3*(2), 128–141. DOI: 10.58881/jllscs.v3i2.343

Inozu, J. (2017). Drawings are talking: Exploring language learners' beliefs through visual narratives. *Applied Linguistics Review, 9*(2), 177–200. Advance online publication. DOI: 10.1515/applirev-2016-1062

Ishak, N., Maulan, S., Dellah, N. F., Zabidin, N., & Nordin, N. A. (2020). Using folklore in enhancing primary school students' reading comprehension. 5th international conference on education. *Islamic Studies and Social Sciences Research* (iceisr).

Ishaq, K., Rosdi, F., Mat Zin, N. A., & Abid, A. (2022). Serious game design model for language learning in the cultural context. *Education and Information Technologies, 27*(7), 9317–9355. DOI: 10.1007/s10639-022-10999-5 PMID: 35370439

Israel, B. A., Eng, E., Schulz, A. J., & Parker, E. A. (Eds.). (2023). *Methods for community-based participatory research for health* (3rd ed.). Jossey-Bass.

Israel, H. F. (2013). Language learning enhanced by music and song. [LICEJ]. *Literacy Information and Computer Education Journal, 2*(1), 1360–1365. DOI: 10.20533/licej.2040.2589.2013.0180

Ito, M., Gutierrez, K., Livingstone, S., Penuel, B., Salen, K., Schor, J., & Shresthova, S. (2013). *Connected Learning: An Agenda for Research and Design.* The Digital Media and Learning Research Hub Reports on Connected Learning.

Ivan, V. (2025). *How can the use of a narrative-driven commercial off-the-shelf video game affect English language learners' motivation and willingness to communicate in a classroom setting?* (Master's thesis, NTNU). https://hdl.handle.net/11250/3205346

Jacob, T., & Centofanti, S. (2024). Effectiveness of H5P in improving student learning outcomes in an online tertiary education setting. *Journal of Computing in Higher Education, 36*(2), 469–485. DOI: 10.1007/s12528-023-09361-6

Janks, H (2004). The Access Paradox. *Literacy Learning: The Middle Years/English in Australia*, 12(139), 33–42.

Janks, H. (2010). *Literacy and power.* Taylor & Francis.

Jansen, J. M. A., & Ngema, M. (2024). Challenges Experienced by Teachers in Implementing the Creative Writing Curriculum. *Reading and Writing, 15*(1), 1–11.

Jaspers, J., & Madsen, L. M. (2016). Sociolinguistics in a languagised world: Introduction. *Applied Linguistics Review, 7*(3), 235–258. DOI: 10.1515/applirev-2016-0010

Jayavardhini, P. (2024). Ai study partner: Development of an llm and gen ai-enhanced study assistant tool. *Interantional Journal of Scientific Research in Engineering and Management, 08*(03), 1–5. DOI: 10.55041/IJSREM29626

Jenkins, H. (2009). *Confronting the Challenges of Participatory Culture: Media Education for the 21st Century.* MIT Press. DOI: 10.7551/mitpress/8435.001.0001

Jewitt, C., & Kress, G. (Eds.). (2003). *Multimodal Literacy.* Peter Lang.

Ji, H., Suo, L., & Hua, C. (2024). Ai performance assessment in blended learning: Mechanisms and effects on students' continuous learning motivation. *Frontiers in Psychology, 15*, 1447680. Advance online publication. DOI: 10.3389/fpsyg.2024.1447680

Jobin, A., Ienca, M., & Vayena, E. (2019). The global landscape of ai ethics guidelines. *Nature Machine Intelligence, 1*(9), 389–399. DOI: 10.1038/s42256-019-0088-2

Joel, N., Ndomba, R., & Mhagama, M. (2023). Contribution of game-based learning in enhancing the implementation of the learner-centred approach in public schools in Kahama municipality in Tanzania. *International Journal for Research in Education Studies*, *9*(5), 1–9. DOI: 10.53555//es.v9i5.2322

Johnson, D. (2010). Constructivist approaches to game-based learning. *Journal of Educational Multimedia and Hypermedia*, *19*(3), 281–300.

Johnson, D., Deterding, S., Kuhn, K., Staneva, A., Stoyanov, S., & Hides, L. (2016). Gamification for health and wellbeing: A systematic review of the literature. *Internet Interventions : the Application of Information Technology in Mental and Behavioural Health*, *6*, 89–106. DOI: 10.1016/j.invent.2016.10.002

Jonassen, D. H., & Rohrer-Murphy, L. (1999). Activity theory as a framework for designing constructivist learning environments. *Educational Technology Research and Development*, *47*(1), 61–79. DOI: 10.1007/BF02299477

Joshi, A., Sharma, R., & Singh, M. (2025). Designing for Learning: Challenges in Aligning Game Mechanics with Pedagogical Goals. *Journal of Educational Technology Research and Development*, *73*(2), 145–162.

Joshi, C., de Azevedo Cunha, M. V., & Dillon, S. (2023). Endangered languages in the digital age: Barriers and opportunities. *Digital Scholarship in the Humanities*, *38*(2), 567–583.

Joubert, A. (2011). Rain songs and the observance of the rain cult amongst the Lobedu people of Queen Modjadji. *South African Journal of African Languages*, *31*(1), 6–16. DOI: 10.1080/02572117.2011.10587352

Julianti, A., Handayani, R., & Handayani, I. (2024). The Effectiveness of Using Lingokids Application toward Young Learners' Vocabulary Mastery at the Second Grade of SD Islam Aviciena Anyar. *PROCEEDING AISELT, 9*(1).

Julita, R. (2024). The impact of gamification on efl students' reading comprehension. *JEFLE*, *4*(2), 136. DOI: 10.26418/jefle.v4i2.74901

Kadenge, M., & Nkomo, D. (2021). Language policy and linguistic human rights in postcolonial Zimbabwe. *Language Policy*, *20*(4), 609–631.

Kafai, Y. B., & Burke, Q. (2015). Constructionist Gaming: Understanding the Benefits of Making Games for Learning. *Educational Psychologist*, *50*(4), 313–334. DOI: 10.1080/00461520.2015.1124022

Kaimara, P., Fokides, E., Oikonomou, A., & Deliyannis, I. (2021). Potential barriers to the implementation of digital game-based learning in the classroom: Pre-service teachers' views. *Technology. Knowledge and Learning*, *26*(4), 825–844. DOI: 10.1007/s10758-021-09512-7

Kaivola-Bregenho, A. (2018). The Riddle: Form and Performance. *Humanities (Washington)*, *7*(2), 1–17.

Kakemo, A. A. (2024). Language preservation: Strategies for indigenous languages. *Journal of Current Issues in Arts and Management*, *5*(3), 1–4. DOI: 10.59298/NIJCIAM/2024/5.3.14100

Kaliwal, A. (2024). The effects of stories on children's cognitive and intellectual development. *Journal of Social Sciences*, *7*(2), 179–192. DOI: 10.62810/jss.v7i2.42

Kallunki, K. P. (2016). *Learning English in World of Warcraft: Perspectives from the players* (Master's thesis).

Kaltsum, H. U., & Utami, R. D. (2015). Folklore as an English teaching medium for young learners. *Proceedings of ISETH (International Summit on Science, Technology, and Humanity)*, 386–392.

Kamal, S. A. (2019). Research paradigm and philosophical foundation of qualitative study. *The International Journal of Social Sciences (Islamabad)*, *4*(3), 1386–1394. DOI: 10.20319/pijss.2019.43.13861394

Kamruzzaman, M., Alanazi, S., Alruwaili, M., Alshammari, N., Elaiwat, S., Abu-Zanona, M., Innab, N., Mohammad Elzaghmouri, B., & Ahmed Alanazi, B. (2023). Ai- and iot-assisted sustainable education systems during pandemics, such as covid-19, for smart cities. *Sustainability (Basel)*, *15*(10), 8354. DOI: 10.3390/su15108354

Kang, J., Kang, C., Yoon, J., Ji, H., Li, T., Hyunmi, M., & Han, J. (2023). Dancing on the inside: A qualitative study on online dance learning with teacher-ai cooperation. *Education and Information Technologies*, *28*(9), 12111–12141. DOI: 10.1007/s10639-023-11649-0

Kaplin, S. (2001). A Puppet Tree, A Model for the Field of Puppet Theatre, in *Puppets, Masks, and Performing Objects*, Ed. by John Bell (TDR Books; The MIT Press, 2001), pp. 18–25

Karabıyık, Ü. (2024). Investigation of the effect of gamified learning on motivation and success in math class. *Journal of Education and Practice*, *8*(1), 32–52. DOI: 10.47941/jep.1645

Kasiyarno, K., & Apriyanto, S. (2025). Influence of globalisation on the shift in local language and cultural identity. *Journal Corner of Education Linguistic and Literature*, *4*(3), 372–383. DOI: 10.54012/jcell.v4i3.435

Katiyar, P. (2024). Ai-driven personalized learning systems: enhancing educational effectiveness. *eatp*. https://doi.org/DOI: 10.53555/kuey.v30i5.4961

Kato, N. M. (2024) 'The role of English language education in multilingual societies', IAA Journal of Arts and Humanities, 11(2), pp. 53–55. Available at: https://www.iaajournals.org/wp-content/uploads/2024/08/IAA-JAH-11253-55-2024.pdf [Accessed 02 February 2026].

Kaxarova, G. S. (2025). Traditional folk songs as a didactic medium for the development of creative competencies in primary education. *International Journal of Pedagogics*, *7*(2), 88–97. DOI: 10.37547/ijp/Volume05Issue05-64

Ke, F., Moon, J., & Sokolikj, Z. (2022). Designing and deploying a virtual social sandbox for autistic children. *Disability and Rehabilitation. Assistive Technology*, •••, 1–32.

Khakpour, A., & Colomo-Palacios, R. (2020). Convergence of gamification and machine learning: A systematic literature review. *Technology Knowledge and Learning*, *26*(3), 597–636. DOI: 10.1007/s10758-020-09456-4

Khater, A., Zaaqoq, A., Wahdan, M., & Ashry, S. (2023). Knowledge and attitude of ain shams university medical students towards artificial intelligence and its application in medical education and practice. *Educational Research and Innovation Journal*, *3*(10), 29–42. DOI: 10.21608/erji.2023.306718

Khumalo, S. (2023, February 21). PabSALB aims to preserve South African languages. *Ekurhuleni News*. https://ekurhuleninews.co.za/pansalb-aims-to-preserve-south-african-languages-2/

Kiili, K. (2005). Digital game-based learning: Towards an experiential gaming model. *The Internet and Higher Education*, *8*(1), 13–24. DOI: 10.1016/j.iheduc.2004.12.001

Kim, S. (2009, June). 3D Virtual Technology, Integrated Language Learning, and Inquiry-Based Educational Curricula for English Language Students in South Korea. In *EdMedia+ Innovate Learning* (pp. 4121-4132). Association for the Advancement of Computing in Education (AACE). https://www.learntechlib.org/noaccess/32077

Kim, B., Park, H., & Baek, Y. (2009). Not just fun, but serious strategies: Using meta-cognitive strategies in game-based learning. *Computers & Education*, *52*(4), 800–810. DOI: 10.1016/j.compedu.2008.12.004

Kim, J. S. (2006). Effects of a Voluntary Summer Reading Intervention on Reading Achievement: Results From a Randomized Field Trial. *Educational Evaluation and Policy Analysis, 28*(4), 335–355. DOI: 10.3102/01623737028004335

Kim, J., & Castelli, D. M. (2021). Effects of gamification on behavioral change in education: A meta-analysis. *International Journal of Environmental Research and Public Health, 18*(7), 3550. DOI: 10.3390/ijerph18073550 PMID: 33805530

King, L. (2025) The impact of multilingualism on global education and language learning. Cambridge Assessment English Perspectives. Available at: https://www.cambridgeenglish.org/Images/539682-perspectives-impact-on-multilingualism.pdf [Accessed 02 February 2026].

King, W. R., & He, J. (2021). A meta-analysis of the technology acceptance model. *Information & Management, 43*(6), 740–755. DOI: 10.1016/j.im.2006.05.003

Kiramba, L. K. (2018). Language ideologies and epistemic exclusion. *Language and Education, 32*(4), 291–312. DOI: 10.1080/09500782.2018.1438469

Kirkland, D. E., & Randolph, A. (2021). Culturally responsive teacher education: Lessons from communities of colour. *Teaching Education, 32*(5), 528–543.

Knowles, M. S. (1975). *Self-directed learning: A guide for learners and teachers.* Association Press.

Kolb, D. A. (1984). *Experiential learning: Experience as the source of learning and development.* Prentice Hall.

Korkut, Ş., & Avcı, C. (2023). The effect of social studies teaching supported by folk songs on gifted students' self-regulation skills and retention of learning. *Journal of Gifted Education and Creativity, 10*(4), 329–343. DOI: 10.5281/zenodo.14878641

Kosonen, K., & Benson, C. (2013). Language Issues in Comparative Education: Inclusive teaching and learning in non-dominant languages and cultures.

Kovach, M. (2023). *Indigenous methodologies: Characteristics, conversations, and contexts* (2nd ed.). University of Toronto Press.

Kramsch, C. (1993). *Context and culture in language teaching.* Oxford university press.

Krashen, S. (1982). Principles and practice in second language acquisition.

Krehbiel, H. E. (1914). *Afro-American Folksongs.* G. Schirmer.

Kress, G. R., Leeuwen, T. V., & Leeuwen, D. of H. and S. S. T. V. (2001). Multimodal Discourse: The Modes and Media of Contemporary Communication. Arnold.

Kress, G. (2003). *Literacy in the New Media Age*. Routledge. DOI: 10.4324/9780203299234

Kress, G. (2010). *Multimodality: A social semiotic approach to contemporary communication*. Routledge.

Kröger, T., & Nupponen, A. M. (2019). Puppet as a pedagogical tool: A literature review. *International Electronic Journal of Elementary Education, 11*(4), 393–401. DOI: 10.26822/iejee.2019450797

Kurniawati, N., Maolida, E., & Anjaniputra, A. (2018). The praxis of digital literacy in the efl classroom: Digital-immigrant vs digital-native teacher. *Indonesian Journal of Applied Linguistics, 8*(1). Advance online publication. DOI: 10.17509/ijal.v8i1.11459

Kusuma, D. A. D. (2022). The Effect of Influent Video Game for Hospitality Students' English Vocabulary Mastery at SMK Kertha Wisata Sawan. *Jurnal Penelitian Mahasiswa Indonesia, 2*(2), 118–122. DOI: 10.36663/jpmi.v2i2.361

Ladson-Billings, G. (1995). Toward a Theory of Culturally Relevant Pedagogy. *American Educational Research Journal, 32*(3), 465–491. DOI: 10.3102/00028312032003465

Ladson-Billings, G. (2006). From the Achievement Gap to the Education Debt: Understanding Achievement in U.S. Schools. *Educational Researcher, 35*(7), 3–12. DOI: 10.3102/0013189X035007003

Lai, K. W. K., & Chen, H. J. H. (2025). L2 vocabulary learning through a COTS adventure game: Individual vs. paired gameplay and the influence of word exposure frequency, word level, and word salience. *Computers & Education, 105343*, 105343. Advance online publication. DOI: 10.1016/j.compedu.2025.105343

Landers, R. N. (2014). Developing a theory of gamified learning: Linking serious games and gamification of learning. *Simulation & Gaming, 45*(6), 752–768. DOI: 10.1177/1046878114563660

Landers, R. N., Collmus, A. B., & Williams, H. (2023). The greatest battle is within ourselves: An experiment on the effects of competition alone on task performance. *International Journal of Human-Computer Studies, 127*, 51–61. DOI: 10.1016/j.ijhcs.2018.09.011

Lantolf, J. P., & Thorne, S. L. (2021). *Sociocultural theory and the genesis of second language development* (2nd ed.). Oxford University Press.

Larsen, M., Gulis, G., & Pedersen, K. (2011). Use of evidence in local public health work in denmark. *International Journal of Public Health, 57*(3), 477–483. DOI: 10.1007/s00038-011-0324-y

Larsson, S., & Heintz, F. (2020). Transparency in artificial intelligence. *Internet Policy Review, 9*(2). Advance online publication. DOI: 10.14763/2020.2.1469

Laudari, S., & Maher, D. (2019). Barriers of ICT use in EFL teacher education courses in Nepal: An activity-theory perspective. *J. NELTA, 24*(1-2), 77–94. DOI: 10.3126/nelta.v24i1-2.27681

Lave, J., & Wenger, E. (2023). Situated learning: Legitimate peripheral participation (Anniversary ed.). Cambridge University Press.

Lave, J., & Wenger, E. (1991). *Situated learning: Legitimate peripheral participation.* Cambridge University Press. DOI: 10.1017/CBO9780511815355

Lee, C. D. (2007). *Culture, Literacy, and Learning: Taking Bloom in the Midst of the Whirlwind.* Teachers College Press.

Legaki, N., Xi, N., Hamari, J., Karpouzis, K., & Assimakopoulos, V. (2020). The effect of challenge-based gamification on learning: An experiment in the context of statistics education. *International Journal of Human-Computer Studies, 144*, 102496. DOI: 10.1016/j.ijhcs.2020.102496

Leggett, N. (2017). Early childhood creativity: Challenging educators to intentionally develop creative thinking in children. *Early Childhood Education Journal, 45*(6), 845–853. DOI: 10.1007/s10643-016-0836-4

Leoanak, S. P. P., & Amalo, B. K. (2018). Teachers' beliefs and perceptions of code-switching in English as a foreign language classroom. *SHS Web of Conferences, 42,* 00034. EDP Sciences. https://doi.org/DOI: 10.1051/shsconf/20184200034

Leonard, W. Y. (2021). Challenging "extinction" through modern Miami language reclamation. *American Indian Culture and Research Journal, 35*(2), 135–160. DOI: 10.17953/aicr.35.2.f3r173r46m261844

Li, N., & Ismail, M. J. (2025). The historical evolution and current development of folk song activities. *Quantum journal of social sciences and humanities, 6*(3), 469-480.

Li, R. and Liu, J. (2022). *Applying gamification in english learning.* https://doi.org/DOI: 10.2991/assehr.k.220504.490

Li, M., Ma, S., & Shi, Y. (2023). Examining the effectiveness of gamification as a tool promoting teaching and learning in educational settings: A meta-analysis. *Frontiers in Psychology*, *14*(1253549), 1253549. Advance online publication. DOI: 10.3389/fpsyg.2023.1253549 PMID: 37876838

Lim, L., Dawson, S., Gašević, D., Joksimovíc, S., Fudge, A., Pardo, A., & Gentili, S. (2020). Students' sense-making of personalised feedback based on learning analytics. *Australasian Journal of Educational Technology*, *36*(6), 15–33. DOI: 10.14742/ajet.6370

Limongi, R. (2024). The use of artificial intelligence in scientific research with integrity and ethics. *Rev. Artif. Intell. Educ*, *5*(00), e0022. DOI: 10.37497/rev.artif.intell.educ.v5i00.22

Lim, W. M. (2023). Philosophy of science and research paradigm for business research in the transformative age of automation, digitalization, hyperconnectivity, obligations, globalization and sustainability. *Journal of Trade Science*, *11*(2/3), 3–30. DOI: 10.1108/JTS-07-2023-0015

Lim, W. M. (2025). What Is Qualitative Research? An Overview and Guidelines. *Australasian Marketing Journal*, *33*(2), 199–229. DOI: 10.1177/14413582241264619

Lincoln, Y. S., & Guba, E. G. (1985). *Naturalistic inquiry*. Sage. DOI: 10.1016/0147-1767(85)90062-8

LingoKid. (2025). *Learning English*. https://lingokids.com/subject/learning-english

Liu, C. H., & Matthews, R. (2005). Vygotsky's philosophy: Constructivism and its criticisms examined. *International Education Journal*, *6*(3), 386–399.

Liu, L. (2024). Survey and analysis of primary school teachers' use of generative artificial intelligence. *Lecture Notes in Education Psychology and Public Media*, *74*(1), 43–52. DOI: 10.54254/2753-7048/2024.BO17693

Liu, Y. C., Wang, W. T., & Lee, T. L. (2021). An integrated view of information feedback, game quality, and autonomous motivation for evaluating game- based learning effectiveness. *Journal of Educational Computing Research*, *59*(1), 3–40. DOI: 10.1177/0735633120952044

Li, Y., & Chen, T. (2022). Blockchain Empowers Supply Chains: Challenges, Opportunities And Prospects. *Nankai Business Review International*, *14*(2), 230–248. DOI: 10.1108/NBRI-06-2022-0066

Li, Y., Leung, F. K. S., & Tan, C. Y. (2024). Developing computational thinking through pop-up storybooks: A multimodal literacy approach in Hong Kong. *Education Sciences, 14*(12), 1377. DOI: 10.3390/educsci14121377

Lo, M., & Fai Li, L. (1998). *Songs as a teaching tool in English language learning.*

Loizou, E., & Olymbiou, O. (2024). Constructive play: Exploring pre-service early childhood teachers' play involvement. *Journal of Early Childhood Research, 22*(3), 329–342. DOI: 10.1177/1476718X231210642

Lomax, A. (1968). *Folk song style and culture.* AAAS.

López, C., & Tucker, C. (2020). Toward personalized adaptive gamification: A machine learning model for predicting performance. *IEEE Transactions on Games, 12*(2), 155–168. DOI: 10.1109/TG.2018.2883661

López-Martínez, E., García-Sánchez, J. N., & Pérez, E. (2022). Gamified learning environments in language education: User-centred design and engagement strategies. *Computers & Education, 180*, 104437. DOI: 10.1016/j.compedu.2021.104437

Lornell, K. (2012). *Exploring American folk music: Ethnic, grassroots, and regional traditions in the United States.* Univ. Press of Mississippi.

Lu, A. (2013). Video Games and Learning: Teaching and Participatory Culture in the Digital Age. *Journal of Children and Media, 7*(2), 277–280. DOI: 10.1080/17482798.2012.724596

Luan, H., Géczy, P., Lai, H., Gobert, J., Yang, S., Ogata, H., Baltes, J., Guerra, R., Li, P., & Tsai, C. (2020). Challenges and future directions of big data and artificial intelligence in education. *Frontiers in Psychology, 11*, 580820. Advance online publication. DOI: 10.3389/fpsyg.2020.580820

Ludke, K. M. (2024). Singing and language learning: The role of repetition and melody in vocabulary acquisition. *Journal of Educational Psychology, 116*(3), 412–428.

Luo, Y. (2024). Innovative research on ai-assisted teaching models for college english listening and speaking courses. *Applied and Computational Engineering, 69*(1), 155–160. DOI: 10.54254/2755-2721/69/20241493

Madondo, F., & Tsikira, J. (2022). Traditional children's games: Their relevance on skills development among rural Zimbabwean children age 3–8 years. *Journal of Research in Childhood Education, 36*(3), 406–420. DOI: 10.1080/02568543.2021.1982084

Madzivhandila, M., Manyange, T., & Mudau, T. J. (2024). Vhavenda traditional children's games as a form of indigenous knowledge; Tshifasi genre. *TWIST International Multidisciplinary Journal, 9*(4), 378–387. DOI: 10.5281/twist.10049652#346

Mafugu, M. T. (2021). Indigenous languages and rural-urban migration in Zimbabwe. *Journal of African Languages and Linguistics, 42*(1), 89–112.

Maggio, I., Ginevra, M., Santilli, S., Nota, L., & Soresi, S. (2021). *Life design for an inclusive and sustainable future.*, 251-270. https://doi.org/DOI: 10.1007/978-3-030-64537-3_10

Magwa, S., & Ngara, R. (2022). Challenges in the implementation of mother tongue education in Zimbabwe. *Journal of Linguistics and Language in Education, 16*(1), 45–67.

Mahardika, I., Nuriman, , Supeno, , Mudakir, I., Wahono, B., & Wicaksono, I. (2023). Science textbook based on merdeka belajar curriculum: Integration of learning implementation for critical thinking skills. *Journal of Education Society and Behavioural Science, 36*(10), 109–115. DOI: 10.9734/jesbs/2023/v36i101273

Mai, X. Q., Luo, J., Wu, J. H., & Luo, Y. J. (2004). Aha! effects in a guessing riddle task: An event-related potential study. *Human Brain Mapping, 22*(4), 261–270. DOI: 10.1002/hbm.20030

Makalela, L. (2015). Translanguaging as a vehicle for epistemic access: Cases for reading comprehension and multilingual interactions. *Per Linguam: A Journal of Language Learning= Per Linguam. Tydskrif vir Taalaanleer, 31*(1), 15–29.

Makaudze, G. (2022). Language policy and linguistic imperialism in Zimbabwe's education system. *Educational Research Review, 17*(3), 89–102.

Makgopa, M. (2022). Parents as pedagogical partners in early childhood centres. *South African Journal of Childhood Education, 12*(1), 1–9.

Makhmudova, O., & Khaydarova, N. (2025). The role of folklore in correcting children's speech. *Academic Research in Education Journal, 10*(3), 120–128.

Makina, B. (2009). Rhythm, rhyme and songfulness: The role of Shona children's gamesongs in education. *Muziki, 6*(1), 49–57. DOI: 10.1080/18125980902931307

Makoe, P., & McKinney, C. (2014). Linguistic ideologies in multilingual South African suburban schools. *Journal of Multilingual and Multicultural Development, 35*(7), 658–673. DOI: 10.1080/01434632.2014.908889

Makoni, S., & Pennycook, A. (Eds.). (2020). *Disinventing and reconstituting languages* (2nd ed.). Multilingual Matters.

Makutoane, T. J. (2022). The people divided by common language: The orthography of Sesotho in Lesotho, South Africa and implications for Bible translation. *Hervormde Teologiese Studies*, *7*(1), a7605. DOI: 10.4102/hts.v78i1.7605

Malinowski, B. (1923). The problem of meaning in primitive languages. In Ogden & Richards (Eds.), *The meaning of meaning*. London: Routledge.

Maluleke, V. L., & Smith, C. (2025). Cultural Perceptions of Folklore in the Grade Nine EFAL Classroom. *Southern African Journal for Folklore Studies*, *34*(1), 1–22. DOI: 10.25159/2663-6697/18867

Malyshkina, E. V., Goroshko, O. N., & Shevchenko, E. M., & NA, L. (2018). Scientific understanding of the functions of repetition in English poetic speech. *Revista Espacios*, *39*(21), 41–59.

Mania, S., Ibrahim, M. M., & Syamsudduha, S. (2024). The impact of traditional games on social-emotional development: A comprehensive review of existing research. *Journal of Learning and Development Studies*, *4*(2), 39–51. DOI: 10.32996/jlds.2024.4.2.5

Mantra, I. B. N., & Maba, W. (2018). *Enhancing the EFl learners' speaking skill through folktales-based instruction*. SHS Web of Conferences, 42, 00017. DOI: 10.1051/shsconf/20184200017

Maori Language Commission. (2024). *Te reo Maori in the digital age: Annual report 2023-2024*. Te Taura Whiri i te Reo Maori.

Maphalala, M. (2019). Indigenous play and learning in South African contexts. *South African Journal of Childhood Education*, *9*(1), 1–8.

Maphanga, C. (2019, June 14). I don't hate Afrikaans. Panyaza Lesufi. *News 24*. https://www.news24.com/i-dont-hate-afrikaans-panyaza-lesufi-20190614

Marsh, K. (2009). *The musical playground: Global tradition and change in children's songs and games*. Oxford University Press. DOI: 10.1093/acprof:oso/9780195308983.001.0001

Martínez-Carratalá, F. A., Miras, S., & Rovira-Collado, J. (2024). Development of multimodal literacy through wordless picture books: A didactic intervention in primary education. *Revista de Investigación Educacional*, *42*(2), 229–247. DOI: 10.6018/rie.563971

Maruma, M. W., & Molotja, T. W. (2018). The Relevance of Folklore in an Indigenous language Teaching and Learning Situation: The Case Study of Sepedi. *Southern African Journal for Folklore Studies*, *28*(1), 1–11. DOI: 10.25159/1016-8427/4293

Mashala, M., & Sanders, D. (2025). The use of translanguaging to support the teaching of literacy: Intermediate phase teachers' perceptions. *International Journal of Multilingualism*, *22*(4), 2876–2893. Advance online publication. DOI: 10.1080/14790718.2025.2502949

Mateus, S. G. (2014). Translanguaging: Language, Bilingualism, and Education. *Bilingual Research Journal*, *37*(3), 366–369. DOI: 10.1080/15235882.2014.965361

Matthew, G., Pelser-Carstens, V., Bunt, L., & Bunt, B. (2025, October). Enhancing Student Engagement and Knowledge Retention Through Game-Based Learning: A Comprehensive Framework Integrating Game Design and Learning Theories. In *Proceedings of the 18th European Conference on Game-Based Learning*. Academic Conferences and publishing limited. DOI: 10.34190/ecgbl.19.2.3873

Mawadza, A. (2021). The constitutional recognition of Indigenous languages in Zimbabwe: Rhetoric or reality? *Language Matters*, *52*(3), 107–129.

Mbunwe-Samba, P. (2012). Oral tradition and the African past. In *Whom Needs the Past?* (pp. 105–118). Routledge.

McCarty, T. L., & Lee, T. S. (2014). Critical culturally sustaining/revitalizing pedagogy and indigenous education sovereignty. *Harvard Educational Review*, *84*(1), 101–124. DOI: 10.17763/haer.84.1.q83746nl5pj34216

McGuire, K. (2022). *Engaging students through wordless picture books during story time. Knowledge Quest*. Retrieved from ERIC.

McIvor, O., Jenni, B., & Stacey, K. (2021). Indigenous language learning games: Engaging youth in language and culture. *Canadian Journal of Native Education*, *35*(1), 127–145.

McKinney, C. (2017). *Language and power in post-colonial schooling: Ideologies in practice*. Routledge.

McLeod, S. (2024). *Vygotsky's zone of proximal development*. Simply Psychology.

McMillan, J., & Schumacher, S. (2014). *Research in education: Evidence-based inquiry* (7th ed.). Pearson Education.

Mehrpour, S., Shavoun, A., Kheiltash, A., Masoomi, R., & Seraji, R. (2023). Evaluating and comparing critical thinking skills of residents of tehran university of medical sciences. *BMC Medical Education*, *23*(1), 133. Advance online publication. DOI: 10.1186/s12909-023-04094-7

Meiklejohn, C., Westaway, L., Ashley, F. H., & Long, K. A. (2021). A review of South African primary school literacy interventions from 2005-2020. *South African Journal of Childhood Education, 11*(1), a919. DOI: 10.4102/sajce.v11i1.919

Merriam, A. P. (1964). *The anthropology of music*. Northwestern University Press.

Merriam, S. B. (1998). *Qualitative research and case study applications in education*. Jossey-Bass Publishers.

Mertens, D. M. (2023). *Research and evaluation in education and psychology: Integrating diversity with quantitative, qualitative, and mixed methods* (5th ed.). SAGE Publications.

Mezirow, J. (2018). Transformative learning theory. In Illeris, K. (Ed.), *Contemporary theories of learning* (pp. 104–118). Routledge. DOI: 10.4324/9781315147277-8

Miao, Q., & Nduneseokwu, C. (2025). Advancing environmental leadership: Education, development, and training. In Miao, Q., & Nduneseokwu, C. (Eds.), *Environmental leadership in a VUCA era: An interdisciplinary handbook* (pp. 467–538). [Publisher not listed]

Mignolo, W. (2011). Epistemic disobedience and the decolonial option: A manifesto. *Transmodernity: Journal of peripheral cultural production of the Luso-Hispanic world, 1*(2). 44-66 https://doi.org/DOI: 10.5070/T412011807

Mignolo, W. (2013). On pluriversality. *Walter Mignolo, 30*, 1–7.

Miles, R. (2015). Complexity, representation and practice: Case study as method and methodology. *Issues in Educational Research, 25*(3), 309–318.

Mina, D. F. C., Muin, A., & Septiana, T. I. (2021). Enriching Students' Vocabulary Mastery by Using Riddle Game. *Indonesian Journal of English Studies, 2*(1), 23. http://jurnal.uinbanten.ac.id/index.php/ijes

Minchen, G. (2024). Scaffolding Learners' Comprehension in Extensive Reading. *English Language Teaching, 17*(11), 1–1. DOI: 10.5539/elt.v17n11p1

Mir, K. (2021). H5P interactive video content in Moodle to improve learners' engagement in online learning. In *34th Annual Conference of the Asian Association of Open Universities - Vol II, 403-414*. https://www.academia.edu/download/89432016/AAOU2021_Volume2_Final_Online_Published.pdf#page=404

Mishra, P., & Satpathy, S. (2020). Genre of Folk Narratives as Rich Linguistic Resource in Acquiring English Language Competence for Young Learners. *Rupkatha Journal on Interdisciplinary Studies in Humanities, 12*(1), 1–10. DOI: 10.21659/rupkatha.v12n1.08

Mislevy, R., Behrens, J., DiCerbo, K. E., & Levy, R. (2012). Design and discovery in educational assessment: Evidence centered design, psychometrics, and data mining. *Journal of Educational Data Mining*, *4*, 11–48.

Mkallyah, K. A. (2022). Songs and Language: Children's Songs and the Learning of Kiswahili in Dar es Salaam, Tanzania. *Umma Journal of Contemporary Literature and Creative Arts, 9*(2). https://www.ijmrd.in/index.php/imjrd

Mkhize, N., & Ndimande, B. (2018). Decolonising knowledge in education: African indigenous perspectives. *Perspectives in Education*, *36*(2), 1–12.

Mlambo, R., & Matfunjwa, M. (2024). The use of technology in preserving indigenous language in South Africa. *Literator-Journal of Literary Criticism. Comparative Linguistics and Literary Studies*, *45*(1), 2007. DOI: 10.4102/LIT.v45i1.2007

Mogavi, R. H., Guo, B., Zhang, Y., Haq, E.-U., Hui, P., & Ma, X. (2022). When Gamification Spoils Your Learning: A Qualitative Case Study of Gamification Misuse in a Language-Learning App. *In: Proceedings of the Ninth ACM Conference on Learning @ Scale (L@S '22)*, New York City, NY, USA, 1–3 June 2022. ACM, 1–14. https://doi.org/DOI: 10.1145/3491140.3528274

Moghadam, S. R., & Barani, G. (2025). The impact of linguistic vs. cultural imperialism on language learning. *Frontiers in Psychology*, *15*, •••. Retrieved February 02, 2026, from https://www.frontiersin.org/journals/psychology/articles/10.3389/fpsyg.2024.1438849/full PMID: 39944707

Mohajan, H. K. (2018). Qualitative research methodology in social sciences and related subjects. *Journal of Economic Development. Environment and People*, *7*(1), 23–48. DOI: 10.26458/jedep.v7i1.571

Mokoena, L. G. (2019). Cultural tourism: Cultural presentation at Basotho cultural village, Free State, South Africa. *Journal of Tourism and Cultural Change*, *18*(2), 1–21. DOI: 10.1080/14766825.2019.1609488

Moldt, J., Festl-Wietek, T., Fuhl, W., Zabel, S., Claassen, M., Wagner, S., Nieselt, K., & Herrmann-Werner, A. (2024). Assessing ai awareness and identifying essential competencies: Insights from key stakeholders in integrating ai into medical education. *JMIR Medical Education*, *10*, e58355–e58355. DOI: 10.2196/58355

Moll, L. C., Amanti, C., Neff, D., & Gonzalez, N. (1992). Funds of Knowledge for Teaching: Using a Qualitative Approach to Connect Homes and Classrooms. *Theory into Practice*, *31*(2), 132–141. DOI: 10.1080/00405849209543534

Moniza Ray, S. P., & Ajit, I. (2024). Digital Game-Based Language Learning: The Impact of Story-Driven Game Life Is Strange 1 on Language Learners' Listening Skills. *Journal of Language Teaching & Research, 15*(2), 448–457. Advance online publication. DOI: 10.17507/jltr.1502.13

Morales, M., Amado-Salvatierra, H., Medina, J., Barchino, R., Hernández-Rizzardini, R., & Teixeira, A. (2024). Personalized feedback in massive open online courses: Harnessing the power of langchain and openai api. *Electronics (Basel), 13*(10), 1960. DOI: 10.3390/electronics13101960

Morgan, D. L. (2023). *Integrating qualitative and quantitative methods: A pragmatic approach* (2nd ed.). SAGE Publications.

Morrison, N. (2022, March 08). The secret to being a better teacher? Be kind to your students. *Forbes newsletter*. https://www.forbes.com/sites/nickmorrison/2022/03/08/the-secret-to-being-a-better-teacher-be-kind-to-your-students/

Mose, P. N., & Kaschula, R. H. (2019). Developing mother tongue as academic languages in primary schools in Kenya: Exploring extent and indispensability. *Journal of Language, Identity, and Education, 18*(1), 329–342. Advance online publication. DOI: 10.1080/15348458.2019.1645605

Moyo, N., & Moyo, T. (2022). Minority language marginalization in Zimbabwe's multilingual education policy. *Journal of Multilingual and Multicultural Development, 43*(8), 723–738.

Mpandashulu, M. (2024). *Investigating teacher practices in integrating indigenous songs for play-based learning in early childhood education centers: A multiple case study, University of Zambia.*

Mphahlele, M. L., & Mammen, K. J. (2022). Exploring the feasibility of outdoor indigenous games and songs to support early childhood education. *Journal of Childhood Education and Society, 3*(2), 120–135. Retrieved August 10, 2025, from https://www.j-ces.com/index.php/jces/article/view/270

Mudau, P. P., Mandende, I. P., & Mushaathoni, M. (2024). Indigenous language preservation: A study of the Tsivenda speech community in South Africa. *Journal of Intercultural Communication, 24*(4), 1–2. DOI: 10.36923/jicc.v24i4.969

Mufanechiya, A., & Mufanechiya, T. (2018). Youth language practices in urban Zimbabwe: Between local and global. *Journal of African Cultural Studies, 30*(3), 344–360.

Mugisha, M., Uwitonze, A., Chesire, F., Senyonga, R., Oxman, M., Nsangi, A., Semakula, D., Kaseje, M., Lewin, S., Sewankambo, N., Nyirazinyoye, L., Oxman, A. D., & Rosenbaum, S. (2021). Teaching critical thinking about health using digital technology in lower secondary schools in rwanda: A qualitative context analysis. *PLoS One*, *16*(3), e0248773. DOI: 10.1371/journal.pone.0248773

Mujahidah, N., Damayanti, E., & Afiif, A. (2021). The role of storytelling methods using hand puppets in early children's language development. *Child Education Journal*, *3*(2), 78–91. DOI: 10.33086/cej.v3i2.2129

Mulaudzi, L. V. (2024). Evaluating the language-in-education policy of 1997: Advancing inclusivity and multilingual education. *Journal for Language Teaching= Ijenali Yekufundzisa Lulwimi=. Tydskrif vir Taalonderrig*, *58*(2), 1–28. https://hdl.handle.net/10520/ejc-langt_v58_n2_a4. DOI: 10.56285/jltVol58iss2a6163

Mundy, K., & Verger, A. (2015). The World Bank and the global governance of education in a changing world order. *International Journal of Educational Development*, *40*, 9–18. DOI: 10.1016/j.ijedudev.2014.11.021

Murodov, M. (2025). Folk songs as a factor in the spiritual and moral education of students. *International Multidisciplinary Journal of Education*, *9*(1), 45–54.

Murray, E. A., Lane, S. J., & Murray, D. G. (2009). Physiological and behavioural differences in sensory processing. *Frontiers in Integrative Neuroscience*, *3*(29). Advance online publication. DOI: 10.3389/neuro.07.029.2009

Murtaza, M., Ahmed, Y., Shamsi, J., Sherwani, F., & Usman, M. (2022). Ai-based personalized e-learning systems: Issues, challenges, and solutions. *IEEE Access : Practical Innovations, Open Solutions*, *10*, 81323–81342. DOI: 10.1109/ACCESS.2022.3193938

Mwinsa, G. M. (2025). Play-based learning: A pedagogical approach for social and cognitive development in early childhood education. ScienceDirect., 10.1016/j.scedu.2025.100123.

Mwinsa, G. M., & Dagada, M. (2024). Efficacy of indigenous games on literacy and numeracy development in pre-schoolers in Zambia. *South African Journal of Childhood Education*, *14*(1), a1555. DOI: 10.4102/SAJCE.v14i1.1555

Mzimela, J. (2016). Exploring the role of teaching using folklore in developing grade R learners' mother tongue. *Studies of Tribes and Tribals*, *14*(2), 129–137. DOI: 10.1080/0972639X.2016.11886740

Nagi, F., Salih, R., Alzubaidi, M., Shah, H., Alam, T., Shah, Z., … & Househ, M. (2023). *Applications of artificial intelligence (AI) in medical education: a scoping review.*. https://doi.org/DOI: 10.3233/SHTI230581

Naidoo, M. (2016). Leisure in Africa. In G. J. Walker, D. Scot, & M. Stodolska (Eds.), Leisure matters: The state and future of leisure studies (pp. 93–100). enture Publishing, Inc.

Naidoo, K. (2024). A review of the effectiveness of educational digital game-based learning on students in tertiary institutions. *European Journal of Teacher Education, 5*(4), 34–47. DOI: 10.33422/ejte.v5i4.1174

Namibia Statistics Agency. (2014). *Languages spoken in Namibian households* [Census data].

Narasid, S. N. K. H., & Rahman, M. N. A. (2025). Application of indigenous traditional songs 'sewang' in preschool teaching and learning. *Cakrawala Dini: Jurnal Pendidikan Anak Usia Dini, 16*(2), 125–136.

Narayanan, K. (2024). Hybrid gamification and ai tutoring framework using machine learning and adaptive neuro-fuzzy inference system. *Journal of Advanced Research in Applied Sciences and Engineering Technology, 42*(2), 221–233. DOI: 10.37934/araset.42.2.221233

Nardi, B., & Kallinikos, J. (2010). Technology, agency, and community: The case of modding in World of Warcraft. In Holmström, J., Wiberg, M., & Lund, A. (Eds.), *Industrial informatics design, use and innovation* (pp. 174–186). IGI Global. DOI: 10.4018/978-1-61520-692-6.ch013

National Center for Education Statistics. (2019). NAEP Reading 2019 Highlights.

NBC Online. (2025, September). *Shortage of qualified teachers for Khoekhoegowab, Setswana, and Afrikaans persists.* Retrieved from NBC News.

Ndhlovu, F. (2023). *Ignored lingualism: The challenges of language marginalisation in Africa.* Routledge.

Ndhlovu, F., & Makalela, L. (2021). Decolonising multilingualism in Africa: Re-centering silenced voices from the Global South. *Multilingual Margins, 8*(3), 7–23.

Ndlovu, M. (2014). Why indigenous knowledges in the 21st century? A decolonial turn. Yesterday & today, 11, 84–98.

Ndlovu-Gatsheni, S. J. (2020). *Epistemic freedom in Africa: Deprovincialization and decolonization.* Routledge.

Neri, L., Robledo-Rella, V., García-Castelán, R. M. G., Gonzalez-Nucamendi, A., Escobar-Castillejos, D., & Noguez, J. (2020). Visuo-Haptic Simulations to Understand the Dependence of Electric Forces on Distance. *Applied Sciences (Basel, Switzerland)*, *10*(20), 1–23. DOI: 10.3390/app10207190

Neuman, S., & Celano, D. (2001). Access to Print in Low-Income and Middle-Income Communities: An Ecological Study of Four Neighborhoods. Reading Research Quarterly - READ RES QUART, 36, 8–26. DOI: 10.1598/RRQ.36.1.1

New London Group. (2000). A pedagogy of multiliteracies: Designing social futures. In Cope, B., & Kalantzis, M. (Eds.), *Multiliteracies: Literacy Learning and the Design of Social Futures* (pp. 9–37). Routledge.

Newgarden, K., & Zheng, D. (2016). Recurrent languaging activities in World of Warcraft: Skilled linguistic action meets the Common European Framework of Reference. *ReCALL*, *28*(3), 274–304. DOI: 10.1017/S0958344016000112

Nguyen, D., & Yukawa, J. (2019). Non-digital game-based learning in EFL classrooms: A case study on student collaboration and motivation. *Language Education in Asia*, *10*(1), 116–132. DOI: 10.5746/LEiA/19/V10/I1/A10/Nguyen_Yukawa

Nguyen, T., Nguyen, M. T., & Tran, H. T. (2023). Artificial intelligent based teaching and learning approaches: A comprehensive review. *International Journal of Evaluation and Research in Education (Ijere)*, *12*(4), 2387. DOI: 10.11591/ijere.v12i4.26623

Nickerson, C. (2024). Interpretivism Paradigm and Research Philosophy. *Simply Psychology*. https://www.simplypsychology.org/interpretivism-paradigm.html

Nicolopoulou, A. (2010). The alarming disappearance of play from early childhood education. *Human Development*, *53*(1), 1–4. DOI: 10.1159/000268135

Niklas, F., & Schneider, W. (2017). Home learning environment and development of child competencies from kindergarten until the end of elementary school. *Contemporary Educational Psychology*, *49*, 263–274. DOI: 10.1016/j.cedpsych.2017.03.006

Nikolajeva, M., & Scott, C. (2013). *How picturebooks work*. Routledge., DOI: 10.4324/9780203960615

Nimoh, S. K. (2014). Indigenous traditional medicine in Ghana tapping into an underexplored resource. In Emeagwali, G., & Sefa-Dei, G. J. (Eds.), *African Indigenous knowledge and the disciplines* (pp. 83–93). Sense., DOI: 10.1007/978-94-6209-770-4

Ningrum, A. K., Riyanti, D., & Regina, R. (2019). *Improving Students' Vocabulary Using Riddles Game: A Classroom Action Research*. Proceedings International Conference on Teaching and Education, 2(2),181-186. ISSN: 2685-1407, FKIP Universitas Tanjungpura. Pontianak, Indonesia.

Nishanthi, R. (2020). Understanding of the importance of mother tongue learning. *International Journal of Trend in Scientific Research and Development*, *5*(1), 77–80.

Nketia, J. H. (1999). *Folk songs as cultural transmission.*

Nketia, J. K. (1974). The musical heritage of Africa. *Daedalus*, •••, 151–161.

Nkomo, S. A., Magxala, X. P., & Lebopa, N. (2023). Early literacy experiences of two children during the COVID-19 lockdown in South Africa: A semi-ethnographic study. *Journal of Early Childhood Literacy*, *23*(1), 141–174. DOI: 10.1177/14687984231154351

Noviana, E., Syahza, A., Putra, Z. H., Hadriana, Y., Erlinda, S., Putri, D. R., Rusandi, M. A., & Biondi Situmorang, D. D. (2023). Why is didactic transposition in disaster education needed by prospective elementary school teachers? *Heliyon*, *9*(4), e15413. DOI: 10.1016/j.heliyon.2023.e15413

Ntwalana, Y., & Matiso, N. H. (2024). Preserving Human Culture in Schools Through Oral Storytelling: Perspectives From Teachers in Eastern Cape, South Africa.

Nxumalo, S. A., & Mncube, D. W. (2019). Using indigenous games and knowledge to decolonise the school curriculum: Ubuntu perspective. *Perspectives in Education*, *36*(2), 103–118. DOI: 10.18820/2519593X/pie.v36i2.9

Nyamayedenga, N., & Makaudze, G. (2021). Language of instruction and academic performance in Zimbabwean primary schools. *International Journal of Educational Development*, *85*, 102456.

Nygren, T., Wassermann, J., Kronlid, D. O., Larsson, E., Guath, M., Novak, J., & Bentrovato, D. (2020). Global citizenship education for global citizenship? Students' views on learning about, through, and for human rights, peace, and sustainable development in England, India, New Zealand, South Africa, and Sweden. *Journal of Social Science Education*, *19*(4), 63–97. DOI: 10.4119/jsse-3464

O'Connell, S. (2022, Sep 22). Heritage Day offers the space to revisit South Africans' painful legacies and tell untold stories of hope. *Daily*

O'Connor, E. (2021). Emotional literacy in early childhood. *Early Years*, *41*(4), 421–436.

Oakes, J. (2005). *Keeping Track: How Schools Structure Inequality*. Yale University Press.

Obeng, P., Brewu, J., & Opoku, E. (2022). Use of Indigenous and Folk-Game Songs for Teaching and Learning in Early Childhood Education Setting. *International Journal for Multidisciplinary Research, 4*(6), 1–36. DOI: 10.36948/ijfmr

OECD. (2013, October 8). OECD Skills Outlook 2013.

Okpokwasili, O. A., & Ekemezie, I. B. (2023). Gendered Media Coverage: Examining the portrayal of female politicians in Nigeria. *IGIRIGI: A Multi-Disciplinary. Journal of African Studies, 3*(1), 102–113.

Olanibi, S. A., Dahiru, W., & Balogun, K. B. (2021). Mother tongue as an instructional medium in Nigeria's lower primary schools: Prospects and challenges. *IOSR Journal of Research and Method in Education, 11*(3), 40–45. DOI: 10.9790/7388-1103034045

Ollerhead, S., & Pennington, C. (2024). Multilingual storytelling as culturally sustaining pedagogy: Reimagining early literacy in diverse classrooms. *Ethnography and Education, 19*(1), 1–18. DOI: 10.1177/14687984241303390

Om, C., Vella, K., Dema, T., Ploderer, B., Murcia, K., & Brereton, M. (2025). Storying-roleplay: A co-design method supporting young children to understand environmental problems. In *Proceedings of the 24th Interaction Design and Children (IDC '25)* (pp. 465–478). https://doi.org/DOI: 10.1145/3713043.3728842

Omidire, M. F., & Ayob, S. (2020). The utilisation of translanguaging for learning and teaching in a multilingual primary classroom. *Multilingua, 4*(11), 105–129. DOI: 10.1515/multi-2020-0072

Onesi-Ozigagun, O. (2024). Revolutionizing education through ai: A comprehensive review of enhancing learning experiences. *International Journal of Applied Research in Social Sciences, 6*(4), 589–607. DOI: 10.51594/ijarss.v6i4.1011

Opland, J. (2018). *Xhosa Literature: Spoken and Printed Words* (Vol. 6). UKZN Press.

Opoku, E. (2020). *Folk songs and early childhood education in Ghan*

Osei-Tutu, A. A. (2022). Developing African oral traditional storytelling as a framework for studying with African peoples. *Qualitative Research, 23*(6), 1497–1514. DOI: 10.1177/14687941221082263

Otero, L., Catalá, A., Morante, M., Taboada, M., López, B., & Barro, S. (2023). Ai literacy in k-12: A systematic literature review. *International Journal of STEM Education, 10*(1), 29. Advance online publication. DOI: 10.1186/s40594-023-00418-7

Palinkas, L. A., Horwitz, S. M., Green, C. A., Wisdom, J. P., Duan, N., & Hoagwood, K. (2015). Purposeful sampling for qualitative data collection and analysis in mixed method implementation research. *Administration and Policy in Mental Health, 42*(5), 533–544. DOI: 10.1007/s10488-013-0528-y PMID: 24193818

Panayiota, M., & Tsilimeni, T. (2021). Developing children's critical thinking through wordless books. *Journal of Literary Education, 5*(2), 54–71. DOI: 10.7203/JLE.5.21392

Papadopoulos, I., & Bisiri, E. (2020). Fostering critical thinking skills in preschool education: Designing, implementing and assessing a multiliteracies-oriented program based on intercultural tales. *Multilingual Academic Journal of Education and Social Sciences, 8*(1), 87–105. DOI: 10.46886/MAJESS/v8-i1/7263

Papastergiou, M. (2009). Digital game-based learning in high school computer science education: Impact on educational effectiveness and student motivation. *Computers & Education, 52*(1), 1–12. DOI: 10.1016/j.compedu.2008.06.004

Pardosi, V., Xu, S., Umurohmi, U., Nurdiana, N., & Sabur, F. (2024). Implementation of an artificial intelligence based learning management system for adaptive learning. *Al-Fikrah Jurnal Manajemen Pendidikan, 12*(1), 149. DOI: 10.31958/jaf.v12i1.12548

Paris, D. (2012). Culturally sustaining pedagogy: A needed change in stance, terminology, and practice. *Educational Researcher, 41*(3), 93–97. DOI: 10.3102/0013189X12441244

Patel, S. (2023). Addressing racial injustice: Examining systems of oppression and promoting equity in contemporary society. *Joura, 1*(2), 13–17. DOI: 10.61963/jkt.v1i2.33

Patton, M. Q. (1990). *Qualitative evaluation and research methods* (2nd ed.). Sage.

Pearce, C., Boellstorff, T., & Nardi, B. A. (2011). *Communities of play: Emergent cultures in multiplayer games and virtual worlds*. MIT Press.

Pendy, B. (2023). Artificial intelligence: The future of education. *Jurnal Indonesia Sosial Sains, 2*(11). Advance online publication. DOI: 10.59141/jiss.v2i11.801

Peristeris, K. (2017). Culturally Sustaining Pedagogies: Teaching and Learning for Justice in a Changing World. *Journal of Teaching and Learning, 11*(1). Advance online publication. DOI: 10.22329/jtl.v11i1.4987

Perley, B. (2012). Zombie Linguistics: Experts, Endangered Languages and the Curse of Undead Voices. Anthropological Forum -. *Anthropological Forum, 22*(2), 133–149. DOI: 10.1080/00664677.2012.694170

Peterson, M. (2010). Digital gaming and second language development: Japanese learners' interactions in an MMORPG. *Digital Culture & Education*, *2*(1), 43–58. DOI: 10.1016/j.compedu.2010.08.003

Petrusly, P. (2024). *The effect of gamification using kahoot on students' critical thinking abilities: the role of mediating learning engagement and motivation.* Kuey., DOI: 10.53555/kuey.v30i5.1524

Pham, T. H. N. (2016). Folktales as a Valuable Rich Cultural and Linguistic Resource to Teach a Foreign Language to Young Learners. *International Journal of Education. Cultura e Scuola*, *1*(1), 23–28. DOI: 10.11648/j.ijecs.20160101.15

Phatudi, N. (2021). Language, culture and play in early learning. *Early Child Development and Care*, *191*(10), 1512–1524.

Phillips, D. C. (1995). The good, the bad, and the ugly: The many faces of constructivism. *Educational Researcher*, *24*(7), 5–12. DOI: 10.3102/0013189X024007005

Piaget, J. (1952). *The Origins of Intelligence in Children*. International Universities Press. DOI: 10.1037/11494-000

Pinedo, R., Garcia-Martin, N., Rascon, D., Jose, C. C., & Canas, M. (2021). Reasoning and learning with game-based learning: A case study. *Current Psychology (New Brunswick, N.J.)*, *41*(3), 1603–1617. DOI: 10.1007/s12144-021-01744-1

Pious, M., & Saishi, A. (2025). The role of traditional ceremonies in the preservation of Zambia's cultural heritage with regards to the Umutomboko ceremony of Lunda-speaking people: A case study of two selected districts in Luapula province in Zambia. *International Journal of Advanced Multidisciplinary Research Studies*, *5*(2), 2407–2418.

Piper, B., Zuilkowski, S. S., & Mugenda, A. (2014). Improving reading outcomes in Kenya: First-year effects of the PRIMR Initiative. *International Journal of Educational Development*, *37*, 11–21. DOI: 10.1016/j.ijedudev.2014.02.006

Pivac, B. (2023). *Game-based learning for culturally diverse students: Designing a conceptual framework for embedding cultural capital into games.* [Unpublished master's dissertation] University of Uppsala. Sweden

Plass, J. L., Homer, B. D., & Kinzer, C. K. (2015). Foundations of Game-Based Learning. *Educational Psychologist*, *50*(4), 258–283. DOI: 10.1080/00461520.2015.1122533

Plass, J. L., & Kaplan, U. (2016). Emotional design in digital media for learning. In Tettegah, S., & Gartmeier, M. (Eds.), *Emotions, technology, design, and learning* (pp. 131–161). Elsevier. DOI: 10.1016/B978-0-12-801856-9.00007-4

Plass, J. L., Mayer, R. E., & Homer, B. D. (2020). *Handbook of game-based learning*. MIT Press.

Plass, J. L., Mayer, R. E., & Homer, B. D. (2020). *Handbook of Game-Based Learning*. MIT Press., DOI: 10.7551/mitpress/12198.001.0001

Polat, E. (2023). Gamification implementation for educational purposes: A scoping review (2013-2018). *Educational Technology Quarterly*, *2023*(3), 367–400. DOI: 10.55056/etq.589

Polleti, G. (2024, March). Building a language-learning game for Brazilian Indigenous languages: A case study. *In Proceedings of the 16th International Conference on Computational Processing of Portuguese*-2 (pp. 18–22). https://doi.org/DOI: 10.48550/arXiv.2403.14515

Postal and Telecommunications Regulatory Authority of Zimbabwe (POTRAZ). (2024). *Abridged annual report 2023*. POTRAZ.

Prah, K. K. (2022). *Mother-tongue education in Africa for emancipation and development*. CASAS Publishers.

Pratama, M., Sampelolo, R., & Lura, H. (2023). Revolutionizing education: Harnessing the power of artificial intelligence for personalized learning. *Klasikal Journal of Education Language Teaching and Science*, *5*(2), 350–357. DOI: 10.52208/klasikal.v5i2.877

Prensky, M. (2023). Digital game-based learning (Anniversary ed.). Paragon House.

Prensky, M. (2001). *Digital game-based learning*. McGraw-Hill.

Probine, S. A., Perry, J., Burke, R. S., & McAlevey, F. L. (2023). An examination of inquiry-based project learning in early childhood settings in Aotearoa/New Zealand. *Early Childhood Education Journal*, *52*(6), 1–11. DOI: 10.1007/s10643-023-01495-7

Purushotma, R., Thorne, S. L., & Wheatley, J. (2009). 10 key principles for designing video games for foreign language learning. Paper produced for the Open Language & Learning Games Project, Massachusetts Institute of Technology, funded by the William and Flora Hewlett Foundation.

Purushotma, R., Thorne, S. L., & Wheatley, J. (2022). 10 key principles for designing video games for foreign language learning. In Reinders, H. (Ed.), *Digital games in language learning and teaching* (2nd ed., pp. 17–38). Palgrave Macmillan.

Quijano, A. (2000). Coloniality of power and Eurocentrism in Latin America. *International Sociology*, *15*(2), 215–232. DOI: 10.1177/0268580900015002005

Rahman, F. (2017). The Revival of Local Fairy Tales for Children Education. *Theory and Practice in Language Studies*, *7*(5), 336–344. DOI: 10.17507/tpls.0705.02

Rahman, R. M. A., Basir, J. M., & Zain, A. (2025). The role of traditional songs in early childhood education: Fostering values, cultural identity, and creativity. *International Journal of Education. Psychology and Counseling*, *10*(59), 264–282. DOI: 10.35631/IJEPC.1059019

Rahmawati, W. T., Harahap, Y. M., & Sembiring, F. W. (2022). The Effect of Riddle Game on Students' Vocabulary Mastery. *PEDAGOGI: Jurnal Ilmiah Pendidikan*, *8*(1), 69–73. DOI: 10.47662/pedagogi.v8i1.277

Rajendran, M., Ray, M., Ilangovan, A., Chokkalingam, V. K., & Singh, A. B. (2024). Commercial video games and english language skills development: A systematic review. *Language Teaching Research Quarterly*, *45*, 57–85. DOI: 10.32038/ltrq.2024.45.04

Rama, P. S., Black, R. W., Van Es, E., & Warschauer, M. (2012). Affordances for second language learning in World of Warcraft. *ReCALL*, *24*(3), 322–338. DOI: 10.1017/S0958344012000171

Ramothwala, T., Segabutla, M. H., Rwodzi, C., & Thokwane, D. (2021). 'Exploring Grade 8 Khelobedu-speaking learners' writing challenges in Sepedi Home Language in Mopani District, South Africa'. *Literator*, *42*(1), a1744. DOI: 10.4102/lit.v42i1.1744

Ramugondo, E. L. (2012). Intergenerational play within family: The case for occupational consciousness? *Journal of Occupational Science*, *19*(4), 326–340. DOI: 10.1080/14427591.2012.710166

Ranalli, J. (2008). Learning English with The Sims: Exploiting authentic computer simulation games for L2 learning. *Computer Assisted Language Learning*, *21*(5), 441–455. DOI: 10.1080/09588220802447859

Randle, O. (2024). The Roles of Riddles, Puzzles, and Narratives as Pedagogy in Video Games: A Case of African-Themed Video Games. *Journal of Black Studies*, *55*(8), 661–683. DOI: 10.1177/00219347241278383

Rasheed, Z., Ghwanmeh, S., & Abualkishik, A. (2023). Harnessing artificial intelligence for personalized learning: A systematic review. *Data & Metadata*, *2*, 146. DOI: 10.56294/dm2023146

Rathore, A., Sultana, N., Zareen, S. J., & Ahmed, A. (2023). Artificial intelligence and curriculum prospects for elementary school. *Pakistan Journal of Humanities and Social Sciences, 11*(4). Advance online publication. DOI: 10.52131/pjhss.2023.v11i4.1909

Reardon, S., & Portilla, X. (2016). Recent Trends in Income, Racial, and Ethnic School Readiness Gaps at Kindergarten Entry. *AERA Open, 2*(3), 2332858416657343. Advance online publication. DOI: 10.1177/2332858416657343

Redecker, C. (2017). *European Framework for the Digital Competence of Educators (DigCompEdu)*. Publications Office of the European Union., DOI: 10.2760/159770

Reed, J., & Lee, E. L. (2020). The Importance of Oral Language Development in Young Literacy Learners: Children Need to Be Seen and Heard. *Dimensions of Early Childhood, 48*(3), 6–9.

Regan, P. M., & Jesse, J. (2019). Ethical challenges of edtech, big data and personalized learning: Twenty-first century student sorting and tracking. *Ethics and Information Technology, 21*(3), 167–179. DOI: 10.1007/s10676-018-9492-2

Regiana, E., Dwiyoga, A., & Prasetya, F. H. (2020). Preservation of Indonesian culture through traditional games application. *Sisforma, 7*(1), 28–37. DOI: 10.24167/sisforma.v7i1.1422

Reinders, H. (2012). Digital games in language learning: Opportunities and challenges. In Hubbard, P. (Ed.), *The Cambridge Guide to Second Language Teacher Education* (pp. 93–101). Cambridge University Press., DOI: 10.1017/CBO9781139046856.012

Reinders, H., & Stockwell, G. (2023). *Computer-assisted second language learning* (2nd ed.). Cambridge University Press.

Reinders, H., & Wattana, S. (2015). Affect and willingness to communicate in digital game-based learning. *ReCALL, 27*(1), 38–57. DOI: 10.1017/S0958344014000226

Reinders, H., & Wattana, S. (2015). Can I say something? The effects of digital game play on willingness to communicate. *Language Learning & Technology, 19*(2), 50–73.

Reinhardt, J., & Sykes, J. M. (2014). Digital Game and Play Activity in L2 Teaching and Learning. *Language Learning & Technology, 18*(2). Advance online publication. DOI: 10.1016/j.system.2013.03.002

Reinhardt, J., & Thorne, S. L. (2023). Digital literacies as emergent multifaceted competencies. In Dooly, N., & O'Dowd, R. (Eds.), *Telecollaboration in education* (pp. 76–94). Routledge.

Remer, R., & Tzuriel, D. (2015). "I teach better with the puppet"–Use of puppet as a mediating tool in Kindergarten Education–An evaluation. *American Journal of Educational Research, 3*(3), 356–365. DOI: 10.12691/education-3-3-15

Rivera, E., & Garden, C. (2021). Gamification for student engagement: A framework. *Journal of Further and Higher Education, 45*(7), 999–1012. DOI: 10.1080/0309877X.2021.1875201

Rizqiyani, R., & Azizah, N. (2019, January). The influence of wordless picture book to improve the ability of storytelling among preschool students. In *Proceedings of the 3rd International Conference on Current Issues in Education (ICCIE 2018)* (p. 74). Atlantis Press. https://doi.org/DOI: 10.2991/iccie-18.2019.74

Rogoff, B., Paradise, R., Arauz, R. M., Correa-Chávez, M., & Angelillo, C. (2018). Firsthand learning through intent participation. *Annual Review of Psychology, 69*, 1–27. PMID: 12499516

Rohmah, N. (2022). A vocational school cutting-edge learning strategy: Examining gamification towards student engagement and achievement. *Jurnal Kependidikan Jurnal Hasil Penelitian Dan Kajian Kepustakaan Di Bidang Pendidikan Pengajaran Dan Pembelajaran, 8*(3), 655. DOI: 10.33394/jk.v8i3.5779

Rojas, V. S., Fuentealba, L. F., & Ranjan, R. (2021). Game-based didactic resources as a strategy in foreign language pedagogy. *International Journal of Teaching and Education Research, 20*(12), 195–211. DOI: 10.26803/ijlter.20.12.12

Rolling, J. H.Jr. (2012). Sacred structures: Narrating lifeworlds and implications for urban arts education practice. *Studies in Art Education, 53*(2), 112–124. DOI: 10.1080/00393541.2012.11518856

Romaine, S. (2021). The impact of language policy on endangered languages. *International Journal of the Sociology of Language, 2021*(267-268), 217–233.

Romanski, N. M. (2019). Reigniting the transformative power of puppets through narrative pedagogy, contemporary art, and transdisciplinary approaches in art education. *Art Education, 72*(4), 36–42. DOI: 10.1080/00043125.2019.1602496

Rudd, R. E. (2007). Health literacy skills of U.S. adults. *American Journal of Health Behavior, 31*(Suppl 1), S8–S18. DOI: 10.5993/AJHB.31.s1.3

Rueckert, D., Pico, K., Kim, D., & Sánchez, X. (2020). Gamifying the foreign language classroom for brain-friendly learning. *Foreign Language Annals, 53*(4), 686–703. DOI: 10.1111/flan.12490

Rugaiyah, R. (2023). The potential of artificial intelligence in improving linguistic competence: A systematic literature review. *Arkus*, *9*(2), 319–324. DOI: 10.37275/arkus.v9i2.313

Rulyansah, A., Ghufron, S., Akhwani, N., & Mariati, P. (2023). Competencies of Teachers in Game-based Pedagogy. *Pegem Journal of Education and Instruction*, *13*(2), 354–370.

Rupere, T., Muzurura, O., Zanamwe, N. & Munyaradzi, M. (2013). Use of a Game in Teaching Early Childhood Learners in Zimbabwe. *International Journal of Computer and Information Technology*, 2(2). ISSN: 2279 – 0764.

Russell, E. S. (2025). Teaching Otherwise: Decolonial Pedagogies in Brazilian Language and Literature Classrooms. *Equity in Education & Society*, 27526461251371310. DOI: 10.1177/27526461251371310

Ryan, R. M., & Deci, E. L. (2000). Intrinsic and extrinsic motivations: Classic definitions and new directions. *Contemporary Educational Psychology*, *25*(1), 54–67. DOI: 10.1006/ceps.1999.1020 PMID: 10620381

Ryan, R. M., & Deci, E. L. (2000). Self-determination theory and the facilitation of intrinsic motivation, social development, and well-being. *The American Psychologist*, *55*(1), 68–78. DOI: 10.1037/0003-066X.55.1.68

Ryan, R., Rigby, C., & Przybylski, A. (2006). The Motivational Pull of Video Games: A Self-Determination Theory Approach. *Motivation and Emotion*, *30*(4), 344–360. DOI: 10.1007/s11031-006-9051-8

Ryu, D. (2013). Play to learn, learn to play: Language learning through gaming culture. *ReCALL*, *25*(2), 286–301. DOI: 10.1017/S0958344013000050

Sakala, M., Kriel, C., Stevens, Y., & Mabala, L. (2025). Leisure education and indigenous knowledge systems in South Africa: A commentary. *World Leisure Journal*, *67*(2), 191–200. DOI: 10.1080/16078055.2024.2438618

Salen, K., & Zimmerman, E. (2004). *Rules of play: Game design fundamentals*. MIT Press.

Samsonov, P. (2025, March). Pre-service and in-service teachers' perceptions of H5P: Results of a survey. In *Society for Information Technology & Teacher Education International Conference* (pp. 2935-2940). Association for the Advancement of Computing in Education (AACE). https://www.learntechlib.org/p/225892/

Samy Alim, H. (2007). Critical Hip-Hop Language Pedagogies: Combat, Consciousness, and the Cultural Politics of Communication. *Journal of Language, Identity, and Education*, *6*(2), 161–176. DOI: 10.1080/15348450701341378

Sardo, M., & Thibault, M. (2024). "I like everything about it" – Perceived educational value of a digital gaming experience with Assassin's Creed Odyssey: Discovery Tour. *Italian Journal of Educational Technology*, *32*(3). Advance online publication. DOI: 10.17471/2499-4324/1399

Savage, C. (2019, August 30). The importance of mother tongue in education. https://www.ie-today.co.uk/Blog/the-importance-of-mother-tongue-in-education/

Schmitz, B., Klemke, R., Walhout, J., & Specht, M. (2015). Attuning a mobile simulation game for school children using a design-based research approach. *Computers & Education*, *81*, 35–48. DOI: 10.1016/j.compedu.2014.09.001

Schön, J., Shaftel, J., & Markham, P. (2008). Contemporary issues in the assessment of culturally and linguistically diverse learners. *Journal of Applied School Psychology*, *24*(2), 163–189. DOI: 10.1080/15377900802089395

Schønning, S. M., & Fløgum, H. (2025). *Fostering joy of writing through a narrative-driven video game: A study of Life is Strange in an L2 English classroom* (Master's thesis, UiT The Arctic University of Norway). https://hdl.handle.net/10037/37349

Schramm, H. (2021). *Implementing a sensory room for preschoolers* [Capstone project, Creighton University]. Creighton University.

Schuler, D., & Namioka, A. (Eds.). (2023). *Participatory design: Principles and practices* (2nd ed.). CRC Press.

Scott, W. A., & Ytreberg, L. H. (2001). *Teaching English to Children*. Longman.

SEAL. (2024) The benefits of being multilingual: How multilingual learning leads to $30 billion economic growth. Available at: https://www.seal.org/news/benefits-of-being-multilingual [Accessed 02 February 2026].

Seddighi-Khavidak, S., Sanchez, B. N., Chan, S. S., & Le-Chan, G. (2025). Game-Based Learning Enhances Engagement and Comprehension in Undergraduate Architecture and Biology Education. *Education Sciences*, *16*(1), 9. DOI: 10.3390/educsci16010009

Seleke, B., Teis, N. J. P., Els, C. J., & Legodu, G. (2025). Indigenous knowledge integration in South Africa's technology education curriculum: Current status, challenges, and future directions. [JELT]. *Journal of Education and Learning Technology*, *6*(1), 120–138. DOI: 10.38159/jelt.2025619

Setiyaningsih, I., Hidayati, H., & Rahmaniah, R. (2023). The use of lingokids game application to encourage the young learners' english vocabularies. *International Social Sciences and Humanities*, *2*(1), 197–203. DOI: 10.32528/issh.v2i1.123

Setyoadi, E., & Patmanthara, S. (2024). Students' goal orientation and gamification in learning for academic performance: A systematic literature review. *Research and Development in Education (Raden)*, *4*(1), 390–403. DOI: 10.22219/raden.v4i1.32630

Shaffer, D. W., Halverson, R., Squire, K. R., & Gee, J. P. (2005). *Video games and the future of learning (WCER Working Paper No. 2005-4)*. Madison: University of Wisconsin–Madison, Wisconsin Center for Education Research (NJ1).

Shaffer, D. W. (2006). Epistemic frames for epistemic games. *Computers & Education*, *46*(3), 223–234. DOI: 10.1016/j.compedu.2005.11.003

Shaffer, D. W. (2006). *How computer games help children learn*. Palgrave Macmillan. DOI: 10.1057/9780230601994

Shah, J. (2024). *Rethinking higher education through multidisciplinary studies*. jes, 20(4s), 2060-2063. https://doi.org/DOI: 10.52783/jes.2309

Shala, D. (2024). Learning styles and motivation: Their role in academic performance. *Journal of Educational and Social Research*, *14*(3), 258. DOI: 10.36941/jesr-2024-0071

Shams, L., & Seitz, A. R. (2008). Benefits of multisensory learning. *Trends in Cognitive Sciences*, *12*(11), 411–417. DOI: 10.1016/j.tics.2008.07.006

Sharma, R., Tan, C., Gomez, D., Xu, C., & Dubé, A. K. (2025). Guiding teachers' game-based learning: How user experience of a digital curriculum guide impacts teachers' self-efficacy and acceptance of educational games. *Teaching and Teacher Education*, *155*, 104915. DOI: 10.1016/j.tate.2024.104915

Shaw, A. (2014). *Gaming at the Edge: Sexuality and Gender at the Margins of Gamer Culture*. University of Minnesota Press.

Shizha, E., & Makuvaza, N. (Eds.). (2022). *Re-thinking postcolonial education in Sub-Saharan Africa in the 21st century*. Sense Publishers.

Shujaa, M. J., & Shujaa, K. J. (Eds.). (2015). *The SAGE encyclopedia of African cultural heritage in North America*. Sage Publications. DOI: 10.4135/9781483346373

Shute, V. J. (2011). Stealth assessment in computer-based games to support learning. In *Computer games and instruction* (pp. 503–524). IAP Information Age Publishing. DOI: 10.1108/978-1-61735-410-620251025

Shute, V. J., Ventura, M., & Kim, Y. J. (2013). Assessment and Learning of Qualitative Physics in Newton's Playground. *The Journal of Educational Research, 106*(6), 423–430. DOI: 10.1080/00220671.2013.832970

Sibanda, R. (2019). Mother tongue education in multilingual township: Possibilities for recognising lok'shin lingua in South Africa. *Reading and Writing, 10*(1), a225. DOI: 10.4102/rw.v10i1.225

Simon, S., Naylor, S., Keogh, B., Maloney, J., & Downing, B. (2008). Puppets Promoting Engagement and Talk in Science. *International Journal of Science Education, 30*(9), 1229–1248. DOI: 10.1080/09500690701474037

Sinha, A. K., & Kumar, R. (2025). The tradition of folk songs: global perspective and comparative study.

Siraj-Blatchford, J., & Brock, L. (2019). How to scaffold learning through free-flow play. *Early Years Educator, 21*(3), 31–33. DOI: 10.12968/eyed.2019.21.3.31

Sitzmann, T. (2011). A meta-analytic examination of the instructional effectiveness of computer-based simulation games. *Personnel Psychology, 64*(2), 489–528. DOI: 10.1111/j.1744-6570.2011.01190.x

Smart Kidz Club, Inc. (2020, March 21). *Namibia Reads* [Mobile app]. Launched on Namibia's Independence Day. https://www.smartkidzclub.app/

Smit, B., & Onwuegbuzie, A. J. (2018). Observations in qualitative inquiry: When what you see is not what you see. *International Journal of Qualitative Methods, 17*(1), 1–3. DOI: 10.1177/1609406918816766

Smith, E. W. (1945). The Realm of a Rain Queen.

Smitherman, G. (1999). *Talkin that Talk: Language*. Culture and Education in African America. DOI: 10.4324/9780203065419

Smith, J., & Sanchez, L. (2015). Collaborative game-based learning in the EFL classroom. *TESOL Journal, 6*(2), 253–271. DOI: 10.1002/tesj.177

Smith, L. T. (2022). *Decolonizing methodologies: Research and Indigenous peoples* (3rd ed.). Zed Books.

Smith, P. L. T. (2021). *Decolonizing Methodologies: Research and Indigenous Peoples*. Zed Books Ltd. DOI: 10.5040/9781350225282

Smith, R., Snow, P., Serry, T., & Hammond, L. (2021). The role of background knowledge in reading comprehension: A critical review. *Reading Psychology, 42*(3), 214–240. https://www.creighton.edu/sites/default/files/2021-12/SPAHP-schrammhannah-3402420-59866244-schramm-hannah-capstone-presentation-2.pdf. DOI: 10.1080/02702711.2021.1888348

Snow, C. E., & Van Hemel, S. B. (2008). *Early Childhood Assessment: Why, What, and How*. National Academies Press.

Soja, E. (1996). *Thirdspace: Journeys to Los Angeles and Other Real-and-Imagined Places*. Blackwell.

Sone, E. M. (2018). The folktale and social values in traditional Africa. *Eastern African Literary and Cultural Studies, 4*(2), 142-159). https://doi.org/DOI: 10.1080/23277408.2018.1485314

Spanellis, A., Pyrko, I., & Dörfler, V. (2021). Gamifying situated learning in organisations. *Management Learning*, *53*(3), 525–546. DOI: 10.1177/13505076211038812

Spolsky, B. (2021). Rethinking language policy. *Language Policy*, *20*(1), 1–15. DOI: 10.1007/s10993-006-9045-0

Stack, M., & Bunt, B. (2023). Developing a game-based learning pedagogy for teaching history using Napoleon Total War. *Yesterday and Today*, 30(1), 9–35. https://doi.org/DOI: 10.17159/2223-0386/2023/n30a2

Statistics New Zealand. (2023). *Te Kupenga 2023: Maori language speakers*. Statistics New Zealand.

Steele, C. M., & Aronson, J. (1995). Stereotype threat and the intellectual test performance of African Americans. *Journal of Personality and Social Psychology*, *69*(5), 797–811. DOI: 10.1037/0022-3514.69.5.797

Steinkuehler, C. (2006). Massively Multiplayer Online Video Gaming as Participation in a Discourse. Mind. *Mind, Culture, and Activity*, *13*(1), 38–52. DOI: 10.1207/s15327884mca1301_4

Steinkuehler, C. (2010). Video Games and Digital Literacies. Journal of Adolescent & Adult Literacy -. *Journal of Adolescent & Adult Literacy*, *54*(1), 61–63. DOI: 10.1598/JAAL.54.1.7

Steinkuehler, C., & Duncan, S. (2008). Scientific Habits of Mind in Virtual Worlds. *Journal of Science Education and Technology*, *17*(6), 530–543. DOI: 10.1007/s10956-008-9120-8

Steinkuehler, C., & Squire, K. (2023). Gaming in educational contexts. In *Handbook of educational psychology* (pp. 674–695). Routledge. DOI: 10.4324/9780429433726-34

Stein, P. (2008). *Multimodal pedagogies in diverse classrooms: Representation, rights and resources*. Routledge.

Stephens, V. (2018). National Library of New Zealand. Feel the rhythm: developing language through rhythm and rhyme. Available at: https://natlib.govt.nz/blog/posts/feel-the-rhythm-developing-language-throughrhythm-and-rhyme (accessed 06 September 2025).

Stoerger, S., Herring, S. C., & Kouper, I. (2007). "Great Job, Quester!" Assessing Language Skills on Quest Atlantis. In *Texas Linguistics Forum* (Vol. 50).

Strauss, A. M., & Bipath, K. (2020). Exploring the influence of parents' home reading practices on emergent literacy. *Journal for Language Teaching = Ijenali Yekufundzisa Lulwimi =. Tydskrif vir Taalonderrig, 54*(1), 195–213. DOI: 10.4314/jlt.v54i1.5

Strauss, A. M., & Bipath, K. (2021). Evolving trends of distance learning for basic education in Namibia: A parental perspective during COVID-19 lockdown. *Journal for Language Teaching= Ijenali Yekufundzisa Lulwimi=. Tydskrif vir Taalonderrig, 55*(1), 57–75. DOI: 10.4314/jlt.v55i1.3

Strauss, A. M., & Marshall, J. (2024). *Rural Undergraduate Students' Narratives of English Language Learning Within Multilingual Classroom Contexts: A Namibian Perspective*. Rural Education Journal. DOI: 10.55533/2643-9662.1517

Strauss, A., & Corbin, J. (2008). *Basics of qualitative research* (3rd ed.). Sage.

Street, B. V. (1984). *Literacy in Theory and Practice*. Cambridge University Press.

Street, B. V. (2014). *Social Literacies: Critical Approaches to Literacy in Development, Ethnography and Education*. Routledge., DOI: 10.4324/9781315844282

Strydom, W., Funke, N., Nienaber, S., Nortje, K., & Steyn, M. (2010). Evidence-based policymaking: A review. *South African Journal of Science, 106*(5/6). Advance online publication. DOI: 10.4102/sajs.v106i5/6.249

Suarlin, S. (2023). Integrating environmental education to form environmental care characters in schools. *Advances in Community Services Research, 1*(2), 44–53. DOI: 10.60079/acsr.v1i2.335

Su, C. Y., Cheng, C. H., & Lin, Y. L. (2021). A systematic review of digital game-based learning in language education: 2000–2020. *Journal of Educational Technology & Society, 24*(1), 250–266.

Sughra, U., & Usmani, A. (2022). Comparison of critical thinking among undergraduate medical students of conventional and integrated curricula in twin cities. *Pakistan Journal of Medical Sciences, 38*(6). Advance online publication. DOI: 10.12669/pjms.38.6.5409

Sunday-Kanu, R. A. (2015). Folk music in child development: A tool for enhanced self-esteem, social responsibility and cultural maturity. [JANIM]. *Journal of the Association of Nigerian Musicologists., 9*, 227–243.

Sun, P., & Sornyai, P. (2025). Mongolian folk songs: Integrating traditional music into contemporary literacy. *International Journal of Education and Literacy Studies, 13*(1), 12–22. DOI: 10.7575/aiac.ijels.v.13n.2p.19

Sweller, J. (1988). Cognitive load during problem solving: Effects on learning. *Cognitive Science, 12*(2), 257–285. DOI: 10.1207/s15516709cog1202_4

Syafii, M. L., Santoso, S., & Hartono, S. (2021). Story-telling technique utilizing puppets to enhance the learners" speaking competence. [IJonSES]. *International Journal on Social and Education Sciences, 3*(2), 304–341. DOI: 10.46328/ijonses.70

Sykes, J. M., & Reinhardt, J. (2023). *Language at play: Digital games in second and foreign language teaching and learning* (2nd ed.). Bloomsbury Academic.

Szalkiewicz, A. (2017). *Why confidence is critical to problem solving?* https://kepner - tregoe.com/blogs/why-confidence-is-critical-to-problem-solving/

Szapiro, D., Kutay, C., Garcia, J., Raffe, W., & Green, R. (2020). *Learning on Country: A game-based experience of an Australian Aboriginal language.* In Proceedings of the International Conference of Innovation in Media and Visual Design. Atlantis Press. game-based learning can support immersion in indigenous oral language contexts that build socio-cultural competence.DOI: 10.2991/assehr.k.201202.054

Takeuchi, L. M., & Sarah, V. (2014). LeveL up Learning: A national survey on teaching with digital games - By &. Retrieved November 12, 2025, from https://www.readkong.com/page/level-up-learning-6779027

Talbot, P. A. (1943). A Study of Lovedu Society.

Tang, J., & Sornyai, P. (2023). The Cultural Treasures of Baima Tibetan Folk Songs in Gansu Province, China, as a Resource for Literacy Education in Chinese Music History. *International Journal of Education and Literacy Studies, 11*(3), 234-243. https://**doi**.org/ AIAC, IJELS.DOI: 10.7575/aiac.ijels.v.11n.3p.234

Tang, H. E., & Othman, N. (2023). Game-based learning in language classrooms: Integrating music and oral traditions for learner engagement. *Education and Information Technologies*, *28*(5), 6123–6140.

Tan, J. P. L., & Teo, T. W. (2021). Preparing for Industry 4.0: Evaluating the Impact of Critical Thinking and Problem-Solving Training in Higher Education. *European Journal of Engineering Education*, •••, 1–17.

Tarhini, A., Hone, K., & Liu, X. (2024). Measuring the moderating effect of cultural dimensions on the Technology Acceptance Model: A study in the context of three Arab countries. *Journal of Educational Computing Research*, *52*(3), 305–328.

Teacher Created Materials. (2024). Wordless books and your classroom—a perfect match. Retrieved from https://www.teachercreatedmaterials.com/blog/wordless-books-in-your-classroom-a-perfect-match

Tegon, R. (2024). An updated systematic review on the impact of gamification in education: Insights from early 2024. In Martinez-Roig, R., Pulido-Montes, C., & Mateu-Luján, B. (Eds.), *Nuevas investigaciones educativas para definir la enseñanza y el aprendizaje* (pp. 318–342). Ediciones Octaedro.

Terralingua. (2022). Biocultural diversity and Indigenous knowledge: Global perspectives. Terralingua.

Thamaga, L. J. 2012, 'IsiNdebele influence on Sepedi learners around the Dennilton Region in the Limpopo Province', MA dissertation, University of Pretoria.

Thangjai, N., & Worapun, W. (2022). Developing inquiry-based learning characteristics of Grade 7 students using integrated 5E's of inquiry-based learning and game-based learning. *Journal of Educational Issues*, *8*(1), 137–150. DOI: 10.5296/jei.v8i1.19547

The New London Group. (1996). A Pedagogy of Multiliteracies: Designing Social Futures. *Harvard Educational Review*, *66*(1), 60–93. DOI: 10.17763/haer.66.1.17370n67v22j160u

The Witness. (2022, March 3). *Mixed opinions on the push to introduce mother tongue instruction in schools*. https://witness.co.za/news/2022/03/21/mixed-opinion-on-push-to-introduce-mother-tongue-instruction-in-schools-20220319/

Thimmanna., Sharma, A.V.N.S., Naik, M. S., Radhakrishnan, S., Sharma, A., (2024). Personalized Learning Paths: Adapting Education with AI-Driven Curriculum. *European Economic Letters (EEL)*, *14*(1), 31–40. https://doi.org/DOI: 10.52783/eel.v14i1.993

Thompson, C., & Parreira do Amaral, M. (2019). Introduction: Researching the Global Education Industry. In Parreira do Amaral, M., Steiner-Khamsi, G., & Thompson, C. (Eds.), *Researching the Global Education Industry: Commodification, the Market and Business Involvement* (pp. 1–21). Springer International Publishing. DOI: 10.1007/978-3-030-04236-3_1

Thondhlana, J., & Kadenge, M. (2023). Linguistic marketplaces and language shift among urban youth in Zimbabwe. *Journal of Multilingual and Multicultural Development*, *44*(5), 441–458.

Thorne, S. L., Black, R. W., & Sykes, J. M. (2009). Second Language Use, Socialization, and Learning in Internet Interest Communities and Online Gaming. *Modern Language Journal*, *93*(s1), 802–821. DOI: 10.1111/j.1540-4781.2009.00974.x

Thorne, S. L., Fischer, I., & Lu, X. (2023). The semiotic ecology and linguistic complexity of an online game world. In Chapelle, C. A. (Ed.), *The encyclopedia of applied linguistics* (pp. 5158–5164). Wiley-Blackwell.

Tierney, J. L. (1995). *Puppetry in Early Childhood Education*" (Doctoral Thesis), University of Massachusetts Amherst.

Tolentino, R., Baradaran, A., Gore, G., Pluye, P., & Abbasgholizadeh-Rahimi, S. (2024). Curriculum frameworks and educational programs in ai for medical students, residents, and practicing physicians: Scoping review. *JMIR Medical Education*, *10*, e54793. DOI: 10.2196/54793

Tolson, M. (2018). The Rising Glory of Africa. *The Patriot Poets: American Odes, Progress Poems, and the State of the Union*, 314.

Tonbuloğlu, B. (2023). An evaluation of the use of artificial intelligence applications in online education. *Journal of Educational Technology and Online Learning*, *6*(4), 866–884. DOI: 10.31681/jetol.1335906

Toshtemirova, K. A. (2021). The role of riddles in teaching logical thinking. *International Journal of Innovations in Engineering Research and Technology*, *8*(3), 24–25.

Trang, N., & Thư, P. (2024). The role of ai in improving student learning outcomes: Evidence in vietnam. *International Journal of Multidisciplinary Research and Analysis*, *07*(06). Advance online publication. DOI: 10.47191/ijmra/v7-i06-48

Travis, B. (2017). *Assassin's Creed Origins' Discovery Tour shows how video games could be an education game-changer.* https://www.standard.co.uk/news/tech/assassins-creed-origins-discovery-tour-shows-how-video-games-could-be-an-education-gamechanger-a3663966.html

Trybus, J. (2015). Game-Based Learning: What it is, Why it Works, and Where it's Going. New Media Institute., Retrieved January 10, 2026, from.

Tsebe, A. (2021). The epistemology of mother tongue(s): What does this mean for language in education? *The Journal of Transdisciplinary Research in Southern Africa*, *17*(1), 1–10. DOI: 10.4102/td.v17i1.1068

Tubino, L. & Adachi, C. (2022). Developing feedback literacy capabilities through an ai automated feedback tool. *Ascilite Publications,* e22039. https://doi.org/DOI: 10.14742/apubs.2022.39

Tucker, L., & Govender, P. (2020). Parental engagement in early childhood centres: Challenges and prospects. *Perspectives in Education*, *38*(2), 72–88.

Tukhtasinova, D. (2024). Importance of Riddles in Language Learning. *Excellencia: International Multidisciplinary Journal of Education*, *2*(3), 1–4.

Tungalag, O., & Narengaowa. (2024). Research on metacognitive strategies of children's self-regulated learning in early childhood education. *Frontiers in Psychology*, *15*, 11368603. DOI: 10.3389/fpsyg.2024.11368603

Tuong Van, B. (2024). The role of family and community in preserving the linguistic identity of the Tay, Nung and Dao people. *International Journal of Education Humanities and Social Science*, *7*(4), 293–302. DOI: 10.54922/IJEHSS.2024.0768

Turin, T. C., Raihan, M., & Chowdhury, N. (2024). Paradigms of approaches to research. *Bangabandhu Sheikh Mujib Medical University Journal*, *17*(2), e73973–e73973. DOI: 10.3329/bsmmuj.v17i2.73973

Tyni, J., Tarkiainen, A., López-Pernas, S., Saqr, M., Kahila, J., Bednarik, R., & Tedre, M. (2022). Games and rewards: A scientometric study of rewards in educational and serious games. *IEEE Access : Practical Innovations, Open Solutions*, *10*, 31578–31585. DOI: 10.1109/ACCESS.2022.3160230

Tzafilkou, K., Perifanou, M., & Economides, A. (2023). Assessing teachers' digital competence in primary and secondary education: Applying a new instrument to integrate pedagogical and professional elements for digital education. *Education and Information Technologies*, *28*(12), 16017–16040. DOI: 10.1007/s10639-023-11848-9

Ubisoft (2025). *All discovery tour curriculum guides.* https://www.ubisoft.com/en-us/game/assassins-creed/discovery-tour/curriculum-guide

Ugwu, C. N., & Eze, V. H. U. (2023). Qualitative Research. International Digital Organization for Scientific Research. *IDOSR Journal of Computer and Applied Sciences*, *8*(1), 20–35.

Ulagammal, S., & Chaluvarayaswamy, R. (2023). Expanding access to mindfulness education in adaptive learning: Enhancing student well-being and academic success. *Thiagarajar College of Preceptors Edu Spectra*, *5*(S1), 81–84. DOI: 10.34293/eduspectra.v5is1-may23.014

UNESCO. (2020). *Education for sustainable development: A roadmap.* UNESCO Publishing. https://unesdoc.unesco.org/ark:/48223/pf0000374802

UNESCO. (2020). *Global Education Monitoring Report 2020: Inclusion and education: All means all.* UNESCO., DOI: 10.54676/JJNK6989

UNESCO. (2020). *Learning through play: Strengthening education through indigenous games*. UNESCO Publishing.

UNESCO. (2022). *Global education monitoring report 2022: Non-state actors in education*. UNESCO Publishing.

UNESCO. (2022). *Global Education Monitoring Report*. UNESCO.

UNESCO. (2023). *Atlas of the world's languages in danger*. UNESCO Publishing.

UNESCO. (2023). *Learning with intangible cultural heritage: Folk songs and oral traditions in education*. UNESCO Publishing. https://unesdoc.unesco.org/

UNESCO. (2024) Multilingual education: A key to quality and inclusive learning. Available at: https://www.unesco.org/en/articles/multilingual-education-key-quality-and-inclusive-learning [Accessed 02 February 2026].

UNESCO. (2024, March 5). *Multilingual education, the bet to preserve indigenous languages and justice.* https://www.unesco.org/en/articles/multilingual-education-bet-preserve-indigenous-languages-and-justice

Unwin, P. T. H. (2009). *ICT4D: Information and Communication Technology for Development*. Cambridge University Press.

Uygun, D. (2024). Teachers' perspectives on artificial intelligence in education. *Advances in Mobile Learning Educational Research*, *4*(1), 931–939. DOI: 10.25082/AMLER.2024.01.005

Valencia, R. (2010). Dismantling Contemporary Deficit Thinking: Educational Thought and Practice. Dismantling Contemporary Deficit Thinking: Educational Thought and Practice, 1–223. DOI: 10.4324/9780203853214

van Dijk, J. A. G. M. (2005). *The Deepening Divide: Inequality in the Information Society*. SAGE Publications.

Van Niekerk, J. (2018). Afrikaans stories of Jackal and Hyena: Oral and written traditions. *Tydskrif vir Letterkunde, 55*(3), 80–97. DOI: 10.17159/2309-9070/tvl.v.55i3.5511

Varas, J., Coronel, B., Villagrán, I., Escalona, G., Hernández, R., Schuit, G., & Achurra, P. (2023). Innovations in surgical training: exploring the role of artificial intelligence and large language models (llm). *Revista Do Colégio Brasileiro De Cirurgiões,* 50. https://doi.org/DOI: 10.1590/0100-6991e-20233605-en

Vasquez, V. M. (2014). *Negotiating critical literacies with young children*. Routledge. DOI: 10.4324/9781315848624

Venkatesh, V., & Davis, F. D. (2023). A theoretical extension of the Technology Acceptance Model: Four longitudinal field studies. *Management Science, 46*(2), 186–204. DOI: 10.1287/mnsc.46.2.186.11926

Venketsamy, A. (2023). Exploring the teacher-learner ratio and its effect on invitational teaching and learning: A South African study. *Journal for Education of Gifted Young Scientists, 11*(1), 1–13. DOI: 10.17478/jegys.1237615

Verger, A., Steiner-Khamsi, G., & Lubienski, C. (2016). The Emergence and Structuring of the Global Education Industry: Towards an Analytical Framework.

Viriri, A., & Viriri, P. (2023). An Afrocentric critique of the language-in-education policy in Zimbabwe. *Educational Research for Social Change, 12*(1), 56–72.

Vos, N., van der Meijden, H., & Denessen, E. (2011). Effects of constructing versus playing an educational game on student motivation and deep learning strategy use. *Computers & Education, 56*(1), 127–137. DOI: 10.1016/j.compedu.2010.08.013

Vygotsky, L. (1978). *Mind in Society*. Harvard University Press.

Vygotsky, L. S. (1978). *Mind in society: The development of higher psychological processes*. Harvard University Press.

Vygotsky, L. S. (1978). *Mind in Society: The Development of Higher Psychological Processes*. Harvard University Press.

Vygotsky, L. S., & Cole, M. (1978). *Mind in Society: Development of Higher Psychological Processes*. Harvard University Press.

Wa Thiong'o, N. (2021). Decolonising the mind: The politics of language in African literature (Anniversary ed.). James Currey Publishers.

Walisundara, D. C., & Ranaweera, M. (2020). Shyamani Hettiarachchi. *Journal of Intellectual Disabilities, 1*, 19.

Wallerstein, N., & Duran, B. (2023). Community-based participatory research contributions to intervention research: The intersection of science and practice to improve health equity. *American Journal of Public Health, 100*(S1), S40–S46. DOI: 10.2105/AJPH.2009.184036

Walsh, C. E. (2023). On justice, pedagogy, and decolonial (izing) praxis. *Educational Theory, 73*(4), 511–529. DOI: 10.1111/edth.12592

Walsh, G., Sproule, L., McGuinness, C., & Trew, K. (2011). Playful structure: A novel image of early years pedagogy for primary school classrooms. *Early Years Journal of International Research and Development, 31*(2), 107–119. DOI: 10.1080/09575146.2011.579070

Walsh, S. (2019). Under the Umbrella: Pedagogy, knowledge production, and video from the margins of the movement. *Educational Philosophy and Theory, 51*(2), 200–211. DOI: 10.1080/00131857.2017.1310018

Walter, Y. (2024). Embracing the future of artificial intelligence in the classroom: The relevance of ai literacy, prompt engineering, and critical thinking in modern education. *International Journal of Educational Technology in Higher Education, 21*(1), 15. Advance online publication. DOI: 10.1186/s41239-024-00448-3

Wang, F. (2016). Role-play activities and ESL speaking competence. *TESL-EJ, 20*(3), 1–18.

Wang, M., & Zheng, X. (2021). Using game-based learning to support learning science: A study with middle school students. *The Asia-Pacific Education Researcher, 30*(2), 167–176. DOI: 10.1007/s40299-020-00523-z

Wang, S., Shen, R., & Novak, D. (2019). Digital vs. non-digital games in language learning: A comparative study. *Interactive Learning Environments, 27*(8), 1077–1092. DOI: 10.1080/10494820.2018.1460964

Warschauer, M. (2004). Technology and Social Inclusion: Rethinking the Digital Divide. DOI: 10.7551/mitpress/6699.001.0001

Warschauer, M., & Matuchniak, T. (2010). New Technology and Digital Worlds: Analyzing Evidence of Equity in Access, Use, and Outcomes. *Review of Research in Education, 34*(1), 179–225. DOI: 10.3102/0091732X09349791

Watkins, S. (2011). Digital Divide: Navigating the Digital Edge. *International Journal of Learning and Media, 3*(2), 1–12. DOI: 10.1162/ijlm_a_00072

Weisberg, L., Kohnen, A., & Dawson, K. (2022). Impacts of a digital literacy intervention on preservice teachers' civic online reasoning abilities, strategies, and perceptions. *Journal of Technology and Teacher Education, 30*(1), 73–98. DOI: 10.70725/926509jtmzpi

Whitebread, D., Basilio, M., Kuvalja, M., & Verma, M. (2012). The Importance of Play. Brussels: *Toy Industries of Europe (TIE)*, 1-54.

Wilson, S. (2022). *Research is ceremony: Indigenous research methods* (2nd ed.). Fernwood Publishing.

Wiysahnyuy, L. F., & Valentine, N. B. (2023). Folktales as indigenous pedagogic tools for educating school children: A mixed methods study among the Nso of Cameroon. *Frontiers in Psychology, 14*, 1049691. DOI: 10.3389/fpsyg.2023.1049691

Wood, E., Ange, B., & Miller, D. (2021). Are we ready to integrate artificial intelligence literacy into medical school curriculum: Students and faculty survey. *Journal of Medical Education and Curricular Development, 8*, 23821205211024078. Advance online publication. DOI: 10.1177/23821205211024078

Wouters, P., van Nimwegen, C., van Oostendorp, H., & van der Spek, E. D. (2013). A meta-analysis of the cognitive and motivational effects of serious games. *Journal of Educational Psychology, 105*(2), 249–265. DOI: 10.1037/a0031311

Wouters, P., & van Oostendorp, H. (2013). A meta-analytic review of the role of instructional support in game-based learning. *Computers & Education, 60*(1), 412–425. DOI: 10.1016/j.compedu.2012.07.018

Xeketwana, S. (2021). *The implementation of language policy for multilingual education, extending the teaching and learning of IsiXhosa for communicative purposes in teacher education*. [Unpublished doctoral dissertation] Stellenbosch University. South Africa

Xiao, M., Amzah, F., & Rong, W. (2023). Experience of beauty: Valuing emotional engagement and collaboration in teacher-child storytelling activities. *International Journal of Learning. Teaching and Educational Research, 22*(2), 165–187. DOI: 10.26803/ijlter.22.2.10

Xu, C., Sharma, R., & Dubé, A. K. (2023). Discovery Tour Curriculum Guides to Improve Teachers' Adoption of Serious. In Champion, E., & Hiriart, J. (Eds.), *Assassin's Creed in the Classroom: History's Playground or a Stab in the Dark?* (pp. 12–35). De Gruyter. DOI: 10.1515/9783111253275-003

Yang, L., Boonsrianan, P., & Karin, K. (2025). Chinese folk music literacy: A case study of Ebian Yi wedding songs. *International Journal of Education and Literacy Studies, 13*(2), 122–134. DOI: 10.7575/aiac.ijels.v.13n.2p.143

Yang, L., Li, R., & Zhou, Y. (2024). Research trends of game-based language learning in K-12 education: A systematic review of SSCI articles during 2009–2022. *Journal of Computer Assisted Learning, 40*(3), 1218–1230. DOI: 10.1111/jcal.12944

Yang, Y. T. C. (2017). Digital game-based language learning: A case study on multiplayer online games. *Journal of Educational Technology & Society, 20*(3), 1–15.

Yang, Y., Chen, H., & Wang, Q. (2024). Game-Based Language Learning in Technological Contexts. *Systematic Reviews*. Advance online publication. DOI: 10.4018/IJOPCD.316184

Yazdanpanah, V., Gerding, E., Stein, S., Dastani, M., Jonker, C., Norman, T., & Ramchurn, S. (2022). Reasoning about responsibility in autonomous systems: Challenges and opportunities. *AI & Society, 38*(4), 1453–1464. DOI: 10.1007/s00146-022-01607-8

Yeboah, R., Amponsah, K. D., Mintah, P. G., Sedofia, T., & Donkor, P. B. (2023). Game-based learning in Ghana primary schools: Listening to the views of teachers. *Education, 53*(4), 1–5. DOI: 10.1080/03004279.2023.2171269

Yende, S. J., & Dhlamini, M. S. (2025). Exploring picture stories and repetition in L2 acquisition through two IsiNguni language songs: A cognitive analysis. *Journal of Second and Multiple Language Acquisition-JSMULA*, 768-786.

Yende, S. J. (2023). Effectiveness of music education in developing and fostering reading and writing for learners. *Reading and Writing, 14*(1), a425. DOI: 10.4102/rw.v14i1.425

Yetman, D. (2000). What is the zone of proximal development? *Healthline.* https://www.healthline.com/health/zone-of-proximal-development

Yin, R. K. (1984). Case study research: Design and methods. *Sage (Atlanta, Ga.).*

Yin, R. K. (2018). *Case Study Research and Applications: Design and Methods* (6th ed.). Sage Publications.

Yongjie, X., & Meesorn, P. (2024). The constructing the Mongolian short songs folk music for Saxophone Quartet Guidebook for teaching first-year students at Wuhan Conservatory of Music in The People's Republic of China. *Journal of Roi Kaensarn Academi, 9*(7), 171–181.

Young, S., & Ilari, B. (Eds.). (2019). *Music in early childhood: Multi-disciplinary perspectives and inter-disciplinary exchanges* (International Perspectives on Early Childhood Education and Development, Vol. 27). Springer. DOI: 10.1007/978-3-030-17791-1

Young, M. F., Slota, S., Cutter, A. B., Jalette, G., Mullin, G., Lai, B., Simeoni, Z., Tran, M., & Yukhymenko, M. (2012). Our Princess Is in Another Castle: A Review of Trends in Serious Gaming for Education. *Review of Educational Research*, *82*(1), 61–89. DOI: 10.3102/0034654312436980

You, X. (2023). Literacy transmission practices for the preservation of Wuyue ceremonial folk songs. *International Journal of Education and Literacy Studies.*

Yuliarsih, Y. (2022). The Use of Riddle Game To Improve Students' Vocabulary. *The Ellite of Unira*, *5*(1), 1–5. DOI: 10.53712/ellite.v5i1.1400

Yumnam, R. (2021). Folklore in English Language Curriculum. Guines Journal. *An Interdisciplinary Peer Reviewed Journal of North East India Studies*. Volume vii & viii (2020-2021): 85-98.

Yusuf, H.O. (2015). Analysis of Nigeria secondary schools students' reading habits: Implication for teacher education curriculum for English as a second language. *African Journal of Humanities,* 2(2), Kaduna state University. Pyla- mak Services Ltd.

Zainal, N. (2023). University students' perspectives on gamification in vocabulary learning: A literature review. *Malaysian Journal of Social Sciences and Humanities (Mjssh)*, *8*(5), e002314. DOI: 10.47405/mjssh.v8i5.2314

Zembylas, M. (2025). Decolonial pathways in education: Walter Mignolo, epistemic delinking, and the risks of ethno-essentialism. *Globalisation, Societies and Education*, 1-15. 1-15. https://doi.org/DOI: 10.1080/14767724.2025.2459110

Zhang, Y. (2023). Preservation and literacy transmission of Xinyang folk songs. A*International Journal of Education and Literacy Studies. 12*(2):66- DOI:DOI: 10.7575/aiac.ijels.v.12n.2p.66

Zhang, F. (2018). The application of a game-based approach in primary school English teaching. *Advances in Social Science, Education and Humanities Research*, *15*(1), 1–13. DOI: 10.2991/emehss-18.2018.120

Zhang, J., & Zhang, Z. (2024). AI in teacher education: Unlocking new dimensions in teaching support, inclusive learning, and digital literacy. *Journal of Computer Assisted Learning*, *40*(4), 1871–1885. DOI: 10.1111/jcal.12988

Zhao, J., Juithong, S., & Nilnopkoon, P. (2024). Effecting an adaptive learning system on academic achievement as regulations for measuring pharmacist qualifications to licensure of pharmaceutical management students. *IJSASR*, *4*(3), 573–582. DOI: 10.60027/ijsasr.2024.4357

Zheng, D., Young, M. F., Wagner, M. M., & Brewer, R. A. (2009). Negotiation for action: English language learning in game-based virtual worlds. *Modern Language Journal*, *93*(4), 489–511. DOI: 10.1111/j.1540-4781.2009.00927.x

Zhou, X. (2024). Sociocultural theory in early childhood education. *International Journal on E-Learning*, *4*(1), 1–12. Retrieved August 17, 2025, from https://www.researchgate.net/publication/380209252_Sociocultural_Theory_in_Early_Childhood_Education

Zimbabwe National Statistics Agency. (2022). *Population census 2022: Preliminary report*. ZIMSTAT.

Zimbabwe, U. N. I. C. E. F. (2023). *Education statistics: Zimbabwe country profile 2023*. UNICEF.

Zou, D., Xie, H., & Wang, F. L. (2022). A meta-analysis of digital game-based vocabulary learning. *Educational Research Review*, *36*, 100446.

Zourmpakis, A., Kalogiannakis, M., & Papadakis, S. (2023). Adaptive gamification in science education: An analysis of the impact of implementation and adapted game elements on students' motivation. *Computers*, *12*(7), 143. DOI: 10.3390/computers12070143

Zulkefli, M., & bin Jamil, A. I. (. (2024). Advancing Islamic Education with Game-Based Learning: Principles, Effects, And Implementation Obstacles. *Journal of Islamic Educational Research*, *10*(1), 1–12. DOI: 10.22452/jier.vol10no1.1

# About the Contributors

**Millicent Ngema** is a Senior Lecturer in the Department of Early Childhood Education at the University of South Africa. She has Doctoral degree in Education (DEd) obtained at the University of South Africa in 2016. With a background in primary education, she has contributed to developing reading materials that have been translated into various African languages. She has also written study materials and articles to help learners transition from their mother tongue to English as an additional language. Her research interests include teacher professional development, literacy in African languages, and early childhood education. She has published articles and presented at national conferences, focusing on practical solutions for teachers and improving educational outcomes in under-resourced areas.

**Nkidi Phatudi** is an Emeritus Professor in the Department of Early Childhood Education, College of Education at the University of South Africa (UNISA). She is the past head of the department of ECD at UNISA. Her research interests are transitions in the early years and the teaching and learning of literacy in the Foundation Phase. She has published articles in transition of children and authored/edited books on language teaching and recently was one of the coauthors of a book in Leadership in ECD: Global Perspectives on Leadership in Early Childhood Education published by Helsinki University Press.

***

**Oindrilla Ghosh** is a Research Scholar hailing from the School of Law at Christ (Deemed to be University) Bangalore, India, focuses her research on health of tribal communities. Her work includes total 39 publications on Neuroscience on Organizational Behavior at IGI Global and also Environmental Disasters that are indexed in SCOPUS and Web of Sciences conference proceedings. She completed her early education at Loreto Day School, Bowbazar and went on to achieve distinction in her undergraduate (B.A/LL.B) and postgraduate (LL.M) studies at Calcutta University. Having served as an Assistant Professor of Law at Kingston Law College,Barasat, Kolkata, Ghosh has actively participated in numerous National Conferences, International Conferences, UN Global Summits, webinars, and seminars organized by prestigious academic institutions. Her expertise lies in health perspectives, environmental studies, human behavior, and related areas. Additionally, she has conducted various workshops, lectures in educational institutions, and is engaged with NGO's to help the needy.

**Xolisa Guzula** is a Senior Lecturer in Applied Language and Literacy Studies at the University of Cape Town. She is interested in emergent biliteracy, literacy as a social practice, language ideologies, third spaces, critical literacy, children's literature, decolonizing language and literacies and multiliteracies anchored in African oral literature. She specialises in linguistic ethnographic research in the field of early biliteracy in African languages and English and in bi/multilingual education. She advocates for justice in the way we use language in education through the bua-lit language and literacy collective which she chairs. Dr Guzula is also a chair of the Western Cape committee of the Literacy Association of South Africa (LITASA).

**Salmita Matshemo Khumalo** holds a Doctor of Education (DEd) degree with a specialisation in Early Childhood Language and Literacy Development from Tshwane University of Technology (TUT). She is currently a Lecturer in the Department of Early Childhood Education in the College of Education at the University of South Africa (UNISA). Dr Khumalo is the recipient of two prestigious teaching and learning awards. She was awarded the Emerging Lecturer of the Year by Tshwane University of Technology and received the Charles Freysen Award from the Independent Institute of Education (IIE) in recognition of excellence in teaching and learning. An emerging scholar in the research field of early childhood education, Dr Khumalo has published in accredited journals and contributed to scholarly book chapters. She has also presented research papers at both national and international conferences. Her research interests include language and literacy in the early years, early childhood education, transformative pedagogies, translanguaging, curriculum development, and teacher development in higher education.

**Nomatter Kufarimani** is an ICT specialist and lecturer at Morgan ZINTEC College of Education. She collaborates her researches in ICT with other disciplines in the Humanities department.

**Binod Kumar** is a graduate student known for his academic excellence, with his total 28 scholarly works indexed in Scopus database on Neuroscience in Organizational Behavior, Neuromarketing and AI Applications on Wildlife

Conservation. Hailing from Ranchi, Jharkhand in India, Binod is currently pursuing a Master of Laws (LL.M) at the prestigious Radha Govind University. His passion for technology and innovation along with climate changes is evident through his high academic performance and numerous projects. Binod has a keen interest in artificial intelligence, machine learning, neuropsychology, climate changes and disaster management, fields in which he has undertaken several research projects. He is particularly fascinated by the potential of AI to solve real-world problems and is dedicated to learning and applying new techniques in these areas. He volunteers at local NGOs, teaching underprivileged children basic computer skills. With a strong foundation in law and a commitment to making a positive impact, Binod Kumar is poised to become a future leader in the legal industry.

**Nilesh Kumar** is a dynamic and dedicated marketing professional with a passion for teaching and research. As a Teaching Assistant and Coordinator- Academics at Amity University Jharkhand, he brings a wealth of industry experience and academic expertise to his role. He is pursuing a Ph.D. in Marketing from Ranchi University, where his research focused on retail marketing and strategies. Prior to her academic career, he also worked for few years in the corporate sector, holding roles in logistics and supply chain. His research has been published in national and international journals and has been cited in the field. Dr. Rodriguez is particularly interested in exploring the intersection of retail marketing strategies, education and information technologies used in business.

**Margaret Malewaneng Maja** is an Associate Professor at UNISA, College of Education. She is teaching the Teaching Practice module for Undergraduates and supervising master's and Ph.D. students. She is a 2020 Scholarship of Teaching and Learning award winner. She leads a community engagement project known as Classroom Interaction Pedagogy in teaching English as a first additional language in the Intermediate Phase.

**Onias Matumbu** is a lecturer in Religion and Social Transformation at Morgan ZINTEC College, an affiliate of the University of Zimbabwe. Holds a Doctor of Philosophy in Religion and Social Transformation from University of Kwazulu Natal in South Africa. Master of Arts in Religious Studies: University of Zimbabwe. Bachelor of Arts Honors in Religious Studies: University of Zimbabwe. Post Graduate diploma in Education: University of Zimbabwe. Research interests encompass a range of topics, including the intersection of religion with HIV and AIDS, mental health, the phenomenology of religion, climate change, gender issues, disability studies, and inclusive education. Serves as the Head of the department of Research, Technology, and Innovation at Morgan ZINTEC College. Founding member of the Zimbabwe Mental Health Initiative, which aims to address mental health challenges within the community.

**Mantsha Modiba** is a Northen Sotho lecturer at the University of Limpopo. Her interests are spelling and orthography and translation.

**Moleboheng Mokhele-Ramulumo** is a Senior Lecturer in the Faculty of Education at North-West University. Trained as a microbiologist, she transitioned into STEM education research, inspired by her sons' developmental delays to explore digital learning tools for inclusive education. Her PhD focuses on early childhood STEM education. She is the creator of Renewable Rangers, a digital game, board game, and wordless picture book that teach children about renewable energy through South African storytelling. Recognized as a Top 50 BRICS Young Scientist, South Africa's Top Young Scientist, and a Top 40 Under 40 Trailblazer, she also chairs STEM-ERA and is a Research Associate at the University of Pretoria.

**Lerato Precious Motaung** is an Intermediate and Senior phase educator with ten years of teaching experience. She holds a master's degree in Education from the University of South Africa. Lerato is a passionate language teacher, committed to fostering learner communication skills and cultural awareness. Lerato believes in the power of language as a tool for communication, cultural identity, and lifelong learning. Beyond the classroom, Lerato enjoys reading, mentoring young girls, and contributing to professional development.

**Anil Kumar Nayak**, Assistant Professor of English at CHRIST (Deemed to be University), Delhi NCR, is a committed scholar with a Ph.D. in English Language Education from the English and Foreign Languages University (EFLU), Hyderabad. He also holds a B.Ed. (English) and M.Ed. from EFLU, as well as an M.Phil. in English Language Studies from the University of Hyderabad. His research interests encompass learner-centred pedagogy, bilingual education, multilingual classrooms, and strategies to support underperforming learners in higher education. A prolific academic, Dr. Nayak regularly presents papers at national and international conferences, publishes in peer-reviewed journals, and contributes to edited volumes. His scholarship engages with critical issues in language education, curriculum design, and the development of critical thinking skills. In his teaching, he offers courses in academic and research writing, business and corporate communication, critical thinking, and language pedagogy. Beyond academia, Dr. Nayak is actively involved in community-based initiatives, including awareness programmes on wildlife conservation and the protection of Ramsar sites, reflecting his deep sense of social responsibility and civic engagement.

**Ayushi Zina** is an Assistant Professor, in the Department of English and Cultural Studies at Christ (Deemed to be University) Delhi NCR Campus. She has qualified UGC NET. and She has been teaching for the past 9 years. She has four books and seven book chapters to her credit. She also has a scopus publication and two of her research papers have been published in UGC Care Listed Journals. She has done her graduation and post-graduation in English literature from St. Xavier's College, Ranchi. Her research areas include, mythological studies, feminism, popular literature, gender studies, soft skills and communication. She is an avid reader and a dynamic speaker. She is a soft-skills expert and has done a certificate course in Enhancing Soft Skills and Personality. She has conducted numerous training workshops for faculty and students. She has conducted Professional Development Programmes for Teaching and Non-teaching staff of BIT Mesra. She has taken courses on Effective Communication, Interpersonal Skills, Presentation Skills, People Skills.

# Index

## B



## C



## D



## E



## F



## G

## H



## I



## L

www.ingramcontent.com/pod-product-compliance
Lightning Source LLC
LaVergne TN
LVHW061526290926
849162LV00004B/688